THE LONG REVOLUTION OF THE GLOBAL SOUTH

# The Long Revolution of the Global South

## Toward a New Anti-Imperialist International

Samir Amin

Translated by James Membrez

Copyright © 2019 by The Estate of Samir Amin
All Rights Reserved

Library of Congress Cataloging-in-Publication Data:
Names: Amin, Samir, author.
Title: The long revolution of the global south : toward a new
  anti-imperialist international / Samir Amin.
Other titles: Eveil du sud. English
Description: New York : Monthly Review Press, [2019] | "A large part of the
  material in this volume was previously published in French in 2008." |
  Translation of: L'beveil du sud : l'aere de Bandoung, 1955-1980 :
panorama politique et personnel de l'bepoque. | Includes bibliographical
references and index.
Identifiers: LCCN 2019001468 (print) | LCCN 2019003986 (ebook) | ISBN
  9781583677759 (trade) | ISBN 9781583677766 (institutional) | ISBN
  9781583677742 (hardcover) | ISBN 9781583677735 (pbk.)
Subjects: LCSH: Afro-Asian politics. | Asian-African Conference (1st : 1955:
Bandung, Indonesia) | Anti-imperialist movements—Developing countries. |
Developing countries—Politics and government.
Classification: LCC DS33.3 (ebook) | LCC DS33.3 .A6513 2019 (print) | DDC
  320.9172/4—dc23
LC record available at https://lccn.loc.gov/2019001468


MONTHLY REVIEW PRESS, NEW YORK, NEW YORK

monthlyreview.org


Typeset in Bulmer Monotype

5 4 3 2 1

# Contents

Table of Acronyms | 7

Prologue: Successive Waves of the South's Awakening | 15

1. The Arab World: Nationalism, Political Islam, and the Predicted Arab Revolutions | 51
2. Africa: African Socialisms, Colonial Disasters, and Glimmers of Hope | 105
3. Asia: Triumphant Capitalism, Dead Ends, and Emergence in Question | 187
4. Latin America: End of the Monroe Doctrine? Popular Advances | 259
5. Eastern Europe, the USSR, and Russia: The End of the Tunnel? | 305
6. China, Vietnam, and Cuba: Fears and Hopes | 331
7. The World Forum for Alternatives and the Social Forums | 365
8. The North and the Question of Imperialism | 403

Appendices | 433

Notes | 463

Index | 467

# List of Acronyms

| | | |
|---|---|---|
| AAPSO | Afro-Asian Peoples' Solidarity Organization | |
| ACP | African, Caribbean, and Pacific Group of States | |
| ADEMA | Alliance pour la démocratie au Mali | Alliance for Democracy in Mali |
| AfDB | African Development Bank | |
| AKFM | Party of the Congress for the Independence of Madagascar | |
| AKP *Norway* | Arbeidernes Kommunistparti | Workers' Communist Party |
| ALBA | Alianza Bolivariana para los Pueblos de Nuestra América | Bolivarian Alliance for the Peoples of Our America |
| ANC *South Africa* | African National Congress | |
| APEC | Asia-Pacific Economic Cooperation | |
| APRA *Peru* | Alianza Popular Revolucionaria Americana | Popular Revolutionary American Party |
| AQIM | Al-Qaida in the Islamic Maghreb | |
| ARENA | Asian Regional Exchange for New Alternatives | |
| ATTAC | Association pour la taxation des transactions financières et pour l'action moyenne | Association for the Taxation of Financial Transactions and for Citizen Action |
| AU | African Union | |
| BJP | Bharatiya Janata Party | Indian People's Party |
| CEAO | Communauté économique de l'Afrique de l'ouest | Economic Community of West Africa |
| CEBRAP | Centro Brasileiro de Análise e Planejamento | Brazilian Center for Analysis and Planning |
| CEDETIM | Centre d'études et d'initiatives de solidarité international | Center for International Solidarity Studies and Initiatives |
| CEMAC | Central African Economic and Monetary Community | |

| | | |
|---|---|---|
| CETIM | Centre Europe-Tiers Monde | Europe-Third World Center |
| CETRI *Belgium* | Centre Tricontinental | Tricontinental Center |
| CLACSO | El Consejo Latinoamericano de Ciencias Sociales | The Latin American Council of Social Science |
| CNID *Mali* | Congrès national d'initiative démocratique | National Congress for the Democratic Initiative |
| CODESA | Convention for a Democratic South Africa | |
| CODESRIA | Council for the Development of Social Science Research in Africa | |
| COSATU | Congress of South African Trade Unions | |
| CPI-M | Communist Party of India (Marxist) | |
| CPI-ML | Communist Party of India (Marxist-Leninist) | |
| CPN (Maoist) | Communist Party of Nepal (Maoist) | |
| CPN (UML) | Communist Party of Nepal (Unified Marxist-Leninist) | |
| CRESFED *Haiti* | Centre de recherche et de formation économique et sociale pour le développement | Center for Research and Economic and Social Training for Development |
| CTA | Central de Trabajadores de la Argentina | Argentine Workers' Central Union |
| CUT *Brazil* | Central Única dos Trabalhadores | Unified Workers' Central |
| DERG *Ethiopia* | Coordinating Committee of the Armed Forces, Police, and Territorial Army | |
| EAM *Greece* | Ethniko Apeleftherotiko Metopo | National Liberation Front |
| ECLAC | Economic Commission for Latin America and the Caribbean | |
| ECOSOC | United Nations Economic and Social Council | |
| ECOWAS | Economic Community of West African States | |

| | | |
|---|---|---|
| EEC | European Economic Community | |
| ELN *Colombia* | Ejército de Liberación Nacional | National Liberation Army |
| EPLF | Eritrean People's Liberation Front | |
| EPRP | Ethiopian People's Revolutionary Party | |
| FALN *Venezuela* | Fuerzas Armadas de Liberación Nacional | Armed Forces of National Liberation |
| FAO | Food and Agriculture Organization | |
| FARC | Fuerzas Armadas Revolucionarias de Colombia | Revolutionary Armed Forces of Colombia |
| FIS *Algeria* | Front Islamique de Salut | Islamic Salvation Front |
| FLN *Algeria* | Front de Libération Nationale | National Liberation Front |
| FNLA | Frente Nacional de Libertação de Angola | National Liberation Front of Angola |
| FPI | Front populaire ivoirien | Ivorian Popular Front |
| FPR | Front populaire rwandais | Rwandan Popular Front |
| FRELIMO | Frente Libertação de Moçambique | Mozambique Liberation Front |
| GIDIS *Côte d'Ivoire* | Groupement interdisciplinaire en sciences sociales | Interdisciplinary Social Science Group |
| IADL | International Association of Democratic Lawyers | |
| IDEA | International Development Economics Associates | |
| IDEP | Institut Africain de Développement Économique et de Planification | African Institute for Economic Development and Planning |
| IEPALA | Instituto de Estudios Políticos para América Latina y África | Latin America and Africa Political Studies Institute |
| IMF | International Monetary Fund | |
| IRD *France* | Institut de recherche pour le développement | Research Institute for Development |
| KLA | Kosovo Liberation Army | |
| LASO | Latin American Solidarity Org. | |

| | | |
|---|---|---|
| M'Pep *France* | Mouvement politique d'émancipation populaire | Political Movement for Popular Emancipation |
| MAPU *Chile* | Movimiento de Acción Popular Unitaria | Popular Unitary Action Movement |
| MAS *Bolivia* | Movimiento al Socialismo | Movement for Socialism |
| MEISON | All-Ethiopia Socialist Organization | |
| MIR *Chile* | Movimento de Izquierda Revolucionaria | Revolutionary Left Movement |
| MPLA | Movimento Popular de Libertação de Angola | People's Movement for the Liberation of Angola |
| MST *Brazil* | Movimento dos Trabalhadores Rurais Sem Terra | Landless Workers' Movement |
| NAFTA | North American Free Trade Agreement | |
| NAM | Non-Aligned Movement | |
| NLTPS | National Long-Term Perspective Studies | |
| NORAD | Norwegian Agency for Development Cooperation | |
| OAU | Organization of African Unity | |
| OECD | Organization for Economic Cooperation and Development | |
| OPEC | Organization of Petroleum Exporting Countries | |
| ORSTOM *France* | Office de la recherche scientifique et technique outre-mer | Office for Overseas Scientific and Technical Research |
| PAI *Burkina Faso/ Upper Volta* | Parti africain de l'indépendence | African Independence Party |
| PAICV | Partido Africano da Independência da Cabo Verde | African Party for the Independence of Cape Verde |
| PAID | Pan African Institute for Development | |
| PAIGC | Partido Africano da Independência da Guiné e Cabo Verde | African Party for the Independence of Guinea and Cape Verde |
| PASOK *Greece* | Panellinio Sosialistiko Kinima | Panhellenic Socialist Movement |

| | | |
|---|---|---|
| PCB | Partido Comunista Brasileiro | Brazilian Communist Party |
| PCI | Partito Comunista Italiano | Italian Communist Party |
| PCRHV | Parti communiste révolutionnaire de Haute Volta | Revolutionary Communist Party of Upper Volta |
| PCT *Congo-Brazzaville* | Parti congolais du travail | Congolese Labor Party |
| PDS *Germany* | Partei des Demokratischen Sozialismus | Party of Democratic Socialism |
| PIDE | Polícia Internacional e de Defqesa do Estado | Portuguese International State Defense Police |
| PIT | Parti ivoirien du travail | Ivorian Labor Party |
| PKK *Turkey* | Partiya Karkerên Kurdistanê | Kurdistan Workers' Party |
| PLO | Palestine Liberation Organization | |
| POLOP *Brazil* | Organização Marxista–Política Operária | Marxist Revolutionary Organization–Workers' Politics |
| POUM *Spain/Catalonia* | Partido Obrero de Unificación Marxista | Workers' Party of Marxist Unification |
| PPS *Morocco* | Parti du Progrès et du Socialisme | Party of Progress and Socialism |
| PRI *Mexico* | Partido Revolucionaario Institucional | Institutional Revolutionary Party |
| PT *Brazil* | Partido dos Trabalhadores | Workers' Party |
| RDA *Burkina Faso/ Upper Volta* | Rassemblement démocratique africain | African Democratic Assembly |
| RENAMO | Resistência Naçional Moçambicana | Mozambican Nat'l Resistance |
| ROC *Burkina Faso/ Upper Volta* | Rassemblement des officiers communistes | Assembly of Communist Officers |
| SACP | South African Communist Party | |
| SAREC | Swedish Agency for Research Cooperation | |
| SEEF | Statistiques et études financières (France: Ministère des Finances) | Statistics and Financial Studies (French Ministry of Finance) |
| SID | Society for Int'l Development | |
| SWAPO [Namibia] | South West African People's Org. | |

| | | |
|---|---|---|
| TANU | Tanganyika African National Union | |
| TWF | Third World Forum | |
| UGTT | Union générale tunisienne du travail | Tunisian General Labor Union |
| UM-RDA | Union malienne du rassemblement démocratique africain | Malian Union of the African Democratic Assembly |
| UNCTAD | United Nations Conference on Trade and Development | |
| UNDP | United Nations Development Programme | |
| UNEP | United National Environment Program | |
| UNESCO | United Nations Educational, Scientific, and Cultural Org. | |
| UNITA | União Nacional para a Independência Total de Angola | National Union for the Total Independence of Angola |
| UNRISD | United National Research Institute for Social Development | |
| UNU | United Nations University | |
| UP *Chile* | Unidad Popular | Popular Unity |
| UPC | Union of the Peoples of Cameroon | |
| USFP *Morocco* | Union Socialiste des Forces Populaires | Socialist Union of Popular Forces |
| US-RDA *Mali* | Union soudanaise du rassemblement démocratique africain | Sudanese Union of the African Democratic Assembly |
| WAEMU | West African Economic and Monetary Union | |
| WFA | World Forum for Alternatives | |
| WSF | World Social Forum | |
| WTO | World Trade Organization | |

# The Long Revolution of the Global South

PROLOGUE

# Successive Waves of the South's Awakening

This second volume of my memoirs offers a detailed account of my activities from 1970 up to June 2014 within the successive frameworks of the IDEP, the TWF, and the joint TWF/WFA.

A large part of the material in this volume was previously published in French in 2008, which covers the period up to the beginning of the 2000s.[1] I experienced the Bandung era from the inside in the exercise of my duties, first in Egypt (1957–1960), then in Mali (1960–1963). I gave an account of that period in the first volume of my memoirs.[2] The exercise of my duties at the IDEP and the TWF occurred during the declining phase of the Bandung era. This report of my activities during those years testifies to this decline.

The contemporary period of the history that I experienced can be divided into three distinct periods: 1) the growth then stagnation of the Bandung era from 1955 to 1980; 2) the restoration of the new imperialist order called "liberal globalization" from 1980 to 1995; and 3) the beginning of the capitalist/imperialist system's implosion in 1995 and the parallel beginning of renewed struggles for "another, better world," particularly in the new "Global South."

The title of the French edition of this volume, *The South's Awakening*, reflects my view of this global history.

The twentieth century witnessed the development of an initial wave of victorious struggles to escape the hold of capitalism and/or imperialism. The victories of liberation from imperialist domination carried in themselves the potential of going beyond capitalism toward socialism.

This first wave exhausted its capacities for development, which led, beginning in the 1980s, to the restoration of a new and savage capitalist/imperialist order, almost tantamount to colonization as pillage for the peoples of the

South. But the new order, inherently unstable, has already been called into question by the rise of a second wave of the South's awakening. The challenge is more serious than ever, but is this second wave, like the first, going to occupy center stage only in the countries of the world system's peripheries, or is it going to start the concomitant transformation of the South and the North, with advances beyond capitalism in both areas of the globalized world?

This work is considered a memoir, a personal account of my activities. But it seems useful to offer in this prologue a synthesis of my analyses of key issues, just as I did in the first volume, without which the reader would have trouble understanding the motivations behind my activities.

First, I present three concise documents that clarify my analysis of the three successive moments of the history in question: 1) Bandung and the first globalization of struggles; 2) generalized monopoly capitalism; and 3) emergence and lumpen-development. I supplement them with a brief exposé of what I understand by Maoism, understood as a form (and maybe stage) of the development of historical Marxism.

Then I offer three documents that summarize my view of the major challenges confronting humanity: 1) the agrarian question (central for the peoples of Asia, Africa, and Latin America); 2) the democratization of societies; and 3) the ecological challenge.

These three documents will spare me much needless repetition because these questions always arise in debates on the radical left, and thus the arguments I have developed in my presentations could not disregard them. This is also true for other questions, such as "international aid," which persistently reappears in debates, particularly in Africa. That is why I also thought it helpful to recall my arguments on these questions in various chapters of these memoirs.

BANDUNG AND THE FIRST GLOBALIZATION OF STRUGGLES (1955–1980)

This text supplements what was presented in the first volume under the title "Deployment and Erosion of Bandung."[3]

The governments and peoples of Asia and Africa proclaimed in Bandung in 1955 their wish to reconstruct the world system based on the recognition of the rights of up-till-then dominated nations. This "right to development" was the foundation of that era's globalization, implemented within a negotiated multipolar framework that was imposed on an imperialism that had to adjust to these new requirements. Bandung's success—and not its failure as is increasingly said without thinking—lies behind a great leap forward for the peoples of the South in education and health, in the construction of a modern state, often in the reduction of social inequalities, and in the path toward industrialization. Undoubtedly the limitations of these achievements—particularly the democratic deficit of national populist governments that "gave to the people" but never allowed the people to organize themselves—must be taken into account when assessing the era.

The Bandung system was linked to two other characteristics of the postwar systems: Sovietism (and Maoism) and the welfare state of the social democratic West. These systems were certainly competing, even in conflict (although any conflicts were completely contained within limits that prevented them from expanding beyond local armed confrontations), but also, consequently, complementary. In these conditions, to speak of the globalization of struggles makes sense since, for the first time in the history of capitalism, resistance occurred in every area of the world and inside of all nations, and thereby formed an initial step toward this globalization.

The proof of the interdependence that characterized these struggles, along with the historical compromises that ensured stability in the management of such societies, was provided, conversely, by the changes that occurred after the parallel erosion in the developmental potential of the three systems. The collapse of Sovietism also entailed the collapse of the social democratic model. Its—quite real—social advances were necessary because they were the only possible way to face the "communist threat." We can also point to the echo of the Chinese Cultural Revolution in 1968 Europe.

The progress in industrialization that began during the Bandung era did not result from the logic of imperialism's deployment, but from the victories achieved by the peoples of the South. Certainly this progress fostered the illusion of "catching up" that appeared to be on the way to realization, whereas, in fact, imperialism, forced to make adjustments to the requirements of development in the peripheries, reconstructed itself around new forms of domination. The old opposition between imperialist countries/dominated countries, which was synonymous with the opposition between industrialized countries/non-industrialized countries, gradually gave way to a new opposition based on the centralization of the advantages derived from the "five new monopolies of the imperialist centers" (control over new technologies, natural resources, financial flows, communications, and weapons of mass destruction).

The achievements of the period, along with their limitations, lead us to reexamine the central question of the bourgeoisie and capitalism's future in the system's peripheries. This is an ongoing question since capitalism's globalized deployment determines the fundamental inequality of the possibilities for bourgeois and capitalist development at the system's center and periphery through the polarizing effects produced by its imperialist nature. In other words, is the bourgeoisie in the peripheries necessarily forced to submit to the requirements of this unequal development? Is it, consequently, necessarily comprador by nature? Does the capitalist path, in these conditions, necessarily lead to an impasse? Or does the margin of maneuver from which the bourgeoisie can benefit in certain circumstances (which must be specified) allow it to pursue an autonomous national capitalist development capable of advancing in the direction of catching up? Where are the limits to these possibilities? To what extent does the existence of such limits force us to characterize the capitalist choice as illusory?

Successive doctrinaire and black-and-white responses have been provided to these questions, first asserting one thing and then its opposite, always adapting ex post facto to changes that were never correctly envisioned in the first place, either by the dominant forces or the working classes. After the Second World War, the communists of the Third International described the bourgeoisie of the South as comprador. Maoism declared that the only possible path to liberation was the one opened by a "socialist revolution by stages," led by the proletariat and its allies (the peasant classes in particular), and above all by their avant-garde mouthpiece—the Communist Party. Bandung was going to prove that this judgment was hasty, that under the leadership of the bourgeoisie, a national populist hegemonic bloc could advance development. The page turned on the Bandung era with the neoliberal offensive of oligopolistic capital from the imperialist center (the triad of the United States, Western and Central Europe, Japan). From 1980, the bourgeoisie of the South again appeared to be subjected to comprador status, clearly visible in the compulsory unilateral adjustment of the peripheries to the demands of the center, in some ways the reverse of the center's adjustment to the peripheries forced on it during the Bandung era. But hardly had this reversal occurred then, once again, in the so-called emerging countries—mainly China, but also in other countries like India or Brazil—a margin for maneuver became apparent, offering opportunities to advance on a path of national capitalist development. Analyzing the potential of these advances, as well as their contradictions and limitations, should remain the focus for debate, and need to be extended and deepened so we can construct effective strategies to coordinate struggles at local and world levels.

## 2. GENERALIZED MONOPOLY CAPITALISM

Contemporary capitalism is a capitalism of generalized monopolies. What I mean by that is that monopolies no longer form islands (important as they might be) in an ocean of corporations that are not monopolies—and consequently are relatively autonomous—but an integrated system, and consequently now tightly control all productive systems. Small and medium-sized companies, and even large ones that are not themselves formally owned by the oligopolies, are enclosed in networks of control established by the monopolies upstream and downstream. Consequently, their margin of autonomy has shrunk considerably. These production units have become subcontractors for the monopolies. This system of generalized monopolies is the result of a new stage in the centralization of capital in the countries of the triad that developed in the 1980s and 1990s.

Simultaneously, these generalized monopolies dominate the world economy. "Globalization" is the name that they themselves have given to the imperatives through which they exercise their control over the productive systems of world capitalism's peripheries (the entire world beyond the partners of the triad). This is nothing other than a new stage of imperialism.

As a system, generalized and globalized monopoly capitalism ensures that these monopolies derive a monopoly rent levied on the mass of surplus value (transformed into profits) that capital extracts from the exploitation of labor. To the extent that these monopolies operate in the peripheries of the globalized system, this monopoly rent becomes an imperialist rent. The capital accumulation process—which defines capitalism in all of its successive historical forms—is consequently governed by the maximization of monopolistic/ imperialist rent.

This displacement of the center of gravity of capital accumulation lies behind the continual pursuit of the concentration of incomes and fortunes, increasing monopoly rents, and captured mostly by the oligarchies (plutocracies) that control the oligopolistic groups, to the detriment of labor incomes and even the revenues of non-monopolistic capital.

In turn, this continually growing disequilibrium is itself the origin of the financialization of the economic system. What I mean by that is that a growing portion of the surplus can no longer be invested in the expansion and strengthening of productive systems and that the "financial investment" of this growing surplus is the only possible alternative for continuing the accumulation controlled by the monopolies. This financialization, which accentuates the growth in unequal distribution of income (and wealth), generates the growing surplus on which it feeds. The financial investments (or, more accurately, investments of financial speculation) continue to grow at breathtaking rates, disproportionate with the rates of "GNP growth" (which itself then becomes largely false) or rates of investment in the productive system. The breathtaking growth in financial investments requires—and sustains—among other things, the growth in the debt, in all its forms, particularly sovereign debt. When existing governments claim to pursue the goal of "debt reduction," they deliberately lie. The strategy of financialized monopolies needs growth in the debt (which they seek and do not oppose)—a financially attractive means to absorb the surplus from monopoly rents. Austerity policies imposed to "reduce the debt," as it is said, actually end up increasing its volume, which is the sought-after consequence.

### *The Plutocrats: The New Ruling Class of Obsolescent Capitalism*

The logic of accumulation lies in the growing concentration and centralization of control over capital. Formal ownership can be spread out (as in the "owners" of shares in pension plans), whereas the management of this property is controlled by financial capital.

We have reached a level of centralization in capital's power of domination, such that the bourgeoisie's forms of existence and organization as known up to now have been completely transformed. The bourgeoisie was initially formed from stable bourgeois families. From one generation to the next, the heirs carried on the specialized activities of their companies. The bourgeoisie was built and built itself over the long run. This stability encouraged confidence in "bourgeois values" and promoted their influence throughout the entire society. To a large extent, the bourgeoisie as dominant class was accepted as such. Its access to the privileges of comfort and wealth seemed deserved in return for the services they rendered. It also seemed mainly national in orientation, sensitive to national interests, whatever the ambiguities and limitations of this manipulated concept might have been. The new ruling class abruptly breaks with this tradition. Some describe the transformation in question as the development of active shareholders (sometimes even characterized as populist shareholders) fully reestablishing property rights. This laudatory and misleading characterization legitimizes the change and fails to recognize that the major aspect of the transformation involves the degree of concentration in control of capital and the accompanying centralization of power. The new ruling class is no longer counted in the tens of thousands or even millions, as was the case with the older bourgeoisie. Moreover, a large proportion of the new bourgeoisie is made up of newcomers who emerged more by the success of their financial operations (particularly in the stock market) than by their contribution to the technological breakthroughs of our era. Their ultra-rapid rise is in stark contrast with their predecessors, whose rise took place over numerous decades.

The centralization of power, even more marked than the concentration of capital, reinforces the interpenetration of economic and political power.

The "traditional" ideology of capitalism placed the emphasis on the virtues of property in general, particularly small property—in reality medium or medium-large property—considered to purvey technological and social progress through its stability. In opposition to that, the new ideology heaps praise on the "winners" and despises the "losers" without any other consideration. The "winner" here is almost always right, even when the means used are borderline illegal, if they are not patently so, and in any case they ignore commonly accepted moral values.

Contemporary capitalism has become crony capitalism through the force of the logic of accumulation. The English term "crony capitalism" should not be reserved only for the "underdeveloped and corrupt" forms of Southeast Asia and Latin America that the "economists" (the sincere and convinced believers in the virtues of liberalism) denounced earlier. It now applies to capitalism in the contemporary United States and Europe. In its current behavior, this ruling class is quite close to that of the "mafia," even if the term appears to be insulting and extreme.

The political system of contemporary capitalism is now plutocratic. This plutocracy adapts itself to the practice of representative democracy, which has become "low-intensity democracy." You are free to vote for whomever you want, which is of no importance since it is the market and not the Congress or Parliament that decides everything. A plutocracy also adapts itself elsewhere to autocratic forms of management or electoral forces.

These changes have altered the status of the middle classes and their mode of integration into the global system. These classes are now mainly formed of wage-earners and no longer of small commodity producers as before. This transformation manifests as a crisis of the middle classes, marked by a growing differentiation: the privileged (high salaries) have become the direct agents of the dominant oligopolistic class, while the others are pauperized.

### *The Profiteers: The New Dominant Class in the Peripheries*

The centers/peripheries contrast is not new. It has been part of the globalized expansion of capitalism from the beginning, five centuries ago. Consequently, the local ruling classes of the peripheral capitalist countries, whether independent or colonies, were always subaltern ruling classes, though still connected to their countries, drawing profits from their insertion into globalized capitalism.

There is considerable diversity in these classes, which are largely derived from those that had dominated their societies before their submission to capitalism/imperialism. The reconquest of independence often led to the replacement of these older (collaborationist) subordinated classes by new ruling classes—bureaucracies, state bourgeoisies—which were more legitimate in the eyes of the people (at the beginning) because of their association with national liberation movements. But here again, in the peripheries dominated either by the older imperialism (forms prior to 1950) or the new imperialism (from the Bandung era up to around 1980), the local ruling classes benefited from a visible relative stability. The disruptions caused by the oligopolistic capitalism of the new collective imperialism (the triad) truly uprooted the powers of all these older ruling classes in the peripheries and replaced them with a new class that I will call "profiteers." The profiteer in question is a businessman, not a creative entrepreneur. He derives his wealth from his connections with the established government and the system's foreign masters, whether representatives of the imperialist states (the CIA in particular) or the oligopolies. He acts as a well-paid intermediary, benefiting from an actual political rent. This is the origin of most of the wealth he accumulates. The profiteer no longer subscribes to any moral and national values whatsoever. In a caricature of his alter-ego in the dominant centers, he is interested in nothing other than "success," in accumulating money, with a covetousness that stands out behind a supposed praise of the individual. Again, mafia-like, even criminal, behaviors are never far away.

The formation of the new class of profiteers is inseparable from the development of the forms of lumpen-development widely characteristic of the contemporary South. But the main axis of the dominant bloc is formed by this class only in the "non-emergent" countries. In the "emergent" countries, the dominant bloc is different.

### *The Dominated Classes: A Generalized but Segmented Proletariat*

Marx rigorously defined the proletarian (a human being forced to sell his or her labor power to capital) and recognized that the conditions of this sale ("formal" or "real" to use Marx's terms) were always diverse. The proletariat's segmentation is not a new phenomenon. The description was more accurate for some parts of the class, like the nineteenth-century workers in the new manufacturing sector or, a better example, the Fordist factory in the twentieth century. Concentration on the workplace facilitated solidarity in common struggles and the maturation of political consciousness, but it also encouraged workerism in some historical Marxisms. The fragmentation of production resulting from capital's strategy of implementing the possibilities offered by modern technologies, without, however, losing control of subcontracted or delocalized production, weakens solidarity and strengthens diversity in perception of interests.

Thus the proletariat seems to disappear just at the moment it has become more widespread. Forms of small, autonomous production, and millions of small peasants, artisans, and small merchants, disappear and are replaced by subcontracting work, large chain stores, etc. Ninety percent of workers, in both material and immaterial production, become, in formal terms, wage-workers. I have drawn certain conclusions from the diversification in wages. Far from being proportional to the costs of training for the required qualifications, this diversification is accentuated to the extreme. Yet this has not prevented a rebirth in the feeling of solidarity. "We, the 99 percent," say the Occupy movements. This twin reality—capital's exploitation of everybody and the diverse forms and violence of this exploitation—is a challenge for the left, which cannot ignore "the contradictions among the people" and yet cannot give up on moving toward a convergence of objectives. This, in turn, implies a diversity in forms of organization and action by the new generalized proletariat. The ideology of the "movement" ignores these challenges. Moving to the offensive requires an inevitable reconstruction of centers able to think about the unity of strategic objectives.

The image of the generalized proletariat in the peripheries, whether emergent or not, is different in at least four ways: (i) the progress of the "working class," visible in the emergent countries; (ii) the persistence of a large peasantry that is, nevertheless, increasingly integrated into the capitalist market and consequently subjected to exploitation by capital, even if indirect; (iii) the extremely rapid growth of "survival" activities resulting from lumpen-development; and (iv) the reactionary positions of large sections of the middle classes when they are the exclusive beneficiaries of growth.

The challenge for the radical left in these circumstances is "to unite peasants and workers," to use terms derived from the Third International, to unite workers (including the "informal" ones), the critical intelligentsia, and the middle classes in an anti-comprador front.

### *New Forms of Political Domination*

Transformations in the economic base of the system and its accompanying class structures have changed the conditions for the exercise of power. Political domination is now expressed through a new-style "political class" and a media clergy, both dedicated exclusively to serving the abstract capitalism of generalized monopolies. The ideology of the "individual as king" and the illusions of the "movement" that wants to transform the world, even "change life"(!)—without posing the question of workers and peoples seizing power—would reinforce capital's new methods of exercising power.

In the peripheries, an extremely caricatured form is achieved when lumpen-development confides the exercise of power to a comprador state and class of profiteers. By contrast, in the emergent countries, social blocs of a different type exercise real power, which derives their legitimacy from the economic success of the policies implemented. The illusion that emergence "in globalized capitalism and by capitalist means" will make it possible to catch up with the centers, and the limitations, in fact, of what is possible in this context, and the concomitant social and political conflicts, open the door to different possible developments, moving either toward the best (in the direction of socialism) or the worst (failure and re-compradorization).

## *Obsolescent Capitalism and the End of Bourgeois Civilization*

The characteristics of the new dominant classes described here are not passing conjunctural phenomena. They strictly correspond to the operational requirements of contemporary capitalism.

Bourgeois civilization—like any civilization—cannot be reduced to the logic of the economic system's reproduction. It includes an ideological and moral component: praise for individual initiative, certainly, but also honesty and respect for the law, even solidarity with the people, expressed at least at the national level. This value system ensured a certain stability to social reproduction as a whole and marked the world of political representations at its service. This value system is disappearing. Taking its place is a system without any values. Ignorance and vulgarity characterize a growing majority in this world of the "dominants." A dramatic change of this kind heralds the end of a civilization. It reproduces what can clearly be seen from other eras of decadence. For all these reasons, I consider that contemporary oligopolistic capitalism must now be unequivocally described as obsolescent, whatever its apparent immediate successes, since the latter are completely absorbed into a path clearly leading to a new barbarism. (I refer here to my study "Révolution ou décadence?" [Revolution or Decadence], already more than thirty years old.)[4]

The system of generalized monopoly capitalism, "globalized" (imperialist) and financialized, is imploding right before our eyes. This system is visibly incapable of overcoming its growing internal contradictions and is condemned to pursue its mad rush. The "crisis" of the system is due to nothing other than its own "success." The strategy used by the monopolies has always resulted in the sought-after results up to this very day: "austerity" plans, the so-called social (in fact anti-social) plans for layoffs, are still imposed, in spite of resistance. The initiative still remains, even now, in the hands of the monopolies (the "markets") and their political servants (the governments that submit their decisions to the so-called requirements of the "market").

Analysis of struggles and conflicts that begin with the idea of challenging imperialist domination allows us to situate the new phenomenon of the "emergence" of some countries in the South.

Yet this autumn of capitalism does not coincide with a "springtime of peoples," which implies that workers and peoples in struggle have made an accurate assessment of the requirements, not to "end the crisis of capitalism" but to "end capitalism" (the title of one of my recent works).[5] This has not happened, or not yet. The gap separating the autumn of capitalism from the possible springtime of peoples gives to the current moment of history its dangerously dramatic character. The battle between the defenders of the capitalist order and those who, beyond their resistance, can urge humanity onto the long road to socialism, viewed as a higher stage of civilization, has hardly begun. All alternatives are thus possible, the best as well as the most barbaric.

The very existence of this gap requires some explanation. Capitalism is not only a system based on the exploitation of labor by capital. It is also a system based on polarization in its development on the world scale. Capitalism and imperialism are the two inseparable faces of the same reality, that of historical capitalism. The challenge to this system developed throughout the twentieth century up to 1980, in a long wave of victorious struggles by workers and dominated peoples. Revolutions conducted under the banners of Marxism and communism, reforms conquered within the context of a gradual path to socialism, the victories of the national liberation movements of colonized and oppressed peoples, all together built relations of force less unfavorable to workers and peoples than previously. But this wave ran out of steam without succeeding in creating the conditions for its own continuation by new advances. This exhaustion then allowed monopoly capital to retake the offensive and reestablish its absolute and unilateral power, while the outlines of a new wave of challenges to the system can barely be discerned. In that crepuscular light of the night that has not yet ended and the day that has not yet begun, monsters and ghosts take shape. Whereas generalized monopoly capitalism is truly monstrous, the responses by forces of rejection are still largely nebulous.

### 3. EMERGENCE AND LUMPEN-DEVELOPMENT

The term "emergence" is used by various people in extremely different contexts and most often without taking the time to clearly define its meaning. Emergence is not measured by an elevated rate of growth in Gross Domestic

Product (GDP), or exports, over a long period of time (more than a decade), or by the fact that the society in question has attained an elevated level in per capita GDP, as the World Bank and conventional economists view it. Emergence implies much more: sustained growth in a country's industrial production and an increase in the ability of these industries to be competitive on the world scale.

Moreover, two further questions need to be clarified: what industries are involved and what is meant by competitive. We should exclude extractive industries (mines and fuels) that alone can, in countries well endowed by nature, produce accelerated growth without drawing in its wake all the productive activities of the country in question. Extreme examples of these "non-emergent" situations are the Gulf countries, Venezuela, and Gabon. It is also necessary to consider the competitiveness of the productive activities in the economy as well as that of the productive system as a whole, and not just the competitiveness of a select number of production units taken on their own. By means of delocalization or subcontracting, multinationals operating in countries of the South can be behind the establishment of local production units (subsidiaries of the multinationals or autonomous units) capable of exporting on the world market, which makes them competitive in the view of conventional economics. The competitiveness of a productive system depends on various economic and social factors, such as general levels of education and training of workers at all levels, and the effectiveness of all the institutions that manage the national political economy (tax system, corporate law, labor rights, credit, public support, etc.). In turn, the productive system in question should not be reduced solely to processing industries that produce manufactured goods for production and consumption (though the absence of these really means there is no productive system worthy of the name), but also includes food and agricultural production, as well as services required for the normal operation of the system (particularly transport and credit).

The concept of emergence, then, implies a political and holistic approach to the question. Therefore, a country is emergent only insofar as the policies implemented by the government aim at the objective of building and reinforcing an inward-looking economy (even if it is open to the outside) and, consequently, capable of asserting its national economic sovereignty. This complex objective implies that the assertion of this sovereignty involves all aspects of economic life. In particular, it implies a policy that makes it possible for a country to strengthen its food sovereignty as well as its sovereignty over the control of natural resources and access to them from outside its national territory. These multiple and complementary objectives are in stark contrast with those of a comprador government that is content to adjust the growth model implemented to the requirements of the dominant "liberal-globalized" world system and the possibilities offered by it.

So far, we have said nothing about the orientation of the political strategy implemented by a particular state and society: is it capitalist or moving toward socialism? Yet this question cannot be eliminated from the debate because a ruling class's choice of orientation has major positive or negative effects on the very success of emergence. The relation between policies of emergence, on the one hand, and the accompanying social transformations, on the other, does not depend exclusively on the internal consistency of the former, but also on the degree of their complementarity (or conflict) with the latter. Social struggles—class struggles and political conflicts—do not arise from "adjusting" to the logic of the state's project of emergence; they are a determinant of what the state does. Current experience illustrates the diversity of and fluctuations in these relations. Emergence is often accompanied by a worsening of inequalities. Yet the precise nature of these inequalities should be spelled out: do these inequalities occur in a context where a tiny minority or a larger one (the middle classes) benefit from policies pursued while the majority of workers are pauperized, or in a context where there is an improvement in the living conditions of this majority, even if the rate of growth in their income is lower than that of the system's beneficiaries? In other words, the policies implemented can link emergence to pauperization or not. Emergence is not a status that a country achieves once and for all. It consists of successive steps— earlier ones, if successful, would prepare the way for the following ones or, if not successful, would lead to an impasse.

In the same way, the relation between the emergent economy and the world economy is itself in constant transformation and part of different overall possibilities, which could support social solidarity in the nation or weaken it. Emergence is thus not synonymous with growth in exports and the rising power of a country measured in this way. A growth in exports hinges on the growth of an internal market that has to be specified (for the working classes, the middle classes) and the former can become a support or an obstacle to the second. A growth in exports can thus weaken or strengthen the relative autonomy of the emergent economy in its relations to the world system.

Emergence is a political project, not only an economic one. An evaluation of its success is thus based on an examination of its capacity to reduce the way in which the dominant capitalist centers continue their domination, in spite of the economic successes of emergent countries measured in the terms of conventional economics. For my part, I have defined these means in terms of control by the dominant powers of technological development, access to natural resources, the global financial and monetary system, means of information, and weapons of mass destruction. I also maintain the thesis that there is indeed a collective imperialism of the triad that intends to maintain, by any means, its privileged position in the domination of the world and prevent any emergent country from challenging this domination. I conclude from this that the ambitions of the emergent countries are in conflict with the strategic objectives of the imperialist triad, and the extent of the violence in this conflict is proportional to the degree of radicalness in the challenges from the emerging countries to the privileges of the center enumerated above.

The economics of emergence also cannot be separated from the international policy of the countries in question. Do they align themselves with the triad's politico-military coalition? Do they, consequently, accept the strategies implemented by NATO? Or do they attempt to counter them?

An authentic project of emergence is the exact opposite of one that includes unilateral submission to the requirements of the globalized capitalism of the generalized monopolies, which can only result in what I call "lumpen-development." I am here freely borrowing the term used by the late André Gunder Frank to analyze a similar development, but in different spatial and temporal conditions. Today, lumpen-development is the result of accelerated social disintegration connected to the model of "development" (which does not deserve the name) imposed by the monopolies of the imperialist centers on the dominated societies of the periphery. It is reflected in the dramatic growth in survival activities (the so-called informal sphere), in other words, by the pauperization inherent to the unilateral logic of capital accumulation.

Among the experiences of emergence, some fully deserve the label because they are not part of processes of lumpen-development. In other words, in these situations, pauperization does not afflict the working classes. Instead, there is an improvement in their conditions of life, whether modest or strong. Two of these experiences are clearly capitalist: Korea and Taiwan (I will not discuss here the particular historical conditions that made possible the success of the emergence project in these two countries). Two others inherit the legacy of socialist revolutions: China and Vietnam. Cuba could be included in this group if it succeeds in surmounting the contradictions it is currently undergoing.

There are other cases of emergence connected to obvious processes of lumpen-development. India is the best example of that. Parts of that country's situation correspond to what emergence requires and produces. There is a state policy that aims at strengthening a sizable industrial system, there is an accompanying expansion of the middle classes, there is progress in technological capacities and education, and there is a foreign policy capable of autonomy on the world scene. But there is also accelerated pauperization for the great majority—two-thirds of the society. This is an example, then, of a hybrid system that combines emergence with lumpen-development. We can even bring out the complementarity of these two faces of reality. I believe, without intending to make a huge overgeneralization, that all the other countries considered to be emergent belong to this hybrid family, whether it be Brazil, South Africa, or others. But there are also—and this is true of most other countries in the South—situations in which the elements of emergence are barely apparent while the processes of lumpen-development clearly are dominant.

## THE CONTRIBUTION OF MAOISM

The "workerist" and Eurocentrist Marxism of the Second International shared with the era's dominant ideology a linear view of history in which all societies have to pass first through a stage of capitalist development, for which colonization—in this regard "historically positive"—planted the seeds, before being able to aspire to socialism. The idea that the "development" of some (the dominant centers) and the "underdevelopment" of others (the dominated peripheries) were inseparable, like two sides of the same coin, both immanent products of capitalism's worldwide expansion, was totally alien to it.

The polarization inherent to capitalist globalization—a major fact with significant worldwide social and political implications—calls for a perspective that leads to the surpassing of capitalism. This polarization is the basis for the possible support of large fractions of the working classes and, above all, the middle classes (whose development is itself favored by the position of the centers in the world system) in the dominant countries for social-colonialism. Simultaneously, it transforms the peripheries into a "zone of storms" (as the Chinese expression has it) in a permanent natural rebellion against the capitalist world order. Certainly, rebellion is not synonymous with revolution, but it is the possibility for the latter. Motivations for rejecting the capitalist model are not lacking, even at the system's center, as the case of 1968, among other examples, illustrates. Undoubtedly, the Chinese Communist Party's chosen formulation of the challenge at one time—"the countryside encircles the cities"—is consequently too extreme to be useful. A global strategy for the transition beyond capitalism toward global socialism must coordinate struggles in the centers with those in the peripheries of the system.

Initially, Lenin distanced himself from the dominant theory of the Second International and successfully led a revolution in the "weak link" (Russia), but always with the belief that this would be followed by a wave of socialist revolutions in Europe. This was a disappointed hope. Lenin then moved toward a view that gave more importance to the transformation of rebellions into revolutions in the East. But it was up to the Chinese Communist Party and Mao to systematize this new perspective.

Maoism made a decisive contribution to a comprehensive assessment of the issues and challenges the globalized capitalist/imperialist expansion represents. It allowed us to place the centers/peripheries contrast immanent to the expansion of the inherently imperialist and polarizing "really existing" capitalism at the center of the analysis, and to draw from that analysis all the implied lessons for the socialist struggle in both the dominant centers and the dominated peripheries. These conclusions have been summarized in a beautiful Chinese-style expression: "States want independence, nations want liberation, and peoples want revolution." States—the ruling classes of all countries in the world when they are something other than lackeys and conveyors of external forces—work to enlarge their space of movement which allows them to maneuver within the (capitalist) world system and raise themselves from "passive" actors, condemned to adjust unilaterally to the dominant demands of imperialism, to "active" actors, who participate in shaping the world order. Nations—that is, historical blocs of potentially progressive classes—want liberation, specifically, "development" and "modernization." Peoples—that is, the dominated and exploited working classes—aspire to socialism. The phrase allows us to understand the real world in all its complexity and, therefore, formulate effective action strategies. It shares the view that the transition from capitalism to world socialism will be long, very long even, and, consequently, breaks with the Third International's concept of the "short transition."

## THREE MAJOR CHALLENGES

### *1. The Agrarian Question*

The agrarian question is at the heart of the problems of development and democracy and other challenges confronting the societies of Africa, Asia, and Latin America. Communist parties and national liberation movements were completely aware of this during the Bandung era. The main issue centers on the rules that regulate access to the use of agricultural land. These regulations must be formulated in a way that "includes rather than excludes," allowing all farmers to have access to land, first condition for the reproduction of a "peasant society." This fundamental right is certainly not sufficient. It must be accompanied by policies that allow peasant family farms to produce in conditions that ensure a marked growth in national production (in turn guaranteeing the country's food sovereignty) and a parallel improvement in the real incomes of all peasants. Here we are talking about implementing a set of macroeconomic policies and concomitant forms of satisfactory political management, and then making sure that negotiations over the organization of systems of international trade are subject to the needs of those policies.

Partisans of the capitalist path ignore the question since for them, in principle, modernity implies private property in land. It is forgotten that this so-called modern land tenure system results from the formation of historical (really existing) capitalism, established through the destruction of "customary" systems of regulating access to the land, beginning in England and subsequently elsewhere in Europe. Access to the land in feudal Europe was based on the superposition of rights over the same piece of land: those of the peasant and other members of a village community (whether serf or free), those of the feudal lords, and those of the king. The attack on this system took the form of the "enclosures" in England, imitated in various ways in all European countries throughout the nineteenth century. Marx quite early denounced this radical transformation that excluded the majority of peasants from access to use of the land—making them into proletarian emigrants into cities by force of circumstance or into agricultural laborers or tenant farmers—which he grouped with other measures of primitive accumulation that dispossessed the producers of property or the use of the means of production or both. This accumulation by dispossession continues in the countries of the contemporary South today.

Capitalist rhetoric about itself—the "liberal" ideology—has produced a myth: the "absolute and superior rationality" of economic management based on private and exclusive property in the means of production, which includes agricultural land. The dominant discourse applies the conclusions that it believes can be drawn from the construction of Western modernity and proposes them as the only "rules" necessary for the progress of all other peoples. To make land everywhere private property in the current sense of the term, such as practiced in the capitalist centers, is tantamount to spreading the policy of "enclosures" to the entire world, that is, to hastening the dispossession of the peasantry. This process is not new. It was started and pursued during the preceding centuries of capitalism's world expansion, particularly in the context of colonial systems. Today, the WTO only envisages accelerating this process, while the coming devastation resulting from this choice is increasingly predictable and calculable, as is the resistance of the peasants and others. Such resistance might make possible the construction of a real and authentically human alternative.

In Africa, land tenure systems are still largely based on different principles than private property. This definition, clearly, is negative—*not* based on private property—and consequently cannot refer to a homogeneous category. Access to the land is regulated in all human societies. But the regulations are managed either by "customary communities," "modern communities," or the state, or more exactly and frequently, managed by a set of institutions and practices that involve individuals, groups, and the state.

"Customary" management (expressed in terms of customary law or called as such) has always (or almost always) excluded private property in the modern sense and always guaranteed access to the land to all families rather than individuals concerned, that is, to those forming a distinct "village community" that identifies itself as such. But it has never (or almost never) guaranteed "equal" access to the land. First, it most often excluded "foreigners" (vestiges of the most frequently conquered peoples) and "slaves" (of various statuses). Further, land was unequally distributed according to membership in clans, lineages, castes, or statuses: "chiefs," "free men," etc. Thus there is no reason to praise these customary rights unreasonably as, unfortunately, a number of anti-imperialist nationalist ideologues do. Progress will certainly require that they be challenged.

Customary management has never—or almost never—been carried out by "independent villages." The latter have always been part of larger state bodies, stable or changing, strong or precarious, depending on circumstances, but rarely absent. The usage rights of communities and the families of which they are composed, then, have always been limited by the rights of a state, which collects a tribute (the reason why I call the huge family of pre-modern modes of production "tributary"). These complex forms of "customary" management, different from one country and time period to another, in the best of cases, exist only in extremely degraded forms, having been subject to the onslaught of the dominant processes of globalized capitalism for at least two centuries (in Asia and Africa), and sometimes five (in Latin America).

India is probably one of the clearest examples. Before British colonization, village communities managed access to the land or, more exactly, their dominant castes—ruling classes, excluding the lower castes—did so; the dalits were treated as a class of collective slaves similar to the helots of Sparta. The imperial Mughal state and its vassals (states of the rajahs and other kings), the collectors of the tribute, controlled and exploited these communities. The British elevated the zamindars, formerly charged with collecting the tribute, to the status of "landowners," thereby forming an allied class of large landowners, in defiance of tradition. However, they maintained the "tradition" when it benefited them; for example, by "respecting" the exclusion of dalits from access to the land! Independent India has not called this unwieldy colonial heritage into question, which lies behind the incredible poverty of the majority of the peasantry and, consequently, its urban proletariat.[6] The solution to these problems and the formation of a viable peasant family economy for the majority requires, consequently, an agrarian reform in the strict sense of the term (see below for the more precise meaning of this proposal). European colonialism in Southeast Asia and that of the United States in the Philippines have resulted in similar developments. Regimes of "enlightened despotism" in the Orient (the Ottoman Empire, Mohammed Ali's Egypt, the Shahs of Iran) also mainly substituted private property in the modern sense of the term for the traditional arrangements, thereby benefiting a new class improperly called "feudal" (by the mainstream currents of historical Marxism) recruited from the higher level officials of the government system.

Consequently, private property in land is now characteristic of the majority of agricultural land—particularly the best of it—in all of Asia outside of China, Vietnam, and the former Soviet Central Asian republics. There remain no more than fragments of degraded semi-customary systems, particularly in the poorest regions, the ones that are the least attractive for capitalist agriculture. This structure is strongly differentiated, juxtaposing large landowners (rural capitalists), rich peasants, middle peasants, poor peasants, and the landless. There is no peasant "organization" or "movement" that transcends these acute class conflicts.

In Arab Africa, South Africa, Zimbabwe, and Kenya, the colonizers (except in Egypt) had granted to their settlers (or to the Boers in South Africa) "modern" private property, in general of the latifundia type. This heritage has certainly been eliminated in Algeria. But here the peasantry had practically disappeared, proletarianized (and turned into vagrants) by the expansion of colonial lands, while in Morocco and Tunisia, the local bourgeoisie took over the land (which was also partly the case in Kenya). In Zimbabwe, the revolution underway has challenged the colonial heritage, benefiting, in part, new, medium-sized landowners, of urban more than rural origin, and, in part, communities of poor peasants. South Africa is still not part of this trajectory. The fragments of the degraded semi-customary systems that still exist in the "poor" regions of Morocco, Berber Algeria, or in the Bantustans of South Africa, are subject to the threat of private appropriation, encouraged by forces from both inside and outside of these societies. In all these situations, the character of peasant struggles (and possibly the organizations that lead them or join forces with them) should be carefully defined: do these movements and demands represent "rich peasants," in conflict with the direction of particular state policies (and the influence of the dominant world system on these policies), or do they represent poor peasants and the landless? Can they form an "alliance" against the dominant (so-called neoliberal) system? Under what conditions and to what extent? Can the demands—whether expressed or not—of the poor peasants and the landless be overlooked?

In subtropical Africa, the apparent continuation of "customary" systems is probably more visible. Here the colonization model was different and referred to as a "trading economy" (*économie de traite*). Management of access to land was left to so-called customary authorities, yet still controlled by the colonial state via authentic traditional chiefs or false ones fabricated by the administration. The aim of such control was to force the peasants to produce, beyond their own subsistence needs, a quota of products specifically for export (peanuts, cotton, coffee, cacao). The preservation of a land tenure system that did not include private property was the result of colonization since no land rent entered into the composition of the prices for the designated products. This system resulted in soil mismanagement, destroyed, sometimes permanently, by the extension of cultivation (as can be seen in the desertification of the groundnut-growing areas of Senegal). Once more, capitalism demonstrated that its inherent "short-term rationality" was well and truly behind an ecological disaster. The juxtaposition of subsistence food production and production for export also made it possible to pay peasants for their labor at rates close to zero. In these conditions, to speak of a "customary land tenure system" is to overdo it considerably. This is really a new system that preserves only the appearances of traditions, often the less valuable parts.

China and Vietnam are unique examples of a system for managing access to land that is not founded on private property or on "custom," but on a revolutionary new right, unknown almost everywhere else: all peasants, defined as inhabitants of a village, have equal access to the land (I emphasize the term "equal"). This right is the greatest achievement of the Chinese and Vietnamese revolutions.

In China—and even more in Vietnam, which was more thoroughly colonized—the old land tenure systems (those I have called "tributary") were already quite eroded by capitalism. The old ruling classes of the imperial system of government largely monopolized agricultural land as private or almost private property, while capitalist development fostered the formation of new classes of rich peasants. Mao Zedong is the first—and probably the only one, followed by Chinese and Vietnamese communists—to have defined a strategy for agrarian revolution based on the mobilization of the majority of the poor, landless, and middle peasants. The victory of this revolution straightaway allowed the abolition of private land—replaced by state-owned land—and the organization of new forms of equal access to the land for all peasants. This organization has certainly passed through several successive phases, including one inspired by the Soviet model of production cooperatives. The limitations of the latter's achievements led the two countries to return to peasant family farms. Is this model viable? Can it produce continuous improvement in production without generating surplus rural labor? Under what conditions? What state support policies are required? What forms of political management can meet the challenge?

Ideally, the model implies parallel rights: of the state as sole landowner, on the one hand, and of the usufructuary (the peasant family), on the other. The state guarantees equal distribution of village lands among all families. It prohibits any use other than family cultivation, such as renting out the land. It guarantees that the product of the investments made by the usufructuary returns to him, in the short term, through his ownership of all of the farm's production (freely marketable, although the state guarantees it by its purchases at a minimum price) and, in the long term, through the inheritance of the usufruct by the children who remain on the farm (the emigrant, when leaving the village, loses the right of access to the land, which returns to the basket of land for redistribution). Since this is certainly about rich soils, but also small (even tiny) farms, the system is viable only as long as vertical investment (a well-organized green revolution—not the one pushed by agribusiness—without large-scale motorization) proves to be as effective in allowing an increase in production per rural farmer as horizontal investment, that is, expansion of the farm supported by intensification of motorization.

Has this "ideal" model ever been implemented? It was probably close to being implemented in China during the Deng Xiaoping era. It remains the case that, while it could produce a strong degree of equality within a village, it had never been able to avoid inequalities among communities, which were a function of soil quality, population densities, and proximity to urban markets. No system of redistribution, even via cooperatives and state marketing monopolies during the Soviet phase, was up to the challenge.

What is certainly more serious is that the system itself is subject to internal and external pressures that erode its social scope and significance. Access to credit, under satisfactory conditions for the provision of inputs, is subject to all kinds of bargaining and interventions, both legal and illegal: "equal" access to the land is not synonymous with "equal" access to better conditions of production. The popularization of "market" ideology encourages this erosion. The system tolerates (even legitimates once again) the leasing of land (tenant farming) and the use of wage labor. The rhetoric of the right—encouraged from the outside—repeats that it will be necessary to give to the peasants "ownership" of the land and to open the "market in agricultural land." It is more than obvious that the rich peasants (even agribusiness) who aspire to increase their property, lie behind such views.

This management system that regulates peasant access to the land has up till now been undertaken by the state and its ruling party. It is clearly possible to envision a system managed by actually elected village councils. That is probably necessary because there is not really any other way to mobilize the majority opinion and reduce the intrigues of a minority who might profit from a more pronounced capitalist development. The "dictatorship of the party" has been proven to be prone to sink into careerism, opportunism, even corruption. There are social struggles underway in the rural areas of China and Vietnam. They are just as prominent elsewhere in the world. But they are mainly defensive, that is, they are committed to defending the heritage of the revolution—the equal right for everyone to the land. Such defense is necessary insofar as this heritage is more threatened than it appears, in spite of repeated affirmations to the contrary by the two governments that "state ownership of land will never be abolished in favor of private property"! But this defense today requires recognition of the right to engage in such practices through organizing those who are concerned—that is, the peasants.

Forms of organizing agricultural production and land tenure systems are too diverse throughout Asia and Africa to construct a single path for the "peasant alternative" that can work for everyone. Hence, agrarian reform should be understood as a redistribution of private property when it is considered to be too unequally distributed. This is not a matter of a "reform of the land tenure system," since this system is still managed by the principle of ownership. Nevertheless, this reform is necessary both to satisfy the perfectly legitimate demand of the poor and landless peasants, and to reduce the political and social power of large landowners. But where it has been implemented, in Asia and Africa after the liberation from imperialist and colonial domination, it was accomplished by hegemonic non-revolutionary social forces, meaning that these reforms were not managed by the majority of poor and dominated classes, except in China and Vietnam. In the latter, there was not any "agrarian reform" in the strict sense of the term, but, as I have said, a suppression of private property in land, an affirmation of state property, and an implementation of the principle of "equal" access to land use for all peasants. Elsewhere, true reforms dispossessed only the large landowners to the ultimate benefit of middle and even (in the longer term) rich peasants, while neglecting the interests of the poor and landless. That was the case in Egypt and other Arab countries. The reform underway in Zimbabwe could very well end up with similar results. Reform is still part of the required agenda in India, Southeast Asia, South Africa, and Kenya.

Even where agrarian reform is an immediate and imperative requirement, it would still be an ambiguous progress because of its longer-term significance. It reinforces attachment to "small property" that becomes an obstacle to challenging a land tenure system based on private property. The history of Russia illustrates this. Changes begun after the abolition of serfdom (1861) and stimulated by the 1905 Revolution, followed by Stolypin's policies, had already produced a demand for property that the 1917 Revolution recognized through a radical agrarian reform. As is well known, the new small landowners were unenthusiastic about giving up their rights in favor of the unfortunate cooperatives organized in the 1930s. Another path to development based on peasant family farming, organized around generalized small property, perhaps might have been possible. It was not attempted.

But what about regions (other than China and Vietnam) where the land tenure system is not (yet) based on private property? Here we are talking about inter-tropical Africa. This is an old debate. Toward the end of the nineteenth century, in his correspondence with the Russian Narodniks (Vera Zasulich, among others), Marx dared to assert that the absence of private property can be an asset for the socialist revolution, allowing the leap to a system for managing access to the land other than the one governed by private property. But he did not specify what form(s) this new system should take, with the qualifier "collective," as true as it is, being inadequate. Twenty years later, Lenin concluded that this possibility no longer existed, eliminated by the penetration of capitalism and the accompanying spirit of private property. Is this judgment correct or not? I will not express an opinion on this question, for which my knowledge of Russia is insufficient. Still it is the case that Lenin was not inclined to give critical importance to this question, having accepted Kautsky's view expressed in *The Agrarian Question*. Kautsky generalized the scope of the modern European capitalist model and concluded that the peasantry was destined to disappear due to capitalist expansion itself. In other words, capitalism would be able to "resolve the agrarian question." This is true for the capitalist countries of the triad (15 percent of the world population), but it is false for the rest of the world (85 percent of the population). History demonstrates not only that capitalism has not settled this question for the 85 percent of the world's population, but even that in continuing its worldwide expansion, it will not be able to settle it (except by genocide—a "beautiful" solution!). It was thus up to Mao Zedong and the Communist parties of China and Vietnam to give an adequate response to the challenge.

The question arose again in the 1960s with the independence of countries in Africa. The continent's national liberation movements, and the states and party-states that resulted from those movements, had benefited, to varying degrees, from the support of the peasant majorities. Their natural propensity toward populism led them to imagine a specifically African path to socialism.

This could probably be described as quite moderately radical in its relationship to imperialism as well as to the local classes connected to its expansion. It nevertheless posed the question of the reconstruction of peasant society in a humanist and universalist spirit. This often turned out to be strongly critical of the "traditions" that the foreign masters had attempted to use for their benefit.

All—or almost all—African countries adopted the same principle, formulated in the "state's right to eminent domain" over all land. I am not one of those who consider this proclamation an error or that it was motivated by extreme "statism." An examination of the real ways that the current system of managing the peasantry operates, along with its integration into the capitalist world economy, allows us to assess the scope of the challenge. The system's management is effected by a complex system that simultaneously calls on "custom," (capitalist) private property, and the rights of the state. The "custom" in question is degraded and serves only as decoration for the speeches of bloody dictators appealing to "authenticity," a fig leaf they believe hides their thirst for looting and treason in the face of imperialism. The propensity to expand private appropriation encounters no serious obstacle other than the victims' possible resistance. In some regions, well placed for cultivating rich crops (irrigated zones, truck farming in suburban areas), the land is bought, sold, and leased without any formal land title. The state's eminent domain, the principle of which I defend, becomes a vehicle for private appropriation. The state can thus "give" the land required for setting up a tourist zone, a local or foreign agribusiness enterprise, or even a state farm. The land titles necessary for accessing the managed areas are rarely distributed with any transparency. In all cases, the peasant families that occupied these lands, and ordered to leave, are the victims of practices that are abuses of power. But to abolish the state's eminent domain to transfer property to its occupants is not feasible in reality (it would require surveying and registering all village territories!), and insofar as it would be attempted, such an operation would allow rural and urban notables to get hold of the best parcels.

The correct response to the challenges of managing a land tenure system not based on private property (or at least one not dominated by it) requires reform of the state and its active involvement in establishing a modernized, economically effective, and (to avoid, or at least reduce inequalities) democratic system to manage access to land. The solution in any case is not a return to "custom," which is actually impossible, and would only serve to accentuate inequalities and open the way to unbridled capitalism.

We cannot say that any of the African states have ever attempted to follow the path recommended here. Mali, the Sudanese Union, following its independence in September 1961, initiated what has been quite incorrectly called "collectivization." In fact, the cooperatives set up were not production cooperatives. Production remained the exclusive responsibility of family farms. They were a form of modernized collective authority replacing supposed "custom" on which the colonial power had based itself. The party that took on this new modern authority had, besides, a clear awareness of the challenge and had set itself the aim of abolishing customary forms of authority—considered to be reactionary, even "feudal." Undoubtedly, this new peasant authority, formally democratic (the leaders were elected), was in reality only as democratic as the state and party. In any case, it exercised "modern" responsibilities: assured that access to the land was "correctly" carried out, that is, without "discrimination," managed credits, distribution of inputs (supplied by state trading entities), and marketing of the products (also, in part, delivered to state trading organizations). Nepotism and abuses of power were certainly never eradicated in this activity. But the only response to these abuses would have been progressive democratization of the state, not its retreat, as subsequently forced by liberalism (through an extremely violent military dictatorship) to the benefit of merchants (*dioulas*). In other areas, such as the liberated zones of Guinea-Bissau (under the influence of the theories advanced by Amílcar Cabral) and Burkina Faso under Thomas Sankara, these challenges were directly confronted, sometimes resulting in unquestionable advances that today are conveniently erased from public awareness. In Senegal, the establishment of elected rural collectives is a response to the principle of which I will unhesitatingly defend. Democracy is a practice that requires an unending learning process, in Europe as much as in Africa.

What the currently prevailing view understands by "reform of the land tenure system" is the exact opposite of what is required to build an authentic and prosperous peasant economy. The view propagated by the propaganda instruments of collective imperialism—the World Bank, most development agencies, but also a number of non-governmental organizations (NGOs) having large financial support—is that reform consists of rapidly increasing privatization of land and nothing more. The objective is obvious: creating conditions that would allow the "modern" pockets of agribusiness (foreign or local) to get hold of lands that are necessary for their expansion. But the additional production that these pockets could provide (for export or the profitable local market) will never be able to meet the challenge of building a prosperous society for everyone, which involves progress for the peasant family economy as a whole.

On the contrary, land reform designed with the aim of building a true, effective, and democratic alternative, based on thriving peasant family production, should define the state's role (main holder of eminent domain) and the role of the institutions, as well as mechanisms for managing access to the land and the means of production. I do not rule out complex and mixed solutions, specific to each country. Private property in land could be accepted—at least where it is established and considered legitimate. Its redistribution can—or should—be reconsidered where necessary through agrarian reforms (in sub-Saharan Africa, South Africa, Zimbabwe, and Kenya). I do not even necessarily, in all cases, rule out opening controlled spaces for the establishment of agribusiness enterprises. But the main point lies elsewhere, in the modernization of peasant family production and the democratization in the process of managing its integration into the national economy and into globalization.

I do not have a blueprint to propose here. I am satisfied highlighting some of the large problems that such a reform raises. The democratic question is the main focus of the response to the challenge we are examining. This is a complex and difficult question that cannot be reduced to the insipid rhetoric of good governance and multiparty elections. The question includes an undeniable cultural aspect: democracy pushes for the abolition of "customs" that are hostile to it—prejudices about social hierarchies, and above all the treatment of women. It includes legal and institutional components: the construction of systems of administrative, commercial, and private law that is consistent with the objectives of social construction and the establishment of adequate institutions (preferably elected!). But above all, when all is said and done, the progress of democracy will depend on the social power of its defenders. The organization of peasant movements is, in this sense, absolutely irreplaceable. It is only insofar as the peasantry is able to speak for itself that advances in the direction of what is called "participatory democracy"—as opposed to reducing the problem to the dimensions of "representative democracy"—will open up.

The question of relations between men and women is a no less essential dimension of the democratic challenge. When we speak of the (peasant) family farm, we are obviously referring to the family, which up to now, and almost everywhere, has been characterized by the structural submission of women and the over-exploitation of their labor power. A democratic transformation will not happen in these conditions without women's organized movements.

Attention should also be focused on the question of migrations. "Customary" rights generally exclude "foreigners"—that is, all those who do not belong to the clans, lineages, and families that make up a village community—from rights to the land, or restrict access to it. Migrations caused by colonial and post-colonial development have sometimes taken on dimensions that shake up the idea of the ethnic "homogeneity" of particular regions affected by such migration. The emigrants—whether originally from outside a particular state, like the Burkinabe in Côte d'Ivoire, or, although formally citizens of the same state, of an "ethnic" origin foreign to the regions where they settled, like the Hausa in the Nigerian state of Plateau—see their rights to the land they have cultivated challenged by narrow-minded and chauvinistic political movements, which benefit from external support. To defeat such "communitarianisms" ideologically and politically, and to unequivocally condemn the para-cultural rhetoric underlying them, has become one of the imperative conditions for authentic democratic advances.

All of the preceding analyses and proposals only concern the status of property and regulations for access to the land. These questions are a major focus in debates on the future of agricultural and food production, peasant societies, and the individuals making up those societies. But they do not deal with all dimensions of the challenge. Access to the land falls short of any potential for social change if the peasant beneficiary is not able to access the necessary means of production under acceptable conditions (credit, seeds, inputs, access to markets). National policies and international negotiations that focus on defining the frameworks in which prices and incomes are determined are another component of the peasant question.

I will limit myself here to outlining two major conclusions and proposals I have reached:

We cannot accept treating agricultural and food production and the land as ordinary "commodities" and, consequently, accept the necessity of including them in the globalized liberalization promoted by the dominant powers (the United States and the European Union) and multinational capital. The agenda of the WTO, which is a direct descendent of the GATT since 1995, must purely and simply be rejected. We must seek to convince public opinion in Asia and Africa—beginning with peasant organizations, but also all social and political forces that defend the interests of the working classes and the nation, particularly the requirements of its food sovereignty, and all those who have not given up a development project worthy of the name—that the negotiations conducted within the framework of the WTO agenda will result in catastrophe for the peoples of Asia and Africa. These simply threaten to ruin more than two and a half billion peasants of the two continents, offering them no alternative other than migration into shantytowns and imprisonment in concentration camps, the construction of which has already been anticipated for these potential migrants. We cannot accept the maneuvering of the major imperialist powers (the United States and Europe) that work together within the WTO in their attack on the peoples of the South. We should be aware that these powers, who unilaterally attempt to impose "liberal" provisions on the countries of the South, always make sure to exclude themselves from such provisions by maneuvers that can only be described as systematic cheating.

Asian and African peasants were organized in the earlier stage of their peoples' liberation struggles. They found their place in powerful historical blocs that created the right conditions for victory over the imperialism of that era. Sometimes these blocs were revolutionary (China and Vietnam) and thus had their main rural base in the majority classes of middle, poor, and landless peasants. Elsewhere, they were led by the national bourgeoisie, or the strata that aspired to be such and had their rural base in the rich and middle peasant classes, isolating the large landowners and the "traditional" leaders who were in the pay of the colonizers.

This stage has now passed. The challenge of the new collective imperialism of the triad will only be met if historical blocs are formed in Asia and Africa that are not remakes of the earlier ones. To define the nature of these blocs, as well as their strategies and immediate and longer-term objectives in these new conditions, is the challenge confronting the so-called alternative globalization movement. This challenge is much more serious than what a large number of these movements involved in current struggles could imagine. New peasant organizations exist in Asia and Africa that drive current struggles. Often, when political systems make the formation of formal organizations impossible, social struggles in the country are conducted by "movements" without leaders, or at least obvious ones. These activities and programs, when they exist, need to be analyzed more. What peasant social forces do they represent, whose interests do they defend? Is it the majority of peasants? Or is it minorities who aspire to find their place in the expansion of globalized capitalism? We should avoid quick responses to these complex and difficult questions. We should beware of condemning some organizations and movements because they do not mobilize the peasant majorities around radical programs. This would amount to ignoring the requirements for organizing broad alliances and formulating a strategy of stages. But we should also beware of subscribing to the rhetoric of "naive alter-globalization," which often sets the tone in forums and encourages the illusion that the world is moving in the right direction solely because social movements exist. This rhetoric, it is true, emanates more from numerous NGOs—of good intentions, perhaps—than from peasant and worker organizations.

## 2. Electoral Democracy or Democratization of Societies?

There is no authentic democracy without social progress. Democracy is both a requirement in itself and a means for the working classes to assert their rights and demands.

Democracy in the general sense involves recognition of the legitimacy of different views of the relations between the individual and society, and the concomitant legitimacy of diverse interests and the institutions necessary to promote their implementation. As such, it is an imperative condition for human emancipation. We cannot imagine such emancipation without a concomitant emancipation of the mind. Democracy provides maximum opportunities for creativity in all areas. But democracy, in the more specific sense of a set of institutions that define and control its practices, is also a means either to facilitate or hinder the advancement of the people's (the working/popular classes) interests. In this latter sense, we should then carefully distinguish the means of popular democracy from those of democracy reserved to the privileged. To describe democracy as "popular" could be taken for a pleonasm since *demos* means "people" in Greek. But the pleonasm is necessary because the democracy that the dominant ideology offers to us was designed and constructed to serve the privileged and not to promote the power of the popular classes.

An authentic democracy is inseparable from social progress. That means it must combine the requirements for liberty with the no less important requirements for equality. These two values are not necessarily spontaneously complementary, but often in conflict. When liberty is combined with property, which is placed on equal footing and sanctified by the economic system, it reduces the space for realizing demands for equality. The property in question is that of a minority; in our era, it belongs to large financial oligopolies. In these conditions, the combination of liberty and property establishes the real power of a plutocracy, reducing democracy to ritual practices without any real significance. However, equality (or at least a certain amount of less inequality) can be—and often was in contemporary history—guaranteed by the government without great tolerance for the exercise of citizen freedoms. Combining liberty and equality is the essence of the challenge that confronts us today.

The institutional democracy that the dominant ideology offers us is an obstacle to authentic democratic progress. Advances in democracy have always been produced by popular struggles, and such advances have always been more prominent in revolutionary periods.

Democracy as we know it was not—and still is not—designed to encourage the expression of grassroot demands, but rather sets up obstacles that are difficult to overcome. Dominant recent tendencies in the institutionalized practice of electoral and representative democracy openly pursue the objective of reducing what their promoters call "the excess of democracy"! The dominant ideology links democracy with "freedom of markets" (that is, capitalism) and claims that they are inseparable: there can be no democracy without markets, thus no democratic socialism is conceivable. This is a tautological and ideological—in the vulgar and negative sense of the term—expression. The history of really existing capitalism as a globalized system demonstrates that this same truncated democracy has always been only the exception and not the rule.

In the centers of capitalism, the progress of representative democracy has always been the result of popular struggles, held off for as long as possible by the power holders (property owners). It is an incontestable fact that such struggles have resulted in the expansion of suffrage (universal suffrage is recent), the strengthening of legislative power against the privileges of kings, aristocracies, and the military high command, and the legalization of limits to the freedom of property owners: labor rights, social security laws, etc.

At the level of the global capitalist system, the link between (truncated) democracy and capitalism is even more clearly without any real foundation. In the peripheries (80 percent of humanity) that are integrated into real world capitalism, democracy has never, or almost never, been on the agenda of what is possible or even desirable for the operation of capitalist accumulation. In these conditions, I will even go so far to say that democratic advances in the centers, while they were indeed the result of struggles by the working/popular classes, were no less largely facilitated by the advantages such societies procured in the world system.

Popular movements and peoples fighting for socialism and liberation from imperialism were behind the authentic democratic breakthroughs initiating a theory and practice that combine democracy and social progress. This evolution—beyond capitalism, its ideology, and the restricted practice of representative and procedural democracy—began quite early in the French Revolution. It was expressed more maturely and radically in later revolutions, in the Paris Commune, the Russian Revolution, the Chinese Revolution, and some others (Mexico, Cuba, Vietnam).

I am not one of those who refrain from severely criticizing the authoritarian, even bloody, excesses and abuses that accompanied the revolutionary periods of history. Explaining the reasons for such practices neither justifies them nor reduces their destructive impact on the socialist future aimed at by these revolutions. Still, we should also keep in mind the ongoing crimes of really existing capitalism and imperialism, the colonial massacres, the crimes connected with the "preventive wars" conducted today by the United States and its allies. Democracy in these conditions, when it is not simply erased from the agenda, is hardly more than a masquerade.

Today, democracy is in decline worldwide. Within the context of generalized and globalized monopoly capitalism, democracy (even in its truncated forms) is not advancing—in reality or potentially—but, on the contrary, is in general retreat. In contemporary capitalism, electoral democracy—when it exists—is combined not with social progress but with social regression. Consequently, it is threatened with loss of legitimacy and credibility. "The market decides everything, the parliament (when it exists) nothing." Moreover, the "war on terrorism" serves, as we well know, as a pretext to reduce democratic rights for the greater benefit of the plutocracy's power in the era of obsolescent capitalism. People then are likely to be attracted to the illusion of retreating into "identities" of various sorts (para-ethnic and/or para-religious) that are in essence anti-democratic and a dead-end.

In the countries of the capitalist/imperialist center, the working/popular classes (and even most of the middle classes, at least potentially) certainly aspire to a more real democracy, more equality, and more solidarity and social security—job security, retirement systems, etc. It is not certain that the ideology of cutthroat competition will be accepted indefinitely. But are the peoples of the North disposed to give up the significant advantages accruing to them through plundering the entire world, which implies maintaining the peoples of the South in underdevelopment? The ecological concern for "sustainable" development should lead to a serious reconsideration of these advantages. For this very reason, it has to be said that the manifestation of this concern seldom exceeds the expression of pious wishes. Here subservience to the democratic farce is internalized by a self-described "postmodernist" discourse that, quite simply, refuses to recognize the extent of such destructive effects. The main thing lies elsewhere it is said; what do elections matter in "civil society," where individuals have become what the liberal virus claims they are—the subjects of history—whereas they are indeed not that at all!

But the democratic farce does not work in the system's peripheries. Here, in the "zone of storms," the established order does not benefit from sufficient legitimacy to allow a stabilization of the society.

The persistence of "backward-looking" aspirations does not result from the tenacious "backwardness" of the peoples involved (the usual rhetoric on the subject), but from an ineffective response to a real challenge. All peoples and nations of the peripheries have not only been subjected to the fierce economic exploitation of imperialist capital, they have also, consequently, been subjected just as much to cultural aggression. The dignity of their cultures, languages, customs, and history has been denied with the greatest contempt. It is not surprising that these victims of external and internal colonialism (Native Americans) naturally link their social and political liberation with the restoration of their national dignity. But these legitimate aspirations, in turn, lead them to look exclusively to the past, hoping to find there the answers to the questions of today and tomorrow. There is a real risk of seeing the peoples' movement of awakening and liberation trap itself into tragic impasses when the "backward-looking" approach is taken as the central axis of the sought-after renewal. This confusion, among other causes, lies behind the "religious renewal." By that I mean the resurgence of conservative and reactionary religious and para-religious interpretations that are "communitarianist" and ritualistic. Here monotheism quite easily is wedded to "moneytheism." I obviously exclude from my judgment religious interpretations that rely on their spiritual sense to justify taking the side of those social forces fighting for freedom. But the former interpretations are dominant, and the latter are in the minority and often marginalized. Other no-less reactionary ideological approaches compensate in the same way for the emptiness created by the liberal virus: "nationalisms" and ethnic or para-ethnic communitarianism are good examples.

In the countries of the periphery, the challenge can be taken up only if, during a long transition period (centuries long), the political systems of popular democracy successfully combine three objectives: (i) maintain and strengthen national independence in a multipolar international system based on the principle of negotiated globalization; (ii) accelerate the development of productive forces without which it is futile to speak about eradicating poverty and building a balanced multipolar world; and (iii) affirm the growing place of socialist values, particularly equality. This challenge involves three-quarters of humanity. Democracy is not a ready-made formula that simply needs to be adopted. Its realization is a continuous process, which is why I prefer the term democratization. The proposed formula—a multiparty system and elections—turns into farce and runs a serious risk that the struggle for democracy will lose legitimacy. Accepting this solution as "less bad" would trap the unsuspecting in a demoralizing impasse. Rhetorics on "good governance" and "reduction of poverty" provide no adequate response to liberalism's destructive effects.

The struggle for the democratization of society is inseparable from the struggle to change the established government. The fight for democratization requires mobilization, organization, choice of actions, strategic vision, tactical sense, and the politicization of struggles. Undoubtedly, these prerequisites of struggle cannot be decreed in advance on the basis of sanctified dogmas. But identifying them is imperative because it is indeed a matter of defeating the system of established powers and replacing it with another one. Undoubtedly, the idea that "the revolution" will replace the power of capital straightaway with that of the people must be given up. In contrast, revolutionary advances are possible, based on new and real powers of the people that push back the power of those who will continue to defend the principles of reproducing inequality.

Abandoning the question of power is tantamount to throwing the baby out with the bathwater. Believing that society can be transformed without destroying, even if gradually, the established system of power, displays the most extreme naïveté. So long as the established powers remain what they are, far from being dispossessed by social change, they are capable of co-opting it and integrating it into the strengthening—not weakening—of capital's power. The sad diversion of ecologism, which has become a new field for capital's expansion, bears witness to that. Evading the question of power is to place social movements in a situation that does not allow them to move on the offensive, and instead restricts them to maintaining a defensive posture and resisting the offensives of those who hold power. In sum, it is to cede the initiative to the enemy.

The movement toward socialism throughout the world, in both North and South, will invent new forms of authentic democracy. Advances must, at each stage of the struggle, include their adequate political and legal institutionalization. The reader will find examples in appendix 2 in chapter 7, "Audacity, More Audacity."

### 3. Ecology and Marxism

The ecological question arises in almost all debates. This is understandable given that the scale of ecological disasters is now clearly visible. Yet these debates rarely get beyond confusion. Only a minority of movements understands that a response to the challenge demands leaving behind the logic of capitalist accumulation. The established powers quickly understood the danger and expended major, supposedly scientific, efforts—which in reality are purely ideological propaganda—to demonstrate that a green capitalism was possible. I talked about this in my analyses of the question of "sustainable" development.[7] I also, in contrast, contended that the works of Mathis Wackernagel and William Rees, to which I referred, illustrate the possibility of calculating (I emphasize the word *calculating*, that is, a quantified measure) use values, on the condition of breaking away from capitalism. François Houtart's book (2010) dissects the hoax of "green capitalism." John Bellamy Foster (2000) has given a masterful analysis of Marx as an ecologist.[8] For these reasons, I believe it might be useful to the reader of my memoirs to know what my viewpoint is on these questions, one that I have tirelessly advocated in many debates. The text that follows is drawn from my book *The Law of Worldwide Value* (2010).

The viewpoint of the dominant currents in environmentalism, particularly in the fundamentalist variety, is certainly not that of Marxism, although both rightly denounce the destructive effects of "development."

Environmentalism attributes these destructive effects to the Eurocentric and Promethean philosophy characteristic of "modernity" in which the human being is not part of nature, but claims to subject the latter to the satisfactions of its needs. This thesis entails a fatal culturalist corollary. It inspires a call to follow another philosophy that emphasizes humanity's belonging to nature, its "mother." With that in mind, supposedly alternative and better philosophies, such as one derived from a particular interpretation of Hinduism, are praised in opposition to so-called Western philosophy. This is ill-considered praise, which ignores the fact that Hindu society was not (and is not) different from so-called Western societies, neither concerning the use of violence (Hindu society is anything but as nonviolent as it claims to be) nor the subjection of nature to exploitation.

Marx develops his analysis on a completely different terrain. He attributes the destructive character of capital accumulation to capitalism's logic of rationality, which is governed exclusively by the pursuit of immediate profit (short-term profitability). He demonstrates that and draws the explicit conclusions in volume 1 of *Capital*.

These two methods of interpreting history and reality lead to different judgments on "what must be done" to meet the challenge—the destructive effects of "development." Environmentalists are led to "condemn progress" and thereby join the postmodernists in viewing scientific discoveries and technological advances negatively. This condemnation leads, in turn, to a method of envisaging what the future might be, which is, at the very least, not very realistic. Thus projections are made in which a particular natural resource will be exhausted (fossil fuels, for example), and then the validity of these—fatally alarmist—conclusions is generalized by the assertion that the planet's resources are not infinite, which is certainly correct in principle, but not necessarily in terms of what can be deduced from it. Thus possible future scientific discoveries that might counter a particular alarmist conclusion are ignored. Of course, the distant future remains unknown and there will never be any guarantee that "progress" will always make it possible to find solutions to unknown future challenges. Science is not a substitute for the belief in eternity (religious or philosophical). In this context, situating the debate on the nature of the challenges and the ways to deal with them would lead us nowhere.

On the contrary, by placing the debate on the terrain cleared by Marx—the analysis of capitalism—we are able to advance in analyzing the challenges. Yes, there will still be scientific discoveries in the future on the basis of which technologies for controlling the riches of nature might be derived. But what can be asserted without fear of contradiction is that as long as the logic of capitalism forces society to exercise its choices on the basis of short-term profitability (which is implied by the valorization of capital), the technologies that will be implemented to exploit new scientific advances will be chosen only if they are profitable in the short term. Consequently, this implies that such technologies will carry an increasingly higher risk of being environmentally destructive. It is only when humanity has designed a way of managing society based on prioritizing use values instead of the exchange values associated with the valorization of capital that the conditions for a better management of the relations between humanity and nature will come together. I do say "better management" and not "perfect management." The latter implies the elimination of the limitations to which all human thought and action are subject. The early critique of Eurocentrism that I advanced (taken up in the second and expanded edition of my book *Eurocentrism*) continues the work started by Marx as a counterpoint to the culturalist, postmodernist, and supposedly environmentalist, discourse.[9]

Environmentalists' choice to debate these questions in a flawed theoretical context traps them, not only in theoretical, but above all in political impasses. This choice allows the dominant forces of capital to manipulate all the political proposals that result from it. It is well known that alarmism allows the societies of the imperialist triad to preserve their privilege of exclusive access to the planet's resources and prevent the peoples of the peripheries from being able to deal with the requirements of their development—whether for good or bad. It is ineffective to respond to "anti-alarmist" views by pointing to the (incontestable) fact that they are themselves mere fabrications of the lobbies (for example, the automobile lobby). The world of capital always operates in this way: the lobbies that defend particular interests of segments of capital endlessly confront one another and will continue to do so. Lobbies for energy-intensive choices now oppose lobbies for "green" capitalism. Environmentalists will only be able to get out of this labyrinth if they understand that they must become Marxists.

# 1

# THE ARAB WORLD
## Nationalism, Political Islam, and the Predicted Arab Revolutions

I am prefacing this chapter on the Arab world with five introductory documents: 1) the contemporary Arab world's historical trajectory; 2) the failure of the *Nahda*; 3) modernity, democracy, secularism, and Islam; 4) the deployment of the United States military project; and 5) the Palestinian question.

These documents should allow the reader to pinpoint my position within the larger context of the Arab debates I am going to summarize. The Arab scene is the site of an ongoing conflict between three groups of political positions that, in turn, leads to three different future possibilities: 1) bourgeois modernism, certainly comprador, but nevertheless motivated by the intention to build "modern" though not necessarily democratic Arab states; 2) reactionary political Islam propagated by the archaic monarchies of the Gulf, the Muslim Brothers, and the Salafists; and 3) a possibly universalist Arab left, which would be part of a movement toward socialism.

We need to examine first what the real reasons are for such fault lines before looking at how they are manifested in current debates. These underlying positions recur with nagging frequency in all Arab debates.

1. THE HISTORICAL TRAJECTORY OF THE CONTEMPORARY ARAB WORLD

The Arab world has gone through three important stages over the past half-century. Nasser's Egypt, Baathist Syria and Iraq, and Boumediene's Algeria were, from 1955 to 1975, major participants in the nonaligned movement and its expansion into Africa. The first conference of African liberation movements took place in Cairo in 1957; it led to the establishment of the Organization of Solidarity with the People of Asia, Africa, and Latin America. The proposed New International Economic Order—the swan song of the non-aligned movement—was drafted in Algiers in 1974. None of these are chance occurrences.

But while the socially positive effects of the "Arab revolutions," which I have called "national populist," were exhausted in the brief time of a decade or two, rising oil profits became dominant after 1973 and encouraged the illusion of an easy modernization. The play on words known by all Arabs, *al-fawra mahal al-thawra* (the spurt, meaning oil, in place of the revolution), captures this transfer of hopes, which is simultaneously the transfer of the center of gravity of strategic decision making from Cairo to Riyadh. Ironically, this occurred at the time when we began to see that this nonrenewable resource was on the way to exhaustion. Within this context, the United States began the implementation of what would become the project for military control of the world, a means for it to ensure exclusive access to this irreplaceable energy resource for its benefit. From 1990, the armed intervention of the United States, now become a reality, completely transformed the nature of the challenges confronting Arab and other societies.

Mired in the *infitah*, the "opening" connected to the petroleum illusion, Arab governments lost the legitimacy from which they had benefited until then. Political Islam rushed into the political void, where it has been in the forefront ever since. As Antonio Gramsci once said, "The old world is dying and the new world struggles to be born; now is the time of monsters."

For someone my age, who has lived through these three periods, the involution associated with this sequence necessarily called for in-depth consideration of the reasons for this dramatic failure. Having experienced this from the inside, I put forward written analyses on the issues involved, which the reader will find elsewhere. I attributed the involution to two sets of causes: those related to the limitations and contradictions of the *Nahda*, the Arab "Renaissance" initiated in the nineteenth century, which were behind the longevity of the political model called the "*mameluk* regime,"[10] and those related to the world geopolitics of the new collective imperialism of the triad (United States, Europe, and Japan) under the leadership of the United States.[11]

## 2. THE FAILURE OF THE *NAHDA*

### *Modernity and the European Renaissance*

Modernity is based on the principle that human beings, individually and collectively, make their own history, and to do that, they have the right to innovate and not respect tradition. The proclamation of this principle was a rupture with the fundamental principle that governed all premodern societies, including those of feudal and Christian Europe. This principle called for renouncing the dominant forms of legitimizing power—in the family, in communities within which ways of living and modes of production are organized, and at the level of the state—that were based up to then on a metaphysics with a generally religious expression. It implies, then, a separation between the state and religion, a radical secularization, which is a condition for the development of modern forms of politics.

Modernity is born with this declaration of principle. This is not a question of a rebirth (renaissance), but a birth as such. The characterization Europeans themselves gave to this moment of history, the Renaissance. is thus misleading. It is the result of an ideological construction in which Greco-Roman antiquity was already supposedly familiar with the principle of modernity, buried during the Middle Ages (between ancient modernity and new modernity) by religious obscurantism. This is a mythical understanding of antiquity, the basis for Eurocentrism, through which Europe claims to inherit its past and "return to the sources," hence re-naissance, while in fact this renaissance is actually a rupture with its own history.

The concomitant birth of modernity and capitalism is not accidental. The social relations that characterize the new production system implied freedom of enterprise, free access to markets, and proclamation of the inviolable right to private property, which is made "sacred." Economic life, freed from the type of supervision by political authorities that characterized the premodern systems, developed into an autonomous area of social life, driven by its own laws. In place of the traditional determination in which power is the source of wealth, capitalism substitutes a reverse causality in which wealth is the source of power.

### *The Arab Islamic Nahda*

The European Renaissance was the result of an internal social dynamic. It was, in effect, the solution provided by the invention of capitalism to contradictions specific to Europe in that era. In contrast, what Arabs called, by imitation, their Renaissance—the *Nahda* of the nineteenth century—was not that at all. It was the reaction to an external shock. Europe, made powerful and victorious by modernity, had an ambiguous effect on the Arab world. It was a cause of both attraction (admiration) and repulsion (through the arrogance of its conquest). The Arab Renaissance took the qualifying term literally. It believed that if, as the Europeans had done (and this is what they themselves said), the Arabs "returned" to their sources, a disparaged time, they would rediscover their greatness. The *Nahda* did not understand the modernity that made Europe powerful.

The *Nahda* did not implement the necessary ruptures with tradition that define modernity. It did not grasp the true significance of secularism, a necessary condition for politics to become a domain of free innovation, thus of democracy in the modern sense of the term. The *Nahda* believed that it could substitute a reinterpretation of religion purged of its obscurantist excesses. Even now, Arab societies are poorly equipped to understand that secularism is not a Western "specificity," but a necessity of modernity. The *Nahda* did not understand the meaning of democracy, understood properly as the right to break with tradition. It thus remained a prisoner of concepts of the autocratic state; it hoped and prayed for a "just" despot (*al-moustabid al-adel*)—not even an "enlightened" one. The nuance is significant. The *Nahda* did not understand that modernity also produced women's aspiration for liberation, thereby exercising their right to innovate, to break with tradition. It reduced modernity to the immediate appearance of what it produces: technological progress. This deliberately simplified presentation does not mean that I am unaware of the contradictions expressed in the *Nahda*, or that some avant-garde thinkers were aware of the real challenges of modernity, such as Qasim Amin concerning the importance of women's liberation, Ali Abdel Raziq on the centrality of secularism, or Abd al-Rahman al-Kawakibi on democracy. But none of these breakthroughs were followed through; on the contrary, Arab society reacted by giving up any pursuit of the indicated paths forward. The *Nahda* is not, then, the moment of the birth of modernity in the Arab world; it is in fact the moment of its failure.

In his magnificent book, *The Arabs and the Holocaust*, Gilbert Achcar dissects the writings of Rashid Rida, the last link in the chain of the *Nahda* in decline.[12] Rida wrote in the 1920s and was one of the original inspirations of the Muslim Brotherhood. The Islam that he proposed, described as a "return to the sources," is utterly devoid of thought. It is a ritualistic, conservative Islam of convenience and communitarian affirmation. The adherence of Rida and the Muslim Brotherhood to Wahhabism, an equally heinous expression of a total lack of critical thinking, which scarcely responds to the requirements of an archaic society of nomads, heralds the advent of political Islam.

## Limits and Contradictions of Modernity

The modernity that developed under the restrictions of capitalism's limitations is, consequently, contradictory, promising much that it cannot produce and thus giving rise to unsatisfied aspirations. Contemporary humanity is thus confronted with the contradictions of this modernity—the only one we have experienced up to now—a modernity that began with the capitalist stage of history. Capitalism and its modernity are destructive of the human being, reduced to the status of a commodity embodying labor power. Moreover, polarization on the world scale caused by capitalist accumulation on the same scale nullifies any possibility for the majority of human beings—those in the peripheries—to satisfy their needs as promised by modernity. For the great majority, the modernity in question is quite simply odious. Hence, the rejection of this modernity is violent. But rejection is a negative act. The inadequacies of various alternative projects eliminate the effectiveness of any revolt and ultimately lead it to submit to the requirements of the capitalism and modernity that it supposedly rejects. The main illusion is sustained by nostalgia for the premodern past. In the peripheries, the backward-looking posture proceeds from a violent and justified revolt, of which it is only a neurotic and powerless form, because quite simply it is based on ignorance of the nature of the challenge of modernity.

The backward-looking position is expressed in various ways, generally in terms of a fundamentalist religious interpretation, which in fact masks a conventional conservative choice, or in terms of an ethnicity adorned with specific virtues that transcend other dimensions of social reality—classes, among others. The common denominator to all these forms is their attachment to a culturalist thesis in which religions and ethnic groups are characterized by transhistorical specificities that define inviolable identities. Even though without scientific foundation, these positions are nonetheless able to mobilize the masses who are marginalized and made helpless by destructive capitalist modernity. They are thus effective means for manipulation that are incorporated into strategies designed to reinforce submission to the joint dictatorship of the dominant forces in capitalist globalization and their local and subaltern transmission channels. Political Islam is a good example of this method for managing peripheral capitalism. In Latin America and Africa, the proliferation of quasi-Protestant obscurantist "sects," supported by North American authorities to hinder liberation theology, manipulates the helplessness of the excluded and their revolt against the conservative official church.

[ABOVE EXTRACTS ARE FROM *THE REAWAKENING OF THE ARAB WORLD.*][13]

### 3. MODERNITY, DEMOCRACY, SECULARISM, AND ISLAM

The image that the Arab and Islamic region gives of itself today is that of societies in which religion (Islam) is in the forefront of all areas of social and political life—to the point that it seems incongruous to imagine that it could be otherwise. The majority of foreign observers (political leaders and the media) conclude from this that modernity, even democracy, must be adapted to the heavy presence of Islam, thereby de facto precluding secularism.

Modernity is a rupture in universal history that began in sixteenth-century Europe. Modernity proclaims that the human being is responsible for his or her own history, individually and collectively, and consequently breaks with the dominant premodern ideologies. Modernity thus allows democracy, just as it demands secularism, in the sense of separation of the religious and the political.

From this point of view, where do the peoples of the Middle Eastern region stand? The image of crowds of bearded men prostrating themselves, as well as cohorts of veiled women, can and does inspire hasty conclusions about the intensity of the religious commitment being expressed. The social pressures exerted to obtain the result are rarely mentioned. The women have not chosen the veil, it has been imposed on them with prior violence. Absence from prayer almost always costs the person in question work, sometimes even that person's life. Western "culturalist" friends who call for respect for the diversity of beliefs rarely inquire into the procedures implemented by governments to present an image that suits them. There are certainly religious extremists (*fous de Dieu*). Are there proportionately more of them than the Spanish Catholics who parade at Easter, or the innumerable fanatics in the United States who listen to televangelists?

In any case, the region has not always presented this image of itself. Beyond differences from one country to another, we can identify a large region extending from Morocco to Afghanistan, including all Arabs (except those from the Arabian peninsula), Turks, Iranians, Afghans, and the peoples of the former Soviet Central Asia, in which the potential for the development of secularism is far from negligible. The situation is different among some neighboring peoples, such as the Arabs of the Arabian peninsula or the Pakistanis.

# THE ARAB WORLD

In this extensive area, the political traditions were strongly affected by the radical currents of modernity. The Enlightenment, the French Revolution, the Russian Revolution, and the communism of the Third International had an impact on thinking and acting and certainly were more important than Westminster-style parliamentarianism, for example. These dominant currents inspired the major models of political transformation that the ruling classes implemented, which in some ways could be called forms of "enlightened despotism."

This was certainly the case in the Egypt of Muhammad Ali or the Khedive Ismail Pasha. Kemalism in Turkey and modernization in Iran proceeded with similar methods. The national populism characteristic of the more recent stages of history belongs to the same family of "modernist" political projects. The model's variants were numerous (the Algerian FLN, Tunisian Bourguibism, Egyptian Nasserism, and Baathism in Syria and Iraq), but moved in a similar direction. The apparently extreme experiences—the so-called communist governments in Afghanistan and South Yemen—were in reality not very different. All these governments accomplished a great deal and, consequently, had very wide popular support. That is why, even when they were not truly democratic, they opened the way to a possible evolution in that direction. In some circumstances—such as those in Egypt between 1920 and 1950—an experiment in electoral democracy was attempted, supported by the moderate anti-imperialists (the Wafd) and fought by the dominant imperialist power (Great Britain) and its local allies (the monarchy). Secularism—admittedly implemented in moderate versions—was not "rejected" by the people. It was, on the contrary, religious figures that were considered obscurantists in public opinion—which most of them were.

Modernist experiments—from enlightened despotism to radical national populism—were not the product of chance. Powerful political movements, dominant in the middle classes, were behind these experiments. In this way, these classes were asserting themselves as full and equal partners in modern globalization, and their "national bourgeois" projects were modernist, secularist, and potentially bearers of democratic developments. But precisely because these projects came into conflict with the interests of the dominant imperialism, the latter fought them relentlessly and systematically mobilized obscurantist forces for this purpose.

The history of the Muslim Brotherhood is well known. The British and the monarchy literally created it in the 1920s in Egypt to counter the democratic and secular Wafd. Also well known is that the CIA and Anwar Sadat organized its mass return from Saudi exile after the death of Gamal Abdel Nasser. Then there is the history of the Taliban formed by the CIA and Pakistan to fight against the "communists" who had opened schools to everyone, boys and girls. Let us also remember that the Israelis supported Hamas at the beginning to weaken the secular and democratic currents of the Palestinian resistance.

Political Islam would have had much difficulty in expanding beyond the borders of Saudi Arabia and Pakistan without the firm, powerful, and ongoing support of the United States. Saudi society had not even begun its transition from tradition when the vast petroleum reservoirs were discovered. The business and political alliance between imperialism and the "traditional" ruling class was immediately sealed, thereby reinvigorating reactionary Wahhabi political Islam. For their part, the British succeeded in breaking Indian unity by convincing the Muslim leaders to create their own state, imprisoned from the very beginning in political Islam. Note that the theory by which this curiosity was legitimized—attributed to Mawdudi—had previously been fully drafted by English Orientalists in Her Majesty's service.

In the same vein, the U.S. initiative to break the united front of Asian and African states established in Bandung in 1955 led to the creation of an "Islamic Conference" immediately promoted (beginning in 1957) by Saudi Arabia and Pakistan. Political Islam penetrated into the region by this means.

The least of the conclusions that should be drawn from these observations is that political Islam is not the spontaneous product of an authentic assertion of religious conviction by the peoples in question. Political Islam was systematically constructed by imperialism and supported, of course, by obscurantist reactionary forces and subservient comprador classes. It is undeniable that the various left forces neither saw nor knew how to confront the challenge, and that is their failure.

### 4. THE DEPLOYMENT OF THE UNITED STATES' MILITARY PROJECT

The United States' project, supported to varying degrees by its subaltern European and Japanese allies, is to establish its military control over the entire world—what I have called the "extension of the Monroe Doctrine to the planet." With that in mind, the "Middle East" was chosen as the region for the "first strike" for at least four reasons: (i) it harbors the world's most abundant petroleum resources, and its direct control by the armed forces of the United States would give Washington a privileged position, placing their allies—Europe and Japan—and its potential rivals (China) in the uncomfortable position of dependence on the United States for their energy supplies; (ii) it is located at the center of the old world and facilitates the exercise of a permanent military threat against China, India, and Russia; (iii) the region is going through a period of weakness and confusion that allows the aggressor to achieve an easy victory, at least in the short term; (iv) imperialism has an unconditional ally in the region with nuclear weapons: Israel.

The developing attack has placed certain countries on the front line: Afghanistan, Iraq, Palestine, and Iran. The first three have been destroyed, and Iran is threatened with being so.

The armed diplomacy of the United States had the objective of literally destroying Iraq well before the pretext given to it on two different occasions: the invasion of Kuwait in 1990, and then after the events of September 11, cynically exploited by the Bush administration with lies worthy of Joseph Goebbels: "Repeat a lie often enough and it becomes the truth." The reason for that is quite simple and has nothing to do with any appeals for the "liberation" of the Iraqi people from Saddam Hussein's bloody dictatorship (which was real enough). Iraq possesses a large portion of the best petroleum resources in the world. What is more, Iraq had succeeded in forming a scientific and technical force that, due to its critical mass, is capable of sustaining a consistent national project. This "danger" had to be eliminated by a "preventive war" that the United States gave itself the right to wage when and where it decided, without the least respect for international law.

Beyond this blatantly obvious observation, several serious questions need to be examined: (i) Why has Washington's plan so easily appeared to be a dazzling success? (ii) What new situation has been created that now confronts the Iraqi nation? (iii) What responses have the different components of the Iraqi people given to this challenge? (iv) And what solutions can Iraqi, Arab, and international democratic and progressive forces promote?

Saddam Hussein's defeat was predictable. Faced with an enemy whose main advantage lies in its capacity to carry out genocide by aerial bombardment with impunity (pending the use of nuclear weapons), the people have only one possibly effective response: resist the invader on the ground. The Saddam regime had worked to eliminate all means of defense available to the people through the systematic destruction of all organizations, all political parties (beginning with the Communist Party) that had made the history of modern Iraq, including the Baath Party itself, which had been one of the major participants in this history. What should be surprising in these conditions is not that the Iraqi people allowed its country to be invaded without a fight or even that certain behaviors (such as its apparent participation in elections organized by the invaders or the explosion of fratricidal conflicts between Kurds, Sunni Arabs, and Shia Arabs) seemed to indicate that the defeat was possibly accepted (which is what Washington had hoped would happen), but that the resistance on the ground has strengthened every day (despite all the serious weaknesses that have been evident), that this resistance has already made it impossible to establish a regime of lackeys capable of maintaining the appearance of order, such that the failure of Washington's project has already been demonstrated.

Nevertheless, a new situation has been created by the foreign military occupation. The Iraqi nation is truly threatened because Washington, incapable of maintaining its control over the country (and pillaging its petroleum resources, which is its number one objective) through a government that is "national" in appearance only, can pursue its project only by breaking up the country. The breakup of the country into at least three states (Kurd, Sunni Arab, and Shia Arab) was, perhaps, Washington's original objective, in line with Israel (the archives will reveal the truth of this in the future). It is still the case today that the "civil war" is the card Washington plays to legitimize the continuation of its occupation. A permanent occupation was—and remains—the objective. That is the only way for Washington to guarantee its control of the oil. Certainly, no one should believe Washington's declarations of intent, of the type "we will leave the country as soon as order has been restored." Remember that the British never said that their occupation of Egypt, beginning in 1882, was ever anything other than "provisional" (it lasted until 1956!). In the meantime, of course, every day, the United States destroys by all means, including the most criminal, a little more of the country, its schools, factories, and scientific capacities.

The response of the Iraqi people to the challenge does not seem to be—at least in the short term—equal to the seriousness of the situation. That is the least one can say. What are the reasons for this? The dominant Western media keeps repeating *ad nauseam* that Iraq is an "artificial" country and that the oppressive domination of Saddam's Sunni regime over the Shias and Kurds is at the origin of the inevitable civil war (which only the continuation of the foreign occupation might be able to avert). The "resistance," in this view, is thus limited to a few pro-Saddam Islamist currents of the Sunni "triangle." It is difficult to believe that so many falsehoods can be assembled at one time.

After the First World War, the British colonialists had great difficulty in overcoming the Iraqi people's resistance. Consistent with their imperial tradition, the British fabricated an imported monarchy and a landowning class to support their power just as they gave a privileged position to Sunni Islam. But despite their constant efforts, the British failed. The Communist Party and the Baath Party made up the main organized political forces that defeated the power of the Sunni monarchy detested by everyone: Sunni, Shia, and Kurd. The violent competition between these two forces, which took center stage between 1958 and 1963, ended in a victory by the Baath Party, hailed at the time as a relief by the Western powers. Yet the Communist project could potentially have led in a democratic direction. That was not true of the Baath. A nationalist party, pan-Arab and favorable to Arab unity in principle, it admired the Prussian model for constructing German unity. It recruited in the modernist, secular petite bourgeoisie and was hostile to obscurantist expressions of religion. As could be predicted, in power it evolved into a dictatorship. Its statism was only partly anti-imperialist because, depending on the conjuncture and circumstances, a compromise could be accepted with the dominant imperialism in the region, that of the United States. This "deal" encouraged the megalomaniacal excesses of the leader, who imagined that Washington would agree to make him its main ally in the region. Washington's support of Baghdad (including the delivery of chemical weapons) in the absurd and criminal war against Iran from 1980 to 1989 seemed to lend credibility to this calculation. Saddam did not imagine that Washington would cheat, that the modernization of Iraq was unacceptable for imperialism, and that the decision to destroy the country had already been made. Saddam fell into the trap (the green light had been given to him to annex Kuwait, which was, in fact, an Iraqi province that the British imperialists had detached to make one of their oil colonies), and Iraq was subjected to ten years of sanctions aimed at battering the country to facilitate the glorious conquest by the U.S. armed forces over what remained.

One can accuse the successive Baath governments, including the last one during its period of decline under Saddam's leadership, of everything except for having stirred up confessional conflict between Sunni and Shia. Who, then, is responsible for the bloody clashes between the two communities today? Certainly, we will someday learn how the CIA (and undoubtedly the Mossad as well) organized many of these massacres. But beyond that, it is true that the political desert created by Saddam's regime, and the example he gave of using unprincipled opportunist methods to achieve his aims, encouraged candidates for government of all kinds to follow this example, often protected by the occupier. Sometimes, perhaps, these people were naive to the point of believing that they could make use of the occupier. The candidates in question, whether religious leaders (Shia or Sunni), supposed "notables" (quasi-tribal), or notoriously corrupt businessmen exported by the United States, never had any real political foothold in the country. Even the religious leaders respected by believers had no acceptable political sway over the Iraqi people. Without the void created by Saddam, their names would not even be known. Faced with this new political world made by the imperialism of liberal globalization, will other authentically popular and national, potentially democratic, political forces have the means to reconstruct themselves?

There was a time when the Iraqi Communist Party encapsulated and embodied the best of what Iraqi society could produce. It was established in all areas of the country and dominated the world of intellectuals, often of Shia origin (I note that Shiism above all produces revolutionaries and religious leaders, rarely bureaucrats or compradors!). The Communist Party was genuinely popular and anti-imperialist, not really inclined to demagogy, and potentially democratic. Is it now called to disappear from history once and for all, after the massacre of thousands of its best militants by the Baathist dictatorship, the collapse of the Soviet Union (for which it was not prepared), and the behavior of some of its intellectuals who believed that it was acceptable to return from exile as appendages of the U.S. armed forces? Unfortunately, this is not impossible, but not "inevitable," far from it.

The Kurdish question is a real one, in Iraq as well as Iran and Turkey. But on this subject also, it should be remembered that the Western powers have always cynically acted with double standards. Repression of Kurdish demands in Iraq and Iran has never reached the level of continual police and military violence as in Turkey. Neither Iran nor Iraq has ever gone as far as denying the very existence of the Kurds. Yet, as a NATO member, Turkey should always be pardoned. NATO, you will recall, is an organization of democratic nations, or so the media constantly reminds us. The eminent democrat Salazar was one of the founding members, and the Greek colonels and Turkish generals were unconditional supporters of democracy!

Iraqi popular fronts were formed around the Communist and the Baath parties in the best moments of its stormy history. Whenever such fronts exercised power, they always found common ground with the main Kurdish parties, which were always, moreover, their allies.

The "anti-Shia" and "anti-Kurd" excesses of Saddam's regime were certainly real: bombardments of the Basra region by Saddam's army after its 1990 defeat in Kuwait and use of gas against the Kurds. Such abuses came as a response to Washington's armed diplomatic maneuvers, which had mobilized sorcerer's apprentices pressured to seize the occasion. Nevertheless, Saddam's reactions were criminal and stupid, since the success of Washington's appeals was quite limited. But should we expect anything else from dictators like Saddam?

The power of the resistance to the foreign occupation, unexpected in these conditions, would seem to be a miracle. This is not really the case because the basic reality is that the Iraqi people as a whole (Arab and Kurd, Sunni and Shia) detest the occupiers and are quite well aware of its daily crimes (assassinations, bombings, massacres, torture). We should then be able to envisage a "United National Resistance Front" (call it whatever you like) proclaiming itself as such, publicizing the list of organizations and parties that constitute it and their common program. Up until now, this has not been the case, mostly because of the destruction of the social and political fabric caused by the successive dictatorships of Saddam and the occupiers. But whatever the reasons, this weakness is a serious impediment that facilitates divide-and-rule policies, encourages the opportunists to become collaborators, and generates confusion about the objectives of the liberation.

Who will succeed in overcoming these barriers? The Communists should be well placed to do so. Already militants—on the ground—are differentiating themselves from the "leaders" (that is, the only ones known to the dominant media) who, not knowing which way the wind is blowing, attempt to give a semblance of legitimacy to their support for the collaborationist government by pretending to complement it with armed resistance! But many other political forces could, in the circumstances, take decisive action toward forming such a united front.

It remains the case that, despite its "weaknesses," the Iraqi people's resistance has already defeated (politically if not yet militarily) Washington's project. This is precisely what worries the Atlanticists in the European Union, faithful allies of the United States. The subaltern associates of the United States today fear the latter's defeat because that would strengthen the capacity of peoples in the South to force globalized transnational capital from the imperialist triad to respect the interests of the nations and peoples of Asia, Africa, and Latin America.

The Iraqi resistance has made proposals that would make it possible to get out of the impasse and assist the United States to withdraw from the trap. It proposes: (i) formation of a transitional administration with the support of the UN Security Council; (ii) immediate cessation of resistance activities, as well as military and police operations by occupation forces; (iii) the withdrawal of all foreign military and civilian authorities within six months. The details of these proposals were published in the January 2006 issue of the prestigious Arab journal *Al Mustaqbal Al Arabi*, published in Beirut. The European media treated this message with absolute silence. Such a response is clear proof of the solidarity of the imperialist partners. Democratic and progressive forces in Europe have the duty to dissociate themselves from this imperialist policy and support the proposals of the Iraqi resistance. Leaving the Iraqi people to confront its enemy alone is not an acceptable option. It reinforces the dangerous idea that there is nothing to expect from the West and its peoples and consequently encourages unacceptable—even criminal—excesses in the activities of certain resistance movements.

The sooner the foreign occupation troops leave the country, and the stronger the support from democratic forces in Europe and throughout the world to the Iraqi people, the greater will be the possibilities for a better future for this martyred people. The longer the occupation lasts, the more dismal the future that follows its inevitable end.

## 5. THE PALESTINIAN QUESTION

The Palestinian people have, since the Balfour Declaration during the First World War, been the victim of a colonization project by a foreign people that has treated it like white settler colonialists in the United States treated "redskins." This is true whether one cares to acknowledge it or pretends to be ignorant of it. This project has always been supported unconditionally by the dominant imperialist power in the region (yesterday Great Britain, today the United States), because the alien state established with that support can only ever be the ally, also unconditional, of the interventions required for the continual submission of the Arab Middle East to imperialist capitalism.

This is completely obvious for all peoples of Africa and Asia. Consequently, the affirmation and defense of Palestinian rights spontaneously unite the peoples on these two continents. However, in Europe, the "Palestinian question" causes division, resulting from the confusions fostered by Zionist ideology, which is often met with favorable support.

Today, more than ever, in conjunction with the deployment of the American "Greater Middle East" project, the rights of the Palestinian people have been abolished. Yet the PLO had accepted the Oslo and Madrid plans and the road map designed by Washington. It is Israel that has openly disowned its signature and continues to implement an even more ambitious expansion plan. The PLO has consequently been weakened: public opinion can rightly reproach it for having naively believed in the sincerity of its opponents. The support by the occupation authorities for its Islamist adversary (Hamas), initially, at least, and the spread of the Palestinian administration's corrupt practices on which the "donors"—the World Bank, Europe, NGOs—are silent, if they are not participants, had to lead to the electoral victory of Hamas, an additional pretext immediately cited to justify unconditional alignment with Israel's policies, "whatever they are"!

The Zionist colonial project has always been a threat, beyond Palestine, for neighboring Arab peoples. Its ambitions to annex the Egyptian Sinai and its effective annexation of the Syrian Golan bear witness to this. A particular place is given to Israel in the project for a "Greater Middle East," to its regional nuclear weapons monopoly and its role as a "required partner" (under the fallacious pretext that Israel has "technological competence" of which no Arab people is capable! Here we have the obligatory racism!).

It is not my intention here to analyze the complex interactions between the resistance struggles against Zionist colonial expansion and the political conflicts and choices in Lebanon and Syria. The Baathist governments of Syria have, in their own way, resisted the demands of the imperialist powers and Israel. That this resistance has also served to legitimize more questionable ambitions (control of Lebanon) is certainly not debatable. Moreover, Syria has carefully chosen its allies from among the "least dangerous" in Lebanon. The Lebanese Communist Party had originally organized resistance to Israeli incursions into southern Lebanon (including water diversion). The Syrian, Lebanese, and Iranian governments cooperated closely to destroy this "dangerous base" and substitute Hezbollah for it. The assassination of Rafic Hariri obviously gave an opportunity for the imperialist powers (led by the United States, with France following behind) to intervene with a double objective: to force Damascus to align with the group of vassalized Arab states (Egypt, Saudi Arabia)—or, failing that, liquidate the vestiges of the degenerated Baathist government—and dismantle what remains of the ability to resist Israeli incursions by demanding Hezbollah's "disarmament." Rhetoric about "democracy" can usefully be called on in this context.

THIS SUMMARY, QUITE UNREMARKABLE for the Arab reader, supplements what I wrote in the first volume of my memoirs concerning the positions taken in May 1948 and subsequently by the Arab states and the main political forces at that time (the nationalists, Islamists, and communists). It is up to the reader to take all this into account.

*These Memoirs*

I experienced the Bandung Conference as an Egyptian, first as a student in Paris and then as a functionary in Cairo.

My analyses never led me to underestimate the responsibilities of the established governments, particularly that of Nasser. Quite the contrary, I attributed decisive responsibility for the failures to the inadequacies of these governments. Without false modesty, I will say that the book that I wrote in 1960, published under an assumed name, Hassan Riad, was prescient.[14] I envisaged that the regime would pass away with a return to peripheral capitalism. The *infitah* gave concrete form to my prediction ten years later.

My return to the Egyptian political scene through my participation in the Egyptian Social Forums beginning in 2002 led me to formulate critical positions with regard to the false alternative of political Islam or "democracy."

Needless to say, my positions are not always shared. Today, political conflicts in Egypt and in the region as a whole involve three sets of forces: those that claim to adhere to the nationalist past (but are in reality only the degraded and corrupt inheritors of the bureaucracies from the national-populist era); those that follow political Islam; and those that are attempting to form around "democratic" demands compatible with liberal economic management. None of these forces is acceptable to a left concerned about the interests of the working classes and the nation. In fact, the interests of the comprador classes associated with the imperialist system are expressed through these three tendencies. U.S. diplomacy works to keep these three irons in the fire, hoping to benefit from their conflicts. Attempting to become "involved" in these conflicts by allying with one or another of these forces (choosing the established governments to avoid the worst—political Islam—or seeking to ally with the latter to get rid of the governments) is destined to fail. The left must assert itself by becoming involved in struggles to defend: (i) the economic and social interests of the working classes, (ii) democracy, and (iii) the assertion of national sovereignty. What is more, all these struggles should be viewed as inseparable.

The "Greater Middle East" region is now central in the conflict between the imperialist hegemon and the peoples of the entire world. To defeat the project of Washington's establishment is the condition for the possibility of successful advances in any region of the world. Otherwise, all these advances will remain extremely vulnerable. This does not mean that the importance of struggles conducted in other areas of the world—Europe, Latin America, elsewhere—can be underestimated. It only means that they should be placed within a global perspective that contributes to Washington's defeat in the region it has chosen for its criminal first strike.

Consequently, the insistence that I place on continuing debates within the Arab left, in particular its Marxist wing, goes without saying.

In Egypt, in the 1950s, I was in favor of Arab unity—like all my communist comrades— without being a "nationalist" (in the Arabic sense of *qawmi*), without accepting its stupidity ("Arabness flows through the blood of Arabs . . ."), without sharing the superficial but common opinion that the division of the Arab world into distinct states was mainly, if not exclusively, the result of "imperialist plots," etc. Rather, we simply thought that liberation and social progress required in our time the construction of large entities, and that the unity of language and culture offered to Arabs a historical opportunity that should be seized.[15]

ONCE AGAIN, I REFER the reader to the first volume of these memoirs for a narrative of my participation in Egyptian political life during the Nasser era. Later, I shall give an account of my activities in post-Nasser Egypt up to the current revolution, which erupted in 2011.

## MY ACTIVITIES IN THE MAGHREB AND MASHREQ

I began my discoveries of the Arab world beyond Egypt with the countries of the Maghreb, which very few Arabs from the Mashreq knew at that time. Within the context of my teaching at the IDEP, I gave myself the objective of closely studying the three experiences of Algeria, Morocco, and Tunisia, still in the initial stages of their development in the middle of the 1960s.

### *Tunisia and Morocco*

It was, I believe, in 1963 that the first opportunity arose to visit the Maghreb. The Plan administration in Tunisia wanted to establish a new framework for its national accounts. It confided this task to two experts: a Syrian statistician, Nazhat Chalaq, and me (recommended by SEEF). We fulfilled our mission, properly I believe, in stays of fifteen days that, for me, were spread over several months. Hussein Zhall and other colleagues at the Plan assisted us with great effectiveness, friendship, and Arab hospitality. Chalaq was a very talented statistician who was able to uncover the contradictions and absurdities in the figures submitted by various people. Having a good sense of humor, he said to me one day: "They cheat everyone, but not to the same extent; the President will have to decide by decree the proportion of compulsory cheating for all services." We pushed the fun to the point of including this proposal in our final report! That report was very well received, and its reception reassured us about the Tunisian administrators' sense of humor.

My stays in Tunis allowed me to meet many intellectuals, professors, and political leaders of the Tunisian left. (These same intellectuals, with well-established reputations, later led teams in the TWF.) Students also asked me from time to time to give them a lecture, a request I never refused. But I did not meet the "big leaders" of the Destourian system, those of the Bourguibist camp or those of the Ben Salahist and Ben Youssefist camps. I met Ben Salah much later, after his release from prison. I only knew of the system's internal contradictions through their interpretation by the left opposition.

Obviously, I visited Tunisia subsequently on numerous occasions and I followed its change of direction—the failure of its attempted insertion into the international system via a strategy of welcoming outsourcing operations in free trade zones—and the rise of fundamentalist Islam. Tunisian society remains, despite everything, one of the least backward in the Arab and Muslim world in an important area: the status of women. In the long term, I believe this advantage is decisive. Habib Ben Ali Bourguiba should be credited with this advance, whatever one thinks of his—quite limited—political views, his illusions concerning the West, particularly the United States, his penchant to autocracy, and perhaps his unbearable vanity. That certainly does not suffice to excuse Ben Ali's odious regime of its everyday villainy.

I began to have a small reputation as a good technician at creating a framework for national accounts tailored to planning needs. This reputation is probably what lay behind the invitation, circa 1964, from the Moroccan Minister of the Economy (or Planning?) Driss Slaoui. I had known the young Slaoui, a communist student in Paris. He had put a lot of water in his wine, but remained, in his own way, faithful to his youthful ideals. The Moroccan comrades with whom I have spent time since this first opportunity, followed by repeated visits, are friends I respect. But despite my respect for the activities of these militants, their party (the PPS) does not appear to me to have succeeded in going beyond the limitations of a narrow elite circle lacking solid grassroots support.

Militants of the left-wing of the USFP—during the heyday of this party— certainly benefited from a much wider popular audience. But all those whom I met left me with the feeling that they would only move beyond the limitations of Nasserist/Boumediennist/Baathist populism with great difficulty. This turned out to be the case, while they gradually and inevitably slid to the right, participating in the great game of the monarchy anxious to expand the system's legitimacy by integrating—beyond the traditional classes that have formed its historical base (the Fassi and Soussi merchants, landed and tribal aristocracies, more recently the new comprador bourgeoisie)—the middle strata of the technocracy and bureaucracy and the urban and rural petite bourgeoisies. From that, there followed the anger and revolt of the new generation in the 1970s, the March 22 movement, and what emerged from various organizations. Their leftism was certainly commensurate with their exceptional courage.

The case of the Western Sahara shuffled the cards even more. The PPS and USFP rallied to the "Green March" bloc, as is well known. Concerning the Western Sahara, my personal viewpoint is not widely shared. Invited by leftist Mauritanians to explain my view of the problem, they suggested that I go say these things "at a higher level," using their connections with the government. The Mauritanian president thus invited me to meet with him. My thesis was simple. We all, I said, are in favor of Arab unity. Then why create an additional Arab state, the Sahrawi Republic? Would this not be tantamount to allowing a small local ruling class to monopolize the earnings from phosphate exports? And if this region has to become part of an existing Arab country, is not Mauritania the best choice? The tribes of Western Sahara are the same ones found in Mauritania. Should not an attempt be made to convince Polisario and the Mauritanian government to make a joint declaration to this effect? And at the same time, why not go further and propose a confederation of Morocco, Algeria, and Mauritania, and begin serious negotiations to provide substance to that proposition? I am sure that the peoples of the three countries would be more than favorable, even enthusiastic. The Mauritanian president seemed to be convinced by these views, although they came too late since the Madrid accords had already been signed, in which Morocco and Mauritania agreed to share the Western Sahara. Some time later, the president perished in an airplane accident. To others, I said: Why don't parties, organizations, and important persons on the left in the three countries adopt this common position? They would be understood and would gain the support of their peoples. None of them would do it. Why?

The Algerian government at the time harbored extravagant expansionist ambitions. It treated its recent Mauritanian ally like a semi-colony. I heard Algerian leaders with my own ears refer to the Mauritanian president as the "*wali* [custodian/helper] of Nouakchott." I laid into them. "Pardon me? Is that how you believe you will achieve Arab unity? Moreover, the Algerian model of which you are so proud is beginning to run out of steam. Is the question of the Western Sahara the major problem for the Algerian people today? Is it not the main priority of the Algerian left [because to cap it all, the statements mentioned above were made by important figures in the Algerian left] to have a closer look at this model and step up efforts to resolve the impasses in which it resulted?"

I never made any public declarations or wrote anything about this affair because I thought that would only throw oil on the fire as long as the leftist forces in the three countries refused to assume their responsibility. But this example illustrates two realities, in my opinion. The first is that the Algerian left had decided to align itself unreservedly with Boumediennism, of which it was no more than one wing. It subsequently had to pay dearly when the regime's legitimacy eroded and then collapsed, to the immediate advantage of the Islamists. In the eyes of the working classes, the Algerian Communist Party did not appear to have a project different from that of the FLN. The second is that the division among Arabs is not only or even mainly the result of manipulation by outside forces. It is the product of the established ruling classes and the opposing forces, of their egotistical ambitions and narrow-minded views.

I subsequently visited Morocco and Algeria on multiple occasions. I must say that I have unfortunately not seen any palpable progress made in any of these areas. There has been no self-critique.

Here is another interesting story. I was invited to Rabat around 1974 to "assist" the Secretaries-General of the Arab League and the OAU in negotiating some difficult issues poisoning Arab-African relations. The OAU had thought of me as a gesture of trust, recognizing that I was no chauvinist and that I placed a united front of Third World countries confronting imperialism above their internal conflicts. I therefore accepted. I listened to each Secretary-General make his case on Eritrea, Sudan, Chad, and Saharan Niger. I presented my personal analyses of these questions in the most neutral language possible, emphasizing the common interests of the peoples concerned and principles for solutions that could strengthen their united front. What I proposed, in short, was: formal respect for borders, democratization of all the countries concerned, complete respect for the rights of minorities, and rejection of any call for outside help in settling these problems. I would like to point out that neither one of the two Secretaries-General had thought of the question of democratization. I stressed the point by saying that, in my humble opinion, none of these conflicts would find a solution without democracy. I am not sure whether I was convincing or that I had any influence, even in the smallest amount, on their future behavior.

*Algeria*

I visited Algeria several times during the 1960s at the invitation either of the Ministry of Planning (notably by Minister Abdallah Khoja and his assistant Remili, later by Minister Hidouci) or universities (by the rector Ahmad Mahiou). Always the same topic: they wanted my opinion on the Plan. I must say that I saw nothing there that went beyond nationalist populism. That was not always easy to explain. The Algerian leadership—many friends among them—was justifiably proud of the glorious struggle led by the FLN. But this pride diminished their critical sense, above all when—this was the case for many—they had only participated in this struggle from afar.

Three major problems worried me. First problem: the attraction of the poorly studied Soviet model of industrialization—with few connections to agricultural development, the primary priority—financed by petroleum revenues, designed by pure technocrats indifferent to the political and social dimensions of choices, poorly justified, among other things, by the theory of "industrializing industries" (a rationalization of the Soviet model that Mao's work "On the Ten Major Relationships" had, in my opinion, destroyed from top to bottom). Second problem: the rapid erosion of vague democratic impulses and the growing rhetoric against the "utopia of self-management," etc. The 1965 Charter appeared to everyone—including the left of the old Communist Party—to be perfect. For me it only reproduced, often to the letter, the Nasserism of 1961. But to say too much would be mistaken for "Egyptian arrogance." Third problem: the fragility of the Algerian nation. For me, that was obvious. Compared to Morocco and Tunisia, which were states before colonization, the Algerian nation was produced by the war of liberation. There is no shame in that. But its legitimacy was consequently fragile and linked to the legitimacy of the FLN government, the populist limitations of which I could clearly see. Subsequent events, with the war unleashed by the Islamists, have unfortunately proved me right. With the collapse of the FLN, basic national solidarity is now called into question. But there again, to say too much might be taken as a reminder of French colonialist rhetoric in which the Algerian nation did not exist. The language question, often cited, is only the tip of the iceberg. In this area, the Algerian government's choice was disastrous: French for the elites, open to modernity and technology, and Arabic for the people, with education handed to the masters of old Koranic schools and supervised by no-less-backward graduates of al-Azhar. (It is a myth that the French wanted to extirpate Islam and thus fought against the Koranic schools. The French maintained the sharia for the native inhabitants; the FLN had attempted to attenuate its scope. By demanding complete respect for the sharia, the Islamists quite simply want everyone to return to the colonial-era practice!) The result is well known. It happened that I was able to assess the extent of the disaster when, invited to make a lecture at a university, I noted that the "Arabic speakers" did not know how to express anything that even remotely made any sense. Words followed one another without any concern for the meaning they carried.

In 1972, IDEP organized one of its large seminars in Algiers. The authorities, both state and university, welcomed us with great pomp by allowing us to use the National Assembly building, whereupon I commented that, for once, it would act as a forum for real debates!

Following this seminar, President Houari Boumedienne received me. It was a long meeting; two hours, I believe. He wanted to talk above all about international and Arab politics, criticizing the Rogers Plan for the Middle East, outlining his view of a "new international economic order" (to which the Non-Aligned Movement gave concrete expression in the declaration of 1974). I was convinced on these areas and attempted to move the discussion toward Algeria's internal problems and my three reasons for worry. This visibly bothered the president, despite my diplomacy—I accused no one, cited no name, took the precaution of first speaking of the "positive aspects" and the "objective difficulties" before broaching the sensitive points. There was nothing in what he told me that was not already known from public speeches. I left convinced that the Algerian government would not find a way out of the foreseeable impasses and would end up falling to the right.

I followed with much sorrow the deterioration of the Algerian system after Boumedienne's death, which had maintained the appearances of a solid construction, but was in fact rotten to the core. Chadli Bendjedid and his senseless opportunist opening to compradors and vulgar excesses prepared the worst: the illusory riposte of the FIS's electoral victory and the criminal excesses of the 1990s. This is a suspect confrontation between two partners who are only competing for comprador government and to be alone in benefiting from it: the old FLN without legitimacy and its generals on one side, and the FIS on the other. The latter was initially able to capitalize on the anger of the working classes and mobilize its minions recruited from among the young *hittistes* (the name given in Algeria to unemployed youth without any prospects). Favored by depoliticization—the usual crime of populist regimes—and supervised by the "Afghans" (the criminals trained in Pakistan and Afghanistan in CIA camps financed by Saudi Arabia), the "Islamists" wreaked the havoc with which we are all familiar. Yasmina Khadra's crime novels are, from this point of view, the best analysis of Algeria's tragedy. Are the Islamists now worn down by the resistance to the former FLN system and the successive maneuvers of Liamine Zéroual (after the elimination of Mohamed Boudiaf—we are still not sure who assassinated him, undoubtedly with the complicity of unknown local and foreign intelligence services) and, today, Abdelaziz Bouteflika? Undoubtedly, putting an end to the killings has become the first priority. But what should be done after that? Here again the historical Algerian left and its intellectuals have a large responsibility. An objective terrain existed, and still exists, to form a "third force" that rejects the Mafia-style management of the former FLN apparatus and the identical one of the Islamists. But this third force has never succeeded in forming. Leadership infighting has probably played a role in this miserable failure. I nevertheless believe that, behind this, there are more fundamental weaknesses, among others the absence of an approach that is able to incorporate the need for democratization of society into the requirements of a socialist renewal. Here again the ideological confusion of nationalist-populist circles, impressed with the Soviet model and their later absurd support for "liberal" solutions, are behind this powerlessness.

I met President Ahmed Ben Bella and his spouse only after his release from prison, rejuvenated by his active participation in the movement to revive worldwide struggle for "another world" freed from globalized imperialist capitalism.

Algeria, Tunisia, and Morocco are quite different in all kinds of ways. And yet, the three systems do converge in a certain way. At least, that was the conclusion of the book I wrote based on my Maghrebi experiences.[16]

## Mauritania

I particularly like the Sahara—its expanses are more varied than those who do not know it imagine it to be; the aridity of its climate; and the elegance, pride, and hospitality of its peoples. I am lucky that my wife, Isabelle, shares these tastes. We thus never passed up the opportunity to travel through these spaces in Mauritania, Algeria, Niger, and Egypt.

Our first travels through the great desert led us from Saint Louis in Senegal to Atar and Chinguetti in the north of Mauritania. There we became acquainted with this "chimerical people"—as one of their finest sons, Abdel Wedoud Ould Cheikh, sociologist and friend, describes them. Invited on several occasions by teachers and students in this country, I came to appreciate their lively intelligence and generous hospitality. I carefully preserve the beautiful chests and *bubus* that were given to me on these occasions.

I verified the accuracy of what Caillé had written on these astonishing tribes. Having arrived at Boutilimit at sunset, ready to sleep, one of the local marabouts welcomed us to his large tent and ordered that a sheep be made ready for our meal. Obviously, that meant that the barbecued sheep would not be ready until two o'clock in the morning! But of course it was impossible to refuse the gesture of hospitality. While waiting, stretched out on the carpets, we attempted to sleep a little. A Maure woman, who saw to our needs, woke me up by pinching my big toe to ask me this astonishing question, in good Hassaniya Arabic: "You know the world, can you tell me how it is?" I no longer know what I tried to splutter in an attempt to satisfy her curiosity—unsuccessfully. In the Maure tribes, there is strict monogamy (the Koran is not interpreted as authorizing polygamy since the condition of equal affection is impossible) and it is the women who are literate—and who transmit knowledge and poetry—while the illiterate men (except for the marabouts) are only there to wield the sword.

At Mederdra, we stopped to drink tea at an administrative camp. The man who prepared it did not have the demeanor of a servant. He was dignified and elegant. Isabelle asked him straight out if he were a servant. No, he said, I am not the servant for this camp. He was an army officer who had participated in a minor attempted coup d'état at Néma (in eastern Mauritania) in 1961.

We had heard echoes of this event in Mali. Some officers, who considered the government to be neocolonial, had attempted to seize the fort at Néma to trigger a general revolt in the country. They resorted to limited means and a naive approach that condemned them to failure. This officer was condemned to death—a sentence commuted, after several years of solitary confinement, to exile in this camp, lost in the sands. We offered to help him escape. "We can take you along in our jeep. We cross the Senegal River in a canoe to a village and then you are free." He was tempted, but upon reflection said, "No, I shall remain in my country." On leaving, we drove very slowly, exchanging repeated gestures of farewell with him, if, by any chance, he was tempted, until he closed the gate to the camp.

Mauritania is not the paradise of the desert. It is, like Sudan, the link and frontier of confrontation between the Arab and black African peoples. The Maure society is slaveholding. This must be said and it must not be accepted. Half of the population is made up of Haratins, descendants of slaves captured in the raids to the south. Brutalized, condemned to perform the hardest labor, despised, and insulted, their fate in no way reflects the soothing rhetoric on "domestic slavery" by which the leaders of the modern state and the intellectuals at their service attempt to justify the supposed "vestiges."

Life in the border region is not as idyllic as the calm countryside of the Senegal River and its Toucouleur and Soninke villages suggest. The river here, as is often the case, is not the border between peoples, but a means of communication. The region is populated on both banks by non-Arab peoples, although highly Islamized for almost ten centuries (unlike Sudan). The Toucouleurs, who in the seventeenth century created their "Islamic republic" (and who themselves practiced slavery within their society, but refused to participate in the slave trade outside it), had centuries earlier produced the glorious Moroccan dynasty of the Almoravids. The ruling classes of the old Moorish country and those of the Senegal River country frequently warred with one another, but they mutually respected each other in their own way. The new "Arab-Berber" (in fact, almost completely Arabic-speaking) ruling classes of modern Mauritania are quite simply racist. This sad reality can be verified over and over. At Boutilimit, the Divisional Commander was Toucouleur (the Mauritanian administration offers a few gestures of concession of this kind for external use). "You are not going to pay a visit to this Negro!" the Maures said to us. "Yes, we are going to do this." And it was at his house that we slept, like it should be. There are principles with which we do not compromise. The Maures accompanied us to the bottom of the sand hill, on top of which the administrative center had been built. But they refused to go any further. We took our luggage and carried it ourselves. Disillusioned, the Commandant said upon receiving us: "How can I carry out my duties in this country?"

The coexistence of the two peoples has been seriously called into question since the serious events of 1988, which led to ethnic massacres in Mauritania and Senegal, and the flight of tens of thousands of peasants from the north bank of the river. Who was behind these massacres? As almost always, they were not "spontaneous," and different peoples forced to live side by side do not generally hate each other to the point of killing each other, even when they harbor serious prejudices that sustain strong barriers in their everyday relationships. The shops of the Maure artisans and merchants, found everywhere in Senegal, were pillaged; their owners were often massacred, not by the "crowd," but by well-organized groups, transported by trucks from elsewhere to the places where the violent incidents took place. A lot of the Senegalese I know protected these unfortunate victims. In Mauritania, well-organized groups massacred the Senegalese and blacks of the river region. Who was behind these organizations? If it were not the established authorities, it could very well have been the segments of the ruling classes, hoping in this way to destabilize the governments and force them to share the advantages of rule, or maybe even replace them. As the African proverb says: "The fish rots from the head down." Fratricidal conflicts are rarely the spontaneous result of unrest among the people. It is almost always the ruling classes, or their segments, that organize such conflicts. That they are exploiting objective realities, more or less poorly managed by established authorities, should never lead us to overlook the strategies of those who are directly responsible for these conflicts. It is true in this case, just as elsewhere in Africa, Asia, or, of course, Europe. In any case, the flight of peasants from the river served well the interests of a new class benefiting from irrigated land, which they seized and wanted to empty of its population to develop agribusiness supported by foreign lenders and the World Bank. These beneficiaries, of course, are all from the Maure (all Arabs) and Senegalese (not necessarily originally from the region) bureaucracies. In some respects, they are as thick as thieves.

### *The Sudan*

A similar tragedy, but on an altogether different scale, has bathed Sudan in blood for thirty years.

I did not visit Sudan, unfortunately, but was only in Khartoum three or four times after 1973, when the situation permitted during one of the short interludes between two dictators. This was always at the invitation of the Sudanese left, the Communist Party and the Popular Front—all were very active at the University, and also in trade unions and other working-class organizations. But they were always victims of the electoral democracy advocated by the popular uprisings they had led. Control of the electoral majorities by the traditional leadership of the Ansar Mahdists inevitably led to the same people in government and then the same chaos led to a coup d'état, be it military, Islamist, or a combination of the two. But what can be done? How can these traditional authorities be abolished and, at the same time, the norms of democracy, even a revolutionary one, still be respected? This was always the unending topic of my very long discussion sessions—the Sudanese can spend the entire night talking—with a large number of the country's militants. I must confess that Sudan exerts an irresistible attraction over me because of its completely successful mixture of Arab (particularly Egyptian) and African cultures.

The question of the civil war was also always at the center of our discussions. And when the circumstances—that is, in moments when a democratic government was in power at Khartoum—allowed the opening of negotiations with the rebels from the south (which often took place in Addis Ababa), I did not hesitate to respond to the confidence the two parties placed in me, not to participate (in what capacity?), but to monitor their progress. The peoples of the south obviously not only have the right, but also have reason to revolt. Democrats in the north share their views. Consequently, the two parties, when they met, really got on well and agreement was sincere. But no agreement could ever be implemented because, each time, the military and the Islamists violently overthrew the democratic government and restarted their war. The Islamists carry total responsibility for the disaster.

This is first of all a disaster for Sudan, which, thanks to the Islamists, no longer exists. Their war exhausted the country's economy, despite the immense financial support received from Saudi Arabia. Consequently, it is no longer only the south that has rebelled; it is the entire country, from Darfur in the west to Kassala in the east. But what is important to these idiotic fanatics is that they can prohibit beer in Khartoum, cut off the hands of small thieves (but not the biggest ones), impose the veil on young girls, etc. Their leader, Hassan al-Turabi, which the Western media are pleased to present as an "intellectual," belongs rather to the group of government criminals. It is amusing to note that his name in Arabic—if a short "a" is substituted for the pronunciation of the long "a"—means "gravedigger." That is what he is called in Sudan.

Sudan's destruction suits the dominant powers in the world and regional systems quite well. For the United States, Sudan is "too large." In fact, for Washington, all countries in the world are too large, except for the United

States. As is well known, the war stopped work on the Jonglei Canal, on which the future of Egypt and northern Sudan depends, however. I am perfectly aware that some environmental movements condemn in principle all major infrastructure projects. In the first volume of my memoirs, I said what I thought of these simplifications concerning the Aswan High Dam.

## *The Gulf Countries*

I also know quite well the countries of the Arab Mashreq. I do not have much to say about the Gulf, which I visited in 1971 and 1974. Kuwait and the Emirates are not nations or even countries. I see them rather as supermarkets. In Kuwait, I met only Egyptians, Palestinians, Syrians, and Lebanese. The native inhabitants pay, but do not work. One day in Dubai, I got the crazy idea to stroll through the city before the meeting I was to attend. Upon entering a telephone store, I saw perhaps three thousand models (a figure provided by the Indian owner, proud of his den) displayed on five rows of shelving in the 100 square meters of the shop. I had neither the need nor desire to buy anything. Later I was told: "No, no, you don't go into a store in that manner. You go with a precise list of everything you want to buy, model X, type Y, color, etc. Obviously, you will find it." The cities of the Gulf are, of course, places where you die of boredom.

Despite the complete stupidity of these U.S. protectorates of the Gulf, there are, all the same, Bedouins capable of making a critical assessment of the situation. What is the future? The few intellectuals from the region deserve admiration for their courage. It is said that things are changing and praise for Dubai's "success" is making headlines. Looking a little closer, I was not convinced. Certainly, there are lively business activities, choice of the city as headquarters for multinational corporations (freed, consequently, from any control), tourism for the rich (for me the place is too boring to be worth the trouble!), skyscrapers, and luxury villas. But there is nothing to indicate any inventive capacity. Dubai remains an opulent relay for a globalization shaped by others.

Bahrain is certainly more interesting. This Arab-Persian bazaar has an ancient history, and while the vestiges of the Qarmatian Revolution—a Muslim millenarian communism—have disappeared, perhaps it has left mental traces that can explain the active political life that characterizes the country, which is quite exceptional in the region.

I was never curious to visit Saudi Arabia, which is the height of horror for me. I know that this country, which presumes to give moral lessons to the entire world, imports half (yes, half—50 percent) of the world's production of pornography. The French sociologist Jean-Louis Boutillier, a friend of great humor, told me about how evenings are spent there: in groups of men (and separately women) seated before five porn movies playing at the same time. I'll pass over the rest.

The south of the Arabian Peninsula is quite different. True societies are found there.

En route to Karachi in 1975, we made a stop for three days in Muscat. It was a difficult but amusing entry into the country. The Dhofar war was in full swing and the Sultanate's English police had undoubtedly made up long lists of undesirable Arabs. The police officer seized my passport, called his supervisor, and told me to wait. While waiting for them to make their decision—after many calls to the Interior Ministry, no doubt—I explained to Isabelle that if they wanted to turn us back, they had a good pretext. Isabelle had no visa on her French passport (as an Egyptian, I did not need one, in principle). I explained to her that she should keep silent about her feminism, remain seated, keep her head covered with a scarf for the occasion, look at her toes, not utter a sound, and refrain from answering anyone who came to speak to her. The cop returned and said: "Go, everything is fine." I thought for a moment, "Do I take out Isabelle's passport?" Then I had a brilliant idea. I took out my identity card and, in the part called "Observations," I wrote in Arabic in this order: *chantatan wa zawja* (two suitcases and one wife!). I got Isabelle's attention with a "psst" and summoned her with my finger. She rose, picked up the two suitcases, and without lifting her head, followed me with small steps, staying behind me as I walked with my head held high. We left the airport, got into a taxi, and then burst out laughing. We fooled them!

*Yemen*

I am not familiar with the former South Yemen, although I have met many political figures of the exceptional left in which we had invested much hope and that I discussed in *Re-Reading the Postwar Period*.[17] Nevertheless, I know North Yemen quite well, having been invited on two occasions (1988 and 1994), after the end of the war and the Egyptian intervention, by the rector of Sana'a University, Abdel Aziz Al-Maqaleh. Everyone knows the superb architecture of Yemeni cities, its mountainous countryside (similar to that of Ethiopia), and even the custom of chewing *qat*. I was invited every day to participate in interesting and intelligent afternoon gatherings. A meeting sometimes brought together men only, or sometimes exclusively women, or even a mixed group (and I was assured that there was nothing exceptional or modern in that). One of the invitees would make a—sometimes lengthy—presentation on a subject that was then freely discussed by the others while chewing *qat* for three or four hours. I was invited to begin the discussions with a presentation on important topics, such as what is socialism; imperialism today; the Arab nation and its problems. I must say that the quite lively discussions revealed unexpected levels of knowledge and thought. Fahima Charaffeddine, who had been invited at the same time as I was, and some other leftist Arab intellectuals, such as the Syrian Issam al-Zaim who worked at that time in Sana'a, confirmed my conclusions: this poor country is not as "backward" as is often believed. In that way, it is just like Ethiopia. Of course, neither I nor the other non-Yemenis could chew with the diligence of the natives, who finished by consuming a bunch big enough to serve a horse. Regular consumption of *qat* ends up deforming the jaws and mouth, changing the cheeks into veritable balls. We were content then to taste the *qat*.

Yemeni hospitality made it possible for me to visit the entire country. I even insisted on going to see the ruins of the ancient port of Moka, which had had its glory days in history. "What a strange idea," said both Fahima, whom I had involved in this adventure, and our Yemeni guide, a professor. We descended from the superb mountains with a delightful climate to low-lying lands, humid and hot. We ultimately discovered that there was nothing left of the vestiges of Moka, just a small square surrounded by wires where archaeologists worked on an ungrateful soil in which they had discovered nothing. Fahima, an elegant Lebanese, had not at all appreciated this little excursion. I, being stubborn, did not regret it since I had seen the site of Moka all the same!

My visit to Yemen helped me to understand the country's importance in Arab history. There were two questions that I always asked and to which I never found answers. Why do the Saudis fear the Yemenis so much? The former are rich whereas the latter are poor. Why do so many Arabs from Morocco to Egypt to Iraq claim that their ancestors came from Yemen? The answer, which several historians offered, but not completely convincingly, in my opinion, is simple. In the entire Arabian peninsula, Yemen is the only area organized as an actual society. Its healthy climate allows for better demographic growth, and every five hundred years or so in ancient times, Yemenis were forced to leave en masse, to emigrate as conquerors. They formed Ethiopia, which shares its language with the ancient Semitic languages of southern Arabia. They provided the largest Arab armies of Islam. The Saudis fear them. They fear their resolution, courage, and capacity for organization.

Upon returning to Sana'a, I was given the opportunity to discuss at length the country's political prospects. Yemeni leaders were strongly critical of the Egyptian intervention, with good arguments. Unfortunately, the problem was not only the well-known arrogance of petite-bourgeois officers—contemptuous toward this "illiterate" people and busy making money by any means to furnish their Cairo apartment—but also, beyond that, the incoherence of Nasser's strategy, not knowing which way to go in relations with the Saudis, the product of a mixture of authentic progressive intentions, useless and absurd expansionist aims, and poor-quality execution. Yemenis—at least those I met—certainly did not come to "anti-Egyptian" conclusions; on the contrary, they remained admirers of Egypt and Nasser, and supporters of Arab unity. But they thought they would not have done any worse acting alone. I believe they were right, knowing that what they did could only be a beginning of modernization, and hardly more. But were they aware of these limitations? It is difficult to say. The imitation of Muammar Gaddafi's populist model through the General People's Congress worried me. There were words, many words, quickly described as "socialist." The progressives among these leaders and militants from the north counted a lot on the support that unity with the south would provide. Subsequent developments proved that the weaknesses of the south's progressive political forces largely quashed these hopes.

### *Iraq, Lebanon, Syria, and Jordan*

I was only in Iraq once—in Baghdad, which I did not leave, to participate in a pan-Arab meeting. That was at the beginning of the Saddam dictatorship in 1980. We spoke freely about the problems on the meeting's agenda, with some prudence as to the vocabulary used. At the back of the hall, four Iraqi participants, with bushy moustaches (I never, or almost never, saw Iraqi men without a moustache; the exceptions stood out) sweated and labored to take complete notes of everything that was said. "Quite figurative" characters, as my friend the Brazilian painter Tiberio would say. I asked to speak. "I see that our brothers, the Iraqi participants, are extremely serious and anxious to derive the maximum benefit from our discussions. Why not facilitate their task by installing a recording device and then we can offer them the tapes? They will then have the possibility of calmly reflecting on exactly everything that we have said." Loud laughter. The proposal was adopted.

Beyond this good joke, the atmosphere was terrible and each day the newspapers reported arrests, sentences, etc. The country was being terrorized. I invented a rather grim *nokta*: every morning, the radio announces the hanging of twenty-five people: five communists, five errant Baathists, five bourgeois liberals, five Islamists, and five with no opinion whatsoever. This way no one will feel secure! My cousin, Mansour Fahmy, who had been a consul in Baghdad, and who had a good Egyptian sense of humor and knew how to imitate the local accent to perfection, told me (he made this up, of course) how a Baathist "culture festival" unfolded. There was a long table with fifteen identical mustachioed men. The first stands up and reads his cultural address. Very brief, one sentence in fact: In May, we killed 50,000. The second stood in turn: In July, we killed 100,000, etc. The last stood: in August, we killed everyone. That's the end, no one can do better. The festival ended.

However, Iraq is full of intellectuals of the highest value and tens of thousands of militants with uncommon courage. Those whom I was able to see dared to speak, in a low voice, only away from their homes, outside and away from any building. What I heard from them testified quite simply to the sheer horror of the Iraqi Baathist political system. Is it then any wonder that most of these admirable intellectuals ended up choosing exile? Unfortunately, most unfortunately, a large number of these intellectuals subsequently believed that it is possible to return to the country in the train of the invader. The tragic sequel to the story is well known.

Lebanon is certainly a small country, but it is captivating and rich in the quantity and variety of its intellectual output. This is certainly a result of both its confessional diversity, which requires of everyone a sense of perspective, and its democratic life—as limited as it is—unequaled in any of the other Arab countries.

I visited Lebanon on several occasions during the civil war, which bathed the country in blood for ten years beginning in 1975, at the invitation of the bloc of democratic and national forces. Everyone knows today that this war was not the spontaneous result of a "visceral" hostility between communities, but rather a complex game played out, on the one hand, between militias—that assumed a monopoly of speech and action in the name of these communities they claimed to defend whereas, in fact, they placed them under their thumb—and, on the other hand, external forces, that is, Zionists, Western powers (the United States foremost, and behind them their Saudi vassal), Syria, Islamist Iran, Palestinians of the PLO) that played this or that card (and sometimes cynically changed partners). The cruelest moment of this period was certainly the Israeli invasion (1982) and the accompanying massacre of Palestinians at Sabra and Shatila, organized by Israel and its acolytes among some Maronite groups. The objective was clearly to break Lebanon apart, fashion a micro-Maronite client state of Israel and the West, and open the south of the country to Israeli conquest and expansion. This plan was defeated, first, it must be said, by the Lebanese people themselves. Giving a big lesson to the Arab world and the Palestinians, the Lebanese civilians did not flee before the Israeli army and fought them by resisting in the occupied territories—a resistance called "terrorist," unfortunately, by the dominant media infused with Israeli views. The later *intifada* of Palestine learned from this earlier experience of popular resistance. Syrian diplomacy also played, with keen intelligence, a decisive role in defeating these plans. This is so whether or not one is favorable to the government in Damascus. In the course of frequent visits to the south of the country, I could see with my own eyes the incredible arrogance of the Israeli occupation forces. They committed daily provocations, such as flights over Beirut and random bombings here and there. But the Western public was, and still is, never informed. The media are not allowed to criticize the Zionist state in any way.

Beirut and Lebanon during the war provided convincing evidence of the exceptional qualities of the Lebanese people, and particularly of its democratic and more or less socialist political segments—in other words, the left. Beirut was a city cut in half, subjected to bombardments by the militias of the two camps and from the Israeli air force; yet it still lived, and did so intensely. Neither water nor electricity was distributed by public services, but there was water and electricity everywhere, supplied through the self-organization of city districts: installation of small generators, the mobilization of water trucks, etc. In Beirut, political and intellectual life continued as if nothing were going on. I gave lectures and held workshops in places where the noise of heavy gunfire could be clearly heard. When the noise from the gunfire got worse, but only then, we decided to go further away, and continue the discussion. Militants from the other side of the front line did not hesitate to attend these discussions. In the mountains—the superb countryside that dominates Beirut—Jumblat's Socialist Party also organized meetings and debates, with my assistance and that of others, some directly about Lebanese or Arab problems, others of a more general nature: the development of world capitalism, the crisis of national and socialist systems, Marxist theory, and the like. I have fond memories of these splendid places and the Ottoman Palace of Deir el-Ahmar. In Beirut and elsewhere, one could only admire the Lebanese passion to live. Damaged homes were immediately reconstructed, without waiting. A comparison clearly comes to mind: a manuscript given to a publisher in Beirut was published at the promised time, whereas in Cairo this was not the case! And it was better printed in Beirut, without mistakes and misprints! When peace returned, it was possible for me to visit in calm all regions of this small country: the Cedars of God Forest, the Bekaa Valley, Tripoli, and Saïda. As always, there were lively conferences.

Of course, the political and social system that forms the basis on which peace was reestablished in Lebanon is far from meeting the expectations of the democratic and progressive forces that form the only solid foundation for this peace. The flourishing real estate speculation, which profits from the capital's reconstruction, will lead to the disappearance of its magnificent historical center—the Place des Canons and the Ottoman buildings close by, of which I, like all those who are familiar with them, have a fond memory. But the city, as ordinary as its so-called modern urbanization might become, remains fascinating. The cafe life, which I have always loved, is certainly one of the most pleasant manifestations of Lebanese sociability.

Greater Syria, from the Gulf of Aqaba and Petra to Aleppo, including the Roman circus in ancient Philippopolis, city of the Roman Emperor, Philip of Arabia—undoubtedly the best preserved of this type of edifice—Palmyra, the historical quarters of Damascus, Homs, Hama, Aleppo, and Lattakia, the Alawite mountains, the fortresses of Salah ad-Din and the Crusaders, overlooking the silk roads, is a beautiful country, both because of the richness and variety of its historical vestiges and because of its scenery.

This wealth recalls the decisive contribution of ancient and Byzantine civilizations to the grand Arab centuries that followed. It is not only that the Great Umayyad Mosque in Damascus is actually an ancient Byzantine cathedral (like Saint Sophia in Istanbul). Ruins of enormous cathedrals, abandoned in a now desert countryside, bear witness to the fact that the region was more densely populated with farmers (replaced today by shepherds) until the tenth century than it was subsequently. The ruins of Palmyra testify to the importance of trade along the Silk Road dating back to Antiquity. Consequently, it is easy to see influences from the East, from Iran and India, in the work of Syrian artisans.

Invited to a cultural week in Damascus, I was struck, but not surprised, by the uncompromising democratic and secular speeches of a large number of high-quality intellectuals. What is more, public speeches were given before audiences of young—students and workers—and not so young militants of diverse tendencies. These speeches would be unthinkable elsewhere in the Arab world, which would get your head cut off by Islamists and a conviction by state courts for an "offense against religion." These are very good signs for the future.

On a different note, the lamentable spectacle, on offer several times, of Khalid Bakdash's almost half-witted son—who apparently inherited the post of General Secretary of the Syrian Communist Party (or shares the responsibility with his mother, the widow)—should only, happily, be found amusing. No one in Syria today is disposed to take him seriously.

### THE PREDICTED ARAB REVOLUTIONS

I owe much to the friends who worked with me in the activities that I am going to report on here.

In Egypt, as president of the Arab and African Research Centre, I led debates organized with a broad spectrum of social and political forces involved in the struggles underway. I shall mention here only the names of Helmy Shaarawi, First Vice President of the Centre, Shahida el Baz, Mostafa Gamal, and Mamdouh Habashi. Ahmad el Naggar's contribution is mentioned in the section "Egypt: Immediate Responses." I can do no more than mention the names of several political men and women with whom I held conversations that are reflected in these memoirs: Hamdin Sabahi, Samir Morqos, Mona Anis, Amal Ramsis, Saad el Tawil (my frequent translator), and Magda Refaa. I am a member of the Egyptian Socialist Party. Some of my comrades are members of the other radical socialist left party and I do not view them as enemies or competitors, but as comrades equal in rights with the others. I have already expressed my opinion on this question of unity and diversity in the movement toward socialism and will not return to that here. I must also thank Madame Fatma El Boudi, editorial director of *Dar el Ain* in Cairo, who unhesitatingly supervised publication over the last three years of four works that I produced very quickly in the midst of the "revolution" then underway.

The decade of 2000–2010 seemed to all of us to be an endless time of darkness. One evening, some of us had imagined a sketch of Egyptian-style black humor, a television program from the year 2500. The announcer presented the latest news about the Islamic Republic of Great Britain and the United Socialist States of North America before coming to Egypt. She then mentioned President Mubarak VI's opening of the 800th construction stage of bridges over the Nile. We were wrong. The same year, Amal Ramsis produced her documentary, which ended with the sentence: "The revolution is tomorrow." She was right. I should add that I sensed the change to come. There were long evening discussions at the "center," the *Markaz*, of which I am the president. While in the 1990s, attendance was made up mostly of older people, beginning in the 2000s, we began to see many young people (25 to 35 years old) in attendance—for whom the Nasser era belonged to Pharaonic antiquity—eager to know and understand, to come and question us. I recognized some of them as leaders in the youth movements that "made the revolution," as they say. Whether or not it is a revolution is not the question. An inscription found on walls in Cairo—"The revolution has not changed the system, but it has changed the people"—perfectly captures the transformation of the country, conducive to possible progress in the end.

In Algeria, we—the Third World Forum networks—benefited from exemplary political and financial support without which I do not know how we would have been able to organize the roundtables we arranged for the World

Social Forums in Dakar (2011) and Tunis (2013), and to prepare for Tunis 2015. Most observers considered these round tables to be of great interest. Here I would like to thank the Algerian Minister of Foreign Affairs, the Algerian ambassador at Dakar, Mr. Abderrahmane Benguerrah, and Madame Khalida Toumi, Minister of Culture. The list of our collaborators in Algiers is too long to recall here. It begins with our major correspondents, Samia Zennadi and Karim Chikh (Éditions Apic), with whom I acknowledge my warm personal friendship here.

The Arab world entered into a period of turbulence beginning in 2011, which was a bit too quickly called the "Arab Spring." I refer the reader to my book on these "revolutions."[18] The strategic objective of the imperialist powers is to destroy the very existence of the state in the countries of the region because they could, with the possible radicalization of popular movements, threaten the established regional and world order. The support given by these powers (the United States, followed by Europe) to reactionary political Islam is the means to obtain this result. The programmed destruction of the Iraqi state begun in 2003, and the decomposition of "post-Gaddafi" Libya are tragic examples. In Sudan, the bloody dictatorships of Gaafar Nimeiry, who became "crazy over God," and his successor, Omar al-Bashir, as well as the systematization of crime "in the name of religion" (!) by Turabi, produced what should have been predicted and feared: the breakup of the country, the independence of the south, and separatism in Darfur and the east.

### *Egypt: Aborted Emergence*

Egypt was the first country in the periphery of globalized capitalism that attempted to "emerge." At the beginning of the nineteenth century, well before Japan and China, Muhammad Ali had designed and implemented a renovation project for Egypt and its immediate neighbors in the Arab Mashreq. This wide-ranging experiment took place over the first two-thirds of the nineteenth century and only ran out of steam during the second half of the reign of Khedive Ismail in the 1870s. An analysis of its failure must include an examination of the violence of the external aggression perpetrated by Great Britain, the major power of central industrial capitalism at that time. Twice—in 1840, then in the 1870s, with seizure of control over the finances of khedival Egypt, which ended with the military occupation in 1882—England relentlessly pursued its objective: prevent the emergence of a modern Egypt. Undoubtedly, this Egyptian project had limitations, ones that were characteristic of the era since it was obviously a project of emergence in and through capitalism, unlike the second Egyptian attempt (1919–67). It is also true that the social contradictions inherent in this project, just like the political, ideological, and cultural concepts that underlie it, played a part in this failure. It remains the case that, absent imperialist aggression, these contradictions could probably have been overcome, as the Japanese example suggests.

Defeated, for nearly forty years (1880–1920) Egypt was forced to be a dominated periphery. Its economic, political, and social structures were reshaped to serve the model of capitalist/imperialist accumulation dominant in that era. The regression imposed on the country affected not only its productive system, but also its political and social structures. There was a systematic attempt to reinforce backward-looking and reactionary ideological and cultural conceptions useful for maintaining the country's subordinate status.

Egypt—its people, its elites, the nation it represents—never accepted this status. This obstinate refusal lies behind the second wave of movements that developed over the following half-century (1919–67). In fact, I interpret this period as a moment of unceasing struggles and important advances. There was a threefold objective: democracy, national independence, and social progress. These three objectives—despite their sometimes limited and confused formulation—are inseparable. In this interpretation, the Nasserist period (1955–67) was only the last chapter of the lengthy moment of struggles begun with the revolution of 1919–20.

The first part of this half-century of rising freedom struggles in Egypt emphasized, with the formation of the Wafd in 1919, political modernization through adoption of a bourgeois form of constitutional democracy and the reconquest of independence. The democratic form that was devised made possible some moves toward secularization—though not necessarily secular in the radical sense of the term—the symbol of which was its flag (combining the crescent and the cross), which reappeared in the 2011 demonstrations. "Normal" elections not only allowed Copts to be elected by Muslim majorities, but even more, it allowed these same Copts to occupy very high posts in the state without that causing the least problem. The British, with the active support of the reactionary bloc, made up of the monarchy, large landowners, and rich peasants, worked to push back the democratic advances of Wafdist Egypt. The dictatorship of Ismail Sedky Pasha in the 1930s (with the abolition of the democratic 1923 constitution) came up against the student movement, which was the spearhead of the anti-imperialist struggles in that era. It is not by accident if, to reduce the danger, the British Embassy and the Royal Palace actively worked together to create the Muslim Brotherhood (1927), inspired by "Islamist" thought in its (backward-looking) Wahhabi *"salafist"* version formulated by Rashid Rida, the most reactionary (anti-democratic and anti-social progress) version of the new "political Islam." The Second World War, by necessity, was a sort of parenthesis. But the struggles resumed on February 21, 1946, with the formation of the student-worker bloc, and its radicalization was strengthened by the entrance of the communists and the workers' movement. Again, the reactionary Egyptian forces supported by London reacted violently and, for this purpose, mobilized the Muslim Brotherhood, which supported a second dictatorship of Sedky Pasha, but without successfully silencing the movement. The Wafd returned to the government, and its abrogation of the 1936 Anglo-Egyptian Treaty and the beginning of guerilla action in the still occupied Suez Canal Zone were only defeated by the 1951 Cairo fire, an operation in which the Muslim Brotherhood was deeply involved.

The first coup d'état of the Free Officers (1952), but above all the second one that started Nasser's control (1954), crowned this period of continual struggles, according to some, or put an end to it, according to others. Nasserism replaced the interpretation that I offer of the Egyptian awakening with an ideological discourse that essentially eliminates the entire history of the years 1919–52. In the Nasserist version, the "Egyptian revolution" begins in July 1952. At the time, many communists denounced this version and analyzed the coups d'état of 1952 and 1954 as aimed at putting an end to the radicalization of the democratic movement. They were not wrong because Nasserism did not stabilize as an anti-imperialist project until after the Bandung Conference (April 1955). Nasserism then achieved what it could: a resolutely anti-imperialist international posture (in conjunction with pan-Arab and pan-African movements) and progressive social reforms (though not "socialist"). The whole thing was organized from above, not only "without democracy," by prohibiting the working classes from organizing by themselves and for themselves, but also by abolishing any form of political life. Political Islam filled the void created. The project exhausted its potential in a brief time—the ten years from 1955 to 1965. The stagnation offered to imperialism, now led by the United States, the occasion to break the movement, which for this purpose mobilized its regional military instrument: Israel. The 1967 defeat marks the end of this half-century of fluctuating struggles. The retreat was led by Nasser himself, opting for concessions to the right (the *infitah*, or the opening to capitalist globalization) rather than radicalization, for which students, among others, fought (the student movement commanded center stage in 1970, a little before Nasser's death, then continued after). Sadat, followed by Hosni Mubarak, pushed this move to the right even more and integrated the Muslim Brotherhood into their new autocratic system.

Nasser's Egypt had established an economic and social system that can certainly be criticized, but it was coherent. Nasser had bet on industrialization as a way of getting out of the colonial international specialization that restricted the country to exporting cotton. This system provided for a redistribution of income favorable to the expanding middle classes, without impoverishing the working classes. Sadat and Mubarak worked to dismantle the Egyptian productive system, for which they substituted a totally incoherent system based exclusively on creating conditions for the profitability of companies that are, for the most part, only subcontractors of imperialist monopolies. This policy resulted in an incredible increase in inequality and unemployment that affected a majority of youth. This situation was explosive; it exploded.

During the Bandung and Non-Alignment period (1955 to 1970–75), some Arab countries were at the forefront of struggles for national liberation and social progress. These governments (Nasser, the FLN, the Baathists) were not democratic in the Western sense of the term, they were one-party states, or in the sense that I give to the term, which implies power exercised by the working classes themselves. But they were nonetheless perfectly legitimate because of their important achievements: gigantic progress in education, which allowed upward mobility (children of the working classes moving into the expanding middle classes), and in health; agrarian reforms; and guaranteed employment, at least for all graduates at all levels. Combined with anti-imperialist policies of independence, these achievements strengthened the governments in question, despite the continual hostility of the imperialist powers and military aggression perpetrated through Israel.

But after having achieved what they could in two decades through the means they gave themselves (reforms implemented from above, without ever making it possible for the working classes to organize themselves by themselves), these governments reached a dead end. The hour of imperialism's counteroffensive had arrived. To preserve their power, the ruling classes then accepted being subject to the new demands of so-called neoliberalism: uncontrolled opening to the outside, privatizations, etc. Consequently, everything they had accomplished was lost in a few years. The rapid erosion of their legitimacy led these governments to resort to increased police repression, supported by Washington. The period of decline (1967–2011) also covered a period of almost a half century. Egypt, subject to the requirements of globalized liberalism and the strategies of the United States, no longer existed as an active regional and international participant. In the region, the major allies of the United States—Saudi Arabia, Israel, and Turkey—were in the forefront. Israel could then move forward with its plan of expanding colonization of occupied Palestine, with the tacit complicity of Egypt and the Gulf countries.

Depoliticization was decisive in the rise of political Islam. This depoliticization is certainly not confined to Nasserist and post-Nasserist Egypt.

It was the dominant practice in all the national popular experiments of the first awakening of the South, and even in the historical socialisms after the initial phase of revolutionary ferment had quieted down. It is responsible for the later disaster. The question of democratic politicization is, then, the core challenge, in the Arab world as elsewhere. Our era is not one of democratic advances, but, on the contrary, of setbacks and decline. The extreme centralization of capital in the generalized monopolies allows and demands unconditional as well as total submission of political authority to its orders. Instead of affirming the presence of active *citizens* capable of formulating projects for an *alternative* society, so-called postmodernist ideology privileges a depoliticized individual, a *passive spectator* of the political scene who merely participates in elections (if that) that have no significance and lead to no real change, "political alternation," a *consumer* modeled by the system, who (wrongly) thinks of him or herself as a *free individual*.

The apparent stability of the regime, praised by Washington, was based on a monstrous police machine that committed criminal abuses daily. The imperialist powers claimed that this regime protected Egypt from the Islamist alternative. That is actually a huge lie. In fact, the regime had completely integrated reactionary political Islam into its power system, by conceding to it management of education, justice, and major media (particularly television). The only authorized speech was that which the mosques gave to the Salafists, thereby making it seem that they formed the opposition. The cynical duplicity of the rhetoric emanating from the U.S. establishment (and on this plane, Obama was no different than Bush) serves its objectives perfectly. In fact, support for political Islam eliminates the capacities of a society to face the challenges of the modern world (it lies behind the catastrophic decline in education and research), while the occasional denunciation of "abuses" for which it is responsible (murders of Copts, for example) serves to justify Washington's military interventions in pursuit of its so-called war against terrorism. The regime could appear "tolerable" so long as the safety valve of mass migration of the poor and middle classes to the petroleum-exporting countries continued. The end of this system (Asian immigrants replacing those from the Arab countries) led to a rebirth of resistance. Worker strikes in 2007—the largest in Africa for fifty years—the stubborn resistance of small peasants threatened with expropriation by agrarian capitalism, and the organization of middle-class protest groups in favor of democracy (the *Kefaya* and April 6 movements), all heralded the inevitable explosion anticipated in Egypt, even if it surprised foreign observers. We have now entered into a new phase of rising struggles for emancipation. We must analyze their direction and chances for development.

Egypt entered a new phase of its history in 2011. The analysis that I have proposed of the various elements involved in the active democratic, popular, and national movement, as well as the strategies of the local reactionary opponent and its external allies, should allow us to examine diverse possible paths to social transformation and determine whether they are promising or dead ends. In conclusion, I note that at this point in time, nothing allows us to say that Egypt is embarked on the path of emergence. But the fight will continue and will, perhaps, allow for an exit from the impasse and the reinvention of an appropriate path of emergence.

### *Crony Capitalism, Comprador State, and Lumpen-Development: The Case of Egypt (1970–2012)*

The Nasserist project of constructing a national development state had produced a model of state capitalism that Sadat was committed to dismantle. State-owned assets were thus sold. To whom? To crony businessmen and those close to the government: senior officers, high government officials, and rich merchants, who returned from exile in the Gulf countries equipped with handsome fortunes (in addition to political and financial support from the Muslim Brotherhood). But these assets were also sold to Gulf "Arabs" and foreign companies in the United States and Europe. At what prices? At ridiculous prices, disproportionate to the real value of the assets in question. In this way, the new Egyptian and foreign "owning class" was formed, which fully deserves the label crony capitalist (*rasmalia al mahassib*, the Egyptian term, is understood by everyone). Property granted to the army transformed the nature of the responsibilities that it carried out in some segments of the productive system (the army factories), which it managed as a state institution. These management powers became the powers of private owners. What is more, during the course of the privatizations, the most powerful officers also "acquired" ownership of many other state assets: commercial chains, urban and suburban land, and housing estates, in particular. The fortunes in question were made by acquiring already existing assets, with no more than negligible additions to productive capacity. Foreign capital investment (Arab and others), which, as a matter of fact, is quite modest, should be viewed within this context. The whole operation culminated in the establishment of the private monopolistic groups that now dominate the Egyptian economy.

> The monopoly of the new crony capitalists has been systematically reinforced by the almost exclusive access enjoyed by these billionaires to bank credit (notably for the purchase of the assets in question) to the detriment

of granting credit to small and medium producers. These monopolies were also strengthened by colossal state subsidies, granted for the consumption of oil, natural gas, and electricity by the factories taken over from the state (cement, iron and aluminum metallurgy, textiles, and others). The "free markets" allowed these companies to raise their prices to match those of competing imports. The logic that underlies the public subsidies that compensated for the lower prices charged by the state sector was broken, and super profits were accrued to the private monopolies.

Real wages for the large majority of unskilled and medium-skilled workers deteriorated through the operation of the laws of the market for free labor and the ferocious repression of union and other forms of collective action. Wages are now far below what they are in other countries of the South with a comparable rate of per capita GDP. The super profits of the private monopolies and pauperization go hand in hand and result in a continual increase in the unequal distribution of income. The taxation system, which rejected the very principle of progressive taxation, systematically reinforced inequality. Light taxation for the rich and corporations, praised by the World Bank because it supposedly supports investment, quite simply ended up as an increase in super profits. These policies also made it impossible to reduce both the public deficit and the foreign trade deficit. They entailed a continuous deterioration in the value of the Egyptian pound, and led to growing internal indebtedness of extreme proportions. This, in turn, provided an excuse for the IMF to demand still more respect for the principles of liberalism.

*Immediate Responses*

Activists responsible for formulating a joint program responding to the immediate requirements undertook a considerable amount of high-quality work for more than a year. The following text owes much to the work of Ahmad el Naggar, to whom I had the pleasure of awarding the Samir Amin Prize in 2011. The Arab and African Research Centre established this prize in my name as a way to encourage radical critical thought. Ahmad did half or more of the investigative work with the various currents and organizations that formed the backbone of the popular protests in Egypt. Here are the salient points:

> The disposal of public assets must be subject to systematic investigation. Detailed studies—the equivalent of good audits—are in fact available for many of these transactions and for the prices corresponding to the

value of specified assets. Given that the "purchasers" of these assets did not pay these prices, ownership of these acquired assets must be legally transferred, following a court-ordered audit, to public limited companies, with the state as a shareholder equal to the difference between the actual value of the assets and the prices paid by the buyers. The principle should be applicable to everyone, whether these buyers are Egyptian, Arab, or foreigners.

The law must set the minimum wage (this was in 2012) at the level of 1,200 LE per month (or 155 euros at the current exchange rate, the equivalent purchasing power of 400 euros). This rate is lower than in many countries with a GDP per capita comparable to that of Egypt. The minimum wage must be linked to a sliding scale and the trade unions made responsible for monitoring its implementation. It will be applied to all activities of the public and private sectors.

Given that the beneficiaries of freedom of pricing, that is, the private sector that dominates the Egyptian economy, have already decided to set their prices closer to those of competing imports, the measure can be implemented and will only have the effect of reducing the margins of monopoly rents. This readjustment does not threaten the balance of public accounts, bearing in mind the savings and the new tax legislation proposed below. Adopting a maximum wage, set at 15 times the minimum wage, will reinforce the proposals made by the movements involved.

Workers' rights—conditions of employment and loss of employment, working conditions, insurance plans for health/unemployment/pensions—must involve major three-way consultations between trade unions, employers, and the state. Independent trade unions established through the struggles of the last ten years should be given legal recognition, including the right to strike (still "illegal" in current legislation). A " survival benefit" should be set up for the unemployed, for which the amount, the conditions of access, and the funding should be subject to negotiations between the unions and the state.

The enormous subsidies granted to private monopolies by the budget must be abolished. Here again, detailed studies undertaken in these areas demonstrate that the abolition of these advantages would not threaten the profitability of the activities in question, but only reduce their monopoly profits.

New tax legislation must be adopted, based on progressive taxation for individuals and a 25 percent increase in the taxation rate for profits of businesses employing more than 20 workers. The extremely generous tax exemptions granted to Arab and foreign monopolies must be abolished. Taxation of small and medium businesses, currently often much heavier (!), should be lowered. The proposed rates for the upper personal income brackets, 35 percent, remains small in comparison with other nations.

A precise calculation was carried out, demonstrating that all of the measures proposed above would not only make it possible to eliminate the current deficit (for 2009–2010), but even generate a surplus. The surplus would be used to increase public spending on education, health, and public housing subsidies. The reconstruction of a public social sector in these areas does not imply discriminatory measures against private activities of the same kind.

Credit must be placed under the control of the Central Bank. The extravagant credit terms granted to the monopolies must be eliminated, and credit expanded for active small businesses or ones that could be created as a result. Detailed studies have been conducted in all these artisanal, industrial, transport, and service activities. It has been demonstrated that candidates (particularly among unemployed graduates) who are willing and interested in taking the initiative in creating businesses and employment do exist.

Concerning the agrarian question, the current demand of the movement is simply the adoption of laws that make it more difficult to evict farmers who are unable to pay the rents demanded of them, as well as to expropriate indebted small-scale property owners. In particular, the movement advocates the return to legislation setting the maximum farm rents (deregulated through successive agrarian reform laws). Organizations of progressive agronomists have produced detailed and well-argued projects for stimulating the development of small-scale farmers. These include improved irrigation methods (drip systems, for example), choice of rich and intensive crops (legumes and fruits), upstream freedom from state control for input and credit suppliers, and downstream freedom for the creation of marketing cooperatives combined with consumer cooperatives. But increased communication between these agronomist organizations and small-scale farmers needs to be established. The legalization of actual farmers' organizations and their federation at provincial and national levels should help move them in this direction.

The plan of immediate action summarized in the preceding paragraphs would certainly begin to stimulate healthy and viable economic growth. The argument advanced by its liberal detractors—that it would ruin any hope of obtaining new capital investment from foreign sources—does not make sense. The experiences of Egypt and other countries, particularly in Africa, who have agreed to comply fully with the strictures of liberalism and have abandoned their own autonomous development plans, show that this does not "attract" foreign capital despite their uncontrolled opening (actually, precisely because of it). Foreign capitalists are simply content to raid the resources of the countries concerned, supported by the comprador state and crony capitalists. By contrast, emergent countries that actively implement national development projects offer real possibilities to foreign investors who are willing to become part of these national projects, where they accept the restrictions imposed by the national state and the consequent adjustment of their profits to reasonable rates.

Mohamed Morsi's government, composed exclusively of members of the Muslim Brotherhood, immediately proclaimed its unconditional support for all the principles of liberalism, took steps to hasten implementation of those principles, and, to this end, deployed all the means of repression inherited from the fallen regime. Public awareness that there was no change ultimately led to the gigantic movement of June 30, 2013, which lies behind the fall of the Muslim Brotherhood. The leading aspects of the program of immediate demands that I have presented here focus only on the economic and social parts of the challenge. The movement also discusses its political aspects: the proposed constitution, democratic and social rights, and the essential affirmation of a "citizens' state" (*dawla al muwatana*) as opposed to the theocratic state (*dawla al gamaa al islamiya*) of the Muslim Brotherhood.

(THIS TEXT WAS DRAFTED BY ME IN OCTOBER 2012 AND DISTRIBUTED WIDELY, IN THE WIDELY READ DAILY *SHOROUK*, AMONG OTHERS.)

## *Algeria: The Impact of the April 17, 2014 Elections*

The two experiences of Algeria and Egypt have many characteristics in common. The ruling class in the two countries, built on the cadres of Boumediennism and Nasserism, respectively, was fundamentally similar. Their projects were identical and, consequently, should be described in the same way. They were genuinely national and popular projects (and not demagogic populist), although not very democratic. It is not important that each described itself as "socialist," which they were not and could not be. In the two cases, the achievements were significant, to the point that they truly transformed the society from top to bottom for better and not for worse. But also, in both countries, these achievements rapidly reached the limitations of what they could deliver and, sinking into their (identical) internal contradictions, could not prepare the radicalization and democratization required to extend those achievements. Yet, beyond these similarities, the differences should be pointed out.

Algerian society had been subjected to major destructive attacks because of colonization. The state and power of the pre-colonial aristocracy had been eradicated. The new Algerian society that was born from the reconquest of independence had nothing in common with that of the pre-colonial era. It had become a *plebeian* society, characterized by a very strong aspiration to *equality*. The Algerian war of liberation had produced, naturally, a social and ideological radicalization. This aspiration to equality is not found, with the same force, anywhere else in the Arab world—not in the Maghreb (just think about the strength of the age-old tradition of respect for the monarchy in Morocco!) or the Mashreq. By contrast, modern Egypt was built from the beginning (starting with Muhammad Ali) by its aristocracy, which gradually became an "aristocratic bourgeoisie" (or capitalist aristocracy), even though this new ruling class had, in the end, to accept submission to imperialist domination, first by the British, then by the United States. The ambiguous 1952 coup d'état came as a response to the impasse of the movement. From these differences comes another, of obvious importance, concerning the future of political Islam. The army and the state, with the support of the nation, defeated Algerian political Islam (the FIS), which had revealed its ugly face. That certainly does not mean that the question has been finally settled.

Bendjedid, Boumedienne's successor, pursued an extreme neoliberal path, similar to Sadat and Mubarak's *infitah*: widespread privatizations throughout the national economy, participation of senior officers in pillaging state assets, dismantling national control of the petroleum sector, uncontrolled opening to multinational corporations, and corruption. But after the defeat of the FIS attempt to impose its project for a reactionary theocracy, also subordinate to the demands of neoliberalism, President Bouteflika initiated a corrective economic policy, going as far as re-nationalizing some large companies. Bouteflika also defeated the Western project to create a "Sahelistan," which would have been formed to the detriment of Algeria, Mali, and Niger. This para-Islamic state, in the image of the Gulf States, would have confiscated the rent extracted from exploitation of petroleum, uranium, and other minerals for the exclusive benefit of its emirs. The project was completely in line with the objectives of the U.S. strategy of domination. Simultaneously, the government made concessions to democratic and social demands, such as those of the Amazighs, unequaled elsewhere in the Arab world. But still, these were timid corrections, and the Algerian people, even when they showed full confidence in Bouteflika's promises, probably expected more.

For these reasons, in the April 2014 elections, the majority supported Bouteflika, despite the handicaps of age and health. These elections also showed the categorical rejection of political Islam's attempt to make a return to the political scene, appearing in the new garb of "national reconciliation." But electors did not make this choice enthusiastically, as can be seen from the rate of participation—only 51 percent, against the 67 percent from the preceding presidential election.

The Algerian model, then, gave obvious signs of stronger consistency than that of Egypt, which explains why it had shown more resistance to its later degradation. Consequently, the Algerian ruling class remains mixed and divided, split between those still holding national aspirations and those submissively giving in to compradorization (sometimes these two conflicting orientations are combined in the same person!). Bouteflika's reelection bought some time and made it possible to avoid the chaos that conflicts within the ruling class would produce. In Egypt, by contrast, with Sadat and Mubarak, this dominant class became completely a comprador bourgeoisie, harboring no national aspirations. Economic, political, and social reforms controlled domestically seem to have a chance in Algeria. The question of democratic politicization is, in any case, the core challenge, in Algeria and Egypt as elsewhere in the world. The Western powers fear a change toward national and popular democracy in Algeria. Also, they have not given up their project of destroying the state and society by means of an alleged "Islamist" government. The support they gave to the Islamist candidate defeated in the April 17 presidential election is clear evidence of that. They have not given up on their objective of breaking up Algeria by supporting a possible secession of the Algerian Sahara and Kabylie. Their rhetoric of "promoting democracy" and "respect for cultural differences" is aimed at hiding the real objectives of their strategy.

The recent history of Algeria and Egypt illustrates the powerlessness of these societies, even now, to face the challenge. Algeria and Egypt are the two countries in the Arab world that are possible candidates for "emergence." The ruling classes and established governments bear major responsibility for the failure of these two countries to reach "emergence." But the societies themselves, the intellectuals, and the militants from the various social and political movements, must also bear some responsibility. Will both parties succeed in rising to the challenge, together and through their conflict?

*Tunisia: The Revolution in an Impasse*

Tunisia initiated the wave of Arab revolutions in December 2010. I heard some of the participants, who arrived with some excitement to share their accounts at the World Social Forum in Dakar (February 2011), in which the World Forum for Alternatives, the Third World Forum, and I, participated.

During the organization of the Tunis World Social Forum in 2013, I had the possibility of hearing more and holding discussions with representatives of a wide spectrum of Tunisian political and social forces (except for the Islamist party Ennahada): the Front Populaire (whose president received me in his office at the Assembly), Mounir Kachoukh, the Parti des Patriotes (whose leader, Choukri Belaid, had just been assassinated by henchmen of Ennahada), Abdeljalil Bedoui, the UGTT, etc. Our sister and friend Hassania had expertly organized many of these meetings.

The impression I got from these meetings is hardly enthusiastic. All or almost all were exclusively concerned with questions of governmental organization and the strengthening of political democracy as well as questions about secularism and women's rights. On these questions, Tunisian opinion appears to be in advance of that of Egyptians. We should not be surprised. Bourguiba had opened up spaces for this, despite his autocratic behavior. Nevertheless, no one or almost no one in Tunisia appears to understand that the insertion of the country into liberal capitalist globalization is the origin of the disaster. All share the same fatal illusions about Europe, from which they expect support! On this level, Tunisia lags behind Egypt and Algeria.

During the World Social Forum in Tunis, Ennahda, like all other movements, had been invited to attend, present its program, and respond to questions. Ennahda abstained and confided to the famous Tariq Ramadan and his supporters (unfortunately from *Le Monde diplomatique*) the task of propagandizing on its behalf. Ennahada, like the Muslim Brotherhood in Egypt, pursues only a single objective: exercise power, all the power. The certificate of conversion to democracy that Europeans have awarded is meant to obscure this reality. Europeans know that the most effective means to guarantee the continuation of their pillage of the countries south of the Mediterranean is to entrust management of these countries to their Islamist friends.

All the conditions necessary to see any Arab country break out of the current impasse are far from coming together, at least in the near future.

The Constituent Assembly resulting from the October 2011 elections in Tunisia was dominated by a rightist bloc that combined the Islamist party Ennahada and numerous reactionary cadres, formerly associated with the Ben Ali regime, still in place, and infiltrated into the "new parties" under the name of "Bourguibists." Both unconditionally support the "market economy" such as it is, a system of dependent and subaltern capitalism. France and the United States do not ask for more: "Everything changes so that nothing will change."

Two changes are, nevertheless, on the agenda. Positive: a political, but non-social democracy, that is, "low-intensity democracy," that will tolerate a diversity of opinions, respect human rights more, and end the police repression perpetrated by the preceding regime. Negative: a probable decline in women's rights. This is, in other words, a return to a multiparty "Bourguibism" with an Islamic coloration. The Western powers' plan, based on the power of the comprador reactionary bloc, will put an end to this transition. They favor a short transition (which the movement has accepted without assessing the consequences), leaving no time to organize social struggles, and will allow the establishment of this bloc's exclusive "legitimacy" through "correct" elections. The Tunisian movement was largely uninterested in the economic policy of the former regime, concentrating its critiques on the corruption of the president and his family. Most of the opposition, even on the "left," did not question the basic direction of the mode of development implemented by Bourguiba and Ben Ali. The outcome was, thus, predictable.

President Moncef Marzouki had been a human rights campaigner and thus a victim of repression. But he seemed unable to make the connection between the poverty of his people and the choice of a liberal economic policy by the state, which he did not question. Curiously, he took the initiative to organize in Tunis in February 2012 an international conference on Syria that provided grist to the mills of the Western interventionists!

It remains the case that sometimes the same causes produce the same results. What will the working classes think and do when they see the continual deterioration in their social conditions, with the accompanying unemployment and job instability, not to mention the probable additional deterioration caused by the general crisis of capitalist globalization? It is too soon to say. But one should not persist in ignoring that only the rapid formation of a radical left that goes beyond the demand for proper elections can make possible a resumption of struggles for a change worthy of the name. This radical left has the responsibility to formulate a strategy for the democratization of society that would go beyond the simple holding of proper elections, combine this democratization with social progress, which implies giving up the current development model, and strengthen its initiatives by adopting a clearly anti-imperialist and independent international position. It is not the imperialist monopolies and their international servants (the World Bank, the IMF, the WTO, the European Union) that will help the countries of the South get out of the impasses they face.

None of these fundamental questions seems to be of concern to the major political participants. Everything happened as if the ultimate objective of the "revolution" had been to obtain elections rapidly. This is to think that power finds its sole source of legitimacy in the voting booth. But there is another, higher legitimacy: undertaking struggles for social progress and the real democratization of society! These two types of legitimacy are likely to have serious confrontations in the future.

*Libya: A Country Erased from the World Map*

Libya never truly existed as a nation. It is a geographical region that separates the Maghreb and the Mashreq. The boundary between these two Arab regions runs exactly through the middle of Libya. Cyrenaica was historically Greek and Hellenistic, and then it became part of the Mashreq. Tripolitania was Latin and became part of the Maghreb. Consequently, there has always been a basis for regionalism in the country. I saved the British atlas used at school by my father in 1913. The region from Kufra to Tibesti was under the rule of the Khedive of Egypt. In 1911, Italy seized Ottoman Libya, which in actuality was only the coastal band. In 1915, to reward Rome for joining the Entente, the British ceded the Saharan regions of Cyrenaica to Italy.

Gaddafi was never anything more than a buffoon whose empty thinking is reflected in his famous "Green Book." Acting in a still archaic society, Gaddafi could allow himself to adopt various positions, without any real significance—"nationalist and socialist" one day, then "liberal" the next. He made the latter choice "to please the West"(!), as if choosing liberalism would have no effects on society.

Gaddafi had insistently invited me, on several occasions, to visit his country. In my twofold role as president of the Arab and African Research Centre in Cairo, and director of the Third World Forum, I had posed one condition: the prior payment of 200,000 dollars to these two organizations, without any conditions on use of these funds. I would then visit the country and present lectures on general subjects, without broaching the discussion of Libyan problems. There was no follow-up, of course.

I also remember that when, following NATO's military intervention, the scandal of the donation made by Libya to the London School of Economics broke—the LSE had awarded, in exchange, an honorary diploma to Gaddafi's son, which all U.S. universities do with their generous donors—I was interviewed in London on the subject and said: "How shameful! This is at least as scandalous as accepting a gift from the Ford Foundation." Obviously, the interview was not published.

Gaddafi's going over to economic liberalism simply worsened the social difficulties for the majority of people. The very large redistribution of the oil revenues gave way to its confiscation by the regime's supporters and Gaddafi's family. The conditions were thus created that led to the explosion we all know, immediately taken advantage of by political Islam and regionalist forces in the country.

It is in this context that the National Transitional Council (NTC) was formed in Benghazi. The president of this Council was none other than Mustafa Muhammad Abdul Jalil, the president of the Libyan Appeals Court who confirmed the death sentence of the five Bulgarian nurses. He was rewarded and named Minister of Justice in 2007, a post he held until February 2011. For this reason, Bulgarian prime minister Boyko Borisov refused to recognize the NTC. The United States and European countries did not accede to this view. There were, perhaps, some more or less confused "democrats" on this Council, but above all there were Islamists—the worst among them, in fact—and regionalists. From the very beginning, the "movement" in Libya was an armed revolt that immediately took over civilian demonstrations. This armed revolt straightaway called for NATO support. France and Great Britain immediately responded to this appeal, subsequently supported by the United States.

The imperialist powers' military intervention certainly did not aim at the "protection of civilians" or "securing democracy," but at the control of oil and groundwater resources, as well as acquiring a major military base in the country. Certainly, the Western oil companies already controlled Libyan oil since Gaddafi's move to support "liberalism." But with Gaddafi, nothing was ever certain. What if he changed sides and brought the Chinese or the Indians into his game tomorrow? But more important than the oil were the Libyan groundwater resources. Initially, it was a question of exploiting them to the benefit of the countries of the African Sahel. This page is now turned. Well-known French multinationals seek to reserve access to these resources and make their exploitation "the most financially profitable" for themselves, probably for the production of biofuels.

Gaddafi had, in 1969, already demanded that the British and Americans evacuate their military bases set up after the Second World War. Today, the United States needs to transfer Africom (the U.S. military command for Africa, an important part of the system for military control of the world, still located in Stuttgart!) to Africa. The African Union refuses to accept it and, to this day, no African state has dared to agree to host it. A lackey placed in power in Tripoli (or Benghazi) would obviously support all of the demands coming from Washington and its subaltern NATO allies. The base would be a permanent threat as it could be a source for interventions against Egypt and Algeria.

The "new regime" has demonstrated its inability to govern the country. Libya's disintegration following the Somali model has begun. Libya no longer exists.

## The Syrian Tragedy

The Syrian Baathist government derived its legitimacy from implementing its non-democratic national popular project. When I visited Damascus, Aleppo, and other Syrian cities in the past, I clearly observed this legitimacy, despite the autocratic practices of the government. I also observed that its policy of secularization had made possible advances in women's rights and allowed freedom in the social behavior of youth, which certainly deserved support.

Then, when the system ran out of steam, opening the way for globalized neoliberalism to go on the offensive and advance its "solutions," the same hard-pressed Baathist ruling class accepted the infitah (the uncontrolled opening to globalized capital), just like the other Arab countries, so as to preserve its political control. The resulting social disaster led to the same consequences as elsewhere: the rise of perfectly legitimate democratic and social protests and increased repression by the government in response. It is almost amusing to note that one leader of the "rebellion"—Abdul Halim Khaddam—was the main architect of the "economic liberalization." The legitimacy of the Syrian people's revolt thus cannot be questioned.

The United States learned from the surprise in Tunisia and Egypt. It thus decided to take the initiative and get ahead of the movement by introducing armed groups that attacked the authorities, proclaimed themselves to be an "army of liberation," and immediately called on NATO to help them. With local collusion and support from the Gulf countries, it was possible to infiltrate armed groups from Jordan (under Tel Aviv's orders), Tripoli (base of "radical" Islam in Lebanon), and Turkey (the Colombia of the Middle East). An important NATO power, Turkey has participated in the conspiracy. The so-called refugee camps in Hatay are actually training camps for mercenaries recruited from terrorist groups (Talibans and others), financed by Saudi Arabia and Qatar. I refer here to Bahar Kimyongur's book.[19]

One would have to be completely naive to be surprised at the silence emanating from the Western governments: silence on the recruitment of "terrorists," silence on the rhetoric of these "liberators"—"Christians to Beirut, Alawites to the grave"—silence about the Saudi and Qatari governments, promoted to the rank of "defenders of democracy," silence on the massacre of demonstrators in Bahrain carried out by Saudi troops, silence on the introduction of al-Qaida into Yemen for the purpose of confronting a possible rebirth of the South Yemeni left! "Terrorism" has a good side: unpardonable when the United States is attacked, welcome when it can be used. This strategy of organized chaos is, moreover, devised with the greatest cynicism by the authorities in Washington.

The possible victory of the Islamists—with or without foreign military intervention—would result in the breakup of the country and the massacre of Alawites, Druze, and Christians. But that is unimportant. The objective of Washington and its allies is not to liberate Syria from its dictator, but to destroy the country, just as the aim was not to liberate Iraq from Hussein and Libya from Gaddafi, but to destroy these countries.

Russia and China's veto in the UN Security Council has fortunately made Libyan-style "humanitarian bombing" more difficult. The Syrian government has, moreover, succeeded in eliminating, it seems, hotbeds of major intervention supported from the outside. It remains the case that the introduction of groups in the pay of foreign powers put the democratic and social movement in an awkward position. The "movement"—diffuse and unorganized—refused to support the so-called liberation committees, obviously manipulated by the imperialist powers, while also refusing to support the government's repression. To respond to the terrorism of imperialism's agents by state terror is not an effective response to the challenge. The solution calls for substantial reforms benefiting popular and democratic forces that exist, and refuse to serve the Muslim Brotherhood. If the government turns out to be incapable of understanding what is required, nothing will stop the tragedy from continuing to its inevitable end.

I have listened to many representatives of the Syrian popular movement, which is extremely divided. Here I should cite Ayssar Midani, Salameh Kailé, Joseph Yacoub, Aziz el Azmeh, Zakaria Khoder, Ahmad Barkaoui, and Michel Kilo. I do not necessarily share their analyses and opinions.

*Sudan: Criminal Abuses*

On a visit to Khartoum in 2010, at the time the south's secession was being prepared, I heard analyses and commentaries (particularly from my very dear friend Haydar Ibrahim Ali and from Adlan Hardallu) that led me to believe that awareness of the disaster perpetrated by Turabi's supposedly Islamic regime was well advanced and, beyond that, that the country's democratic and progressive forces were preparing a counteroffensive.

It was too late. The people in the south chose independence by an overwhelming majority in the referendum. But the imperialist powers, probably working through the Mossad, had taken the precaution of assassinating John Garang, the only leader capable, not only of uniting the peoples of the south, but also of working with the democrats from the north to change the state of relations between the two states. The outcome was fatal. The south has become another Central African Republic given over to conflicts among mediocre local potentates for control of the country and has descended into civil war. This is the only way for the politicians in question to attract supporters in their pay.

### *Yemen: Ally of the United States?*

The United States supported the Ali Abdallah Saleh regime. The reason is their fear of the Yemeni people, above all in the south of the country. The latter had had a progressive Marxist government, which derived its legitimacy from its large popular support. Today, those forces are active in the social protest movement. Washington and its allies thus fear a breakup of the country and the reestablishment of the progressive government in South Yemen. Consequently, in allowing al-Qaida—largely controlled by the United States—to occupy the cities of the south, with U.S. support, the Yemeni regime wants to create fear among the progressive forces so that they can be pressured to accept the continuation of Saleh in power. The friendships that I have maintained with a large number of leaders from the former South Yemen have provided me with some insights into the nature of the issues facing this country.

# 2

# AFRICA
# African Socialisms, Colonial Disasters, and Glimmers of Hope

Independent Africa was divided into two camps from 1960 to 1963: the Casablanca group (Egypt, Morocco, Guinea, Ghana, and Mali), who considered that the independence "granted" by the colonizers had not settled the question of liberation, and the Monrovia group (the other countries) that accepted their situation, described by the former as neocolonialist. African countries are united in the Organization of African Unity (OAU), created in 1963 on the initiative of Haile Selassie. All countries of independent Africa belonged to the Non-Aligned Movement, founded in Bandung in 1955. The spirit of the Bandung Conference had a wide enough resonance to attract not only the African peoples, but also the ruling classes and governments.

Having personally been involved in the continent's intellectual and political life from that era and even before, I believe that the overview I am going to offer to the reader in the following pages might help in better understanding the vicissitudes of Africa's attempts to overcome the burdens of colonialism.

The new Africa is fragile precisely because of the miserable heritage of this colonialism. Most African societies are threatened with disintegration, and several of them are now quite far along in this terrible process. The dominant narrative on the subject attributes responsibility for this state of affairs to the "insufficient maturity" of these societies, with the implication that they were decolonized too quickly. As a result, the true cause of the tragedy is ignored: the market. The market itself always works as a centrifugal, disintegrating force. It is only when it is regulated by the state that it ceases to be so. In economies as fragile as those that Africa inherited from the colonial period, this disintegration effect is even more devastating than elsewhere. Here there is no productive system worthy of the name. The market does not create such a system; it has never done so anywhere. It is the state—acting as an instrument of society and of the social compromises that characterize it at each stage of its evolution, including the capitalist stage—that is responsible for creating a productive system consistent with social development. In the absence of this, the market forces quite simply exploit the scattered fragments of a system that cannot offer any resistance since it does not exist as such. Compradorization is the social, political, and ideological form through which this absence of a state is expressed. There is not "too much state" in Africa; there is only a bad comprador administration that is not even a real state. In ideological terms, this situation results in the triumph of individual interests or those of clans and their patronage systems, the absence of a sense of solidarity (class or national), and the restriction of political struggle to vulgar opportunist practices—which in turn depoliticize the people and retard the formation of responsible citizens, an essential condition for democratization.

Neocolonialism, then, develops only on the basis of permanent crisis. It is itself in permanent crisis. That is why different movements have continually challenged it, in various times and places. Even if these movements have not attained the consistency and strength necessary to form an effective and viable alternative—as has been the case up to now—they nonetheless prefigure the requirements for a better future. That is why the waves of what I call national populist (rather than socialist) responses continually follow one another in Africa. The first of these waves—Kwame Nkrumah's Ghana, Modibo Keita's Mali, Guinea, the Congo—had barely run out of steam before a new attempt was made in West Africa, Benin, then Burkina Faso, while a rebirth began, perhaps, in Ghana and Mali, Tanzania, Ethiopia, and Madagascar in East Africa, then southern Africa. I closely followed all these attempts to construct an alternative to neocolonialism in crisis.

Has this been a failure on the part of Africa? No. We should say that it is a failure of capitalism, which is unable to offer Africa anything acceptable. Today, the Bandung era has come to an end, and the impasse is more desperate than ever. The frontal attack on the peasantry promoted by the WTO's liberalization project has only accelerated the transformation of the continent into a world of abandoned rural areas and overcrowded urban slums. The inevitable consequence is the rising migration pressure—the new "boat peoples"—while the Europeans persist in not wanting to recognize their overwhelming responsibility.

I shall offer in what follows a sequential picture of the experiences of

African socialism and, in contrast, an overview of the miracles without a future, the neocolonial quagmires and disasters.

THE EXPERIENCES OF AFRICAN SOCIALISM

I lived through my second experience of Bandung in Mali (and supplemented this with visits to Nkrumah's Ghana and Ahmed Sékou Touré's Guinea). I reviewed this in the first volume of these memoirs. I shall not then return to this stage of the story. The following pages deal only with Mali after Modibo Keita and Ghana after Kwame Nkrumah.

## *Mali after Modibo*

The IDEP had organized one of its seminars in Bamako in 1972. This was an important event since we discussed both the experience of Modibo's government and the policies implemented after his fall in 1968, without making any concessions in criticizing either the past or the Moussa Traoré government. The seminar took place in the famous motel of that era, a rudimentary establishment near the old airport on the banks of the Niger. At the request of our partners, we (willingly) held additional lectures every evening, attended by most of the old and new leadership.

I regularly saw former leaders Mamadou Gologo and Madeira Keita after their release from prison. From time to time, Keita came to Dakar for medical treatment and contacted me on each of these occasions. Although he was the type of person who forgot nothing and learned little, I always enjoyed our conversations immensely. He was a man of remarkable honesty and courage, endowed with great warmth. He never forgot his old friends. His death pained me a lot. He is the uncle of Ibrahima Keita, one of the leaders of the youth revolt against the dictatorship, who became prime minister in the Konaré government. One day, Ibrahima said to me, in the presence of Madeira: "My uncle asks me why I am not a member of the Union Soudanaise, but rather a supporter of ADEMA" (the new democratic movement); "I believe he thinks that the Union Soudanaise genes are indestructible!" Beyond the older generation, I became acquainted with the new generation of militants from ADEMA, CNID, and the feminist movement (Aminata Traoré), and with many other youth who were mobilized during this time. This generation was certainly more promising than the "young cadres" of the first wave from the early 1960s, whom I criticized rather severely, on the whole. Amadou Toumani Touré, who was the astute and open democratic-minded soldier who oversaw a remarkable transition and who received me after the fall of Moussa Traoré, convinced me that the "Marxist" education given to the army during the Modibo era, despite all of its outrageous dogmatic simplifications, had some good effects, since it produced a military corps that did not behave with the usual savagery found in most Third World armies. I saw Amadou Toumani Touré again behind the scenes in Cairo on the occasion of the Euro-African Summit in 2000. He developed a coherent viewpoint on security questions, conscious both of the ravages of the depoliticization resulting from the neoliberal social disaster, and the dangers of the imperialists using this situation. He believed that geostrategy and geopolitics are dimensions of reality that we are always wrong to ignore. That is also my view.

The victory won by the Malian people, which succeeded through its courage alone, without external support—on the contrary, the Western powers lined up behind the dictator, despite their "democratic" pretensions—had, naturally, aroused the enthusiasm of the working classes and even the majority of the middle classes and intellectuals. We expected, among other things, that the new president, Alpha Konaré, would listen to the strong democratic movement that had mobilized the Malian people and begin a new style of leadership and management in the country. These hopes were disappointed. Beyond the possible responsibility of individuals, I attribute the failure to the overwhelming force the world system brought to bear on Bamako's choices, compelling unconditional submission to the neoliberal diktat. Once more, the combination of democracy and neoliberal choices produced only social disaster and, in the end, turned out to be essentially anti-democratic. The crisis that hit Argentina in 2002 is the most convincing and dazzling example of this. The social disaster is visible to the naked eye. When I visited Bamako for the African Social Forum in January 2002, I saw that it had become a miserable metropolis, its center devastated by widespread "informal" employment, which is the only means of survival that capitalism now offers to people.

Nevertheless, there are glimmers of hope on the horizon that foreshadow the appearance of new struggles in the future. The birth of a peasant movement independent from the government and opportunist "parties" is a change that would have been difficult to imagine ten years ago. "Control" of the peasantry by national liberation movements and the subsequent state administrations was widespread in Africa, and appeared unshakeable. In all the Francophone countries of West Africa—and particularly in Burkina Faso (which was behind this change, the heritage of Thomas Sankara), Senegal, and Mali—the peasantry began its emancipation from this supervision. In Mali, the first peasant strike—refusing to cultivate cotton—forced negotiations on the government and foreign capital (French, in this case), which controls the "cotton sector" and imposes its conditions, including paltry prices.

The organization of a session of the Social Forum in Bamako in 2006 confirmed my hopes. The enthusiastic support of all the popular forces that have again emerged in Mali guaranteed the success of the undertaking. Here I would like to extend a sincere thank-you to all the militants of the Comité Malien and to Aminata Traoré. The Bamako Appeal, which came out of this session, opens new horizons for the development of a worldwide movement to challenge the imperialist liberal order. Africa has once again found its place in the globalization of struggles for an alternative.

*Sahelistan: Whose Interests Does This Project Serve?*

My repeated visits to Bamako beginning in 2005 allowed me to follow with my own eyes the continual deterioration in the social conditions of the Malian people, subjected by the Western powers, Europe and France in particular, to an austerity regime more severe than what was imposed under Moussa Traoré's dictatorship. The cuts in an already pitiful budget ended in the abandonment of the northern part of the country. In these conditions, the conquest of democracy lost its meaning, opening the way to the rise of political Islam, financed by the Gulf countries. Respectable intellectuals, whom I had known as fighters for democracy and progress, passed over to Wahhabism. I discussed all that with my numerous Malian friends, the marvelous Aminata Traoré, always available to facilitate my visits, Issaka Bagayogo, Mamadou Goita, and Assétou Samaké, as well as the leadership of the political parties that had honored me by inviting me to their grand commemorative celebration on the 1960–65 Malian Plan. I continued these discussions with my friends from Niger, Abdou Ibro in particular. My growing unease was reinforced even further when the Malian army was chased out of the north in 2013 by al-Qaida in the Islamic Maghreb, which did not surprise me.

I then immediately drafted the following text. Welcomed by some, violently rejected (occasionally with insults) not only by those who had joined the Islamic opposition (not surprising), but also by others who went no further than the simple principle that the French intervention served Paris's colonial interests. I was not unaware of this. Yet these critics ignored the impact of the Sahelistan project and acted as if this project only challenged French colonial interests. In short, they ignored the fact that the success of this project would quite simply lead to the destruction of Mali on the model of Somalia.

I reproduce this text here.

De Gaulle had entertained the idea of a "Grand French Sahara." But the tenacity of the Algerian FLN and the radicalization of Mali under the Union Soudanaise of Modibo Keita put an end to the project for good in 1962–63.

Today, the Sahelistan project is not French—even if Nicolas Sarkozy did come to support it. It is a plan formulated by a loose nexus of political Islamist groups and benefits from the possibly favorable view of the United States, followed by its European Union lieutenants.

"Islamic" Sahelistan would allow for the creation of a large state covering a good part of the Sahara found in Mali, Mauritania, Niger, and Algeria, an area endowed with important mineral resources: uranium, oil, and gas. These resources would not be available mainly to France, but primarily to the dominant powers of the triad (the United States, Europe, and Japan). This "kingdom," modeled on Saudi Arabia and the Gulf Emirates, could easily buy the support of its scattered population, and its emirs could transform the fraction of the rent left to them into vast personal fortunes. The Gulf remains, for the triad powers, the model of the best ally/useful servant, in spite of the fiercely archaic nature of its social system, based in part on slavery. The established governments in Sahelistan would refrain from supporting acts of terrorism on their territory, without necessarily refraining from possibly supporting them elsewhere. France, which had succeeded in preserving out of its abandoned "Grand Sahara" project control over Niger and its uranium resources, would have only a secondary place in Sahelistan. The Algerian government showed that it understood the aim quite well. It knows that the formation of a Sahelistan aims to include southern Algeria and not just northern Mali.

I wish and hope that the Sahara war will be won, that the Islamists are eradicated in the region (Mali and Algeria in particular), and Mali's territorial integrity restored. This victory is the necessary but far from sufficient condition for a future reconstruction of the Malian state and society. This war will be long and its outcome uncertain. Reconstruction of the Malian army is entirely feasible. Modibo's Mali had succeeded in building a competent army that was devoted to the nation, sufficient to deter aggressors like the Islamists of AQIM today. This army was systematically destroyed by Moussa Traoré's dictatorship and his successors did not reconstruct it. But since the Malian people are quite aware that their country has the obligation to be armed, reconstruction of its army would benefit from favorable public opinion. The obstacle is financial. To recruit and equip thousands of soldiers is not currently within the means of the country, and neither will other African states or the UN agree to compensate for this lack of means. Not much can be expected from the countries of the ECOWAS. The Praetorian Guards in most of these countries are an army in name only. Certainly, Nigeria has numerous, well-equipped forces, but unfortunately not very disciplined, to say the least. Most of its senior officers have no other objective than to pillage the regions targeted for intervention. Senegal also has a competent and disciplined military force, but it is small, on the scale of the country. Farther afield in Africa, Angola and South Africa could provide effective support, but their geographic distance, and maybe other considerations, might dissuade them from running the risk of any commitment.

Mali's reconstruction can only be done by the Malians themselves. Still it would be desirable to help them rather than erect barriers that would make such reconstruction impossible. French colonial ambitions—to make Mali a client state like several others in the region—certainly motivate some of the administrators in Paris responsible for Malian policy. Françafrique still has its mouthpieces. But they are not a real danger, let alone a major one. A reconstructed Mali will also quickly affirm—or reaffirm—its independence. However, a Mali wrecked by reactionary political Islam would before long be unable to find an honorable place on the regional and world scene. As with Somalia, it would end up being erased from the list of sovereign states worthy of the name.

During the Modibo era, Mali had made economic and social progress, asserted its independence, and achieved some success in uniting its diverse ethnic groups. The Union Soudanaise had succeeded in uniting in one nation the Bambara from the south, the Bozo fishers, the Songhai peasants, and the Ikelan (Bella) of the Niger Valley from Mopti to Ansongo (it is forgotten today that the majority of the inhabitants found in northern Mali are not Tuaregs), and had even made the Tuaregs accept the emancipation of their Ikelan (Bella) serfs. It remains the case that for lack of means—and lack of will after Modibo's fall—successive governments in Bamako have abandoned development projects in the north of the country. Some of the Tuareg demands are, consequently, perfectly justified. Algiers has demonstrated a clear understanding of the situation. It recommends making a distinction in the ranks of the rebellion between the Tuaregs (now marginalized), with whom discussions should take place, and the jihadists who have come from elsewhere, often quite racist in regard to the "blacks." The limitations in Mali's achievements under Modibo, but also the hostility of the Western powers (and France in particular), lie behind the project's failure and the ultimate success of Moussa Traoré's odious coup d'état (supported to the end by Paris). That dictatorship bears the responsibility for the decomposition of Malian society, its pauperization, and its helplessness. The powerful revolt of the Malian people succeeded, at the price of tens of thousands of victims, in overthrowing the dictatorship. It gave rise to great hopes for the country's rebirth. These hopes were disappointed. Why?

Since the fall of Moussa Traoré, the Malian people have benefited from unequaled democratic freedoms. Yet that seems to have served no purpose:

there have been hundreds of phantom parties with no program, impotent elected members of parliament, and widespread corruption. Analysts who are not always free from racist prejudices have been quick to conclude that these people (like Africans in general) are not ready for democracy! It is left unacknowledged that the victory of the Malian people coincided with the "neoliberal" offensive that imposed on this extremely fragile country a form of lumpen-development advocated by the World Bank and supported by Europe and France. The result was social and economic regression and unlimited pauperization. It is these policies that bear the major responsibility for the failure of democracy, now discredited. This involution has created, here as elsewhere, favorable terrain for the rising influence of reactionary political Islam (financed by the Gulf), not only in the north, captured subsequently by AQIM, but also in Bamako.

The resulting decay of the Malian state lies behind the crisis that led to the destitution of President Amani Toumani Touré, to Amadou Sanogo's reckless coup d'état, and then to putting Mali under the supervision of the ECOWAS, which "nominated" a "provisional"—so-called transitional—president. The ECOWAS president is the Ivorian president, Alassane Ouattara, who is nothing more than a functionary of the IMF and the French Ministry of Cooperation. It is this transitional president, whose legitimacy is close to zero in the eyes of Malians, who called for French intervention. Above all, Mali's reconstruction now requires the pure and simple rejection of liberal "solutions" that really lie behind all its problems. On this fundamental point, Paris's ideas are the same as those current in Washington, London, and Berlin. The concept of "development aid" coming out of Paris does not go beyond dominant liberal platitudes.

## *Ghana After Nkrumah*

After Nkrumah's fall, I had only passed through Accra several times. But my colleague Kwame Amoa, assistant director of the IDEP, frequently visited the country. He regularly had contacts with the two popular movements that, during the 1970s, created conditions favorable for the army's intervention, under Jerry Rawlings's leadership. I deliberately say "intervention" and not "coup d'état." The army movement here worked with the two avant-garde popular movements. Certainly, problems arose between the two branches of the movement that rejected the business-friendly compradorism of the civilian and military regimes that succeeded one another from 1966 to 1980.

Amoa and I were then invited to meet Rawlings's new team in 1981. Our main mission was to clean up the Treasury accounts, left in a state of total confusion by the chaos of the preceding regimes. The IMF and the World Bank used the situation, as always, to the advantage of the multinationals—the only institutions toward whom they feel any sense of responsibility. The IMF and the World Bank then presented the populist regime with an unpaid bill. They had never demanded any settlement of this supposed bill from their recently overthrown corrupt servants. This consisted of extravagant foreign debts. I had developed, as I have said, a certain competence in this area and always find pleasure in disentangling a confusing mass of details in situations of this kind. Amoa and I were able, with the assistance of numerous comrades on site, of course—notably P. V. Obeng, a sort of prime minister in the provisional government, and Kwesi Botchwey, subsequently named Minister of Finance—to produce a large report that, I believe, had its usefulness. It provided support for a considerable reduction in the claims of the IMF, the World Bank, and multinationals, and established their share of responsibility. These institutions had actively supported numerous bad projects that were behind the disaster. Their functionaries should also have known that these projects were the source of the misappropriation of funds that led to the gigantic fortunes of their friends in government. And if they had not seen anything amiss—as they wanted us to believe by presenting the naive face of being great destroyers of corruption—they should have been dismissed for gross incompetence. Of course, our work was not going to win us any friends in Washington!

But we were also given more directly political objectives. Could we contribute to a calmer exchange of views between the different parts of the movement? The grassroots organizations, the Committees for Defense of the Revolution and others, established and led by cadres, many of whom came out of local Maoist circles, were certainly not without roots or some resonance in the working classes. But they did not always have a coherent strategic vision, and the demands put forward here and there as priorities were sometimes conflicting, or "leftist." There is no reason to be afraid of this. It is difficult to see how a genuine people's movement would otherwise begin. Nevertheless, I am one of those who continue to believe that coordination and organization are essential if one wants to prevent a movement from stagnating, thereby preparing the conditions for a reactionary counteroffensive. Yet any such organization should promote democracy and actually practice it in its own affairs. This is never easy. It is even less so when it is necessary to work with a wing of the movement that holds critical positions in the government—here meaning Rawlings, his group (in particular, P.V. Obeng, head of the civil administration, Kojo Tsikata, a remarkable soldier, head of the secret services who also maintained political control over the army, and Emmanuel Hansen, the group's ideologue), and his army. Rawlings, Obeng, Hansen, Tsikata, Amoa, and I held long discussions that convinced me that the Rawlings group belonged to a new generation that was much more aware than the earlier national liberation leaders of the minimal requirements of democracy, and more in touch with the expressed demands of the working classes. But they were also, as is often the case in English-speaking lands, limited by pragmatism. The central question dealt with which strategy to adopt, in relation to the Ghanaian bourgeoisie, both its corrupt comprador-bureaucratic wing (an enemy) and its active economic wing (the affluent planters, the merchants). Neutralize them? Integrate them into the system? What democratic forms should be constructed—multiple parties, grassroots movements, election procedures, organization of powers—to move forward and strengthen the real weight of the people while avoiding economic chaos?

Ghana does not lack leaders. At the University of Legon, the group that has since led debates at the Forum asked me to lecture and participate in debates, which I never refuse, and also carried out active functions in the movement's internal discussions. There was a diversity of opinion that could have gradually evolved over time as the regime became stabilized around the center right in a difficult world and regional conjuncture, which should encourage some prudence in passing judgment. None of this precludes either a more consistent move to the left in the future or a return to compradorization in the service of dominant capitalism.

### *Congo-Brazzaville*

Following the fall of the clown Fulbert Yulu in Brazzaville in 1963, comrades (as they called themselves) from the popular movements that lie behind the change invited me in 1968–69 to discuss their economic strategies. I then got to know this group of young radicals: the brothers Antoine and Joseph Van den Reysen (we have since developed a strong personal friendship), Ambroise Noumazalaye, Pascal Lissouba, Da Costa, Pierre Nzé, Aba Ganzion, Henri Lopez (who subsequently became assistant director general of UNESCO), Charles Ganao (a diplomat of the first order and defender of the collective interests of Africa in many international forums), and Ange Diaware (head of the youth militias, organizer of a resistance movement), who was subsequently murdered in atrocious circumstances. The analyses of Pierre Philippe Rey, at that time assigned by the ORSTOM, now the IRD, to Brazzaville, were also very useful to me.

My first stay allowed me to get right to the heart of this country's complicated political life, impossible to reduce either to the cliché of "tribalism," so dear to many anthropologists and political scientists, or to the "class analyses" put forward by the various conflicting tendencies within the movement: trade unionists, activists from the revolutionary youth, intellectual leaders, and bureaucrats. I followed for numerous years the chaotic evolution of the Congolese movement and the country's economy.[20]

The IDEP then organized a good seminar in Brazzaville in 1974 at an important moment, characterized by the intensification of debates. What exactly should be done in the economic area? The temptation was strong to give way to the easy possibilities offered by income from the exploitation of oil resources to finance the growth of public administration, but also the development of education (in a country already well educated in 1960) and the improvement of social services. But the question then was how to complement this approach with a serious plan to increase agricultural production and a specific kind of industrialization, one that takes into account the extremely limited economic space of this demographically small, but geographically large country? The collective audience that the president granted to us revealed nothing except for the unfortunate impression of an appetite for unlimited power.

I subsequently visited this friendly country from time to time, despite its tragic political evolution. Pascal Lissouba, then prime minister, hoped that I could give him some proposals to, at the very least, make some minimal improvements in the management of the public sector. This was a pertinent question. I then had to make on-site visits to a group of ailing companies, from Fort Rousset and Makoua in the north, to Niari and Pointe Noire. I was given an all-terrain vehicle, a driver, and a guide. I was able to see the large equatorial primary forest, its gigantic trees and impenetrable undergrowth. It was beautiful, very beautiful, but terrifying. Along the road, when we stopped to eat, the Pygmies, who seemed to come from nowhere, immediately appeared and offered us the only product they had: monkeys. The guide, a good and jovial cook, grilled and sautéed them in a frying pan, then flambéed them— in the Parisian style, he said—with whisky. I also saw an incredible scene of Pygmies exploited by the Bantu planters. The Pygmies came to work—hard— for several days to harvest coffee and were paid in low-quality red wine, drunk in unlimited quantities from a cistern with a rubber hose. The Pygmies drank for one or two hours, after which, dead drunk, they slept on the ground, disappearing the next day into their great forest until the next harvest, a year later.

I realized after visiting the country how difficult it was to start any sort of agriculture in this underpopulated country. Farmers isolated in pockets of the forest could, at best, deliver to market only a few sacks of produce that they had to transport over hundreds of kilometers on terrible roads. Should the farmers be brought together? But they did not want to hear that. I also realized that the "industries" could hardly be designed and managed without taking into account all types of conditions specific to the country.

I was in Brazzaville, en route to Luanda, two days after the presidential election in which Lissouba was victorious. Lissouba, who met with me, had made a good impression. He spoke about democratization, surpassing ethnic divisions, and reconciliation with the militants of the PCT, who had just lost power. I had not been surprised by this defeat. Gradually, sustained by oil revenues, the state bureaucracy—in which the majority of intellectuals was integrated—had absorbed the so-called Marxist-Leninist party, suppressed the autonomy of working-class organizations, and massacred young rebels. The army had become an essential component of this rather ordinary form of authoritarian statism. All efforts to develop agricultural and industrial production were abandoned and replaced by simple social redistribution of oil revenues sufficient to ease popular discontent. The movement for democratization, which began in 1990 with all sorts of ambitions, waved the multiparty flag to begin the attack on the decrepit machinery of state power. But this was a farcical democratization that worked for dominant transnational capitalism through globalized neoliberalism. It would effectively put an end to the chance—as small as it was—for a renewal of the left and would liquidate the vestiges of statism and its vague desires for independence without threatening the interests of the multinational corporations. Such a democracy would combine perfectly with the compradorization of the local system. In these conditions, Lissouba's election only emphasized the uncertainty of the future. Had he been elected to set up this farcical comprador democracy? Or had he been elected against this farce, whose real candidates—the horrible Paul Kaya, former lackey of Fulbert Yulu, and the disturbing Thystère Tchicaya, former member of the PCT, a convert to liberalism who proposed particularly violent repressive measures to settle all problems—had been soundly beaten when voters ultimately split their votes between Lissouba and the PCT? I personally hoped that the second hypothesis offered the correct explanation. I discussed all this with several former leaders of the PCT and received varying opinions. Subsequent history showed that Lissouba really intended nothing other than to assert his personal power and, for that purpose, to select the worst means: ethnic chauvinism, thereby preparing the most favorable conditions for violent confrontations on ethnic terms. He unreservedly accepted neoliberalism without discussion, but he believed he could secure his monopoly on power as a privileged *interlocuteur* of the West through opportunistic advances to various parties. Denis Sassou Nguesso easily succeeded in uniting behind him the army and public opinion, undoubtedly tired of Lissouba's megalomania, but at the price of thousands of civilian victims.

## *Benin*

The 1970s and 1980s in Benin were characterized by an attempt to "do something." In the unanimous opinion of Beninese analysts, whether favorable to or critical of President Mathieu Kérékou's government, the 1960s had been a real farce: a non-state, in fact, a bad colonial administration that had survived the proclamation of independence. This was an administration managed by politicians in the most vulgar sense of the term—their names: Apithy, Zinsou, and Maga—for their personal profit and that of their small, microregional supporters. It is not surprising, then, that in these conditions, the populist project of the army and its leader, Kérékou, had a real and immediate resonance with the people of the country, even if—with some perceptiveness and maybe a little sectarianism—the Marxists of the Communist Party of Dahomey had quite quickly seen the contradictions and limitations of this project.

At the beginning of this period, in 1975, the IDEP organized a large seminar in Cotonou with really ambitious objectives defined in cooperation with the state's economic management institutions (that our friend Justin Gnidéhou coordinated) and academics—to contribute to the definition of the social project, the identification of the difficulties it would confront, and the elaboration of a phased approach to push the program forward. I believe that this seminar has remained an important date in the country's history in the memory of all participants. Not that the responses given to the initial questions were in any way final ones. Far from it. But a full, serious, even contentious debate had tackled them all head on. President Kérékou came himself to close the seminar, not with a formal speech, but as a direct participant in the concluding debate. He then agreed to respond to questions put to him, without knowing those questions in advance. Say what you want, but I have not known too many presidents—in Africa or elsewhere—who would have accepted a challenge of this type. Although the atmosphere was somewhat tense—which proves that the debate was real and serious—I believe that this confrontation was not negative and useless, even if what happened after in practice did not have the desired positive effects.

Personally, I do not criticize the project for not having been "truly socialist"—besides, there still needs to be some agreement on the meaning of this label. A national popular project seemed to me to be the best that could be achieved in the conditions of this small, vulnerable country. Of course, we need to understand that "national popular" is more than populism because, faced with the predictable attacks from the enemy, there are not, in my opinion, any better ramparts than the autonomous and democratic organization of the working/popular classes. The system remained populist and even slid gradually toward authoritarianism. But it was not terrorist. The Western media, once again, presented a distorted image of the country during this time. The Benin government did not commit criminal acts of repression like its neighbor Togo, which, under the Gnassingbé Eyadéma dictatorship, commonly carried out such acts. Kérékou was presented as a bloodthirsty monster—since he said he was a Marxist-Leninist—while the "liberal" (that is, someone who allows the compradors and multinationals to do what they want) Eyadéma's continual crimes were passed over in silence.

The balance sheet from the Kérékou's decades is certainly mixed. Its positive aspects (the decline in regionalism, positive economic growth, reduced social inequality) can certainly be contrasted with its negative ones (inefficient management, public deficits, administrative disorder, even corruption). In this assessment, we should also take into account what happened in the country after the end of the populist government. A well-manipulated "democratization" operation led to a showy system of "multiple parties" and "elections." Many Beninese intellectuals decided to play the game, even some of the best. They can be excused because of the absurd abuses of power to which the populist regime had subjected them and maybe because of their naive faith in electoral democracy. The result was the "Soglo" episode. Governed by a president-functionary deprived of any political sense who was pushed into the position by the World Bank, handed over to the diktat of structural adjustment presented as a "corrective for past errors" (which, of course, it is not, neither in Benin nor elsewhere, since it is only a project for unilateral subjection to the requirements for managing the crisis of world capitalism), and subjected to the nonsense of neoliberal ideology, Benin has since experienced only a decline in the condition of the masses. And the old Kérékou was reelected! But obviously this was in conditions that would hardly allow for any exit from the impasse. Defenders of the principle of this idiotic liberalism are quick to say that the failure is due to the vulnerability of this small country to the external conjuncture. But is the same vulnerability also not largely responsible for the failures of the populist project?

I visited this small, captivating country on several occasions. Its history is a tragic one, though, since it was one of the places where the slave trade flourished the most. And this produced a contradictory mix of local political systems, some of which were part of the slave-trading system and others of which resisted it. One cannot visit without emotion the Ouidah Fort over which the Portuguese flag continued to fly until I don't know exactly when. In the Abomey Palace, I was able to assess the actual effectiveness of the methods of hypnosis (probably) that the "sorcerers" of the place practice. Benin is a country rich with both astute modernist intellectuals and feared fetish-priests throughout the whole region.

### Burkina Faso

In the first period after the independence of Upper Volta, the moderate RDA—following the lead of Côte d'Ivoire, of which it was only an economic subsidiary—had prevailed. "Colony of a colony," Upper Volta provided through emigration the bulk of the workers who built the Côte d'Ivoire's colonial economy, while the villages of origin of these builders of prosperity survived only on crumbs. In general, emigration impoverishes the regions of departure, which support the cost of raising and training the workers from their birth to their departure. Often these same regions bear the cost of supporting the older workers when they return to the country. But emigration enriches the ruling classes of the host countries that benefit from the labor of immigrants, generally at low wages. This is the exact opposite of what the neoliberal theory claims, echoed by the media, which thereby almost always tailors a hostile prejudice toward immigrants. Côte d'Ivoire, then, had a vested interest, under such conditions, in having this country be "independent," in being relieved of the burden of supporting it (most of Upper Volta had been part of the colony of Côte d'Ivoire until 1947). If the two countries are examined together, which actually corresponds to the reality of the unequal economic partnership, the figures of the Ivorian "miracle" should be halved.

This situation was always well understood by the Burkinabé people and intellectuals. They revolted against it spontaneously. Discussing this problem during a lecture at the University of Ouagadougou, I responded to a mischievous question from a student. I said bluntly: "Take your bicycles"—the Burkinabé are the only people in Africa to make extensive use of bicycles and Ouagadougou resembles Beijing in this regard—"and ride down to Abidjan to proclaim the unity of the two countries. Two problems will be solved at the same time: the economic problem of Upper Volta and the political problem of Côte d'Ivoire!" I was applauded as never before. This revolt is, perhaps, one of the reasons why the Burkinabé intelligentsia was, and remains, dominated by the left. Everybody, or almost everybody, belongs or belonged to one of the communist movements, the original PAI or the Maoist movements (the PCRHV and other organizations). It is not surprising, then, that this influence extended into the army and that a group of officers even dared to take on the name Rassemblement des Officiers Communistes (Assembly of Communist Officers).

The masquerade of the neocolonial administration by Maurice Yaméogo's RDA could not, then, last. But the radicalization of the response was not determined in advance. Urban unrest was led by the powerful unions, which refused to be domesticated by the one-party government (this setup is not characteristic solely of "socialism," given that the one party of the Côte d'Ivoire, applauded by the Western powers, had domesticated the unions). Yet they were confined by the limitations of their support from the petite bourgeoisie (teachers and functionaries) and were lacking a base among industrial workers. Initially, they had only paved the way for the weak and indecisive Sangoulé Lamizana military government. Then the ROC, led by Thomas Sankara, took over.

Immediately, the standard problems of such situations arose: What to do? Go beyond populism and encourage the peasant and urban masses to organize themselves freely or attempt to "manage" them to the point of eliminating all potential strength? What relations should the government establish with revolutionary Marxist organizations? Should it seek to absorb them into a new single party or accept a more democratic approach of a real united front tolerating different viewpoints and open to debate? Such was the focus of repeated discussions with Sankara, who invited me in 1986 to give my viewpoint. I must admit that Sankara was a likable person. He was quite modest, direct (even in his frank look), open, and listened to what you said and responded without abusing his leadership position. Moreover, he was a real feminist and insisted on the importance of changing habits to support the equality of the sexes, which is quite rare among great men. He was also educated, having read the classics of Marxism with the same care as a good civilian intellectual. I personally felt quite at ease with him and, if he had not been a head of state, would have unhesitatingly become his friend. His assassination upset me greatly.

Concerning the "strategy of economic and social development," Sankara was, in my opinion, right—at least in theory. As a first step, he thought it necessary to start with "small projects," that is, projects that quickly improve the production conditions of rural communities, and do so with the least expense possible. The profits from this improvement would be completely returned to the communities in question. This choice was not motivated by the dubious philosophy of "small is beautiful," but rather by realism (what is immediately possible) and political sense (through this type of activity, the organization and democratization of rural life could be initiated). Moreover, Sankara had decided—inspired, perhaps, by the Chinese model—to send functionaries and technicians to undergo training at the base, that is, in the villages. The hope was that "they would learn from the masses" (know their real problems) and "teach the masses" (by providing the latter with their knowledge as agronomists, veterinarians, doctors, teachers, and accountants). I certainly had nothing to reiterate or add to a plan of this type. I then said to Sankara that I only hoped to see—at least a little—how this was working in the field. I had the impression that he was expecting this question. But his response was even better: you can't see everything; you would have to stay a year for that. But make your choice, go see your friends (everyone knew that I visited the entire Burkinabé left) and choose according to what they will tell you (many of them had misgivings and would probably choose examples of failure). That is what I did. I shall not be so bold as to claim that I could have made a serious report based on my observations, which were quick and impressionistic. I will only say that my impressions were rather favorable. Perhaps this was from ignorance of the true difficulties and realities since I had to accept at face value what the two or three persons at each place I visited were in a position to say and analyze. But the very fact that, perhaps, a third of the functionaries and technicians I met in the field were happy with their lot (material life is much harder than in Ouagadougou, but much is learned and one feels useful!), I felt it was a success. Perhaps two-thirds of these (silent) "deportees" had a different opinion. But one-third was much more than I had imagined (I thought 10 percent at most). This reminded me of Amílcar Cabral's observation about the suicide of the petite bourgeoisie as a class. In any case, the material results of the project—an increase in production, self-consumption, and sales—showed at least partial success, which could have been improved with time.

Concerning the second aspect—relations with revolutionary organizations—things were more difficult. Sankara knew that I would see my friends. He even wished and, I believe, hoped that I would play the role of official intermediary. I insisted on maintaining my place: a foreigner too ignorant of many of the underlying realities to set myself up as an arrogant sermonizer. I certainly met everyone, or nearly so, and listened to their analyses—which, incidentally, were quite diverse and often even opposed: Basile and Joséphine Guissou, Talata Kafando, Arba Diallo, Phillippe Ouedraogo, Taladie Thiombiano, and many others (without counting moderate political figures like Joseph Ki Zerbo and Charles Kaboré, and economists like Pierre Damiba, and others). The government had set up its own organizations—Committees for Defense of the Revolution, and others. Their behavior, their degree of organization and possible control, and their relations with the militants of the revolutionary organizations—none of these were clear enough (at least for me) to reach any conclusions about political strategy, either for the government or the revolutionary organizations. The leaderships of the latter, which I normally met with separately, had viewpoints that I was content to listen to. My only intervention was to say to everyone—the revolutionary organizations and Sankara: keep your differences and respect each other, if that is possible, but also try to work together on points of convergence. After all, there are some. And that is what I really thought.

Burkina Faso's experiment stalled and went wrong. People close to Sankara assassinated him, as is well known. Since then, the country has not left the well-worn path of ordinary neocolonialism. But the future remains open and a return to the left is still possible if internal and external conditions permit. Burkina Faso, like Mali and Ghana, is in a holding pattern.

## *Tanzania*

Accra had been a sort of capital of Africa from 1958 to 1966. The importance that Nkrumah attached to the prospect of African unity—"Africa must unite"—and the fact that representatives from liberation movements of countries still struggling for independence, and from radical movements hounded out of their own countries, found a safe space in Accra gave it an importance that it lost with Nkrumah's fall. But the baton was immediately taken up by Dar es Salaam. Two major events began Tanzania's glorious decade.

The first was the revolution in Zanzibar in 1964. In Zanzibar—or the Arab Antilles, as I have called it—we could find slavery plantations producing cloves for all the peoples of the Indian Ocean; Arab planters who came from the south of the Arabian peninsula; and black slaves captured in eastern Africa. For a time, it was the capital of the Sultanate of Oman. A visit to Bagamoyo, a small Tanzanian port that faces Zanzibar and was the landing place for slaves, immediately gives rise (at least in me) to a profound sadness. Like the Nazi concentration camps, these are places that must be visited so that we will never forget the infamy of which humanity is capable, even today. The party led by one of my oldest friends, Babu, had made the revolution. I have already spoken of how we first met in London in 1953 and then later cooperated on the periodical *Révolution* in 1963.[21] After Babu died, his Anglo-Indian partner, Amrit Wilson, invited me to trace the stages of his life at the remembrance ceremony one year later. Babu had promised to write his memoirs. He left only a few notes. But I believe I knew his intellectual and political development, parallel to my own, sufficiently well to fulfill my mission honorably. The Zanzibar revolution was brief, but terrible. The sultan and landowners, who had remained quasi-slaveholders—despite their legally free status, the peasants continued to be treated as slaves—were all cruelly massacred. That was inevitable: three centuries of oppression in the most odious forms imaginable can only be obliterated in an explosion of victorious hate.

But Zanzibari society remained a Creole society with all its stratified color prejudices. Eager to get rid of this stupidity from the legacy of the past, the mayor of Zanzibar (it was he who told me the surprising story that follows), observing that whites married only among themselves, just like the blacks, or the various so-called mixed races (half, quarter, etc.), he decided to force them to mix: You there (to a white in the line), you marry this one here (a black), etc. And on paper the mixing was registered! I shall refrain from any comment.

Here is an amusing story concerning the island. It had a mini-government, one of whose "ministers" said to me, "We are requesting external aid by selecting partners based on their competence: the Russians for heavy industry [in Zanzibar!], the East Germans for the police, and the Egyptians for propaganda." "That is a recipe for guaranteed failure," I responded. I do not think he understood.

The second event was the Arusha Declaration in 1967 in which the party of the national liberation movement for the former Tanganyika (TANU) and its leader, Julius Nyerere, proclaimed their wish to get off the well-worn paths of neocolonialism and move onto a socialist path. What resulted, here again, did not go beyond populism. That was the case despite the existence of numerous cadres quite aware of the problem.

Dar became, as I said, the capital of Africa. On this level, Nyerere's choice was quite remarkable and made him one of the positive personalities of African history. Dar welcomed all the liberation movements of southern Africa: the MPLA in Angola, FRELIMO in Mozambique, and the freedom fighters of Zimbabwe (then Rhodesia) and South Africa. Tanzania had become the rear base for rest and training of guerillas. Nyerere was behind the formation of the Front Line States, anti-apartheid and active on the international level when the Western nations were silent (as Nelson Mandela reminded Bill Clinton). Tanzania also welcomed the scattered forces of Lumumbism and encouraged them to take up the fight to liberate Zaire, exploited by the horrible Mobutu Sese Seko. It also welcomed the more or less radical, but at least honest sections of the national liberation movements of Uganda, Kenya, and Malawi.

I frequently visited Dar from 1972 to 1975. The IDEP organized a double seminar there of great importance, in my opinion. Half of the seminar focused on the economic and political strategies of Tanzania. There was open debate in which the government's viewpoint was presented directly by the ministers Amir Jamal and Wilbert Chagula, the best functionaries and technocrats of the economy. Some of the most prominent political organizers of the state and party (such as Kingunge Ngombale-Mwiru and others) made their presentations, specifically concerning the social project (Ujamaa) and its implications. Academics of the highest quality, such as Justinian Rweyemamu, Haroub Othman, Issa Shivji, C. S. L. Chachage, Simon and Marjorie Mbilinyi, and many others presented particular aspects of the situation. Students formed the largest group of participants, but many urban activists—trade unionists, among others—had also decided to participate in these debates and share their experiences.

The debate revealed a real divide. On one side were those who did not see beyond populism, always disposed to accept the state's proposals without much discussion—even the most debatable ones, such as bringing together the rural population into collective villages, the results of which turned out to be disastrous, and which caused TANU to lose the popularity it had gained during the national liberation struggle, with a dramatic consequence in the end: a depoliticization that made new advances in democracy impossible. There were intellectuals, militants, and agents of the state or party in all groups. On the other side were those who saw quite clearly the limitations of the system. Their alternative proposals were not necessarily "leftist"—a facile accusation made by those who were "satisfied with the government." The emphasis placed on workers' and peasants' democracy (autonomous unions, worker participation in management of the public sector, no forced resettling of rural populations, genuine local elections) was not—in my opinion—"dangerous," but, on the contrary, the correct response to the challenges. These comrades were also to be found in all groups, but Babu was incontestably the most experienced politician among them, as well as the most constructive in his analyses and proposals.

Nyerere chose the first version of Ujamaa. He had no doubts on the subject. Can this be explained by his personal makeup? Perhaps it can, at least in part. Nyerere was a pastor and had never read much beyond religious and moral texts. All of my Tanzanian friends who interacted with him—Babu in particular—all told me that he had never read anything of Marxism except an English pamphlet. His speeches—delivered in a preaching tone—had been effective in mobilizing the people in favor of independence, and even socialism, defined simply in moral terms: justice, equality, respect for individuals, etc. The positive aspects of his convictions—horror of "tribalism," horror of supposedly nationalist demagoguery directed at the minority of Indian origin (who never suffered in Tanzania the exclusion to which it was subjected in Kenya and Uganda)—are to his credit. But there were limitations to his moral perception of social relations. Babu said of him: he does not understand the difference between the word "popular" and the word "populist." Babu paid dearly for his deep disagreement with Nyerere's approach to Ujamaa.

Babu was arrested in 1972, a few days after the assassination of Karume, vice president of Tanzania and president of Zanzibar. Accused without proof of participating in this "plot," he was thrown into prison and was not released until 1978. In the too brief memoirs he left behind, Babu explains how he had found in prison many militants from the liberation movements established in Dar whose leaders wanted to be rid of them for one reason or another (generally because the leftist line of these militants bothered them or for more ordinary reasons such as power struggles). The Tanzanian authorities carried out, without discussion, the decisions of the leaderships of these movements—MPLA, FRELIMO, ANC, SWAPO, Lumumbists, and others. Consequently, and whatever his personal qualities, Nyerere largely bears responsibility for the turnaround that ended with a re-compradorization—led, in part, by the party (which had degenerated) and, in part, by the right's machinations, supported by the democratic West, as always. But in Tanzania, as in Burkina Faso and several other countries, the forces of the left are still present on the ground. This country, too, is in a holding pattern. Some foreign observers, who not long ago were admirers of the "Kenyan miracle" and happy with the breakdown and failure of socialism in Tanzania, have today discovered that the potential of this country remains high, while the extent of the disaster in Kenya is extraordinary.

The second part of the seminar concerned more general problems—the construction of socialism in Africa—and the problems of liberating southern Africa. This part of the seminar benefited from the participation of movements that were well established in Dar and numerous intellectuals who were refugees in Tanzania. There were Kenyans and Ugandans: Mahmood Mamdani, Ahmad Mohieddine, Yash Tandon, Dan Nabudere, Yoweri Museveni (the future president of Uganda), and Abdallah Bujra (whom I recruited to help me establish CODESRIA in Dakar). From Zimbabwe, there were Ibbo Mandaza, Nathan Shamuyarira, and Tekere, whom we will encounter later. I shall return to the positions taken by comrades from the Portuguese colonies present at that time. Numerous English-speaking West Indians had chosen Dar, just as French-speaking ones were found in Francophone Africa. Walter Rodney, subsequently a popular leader in Guyana, was assassinated by a gang working for the reactionaries of his country, as is well known. He had a brilliant mind and great courage.

The discussion was tense. The reason was obviously the weight that the official Soviet view had on all these questions. In this area, Nyerere and his government were quite prudent. It is well known that they were considered "pro-Chinese" (thus anti-Soviet) by foreign governments. This was a bit flimsy, even if the Chinese had a presence. China financed the only large-scale project that changed the geopolitics of the region in favor of liberation: the Tanzam railway that opened up Zambia and freed it from the grip of South Africa. Ruth First, the wife of Joe Slovo, General Secretary of the South African Communist Party, systematically and fiercely defended the official Soviet view on all levels. What is socialism? It is the USSR, which is perfect; the defects are secondary and correctable human errors. What is liberation? It is the "non-capitalist way," that is, populism, the forms of which, however— from Egyptian Nasserism to Nkrumahism and Ujamaa—clearly demonstrated its contradictions and limitations. Any other opinion, First said with calm assurance, is at best only a deviation, and perhaps an infiltration of imperialist propaganda. Simple. Whatever the undoubted talents of this militant (and she had more than enough), despite her strong and, in many respects, even agreeable personality, as well as her undoubted courage, the speech not only did not convince me personally, but irritated half the participants.

As the organizer of this debate and one in charge of the meeting between "the two schools," I tried to maintain the correct balance in formal terms— freedom of expression for both sides, etc. Yet I did so without refraining from presenting my own view—in neutral terms, of course, never polemical or even insulting. Following this seminar, I immediately wrote an article on "The Future of Southern Africa."[22] I deliberately did not refer to the positions of the South African Communist Party (this was not the moment to polemicize against one of the forces on the ground fighting against apartheid). But I did allow myself to say that an imperialist solution to the region's contradictions was not impossible. The later Lancaster House Agreement for Zimbabwe and the results of the fall of apartheid in South Africa did not invalidate my analysis. In fact, when I met Slovo in liberated Johannesburg (Ruth had been assassinated in exile in Maputo by a letter bomb sent by the South African police), he fell into my arms and said, "Our quarrels belong to the past." "The Soviet Union no longer exists," I said to him, "and I am not happy about that." I always had hoped that the system would fall to the left. It fell to the right, as I feared it would.

A coastal country, Tanzania is very pretty. Isabelle and I visited the magnificent Kilimanjaro region and the gorgeous Ngoro Ngoro Park, situated in the crater of an extinct volcano. This is one of the most beautiful nature reserves in the world. I also had the opportunity to travel many kilometers with Babu. He was a real force of nature, always laughing at everything. He was endowed with a wonderful sense of humor and was a sharp social critic. Yet he was serious in his analyses and courageous and persevering in his militancy. I can attest to the fact that everywhere we went, he knew the people and the problems. He was a true popular leader.

## Madagascar

I was not surprised by the fall of Philibert Tsiranana's neocolonial regime in Madagascar. Rather, it was its existence that was an aberration, which can only be explained by the 1947 colonial massacres that had decapitated a young and powerful national movement. But unlike what happened elsewhere in similar situations, national sentiment remained strong and allowed a rapid resumption of the movement. Tsiranana was not accepted; he was the symbol of defeat and capitulation. The French media explained his lack of popularity by the fact that he was "Sakalava," a coastal group despised by the Hova aristocracy of the plateaus, which dominate the country. This explanation is not worth much. Didier Ratsiraka, who became the "socialist" president of Madagascar and was reelected following the failure of the first neoliberal farce, is himself from the coastal region. Madagascar is a nation organized around its unifying language and its historical royalty, which, with the means of the time and thus within the limitations of its real power, governed the whole island. A mixture of immigrants from Indonesia—historians are uncertain as to their origin; Sumatra, perhaps—and Bantu Africans created this nation. The former first landed on the coast of East Africa. Later, when they moved to the island, they either brought the latter from the mainland as slaves or accepted them as migrants. Of course, as almost always, such mixing gave rise to physical types and skin colors that run from so-called yellow Asian to so-called black African. Yet the physical characteristics do not at all have the same value here as they do in Creole societies. More important is regional origin (either from the plateaus or the coasts) and, above all, social status: Hova nobility, free peasant, or dependent of inferior status. In this sense, the Malagasy nation can actually be viewed—from the outside—as weakly integrated. But that is the case for all premodern nations and even for many so-called modern nations. French colonization exacerbated these differences, dividing in order to conquer and control, as always. But it never succeeded in eliminating the strong unifying national sentiment of all Malagasy. It is this failure that explains both Tsiranana's fall and the precocity of the independence movement (the leaders who dreamed from the beginning only of independence, even if that were accompanied by some kind of link to France, whereas many others in continental Africa at that time never dreamed of such a thing, as I said earlier).[23]

The successive governments of the island since then have been confronted with a major question, still not resolved. Is it solely a question of achieving the national objective: govern Madagascar as an independent country, as it had been for its entire pre-colonial history? Or is it actually a question of social, political, and ideological transformations brought about by insertion into the modern world such that the social content of the Malagasy government must be adapted to those changes? In other words, it is the class struggle that defines this content. As with other societies, Malagasy society was profoundly transformed by colonization. The relations between the old ruling classes—supposedly feudal, whether the term is correct or not—and their peasants have become, to various degrees, relations between landowners and tenants or agricultural workers, whose products are, in large part, commodities. In addition, a class of wealthy and middle-income free peasants was formed. There are also now a large number of salaried city dwellers and a petite bourgeoisie of employees, functionaries, and other categories: the urbanized "poor," resulting from the rural exodus; a comprador bourgeoisie of merchants and intermediaries; and an educated national "elite," which sees itself as the natural heir of the national governing class.

I had been invited by the government after the fall of Tsiranana, in 1974 and 1975, for the same mission I had become well known for among technocrats: assess the public finances, left in extreme chaos by the mismanagement of the overthrown neocolonial government. I carried out this mission. At the same time, it was obviously an opportunity for me to get acquainted with this unique Afro-Asian society that is really quite fascinating in the way it has successfully synthesized characteristics originating among Asian rice growers (skilled movement, delicate craftsmanship, artistic taste, intense labor, etc.) and African peasants (taste for freedom, sense of equality, etc.). Also, I used the opportunity to learn about the state traditions of this country, proud of its monarchical history. The monarch was often a woman. The queens of Madagascar sometimes eclipsed the kings and princes consort, and exercised real decision-making power. This characteristic is found throughout the society, where the place of women is less subordinate than in many other countries. No one should be surprised in this context that the head of the AKFM, the radical party that came out of the 1947 insurrection, was an energetic and intelligent (and quite pretty) woman, Gisèle Rabesahala. Tradition also always seems to call for what the intelligentsia of the country call the "Queen of Madagascar." Successive presidents have all had muses, who were not mistresses without any real political clout, even if, in many cases—in Africa and elsewhere—these women know perfectly well how to use their charm to exercise a certain influence (particularly in nominations for important posts). But the Malagasy muses are above all political councilors. These are strongly politicized, cultivated, and generally intelligent women. Now it happened to be the case that successive Malagasy muses had all been my students, conspicuous by their intelligence and willingness to work!

The Malagasy intellectual and university community is politicized and active. It has produced some of the leaders of powerful popular movements and parties, such as Manandafy Rakotonirina. He was on the extreme left and worked effectively to mobilize the destitute urban population (the lumpen for some people, the real masses for others). He made a career and moved toward the right. After Ratsiraka's electoral defeat, he decided to go along with neo-liberalism without too many reservations. But the university is not the only place where popular leaders are produced. Monja Jaona, the old leader of the powerful peasants' movement from the south of the island, is a Protestant pastor.

The place and role Christian religions occupy in Malagasy society are rather special. In the nineteenth century, the Malagasy monarchy was officially converted to Protestantism at the instigation of English pastors. Their official Protestantism was subsequently a way for the Hove ruling class to differentiate itself from the French colonial government, which dominated the army and the colonists through Catholic influence, despite the secular nature of the state. Catholic missionaries had to focus their efforts on the working classes, not very Christianized up to then. But Catholic or Protestant, the Malagasy people synthesized Christianity with their earlier religious beliefs. The tradition of "turning of the bones," in which families annually disinter the bodies of their departed loved ones for a period of many years, bring them home, share a meal in their presence, and then return them to their tombs, is one of the most well-known manifestations of this synthesis.

It was normal that I would think of Madagascar as the site of IDEP's Afro-Asian conference.[24] Academics, activists, and government functionaries I knew (Willy Léonard, François Rajaona—subsequently rector—my student Céline Rabevazaha, Léon Rasolomanana, and others) were collaborators and effective organizers in this undertaking; I owe them much. The conference was a great success, I believe. First, because it was an opportunity for the intellectuals of each continent to discover each other and get to know currents of thought previously unknown to them. Second, because they discovered that Afro-Asia existed and Madagascar was the symbol of its reality. This reality was striking, and it reinforced the solidarity of the non-aligned—which are Asians and Africans. I was told several times on multiple occasions by the secretariats of the Non-Aligned Movement that this conference had more influence on that generation of intellectuals than can be imagined. I am, without any false pride, quite proud of this achievement.

I was also obviously interested in the Malagasy political and social project, an ongoing topic of my discussions with leaders of all persuasions. Some—from the extreme left—had supported Richard Ratsimandrava's attempt to radicalize the class struggle by organizing the poor peasants around a program of radical agrarian reform. The period of Ratsimandrava's government was very brief and its leader assassinated for reasons that have never been clarified, but are obvious: the property-owning classes, with a powerful presence in all parts of the state, could not accept anyone getting involved in agrarian reform.

What happened subsequently was predictable. The radical approach was replaced by a vague project based around cooperatives, reviving a real, or allegedly real, tradition: the *fokolonana,* or village communities. The accompanying rhetoric was well known: a socialism that would sink its roots into national tradition. In fact, it was a way to dilute the seriousness of the problems. Of course, there were nuances. Some basically wanted to do nothing, and were content with ideological rhetoric. Others thought it possible to use the contradictions of the project to advance peasant struggles. At the same time, succeeding Malagasy governments, above all after Ratsiraka's stabilization, advanced national construction through the Malagisization of education, nationalizations, leaving the Franc zone, opening up to cooperation with countries from the East and China, adopting a consistent non-aligned diplomatic line, etc. Also within this context, various positions confronted one another in urban conflicts. Many were satisfied with the system as it was—it offered a field of expansion to the educated petite bourgeoisie, posts and promotions, and, later, even less legal opportunities for enrichment. Others were impatient and saw that the natural development of this system could not really lead the country out of the neocolonial trap. In my opinion, they were right. But what social forces should be mobilized, and how, to reverse the course of things? Should it be the radical petite bourgeoisie—youth, students—backed by the unions? Or should it be the poor masses of the city? Consequently, violent and bloody conflicts sometimes erupted in the capital.

I had the opportunity to hear all these points of view extensively argued by their defenders. I also had the opportunity to discuss these issues more directly with the government's main leaders, including the "queen" of Madagascar and President Ratsiraka. French media often presented Ratsiraka as a dangerous megalomaniac. That is not at all the image I had of him. On the contrary, he was a reasonable political man. He was cultivated; he was well acquainted with Marxism (but perhaps that is a vice in the eyes of the media). He was moderate in the sense that when it came to the historical experiences of the USSR and China, I heard him make only restrained and reflective comments, informed neither by stupid ideological submission nor systematic denigration. He was neither pro-French in the manner of colonial lackeys nor neurotically anti-French. He was a man who knew France, loved its culture and its left, but did not at all like its colonists and its imperialism. The commemoration of the 1947 massacres did not give rise to nationalist verbal violence, but to internationalist rhetoric, recalling the solidarity expressed by the French Communist Party. Internally, Ratsiraka was in favor of adopting a middle line. That seemed to me the only line possible, leaving the future open. But it must be acknowledged that this line was not imposed, at least with sufficient enough force, to prevent later deviation. His government, which was far from being absolute but had to rely both on social forces from the right, with positions of control, and active left opposition, did not succeed in implementing the advocated middle policies. The public sector became a field for competition between bourgeois clans and sectoral or regional interests. All of that, on the background of a weak and vulnerable economy, could only lead to worsening deficits. The makeshift means used to deal with the deterioration of the economy—external debt, delays in maintaining infrastructure, etc.—ultimately only worsened the situation. The day thus arrived when, with the world crisis worsening, capitalism moved to the offensive everywhere in the world, as we all know. Structural adjustment programs coincided with the collapse of the USSR. The political weapon mobilized to serve the imperialist strategy was "democracy." Obviously, this was understood as a cheap and showy multiparty setup that led to fractions of the bourgeoisie—the same bourgeoisie that had strengthened its position within the context of the populist project—being played off against one another, thereby offering to foreign interests an expanded field for intervention. Ratsiraka was beaten. The so-called democratic government that followed corrected none of the past "errors." The deficits worsened and Ratsiraka returned, reelected. But he was old, and the internal and external conditions were not those of the 1970s. Here again is another country on hold.

The recent questionable presidential election brought the usual practice of an alternating changeover to the forefront, under the leadership of the mayor of Antananarivo, Marc Ravalomanana. He is a U.S.-style businessman, pro-liberal and with no real experience other than what "managing the market" (for yogurt, as it happens) can teach him. Like Laurent Gbagbo of Côte d'Ivoire, he seems convinced by one of the U.S. sects that ravage Africa. His victory ended in a new disaster that the combination of democracy and neoliberalism necessarily produces. But from another perspective, Ratsiraka's stubbornness had put a considerable damper on an independent recomposition of the left, which still has considerable historical resources in the country.

One aspect of the question that, in my opinion, is of central importance for the future of the entire Indian Ocean region, and thus concerns not just Madagascar, but also the Comoros and Seychelles, is its geopolitical importance. That is an aspect that economists generally ignore—wrongly, in my view.

The region's less naive political leaders (the "market" is not everything!) have always mentioned the geostrategic dimension of the Indian Ocean, whether that be in Madagascar, Tanzania, Sri Lanka, or India. The question was on the agenda of the Non-Aligned Movement summit in Colombo. The British offered to Washington the opportunity to set up the gigantic U.S. nuclear and marine base on Diego Garcia, which threatens the entire Middle East, South Asia, and East Africa. In doing so, the British simply abused their rights since the island legally belongs to Mauritius.

*Ethiopia*

I went to Addis Ababa for the first time in 1962 to participate in the team that set up the IDEP. Ethiopia is a country that I found I needed to get to know better. Just like Yemen across the Red Sea, but on a larger scale, the country is poor, but is nevertheless a cohesive society full of potential. Third-largest country in Africa by population (today 80 million), Ethiopia has been a state for two thousand years. It had the opportunity to avoid complete colonization in the nineteenth century, although it has recently lost its maritime province (which became Eritrea). Ethiopians are certainly proud of the antiquity of their state, which legend dates back to the queen of Sheba (this legend is really nothing more than the expression of the Yemeni origin of its people). There is a story of a foreign journalist who asked a question of the Emperor Haile Selassie at the beginning of the 1960s. Now, this was at a time when most heads of African states claimed that their societies were "without classes," following the supposed African tradition. "And are there classes in your country?" the journalist asked. "Of course," answered the Negus, "we are civilized!"

During my trips around the country, I had the opportunity to become acquainted with the Falachas or Beta Israel. The Falachas, who are Ethiopian Jews, poor peasants like the others, producing the same pretty pottery as the Copts (distinguishable only by the Stars of David used as a decorative motif), had never been subject to any particular discrimination. Their Judaism, the Coptic Christianity of the majority, or the Islam of some communities, were and still are lived by all sections of this peasant people as variations, with fluctuating and indistinct boundaries, of the same "true religion." Fanaticism—which now exists—is a product of modernization and of the urban petite bourgeoisie. It required all the cunning of Zionist agents—backward Polish rabbis who saw in the Ethiopian Jews an unsophisticated population that they could recruit into their fundamentalist groups, soldiers in the German tradition who saw in them future soldiers, and Americanized businessmen who saw a potential low-wage labor force—to uproot these unfortunate people from their country and induce them to move to Israel where they now occupy the lowest rank in that country's social hierarchy.

Whether it can be described as feudal or something else, the exploitation of Ethiopian peasants was particularly violent. I saw groups of peasants chained by their owners, led I do not know where to be punished, probably for not having paid the exorbitant farm rents demanded of them. The agrarian reform that reduced these rents is to the credit of the DERG government. But will this reform—and its positive effects in terms of improving self-consumption of peasants and even marketing—be able to resist the dominant force of liberalism? The tradition in this country is that everyone is armed: landowners and bourgeois with revolvers in a shoulder strap under a jacket (as I saw when at a restaurant; in the country, they remove the jacket) and the peasants with old rifles. Generally speaking, Ethiopian society is violent. Political conflicts, even strictly ideological ones, can easily be settled by execution.

The fact that Ethiopia maintained its independence until 1935 led the society and even its successive ruling classes to behave in a way that was not at all welcome in Western capitals, where it was normal to treat African peoples as potential subjects for colonial submission. Like all ruling classes, those of imperial Ethiopia and "socialist" Ethiopia (from 1975 to 1991) were realistic and not averse to compromise alliance with dominant external forces, or even submission to them, if necessary. They always wanted to be allies and not agents, whether that be Emperor Haile Selassie in his relations with the U.S. protector, or Mengistu in his relations with Moscow.

Ethiopia is a multiethnic society, as were all states that encompassed more than one village in all pre-capitalist eras in all regions of the world. The very concept of ethnicity is here as fluid as elsewhere. Nevertheless, since it is in question, it should be noted that modern Ethiopia is 28 percent Amhara, 28 percent Oromo, and 10 percent Tigray, while the rest consists of a large number of scattered ethnicities and linguistic groups. Sixty-one percent of the population are Coptic Christian and 33 percent Muslims.

In this ethnic panorama, Eritrea has no distinct identity. It is populated mainly by Tigray people—also found on the other side of the colonial boundary in the province of Tigray. The majority of the population are Coptic Christians. As with all colonial borders, those of Eritrea have no historical foundation. Even the name "Eritrea" is a European invention unknown in the languages of the peoples who live there. The Eritrean "personality"—if such exists—would only, then, be the result of this colonization. This is not, of course, a new cultural identity—colonial Eritrea remained as diverse on this level as all colonies—but only the expression of the new petite bourgeoisie's aspiration, produced by colonial capitalism, to take over from the foreign administration and take on the same fundamental functions, that is, those that favor the integration of the country into world capitalism. The legend has it that consequently Eritrea was "in advance" of the rest of Ethiopia. This was not at all true, except for superficial appearances. Eritrea's subsequent growth from 1960 owes much precisely to its integration into Ethiopia, which provided a large market for it. But the Eritrean province by itself remains a poor province. Its agriculture is hampered by the increasing aridity of the Sahel.

The ethnic question in Ethiopia is certainly not an artificial invention of foreign governments. But it is not as determinant, in the current phase, as claimed by the media that orchestrate world opinion. Did the imperial regime and its successor, the DERG, maintain the domination of the Amhara and the oppression of the other ethnic groups? The terms used are misleading and project onto Ethiopian society practices that should be analyzed in their true historical context. As almost always in pre-capitalist states of any size, the ruling class goes beyond its ethnic origins to assert its imperial power over (ethnically) diverse peasant communities, all equally subject to its equally unrestrained exploitation. The Ethiopian monarchy is not exempt from the rule. The dominant class integrated, without any difficulty, people from diverse origins. The modernized monarchist state, followed by the republican state, continued this policy. The civil service, army, police, and decision-making centers at the highest levels never practiced the least discrimination in favor of the Amhara. And while the Oromo or Tigray peasants, and the Somali or Afar herders were odiously exploited, the Amhara peasants were no less so.

The Amharic or Amharinya language remained, nevertheless, that of the state and school. In this respect, can one speak of cultural oppression? Such a judgment must be placed in its correct historical context. Whether anyone likes it or not, Amharic has also become dominant because of its cultural lead, to the extent that if Ethiopia were to break up into ethnic states, they would probably be unable to use their "national languages" and would have to maintain the use of Amharic as the language of administration and communication, or would be forced (like other African states) to adopt, perhaps, English, or maybe Italian, in its place. It remains the case that the development of schools and urbanization has created a new problem. In the illiterate peasant society of the past, the linguistic question was of little importance. The peasants spoke their language and the administration could use another; it hardly ever intervened in daily rural life. Modernized society is different. The school and the city require a considerably heavier use of the written language. The new educated petite bourgeoisie experiences the linguistic situation in all of its dimensions and tends to interpret the new situation as if it involved real "cultural" discrimination.

That said, in some circumstances, the ruling class, leading the hegemonic bloc that it forms around itself (which here includes the new urban petite bourgeoisies), does not play the ethnicity card, but, on the contrary, emphasizes "national" unity (of the state). Yet, in other circumstances, it adopts a different attitude and rallies around ethnic difference. Why? Now, that is the real question. Why, then, did the political and social forces in Eritrea, then in other regions of Ethiopia (notably in Tigray province), choose the path of separatism? The war in Eritrea goes back to the 1960s, the years of Ethiopia's accelerated modernization. At the beginning it was only a limited regional (non-ethnic), if not artificial, problem produced by the overweening ambitions of a fraction of the Eritrean middle classes that refused to be integrated into a national hegemonic bloc. The encouragement and support from the great powers (the United States and USSR), always cynical in their changing short-term calculations, as well as neighboring states (Arab ones, in this context), with views dominated by short-term opportunism or religious fanaticism (Nasser was an exception here), also played a non-negligible role in this history. But of course the responsibility for the continued worsening of the situation lies mainly with the central Ethiopian government. Its response to Eritrean regionalism was military repression. There again, the Ethiopian case is not an exception to the rule, but confirms it. All autocratic governments are almost by nature unable to respond to the least challenge in any way other than by brutal violence. The practice of compromise—characteristic of democracy—is alien to them.

The overthrow of the Ethiopian monarchy in 1975 could have been the beginning of a salutary change. Unfortunately, the weaknesses of the movement (triggered not by a coup d'état, but by a military mutiny), and the encouragement given to the DERG government by the USSR—the promise to help it gain a "military victory" in Eritrea—resulted in a lost opportunity. Subsequent events became tragic: exhaustion of the army, worsened by successive purges (useless liquidations of officers, a sort of repeated vengeance of mutinous soldiers); the fragmentation of the ruling class and the petite bourgeoisie first into diverse factions (including revolutionary ones, at least in principle), then into ethnic clans. It is in this context that the "Tigray guerilla" movement was born, which was not the result of Tigrayan ethnicism, but a by-product of the continual deterioration of the situation. In the same way, the "liberation fronts" of the Oromo and others, far from having any real foundation in their respective "peoples," were really just simple reorganizations within the petite bourgeoisie. This deterioration occurred at the moment in which the accumulation crisis had already put an end to the earlier modernizing period of growth: the 1970s and 1980s saw increasing aridity, famines, etc.

I followed the development of the Ethiopian situation as closely as possible, especially after 1974. The DERG's views on socialism never went beyond an autocratic statist nationalism with populist overtones. In fact, it was very close to Nasserism in many respects. But the Ethiopian intelligentsia was different. It was large, active, well educated (Addis Ababa had one of the continent's best universities), cultivated, and critical. All observers noted the dominance of Marxism among Ethiopian students, whether in Addis or abroad. Ethiopian communists have always had incredible courage, active in situations where just the suspicion of communist activism merited a certain death sentence. But it was also always divided into competing organizations, a little like Egypt. Here again, the criteria of the dividing lines were not easy to identify. The opposition between the Soviet line and Maoist line, for example, was diffuse and was found, it seems to me, within the two main organizations: the MEISON and the EPRP. The question whether to cooperate with the DERG or fight it, of course, underlies internal debates. This was especially true since the DERG proclaimed itself, with Mengistu Haile Mariam, to be Marxist-Leninist, and Moscow treated it as such. I listened to the arguments of both groups at length and I have much respect for most of the numerous militants I met, whether or not their viewpoints seemed reasonable to me. I am not their judge. Besides, I have always refrained from taking any public position whatsoever "in favor" of one line or another, although I was invited frequently to speak in public in Ethiopia by the university and by state agencies.

The entry into Addis Ababa in May 1991 of the Tigray guerillas, and into Asmara of the EPLF, did not crown a real military victory, but rather the collapse of the DERG army, abandoned by a moribund Soviet Union. Washington dictated the solution: Eritrea would be administered by the EPLF as a single party (an exception to the rule that Western powers always supported a multiparty system in principle); the rest of Ethiopia would be divided into fourteen pseudo-ethnic regions and elections held on that basis. In other words, "democratization" was here captive from the beginning to ethnicism and its function was to provide legitimacy to the breakup of the country along ethnic lines. However, a large part of the country wanted nothing to do with that, not only the "traditionally chauvinist Amhara," as the media proclaimed. The Tigray, Oromo, and other peasants were not consulted to find out if their true desire was to create their ethnic "state" or if they considered their real problems to lie elsewhere. When city dwellers expressed their concern and their wish to maintain the unity of the country, they were brutally repressed, as in the massacre of students in January 1993. In Eritrea, a truly open and democratic discussion was prohibited out of fear that the a priori decision in favor of independence would be called into question.

The danger of criminal abuses was worsened by all the measures adopted by the established authorities, dictated by Washington. The demobilization of the Ethiopian army threw tens of thousands of soldiers with no means of support into the countryside, which the clans warring for power remobilized in their service. Thus a Somali-type situation was deliberately created, one that the Western powers will undoubtedly wash their hands of tomorrow. The government wants to force the formation of "ethnic parties" and impede the formation of parties that refuse to be part of this "ethnicization" process. A glance at the fourteen pseudo-ethnic regions drawn on the map (which, interestingly enough, has similarities with that of Mussolini's plan for ruling eastern Africa) shows that we are heading straight toward a permanent civil war, huge population transfers, etc. In this way, the country's decomposition is organized along pseudo-ethnic lines, just like in Yugoslavia and Iraq.

In Eritrea, the difficulties will be immense and the new comprador state will only survive if it succeeds in "selling" its existence to outside interests. Did the ruling class count on selling its opportunist support to one outside group (Arab money?) or another (American base, Israeli base?) based on circumstances or possibilities? It remains the case that we must ask why and how the "revolutionary" groups (the Eritreans and Tigrayans had initially adopted Marxist-Leninist language) could deviate so far from their supposed original project. History demonstrates that such deviations are possible and frequent when the "avant-garde" in question errs in its historical assessment of the nature of the social forces that it claims to mobilize and the objectives those forces can realistically set for themselves. Deprived of a social basis consistent with their rhetoric, these avant-gardes can degenerate toward pure and simple adventurism. That is the case in Ethiopia.

Will a sudden burst of patriotism and reason on the part of the ruling classes, intellectuals, and leaders of the active political forces in Eritrea and Ethiopia defeat the nightmare scenario envisaged here? There are happily some indications that this might be the case. The government in Asmara quickly had to confront huge difficulties: Eritrea is not a viable country, the hoped-for external financial support is only an illusion, and Sudan (and behind it, Saudi Arabia) continually carries out destabilizing operations. Asmara, then, seems to have understood that it must reconcile with Addis Ababa, maintain the economic unity of the two countries, and move in the direction of some type of confederation. In Ethiopia, the most diverse political forces refuse to play the game of "ethnic elections," widely boycotted. But the fragile regime governing in Addis Ababa is unable to disobey orders coming from Washington, which pursues its ultimate objective: destroy the power of the state and break up the country. All of this is justified in the name of democracy (!), but in fact it leads straight to economic collapse and a civil war. But this is also undoubtedly the most effective way for Washington to "manage the crisis" of global capitalism and continue its hegemony. It is in this context that the highs and lows of Ethiopian-Eritrean relations should be placed. It remains the case, in my opinion, that the major responsibility for the deterioration of these relations (culminating in the resumption of war in 1999) lies with Asmara, in desperate straits. Furthermore, the recent Ethiopian intervention in Somalia cannot end well.

The United States' active intrusion into Ethiopia throughout all of contemporary history, well analyzed by the co-author of my work on the ethnic question, should surprise no one.[25] The geostrategic importance of the countries of the Horn of Africa is decisive for the political strategy of the United States. When he visited the region, Fidel Castro said that the solution to the problem is to establish a confederation of five or six countries: Ethiopia, Eritrea, Somalia, Djibouti, and Yemen (South and North). All say they are socialist, some even Marxist-Leninist. Such a confederation would balance relations between Muslims and Christians, Arabs and others, which would, in turn, encourage tolerance and democracy. It would control a key geostrategic region and could rebuff any imperialist intrusions. This was worth saying, even if, obviously, the basic conditions for starting a change in this direction do not exist, to the benefit of the imperialists.

## The Portuguese Colonies

Whereas France, Great Britain, and Belgium accepted the principle of political decolonization in 1960, Portugal, on the other hand, rejected it. Thus the only option for the national liberation movements was to begin wars of liberation. War always inspires both real possibilities for radicalization of politics and romantic illusions. A large proportion of those who supported these movements, both in Africa and outside the continent, particularly among Western Third Worldists, held such illusions. I certainly do not reproach them for that: their manifest internationalism and their respect for the rights of colonized peoples are sufficient motives to express gratitude to them; their courageous actions are to their honor.

I obviously knew most of the leaders and militants of these movements who wished to discuss with me all sorts of questions concerning the future of their country, Africa, the world system, and socialism. I always accepted the responsibility that such discussions inevitably entail. I gave my viewpoint freely, knowing full well that history is not made by intellectuals and ideas—neither mine nor those of others—but results from the confrontation of objective forces. Ideas are, at most, only the expression of views and strategies.

## Cape Verde and Guinea-Bissau

Amílcar Cabral was probably one of the best thinkers of our era, not only in his small country, but also in all of Africa and beyond. He was also a true militant, that is, a person who wants to understand the world in order to change it. I had the opportunity to discuss two major questions with him.

The first concerned his thesis of the "suicide of the petite bourgeoisie as a class." Undoubtedly, the conditions created by war often encourage the blossoming of human qualities, of which the petite bourgeois are not deprived "by nature." Courage, solidarity, and continuing contact with the real peasant masses can contribute to getting rid of initial prejudices and ignorance. But I remained unconvinced that, once independence was achieved, social realities—that is, the advantages procuring from leadership positions, inevitably reserved to a minority even when some of them come from the base—would cease to reproduce social inequalities. The struggle for socialism is, for me, a long-term process. One can already see hierarchies at work and all the usual accompanying intrigues, even within national liberation parties, beyond their unquestionably progressive historical role. The model of Soviet-style communist parties encouraged these behaviors. Around the leader, or local leaders, how many militants—even courageous ones—would behave, more or less unconditionally, as followers, sometimes even as sycophants? What I did not say to Cabral is that some of those whom I knew to be among the best militants, working the most sincerely with the people, the most courageous in military terms, were sent to the front lines—sometimes to certain death—by others, "leaders" well hidden from the outside in their positions. I already saw that the petite bourgeoisie was not ready "to commit suicide."

The second question concerned the national problem in Guinea-Bissau and Cape Verde. I did not believe that the peoples of these two colonies formed "a single nation." Guinea-Bissau is a piece of West Africa similar to the others, a potential multiethnic African state. Cape Verde is quite different. It is in the Cape Verde islands, inhabited by the Portuguese during their discovery, and where they developed the system that was going to build America: the slave plantation colony, a central component of the Euro-Atlantic mercantilist system. It was the (truly inventive) founders of the Portuguese—and later Spanish, British, and French—conquest of the Americas who established this system. It was defined in all of its dimensions: the slave trade, colonization, creolization of the colony, and administrative forms. Cape Verde is the ancestor of the Antilles and Brazil.

I visited Cape Verde much later, in 1987 and 1991, after the PAICV had lost power. Isabelle and I roamed around these captivating islands, each one different from the others: Santiago, with the largest population of African Creoles; San Vincente, rocky and barren with its pretty port Mindelo opposite San Antao; Fuego, with its incredible volcano at the summit of which is found a strange village of "French." They are descendants of castaways from a shipwrecked royalist ship that was fleeing the Vendée during the Revolution. They drink the cheap wine produced from the miserable vineyard they continue to cultivate and have become degenerate through alcoholism and endogamy within the small population.

That the PAICV lost the elections to precisely the Creole petite bourgeoisie—and bourgeoisie—that had not taken part in the liberation struggle, calls into question what kind of society this really is. It is certainly sad because whatever may have been the limitations and errors of the PAICV government, Cape Verde owes its existence to that organization; and it is the PAICV that gave land and schools to its hungry and barefoot people. Then how can we explain the defeat? Certainly, part of the explanation lies with an underestimation of the Church's role. But another factor must be the arrogance found in the petty daily behavior of former courageous militants who had become leaders in the administration. Pedro Pires himself, General Secretary of the PAICV, explained it to me in that way. However, the PAICV government could rely on remarkable supporters, in relatively much larger numbers than in many other African countries. I would say as much of the PAICV's "left opponents" who, having adopted a Maoist line during that time, had been viewed rather dimly by the PAICV government to the point that many of them were forced to go into exile in Portugal, returning to the country later. These quarrels should be closed today. The important thing now is to rebuild a force of the popular left, unified around a minimum program, but maintaining its diversity within the mutual respect of the partners. I do not hesitate to say that some of the elements that contributed to the victory of the right, out of spite and forced by the PAICV's triumphalist sectarianism, could find a place in this democratic and popular alternative.

But—to return to the national question—I must say that Cabral had not been happy with my viewpoint. However, intelligent and cultivated man that he was, he could not doubt its correctness—which was blatantly obvious. Yet he knew that I would never say anything publicly. And, up until the victory and even after, when the Cape Verde-Guinea union had broken down, I was silent. But the sycophants who surrounded the Partido Africano da Independência da Guiné e Cabo Verde (PAIGC—African Party for the Independence of Guinea and Cape Verde) leadership, knowing about my discussion with Cabral on the subject, used it to make me into what I am not: a saboteur of the union! My viewpoint was acknowledged in Bissau, when I visited in 1986.

## Angola and Mozambique

Angola's problems were no less difficult, although of an entirely different nature. I knew the veteran leaders of the MPLA, Mario de Andrade and Agostinho Neto, from their days in exile, but I met the actual founder of the party, Pinto de Andrade, only much later, in Luanda. I also knew well the representatives of the left in the MPLA, Viriato da Cruz and Lúcio Lara.

Neto behaved as a king, the type who speaks very little because each of his words is inevitably correct and important. I felt it was impossible to have a discussion with him. Besides, he did not wish it anyway. Mario de Andrade told me that, in fact, he had discussions with no one. He was, then, a little Stalin, which, unfortunately, the communist parties of that time seemed to produce quite easily. Mario de Andrade was a completely different type of person; he was head of the MPLA for only a brief period of time, "thrown out" by the bloc of sectarians that monopolized the leadership and sent to "make war." That is what he did. "It was a war that I fought against the mosquitoes above all," he told me with his light humor. This does not lessen his courage, but rather demonstrates his modesty. He was too modest to be a "great leader."

With Mario, then, I could discuss the Angolan disaster then brewing. For various reasons that in no way reduce the historic merits of the MPLA, it was not the sole representative—real or pretended—of the country's political forces. Whatever one may think of them, Holden Roberto's FNLA among the Bakongo in the north and UNITA among the Ovimbundu in the south did exist. The MPLA was well established in the capital and particularly in the better-educated classes—often of mixed race—which the demagogues of anti-white/anti-mixed race nationalism made sure to exploit. It was also a party convinced that only a socialist approach met the expectations of the people, and counted in its ranks a large number of militants formed in the Portuguese Communist Party. The FNLA and UNITA were only tribal organizations with no program whatsoever, built around an absolute, demagogic leader. Not only, then, were they anti-communist, of course, but also ready for any compromise with Washington, Mobutu, and even the PIDE, which knew how to use them, if need be, against the MPLA. Later, when elections gave Angolans a choice between the MPLA and UNITA (the FNLA had disappeared earlier), the voters said they preferred the "thieves" (the MPLA) to the "murderers" (UNITA). And this was true. The MPLA, in power for fifteen years in Luanda, had changed and corruption was widespread; but the henchmen of UNITA were genuine murderers in the areas they controlled. None of that prevented the Western media from detesting the MPLA leaders—they were not democrats (which was not untrue)—and heaping praise on Jonas Savimbi, leader of the murderers (is he a democrat?). Nevertheless, the FNLA existed and UNITA still exists.

A stormy meeting had shaken the OAU when, following 1974, it had to recognize an Angolan representative from the national liberation movement. I did not participate in this meeting; I had no valid reason to do so. But I had been invited, separately, as a "knowledgeable person" (a "sage," says the French original) whom the OAU could "consult." I was not old enough to be a "sage," still less did I have the physical appearance. But there was a kind of recognition that my writings had some resonance. I made clear that I would have nothing to say about the actual representativeness of any particular organization or its presence on the ground. That should be within the purview of the African political investigators duly mandated to deal with those questions. Also, I would not play the irresponsible journalist of which, unfortunately, there are all too many. It was agreed. Then what was my role to be? It was rather vague, but came down to listening. I then understood. And said nothing. But then I observed the loud interference of the Soviets, with a massive presence in the corridors. They and some allied African states directly asserted that only the MPLA existed on the ground and that it alone had the right to form the legal government of the country. In my opinion, this assertion hindered rather than helped, because it was false and everyone knew it. The United States took a more subtle approach and pointed this out via friendly states. China then entered into the fray. At that time, it never allowed the Soviets and Americans to take the stage alone. The Chinese suggestions—very informal—were initially reasonable, in my opinion: form a coalition government with the three organizations to avoid civil war. I heard with my own ears a Chinese ambassador say quite simply that if the MPLA were really so strong, it would absorb the others and come to terms with them; if it were not, then a coalition government would be even more necessary.

That being said, anti-Sovietism caused China's attitude to veer onto slippery ground a little later. An MPLA government was established in Luanda, but controlled only part of the country. It accepted the prospect of going to war to defeat UNITA and received Soviet military aid for that purpose (Cuban support did not happen until later). As a result, China decided to continue its support for UNITA (as it had done before 1974, supposedly so that the pro-Soviet MPLA would not be the sole force on the ground), thereby finding itself side by side with the United States and South Africa, which were not skimping in their financial and military support for Savimbi, the murderer. Discussing this entire history much later with Mario de Andrade, he told me that the solution of a coalition government had been the best. But he was not sure what had been possible at the time. Washington was anxious to sabotage it. I believe that is true. Still, if it had been possible, a compromise would have avoided seventeen years of useless war. At the end of this tragedy, the USSR no longer existed, Cuba had withdrawn (after having beaten the South Africans, which was magnificent), apartheid had disappeared, the MPLA no longer feared Washington (although the United States never forgives and always remains full of hatred toward those who have resisted it), and Savimbi's heirs were also still there. Hence it was still necessary to accept negotiations and even a coalition government. What a sad end.

Things appeared simpler in Mozambique. The FRELIMO led the war of liberation alone. The Dar es Salaam base was obviously the place for frequent meetings, particularly with Marcelino dos Santos, future vice president; Aquino de Bragança, who died in the same airplane accident as President Samora Machel; and Sérgio Vieira, the party's ideologue. I do not remember very much of these discussions that were, I believe, quite mundane.

The problems arose after liberation. The FRELIMO was established only in the north of the country and was not adequately prepared to control the situation in Maputo and absorb the influx of petite bourgeoisie who had hardly participated in the war but provided most of the cadres that were rapidly promoted to take the place of the Portuguese, who left en masse. The response to the challenge came in the form of a "shift to the left"—unpopular collectivization, and the like. To this was added a new war led by the RENAMO, with South African support. Although the supporters of this party, which had the good fortune of pleasing Western "democrats," were only vulgar murderers without any program, their very existence was made possible only by FRELIMO's errors. The capitulation that followed the Nkomati Accord (1984) with South Africa, and the opening of negotiations with the RENAMO and the adoption of a multiparty system had the expected disastrous effects: collapse. The triumphant ideology of the "NGOs—representatives of civil society" wreaked havoc, which was forcefully denounced by the Swede (Abramson). It is obvious that reactionary external forces (promoters of the "new neoliberal order," without a state!) implemented, manipulated, and formed these NGOs as additional instruments, with the internal support of the corrupt bourgeoisie. They were in no way the autonomous expression of the working classes. But I only know all that from my readings and from the discussions that the Forum began to organize around a small team led by economist Eugenio Macamo, with our friends Carlos Machili, who was a rector, and Maria do Ceu Carmoreis.

## Zimbabwe

After 1960 and 1975, 1980 is the third great liberation date in Africa. The collapse of the white minority regime that had proclaimed the "independence" of Rhodesia in 1965 heralded the disintegration of the entire system of "reserves" in southern Africa. But the liberation movement in Zimbabwe had been forced to accept a compromise, as did South Africa ten years later. The Lancaster House Agreement made a radical agrarian reform impossible. The peasants that the white colonists of the highlands had forced onto unproductive land would remain there. This Agreement began the process of establishing what my friend Ibo Mandaza calls a "schizophrenic regime": a government formed from a party the program and ideology of which are on the left, which most of the cadres and militants sincerely support and which are continually appealed to in the rhetoric, but is counterposed to policies that do not implement this program. Time passes, and the working classes lose their faith in the system, which they judge with cynicism, while a new African bourgeoisie continues to grow stronger. There is minimal agrarian reform, which reduces pressure a little on the peasants, but above all new African landowners take over some of the previously colonized land. That is just like what happened in Kenya. To that is added the difficulty in reconverting manufacturing industries developed by the minority regime of Ian Smith, which had benefited from the protection resulting from the international boycott. Urged to become "competitive" and no longer benefiting from the advantages formerly available to them from state subsidies, they are today seriously threatened by structural adjustment policies. Simultaneously, of course, the condition of the working class is deteriorating and unemployment is increasing.

In the course of my travels through the country in 1986, I concretely verified how the reserves system, about which I had written, had been very systematically organized. On colonized lands with a low-population density, there were good paved roads, telephones, electricity, and running water. As soon as one entered the overpopulated reserves, there was nothing, no roads or basic services. Thus, the reserves—the Bantustans—are condemned to provide cheap labor for the colonized lands, mines, and industries. This is a horrible system, which was not invented by the Boers (though it is attributed to them), but by the British—Cecil Rhodes, in particular. A similar situation is found in the colonization of Algeria and in Israel-Palestine.

The Lancaster House compromise, to which Zimbabwe's national liberation movement had consented in 1980, was from the beginning an additional barrier to any possible radicalization of the government, which, moreover, the general conjuncture—no longer in the 1980s what it had been in the 1960s and 1970s—hardly favored in any case. The populist rhetoric of the regime quickly lost credibility while its intransigence could only reinforce an opposition almost nonexistent in dominant African opinion at the beginning. Yet, far from forming a coherent left alternative, this opposition defends both multiparty democracy and neoliberalism and, as in Zambia, a victory of this pro-U.S. right would obviously not only provide no solution to the social problems of the working classes, but quite the contrary, would worsen the tragedy.

Robert Mugabe has chosen to pursue his counterattack in the area of agrarian reform, a little late and with debatable methods. But none of that should obscure the hypocrisy of the British government, which has never respected its commitment to cover the cost of necessary agrarian reforms by taking on "compensation" of the white farmers, beneficiaries of hundreds of thousands of hectares of land given to them for free by London's colonial government, at the price, obviously, of expelling the indigenous population that lived there. The counterattack adopted, as is well known, rather brutal methods, thereby facilitating the mobilization of "sensitive" Western public opinion, which was, at the same time, bombarded with the repeated message that the "agrarian reform" would inevitably be an economic disaster and would deprive the country of its "efficient" farmers. This is an argument, obviously, that African peasants, victims of the history here, have no use for. Moreover, the argument does not hold water: the financial profitability of the white latifundia has, as a counterpart, the necessary exclusion of millions of rural Africans condemned to famine and the overexploitation of capital in land (an argument convincing to Western Greens in other places, but curiously not here!). The best analysis of the question has been made by Sam Moyo as part of a working group of the Forum.[26]

In any case, here as elsewhere, the Western powers support "alternation," which suits them quite well since it ensures that the supposed "democrats" will accept not only the neoliberal diktat, but also the indefinite postponement of agrarian reform. The sad thing is that a sizable portion of the left—unions and intellectuals—has rallied to this kind of opposition to Mugabe. The least that can be said here is that the future remains uncertain. This is all the more the case because the crisis in Zimbabwe runs the risk of spreading to South Africa, where the same problem is encountered in similar terms and historical conditions. In the 1930s, the South African Communist Party had the courageous intelligence to make the anti-colonial, anti-capitalist peasant revolution one of its fundamental policy principles along with the revolution of the working class against the imperialist mining monopolies. By giving up that principle (in the 1960s), it left the question open, a question that capitalism will never resolve.

### SHORT-LIVED MIRACLES

### *Côte d'Ivoire*

When I was at the IDEP, I set myself the objective of personally studying more closely some neocolonial experiences—the success of which had been trumpeted by the World Bank and others, above all in Côte d'Ivoire, which I visited on several occasions between 1963 and 1973.

During 1963 and 1964, I was welcomed at the Planning Ministry by the then-minister, Mohamed Diawara. I collected information from which anyone endowed with a minimum sense of reality—not even any acute critical sense— could only conclude that the "miraculous growth" was nothing more than a remake of what Ghana had experienced thirty years earlier, with no originality. But the mediocre econometricians of the French Development Agency, World Bank, EEC, and UNDP were united in ecstasy and, carrying out the facile exercise of making a simple mechanical projection, did not hesitate to promise a radiant future to the country's leaders. Project a 6 percent—or even 10 percent—annual growth for 20 (or 30!) years, and you inevitably conclude that Côte d'Ivoire was destined to "catch up" to Europe. I discussed this with Ivorian leaders and tried to show them how they were being deceived. I suggested looking at Ghana to better see the real problems that would be encountered in fifteen or twenty years. This was rather in vain since the success intoxicated almost everyone. A few critical intellectuals—Memel Foté, Moustapha Diabaté, Ali Traoré, and Charles Waly Diarrassouba (at that time)—were just about the only ones to hear something other than a hymn to the glory of colonial capitalism. Later, when the rhetoric of the "Ivorian miracle" was finally buried, a new democratic opposition began thinking about the real problems of their society. It could then be hoped that Laurent Gbagbo and Dramane Sangaré of the FPI, and Francis Wodié of the PIT, who were part of this opposition, would put their country back on the right path.

The widespread stupidity of the Third World nouveaux riches shows itself in daily demonstrations. One day, I met a friend, Melle Garnier, who had been professor of economy at the University of Brazzaville. "What are you doing today?" she asked me. "Nothing," I responded. "Well then, I'll take you to the Hotel Ivoire where an amusing ceremony will be happening; I have an invitation for two." The Club des Riches—that was its real name—was celebrating the anniversary (I do not remember how many years) of its creation.

From each of the black Mercedes in a long line exited a thin Burkinabé chauffeur in khaki shorts who opened the rear door of the vehicle. A large man in a dark three-piece suit wearing a fedora and carrying an umbrella—the usual uniform—emerged. Always the same figures, "a well-polished Negro," as my Senegalese friend, Samba Ndiaye, would say of them; a little fat, with a rather unintelligent look. Assembled in an ultra-air-conditioned room of the hotel—so they would not regret wearing the three-piece suit—the rich in question listened to the welcome speech by a very prominent person from the Republic, Auguste Denise. A simple and repetitive speech, saying almost literally: "You are rich, that means everything is going well, that Côte d'Ivoire is growing richer!" Then, when the speech had ended, an army of servants entered with bottles of champagne—there must have been hundreds—opening them noisily and poorly so that half of the beverage spurted in jets of foam straight onto the face. Everyone was drinking and drinking without conversation—these gentlemen probably did not have anything to say—but with many resounding and stupid laughs. Then everyone left. The Festival of the Rich was over. This type of ruling class might please the racists of Europe and the United States, and might cause the Rastignacs of the local petite bourgeoisie to drool with envy. The common people view it as strange, which it is. The ironic intelligence of the people of Côte d'Ivoire is displayed on each occasion, as Ahmadou Kourouma's novels illustrate better than so-called sociological inquiries.

Abidjan is also the headquarters for numerous African institutions, which gave me some additional opportunities to go there. The African Development Bank organized a conference on African monetary questions there, to which I was invited. It was on this occasion that President Félix Houphouët-Boigny received us in his palace, and that I chatted with the *djinké* (a traditional hetaera) whose judgment on "rich old fools" I recounted in the first volume of my memoirs.[27] Before reaching the garden, we passed by a large hall in which a wall was decorated, so to speak, by a golden plaque upon which a spotlight was shining. It was so bright that we regretted not having our sunglasses. Later on I also visited the absurd project of Yamoussoukro—the village where Houphouët was born—promoted as the future capital with its avenues as wide as airport runways leading nowhere, a basilica of Italian marble of the size of St. Peter's in Rome, etc. It was a Sunday and to make sure there were attendees at the service other than the dozen tourists, who would not, in any case, stay for the whole thing, cars had collected fifty children from neighboring villages. A band of clerics—Polish and Italian, judging by the accent—showed us the monument, accompanying their comments with racist remarks (they did not imagine that a "white," at least in appearance, would not share their ideas—I benefited from this treatment in Zaire, at the Bakwanga Mine, but I'll share that story later). I listened to these words in silence, to see how far they would go, even if it meant saying what I thought only in three words. I concluded our visit by a brief remark to our clerical guide: "Thank you, in a few moments you have succeeded in making your interlocutor anti-Christian, and in convincing him that the white race produces the most imbecilic specimens of the human race."

These are aspects of really existing capitalism that are not often spoken about. These are the same aspects that are particularly pleasing to some—a large number of "experts" who roam around Africa. One of them, an American employed by the World Bank, not suspecting that a "white" would not naturally be racist, told me that there were only two "livable" countries in Africa: South Africa (this was during the apartheid era) and Côte d'Ivoire. It is true that an Ivorian minister who had had the audacity to go to South Africa during that time and had gone to a soccer match had accepted being "caged." It was common practice then to separate white and black spectators with a wire fence!

The question of economic relations among the countries of the CEAO brought me to accompany the Senegal president, Léopold Senghor, to a summit in Abidjan that was to decide on the method of calculating the transfer of customs duty from the coastal countries to the inland countries. Senghor had given me the file to read on the plane. It was a pointless econometric exercise to legitimize a simple political decision. I gave my viewpoint, saying that the (modest) pseudo-scientific result could be divided by three or multiplied by six with no problem. President Senghor repeated this argument at the summit, to the great astonishment of the technocrats, who were forced to agree. It was on this visit that I was told that President Houphouët had said that what I had written in my book on Côte d'Ivoire was quite right. But I had not needed to write it, only report it to him orally, whisper it into his ear. That is not the method I advocate to advance critical thinking in any country whatsoever, I simply responded.

Yet, things seemed to begin to change in Côte d'Ivoire. The "miracle" was over, which I had the possibility to verify when I was invited first by the GIDIS (an independent association of social science researchers in Côte d'Ivoire directed by Memel Foté) in 1994, then by the NLTPS program, the UNDP group charged with future-oriented research in Africa, at that time headed by José Brito, who was succeeded by Alioune Sall. On this occasion, the economic managers of the country consulted me "like a seer," as I said in recounting this story in volume 1.[28]

The Ivorian miracle, like almost all miracles of this kind, was destined to lead to a real political disaster when its foreseeable end came to fruition. The systematic depoliticization fueled by the illusions of the prosperous years meant that neither the working classes nor the leadership—including that of the opposition—was prepared to confront the new difficulties. Côte d'Ivoire was not only trapped in an impasse, it was sliding down the slippery slope of a regressive and demagogic rhetoric about "Ivorian identity" and systematically mobilizing hostility toward immigrants (from Burkina Faso and Mali), without which the "miracle" itself would never have occurred. But while Houphouët—perfectly aware of the key contribution of these "foreigners"—had opted, consequently, for an intelligent policy of legal assimilation, his successor, Henri Konan Bédié, known for his remarkable stupidity, chose, on the contrary, to flatter the "Ivorian identity" of the "authentic" children of the country. The military coup d'état that overthrew him in 1999 could have given hope that an end would be made to this odious policy. Unfortunately, the aspiring dictator—General Robert Guéï, and behind him, Laurent Gbagbo and the opposition parties—decided to push the policy further.

Since then, Côte d'Ivoire has foundered in unending conflict with no apparent end other than the society's self-destruction. The abuses of the FPI did not terribly surprise me, despite the hope placed rather too rapidly by many in the person of its leader. I learned later that Gbagbo belonged to one of those Protestant sects whose establishment in Africa is supported by the United States. This is a planned strategy that aims at nothing less than eliminating any hope of getting out of the impasses caused by the continent's globalization. The dice have been thrown and I do not see how this country could one day be reconstructed. Côte d' Ivoire has gone under, as I feared. This can surprise only conventional economists—such as the French professors based in Clermont-Ferrand who "specialize in Africa"—who claim, in response to my criticisms of the Ivorian model, that the country was on the point of becoming a second Korea! Unable to understand the significance of social transformation, they could not see the stupidity of this argument provided by World Bank managers!

*Kenya*

Kenya's economic development was praised as thoughtlessly as that of Côte d'Ivoire. It was another "miracle," simply because primary agricultural exports registered high growth rates for several years. As a result, there was total silence on the dictatorships of Jomo Kenyatta and Daniel Moi, but there were praises for stability, a value at the time deemed to be higher. The praise became extravagant concerning Kenya, initially equipped with a few more industrial plants than Côte d'Ivoire. Here was a country, it was said, where an enterprising national bourgeoisie would finally take shape, in the name of which all the rest seemed acceptable: awful social inequalities, among other things. Teams of economists from the repentant left, Britons from the *New Left Review*, and naive former Third Worldists from Scandinavia won over to liberalism (like Göran Hydén), saw in Kenya proof of the error in the thesis of global capitalist polarization. The results achieved by this enterprising national bourgeoisie are really quite poor. In fact, that bourgeoisie differs so little from the comprador bourgeoisie that we would need a magnifying glass to make out its positive originality. In fact, today, tourism (beaches and safaris in the nature reserves) is becoming the country's main resource. Fantastic!

Nairobi is a capital that hosts a large number of African and international institutions, such as the UNEP and the African Academy of Sciences (headed by Professor Thomas Odhiambo). It also has a good university. Dharam Ghai, subsequently director of the UNRISD, Peter Anyang, Michal Chege, Apolo Njonjo, and others who have often been active in the Forum's networks. The women's movement is particularly active in the university community here (led by Patricia MacFadden, among others). Nevertheless, the Kenyan intellectual community, just like the country itself, is divided into three large cultural groups: Kenyans of Indian origin, gradually pushed to emigrate; Africans belonging to the main ethnic groups from the interior (Kikuyu and Luo); and the Swahili Muslims of the coast, often attracted by the culturalist rhetoric that "emphasizes the difference" separating them from the peasant and worker majority. Ali Mazrui, an ideologue of culturalism, is consequently more popular in the United States, where there is a public fondness for cultural specificity, than in his own country. The others, such as our colleague and friend Abdallah Bujra, who was Executive Secretary of CODESRIA, have never lapsed into this type of rhetoric. In 1993, the Forum organized one of its working groups in Kenya, near Mombasa.

The convening of the World Social Forum in Nairobi in 2007 forced us to become aware of the other face of the reality: the popular resistance movements, mobilized by Wahu Kaara, a popular woman of great eloquence. But these movements remain, as a whole, stuck in Anglo-American pragmatism, poorly prepared to understand the nature of the problems.

*Malawi*

I had the opportunity to visit Malawi in 1997, after the end of the dictatorship of Hastings Banda, and when a local team of the Third World Forum—led by Chinyama Chipeta and Mjedo Mkandawire—conducted an important study on the failed "miracle" (another one) and put forward alternative proposals. The miracle was based on a simple formula: place all of the country's resources at the exclusive disposal of expanding the agricultural export sector, specifically for tobacco. This benefited the large growers, that is, colonists and citizens, as well as the multinational cigarette oligopolies—which obviously led to the World Bank's wild enthusiasm that this "success" entailed the decline of food-crop production, the impoverishment of the peasantry, and the exercise of a violent dictatorship by a "single party" (but fortunately anti-socialist!)—and did not bother in any way those who later were going to start the new rhetoric on "poverty" and "multiparty democracy."

In these conditions, the government that resulted from elections attempted nothing more than continuing the dictatorship's economic policies, even though they were already visibly exhausted. As in Zambia, the democratic option is acceptable—for dominant transnational capital and Western governments—only if it proposes nothing new and accepts complete subjection to the aims of liberal globalization. The disappointment of voters is then expressed by disillusioned jokes: "We miss the single party because we knew whom to go and see, how much to give, and we were assured of the result. While with the multiparty system, we no longer know whom to seek out, we pay more, and we are not even sure of the result!"

But while Kenyan and Malawian societies have succeeded in offering a minimal resistance front to the attacks of comprador liberalism, the same cannot be said of other African societies, more fragile and vulnerable, which have fallen, body and soul, into a downward spiral leading to the complete disintegration of their social fabric. This is obviously the case with Sierra Leone, Liberia, Rwanda, Burundi, and Somalia.

THE QUAGMIRES OF NEOCOLONIAL EXPERIENCES

### *Central Africa*

Central Africa is characterized by the violence of its political life. The most common explanation—that this is due to the tribalism or even to the "savagery" of its peoples, an explanation marked by a thinly disguised ordinary racism—does not hold water. It ignores the incredible destruction caused by colonization in this region. Catherine Coquery emphasizes the particular forms of colonial intervention—in this case "concessionary companies"—and identifies the essential point: the incredible disarticulation of these weak and vulnerable societies by colonial pillage, which was particularly primitive. Colonial practices here, in the twentieth century, recalled those of the fifteenth century that decimated Native American societies. André Gide, upon returning from the Congo, used all his talent to describe the horror of this colonization. After being dismantled, the societies in the region can then be bled dry by common criminals (like Mobutu) or clowns (like Emperor Bokassa or Fulbert Yulu), while the dominant media do not report the most important thing: that these criminals and clowns are the West's best "friends," often put in place and supported by its financial or even military interventions. But at the same time, this region is the site of potentially radical explosions, among the most violent of our modern world. It is not by chance that Cameroon gave rise to the UPC, Congo-Brazzaville to socialist hopes, and the Democratic Republic of the Congo (called Zaire by Mobutu) to an uninterrupted series of peasant rebellions. But it is also not by chance that all these possibilities have been stifled. Poor clowns or rich clowns (financially), they were dictators in any case, sometimes to the extreme limit of criminality. To the savage violence of the ruling classes, I unhesitatingly counterpose the intelligence found in the multiple forms of resistance mounted by the majority of peoples to limit the damage (ignoring the small cliques of enforcement officers recruited by beleaguered governments).

I was the director of the IDEP when a curious invitation from the president of Gabon reached me in Dakar—with no indication of a motive other than "special consultation." I thought about it and then accepted. Traveled in first class, red carpet upon arrival, taken to a villa, but still no indication about the subject of the consultation. My friend Ntogolo, whom I telephoned, did not himself know, though since he was the head of the Planning Ministry, I suspected (wrongly) that he might be behind the mission. "You will be received by the President tomorrow morning at 10:00 and will know the aim of the mission at that time." Understood. The next day at nine, I was taken to the palace, put in an office adjoining that of the president, and was told "monetary questions." I thought about that for around ten minutes. Then somebody came to move me to the presidential office, placing me on a low sofa facing a desk on a raised platform. "The President," shouted an assistant. I rose. The President appeared. I began: "Mr. President, as far as monetary questions are concerned . . ." and I launched into a simplified course on the franc zone system. The President stopped me and said: "That is not what I want to know. Can I have my picture on the banknotes?" "Mr. President, you can print whatever you want on the banknotes; that does not change any monetary issue." "That is what I thought and I thank you for confirming it, but the French told me just the opposite." "Mr. President, they misled you." Three months later, Gabon issued its CFA notes, decorated with the image of its president.

Isabelle and I were in the Central African Republic in 1972. Jean-Bédel Bokassa was still president for life. The later farce of his imperial clowning gave rise to a torrent of facile commentaries making fun of the country's people, without saying that the emperor had overthrown a slightly more normal regime—that of David Dacko—which had only had the preposterous idea of requesting aid from the People's Republic of China, and that this roughneck soldier of the colonial government was Paris's friend. These commentaries also avoided pointing out which of the two was the most contemptible: the roughneck soldier in question or the French president, who accepted the former's diamonds, or played at being Tartarin hunting lions (these hunts were undertaken with drugged lions placed three meters from their executioner). The Central African people are peasants who make pottery full of humor and, rightly, make no major distinction between an autocratic president and an emperor cast in the same mold. We knew a Central African made ill and then hospitalized by the blow inflicted on his people by his emperor's ridiculousness. How many French people were made ill by the clowning around of their president in Bangui?

Cameroon has suffered, since the defeat of the UPC-led rebellion by the French colonial army, a savage dictatorship uninterrupted for forty years. That has never much bothered the official democrats of the West any more than did Suharto in Indonesia. Paul Biya followed Ahmadou Ahidjo in power, and he was almost worse. Yet he was presented as the hero of the new "democracy" (a real farce, then). The IDEP organized a good seminar in Douala in 1974 in collaboration with the PAID, ably directed at the time by Cosme Dikoumé. This was a Christian institution that trained mid-level cadres for rural development. This was the best possible setting in the country since the government was busy preventing the university from moving beyond the threshold of the greatest mediocrity. The results of such an education are obviously easier to domesticate, buy, co-opt, corrupt, or simply terrorize.

On another occasion, I traveled through the country by car from Yaoundé to the border with Chad. Fort Lamy at that time was dreadful. The French intervention, before that of the Libyans in the north, was in full swing. Drunk and loud ruffians from the French Foreign Legion occupied the city. The Chadians hugged the walls in silence.

*Congo-Kinshasa*

The Belgians made a mess of the decolonization. As a result, from 1960 to 1963 the Democratic Republic of the Congo was the site of a tragic contest. The national liberation movement was belatedly established here and thus was radicalized in difficult conditions around Patrice Lumumba. Cadres were almost totally nonexistent. In 1960, there were only nine Congolese in the country who had attended university, six of them in theology. Congo-Brazzaville had fifty times more senior managers for a country twelve times less populated! The hastily formed united national liberation movement then encountered centrifugal regional and ethnic forces, as well as neocolonial plans hatched by Brussels. Albert Kalonji, leader of the Baluba—who was proclaimed emperor—called on his people to create their state in Kasai, around the diamond mines. Moise Tshombe pushed for the secession of Katanga, not on an ethnic basis, which was somewhat impossible in this province populated by migrants from various countries, but to place his puppet state under the direct control of the mining companies of the "Copper Belt." Brussels supported these movements, but at the same time counted on successfully placing its men at the head of the unified movement and getting rid of Lumumba. Mobutu, who had begun his career as a police informer, was chosen for this purpose. Chaos resulted from these confrontations. Simultaneously, and independently from the ethnic-based movements, peasants rebelled in several of the country's provinces. As usual, the peasant rebellions appeared to be regionalist because they took place within a population attached to their region. But the ideology and demands of these rebellions clearly indicated there was nothing ethnic about them; they were peasant in the content of their objectives. This was particularly the case for the rebellion in Kwilu, led by Pierre Mulele, and also for those in the east of the country.

We closely followed these serious events. I visited the Democratic Republic of the Congo on numerous occasions during this time. The new university, still called Lovanium—a branch of Louvain—was bustling with activity. A little after the surrender of Kasai, I decided to make a visit in 1967. Very few state officials had dared to go to Mbuji Mayi, the new capital founded by the Baluba at the base of Bakwanga hill. It was an incredible discovery. The city had been built piecemeal, without any urban plan, although it already had 300,000 inhabitants. Each immigrant had consulted a soothsayer who had told him: the diamond is there below you. He built his hut on the spot and began to dig a mineshaft in his courtyard.

The hotel consisted of rooms around a large square courtyard with a "dancing bar" just as large. In the latter were found an armchair in good condition, a sagging one, and other chairs. I went to sit in the good armchair. "No," the owner said to me, "it is reserved for the governor who comes later." "For you, distinguished guest, the sagging one." Later in the evening—around ten or eleven—the diamond merchants arrived, one after another, big and strong, in large *boubous*; the last—a little thin—carrying an enormous new leather briefcase. They all sat together on the same bench. They were brought lemonades; all the others, the Congolese, were brought beer. The governor was brought the "large platter" (three bottles of whisky, six bottles of beer) and I was brought the "small platter" (one bottle of whisky, two bottles of beer). The Congolese were miners who came to sell their diamonds. The measure was a bottle of Coca-Cola (we're talking about raw industrial diamonds here). The merchants examined the diamonds then decided on the price, which was paid in bills taken out of the leather briefcase. The seller went to the governor and paid him his percentage (3 percent). Little by little, the proceedings came alive. Many of the sellers, now richer, spent their earnings freely, causing the price of beer to increase. An army of women and young girls, looking to share in the fun, invaded the premises. There was inflation hour-by-hour, music, joyous dancing. The merchants left as soon as the purchase transactions ended. I drank with the governor and several happy miners. The governor explained to me that the 3 percent fee did not belong to him (at least completely). He had to pay the functionaries that Leopoldville forgot and maybe (I suspected) had to send some to the capital. My calculations led me to the conclusion that even if he were to retain only a third or a quarter of the fee, his fortune would be guaranteed in one year. As for the miners, they were "lucky," as was said there, or not. The small-scale mine was horrifying. Many lost their lives. I calculated that while the proceeds of the sale were distributed by chance, nightly inflation redistributed the income widely. In the morning, drunk, most of the lucky miners left as poor as they had arrived. They settled debts, "lent" to neighbors, parents, and others, and paid large sums to the "hostesses." In sum, the entire city benefited from the evening sales.

I also visited the Bakwanga Mine. This was something else entirely, a real concentration camp. Barbed wire fences, surveillance by helicopters piloted by armed mercenaries who shot on sight anyone who attempted to enter. It was a Belgian mining village, perfectly round, with a church and community hall at the center. The mineworkers were adolescent boys recruited from villages, almost purchased from their parents (price: usually a bicycle), sort of educated and trained at work by clerics. They were there for their whole life. Young girls from their native villages were brought in and offered as spouses. They believed they led a happy life: running water and the company mill provided them with manioc meal. They were thereby freed from two major chores. Distractions? After Sunday Mass, educational films of the type "miracle of saint someone or other." And, of course, there were the beer-drinking sessions. At retirement age, the elderly were returned to their native villages, with a small gift: some money (very little) and a bicycle. At some distance from the village were found all the villas of the Belgian managers. Received by the director, I heard the usual racist patter. No comments from me; I wanted to see everything, down to the last detail.

At Kinshasa, in 1972, colleagues and friends from the university and I discussed all these problems in the evenings. This included, above all, the peasant rebellions, about which Benoit Verhaegen and Lemonnier could talk forever. I learned many things from these discussions. I supplemented my information later upon meeting Mulele in Brazzaville. Mulele was shamefully turned over to Mobutu and executed. The hidden aspects of this affair remain obscure. Mulele impressed me as a true popular leader, level-headed, someone who was quite familiar with the demands of his peasant people, their strongpoints and weaknesses. Perhaps he was optimistic in thinking that the small circle of his rebellion could become the "Yan'an" of the Congo, and his army of resistance fighters the future people's liberation army. I met later, in Dar es Salaam in its heyday, some of the Lumumbist politicians—Soumialot and others—refugees in Tanzania after the fall of their government in Kisangani. My impression was rather negative. They led a merry life, but financed by whom? They were true urban politicians—well informed about "politics on the grand scale," as well as the machinations and plans of the powerful and friendly African states (on which they counted too much). But they were not very interested, it seemed to me, in the problems of their people. Some of them expressed the desire to "do something," that is, to open a front and establish resistance fighters in the east of the country. Laurent Kabila was one of these. Che Guevara had a negative opinion about him and his friends, as we now know. My opinion was less negative. I assessed the distance that there could be between the desire to establish a group of resistance fighters and the difficulty in doing so effectively. It was not entirely their fault if the strategic vision remained vague.

Mobutu's power gradually deteriorated into both a corrupt autocracy and institutional nothingness. The man was not content with pillaging his country, amassing a personal fortune equal to Zaire's foreign debt. The World Bank and the IMF did not suggest that if he were to offer this fortune, which he had not received as an inheritance from his parents, as a gift to the country, the debt problem would be settled. Mobutu had chosen a scorched-earth strategy. Destroy everything, every institution, beginning with the universities. Several years later, it had become useless to return to the country: there was no one to see. All the worthwhile intellectuals had been forced to choose exile. The others had become the president's flunkies, rewarded mainly financially. But Mobutu had also destroyed any form of administration in the country. The rural zones had been abandoned to self-subsistence, with neither schools nor hospitals. They had, perhaps, been freed from taxation—though not from the army's abuses of power—but also left without the most basic services. The east of the country—Kivu and Lake Tanganyika—lived from "illegal" trade with East Africa. Though it was not actively rebelling, the region escaped Kinshasa's control. Mobutu's regime survived on taxes collected from the mining enclaves, supplemented by financial support from the West, not very discriminating in this regard. That sufficed to maintain a Praetorian Guard and sustain a world of corrupt politicians, all established in Kinshasa since they had no real base in the country. These were the future "democrats."

The collapse was predictable. The regime was rotten to the core. It did not take much for it to disappear. The occasion arose in connection with the Rwandan tragedy. After the genocide organized by the so-called Hutu neo-colonial government—supported to the end by the Western powers, France and Belgium in particular—the army of murderers was forced to flee from the liberation army (it is not important here that the latter was a minority—mainly composed of Tutsi refugees from Uganda—and supported by East African countries) over the border into Kivu, where it settled. The possibility that this army would go on the offensive and return, with outside support from the French base in Bangui, was a real threat. Goma, a small Zairian city in Kivu, was the strategic key of the system. Why not take it—or liberate it—and, as a result, isolate the Hutu army of the genocide from the border with Rwanda? The leaders of some East African countries—Uganda and Tanzania—thought that possible. History proved them right. Did not Kabila have a small base of resistance fighters in the area? Could he not seize Goma with a small army? The move succeeded with surprising ease, which should not be surprising. He entered Goma with some armed men. At the first shot, Mobutu's army cleared off, but not without first pillaging the population they were supposed to be defending. It is not surprising that Kabila was received as a liberator, even though no one knew who he was and what he wanted. Since it had been so easy, why not continue the march right to Kinshasa?

Liberation achieved in these conditions entails limitations and poses problems. It was not the result of a struggle by the masses in revolt. It was received favorably because no Congolese would defend the horrible Mobutu regime, missed only by its Western backers. But in Kinshasa, political machinations resumed. The corrupt politicians that dominated the city (but not the country) converted quickly from "Mobutism" to "democracy," offering to foreign powers an ideal terrain to cut short any desire for serious change. Kabila himself, together with his small coterie of friends, long exiled, might be tempted by the inexorable appeal of autocracy, which only the rapid organization of autonomous people's forces could prevent. Or they might believe it possible to play the foreign powers off against each other, and since Mobutu was the darling of Paris, play the U.S. card.

Established in Kinshasa, Kabila was immediately challenged by problems that neither he and his team nor the Congolese people as a whole were ready to deal with: the systematic hostility of the Kinshasan political class, which had been the beneficiaries of Mobutu's largesse, but now played the "democratic card"(!) with the support of the Western powers, who wanted everyone to forget their support to the fallen dictator; the apathy of the Congolese people depoliticized by thirty-five years of bloody dictatorship; and the intervention of armies originally allied with Kabila (Tutsi Rwandans and Ugandans), who pursued their own objectives (destroy the Hutu military bases) by debatable means. The intervention of Kampala and Kigali, on the one hand (which South Africa came to support), and the intervention of those who supported Kabila (Angola and Zimbabwe), on the other, posed problems.

Kabila chose to be the head of all of Congo and preserve its unity and not act solely as the head of an ethnic-regional group from the eastern part of the Congo, to which he belonged by chance only. This is a choice that can only be applauded. In fact, Congo could have fallen apart, and there were malevolent attitudes in Western diplomatic circles that desired that outcome and believed it possible to justify their behavior by adopting the rhetoric of "Africa's primordial ethnicism," which some backward anthropologists reveled in and the dominant media unthinkingly repeated. The Congolese people gave a good lesson in this regard, refusing to play the game and protecting the unity of the country and its future.

The Kampala-Kigali bloc chose to support the breakup of the Congo, a means—in their opinion—of guaranteeing their "security." Savimbi's UNITA sided with them, for easy to understand reasons: like Lissouba, Savimbi was in desperate straits in Brazzaville. That South Africa joined them is astonishing. In a study on the alternatives to regionalization in southern Africa, Hein Marais, the Forum's coordinator for the region, concluded that Pretoria considers that its African neighbors are a privileged area for its expansion, reproducing the traditional unequal regional development model. The very title of the study, *Reinforcing the Mould*, summarizes the conclusions of the analysis. The fact that serious opponents of the Mobutu dictatorship, such as our friend Wamba Dia Wamba, have rallied to this camp coupled with their aerial landing at Matadi is equally astonishing. It is understandable that Angola of the MPLA and Zimbabwe have come to the aid of Kabila, that is, have opted to support maintaining Congolese unity.

Given all of this, the situation remains dangerous, especially given the devastating effects of Mobutu's regime. There are serious phenomena that clearly indicate the people's feeling of helplessness. For example, many have found refuge in so-called salvation sects that have proliferated more than ever under the control of U.S.-style televangelists. These sects, which preach submission while awaiting the apocalypse, play directly into the hands of reactionary forces, of course. They are the exact opposite of what liberation theology is elsewhere. An autocratic turn by the new government is entirely possible.

This entire tragedy is the result of Mobutu's bloody dictatorship. It succeeded in destroying—at least temporarily—the potential of an entire people. This is similar to what has happened elsewhere every time a people's movement has been crushed in a bloodbath. The destruction of the UPC in Cameroon or that of the Mau Mau in Kenya guaranteed stability in an astonishing mediocrity for three decades or more. Suharto's dictatorship, built on the bodies of 500,000 victims, is a success of the same type. It is only when the economic and social failure of these neocolonial regimes, established with the West's active support, bring an end to their apparent stability that the diplomats of the Western powers rediscover the virtues of democracy—the absence of which they had probably not noticed for thirty years! Democracy in these conditions does not appear to them to be dangerous. It can be the means to continue to do the same thing: manage the crisis and create obstacles to the organization of the working classes. The long list of failures and stagnation-in-mediocrity that I have presented in the preceding pages could encourage the greatest degree of pessimism. The possibilities of entire peoples have been systematically destroyed (Cameroon, Congo, Kenya), or the projects for liberation and social progress have gotten bogged down in a populism that they were unprepared to go beyond (Modibo's Mali, Guinea, Nkrumah's Ghana, the PCT's Congo-Brazzaville), or the opportunities to revive the movement have run up against an extremely hostile world conjuncture (Rawlings' Ghana, Konaré's Mali). None of this has prevented waves of popular discontent from arising all over the continent, from north to south and from east to west, throughout the last forty years.

If that is so, it is because the neocolonial project is itself in crisis, even in permanent crisis. It is not only national liberation and socialism that have suffered a series of undeniable failures. The capitalist alternative, and particularly its comprador variant, is itself a false alternative, unacceptable and unaccepted—rejected by peoples everywhere. When circumstances favor the continuation of its program, then the crisis and collapse are often more serious, sometimes even leading to the total dissolution of the society and the disappearance of the state.

## *Niger and Nigeria*

Niger is the result of a rather absurd case of drawing colonial boundaries. Moreover, it has never succeeded in extricating itself from the dead-end of impoverished colonial era extroversion. It has not totally fallen apart—an ongoing threat it would be foolish to ignore—due to the wisdom of its people and also many of its leaders. But it was very close to doing so several years ago when so-called democracy was all the rage. The multiparty system ended quickly with the formation of small groups contending for power, all reduced to clans of small urban bourgeois politicians seeking to create support on an ethnic and regional basis, particularly by making alliances with dubious rural notables. The military coup d'état that ended this game—fortunately without repression that would have prevented the continuation of debates and discussions—appeared to me (and to numerous Nigerien political friends) to be a beneficial event, when all was said and done. Real democratization—a necessary condition for any progress off the well-worn paths—cannot be reduced to a choice between the autocracy of the single party and a "tin-pot" multiparty system.

I discovered Niger for the first time during the 1960s. The UN was responsible for a study on the viability of a trans-Saharan highway. A group of three "experts" had been formed for this task: Alain Savary (French politician), an Austrian road engineer whose name I forget (he had been a tiger hunter in Bengal), and me. A small airplane (four seats) had been put at our disposal with which we traveled along the entire southern edge of the Sahara, from Dakar through Saint Louis, Kaedi, Kayes, Bamako, Mopti, Gao, Niamey, and Zinder to Fort Lamy. A magnificent journey: we flew at an altitude between 500 and 1,000 meters and the views of the scenery were much better than from the road. At Niamey, Boubou Hama received us, with all the refinement characteristic of the learned and powerful in the Sahel. There were no tedious speeches upon arrival at the airport. We were led directly to a villa so we could bathe, eat (caviar!), and drink (champagne!) before the *méchoui* (lamb barbecue) reception at nightfall. We exchanged views with this cultivated man who wished to reestablish the historical relations between the peoples who live along the edges of the Sahara, north and south—relations destroyed by colonization, which had redirected trade from the Sahel exclusively toward the coast of the Gulf of Guinea.

Our report was quite simple to write, and really did not require the journey we had made. But international money must be wasted for prestige. And I do not regret this magnificent journey! We said that three good north-south road links could be justified, even if the then dominant view privileged outward-looking development and made immediate use quite limited. But neither we nor the countries concerned—officially at least—adopted this dominant view. A day will come when the real implementation of African integration, even if it takes different forms in different contexts, will correct the distortions resulting from the colonial heritage. Thus the trans-Saharan highway would fulfill functions similar to those of the transcontinental railroads in North America and Russia. This would make good historical sense, if nothing else.

On another occasion, Isabelle and I had the pleasure of a tour through the country guided by Michel Keita, who led us into the heart of the Aïr Mountains region. Lying in the middle of the desert in Niger, this region is not only one of the most beautiful in the world, in my opinion, but also unique. As the Sahara dried up, many of the fauna and flora from earlier times, which disappeared elsewhere, survived here. Waterfalls, unexpected in this part of the world, can be found next to vegetation unlike any elsewhere.

At the end of the 1970s, I had had at Paris Vincennes a group of African students of exceptional quality: Oumar Blondin Diop, Michel Keita, Abdussalam Kane, and Alioune Sall. They were intelligent, curious, cultivated, and politicized. Unfortunately, three of them came to a tragic end. Blondin was killed by prison guards in Gorée, Kane died in an auto accident in Mali, and Keita was burned to death in his automobile, which was carrying a gas cylinder that exploded. I remember having had to give Michel Keita an oral exam at Vincennes. I knew his capabilities so well that I felt the exam was a useless formality. I said to him straightaway, without posing any questions: "What score should I give you, 18 or 20? Quickly." I prefer to spend more time with students for whom it is necessary to verify more seriously if they know more than they appear to, those whom shyness paralyzes, for example. Modest, Michel responded: "Oh! 18 would be wonderful."

It was the end of the day on the road to the Aïr Mountains and we thought it was time to begin thinking about making camp for the night. There was nothing on the horizon, except three camel drivers coming into view. We decided to head for them. When we got close enough to talk to them, we exited the car. There were the customary lengthy greetings. It was cold in the mountainous Sahara. Michel tried all the many languages he knew: Hausa and Targui, I tried Arabic. Mischievous, the Tuaregs remained silent, allowing us to get more and more worked up. Then, in superb French, one of them said: "We don't know the area; we are here for the weekend." All the same, they helped us find a shack of sorts where, piling up and sharing our blankets, we spent a not very warm night. They also offered us wonderful Tuareg-style crêpes, a delight, especially when hungry. When we departed in the morning, we came across a pretty young woman asleep next to her camel and its young one. What a wonderful scene. When we reached the end of our journey, we were received with great hospitality at the main administrative center. We were offered what was fed to the hungry: a thick paste made from dates, almonds, and dried cheese pounded together. It was delicious, but a block in the stomach that filled us for three days. We just had to drink tea on top of that every two hours, which slowly dissolved the food reserves and provided us with what we needed to survive. But since we were not Bedouins, who only eat occasionally, like their camels, we found it difficult to digest. Also on the highway, at the foot of the Aïr Mountains, there is the uranium mine of the French Commission for Atomic Energy. We visited this terrible place where the miners are quickly contaminated by radiation. We also visited an absurd garden in a greenhouse, air conditioned so the French gardener would not suffer too much from the heat. Tomatoes were grown there for the managers, at an actual cost that must have been the highest in the world. The Tuaregs, of course, grow tomatoes directly in the sun and their women sell them in the market.

President Hamani Diori thought it would be desirable to reform the monetary system of the French CFA-franc zone and, knowing that I was one of the few people who shared this viewpoint and also had a fairly good knowledge of the economic problems of the region, he invited me in 1969 to present my views. My opinions on the subject were well known and I presented some essential principles. First, monetary management is never the primary aspect of the problem; it comes after, not before, fundamental social choices and the corresponding economic strategies. Then, if the countries concerned wanted to break with the outward-directed colonial model and move onto the path of self-reliant development at the level of individual states as well as on a regional level (by implementing a real integration), the franc zone system such as it existed would not be suitable. Of course, I had the intention of aiding a reform, not of proposing "all or nothing." I then developed a project that seemed acceptable to me in the sense that it would open room for movement for those countries that wished to embark on stronger social development and regional integration, without hampering the others.

Also, in France and within the European community, it could be possible to find allies supporting the project, which would be unacceptable only for ultras nostalgic for the colonial period. The project envisaged a national currency for each country of the group, with fixed exchange rates, but adjustable between these currencies and the franc as well as other currencies. In fact, I thought that the CFA was overvalued, but in already varying proportions from one country to another and would be increasingly so since the national development policies and their results differed. I insisted that it should be understood that a devaluation is not in itself a disgrace, but that it is necessary to control it and not be placed in a situation where it is imposed by the "market," the French Treasury, or the IMF. The system would retain a strong regional dimension, which I proposed to strengthen gradually by a customs union, the adoption of taxation systems as close to one another as possible, the possible joint management of a fraction of the currency reserves, and the freedom of transfers. It would also remain open and retain a privileged link with the franc zone; the French Treasury would guarantee the freedom of transfers and the fixity of exchange rates, but its guarantees would be negotiated and conditional. I proposed to open the system in two directions: by the possible membership—complete or limited—of, on the one hand, countries outside the CFA zone (Nigeria and Ghana), and, on the other, the treasuries of other European countries and/or by the adoption of a clause in the Yaoundé convention (the Lomé Convention was then only in the preparation stage) establishing a Euro-African monetary institution charged with negotiating these collective guarantees. I believe that if I had to offer proposals today concerning the future of monetary relations between the CFA, other African currencies, and the euro, I would not deviate too far from this forty-year-old project!

Diori was personally convinced by my analysis. But Côte d'Ivoire and Senegal had to be convinced and their responses were unreservedly negative. France's response at the time was negative as well. The project then fell apart, and the slow but steady movement toward disaster continued. Today, no one is prepared, in France, the European Union, in the countries of WAEMU and CEMAC, or in other African countries, to confront the unknown future of the euro, its relationship to the dollar, and its internal solidity. And no one knows how the new Cotonou Convention will deal with these problems, or, since the latter were excluded from consideration during the negotiations, how "things" will develop. The disorderly breakup of current African monetary zones is quite probable, on the occasion of the next devaluation, which has a good chance of being as poorly handled as the last one.

Nigeria always reminds me of a sort of sea monster or prehistoric animal, or even of an Albert Dubout-style factory. It is important not only because of the size of its population, equivalent to that of fifteen other African countries combined, but above all because of its significant density. This is not the result of chance, but the legacy of the history of the former states that formed its territory and showed great potential, up until now totally wasted. It is more like an enormous antediluvian machine with almost no output, a conglomeration of interests that are not inherently in conflict (otherwise the federation would disappear), but independent from one another and, consequently, reduce the central power to their almost nil common denominator. This is, in its own way, a model of the space for a market without a state, the ideal for the laissez-faire of liberal capitalism, here of compradorism. State interventions are not absent in appearance. But they are always possible to circumvent because the state is privatized. It is itself the space of confrontation and bargaining between these interests, of their "competition." A system that impedes politics only encourages demagogy, accompanied by mafia violence.

Nigeria is a country always fascinating to visit, but, at the same time, it always leaves one (or at least me) with a bitter feeling of waste and the impossible. Lagos, dominated by rackets of all kinds, from the customs officers at the airport to the taxis and the hotel-keepers; Ibadan, where the IDEP organized a seminar on its very British campus in 1973, isolated and ignorant of what is happening in the city, on the other side of its protective walls; and Kano, like Djenné, Timbuktu, or Zinder, but on a scale ten times larger, which reminds the ignorant that there were cities here before colonization—none of them can go unnoticed.

Yet neither organized popular forces (including trade unions) nor critical intellectuals are absent or inactive. The weight of these grassroots and ideological counterforces has preserved the Federation from breaking up, even during the horrible Biafra war, far more than the oil revenues that, on the contrary, more readily sustain the regionalism of those who hope to capture them, with the blessing of transnational capital.

### Uganda and Zambia

Tanzanian advances, despite their limits, have played a positive role, encouraging change in Uganda and Zambia.

Uganda is an extremely complicated country. The British successfully manipulated a curious conflict between Catholics and Protestants in this region, between the Kingdom of Buganda and the Nilotic peoples that had no state. They made a system of laws, administrative forms, and a constitution such that nothing could work after their departure. This led to the successive farces of the first Milton Obote regime, the famous Idi Amin, then the return of Obote with the Tanzanian army. It remains the case that Ugandan comrades, refugees in Dar, and primarily the one who asserted himself as leader—Yoweri Museveni—worked out and implemented the beginnings of a progressive response to the "Uganda challenge." They organized a guerilla war, crossing Lake Victoria at the risk of their lives, and ultimately liberated the country. The political formula for managing the country was original and could open up interesting possibilities. The formula was no single party (that would inevitably be created from above and bureaucratized from the beginning); no multiparty system (that would necessarily be captured and manipulated by the small bourgeois clans of traditional Uganda politics). Instead, factions of the people were encouraged to organize, elect representatives, etc. I have not visited Uganda since, except on the occasion of the CODESRIA assembly in 2002. But everyone knows that this "project" has never been implemented. Among my Ugandan friends, Mahmood Mamdani and Dan Nabudere are strongly critical of the situation, with good arguments.

Under the leadership of another Protestant pastor, Kenneth Kaunda, Zambia also introduced "African socialism" in its populist version, obviously, but it seems little contested by the left, despite the apparent power of the copper miners union. Our critical intellectual friends Derrick Chitala and Gilbert Mudenda were, consequently, rather isolated.

All the same, we organized a colloquium in Lusaka, in cooperation with the Southern Africa Association of Political Science—the most active branch of the African Association of Political Science in the hope that it would contribute to starting discussion and debate. We—Isabelle, Amoa, I, and a few others—arrived in Lusaka on a Friday and the colloquium began the following Monday. Lodged on campus, far from the city as would be expected, we needed a minibus to be able to visit Lusaka during the weekend. "There is nothing to see," said the driver. "All the same, we want to go." We can verify that the driver was right. The two bakeries at the city center (there were no cafés) were closed on Saturday and Sunday, as were other public places, except for the churches, which were open, but did not interest us much. As for the working-class areas, they were designed by the English so as to kill any possible social life. The residential complexes were totally monotonous, each one designed for a quite specific social category and only one "ethnic" group authorized to live there. They were totally devoid of any means of social life—not even bars, nothing, except a church. This was the perfect model of the so-called communitarian ideal. To each community its difference and its living space! There was no mixing of classes or peoples. Each person had his or her own home and nothing more. It was a horror, then, which should give cause for reflection to all defenders of fashionable communitarianism. Obviously, the only distraction, then, is to drink beer, seated on the edge of the sidewalk in front of your door, chatting, or quarreling with your neighbor. This "urban" model is widespread in southern Africa. I have seen other examples in Windhoek (Namibia) and Cape Town (South Africa).

Holding a session of the African Social Forum in Lusaka in 2004 confirmed my fears. There were no genuine Zambian people's organizations to participate, only questionable NGOs, often supported by the "black diaspora in the United States"—and behind it, the CIA! The devastating effects produced by the spread of the "new churches," all also exported by African-Americans, added to the sad picture.

## THE NEOCOLONIAL DISASTERS

The list of countries that are currently victims of the colonial disaster caused by the new globalization, which only serves the financialized monopolies of the triad, is quite lengthy: it involves four-fifths or more of the world's countries. I have thus carried out a severe selection, reducing the list to three examples: the West African Sahel (to which I referred above), Somalia and the Horn of Africa, and Rwanda and the Great Lakes-Congo region. I have participated in several important debates about the problems of these regions.

Africa is above all a region doomed by the dominant system to be only a reserve of natural resources (oil, minerals, agricultural land, water) for the imperialist triad. While "Africa" is important, the African peoples, on the other hand, are more an obstacle than anything else. Since the Treaty of Berlin (1885), the strategy (colonial and then post-colonial) has been to destroy all attempts at industrialization on the continent. Industrialization, of course, is an imperative condition for any development worthy of the name. The neocolonial systems—the subject of my analyses in these memoirs—have succeeded in maintaining Africa in this fatal preindustrial state. The Development Assistance Committee, the group of Western "donors" managed by the OECD, designed the system of "aid" for that purpose. I refer the reader to the decisive critique that Yash Tandon (2008) has made of the function of aid in imperialist strategy.[29] Imperialism has nothing to offer to African peoples other than a lumpen-development that lies behind their continuing pauperization. This process, in turn, encourages the breakup of states. Imperialism is making every effort to establish a system of military control over the continent as a response to the explosions of anger by African peoples. Consequently, the objectives of the United States Africa Command (U.S. AFRICOM—African wing of the American military command) have acquired a central place in the contemporary world system.

The secession of the northern part of Mali, made possible by the destruction of Libya, is an indication of this sad future. It is the best pretext to allow the permanent military presence of NATO in the region and thereby guarantee control of uranium in Niger, which is maintained in a state of powerlessness by immiserating aid. The civil war in Côte d'Ivoire was the predictable result of what I had feared (refer to my analyses above on this country). Yet the apparent success of the government of bureaucrats and technocrats established in Abidjan on the orders of Washington and Paris is far from being able to assure stability. The breakup of Somalia is accomplished. That still poses a threat to Ethiopia, which has probably entered into a period of turbulence following the death in 2012 of its pro-U.S. dictator (Zenawi).

The Rwandan genocide is certainly among the most unpardonable horrors of modern times. But the establishment of a new regime, dominated by the Tutsis, whatever one may say, and supported by Uganda and the United States, is far from having settled the central question of the necessary coexistence of peoples in the region. This is even more the case since the Kigali and Kampala regimes harbor expansionist ambitions in the Congo's eastern provinces and the Kabila government in Kinshasa is poorly equipped to resist. The democratic question is here at the center of the challenge, and none of the governments in the region is able to ensure progress in this matter. Will the revolts by the victims succeed in developing a common alternative strategy combining democratization of society with social progress? Will they be up to the challenge presented by the necessity to: (i) create a large alliance of states in the region, which alone would allow them to confront jointly the pillage of their important natural resources by the imperialist powers; (ii) overcome lumpen-development; and (iii) assure the coexistence of ethnic groups on the basis of their common interests?

### SIERRA LEONE AND LIBERIA

The International African Institute (IAI), based in London, had organized in 1969 in Freetown a conference on the topic of the African bourgeoisie to which I was invited. Later, an exchange of views between this institution and the IDEP was continued in Dakar on the topic of internal migration in West Africa. Thus I had the opportunity to look a little more closely at this curious British colony, the capital of which—Freetown—had been a welcome center for freed slaves. This is a country that has never, at any moment of its history, had the strength to challenge its effectively colonial status in globalization. I have only a semi-tourist memory of my visit, inasmuch as the discussions with the Anglicized intellectuals of Fourah Bay—the oldest university on the coast of the Gulf of Guinea—were of little interest.

Sierra Leone has entered into an unending process of breaking apart. But no one in the dominant media suggests that this is the effect of the ongoing crisis of neocolonialism since here socialism cannot be held responsible for the disaster.

Liberia is another example of the same kind. In its semi-colony, the United States, lacking the ability or willingness to go a little beyond the usual unrestricted practices of economic liberalism, has not succeeded in establishing a minimum set of functional public institutions. Everything is private and, as a result, nothing works. The result is the ongoing breakup of the society, today given over to mafia gangs none of which are better than the others and which, since the only objective is to capture control of the government, end up killing one another. Long live liberal capitalism! I had made a brief visit to Monrovia in 1971 on the occasion of some West African ministerial meeting to which I had been invited. It was a dull meeting. The amusement came at the president's reception. His large, North American police-type bodyguards, armed with weapons, surrounded him. Each time someone approached the president, they moved their hands to their revolvers. The president himself remained silent. But a small whisky bottle could be seen bulging from the rear pocket of his pants! Very American!

As with Sierra Leone, Liberia has begun to fall apart. The American establishment has demonstrated here that it is incapable of creating the concepts and methods for the effective management of a small colony. The unimaginative and naive rhetoric on "good governance" that the United States, with all its well-known arrogance, offers to the entire world today should simply make us smile.

*Rwanda*

Rwanda is a tragic example of criminal management by comprador neocolonialism. I had always felt an instinctive revulsion for the Nazi option of the so-called Hutu comprador petite bourgeoisie, using an anti-Tutsi racism to legitimize its power and dominate public speech in the name of the "Hutu masses," but in reality exploiting them. That it had to lead to genocide—planned, no less—was more than obvious. But apparently none of that bothered Western diplomacy, satisfied with the economic liberalism of this criminal government. I had discussed the Rwanda situation on the occasion of visits to Kampala and Dar es Salaam where, it is true, I met only intellectuals among the Tutsi refugees. The Tutsis are only a minority in Rwanda, but that is not an acceptable reason to massacre them. We came to the conclusion that the solution to the problem was to dilute the Hutu-Tutsi opposition by incorporating the two countries (Rwanda and Burundi) into a larger entity such as Tanzania (that would be a return to the borders of German Tanganyika) or Uganda, or even a federation of the four. In such a context, Hutu and Tutsi (whether they actually are two different ethnic groups is no longer the problem) would be two among ten other peoples (call them ethnic groups or tribes, if you want) and the confrontation would lose its intensity. Moreover, the Hutus and Tutsis in neighboring countries (there are some) do not kill each other for that reason. After the genocide, this solution is more than ever the only human one imaginable. But neither the local comprador ruling cliques, whose interests inevitably depend on their access to power, nor Western diplomacy, which always hopes to gain something by manipulating the opposing parties, accepts the idea of these two states disappearing. It is difficult to see how any model of development other than the prevailing neocolonial model could take shape in these countries so long as this precondition has not been met.

*Rwanda: Twentieth Anniversary of the Genocide, 1994–2014*

My visits to Kigali in the past had never convinced me of the benefits of the regime that stemmed from what it claimed was the "Hutu peasant revolution." The 1994 genocide did not surprise me. But twenty years later, the odious military dictatorship of the Tutsis under Kagame hardly seems better to me, as I explain in the following text, which I immediately sent to democrats and progressives in Dar es Salaam:

Twenty years after the event, we still do not have a clear idea of the specific circumstances in the attack against the plane of Rwanda's former president, Juvénal Habyarimana. This event was immediately followed by the genocide of the Tutsis by Hutu militias.

Two hypotheses still remain possible: 1) the plane was shot down by Hutu extremists, a pretext both for launching the planned ethnic cleansing and getting rid of the Rwandan president who, after the Arusha Agreements (which had brought to life a transition government), logically had to oppose any such plans; or 2) the plane was shot down by members of Paul Kagame's FPR, who wanted to eliminate Habyarimana, one of the key players in the rise of anti-Tutsi racism and the war against the FPR—and who could, moreover, have benefited from the reconciliation promoted at Arusha and hope to see his party or his Hutu allies maintained in power after the multiparty elections. If the second hypothesis is correct, then Kagame and the FPR must have done so knowing that it meant taking the risk of triggering reprisals against civilian Tutsis, the possible extent of which they underestimated, but also knowing that it would justify a break with the peace agreement and an offensive against the Kigali government from Ugandan territory.

This tragedy is not an ethnic war, as is usually said. Hutus and Tutsis belong to the same nation, speak the same language, have the same religion. Hutu is the name given to the majority (85 percent) of the peasants subject to the Tutsi aristocracy, which the German colonizers, followed by the Belgians, saw fit to consolidate as the dominant group. Exempt from agricultural work, they owned the cattle and devoted their time to administering the country. The system is similar to that of Hindu castes, without being as extreme: mixed marriages were possible. The national liberation movement was, for this reason, a bit disoriented. As almost everywhere, the local privileged classes (here the Tutsis) embraced demands for independence in the hope of maintaining their dominant position, while numerous Hutu leaders combined their demand for independence with social demands that aimed at the elimination of Tutsi privileges. In Burundi, a compromise was (momentarily) found between the two parties, but not in Rwanda, where a little before independence, the Hutus seized power with the last-minute support of the colonial power, which hoped in that way to encourage the future stability of the country, now in the hands of the majority of its citizens. What followed were anti-Tutsi pogroms and the exile, in successive waves, of thousands of Tutsis in neighboring countries, particularly Uganda, where, thirty years later, an "army" for Rwanda's liberation was formed, with the support of the host country and the United States.

France, Belgium, and the United States were active in the region and thus share responsibility for this tragedy. This is particularly true of France and Belgium, which supported the Hutu regime in Kigali and could certainly not be unaware that extremists planned a genocide, numerous signs of which were already clear. The Arusha Accords, signed in August 1993, certainly allowed power sharing in all public institutions, including integrating the FPR army into Habyarimana's Rwandan army on an almost equal basis, but it would have led to an inclusive electoral process that the FPR could not have won. Now, under different pretexts, Kagame still does not accept democratic procedures and runs his government with an iron hand.

The Western powers do not seek the modest wealth of Rwanda, but rather the immense resources of the Democratic Republic of the Congo, which possesses many rare minerals. Effective and combat-hardened, the Rwandan army, which has long had direct or indirect control over the eastern areas of Congo, can thus be an asset for those who have designs on the wealth of these regions. There were tensions between the United States, France, and Belgium until the Europeans seemed to accept a U.S. command over the region. But this arrangement could be called into question. African countries are themselves divided on the role of Rwanda. Supported above all by Uganda, Washington's main ally in the region, Rwanda is losing the support of countries like South Africa, at present aligned with Zimbabwe and Angola, which openly tilt toward Kinshasa.

The case of Rwanda is, in any event, striking. There is no sign that the entire region can, one day, leave the wars and chaos behind, which justifies the ongoing imperialist interference and pillage of natural resources, particularly from Congo. The only acceptable solution would be to dilute Rwanda's heritage of violence through the construction of some sort of vast "confederation" of the Great Lakes region. It would include Rwanda, Burundi, Tanzania, Uganda, and Congo (there are Hutu/Tutsi minorities in all these countries), with a joint sovereign project as distant as possible from the Western powers. This is an immense task for the popular democratic forces of the region. We have returned to square one. Today, we go back to what we already thought was the only reasonable solution for the region thirty years ago, as reflected in debates in Dar es Salaam.

The Rwandan mess does not involve only this country. It is part of the "shifting sands of neocolonialism," the term I use to characterize the typical form of political management in Congo and the region as a whole. Kabila's reconquest of Congo is part of this context. None of the governments in the region has ever dreamt of expelling the imperialist financial-mining monopolies intent simply on pillaging the region's resources. They simply believed they could play off these monopolies against one another in order to line their personal pockets (not even the state coffers) with the bribes that inevitably accompany the successful profits. I have had numerous discussions on these subjects with, among others, George Ntalaja Nzongola and Kankwenda Mbaya. François Houtart, who closely follows the development of popular movements in the Congo, can say more about this.

The recent explosion of the so-called civil war (fighting between militias devoted to one group or another) in the Central African Republic is nothing more than an additional example of the impasse in which imperialist pillage has trapped the countries of the region.

## *Somalia*

Somalia is another tragic example of a fragile society that compradorization broke up to the point of causing the disappearance of a minimum level of national solidarity, without which no progress is possible.

However, Somalia had, at the beginning, two significant assets. The first is that its population, although divided into tribes and clans, is a strong ethno-linguistic whole. This ethno-historic entity is not Arab, though it is Muslim. It is Somali. The choice to use the Arabic alphabet for the Somali language was likely to strengthen national sentiment, and for that reason I believe it was a positive choice. The disaster began when the comprador ruling class had Somalia join the Arab League, and proclaim itself "Arab." The motive was strictly opportunist: to benefit from the influx of Saudi capital! But the effects were disastrous. The proclamation of the "Arabness" of the nation sowed confusion and destroyed the sense of belonging to the Somali community, and thereby even restored excessive importance to tribal and clan identities.

False Arabness could not act as a unifying force as well as Somali identity could. To the contrary, it immediately acted as a centrifugal force. The second asset was the so-called socialist option, certainly fragile, but perhaps, despite all its limitations, conducive to a possible strengthening of a sense of national community by giving it a dimension of social solidarity. This option was not going to be able to resist the artificial choice of Arabness and the Saudi pressures associated with it.

The seminar that the IDEP organized in Mogadishu was one of the sites of serious debates about this twofold (national and social) challenge. It was, consequently, a conspicuous date in the country's intellectual and political history. The best Somali political thinkers—Mohamed Aden, Ibrahim Meygaag Samatar, Weira—quite remarkable ideologues and organizers of the nation's modernization, truly educated us about the underlying problems that are never spoken of. These militants combined their view of the Somali nation with a progressive social vision, and paid for their convictions with long prison terms. Then Siad Barre, having to face Ethiopia—at that time (before 1974) governed by the Negus and supported by the United States—believed it possible to gain the USSR as an ally by suddenly claiming he was "socialist." The fragility of all this hodgepodge of opportunism—verbal socialism, artificial Arabness, Soviet military support, Saudi financial support—is behind the disaster. Besides, the very day that Ethiopia declared itself socialist, Siad Barre officially repudiated the socialist label and passed over to the U.S. camp.

In these conditions, economic dissipation, produced as a matter of course by the neocolonial economy, was reinforced by the collapse of the attempt to construct a nation with a minimum of social solidarity. Clan warfare began. Siad Barre, always a total opportunist, chose to enter the fray by giving his clan a monopoly of power. And the decomposition continues. I had been invited to Mogadishu a second time on the occasion of the OAU summit. I no longer remember much about this summit since it was so dull. The essential questions I had been invited to discuss with other African intellectuals were all removed from the agenda. The consequences are well known. Exhausted by the fighting among the warlords, Somalia became fertile ground for a takeover by political Islam, pushing the country even deeper into chaos.

*Somalia: A Country Erased from the World Map*

I earlier described the course followed by the Siad Barre government as a "colonial disaster." The following text simply says more about what is known about the obliteration of the Somali state and nation.

The first republic, from 1960 to 1969, was a multiparty electoral democracy, though neocolonial. It disappointed all those who expected more from independence. Siad Barre's coup d'état (1969) was, consequently, welcomed in the country.

The regime was "nationally popular," and its achievements from 1969 to 1982 were the basis of its legitimacy. The regime established the foundation for a renovation of the Somali nation by fostering education in the national language. This was, in effect, recognition of the fundamental reality of national identity: the Somalis are not "Arabs"; they are an African, and Muslim, nation with its own unique language and culture. Economic development—as modest as it was—primarily of administrative and social services, provided a basis for the formation of a middle class, which consequently gave the regime a good deal of legitimacy. Certainly this regime was not "democratic" according to Western criteria, since it was based on a single party, but it was also not completely open to capitalism as were other single-party African regimes (such as Côte d'Ivoire and Malawi), which were not characterized as non-democratic. But the regime was not "democratic" in a higher sense. It was confronted with a historical reality: the importance of clans in the definition of the Somali nation's multiple identities. As with many other regimes confronted with ethnic diversity, the regime was content to deny the fact and deal with "clan" resistance by repression. It was the same with Islam, to which the regime—without being secular in the true sense of the term, despite advances in this direction on more favorable treatment of women in the family code—denied the right to be political. This "enlightened despotism," if it had been supported from abroad—instead of attacked—probably could have created more favorable conditions for a possible evolution of the country toward democratization of society and politics.

At that time, Mengistu Haile Mariam's Ethiopia, South Yemen, and the Eritrean resistance all shared a common denominator—anti-imperialist and popular—that could have served as a basis to bring them closer together. Fidel Castro had proposed that a grand "confederation" (Ethiopia, Eritrea, Somalia, Yemen) be built, balanced in national and religious terms. Advances in this direction would have strengthened the position of this region in its confrontation with the ambitions of the imperialist powers and increased the size of its development base. That was not the path chosen by the potential partners in the region. In response to the rapid exhaustion of their possibilities, the regimes chose the narrow nationalism card to boost their opportunities, becoming involved in the Ogaden war in 1981. It was then that Siad Barre suddenly changed sides and abandoned "socialism" (and Soviet support) in exchange for support from Saudi Arabia and the United States.

The second period of the Barre regime (1982–92) should not, then, be confused with the first. The regime slid toward "opening" (particularly to Saudi capital), much appreciated by the imperialist powers. At the same time, these powers stopped criticizing him for violent repression, which actually worsened, leading to the revolt of clans excluded from power. The penetration of political Islam, supported by the new Saudi ally, blossomed with, once again, Washington's blessing.

What followed was inevitable: the collapse of the state, clan wars, warlords, the consolidation of political Islam, deterioration in basic conditions of life; destruction of the middle classes, and ultimately piracy. The United States attempted a direct intervention. But that only demonstrated their military and political inability to undertake this "police operation" successfully. Twelve GIs were killed, and it was chaos! Washington then turned to Ethiopia, which had passed into its camp after Mengistu's fall. But even though the entry of Ethiopian forces into Somalia encountered no serious obstacle, the new occupiers, who turned out to be unable to establish a stable government, were, in turn, forced to withdraw. The results of all these attempts to "stabilize" Somalia were, then, nil. Undoubtedly, piracy in the Indian Ocean was a problem. Still, it should be remembered that this piracy came in response to another that preceded it: pillage of marine resources and their destruction due to ocean pollution, now unrestricted because there was no Somali state to enforce international laws. Somali fishers, who are the victims of all this, had hardly any other alternative than resorting to piracy. Certainly, in the chaotic conditions of the country, the warlords were able to extort money from this piracy.

Unending chaos with no solution appears to be the situation in Somalia for the foreseeable future. Then what to do? Could the "international community" impose another solution? I strongly doubt that. This self-proclaimed "international community" is nothing more than Washington supported by its subaltern European and Japanese allies. The African community, in particular the community that could be formed by the countries of the region, can provide the only possible solution to the Somali chaos. The proposals that were made by Fidel Castro a long time ago consequently still appear to have some obvious relevance to the situation. Yet the conditions are no longer what they were at the time the proposals were originally put forward. In the current state of things, Addis Ababa is not interested in the reconstruction of a viable Somali state. Ethiopia is, and will remain, the center of gravity in the region. It is the only state worthy of the name because of its size and the tradition of its political culture. Proof of that can be found in the failure of the attempt at breaking up the country along "ethnic" lines, as Washington had hoped, which was defeated by the Ethiopian people. Consequently, a rebirth of Ethiopia remains possible. Although it might appear paradoxical to put it this way, the reconstruction of a viable Somali state greatly depends on the rebirth of a united, strong, and independent Ethiopia, capable of moving forward on a line of development favoring the people, an Ethiopia capable, consequently, of taking the initiative and bringing other countries in the region along this path.

### SOUTH AFRICA AFTER APARTHEID: AN EMERGENT NATION?

South Africa is a sort of microcosm of the world capitalist system, combining on the same territory the specific characteristics of each of the four "worlds" of the world system. It includes a white population that, by its mode and level of life, belongs to the "first world." A humorist would have noticed that the strongly "statist" behavior of the white minority could be compared with that of the second world, today collapsed, which used to be called socialist. As for the populations of the cities reserved to blacks and the "mixed" races, they belong to the modern industrialized Third World, while the peasants described as "tribal" and shut away in the Bantustans do not differ substantially from peasant communities of what is now called the African "fourth world."

After the Second World War, the Boers took over responsibility for managing this system by taking over state power. They gave it a name—apartheid—and, what is more, an ideological justification to conceal the racist practices already in force and codified into law. In the following period, the half-century now ending, a process of industrialization in the peripheries of the global system took place. In South Africa, the ruling class developed, in this context, its own program of advancement in the world system by means of industrialization that was protected and supported by the state. Apartheid was, in this respect, completely rational. That the labor force was paid very little would not necessarily create a problem for ensuring outlets for production. Demand can be created by increasing the income distributed to the nonproductive or not very productive minority and by increasing exports to pay for the imports required for the overall efficiency of industry. The liberal theory that presented apartheid as if it were in conflict with capitalism—as if capitalism were the equivalent of liberty and equality!—was totally irrelevant.

In fact, the economic results of the South African "historical" project are not very outstanding: South African industry has completely failed in its quest for "competitiveness." Its (non-mineral) industrial exports are negligible, aimed at the captive markets of southern Africa. And yet the South African regime, despite its ignominy, benefited from exceptional support, financial as well as economic, political, and military, from the United States, Great Britain, and all of Western Europe. I see no explanation other than racist prejudice, which can shed some light on the fact that the failure of South African industrialization is not recognized by international institutions, such as the World Bank, while failures of this type on the part of other countries that attempted it while encountering the hostility of the Western powers—for example, Egypt and Algeria—are commented on *ad nauseam* by the dominant media. Ultimately, from the perspective of the global system, South Africa continues to be an exporter of raw materials. At the same time, the Bantustans remain among the most miserable zones of the "fourth world," incapable of guaranteeing even a minimum level of survival for their inhabitants. This failure has essentially been due to the growing resistance of the black working class, at workplaces and in the cities, and to the political capability of its organizations (the ANC, the SACP, unions of COSATU, and others) which have acted effectively and created obstacles to all attempts to "legitimize" the Bantustans, including in the opinion of the inhabitants of these territories.

Now that apartheid has ended, there are and will be for a long time to come two opposed lines. Dominant capital, both foreign and local, along with its new allies (the developing black bourgeoisie) claim that, with non-racial political democracy, all problems are settled. The black working class is now called on to "accelerate" the march toward "competitiveness." What capitalism, with the active support of the entire West, could not succeed in doing, the working class should now do as quickly as possible and, of course, bear the main costs!

In opposition to this program, the progressive forces continue the fight for a true democracy that can be the means for achieving social changes—even if such changes will be difficult and will take time, perhaps thirty to fifty years. The conditions for such changes are the following: 1) A sufficiently unified interpretation of the constitution that permits the reallocation of income and investments at the Republic level. 2) A considerable effort at development in the backward rural areas, which should go hand in hand with the long-term prospect of an internal redistribution of the population. That is absolutely indispensable for creating a united popular front of workers and peasants and defeating any attempt at sowing conflict between them. 3) An agrarian reform in the rural zones occupied by white farmers, to the benefit of the rural African proletariat, and support for an expansion of small black farms. The "success" of white agriculture in South Africa that the media praise so much is, in reality, based on the exploitation of a labor force practically reduced to a condition of slavery and on the enormous ecological disaster resulting from an enormous waste of land. 4) A redistribution of income to the benefit of the black workers, who provide the productive labor, simultaneously with an improvement in their living conditions, particularly in the area of education, which is in a deplorable state; the eradication of AIDS, which is the first priority of any public health program; and all this offset by a reduction in the costs of supporting a large number of unproductive individuals of the white minority. 5) A gradual restructuring of the country's industrial sector, but not with the aim of increasing competitive exports. The priority should be quite different. The productive system needs to be restructured to allow it to respond to social changes related to income redistribution. In other words, supply more consumption goods to the mass of people, be able to satisfy needs arising from a better productive system in rural areas, and develop a better capacity to satisfy the housing needs of the masses. But also, there should be less wasted production to satisfy the consumption needs of the minority, for example, the senseless production of private automobiles and other luxury products. Without excluding the launch of needed changes to improve the country's exporting capacity, it is necessary to acknowledge that the objective of competitiveness can reasonably only be attained in the long term. In the interval, the political economy of a real democratization implies what I call "delinking," like it or not. These are, in my view, the issues involved in any real democratization. The other proposed alternative is based on two essential pillars: more "openness" and a quasi-federal political solution. These were exactly the two components of the Yugoslav political economy that the World Bank enthusiastically hailed. We can see today where they led.

I have already been to South Africa several times since it was possible for me to go there, after 1991. Invited by the African partners of CODESA (which negotiated the new constitution with de Klerk's transitional regime)—the ANC, the SACP, and COSATU—I then had the opportunity of discussing the problems outlined above with numerous comrades of these organizations as well as with activists of numerous people's organizations. Also invited by the Universities of Johannesburg, Cape Town, and Durban, notably on the occasion of the Congress of Sociology held at Umtata, and also by intellectuals involved in political struggles, I also pursued these discussions in these diverse circles. Hein Marais, active within the Third World Forum, is the author of a quality work dealing with all these debates.[30] None of these debates is closed. The struggle continues in South Africa.

The World Conference against Racism organized by the United Nations in Durban, September 2001, was the occasion for a manifestation of spontaneous solidarity by African and Asian peoples, particularly with Palestinians, which rubbed the Western powers and their servants the wrong way. On this occasion, the speech I gave to the so-called civil society conference—which I had titled "Globalization or Apartheid on the World Scale?"—had, I believe, an effect, as can be seen in the text of the final resolutions, but above all in the honor the South African Parliament gave to me when I was invited to present it at one of its sessions in Capetown. That was precisely on September 11, 2001.

South Africa, freed from odious apartheid, is now confronted with a truly formidable challenge: how to go beyond the facade of multiracial democracy to transform society profoundly? The choices of the ANC government have, up to now, evaded the question and, as a result, nothing has changed. South Africa's sub-imperialist role has been reinforced, still dominated as it is by the Anglo-American mining monopolies. The magnificent work of our colleague Hein Marais, to which I referred above, analyzes the impasse represented by this choice. Is a change in the offing? Is the 2012 massacre of striking miners—carried out by order of the government implementing the same odious apartheid laws that permit such an action—going to put an end to the confusions of the working classes, which have lived during the last twenty years in the illusion that the abolition of apartheid opened a royal road to settling questions of the future without any great obstacle?

The submission of the ANC governments to all the demands dictated by the imperialist monopolies—unfortunately, not called into question by the May 2014 elections—was indecently hailed during Mandela's funeral. We then saw the entire panoply of heads of state from the Western powers strut through Johannesburg to hail South African democracy. These are the same Western powers that had supported apartheid, trained its police, sometimes lavished their advice concerning torture, and not lifted a little finger to defend Mandela in prison, while the countries that had really supported the South African people were absent.

There is no sovereign project in South Africa. Its economic system remains under Anglo-American control. What are the conditions for the emergence of a sovereign project in the country? What new relations with Africa would such a project imply?

I have paid particular attention to these questions, which I have discussed on several occasions during my visits to South Africa. I participated in several important debates put together by work groups organized around Patrick Bond, Dot Keet, Ben Turok, Hein Marais, Langa Zita, Oupa Lehulere, Ari Silas, and others, at the Universities of Johannesburg, Cape Town, and Durban, as well as in meetings of civil society, unions, the ANC, and the SACP.

South Africa, as everyone knows, is a beautiful country. The Cape peninsula undoubtedly counts as one of nature's marvels. It is too bad that the city of Cape Town has been "urbanized," if you can call it that, along the odious principles of "communitarianism," on the model of Lusaka or Windhoek. Truly, an urban horror in an unparalleled natural setting, it must be said. A group of (mixed) youth acquainted me with the turbulent history of this old colony, populated by Boers, French Huguenots, Hottentots, persons of mixed race, descendants of slaves (and "free" laborers) imported from Malaysia, and later the English and Africans from the Bantu civilization. I learned, with horror, about the Bantustans, barren and without built villages, an arid landscape with scattered slum-houses, inhabited by the elderly, women, and children in rags. Almost all of the adult male population had emigrated to the industrial cities and the mines.

## GLIMMERS OF HOPE

The barbaric violence of a colonialism of pillage and the implosion of globalized neoliberalism have not only given rise to explosions of anger without any clear strategy, stuck in the cul-de-sac of regressions, they have also opened the way to actual advances toward building positive alternative strategies that offer glimmers of hope for the future.

Everybody knows about the popular advances that began in some South American countries (Venezuela, Bolivia, Ecuador) over the last twenty years, as well as the prospects opened in Nepal since 2008. Moreover, the exhaustion of the globalized neoliberal order has opened margins of maneuver to countries that remain attached to the socialist vision (Vietnam and Cuba). This should allow them to undertake appropriate and positive reforms and avoid capitulation. Having personally participated in important debates in the countries concerned, I report on them in these memoirs.

But beyond these experiences of relatively more advanced struggles, glimmers of hope are apparent elsewhere, even if only tentative. I offer here a report of my contribution to the debate in Zambia on an alternative strategy that could open the way to the beginning of an authentic African revival.

I had visited Zambia at the end of the Kenneth Kaunda era. The stagnation of his national-popular model, implemented tentatively, had opened the way to a brutal colonial restoration. The best copper mines (the country's wealth) were sold for a song to the mining monopolies, while permission given to anyone to engage in mining the ore opened the doors to gigantic waste and ecological disaster. The Tanzam railway—built by China—was "privatized" and entrusted to an Israeli firm. Given the responsibility to renovate the railway, this company failed to do that and instead simply stole the rails (there is no other way to describe it) and sold them as scrap before disappearing without leaving an address. When I asked: "Why not sue the state of Israel, home country of the company?" the response was, "Impossible, our European friends would treat us as anti-Semites!"

In 2012, a Patriotic Front, uniting all the forces tired of corruption in the established regime, won the elections. Vice President Wynter Kabinda invited me in 2013, through the Policy Monitoring and Research Centre, a public institution directed by Michelle Morel. After I arrived in Lusaka, I discussed with officials and their adviser, professor Donald Chanda, the main axes of a new development strategy. We agreed to emphasize management of the mines, industrialization, cooperation with China, and sub-regional integration. To be brief, I will say that we envisaged various possible forms of balanced cooperation: access of China to copper (mixed companies, long-term trade agreements, state level accords, making it possible to be freed from manipulations of the market by the mining monopolies) balanced with the construction of infrastructure and industries (which the Western powers stubbornly refuse to do). We also discussed the desirable opening of negotiations with neighbors (Tanzania, Angola, and Zimbabwe, and later with Congo if it could succeed in overcoming its difficult situation) that would give meaning to collective industrialization. I do not know if my Zambian colleagues got anything out of my observations. But I know that I learned much from them as they had mastered the issues with a high degree of competence.

Can we say more? We know that the government of South Africa had proclaimed several years ago, with great fanfare, the "Renaissance of Africa." Certainly, the revival of this continent is desirable and possible. But has it already begun? No. Invited to participate in a "committee" charged with "inspiring" this rebirth, I declined. I knew that the committee, made up of persons designated by governments that accept the globalized neoliberal order without batting an eyelid on the pretext that "there is no alternative outside this context," could not generate any ideas for an actual positive alternative. I was not mistaken. The project was quite rapidly transformed into a "Euro-African partnership" for development. There is no partnership possible between the victims of colonial pillage and those who intend to continue it.

This was nothing more than a maneuver to impress the naive and reinforce their neoliberal reformist illusions. This was quite similar to the objectives of the Stiglitz Commission to which I referred in the first chapter of these memoirs. The propaganda centers of imperialist monopoly capitalism—the World Bank, the European Commission—are, in fact, worried and have taken note of the growing rejection by people of their imposed world order. They must, then, propose reforms that are such in name only, implying that "capitalism with a human face" is possible and that that is what they want.

## Appendix to Chapter 2: Africa

*Development Aid on Behalf of Pillaging the South's Resources*

In countries ravaged by the colonialism of pillage, the question of "foreign aid" continually and insistently cropped up in our debates. The extreme vulnerability of the economies in question can probably explain this seeming inevitability. "We can't get by without aid." And the illusions concerning the "generosity" of the international community, and Europe in particular, the wishful thinking in this regard, do not fuel only the rhetoric of the high officials responsible for the decisions in this area. Most organizations and popular movements, even leftist political parties, share these illusions. It is incumbent on us—on me personally—to return continually to this question in our discussions, analyze the functions that Western aid such as it is (and it cannot be any other way) fulfill. I am indebted to Yash Tandon for having convincingly done this in his lucid analysis of this sad reality. Including this text on aid in an appendix thus is justified. But we must also put forward alternative proposals, emphasizing the possibilities for solidary cooperation of the countries of the South.

I claim that "aid" is a strategic instrument for imperialist domination, designed to weaken the most vulnerable countries of the globalized capitalist periphery. In opposition to this form of aid, today popularized in the name of insipid and misleading humanitarian ideals, I vigorously propose "another aid," based on the principles of people's internationalist and anti-imperialist solidarity.

If, as it is claimed, there are two "partners"—in principle equal—in the aid relationship, the donor country and the beneficiary country, the architecture of the system would have to be negotiated between these two sets of states. Nothing of the sort happens. The debate on aid has been trapped in a straight-jacket, the architecture of which was defined in the Paris Declaration on Aid Effectiveness (2005), drafted within the OECD, and imposed on the beneficiary countries by the Accra Action Agenda (2008). From the very outset, then, the procedure was illegitimate. The general condition, defined by alignment on the principles of liberal globalization, is omnipresent: encourage liberalization and the opening of markets, and thereby become "attractive" for foreign private investments. In addition, the triad's means of political control were reinforced by the addition of a political condition: respect for human rights, electoral multiparty democracy, good governance, spiced up with insipid rhetoric on "poverty." The Paris Declaration is, then, a retreat in comparison to the practices of the "development decades" (1960–1970) when it was generally accepted that the countries of the South could freely choose their economic and social system and its accompanying policies.

*Poverty, Civil Society, Good Governance: The Impoverished Rhetoric of the Dominant View on Aid*

The very term "poverty" belongs to the language of charity, which existed prior to the advent of the language developed by modern social thought.

As it is offered to us, "civil society" is linked with a two-part ideology of consensus: (i) that there is no alternative to the "market economy" (itself a commonplace expression serving as a substitute for any serious analysis of "actually existing capitalism"); and (ii) that there is no alternative to representative democracy based on multiparty elections, which serves as a substitute for the conception of a democratization of society, itself an unending process. The genuine concept of civil society must restore the rightful place of workers' unions, peasants', women's, and citizens' organizations. Thus, it includes, and does not exclude, the movement's political parties, reformist or revolutionary. "Aid" rhetoric gives preeminence to NGOs in their place. This choice is inseparable from another side of the dominant ideology, which sees the state as an inherent opponent of freedom. In current conditions, this ideology amounts to legitimizing the "business jungle," as the current financial crisis illustrates.

"Governance" was invented as a substitute for "government." The opposition between its two qualifiers—good or bad governance—recalls Manichaeism and moralism, which act as substitutes for analysis of reality. Once again, this approach comes to us from across the Atlantic, where sermons dominate political discourse. The underlying visible ideology is used to evade the real question: the established government, whatever it may be, represents and defends what social interests? Of course, it should be understood that the multiparty electoral system has proven its limits from this point of view and, in actual practice, the diplomacy of the imperialist triad follows an unscrupulous policy of double standards, particularly concerning "human rights."

*Aid, Geoeconomics, Geopolitics, and Geostrategy*

Aid policies, choice of beneficiaries, and forms of intervention are inseparable from geopolitical objectives. The different regions of the world do not fulfill identical functions in the globalized liberal system. Africa is not "less integrated" into the system of globalization than other regions of the South, it is integrated differently.

The geoeconomy of the region is based on two groups of products that form its structures and define its place in the global system: (i) "tropical" agricultural products for export—coffee, cacao, cotton, groundnuts, fruits, palm oil, etc.; and (ii) hydrocarbons and mineral products—copper, gold, rare metals, diamonds, etc. The first are means of survival, beyond food production for the peasants' subsistence, which finance the grafting of the state onto the local economy and, on the basis of public expenditures, the reproduction of the middle classes. These products interest the local ruling classes more than those of the dominant economies. What really interests the latter are the continent's natural resource products. Today, that means hydrocarbons and rare minerals. Tomorrow, it will be reserves for the development of biofuels, solar resources, and water.

The race for control over rural territories to be converted to the expansion of biofuel production is underway in Latin America. Africa offers gigantic possibilities in this area. Madagascar has begun moving in this direction and has already granted large areas in the west of the country. The implementation of the Congolese Rural Code (2008), inspired by the Belgian Development Agency and the FAO, will undoubtedly allow agribusiness to take over large tracts of agricultural land to "develop" them, just like the Mining Code not long ago allowed the pillage of the colony's mineral resources. The peasants will become useless and will bear the costs. The increased poverty that awaits them might interest humanitarian aid organizations of tomorrow and "aid" programs for the reduction of poverty!

The new phase of history now opening is characterized by a sharpening of conflicts for access to the world's natural resources. The triad intends to reserve exclusive access to this "useful" Africa (the reserves of natural resources) and prevent access by the "emergent countries," which already have considerable needs in this regard that will only grow in the future. Guaranteeing exclusive access requires political control and reducing African states to "client states." In this context, foreign aid fulfills important functions in maintaining the fragility of these states.

It is not, then, excessive to consider that the objective of such aid is to "corrupt" the ruling classes. Beyond the diversion of funds (well known, unfortunately, and we are expected to believe that the donors have nothing to do with it!), aid becomes "indispensable" (since it becomes an important source of financing budgets) and fulfills this political function. It is, then, important that this aid not be reserved exclusively and completely for people in positions of responsibility, to the "government." It is also necessary that this aid involve the "opposition" that might succeed this government. This is where so-called civil society and NGOs fit in.

For the aid in question to be politically effective, it must also contribute to maintaining the insertion of the peasantry into the global system. This insertion is another source of revenues for the state. Aid must also, then, focus on the progress of "modernizing" the production of export crops.

The case of Niger illustrates to perfection the articulation among strategic mineral resources (uranium), "indispensable" aid, and maintaining the country in a client state status. This country receives an exceptionally large amount of "aid" (50 percent of its budget) and yet remains on the list of the poorest countries in the world. Is this due to a failure of the aid? Or rather is it a failure of the development model imposed by this "aid"? A team of the Third World Forum in which I participated, in cooperation with our friends Abdou Ibro, Moussa Tchangari, and the IRD team in Niamey, studied the case of Niger.

In an excellent article, Anna Bednik (2008) persuasively established this link.[31] Niger is, for the Western powers, a "uranium country" above all. The diplomats of the triad are aware of this and Niger's geographical situation causes them to fear the worst. That is why the specter of the "Tuareg rebellion" is cynically used here. The conflict around the concessions, formerly an exclusive monopoly of France, reveals the reality of the threat (by China's entry into the contest).

### Outline of an Alternative Aid Worthy of the Name

Drawing up a global vision for aid cannot be left to the OECD, the World Bank, or the European Union. This responsibility belongs to the UN and to it alone. That this organization is, by nature, limited because of the monopoly of control exercised by states, which are supposed to represent peoples, is true enough. But this is just as true for the organizations serving the triad. That we should propose to strengthen a more "direct" presence of peoples in the UN next to that of states is also true. Possible forms of this representation merit attention and discussion. But this presence must be designed to strengthen the UN. It should not consist of the participation of (handpicked) NGOs in conferences designed and managed by the North (and inevitably manipulated by the North's diplomats). That is why it is necessary to support the 2005 initiative of the ECOSOC to create a Development Cooperation Forum (DCF). This initiative envisages the construction of genuine partnerships with a view to constructing a multipolar world. The initiative has been poorly received by the triad's diplomats, as could be expected. But it is necessary to go further and dare to cross a red line. We should not focus on "reforming" the World Bank, the WTO, or the IMF, nor should we limit ourselves to condemning the tragic consequences of their policies. Rather, we should propose alternative institutions, define their tasks in positive terms, and lay out their organizational contours.

The choice of an alternative aid is inseparable from the formulation of an alternative development. The important principles that should orient development are, at the very least, the following:

Development requires the construction of diversified productive systems, and first of all a process of industrialization. We can only draw attention to the persistent refusal to recognize the necessity of this approach for subtropical Africa. How can we otherwise understand such statements as the "crazy trend toward industrialization"—which should be cause for laughter; after all, what country in Africa is actually "overindustrialized"?—unfortunately sometimes taken up by friends from the "alter-globalization" movement. Is it not clear that it is precisely those countries that are committed to this "crazy" path that are today the so-called emergent countries (China, Korea, and others)?

Diversification and industrialization will, in turn, require the construction of appropriate forms of regional cooperation. Such forms must be reinvented to be consistent with the development objectives outlined here. Regional "common markets," which dominate established institutions (when they exist and function), do not fall into this category since they were designed as constitutive blocs of liberal globalization. South-South cooperation must be the focus. Moreover, the donor countries of the South have refused, for good reasons, to participate in the "donors club" of the imperialist triad.

The problems of the rural world and agricultural development must be placed at the very center of defining a strategy for an alternative development. The Paris Declaration does not go beyond the perspective bequeathed from colonization, that is, agriculture based on the export of tropical products, which should be beneficial according to the conventional theory of "comparative advantage." As opposed to that, priority must be given to food crops with a view to food sovereignty and not food security, which lies behind the current "food crisis." This priority implies the implementation of policies based on maintaining a sizable rural population (slowly, instead of rapidly, declining). This conception of peasant agriculture also implies that access to the land and to the means of farming it properly be as equal as possible. That, in turn, implies agrarian reform, the strengthening of cooperation, and overall appropriate macroeconomic policies (credit, supply of inputs, marketing of products). These measures are different from the ones that were implemented in Europe and North America under historical capitalism, based on appropriation of the land, its reduction to a commodity, increased social differentiation within the peasantry, and the rapid expulsion of the "useless" surplus from the rural populations. The choice advocated by the dominant system, based on financial profitability and short-term productivism (rapid increase in production at the cost of expelling the surplus peasantry) certainly responds to the needs of the agribusiness multinationals and a new class of wealthy peasants, but not to those of the working classes and the nation itself. The alternative implies a radical challenge to the globalized liberalization of production and international trade in agricultural and food products, as Jacques Berthelot persuasively demonstrates (www.solidarite.asso.fr). It requires national policies for the construction/reconstruction of national funds for the stabilization and support of the products in question supplemented by the establishment of joint international funds for basic products that allow an effective alternative reorganization of international markets for agricultural products.

The alternative development model outlined here requires real control over external economic relations, which implies, among other things, getting rid of the "free trade" system that is supposedly "regulated by the market," and building national and regional systems of controlled trade. It is based on the principle that priority should be given to internal (national and regional) markets and, within this context, primarily to markets that respond to expanding demand from the working classes, not to the world market.

# 3

# ASIA
# Triumphant Capitalism, Dead Ends, and Emergence in Question

I belong to that region of the world that today is the most disadvantaged. Africa and the Arab world as a whole make up the majority of the countries in the so-called fourth world, those that have not succeeded in entering into the industrialized era and thereby establishing a presence in world markets. By contrast, East, South, and Southeast Asia, as well as large Latin American countries are on the road to a triumphant capitalism to the point that it could be argued that their success refutes the theory of global capitalism's immanent polarization. I do not see it that way. These countries have achieved, at best, a partial "emergence." The elements of emergence, when they exist, are here combined with characteristics of lumpen-development and the continuing pillage of their natural resources. This is the case for the countries of Southeast Asia. (This chapter focuses on all the Asian countries except China, Vietnam, and Japan.)

My fundamental principles had always led me to see the two continents—Asia and Africa—as forming a single whole: historically non-European societies that, having been colonized, have the same enemy—the imperialism of the capitalist centers. I have thus followed the vagaries of economic and political developments in the Asian countries with as much passion as those of my African continent.

### TURKEY

Turkey is not only one of Africa's immediate geographical neighbors, but also the heir of the Ottoman Empire to which the Arab World had belonged. But we had fewer reasons to go there because of the European choices of this country's ruling class since Ataturk. So many of the intellectuals and leaders of all political and social forces in the country claimed to have nothing to do with the scorned Third World, excluding themselves from the area covered by our Forum. Thus Isabelle and I visited Turkey purely as tourists. The first time was in 1973, when we stopped over in Istanbul for a few days on our way from India to Paris.

What struck me was the violent trauma imposed on the Turkish people by the abrupt break with its past, among other things by the hasty Romanization of the written language. On a visit to the Topkapi Museum in Istanbul, I saw adolescents led by their teachers looking at photographs from the beginning of the twentieth century—of their grandparents—as if the people pictured were completely unknown. When I read to them the captions written in Ottoman Turkish—with Arabic letters—they looked at me as if I were a being from another planet!

The Ottoman Empire was what it was, neither better nor worse than other societies in the premodern world. What is certain is that its description as a "Turkish" empire is a misleading reduction. Turkey, on the other hand, is indeed Turkish, although perhaps a third of its inhabitants are Kurds. The creation of this new nation of Anatolian peasants has certainly entailed unquestionably positive aspects and opened the way to a capitalist development that, even though peripheral, provided a model, thirty years in advance, to the Nasserist and Baathist Arab Middle East. But this development also intensified certain violent characteristics wrongly attributed to the nature—the "atavism"—of the Turkish people. In fact, in the distribution of tasks and responsibilities within the Ottoman Empire, the Anatolian peasants provided most of the manpower for the army—which explains the description of the Empire as "Turkish." Submission and brutality are mainly the result of this specialization. But in the Empire, the Anatolian peasant origin of the army was, at least in part, balanced by the cosmopolitan refinement of the ruling classes, which were multiethnic in origin, and the cultural and religious diversity of the peoples that made up the Empire. Hence, to describe the Empire as "Turkish" is true only in a relative sense. The disappearance of these characteristics simultaneously with the disappearance of the Empire itself was not compensated for by the formation of a new bourgeoisie. The latter, weak and peripheral, in the sense I give to the term, has not even produced a democratic culture. It has thus never gone beyond the horizons of nationalism, which, as everyone knows, is easily satisfied with autocracy and brutality.

Since the Turkish "miracle" (celebrated in its time by the World Bank) and the illusion of catching up and Europeanization have run out of steam, things have begun to change, for better (there are signs of the beginning of a deeper analysis of the limits of capitalism and nationalism and a critique of the autocracy that accompanies them), but also for worse (space seems to be opening up for the resurrection of a backward-looking Islamist utopia). The existence of a Turkish intelligentsia that is comparatively advanced in relation to what it is in many other countries of the region, one of the positive results of Kemalism, and that offers a critique of capitalism without any backward-looking nostalgia (the intelligentsia is fairly secular) is, for me, one of the main forces that make a progressive exit from the current impasse possible. The other is the presence of an exceptionally courageous communist tradition, which has never been eradicated by successive dictatorships. This tradition is certainly sometimes a bit worrying with its "Stalinist" dogmatism, accentuated perhaps by its strong relationship with the rebellious Kurdish peasantry—symbolized by the PKK. Some exchanges of views with its leaders, who had invited me to Ankara and Istanbul, left me with some uneasy memories. But I also value the subtlety of the analyses and the reality of the socialist and democratic convictions of the intellectuals (Fikret Başkaya subsequently spent two years in prison for the crime of writing!). They invited me in 1991 to lead debates in the two capitals, and took the initiative to create a branch of the Forum for non-Arab western and central Asia. Their hospitality, kindness, and fine manners (and the truly succulent Turkish cuisine), the visit to the astonishing region of Cappadocia in their company (in the middle of winter—I don't regret it—cold Cappadocia is brutal and certainly very different from what summer tourists experience), all these remain fond memories for Isabelle and me. Our friend Yildiz Sertel, long a communist political refugee in the USSR, later in Paris (she taught at Vincennes), had already acquainted us a bit with the nuances of Turkish politics from the inside. The international tribunal formed to examine the crimes involved with the invasion of Iraq, led by Ayse Berktay, held its closing session in Istanbul in 2004. The publicity given by the Turkish press to the event, passed over in silence in Europe, is, for me, a good sign of anti-imperialist sentiments, still powerful in Turkey.

### *Turkey's Aborted Emergence*

I have close friends in Turkey—Başkaya, in particular. Most of my works have been translated into Turkish. The left press, in particular the journals *Toplum ve Utopya, Aydinlik,* and *Redaksyon,* frequently interview me. I submitted the following text to them and took into account their observations when it seemed necessary. Nevertheless, I alone am responsible for the ideas developed here:

*Is Turkey "European"?*

Debates on this question are generally polemical in the extreme and, consequently, lack a solid scientific foundation. It is important to know that the ruling class of this country has considered itself to be European for a long time, back as far as the Ottoman era and even to 1453, when Mehmed the Conqueror (who conquered Constantinople) hesitated, it is said, and thought to proclaim himself the "(Orthodox) Emperor of Byzantium/Constantinople," but then gave up that idea since his soldiers, who had fought under the banner of Islam (as *ghazi*, or "conquerors"), would not have accepted it. In the nineteenth century, Ottoman Turkey was involved in a reform of its state organization known as the *Tanzimat*—"reorganization, or "perestroika," one could say—the intent of which was quite clear: to make Turkey into a "European" country. Did Ottoman/Turkish society really advance in this direction or did progress remain insignificant? This is a question that a number of historians have examined. Toward the end of the nineteenth century, a good number of Ottoman intellectuals and politicians (Turks and others) assessed the situation and, finding progress insignificant, organized under the name *Young Turks* with the aim of increasing the pace of change, even if this meant getting rid of a sultan considered to be incompetent. They did not, however, envision either the overthrow of the caliphate/sultanate or the abandonment of its imperial Ottoman character (control of the Arab Mashreq). Yet, echoing the nationalist ideology of modern European peoples, they decided to openly describe themselves as Turk (and no longer as Ottoman). The 1914–1918 world war created the conditions in which the Young Turks project, led by Mustafa Kemal (Ataturk), could unambiguously move forward. The Arab provinces were lost and the Caliphate/Sultanate abolished, while the war was won against the intervention of the Entente powers. The new Turkish Republic had reason to believe that it was moving on the way toward triumphant Europeanization.

It was unquestionably a project of emergence. Still, it should be emphasized that it was conceptualized in the way common at the time: emergence by means of a capitalist transformation of society. It was believed that it was enough to want it to be able to do it. The idea that the logic of globalized capitalism—through the creation of a centers/peripheries polarization between partners integrated into the world system—would not allow such emergence was still quite alien to thinking at the time. Yet the concomitance of the Atatürk project and the Russian Revolution might have suggested that the capitalist path was problematic. But Atatürk and his friends did not think that, and Turkish communists of the time did not have very clear ideas on the question.

Social reality was going to impose itself and shape the development of the new attempt at emergence. To understand this, we need to know, without oversimplifying the realities in question, that a capitalist "bourgeoisie" in the true sense of the term had, at best, achieved only an embryonic existence in the Turkey of 1924. But there was a large class of intellectuals, statesmen (no women at that time), and military officers capable of taking on responsibility for leading the country. This class was recruited from the west of the country—Istanbul, Edirne, Smyrna—which was called (and called itself) "Rumelia." The root *Rum* (Rome, that is, Byzantium) is a good indication of the cultural aspirations in question. The east—Anatolia—was exclusively peasant. The Turks of that time recognized themselves either as Rumelians, hence "civilized" and "European," or Anatolians, thus barely civilized poor wretches. Of course, the Rumelians were secular or, for many, atheist. In contrast, the Anatolian peasants could not imagine themselves as anything other than practicing Muslims.

The Rumelian/Ataturkist ruling class was nationalist in the intolerant and chauvinist sense of the term. It never wanted to recognize the reality of the Armenian genocide or even the horrible treatment of the rare Armenian children spared—Islamized by force, and discriminated against—any more than it would recognize the Kurdish reality or that of the Arabs of Hatay. All the governments in Ankara, including that of the Islamists today, have shared this chauvinism. Whereas the ideologues of "Arab" political Islam privilege Islamic identity to the point of aspiring to consign any other identity (Arab or Amazigh, for example) to oblivion—"We are not Algerians, Arabs, or Berbers, we are only Muslims," proclaim these ideologues—Turkish political Islam is asserted as such: a Turk (and there is no "Kurd") is Muslim, but also Turk.

The only model of development and modernization thinkable and possible in these conditions was state capitalism, on the economic plane, and an enlightened despotism, on the political plane. Incidentally, the working classes, both peasant and urban, did not demand that this be put into practice. Insofar as the implementation of the model brought them real benefits, more in terms of rising in the social hierarchy through the education of children than in terms of perceptible improvements in living standards, enlightened despotism benefited from an unquestioned legitimacy in the eyes of the peoples concerned. This was even truer when it was combined with flaunted anti-imperialist positions.

## Differences from the Arab Countries

It is precisely on this point that the Turkish attempt at emergence can be distinguished from similar attempts in the Arab countries. The national governments in the latter were, as can be seen with Nasserist Egypt, systematically fought against by the imperialist powers. This was never true for the Turkish governments. This was both its strength and weakness. From 1945, Turkey—then still Kemalist—opted for an alliance with the West against the Soviet threat (concretely embodied by Stalin's inconvenient demands in 1945 concerning Kars and Ardahan and the status of the Straits of Bosphorus). Turkey was a founding member of NATO at a time when its members were not required to mouth any declaration of democracy.

The weakening of Kemalist state capitalism provided an opportunity for the United States (an ally, not an enemy) to reintegrate Turkey into postwar globalized capitalism. Washington "advised" Ankara to hold "elections" that, in 1950, brought Adnan Menderes to power. His electoral victory transformed the relationship of forces between the Rumelian Kemalist elite and the Anatolian peasantry. Menderes received his support mainly from a new class of wealthy Anatolian peasants, produced by the development of agriculture, even though that development had been modest up until then. The end of the privileged position of the Rumelian/Kemalist elite became apparent and the situation was going to increasingly develop in that direction. The new model, suggested and supported by the United States, the World Bank, and all the rest, emphasized the development of a capitalist agriculture. But the wealthy peasant class that benefited remained "Muslim" and asserted itself as such against the Kemalist state. The compradorization of Turkey's mode of development was gradually and fully affirmed: capitalist agriculture, opening to industrial subcontracting, privatization of segments of what was originally part of the state capitalist sector, safety valve of massive emigration of poor peasants from Anatolia, etc. The new business class, associated with and beneficiaries of the compradorized development, now recruited mainly from the children of the wealthy peasantry of Anatolia.

On the political plane, the last defenders of Kemalism, that is, the army, drifted from defeat to defeat (despite the restoration of its dictatorship on two occasions) up to the day, only a few years later, when Anatolian Turkish political Islam took over as the dominant force in the society.

This change, which I define as a re-compradorization that put an end to the Kemalist project of emergence, was accompanied by the firm assertion of continuity on the essential point: membership in NATO, that is, support for the imperialist triad (United States, Western Europe, and Japan). This consideration is what lies behind my response to a question from Ecuador's President Correa: "Turkey is the Colombia of the Middle East." The message was immediately understood.

Of course, the Turkish ally of the United States remains a candidate for membership in the European Union because there is no contradiction but, on the contrary, a great continuity between belonging to the EU and to NATO. This project of "Europeanization," which encourages the illusion that the new Turkey is still the heir of Kemalism, is a real question, although a minor one. That some political forces in the European Union favor Turkish membership whereas others oppose it, using polemical arguments as a justification (a "Muslim" country in "Christian" Europe? Never!), are also real, but all the same secondary questions. But the compradorization (the exact opposite of emergence) of contemporary Turkey ends up still using the enthusiasm of supporters of "Europeanness." Is Turkey going to rediscover an "Oriental" or even "Turanian" way forward? And what would be the possible significance of such a change in course?

*What Role in the Middle East?*

Turkey is active in the Middle East. It intervenes there as an ally of the United States and not as an autonomous emergent power. That is not new. Earlier, Turkey had been the center of the "Baghdad Pact" rejected by Nasser and later by the government that emerged from the Iraqi revolution of 1958. Turkey is—and remains—Israel's military ally. It is intervening today in Syria on behalf of Washington. The Turanian alternative to European rejection was outlined initially in 1918, and Enver Pasha had attempted to follow this path. The Soviet construction had put an end to these rather crazy ambitions; yet the collapse of the project seems to have created conditions for its rebirth. But Turkey here again can hardly fulfill any ambitions that go beyond its supporting role as subaltern ally of the United States.

The Kurdish population began an armed rebellion in response to an absolute negation of all its collective rights without comparison, in terms of continuity and violence, to the discriminatory practices implemented in Iraq and Iran in some circumstances by some of their governments (not all). But, beginning in 2010, the leadership of the movement decided to end armed struggle in favor of fighting for a single nation that would include both Turks and Kurds. I do not know the motivations behind this reversal, and I shall refrain from making any comments, which would be irresponsible.

The political positions taken by existing governments in the countries of the South are not neutral in their effects on the direction of economic development. Accepting the geostrategic choices of imperialism is naturally linked with capitulation to the requirements of economic compradorization, the very opposite of emergence. Turkish political Islam is, like that of the Arab countries or Pakistan, reactionary in its social positions. It is openly opposed to the struggles of workers and peasants. This is why it is accepted by the Western powers, always ready to award it a certificate of democracy.

The emergent countries must inevitably come into conflict with imperialism, even if this conflict remains muffled and its intensity varies from one country and one moment to another. But conversely, is it enough to be treated as an opponent by the imperialist powers to become a possible candidate for emergence?

IRAN

Like the Ottoman Empire and China, the Persian Empire had escaped violent colonization, even though it was semi-colonized by the unequal treaties that the imperialists imposed on it. We should not be surprised to see that its ruling classes in the 1920s had also attempted to lead a modernization process controlled from above. As in China and the Ottoman Empire, reforms, motivated by a nationalist reaction, were combined with popular and peasant movements, which the early communist parties attempted to move in a revolutionary direction, strengthened by the proximity of the Soviet Union. But in Iran, modernization was carried out through a simple dynastic change and did not break with history, as was the case in Turkey. I verified the acute awareness Iranian intellectuals have of this issue when, having posed the question of the possible Romanization of the Persian writing system—using the same argument as had been advanced by Atatürk, namely, that the Persian language is not Arabic, so the choice of using Arabic letters is itself as artificial as using Latin letters—all of them, whether on the right or the left, responded: "Never. We will not break with our history; look at the cultural disaster that produced in Turkey."

After the passing of the "Soviet" threat of the immediate postwar period, the populist crisis of the 1950s, and the fall of Mohammad Mossadegh organized by the CIA, the Shah's bloody dictatorship rushed into a hurried modernization, the prototype of the one that South Korea entered into around the same time. It had a remarkable success, in spite of its appalling political and social aspects. I obviously had had many friends among the militants in the Tudeh Party: Iskandari, collaborator in the journal *Moyen Orient*; Ekbatani, leader of the Union Internationale des Étudiants (UIE), the headquarters of which was in Prague; Vazguen Ovanissian, student at the Lycée Henri IV at the same time as I, who was murdered in prison by Savak. It had been difficult for me to go to Iran during the harshest periods of the Shah and CIA's dictatorship. But the opportunity arose in 1975. Having succeeded in dismantling any form of organized resistance, the regime softened (to speak of democratization as the dominant media proclaimed at the time was truly farcical), and many intellectuals adopted "moderate" attitudes, hoping to push the regime gradually in the direction of a minimum of democratization, without calling into question the strategic choices of a capitalist development that they believed was ultimately able to "catch up" and thereby establish the national autonomy of the country in the global system. They invited me to Tehran and I accepted, having in mind the creation of a cell for the Forum in this important country.

One could already feel the beginnings of the Islamist popular reaction and I pride myself on having foreseen its victory, in which neither the CIA nor the KGB believed, both obsessed by the apparent power of the government. The aristocratic and bourgeois ruling class was certainly not democratic, except perhaps on some of its intellectual fringes. It was not secular, but only secularizing, as were the ruling classes of the entire pre-populist Arab Middle East, in the sense that these classes had understood that the theocratic concept of power had become a cultural obstacle to modernization, the only means to face the challenge presented by the imperialist West. Incidentally, even Kemalism had never been secular in the radical sense of the term. Islam in this context is linked with nationalism—to the very definition of the nation (one cannot be a Turk without being socially a Muslim, even if one is agnostic or even atheist). This nation is, moreover, defined in ethnic terms—a phenomenon current in modern societies that have not made a bourgeois democratic revolution (the same concept of the nation is found in Germany for the same reasons). In Turkey, the Turanian ancestor is, therefore, officially and insistently celebrated, as was the pre-Islamic imperial civilization among the Iranians. In Iran, this celebration had taken on the dimensions of caricature, as is well known, symbolized by the Hollywood farce of the 2500th anniversary of the Achaemenid dynasty organized at Persepolis. It was not only the waste occasioned by this event that shocked the Iranian people, it was also the contempt for the Islamic conviction that the cult of these polytheist ancestors should be banned. Passing through the region of Persepolis and Pasargadae to visit the ruins of ancient Persia, we saw on Cyrus's tomb, lost in the arid and rocky terrain, a vengeful inscription that spoke volumes about what the people probably thought of the farce in Persepolis: "You too, Emperor, are only dust."

Over the course of this trip, we had other opportunities to assess the hostility this modernization was facing. In the city of Isfahan, we toured the historical districts on foot. Exhausted by the heat, the noise (from the autos and construction and demolition work), and the dust, we decided to enter a garden of one of the pretty mosques for a little rest on a bench in the shadow of orange and other fragrant trees. A mullah approached us and I began a discussion with him (he spoke Arabic reasonably well). "What are you doing here?" he asked kindly. "Nothing in particular, we are seeking a respite from the infernal noise of the city and enjoying the calm and beauty of this place." "You are right," he said. "Here is Iran. Outside is capitalism" (this was the term he used). In the Shiraz region, we had decided to visit some neighboring villages and negotiated with a taxi for the day's drive. We were able to assess the absurdity of some aspects of the commercial modernization imposed on the country. In one of these villages, there was a magnificent watermill, built during the Buyid era. The mill, paid off centuries ago but still in working condition, used to allow the villagers to come and grind their grain for free. The authorities had closed it and built, a short distance away, an oil-powered mill, forcing the peasants to pay for its services! On the road, we passed a mullah who made a hitchhiking sign. We took him on board. Dressed in his impeccable large black robe, he held a large leather briefcase. We chatted. "Do you know what I am carrying?" he said. "No." "It is money." He opened it and it was, in fact, full of bundles of banknotes. "The government takes money from the poor to give to the rich. We do the opposite. We collect it from the rich to distribute it to the poor." "With that much money," I said to him, "you could pay for a taxi. Why do you travel on foot?" "This money is not mine. It belongs to the people and I do not have the right to touch it."

These small stories helped me to understand how the Shia church had actually succeeded in crystallizing around itself popular opposition to the social and cultural destruction, resulting from capitalist modernization as devised and implemented by the government. But this close link between populism and religious assertion would not have been possible without the systematic destruction of the left alternative represented by Tudeh, in spite of all its inadequacies. Anti-communism here, as in Nasserist Egypt, Baathist Syria and Iraq, and Boumediennist Algeria, opened the doors to backward-looking fundamentalist Islam. This was so to the extent that the most determined fringe of rebellious youth chose to be part of the large Islamist current. The Mujahidin and Fidayin organizations were the spearhead without which it is probable that the Shah's regime would not have been overthrown. They were poorly rewarded for their efforts: massacred, in the proper sense of the term, following Ayatollah Khomeini's victory by bands of Pasdaran, which were hurriedly recruited from lumpen elements and organized by the Islamic authorities to fulfill this function. When, years later, I discussed this with former militants of these movements, they acknowledged that they had not seen the danger and realized only too late that the Shia church was not a vehicle for any social project worthy of the name, but only backward-looking nostalgia.

What has followed since is, then, an unspeakable disaster. Iran, which could have become another Korea, moves further away from that every day. Of course, the Korean option is not, for me, the "only possible one," or even acceptable, as I will discuss later. But it leaves the future open by preparing the conditions that allow it to confront challenges on new foundations with new possibilities. The backward-looking option destroys, nothing more. The Iranian Islamist regime has ultimately turned out to be more reactionary than that of the Shah, even returning to the agrarian semi-reform of the so-called White Revolution. But it has long derived—and can still derive a bit longer, under the form of what has become a legend—benefit from the ambiguity of its origins. The open pro-Western bias of the Shah's regime allowed an anti-imperialist nationalist populism to be carried by the fundamentalist religious current, while in the Arab countries populism had triumphed in a different way—through various coups d'état by petite bourgeois soldiers. In spite of this difference, the results have ultimately not been very different, populism opening the way to the Islamist ascent.

Iran's so-called Islamic revolution has, perhaps, entered into the final phase of its decay. The 1999 elections opposed the hardliners, the leaders of theocratic power, to the reformists. The constitution requires that the electoral contest take place within pre-established limits in which all candidates accept the Islamist "principle." Hence, behind the vote in favor of the reformists—who obtained an overwhelming majority—are found a large range of opinions that cannot all be fit within the required limits. There is a common denominator in all the protests: the deplorable results of the system, which are in no way different from those found elsewhere in systems that have accepted identical liberal economic management principles (worsening of inequality, pauperization, etc.). But behind this common denominator there are conflicting viewpoints and interests—those of a fraction of the comprador bourgeoisie, tired of the incompetence of the mullahs and their excesses, and those of the disappointed working classes, depoliticized by the successive dictatorships of the Shah and the religious leaders, but now impervious to the dominant rhetoric.

What future can emerge from such confusions? It could be the worst or the best; neither one is impossible. The worst would be that the comprador bourgeoisie would maintain continuity in succession, in one way or another, and that the mullahs would accept the path of a straightforward dictatorship like Pakistan or Saudi Arabia. The U.S. establishment favors this option, of course. The best would be that the working classes, without necessarily succeeding in formulating a clear alternative project as part of the long transition to socialist democracy, would force a democratization that would necessarily be secular (or at least secularizing) and social.

It is not my intention here to develop the analyses called for by the "Islamic revolution."[32] Was it, as it proclaimed itself to be and as it was often seen by many in the camp of political Islam as well as by "foreign observers," the herald and point of departure for a development that, in the end, must take over the region, even the whole of the "Muslim world," renamed for the occasion "*umma*," or "nation," which it has never been? Or was it a unique event, particularly because it resulted from a combination of interpretations of Shia Islam and the expression of Iranian nationalism?

In terms of what is of interest, I shall make only two observations. The first is that the regime of political Islam in Iran is not by nature incompatible with the integration of the country into the globalized capitalist system as it is (the principles on which the regime is based find their place within the limits of "liberal" management of the economy). The second is that the Iranian nation as such is a "strong nation," that is, the major components of that nation, if not all of them—working classes and ruling classes—do not accept integration of their country in the globalized system as a dominated entity. There is obviously a contradiction between these two dimensions of Iranian reality, and the second accounts for Tehran's foreign policy orientations, which clearly manifest a desire to resist foreign diktats.

It is also Iranian nationalism—powerful and, in my opinion, historically quite positive—that explains the success of the "modernization" of scientific, industrial, technological, and military capabilities undertaken by the successive regimes of the Shah and Khomeinism. Iran is one of the rare states from the South (with China, India, Korea, Brazil, and maybe a few others, but not many) to have a "national bourgeois" project. Whether this project is achievable in the long term or not (and I do not think it is) is not the focus of this discussion. Today this project exists; it is in place.

It is precisely because Iran is a critical mass capable of attempting to assert itself as a respected partner that the United States decided to destroy the country by a new "preventive war." As is well known, the "conflict" is ostensibly about Iran's development of nuclear capabilities. Why should this country—like all others—not have the right to become a nuclear military power? By what right do the imperialist powers, and their Israeli toy, claim a monopoly of weapons of mass destruction? Can we grant any credence to the rhetoric that "democratic" nations would never use such weapons unlike "rogue states," especially when we know that the "democratic" nations in question are responsible for the most extensive genocides of modern times, including that of the Jews, and that the United States has already used nuclear weapons and today refuses an absolute and general prohibition on their use?

All societies in the Middle East—Arab, Turk, and Iranian—have regressed because of this tragic history and the backward-looking illusions that delay awareness of the requirements for a democratization of society. There is a retreat from nationalism in the healthy sense of the term (solidarity of peoples within the borders history has left them) to the evident benefit of a vague and powerless pan-Islamic identity. This retreat is expressed in the systematic obfuscation of the complete historical identity of the peoples in question. For example, the official history taught in Egypt has now eliminated antiquity and the Coptic period from its texts, as if Egypt had not existed before the seventh century. Struggle on the field of real challenges—political, economic, and social—has been abandoned and instead attention is focused on the evasion known as "cultural" identity, itself reduced to the submission to religious ritual while the compradorized submission to world capitalism is accepted without discussion.

MY WORKS ARE SOMETIMES PUBLISHED in Farsi by translators who work in prison! The following text was submitted to Iranian friends in forced exile, in particular "Foad."

## *Iran's Aborted Emergence*

Iran is an old and great nation, proud of its history, which reacted quite early to threats from Europe (England and Russia). From 1905 to 1907, there was a revolution against the regime of the decadent Qajar dynasty, considered incapable of resisting foreigners. The Iranian constitutional revolution was the first of its kind in the Middle East. It began the modern era in Iran. What is more, the intellectuals who had been educated in the Russian Caucasus within the Russian Social Democratic Workers' Party (out of which the Bolsheviks arose) played an important role in this revolution and provided the Iranian avant-garde with a more accurate understanding than elsewhere of the issues involved in the relation between imperialist domination and the local power of the old exploiting (feudal) classes.

## *The First Attempt at a Real Emergence*

The new government of the Pahlavis, established in 1921 (although Reza Shah did not become the Shah of Iran until 1926), thus took on a particular character: it was reactionary on the level of its social positions, yet it refused to become the lackey of dominant forces on the international level. Reza Shah abolished in 1928 the unequal regime of "capitulations" that the European powers had imposed on Iran. He created centralized state power that put an end to the traditional tribal regime of management (*Molouk al tavaef*). He promulgated a civil code, created a national army and police force, established compulsory military service, established a state postal service, opened highways and railways, and initiated the first real network of public schools for boys and girls, independent of the clergy. The state also took the initiative of creating the first industries: textiles, canning, and sugar refining. Nevertheless, Iran respected the best interests of Great Britain (particularly in the petroleum sector) and the government declared itself to be anti-communist (a 1931 law prohibited spreading "communist" ideas). Reza Shah's pro-Nazi sympathies forced the Allies (Britain and the Soviet Union) to depose him and replace him with his son, Mohammad Reza.

The emergence of a powerful anti-imperialist and socialist party (the Tudeh) and the nationalist position taken in 1951 by Prime Minister Mossadegh, who dared to nationalize the oil industry, could not be eliminated by the CIA-supported coup d'état that allowed Mohammad Reza to change tack and rejoin the Western camp. To deal with the challenge of democratic, nationalist, and progressive forces, Mohammad Reza then initiated the "White Revolution" in 1962, combined with a "neutralist" international position. Certainly, the agrarian reform was one in name only; it did not reduce the power and wealth of the large landowners by much, although it did encourage them to modernize, and it did facilitate the emergence of a new rich peasantry. In addition, there was a modernization of customs (notably in favor of women) and efforts made in the field of education. The neutralist position—the rapprochement with the USSR (in 1965) and China (in 1970)—and the recovery of control over the petroleum industry (in 1973) were, in these conditions, accepted by the Western powers, with no better alternative available. It was a police regime in the extreme—Savak, the political police, has a deserved reputation for the crimes it committed—and the only guarantee for maintaining the reactionary social order. Simultaneously, the Tudeh Party abandoned its original radical positions and went as far as supporting the Shah's reforms, just as later it would rally to the Khomeini regime, thus beginning its loss of credibility with the working classes and the revolutionary intelligentsia. Ultimately, Mohammad Reza's project was one of emergence, although devised within the context of capitalism (partly a state capitalism). Its limitations and contradictions were the result of this fundamental choice.

This system retained a marked comprador character, reinforced by petroleum revenues. These revenues encouraged easy imports, which competed destructively with local industries (textiles, cement). Agriculture itself suffered from the massive imports of surplus U.S. wheat, a system that impoverished hundreds of thousands of peasants from the arid regions that were ancestral producers of wheat. Moreover, Mohammad Reza feared the emergence of a true national bourgeoisie and preferred to rely on the traditionalist conservative commercial bourgeoisie. Tudeh's destruction by police violence, and its opportunist shift, created a large political void and opened the road to a new force in opposition to the regime, organized around the Shia Mullahs and their leader, Ayatollah Khomeini.

## *The Contradictions of Government by the Shia Mullahs*

The Islamist regime that resulted, established in 1979, has been undermined by its internal contradictions. In terms of the conceptions of the society to be "reconstructed," the regime was fundamentally reactionary, not only in its cultural positions (the veil for women, etc.), but also in its relation to economic and social life. Two reactionary social classes provided most of its support: the "bazaaris," that is, the traditionalist commercial/comprador bourgeoisie, and the new rich peasantry. The regime inherited a partial state capitalism managed by "technocrats" who had rallied to the Shah's dictatorship. What the regime did was simply replace "civil" with "religious" management. Mullahs were everywhere in management positions, enriching themselves, of course, with no concern to provide any overall coherence to the Shah's modernization project—now controlled by clerics—itself flawed by its limitations and contradictions. But at the same time, because the Shah's regime had been "pro-Western" (despite its neutralist positions), the new regime could adorn itself with a flashy anti-imperialism confused with anti-Westernism.

Confusion is extreme, and explains why many Western analysts believe it is possible to describe the system as "modernist": "modernist Islam," they say. They base themselves on real changes in order to prove it, but these changes do not have the meaning they attribute to them. Yes, the marriage age for women has been raised; yes, there is a growing number of women who work, some of whom even occupy posts of responsibility. But these changes are found everywhere in the South (except in the Gulf countries!) and in the North (because the world always "changes," of course). Modernity—without speaking of emancipation—requires much more.

Washington had supported the Shah until the very end, and its reaction motivated, in turn, an expected Iranian position; a nationalist one, of course.

At that point, Washington thought it could mobilize its ally at that time, Saddam Hussein's Iraq, to launch a criminal and absurd war that lasted ten years, beginning in 1980. The creation of an "Arab" camp (the Gulf supporting Iraq) under Washington's leadership was the beginning of open hostility between Iran (Shia) and the Gulf (mainly Sunni and monarchical)—hostility that is ostensibly atavistic. It is hardly that, and it does not run through the entire history of the region as it would if it were an immanent, invariable, and constant reality. But it can, with the help of generalized stupidity, appear to be so because the reactionary and backward political Islams on both sides use it that way.

*Aborted Emergence*

Within this context, Iran (Islamist, Shia, Khomeinist) became the enemy of the Western powers, although it did not want to. Khomeinist Iran did not imagine managing its economy other than by the simple rules of the market and capitalism as it is, that is, a dependent capitalism. A modus vivendi would have been easy to work out between this local system and the dominant globalized capitalism. The mullahs—in particular the supposed reformers—sought that very thing. But the Gulf worked to undermine their attempts, spurring on Washington.

Tehran's nuclear program could, then, only poison the atmosphere. This was actually not something that began with the Khomeini regime. It was Mohammad Reza who had committed his country to this path. At the time, Washington had no complaints about it. The Khomeini regime only continued along the same path. It is difficult to criticize it for that decision, even if the risk of nuclear weapons could be looming behind civilian nuclear energy. There is truly no reason to accept the viewpoint of Washington and its subaltern NATO allies on the issue of "proliferation." This is only considered dangerous when a potential opponent of the imperialist powers might benefit. The silence about Israel's huge nuclear arsenal expresses the Western powers' usual double standards. If denuclearization should be set in motion (which would be more than desirable), then that could only be done if the country that most threatens the entire world—the United States—were to begin the process. The threat of aggression against Iran is brandished and to that end there is a great deal of baying from Tel Aviv about the Iranian threat.

The situation is now all the more complex since the occupation of Iraq by the United States and the quagmire of the war in Afghanistan have not resulted in what Washington expected. Certainly, Iraq was destroyed, not only its state (de facto broken apart into four states: Sunni, Shia, Kurdish no. 1, and

Kurdish no. 2!) but its society as well, including, among others, all its scientific personnel, who were murdered on order of the occupiers. But Iraq's destruction has, at the same time, given Tehran a card to play, now able to mobilize its "Shia" friends if necessary. To get around the problem, Washington then decided to weaken Iran by destroying its regional allies, beginning with Syria. All that confirms that the political conflict between Iran and the United States is quite real. But this fact changes nothing in the question being posed: Is Iran on the way to emergence? My answer is purely and simply no. Nothing in the development of Iran's economic system will allow the country to emerge from the "lumpen-development" in which Khomeinist political Islam has trapped it. It does not suffice to be considered by the imperialist powers to be one of their enemies to become thereby—miraculously—an emergent country.

## AFGHANISTAN

En route from India to Europe in 1973, we made a stop in Afghanistan. This was the time of the recent republic, moderately reformist and ferociously attached to the country's independence. It was suspicious of the Western powers. In the nineteenth century the British had attempted to extend their Indian empire up to the Russian frontier and had succeeded in cutting off Kabul's access to the sea by establishing their rule in Baluchistan. Less suspicious of the Soviet government, which had given evidence of its scrupulous respect for the country's independence, the reformist Afghan government had thus opted for an active neutralism, with a tilt toward Moscow, justified since the Soviets supported the neutralism of the Bandung group, while the Western powers worked to destabilize the governments in this group. For the Western powers, the model "friend" was the Pakistani regime—even if it were odiously repressive.

Pakistan was, moreover, an enemy of Afghanistan, since the British had succeeded in including the Pathan (Pashtun) populations, to which Kabul's ruling families belonged, into its Indian empire. But as a result the friendship linking the republican government and Moscow marginalized the radical wing of the intelligentsia, who were attracted by the progress achieved in Soviet Central Asia (all the more so since northern Afghanistan is populated by Uzbeks and Tajiks) and thus became "communist." The "party" consequently was divided into two tendencies—Khalq and Parcham—one rather pro-Soviet, despite Moscow's official support for the republic, and the other more suspicious and assertive in its autonomy.

I knew militants from this party and found them to be brilliant intellectuals, courageous and cultivated, and not at all cut off from their people by a destructive Westernization. I thought they had a clear future, although they had not yet succeeded in building large grassroots alliances without which they were condemned—like the other parts of the republican ruling class—to remain reformers from above. As opposed to the moderate republicans, who did not dare to confront the "feudal lords" and undertake an agrarian reform, the radicals were not wrong to think that such a reform was absolutely necessary to establish a real modernization of society. Circumstances allowed them to seize power—through a kind of coup d'état/palace revolution within the modernist ruling class—without Moscow's support at that time (it should be remembered), but before having succeeded in building an alliance with the peasantry. Left to themselves, the Afghan "revolutionaries" would probably not have developed too badly. They would undoubtedly have been violent in implementing the reforms, but these were necessary. Should they be criticized for having opened schools, for having accepted girls into them, and for daring even to offer posts of authority to women? The Western powers, in any case, immediately declared their hostility to the new government in Kabul, pointing to its "non-democratic" character (passing over in silence the incomparably more anti-democratic nature of the government of their Pakistani ally!), criticizing its "brutality" (toward whom?—the fathers of families who refused to send their daughters to school?) while the brutality of the Islamists (toward women, for example) was attributed to "cultural tradition," acceptable since it was part of an "identity." Militant Islamism, which had not existed in Afghanistan up to then, was supported with millions of dollars and training camps financed by the CIA, Pakistani military cliques, and drug-trafficking warlords. Washington, London, Paris, Bonn, all the capitals of the democracies, recruited defenders of the "right to difference" and the "rights of peoples," and even feminists (!) to oppose the Afghan government while their intelligence services recruited ideological instructors from al-Azhar and the rebellious youth lost in the ghettoes of Cairo and Algiers whom they made into the killers of the Algerian Islamic Salvation Front, not by chance called "Afghans." What a wonderful fight for democracy by the West! The Afghan case is a good example of the total lack of credibility accruing to this manipulated rhetoric.

The Soviet intervention was, at the beginning, completely useless. It even ended up creating additional difficulties for the Afghan government, which was, in my opinion, radical reformist rather than "communist." But ultimately, it served as a pretext to give a semblance of legitimacy to the support given by the Western powers to the worst enemies of the true liberation of the Afghan people. On the Soviet side, the reasons for this intervention remain unclear. On the Afghan side, we can only be rather severe toward those who, among the radical reformers (and they were far from being the majority) believed it intelligent to appeal to Moscow for assistance. History has condemned them.

Yet it is the case that, once the Soviets left, the reformist government was the target of repeated attacks by a general military offensive no less supported from outside the country, without which the Islamists would not have been able to seize Kabul. The result of the installation of the Islamist government was quite visible: an unending war among the warlords. But Western opinion was no longer entreated and the media no longer called for defending democracy in Afghanistan. The objective had been attained and the chance that the Afghan people could emerge from the darkness was eliminated. Washington could catch its breath. The Afghan episode had sealed the strategic alliance between the United States and the Islamists, aimed at establishing the hegemony of globalized neoliberalism and sinking the Muslim peoples even more into decline and marginalization.

The Islamists—specifically, the odious Taliban—were (and remain) among the preferred allies of the North American establishment up to the day when, for reasons that have yet to be clarified, their guest Osama Bin Laden revolted against Washington. It remains to be seen if he organized the September 11 attacks (doubtful, in my opinion), or if the operation involved some degree of complicity with the CIA and the Mossad (which appears highly probable to me). What followed is too well known to be recounted here: the massacre of the Afghan people by U.S. terrorist bombings, the use of September 11 to justify, through conflation, the establishment of a new McCarthyism in the United States, and the use of "anti-terrorism" by the criminal Ariel Sharon to justify the massacre of Palestinians. Simultaneously, media campaigns were orchestrated to lead Western public opinion to "discover" the horrors of the Taliban regime (particularly toward women). The reopening of schools for girls was hailed as a new idea, something the "communist" regime had done in its time, which had been denounced because it did not "respect traditions"!!! The "Northern Front" was praised. Yesterday, they were warlords. The idea of returning to the monarchy was revived, which the Afghans themselves had already eliminated. But apparently nothing is ever ended in Afghanistan. I have no doubt that this people will redouble the intensity of its liberation struggle against the new occupiers—the United States and their subaltern allies.

Afghanistan experienced the best moment of its modern history during the time of the so-called communist republic. It was a modernist regime of enlightened despotism that opened educational opportunities to the children of both sexes and was an opponent of obscurantism, thereby gaining decisive support within society. The agrarian reform that had been undertaken consisted mainly of a group of measures aimed at reducing the tyrannical powers of the tribal chiefs. The—at least tacit—support of the peasant majority guaranteed the probable success of this well-begun development. The propaganda conveyed by the Western media and by political Islam presented this experience as a "communist and atheist totalitarianism" rejected by the Afghan people. In reality, the regime, just like that of Ataturk in its time, was far from being "unpopular."

The United States in particular, and its allies in the triad in general, have always been persistent opponents of Afghan modernizers, whether communist or not. They are the ones who mobilized the obscurantist forces of Pakistani-type political Islam (the Taliban) and the warlords (the tribal leaders successfully neutralized by the so-called communist regime), trained them, and armed them. Even after the Soviet retreat, Mohammad Najibullah's government demonstrated the capacity to resist growing attacks and would probably have won if not for the Pakistani military offensive in support of the Taliban and, increasing the chaos, the offensive of the reconstituted forces of the warlords.

Afghanistan has been devastated by the intervention of the United States and its allies and agents, Islamists in particular. Afghanistan cannot be reconstructed under their government, formally led by a clown without roots in the country who was parachuted in by a Texan multinational of which he was an employee. The supposed "democracy," in the name of which Washington, NATO, and the UN called for help, and which they persistently use to justify the continuation of their "presence" (in fact occupation), was a lie from the very beginning and has become a crude farce.

There is only one solution to the Afghan "problem": all foreign forces must leave the country and all powers must be forced to refrain from financing and arming their "allies." To all people of good conscience who fear that the Afghan people will then tolerate the dictatorship of the Taliban (or the warlords), I respond that the foreign presence has been up to now and remains the best support for this dictatorship! And I would remind these people of good conscience that the Afghan people were moving in another direction—one of great potential for a better future—at a time when the "West" was forced to intervene less in its affairs. As opposed to the enlightened despotism of "communists," the civilized West always prefers obscurantism, infinitely less dangerous for its interests!

## PAKISTAN

The holding of the founding congress of the Third World Forum in December 1974 in Karachi gave me the opportunity to get to know the country better, beyond what I had learned through reading and discussions with exiled intellectuals. Pakistan is a criminal creation of British imperialism, part of the political strategy of undermining Indian unity. Whatever one may think of the Congress Party—and I am strongly critical of it—it should be recognized that it succeeded in defeating this strategy and creating a multinational Indian union managed through a secular electoral democracy. It was successful all along the line except with the Muslim Indians. The fundamental alliance of imperialism and fundamentalist theocratic Islam is thus the origin of the separation of the two Pakistans (West and East; the latter later became Bangladesh). What resulted was this absurd, ultra-reactionary state, always managed by Islamo-military dictatorships, yet faithful friends of Washington, which took over from the British as the dominant imperialist power. Here is yet another reason to doubt the sincerity of the Western powers' rhetoric about "democracy."

Pakistanis are nothing other than Muslim Indians who share history, territory, languages, and civilizations with other Indians—the Hindu majority. However, the majority of this country's intellectuals have internalized the views of theocratic Islam, to the point of forgetting the country's origin and believing it to be the authentic product of the unchangeable "specificity" of Muslim civilization. This theory, cherished by all of contemporary Islamic fundamentalism, had originally been elaborated—in fine detail—by "experts" of the British intelligence services from which Maulana Maududi, one of the key figures of contemporary fundamentalism, derived much of his inspiration. Entire fragments, taken word for word, from the British reports can be found in this ideologue's works. The reports suggest propaganda topics to develop systematically with the aim of breaking the unified Indian national movement: that Islam is not susceptible to modern interpretations based on the separation of politics and religion, or that the idea of evolution and adaptation is alien to Islam, or that Islam does not allow the coexistence of a Muslim minority and others in the same state.

But the aim of gathering all "Muslims" in the same state, with no respect for any other dimension of identity—linguistic and historical—has not stood the test of time. Bangladesh separated from West Pakistan and ended up acknowledging what it is: Muslim Bengal. Modern Pakistan's ruling classes have, moreover, treated the people just like their political ancestors—conquerors of northern India—had done in the past: as a conquered and dominated people, whether it preserved its original religion or embraced Islam.

In Pakistan, these same ruling classes gave themselves an additional "specificity" of dubious origin. I verified this more than once, saying to them, somewhat provocatively, that Pakistanis are nothing other than Muslim

Indians and, moreover, that Muslims are as numerous in India as in Pakistan. The response I received was always the same and quite instructive: "No, we are not Indians, we are from Central Asia!" I pointed out to them that this origin in Central Asia was indeed that of the Turko-Mongol conquerors of all of northern India—not only the northwest—but these conquerors had never been more than a tiny minority who dominated a people that had remained Indian. The proof is that Pakistan's official language, Urdu, is nothing else than Hindi written with the Arabic letters of Persian, and that no people of Pakistan speaks a Turkic language of any kind from Central Asia. But Pakistan needs this absurd origin myth to appear "different," just as it needs the theocratic Islamic theory to reject the idea of a pan-Indian state.

The impasse in which the Pakistani ruling classes have trapped their people is tragic. Cheap compradorization and an obstinate rejection of democratization (under the pretext that this idea is "foreign") are an expression of that. An Islamo-military dictatorship is, then, the rule. The attempts to escape from that tradition—implemented by Zulfikar Ali Bhutto in the middle of the 1970s and later by his daughter—have always been cut short. Benazir Bhutto, who is presented in Western media as a heroine of democracy and sometimes of secularism, had nevertheless chosen to provide resolute support to the Afghan Taliban, without which they probably would never have conquered Kabul. She was badly rewarded for it. She had not understood that Islamists wanted nothing other than all the power for themselves alone.

I shall not pretend to know how the people of this country live with these problems today. (Feroz Ahmad and Eqbal Ahmad have produced excellent analyses on these questions.) Pakistan is just as multinational as India. It is made up of four distinct nationalities—Punjabis, Pathans, Sindis, and Baluchis, without counting the Tibetan peoples of the Pamir Mountains. To these four peoples should be added the Muhajir, that is, the Indian Muslims who immigrated to Pakistan—willingly or under duress—since the partition in 1947. The large number of these refugees in Karachi reduced the Sindis to minority status in their own province. The latter, of course, do not want to accept that change in their status; and a permanent civil war, latent or open, between these two communities has continued to wreak havoc for the past fifty years. The Baluchis have also revolted against the de facto domination of the Punjabis and Pathans. A nomadic people of small numbers, they were exterminated and it is not the least of the paradoxes that this actual genocide was perpetrated by the Ali Bhutto government, anxious to make gestures of goodwill to the ultras of the military-Islamic clique. That did not bring him good fortune since he was later, in 1979, forced out of office and hanged by this same clique. The void created in Baluchistan was later filled by an influx of immigrants (Pathans) from Afghanistan, who today dominate the province and are in a state of quasi-secession. The Bengalis of the former East Pakistan straight out seceded, as is well known.

India is recognized and constituted as a multinational state. Pakistan refuses to do that because its absurd theocratic Islamist ideology will not recognize any identity other than Muslim, and denies nationality. The result is appalling and is here, like elsewhere in political systems that claim to adhere to Islamism, an almost certain guarantee of permanent civil war and social decomposition. This is the case, for example, in Sudan or in Algeria, where the Islamists claim that there are neither Arabic speakers nor Berber speakers, but only Muslims!

The alternative to the criminal partition of British India had been the creation of a large, multinational federal state. That is what India is, despite the limitations of its political and social system. In most Indian states, while the Hindus are in the majority, Muslims make up a not insignificant minority (12 percent for all of India). The former northwest province Sind and Baluchistan would have formed three Indian states with a very large Muslim majority. Greater Punjab, like greater Bengal and Kashmir could have been three other states that would have been half Muslim and half Hindu or Sikh. Reasonable proposals like this were made at the time. But the Muslim leaders, who claimed to speak on behalf of the people (and were supported by the imperialists), preferred partition. All non-Muslims were mercilessly chased out of Pakistan (following the theory of the theocratic state). India did not respond in the same way, although obviously the ill treatment suffered by Muslims at the hands of fanatical Hindu groups was partly responsible for the exodus that followed partition.

Certainly Islamism is not always accompanied by the negation of the nation. When a regime that claims to be Islamist governs a strong and ancient nation, as is the case in Iran (or in Turkey), Islamism can coexist with a heightened nationalism, here "anti-Arab." This is all the more so in the case of Iran where there is a coincidence between Iranian nationality and the Shia form of Islam, organized into a quasi-national church. But such coincidences are never acknowledged because they conflict with theocratic dogma. The latter is invoked, in turn, to deny the rights of minorities in Turkophone Azerbaijan and in Kurdistan.

Militant Islamism has another disastrous effect: the negation of the pre-Islamic history of the peoples in question. In Egypt and Iran, attempts are made to convince the people that their history did not exist before the seventh century by lumping all previous eras into one indistinct mass called *jahiliya* (era of ignorance), while Pakistan is proclaimed to be "non-Indian." Critical sociologists and political scientists from these countries have forcefully analyzed the ravages of these jarring disjunctions. The pre-Islamic past is not only in a past that, as glorious as it was, has completely disappeared. The ancient civilization of these countries was transmitted to really existing Islam and even shaped it to a large extent. Without this past, there would not have been an Islamic civilization. Attempting to extirpate it is tantamount to impoverishing the societies in question. Yet that is exactly what the fundamentalists propose to do. Do they not condemn the Arab Islamic philosophy of the brilliant centuries of the Abbasid Caliphate because it had not broken with Hellenism? If this philosophy was as rich as it was, that is precisely because it had not ignored the centuries of the supposed *jahiliya*.

It should be no surprise that an ideological hodgepodge of this type must be accompanied by forms of exploitation, themselves archaic and savage, which are forbidden to be questioned since they existed in the Islamic past, and thus are not prohibited. Pakistan provides the most striking example of this where there are entire regions (like Bahawalpur), in which serfdom and a particularly harsh treatment of serfs are still in place. Unquestionably, no less violent forms of exploitation exist elsewhere, such as India. But social movements can challenge these and their right to do so cannot be negated by any theocratic dogma. It is important to note here that theocratic dogma, with all that it implies concerning the negation of national identities or attempts to erase history, is not a monopoly of Muslim history. The church in medieval Christianity did not behave any differently. But it must be recognized that, in the contemporary world, only Islamic theocratic dogma has sufficient political power to establish itself in an actual absolute government.

How can this be explained? I connect it closely with the rise of new "middle classes" produced by the expansion of peripheral capitalism. Doomed to be no more than comprador social classes with subaltern status in the world system and willing to accept this fate as compensation for the material advantages that it procures for them, these uneducated and traumatized classes are victims of an incurable dissonance. They want to benefit from the material advantages of the modern world—under the most vulgar form of consumption—but reject freedom of thought. The backward-looking religious illusion is not the only means by which they succeed in reconciling a compradorized submission to dominant capitalism and protection of a supposed "identity." Ethnic chauvinism can fulfill the same functions. All forms of populism have prepared the terrain for this slide into an impasse with no way out, even when, as in the Arab countries, this populism accomplished real reforms that were indispensable and attenuated the violence of exploitation. Here we must speak of an Islamist regression that has arisen as a response to the crisis of an earlier populism (as in Turkey). This regression was greatly encouraged by the increase in petroleum revenues. Archaic Saudi Arabia, poor in olden times, could not exercise any attraction over the new Arab bourgeois classes. It should not be forgotten that Egypt traditionally used to subsidize Mecca and Medina, which were incapable of welcoming pilgrims with their own resources. The combination of the sudden fortune accruing to the Gulf from the petroleum industry and the permanence of the archaism that no local force threatened, to the great satisfaction of the imperialists, gave rise to an incredible myth: the fortune was precisely the result of the archaism.

Theocratic Islamism—like other forms of the dissonance found in the comprador classes of the modern periphery—argues for the reconstruction of states on homogeneous foundations that would supposedly be guaranteed by religious or ethnic unity, even if it is accomplished by "ethnic cleansing" or the extermination of religious minorities, and the fragmentation of the world into appallingly anti-democratic political systems built on these foundations, all of which would be integrated into the world capitalist market. This project is the exact opposite of the internationalism of peoples, the humanist response to the cosmopolitanism of capital. In fact, this is imperialism's plan, even if it be presented under the insidious form of "respect for communities" (of which Anglo-American racist ideology is particularly fond). It is the basis of the strategic alliance between the hegemonists of Washington and the religious or ethnic reactionaries of the periphery. This is the program followed by the Third World's comprador classes. The popular classes have nothing to do with it. They are the unfortunate victims, easily manipulated up to now for various reasons.

## CENTRAL ASIA

Central Asia has always strongly attracted me. This is so, not only because of its magnificent landscapes, but also because I want to know a bit more about its peoples, who succeeded in conquering China, India, Europe, and the Middle East, strongly affecting Islamic civilization. These peoples are frequently treated as "barbarians" in official histories and in popular consciousness, but they are certainly deserving of a more nuanced assessment. Reading the great Russian historians—the only ones, in my opinion, who have studied the region with subtlety and attentiveness—had convinced me that to understand their role in the shaping of the world was an important question for advancing historical materialism.

An opportunity was offered to me by UNESCO's Silk Roads program. Directed by the Senegalese Doudou Diène—his organizational and diplomatic skills are remarkable as is his subtlety—this program allowed me to visit Sinkiang (Summer 1990), Central Asia—still Soviet at that time (Summer 1991)—and Mongolia (Summer 1992). Isabelle accompanied me for the last two parts of the program, each of which lasted one month. These were not occasions for rambling as tourists, but serious study trips. The excellent historians who participated in these programs—more specifically, the Russians (and other Soviets of the time) and the Chinese—led discussions of the greatest interest. The analysis that I offer of the ancient system of globalization—the one that capitalism had dismantled and then replaced with the modern system dominated by Atlantic Europe—owes much to these discussions.[33] Too many Westerners in the group, however, fell too easily into exoticism. Journalists and television crews behaved as if that were too often the case, with a lot of arrogance despite their ignorance—maybe a way of hiding it. There were also some remarkable specialists. For example, there was an expert in Buddhist art (the conservator of the Guimet Museum in Paris) and also an expert in Mongol singing (an extraordinary—and beautiful—way of singing in which the sound comes from the lungs and the throat by I don't know what kind of technique, so unique that the Mongols could not believe their ears when a Frenchman reproduced it to perfection). There were also spies: an Israeli charged with contacting the Jewish communities of Soviet Central Asia, as well as Americans and Japanese who did not have any historical knowledge, but were specialists in communication strategies or mineral wealth. I was sorry that Easterners (Arabs, Turks, and Iranians), who should have been among those most interested in the region, were absent. The UNESCO team supporting Doudou Diène was highly competent and extremely kind, making the trip relaxed and enjoyable, and helping us forget the strains of the difficult roads.

But, beyond learning about the region's historical past and contemplating the scenery, the trip allowed me to discover some interesting aspects of its modern problems. The contrast between the perfect organization of the trip in China, the disorder of the one in the Soviet Union, and the total absence of any form of organization in Mongolia, while it is almost a caricature, is nevertheless significant.

## *Xinjiang*

I arrived in Beijing late. I thus joined the caravan, which was already at the doorsteps of Xinjiang, at Dunhuang, at the end of the corridor that connects China proper—the province of Gansu—to Mongolia and Xinjiang. I went as far as Lanzhou by plane, then from there, thanks to the kind assistance of my

Chinese friends in the Academy, I traveled by automobile to meet the caravan. The trip was quite educational for me. My visit to the capital of this interior province, among the poorest in China, provided an opportunity to assess the incontestable progress made due to the effective redistribution of the means of accumulation mainly financed by the wealthier coastal provinces. This is an aspect of the strategy of interprovincial integration often ignored by both defenders and critics of the "capitalist path" followed by the government. This impression was strengthened when I traveled through villages at the slow pace of car traffic in China. My guide-interpreter (from the Academy) was a very friendly young man and we chatted about everything—including politics, obviously, and quite freely, as is the case in China. We stopped unexpectedly here or there in a large village to drink tea or eat something in some sort of "café-restaurant-general store" (I don't know exactly what to call this type of "store" that is found everywhere in China), generally managed by the commune. People were always welcoming, the peasant clients were jovial and curious (coming up to me and asking where I came from, who I was, if I like the local cuisine, did I like the village, etc.). These places were relatively clean (except for the toilets, of course). The impression I had—from the quality of the buildings and the accommodations—was of poor Europe in the nineteenth century, but not desolate scenes as elsewhere in the capitalist Third World, even in countries that are considerably wealthier.

The UNESCO caravan had left Xian, one of the capitals of ancient China, starting and ending point of the long-distance trade of that time. I had had the opportunity in an earlier trip with Isabelle to visit Xian and admire its vestiges—murals and old temples—and the incredible cemetery of giant statues of the imperial army, an artistic and historical treasure of China. The corridor formed by the "Western finger" of Gansu offers an unforgettable scenery. On the left side, heading west, we passed the high peaks of the Qinghai, towering up to more than 5,000 meters, while on the right was the Great Wall—which we continually approached or veered away from—separating rural and peasant China from the Gobi Desert and Mongol herders. In Dunhuang, I marveled at early Buddhist caves. There I joined our group.

At each of our stops, we were urged to participate in a three- or four-hour discussion that Chinese historians presented about different aspects of the region's history and the role it played in the relations between China proper, India, and the Byzantine and Islamic Middle East, such as the formation of the Uyghur peoples and states, religious developments—Buddhism, Nestorian Christianity, Islamization—social structures, modes of agricultural production (irrigation) and trade, technology transfers, artistic styles, etc. In other words, it was good historical materialism as a whole. What struck me—and perhaps others as well—was the extent of the vestiges of enormous cities that had disappeared.

In Turpan, we descended to an oasis located at the lowest point on the planet—168 meters below sea level. This marvelous small city presented a distinctive characteristic that I have found nowhere else: some of the streets, even some of the widest open to automobile traffic, were entirely covered by a trellis bearing grapevines. Traveling around, then—on foot, by bicycle, or in a horse-drawn carriage—was done in the shade and it was even possible to collect a few refreshing grapes from above one's head in passing.

Kashgar, last stop on the trip, was the historical capital of the Uyghur Turks, in close contact with western Turkestan of the Uzbeks and Tajiks and, through them, with Persia and India. To the east, Kashgar commanded the two roads that lead to China proper, bypassing the terrible, impassable Taklamakan desert by either the north or the south. To the west, it commanded access to the main passes that allow a traveler to bypass the Pamir Mountains through the roads of Afghanistan leading to the Khyber Pass to Peshawar. This entire region of very high mountains and pleasant valleys was closed to our expedition. To visit Afghanistan had become, of course, quite impossible. The heart of the Kushan state, where the three roads from Iran, India, and China met, was thus off limits to us. Fortunately, Isabelle and I had traveled through this area in 1973. Kashgar is a pretty city full of history and charm. We also visited the former pre-1914 "consulates" of Russia and Great Britain—odd places—that had been active centers for espionage and intrigue between the two powers, which watched each other carefully and fought each other for control of the region.

Throughout the trip, I talked about everything—the past, Marxism, international and Chinese politics—with Chinese colleagues. But, as almost always in China, at exactly twelve noon, regardless of the interesting discussion, we had to stop. At midday, it was time to eat. The Chinese stopped all activities, whatever it might be. Extremely fond of food, for them there was nothing that could justify being late—for example, there was a terrible risk that the food might get cold. And during the meal, it was forbidden to talk of anything other than the food. You tasted, commented, critiqued. The interrupted discussion was only resumed once the meal was over—starting from the middle of the last sentence uttered before we ate, I noted with amusement.

In Kashgar, I had a strong urge to climb up the Pamirs. Peaks of more than 7,000 meters surrounded us. I discussed at length a car trip by the highway that led to Pakistan. There was almost insurmountable resistance by the Chinese with all possible and imaginable pretexts. The fears were not political—the highway was open to commerce and tourism—but simply the expression of the incredible fear the Chinese (in this case, peasants from rice-growing plains) had of high mountains: there were landslides, it was too cold, the road was too dangerous, etc. But I was stubborn and succeeded in getting what I wanted: a car and a driver. A Chinese accompanied me the whole trip—three or four hours of a steep climb, the same amount of time to go back down—seated next to me, eyes closed, paralyzed with fear! The Chinese soldiers at the last stop before the pass leading to Pakistan laughed—as I did—rousing him, saying "it's over" and giving him some tea, which he drank with shaking hands, without daring to look at the incredibly beautiful peaks. I believe he will never forgive me for having persuaded him to accompany me!

Xinjiang is an autonomous province, originally inhabited exclusively by Muslim Turkic-speaking Uyghurs, today living next to Chinese immigrants who are dominant in the vast areas opened to agriculture by large-scale irrigation works. This coexistence is not without problems and I am not one of those who deny its reality. The administration is certainly often arrogant in its behavior, but that is just as much the case in China proper. Even though as many Uyghurs as Hans carry out administrative work in Xinjiang, it is certainly experienced as "Chinese" by the majority of indigenous inhabitants. The progress achieved thanks to the government, in education and health, although it has made it possible for this people to escape from incredible poverty and terrible (so-called feudal) forms of exploitation, does not always compensate for offended nationalism. Most of the Western visitors who were part of our caravan endlessly protested and straight-out insulted the Chinese, whom they treated as imperialists. This was unbearably arrogant, all the more so since some of them were visibly intelligence agents of the real imperialist powers. I found this same behavior from the defenders of the "rights of peoples" in Soviet Central Asia and Mongolia.

The official who was in charge of our caravan was himself Uyghur. He had studied Arabic in Damascus and spoke it perfectly—with a pronounced Syrian accent. (In Nanjing, I met a Chinese woman who had studied Arabic in Cairo and spoke *baladi*, or "native" or "local" Egyptian Arabic, to perfection; she had even adopted the appearance of an Egyptian woman! The official did not know any Western language (he spoke only Chinese, Uyghur, Russian, and Arabic) and that made a good number of the Westerners in the caravan furious. "So, you don't speak any foreign languages?" "Well, yes, for us, Arabic and Russian are foreign languages." I discussed with him, and other Chinese, the problem of Xinjiang without the least discomfort. I told them what I really thought. I did not defend Chinese policies "unreservedly," but, on the contrary, expressed my fear that the government was incapable of resolving the national problem in Xinjiang and Tibet correctly. Yet I remained completely hostile to Western views that support the "separatists" of these two countries. The government of the People's Republic has freed the Tibetans and Mongols from a slavery (in the proper sense of the word) that supported the ruling class of Buddhist monks (the Dalai Lama in the lead). Just like earlier, the "democrats" of the West supported the Islamists in Afghanistan, today they are instruments in the U.S. hegemonic strategy of attempting to break up China. The interests of peoples have nothing to do with it. The U.S. hegemonists have proven that point themselves, with their unconditional support for the worst regimes—the most criminal imaginable. Their rhetoric about "democracy" and "rights of peoples" has no credibility. The possible independence of Tibet and Xinjiang would inevitably end in unbelievable social regression and a strategic (perhaps even military) takeover of these countries by the United States. This is the actual aim of the strategy pursued by Washington and its European and Japanese allies.

*Former Soviet Central Asia*

Our visit to Soviet Central Asia took place in quite different conditions. This was in July 1991, one month before the attempted coup d'état against Mikhail Gorbachev, his defeat, the collapse of the government, and the breakup of the USSR. The UNESCO caravan had departed from Merv, last stop of the Turkmen nomads, gateway to the Silk Road leading to Persian Khorasan with its historic cities of Mashhad and Nishapur. Having left Paris late, Isabelle and I joined the caravan in Khiva by plane via Moscow.

Traveling on acceptable roads in a caravan of autos, we visited historic cities: Khiva, Bukhara, and Samarkand. These cities were certainly interesting—and beautiful in their way. Our colleagues, Russian and other Soviet historians, were very likable and the best guides one could have. The discussions they led at the sites we visited, and above all later in the evening at the hotel, were of the highest quality. Having read the best Russian and Soviet works on the region and its history translated into French or English, I always had questions to pose. I believe I received the best answers possible. Renovation of the monuments was impressive, too much in a way, since some of them—notably Tamerlane's gigantic constructions in Samarkand—were practically redone. Although these renovations had scrupulously respected the originals, the impression they gave is of something "too new." I only saw something similar in Luxembourg where the—superb—old city has been renovated so well, so properly repainted, that the impression given was that of an "imitation" of an old city recently constructed, which was not the case. But, as impressive as these monuments were, they remain—to my taste—a little too much like a "caravanserai," having borrowed their styles here and there. They did not have the subtlety of the Persian monuments of Qom, Isfahan, and Shiraz. These Central Asian monuments embodied the relationship that existed between the culture of the Turkic nomads and the Persian source of its inspiration: the same thing, but less delicate.

From Samarkand, we branched off to the south, toward Amu Darya (Oxus River), which we met at Termez, the gateway to Afghanistan, that is, the ancient Bactria of Alexander the Great, later the Kushan state, hub of Persian-Indian-Chinese relations. This was the setting of the route of the "Iron Gates" traveled by Alexander, all the more impressive since a violent storm accompanied us the whole length of this part of the journey. The long discussions that followed helped me to realize the importance this region had in the pre-capitalist past, and made me understand why Transoxiana—the Khorezm of Islamic civilization—which is always wrongly thought of as a semi-barbarous periphery of the Caliphate of Baghdad, produced many thinkers—philosophers and scientists—of the highest quality.

Traveling back toward the north, we reached Dushanbe, the Tajik capital huddled up against the feet of the Pamirs—a modern, Soviet-style city of no great interest—and then descended down to the garden-like Ferghana Valley from Kokand.

Despite the best efforts of Doudou Diène and the entire efficient and friendly UNESCO team, the trip's organization was chaotic. Everyday we left very late—two hours or even more. Something was always missing: fresh water, gasoline, a driver, two guides, or three papers. Soviet-style. Consequently, we obviously always arrived everywhere late—but whatever. People at our destination either waited for us or did not do so. The "plan"—always extremely detailed and distributed at the outset—was continually revised. That reminded me of my Syrian friend Shalaq's witty remark, which, in turn, reminded me of an Arab proverb: All action is made according to a plan, but the plan is improvised! At dinner, it was always the same "surprise"—the same pilaf (fatty rice with mutton)—pompously offered to us as the delicious local specialty (the same specialty everywhere then!). It could be hot, cold, or reheated. But when you were hungry, it was edible. The Chinese would never dream of traveling without a cook (professional or advanced amateur). The Russians, on the contrary, hardly ever think of these things. Many others think of them even less than they do.

Notwithstanding this, Soviet Central Asia was not the hell that the contemporary dominant media wanted us to believe. It takes a remarkable degree of bad faith to conveniently forget that, in 1917, Russian Central Asia was more destitute and squalid than Bangladesh. Today it looks like a poor

Europe. But of course it is suggested that it should be compared to Germany to properly assess the socialist disaster! For more than a half-century, the most advanced regions of the USSR—Russia and Ukraine in particular—financed the improvement that, as relative as it was, should be credited to the system. The Western powers have done the exact opposite: they have never stopped pillaging their dependent peripheries. The Karakum Desert south of the Amu Darya and the Kyzylkum Desert between the latter and the Syr Darya are among the most arid regions in the world. Gigantic irrigation works have made their valleys into a new Egypt. Plantations of prickly shrubs and cacti, seeded by airplane along agricultural areas to protect them from drying winds, have transformed a large portion of the deserts we crossed into steppe. If any European colonialism could be credited with even 10 percent of such achievements in Africa, there would be no end of harping about its successes. Thus emphasis is systematically placed on the environmental destruction associated with this type of "development": too much water used by irrigation, which increases the drying up of the Aral Sea; too many chemicals used for agriculture; overfishing in the inland seas, etc. All of that is correct. It is also the case that the Soviet system completely ignored all considerations of this type. Moreover, it shared with capitalism this disregard for nature—in which it saw only a resource to exploit—which has been no less destructive in Japan or the northeastern United States. As a version of the development of what I call "capitalism without capitalists," the Soviet system did not sin from "too much socialism," but, on the contrary, by ignoring the principles of socialism. At the outset, it had to work under the conditions of a poor country. Consequently, it left striking images of ugliness, each of its large cities surrounded by a cemetery of all kinds of detritus, old material thrown there any old way.

Could it have been done differently or better? I believe so, and I think we should never stop trying to do better. That being said, it remains the case that without the irrigation works, the region would not be able to support the population that today makes up its nations. The reproach that Russian reactionaries now make to the Soviet regime is that it "spent" too much on Central Asia. On the political and social plane, Central Asia was certainly no better than the rest of the Soviet Union. The autocracy that predominated there, far from being the result of socialism, was instead its negation. But once again, we must not confuse a left critique of the system with the right critique offered by the dominant media.

The nationalities policy implemented in the region was not above suspicion. Great Russian arrogance was a reality. Yet the borders of the republics were designed not to create problems, as some would like us to believe, but to resolve them. These borders—purely administrative as in Yugoslavia— were not intended to become the borders of independent states. They could thus be designed to resolve different kinds of problems. Separating territories populated by Turcophone Uzbeks from Persophone Tajiks was aimed at ending their mutual hostility (all of Transoxiana was Persian and it was "Turkified" by a nomadic conquest that had not yet ended on the eve of the Russian Revolution). The alternative to these complicated borders (or enclaves as in Armenia and Azerbaijan) would have been the transfer of the populations involved (an attenuated way of saying ethnic cleansing). The complicated line of the borders did not hinder transportation, communications, and economic integration. It also did not prevent the creation of an immense state, like Kazakhstan, to give dignity to the unfortunate nomads of the steppe, even though much of its territory had already long been Russianized. It is the breakup of this region into five states that presents a problem and will present more tragic ones in the future.

It is not my intention here to discuss the new problems now confronting the peoples of the region due to the intervention of the United States and its attempt to control the region's petroleum resources. I shall only say that, in my opinion, the best and probably only acceptable solution—but it is far from being the only possible or even the most probable one in the immediately visible future—requires the reconstruction of a genuine Commonwealth of Independent States (CIS) and a rapprochement with Russia.

The journey through the region was, on all these levels, quite educational—at least for me. The tensions—quite visible (such as the absurd controls at the pseudo-frontiers of the era)—were mollified due to Doudou Diène's immense diplomatic skills, but also due to the efforts of many of our Soviet partners. There was an Uzbek politician—a member of the Communist Party at the time, as he had to be (today he would have to be in the government's party, always the same)—who was skillful and, well, nice. He was undoubtedly calculating, but relaxed, and called on us to get back into our vehicles by crying out in Russian "To your horses!" There was a driver who read *Les Rois maudits* (*The Accursed Kings*—translated into Russian, of course—a series of seven historical novels by Maurice Druon) during our long walks. How many drivers in the West would have the same curiosity?

## *Mongolia*

In the following summer, in 1992, Isabelle and I participated in the third stage of the Silk Roads program. From Ulan Bator, to where we flew via Beijing, we traveled through the western part of Mongolia to Kobdo. The outbound and return trips were by different routes—4,000 kilometers in all—the driving surface neither asphalted, of course, nor even covered with earth! No silk road ever passed through Mongolia. But, for diplomatic reasons, UNESCO had granted the request of this country to be part of the program. The trip was still interesting, though for different reasons, primarily to make the acquaintance of this unusual country.

Of the three teams, this was by far the worst organized; I would even go so far as to say that it was not organized at all. The fault certainly did not lie with UNESCO, but completely with the local authorities. The so-called communist government had just given way to a victorious "liberal" coalition in the first round of multiparty elections. Later, this same coalition would give way to a return of the former "communists."

Traffickers of all sorts, who had come to draw the quickest profit from economic "liberalization," had invaded the hotels in Ulan Bator. The reservations made for our caravan had not been honored. We were lodged in a sort of vacation resort for young people located about ten kilometers from the city. It was a nice place, although of limited comfort (shared bathrooms and showers, the water was rather cold than hot). Above all, there was the loss of time for those of us who wished to see more of the capital. We visited it all the same, of course. It was a Soviet-style city without any great architectural interest. But the end of our return trip coincided with a pseudo-national festival dedicated to the rehabilitation of Genghis Khan, who definitely would not be in favor with the Soviet regime. As a feudal conqueror, he represented what the revolution had aspired to combat. The new regime attempted to substitute legitimacy based on nationalism for the preceding one whose socialist values had exhausted their mobilizing potential. The "Genghis Khan celebration" was a grand spectacle of Mongol horsemen, superb on their small horses, dressed as during the era of the great Khan. It was a very beautiful spectacle certainly, but devoid of any political or social content.

We discovered that the country lacked tourist facilities to the extent that we would have to camp. A Canadian tent and a single blanket were given to each of us. The nights in Mongolia, even in summer, can be very cold. We discovered later that there was a supply of blankets, but that the Mongol staff had undoubtedly intended to steal them. After much grumbling and almost a revolt, we prepared to attack the truck where they were hidden. In the end, we were given extra blankets.

Everything was in keeping with this. The "field kitchen" was a real antique piece, which would have been at home in a military museum: it was a rolling cast-iron stove, equipped with a high chimney, fueled with wood and weighing I don't know how many tons. It must have belonged to an imperial army of the nineteenth century—Russian or Chinese! This field kitchen did not leave before us, it left with us, pulled by a truck. That meant that it would only join us at the campsite chosen for the day—two, three, or even five hours later. We then had to wait much of the night before being able to eat something, or wait to eat the evening meal for breakfast the next day.

It is actually not accurate to call it a meal. There was no proper cook, but simply a man (or woman) responsible for lighting the stove and boiling an old and poorly butchered sheep in the cauldron, garnished with some old cabbages. We had each been given a bowl at the outset, into which this disgusting "soup" was served—the only utensil we had for everything: eating, washing, brushing teeth, shaving, possibly even for use for other nightly needs. It was up to us to wash it in the stream not far from the campsite. A Swiss woman who was part of this adventure—what was she doing in this hell?—ultimately cracked up and cried, shouting: "I wouldn't give this to my dog to eat!" But eat it we did, since there was nothing else. Isabelle and I were the type of people who knew how to adapt to anything, or almost anything. In any case, we were more resistant than most. The "young people" in the group—pretentious journalists—looked at us scornfully at the outset. These old people would not hold up, they thought. But they were the first to complain of the difficulties imposed on them by their profession. A poor Indian journalist who was a vegetarian stoically ate biscuits for one month. She was a charming woman, full of humor, and also quite adaptable.

In China, I had eaten a delicious dish: a hotpot of mutton with legumes, spices, and other ingredients, accompanied by fine rice noodles. The dish was called the "Mongol pot." Upon returning to Beijing, I said to a Chinese friend that I had never eaten the "Mongol pot" in Mongolia. He told me that it was a dish from northern China. "So why is it called that then?" "The Mongols have never invented anything in culinary matters so it was necessary to attribute something to them," he responded. In any case, the Mongol "meal" in question was served—as soon as it was ready—at any hour and thus served as breakfast, lunch, or dinner. Many of us had taken the precaution of bringing along boxes of Nescafé and tea and some biscuits, which provided some relief from the everyday fare.

We traveled in three types of vehicles: U.S. jeeps, Soviet jeeps (GAZ), and ordinary (city) buses. This was the opportunity to discover the extraordinary qualities of Soviet equipment. These ordinary buses went everywhere, climbed up rocky slopes at a 45-degree angle and crossed rivers, with the water rising up to our feet in the vehicle! It was continually necessary to repair the sophisticated U.S. jeeps, even tow them, but obviously in the buses the seats were of wood and the backs were rigid.

The Mongols who accompanied us were not particularly interesting people, fairly ignorant. Half of them got drunk on vodka beginning in the morning, shouted and groaned, sometimes violently quarreled. The "chef" himself did not display any exemplary sobriety. Toward the evening, when it was time to look for a campsite, our Mongol "guides" were only relatively helpful. All of that would have turned into drama without Doudou Diène's extraordinary competence. Setting up the tents took all the more time since we were not all, at the outset, experts in the activity. In any case, I was not. The country's climate was always extraordinarily violent and changed quite abruptly. One day we camped near a large and beautiful lake. There was beautiful weather, but then, all of a sudden, a wind of unbelievable power appeared. The lake was transformed into a stormy ocean. We tried to keep our tents upright, standing in front of their doors, firmly holding the pegs. Isabelle's tent, solidly anchored, held. But mine did not. The wind passed, the night came, and everything had to be redone.

On the scientific side, there was nothing comparable to the quality of information gathered in China and the USSR. The Mongol group did not include historians comparable to the Chinese or Soviets. Only one of them—an old "communist" in plain clothing who refrained from drinking—had something to say. I talked to him, then, in a sort of Anglo-Russian pidgin, occasionally calling on the few (and bad) interpreters. He was an administrator rather than a scientist, but he knew his country well, its problems and history. As far as the other foreigners were concerned, they were frankly mediocre. There was a West German woman—actually a specialist in Mongol history—who was reactionary enough to tremble with excitement over the worst stories of Genghis Khan's "conquests" and massacres. If she had been a little older, she would have reacted the same way to stories of the victories of Hitler's panzers. No doubt about it. There was also a stupid and ignorant American woman who probably would not have been able to find Mongolia on the map of Asia before the trip. What was she doing there? UNESCO had not rejected her application because, while the United States boycotted the organization, UNESCO fell over itself to indulge the Americans. This was a lame attitude. This American monopolized the use of a more comfortable U.S. jeep. There were a couple of quiet and unbearably egotistical English people. There was a very competent French musicologist—he is the one I mentioned earlier who perfectly imitated the Mongol songs—who was quite likeable. Also in the group was the charming Indian journalist I mentioned above. And, of course, there was Doudou Diène's secretarial team—Isabelle Moreno and others—who were remarkably polite and efficient. These friends made the trip, which could have been quite difficult, pleasant and enjoyable.

The impression I had of the modern society was that the progress achieved by the government that resulted from the 1920s revolution was rather modest, once the people were freed from the slavery in which the Buddhist church had held them. Of course, there was nothing democratic about the government. But the administration, as arrogant as it was, did provide some services, which abruptly disappeared with the capitalist "liberalization." No more schools, no more community clinics, even no more commercial services. The private sector did not take over from the abolished state trading enterprises, as anyone endowed with the least bit of good sense could have predicted. What is more, the stock farmers no longer found the minimum of essential products—a little tea, some matches, or oil for their lamps. In return, they no longer marketed the surplus from their herds. And to cap it all for this country that has many more goats, cows, and sheep than people, there was no more meat in the markets of Ulan Bator! Who can be surprised that the Mongols had reelected the former communists to lead their country? The misery caused by this disappearance of trade was attenuated a bit by the sudden appearance of itinerant Chinese traders—as in the eighteenth century (but it is better than nothing!). Thanks to one of them—who had spotted our caravan from far away and had rushed to join us—we were able to replenish our stock of tea and biscuits. In addition, I bought a magnificent and super warm down jacket that increased my comfort during the cold nights.

In spite of everything that I just wrote, Isabelle and I do not regret making this beautiful trip. The reward was worth the strain. The scenery was incomparably beautiful and difficult for me to describe. In any case, it was unmatched in many ways—the color of the Altai Mountains and of the sky, etc. There were herds of wild goats and herds of Asian camels (with two humps). All of that would be impossible to see without traveling thousands of kilometers off of any roads. But it was also the only way to get to know the Mongol people a little. It is well known that the Mongols are equestrians. But you have to see them living in their own environment to understand the unity of the man or woman and his or her mount, their shared life. There was a children's race (from five to six years old)—boys and girls seated on their horses, without saddles, their braids flying, covering fifty kilometers at full gallop. This is difficult to picture when you have not seen it. In the camps, we tasted cheese, hard as a rock, but so good after the daily fare of old mutton. Some appreciated the fermented mare's milk, but not I. Doudou Diène, in his capacity as a leader, was invited to eat sheep's tail—pure fat, no meat. This wealth of delicacies (for the Mongols) is, as one probably can imagine, rather repugnant, despite its utilitarian nutritional functions for the severe cold. Doudou submitted to this preferential treatment with incomparable self-control. As everywhere, human beings, behind their faces hardened by the conditions of their life, are nonetheless sensitive. A young Mongol running through the countryside returned carrying wild berries, which he offered to Isabelle. Another wanted to give her a wolf cub with which he was playing. Isabelle almost gave in, but there could be no question of crossing the frontiers with this wild animal.

There was much nature, but very little in the way of monuments. There were a few abandoned Buddhist monasteries that the new government was proposing to restore and revive. Most of our Western fellow travelers were enraptured by the Buddhas crammed into these monasteries and were indignant that they had been closed by the "communist terror." I was not the only one to be irritated—along with Isabelle—by these attitudes. Numerous Mongols—old and young—were no less so and reminded these Westerners that the monks who lived well without working held their people in slavery and subjected them to untrammelled exploitation; that their power had been overturned by a popular revolution; and that if the monasteries were closed it was because from the moment monks had been required to work in order to eat there were no more candidates to the monastic life.

The ruins of Genghis Khan's capital, Karakorum, are quite modest in size and do not compare with the dead cities of Xinjiang or with the vestiges of cities in Uzbekistan, which shows the modest role of Mongolia in history. There were large conquests to be sure, but short-lived. Marco Polo, who visited Karakorum in its heyday, made clear that the city had only thirty thousand or so inhabitants. This is also confirmation that the Silk Roads did not pass by there. Upon returning to Ulan Bator, we had the possibility during a brief meeting with critical intellectuals from the center for history (who had been excluded from the trip) to supplement a little—and more seriously—our information on the country.

### INDIA

There are very few other so-called emergent countries beyond China, if we exclude from the list the certificates of convenience issued by the World Bank. Due to their continental size, India and Brazil weigh heavily in the development of the international balance of power. South Africa, finally rid of political apartheid, already exercises a marked influence in southern Africa. Thailand and Malaysia and others are committed, it is said, to development paths that should not be reduced solely to the implementation of neo-liberal formulas.

India, like China, is a continental country that cannot be ignored if we are interested in the future of the world system. Fortunately, the Indian intelligentsia—dominated by the left in the broad sense of the term—has often produced high-quality analyses that are, moreover, easily accessible since they are published in English. A good number of these intellectuals are acquaintances or even personal friends, sometimes active in Forum networks, and it is always a pleasure to have a discussion with them. But I have always believed it necessary to supplement knowledge acquired in this manner with site visits. I thus give much importance to the impressions that I have retained from multiple trips to India during the 1970s, 1980s, and 1990s during which I visited some of its large cities (Delhi, Varanasi, Patna, Mumbai, Bangalore, Madras, Hyderabad, Kolkata, and their monuments and palaces, but also their slums) and also saw the countryside in the Ganges Valley and in the Deccan. Even if these visits were always relatively brief and certainly did not deserve to be called study trips, the fact of having often been accompanied by intellectuals of worth—the best guides possible—is an advantage from which most other visitors to India have not had the opportunity to benefit.

Current Indian society is, for me, totally unacceptable. I am certainly not one of those—numerous among Westerners—who admire Hinduism and its rhetoric on "nonviolence." I share the opinion of critical Indian intellectuals who emphasize the social disaster associated with the domination of the concept and practices of dividing society into castes. It is not my intention here to offer any sort of analysis of this fundamental dimension of India's history, culture, and social organization, as well as its relations to ancient and modern social classes and forms of exploitation, its interweaving with modern colonial development and contemporary peripheral capitalism, and its functions in the system of governments and in political life. An abundant and serious literature exists on all these subjects. I will only say that this cruel reality invalidates all rhetoric about nonviolence. Indian society is, in fact, particularly violent.

British colonialism bears major responsibility for the persistence of the caste system, unparalleled in the modern world. With its characteristic cynicism, British imperialism systematically reinforced the power of the traditional dominant exploiting classes—rajahs, zamindars, and others—and integrated them into the general system dominated by capital. Without such an alliance, it would have been impossible for the English to govern and exploit this immense country for their benefit. With their well-known hypocrisy, the British attempted to justify these villainous alliances by praising local "specificity," particularly the caste system, and "respect for traditions"—the worst, of course.

The result is that India presents scenes of human misery on a scale rarely seen elsewhere, except for Pakistan and, of course, Bangladesh. The rhetoric praising Indian "democracy" in contrast with its absence in China passes over this major fact in total silence. No statistic is necessary to know that, thanks to its revolution, China presents no comparable spectacle. It suffices to travel by road through the two countries—which I have done often—to be convinced of that, if one is honest. India's dreadful poverty is such that, during her first trip there in 1973, Isabelle found it difficult to bear the strong emotions produced by this spectacle. We were in Delhi in the summer, staying in a magnificent hotel (whose name I have forgotten), which was a veritable fortress, isolated from the real country. Leaving the hotel simply to see the city, we came across a child literally dying from hunger who grabbed my foot, imploring us for something. What could we do except flee from the scene, powerless, ashamed, and in tears. The next day, we took the plane to Kabul.

Such realities especially limit the meaning and impact of electoral democracy and the achievements made by the Indian national bourgeoisie, which founded and led the Congress Party. Here again, in contrast with the enthusiasm that most Third World anti-imperialist nationalists, including on the left, show toward the Indian ruling class, one of the leading lights of active nonalignment in the Afro-Asian world (and there are positive aspects to this stance, of course) Indian intellectuals have never been the victims of such blindness. By emphasizing, on the contrary, the class conflicts of contemporary India, the ambiguities of bourgeois nationalism in its relations with dominant international capital, these intellectuals have often been more perspicacious than most of India's "admirers," both Westerners and Third World nationalists, anticipating long in advance the fatal consequences of the Congress Party's erosion: the rise of Hindu fundamentalism and regionalisms, the spread of corruption and the formation of mafia-like groups, and the pro-Western capitulation of the middle classes. Having had the opportunity to visit India frequently during the last three decades, I could see these changes spread almost physically in the change of style in successive generations of the ruling classes. The parents dressed in the traditional manner or in a plain Western style, ate Indian food, cultivated politeness, and hid their fortunes. The children arrogantly displayed their wealth and imitated the American middle classes in their style of dress, speech, and life.

Whereas the comparison between India and China is largely favorable to China—and consequently, we can only conclude that the "revolution has yet to be made" in India—the comparison between India and Pakistan is quite in favor of India. India of the Congress Party had chosen the principle of a secular, multinational state. Whatever the limitations in the implementation of this principle in the Indian social context, it nonetheless holds potential for changes in a favorable direction, in contrast with the impasse that the dogma of the theocratic state has made for Pakistan. Hindu fundamentalism itself is not—or not yet—comparable with the fundamentalism the "Islamist" ruling classes impose on Pakistan—and elsewhere. It is even, in large part, a reaction to the opposing fundamentalism. As I have already said, there are no Hindus in Pakistan (they were all expelled), but there are many Muslims in India (the majority of those who lived in what became India remained there). The Indian state has declared itself to be secular. Thus it does not prohibit the construction of mosques. Something I saw for myself is that in regions where the Muslim minority makes up less than 5 percent of the population that minority never hesitates to build mosques as large as possible, close to all the Hindu temples, and to install powerful speakers in them. Can you imagine the Christian minority in Egypt doing likewise? Even after protests by Hindu parties, the Indian government has always had only one response: the state is secular, religious communities have the right to build as many religious buildings as they want and where they want them.

Indian secularism is nevertheless threatened today by the Hindu right's access to the government. India was built on the principle of Bharatva (from the country's name, Bharat), a concept of citizenship-nationality affirming the community of nations and linguistic groups of the subcontinent. The right's intention is to replace that principle with the principle of Hindutva, which refers to the community of Hindus, thereby excluding Muslims and Buddhists. The left and a good part of the Congress Party have been fighting with determination against this "religious fascism." They succeeded in getting an inquiry into the massacres of Muslims in Maharashtra, which openly revealed the complicity of the administration. We can only compare with sadness the boldness of such an inquiry with the pusillanimity of the "denials" that the Egyptian authorities always produce during similar incidents in which Copts have been the victims.

What I have attempted to summarize in the few paragraphs above is not only the result of my impressions from traveling in India and from my readings. It is also the product of long discussions with numerous Indian intellectuals, taking advantage of the invitations that I frequently received from universities—especially Jawaharlal Nehru University in Delhi—but also from grassroots organizations, unions, the Communist Parties (both Marxist and Marxist-Leninist), particularly during the electoral campaign in February 1998, journals and reviews (*Economic and Political Weekly* in Mumbai, *Frontier* in Kolkata), or publishers (Rainbow Publishers, for example). The list of my Indian interlocutors, who are often friends as well, is long.[34]

Hyderabad hosted the Asian Social Forum in January 2003 and Mumbai was the host for the World Social Forum in 2004. At the Hyderabad and Mumbai Forums, I was impressed by the strength of the grassroots organizations that participated (unions, peasant organizations, associations of dalits—the "untouchables"—in other words, something other than NGOs!), as well as by the scope of the debates and the seriousness of the participants. India will certainly be at the center of the reconstruction of a front of Asian and African peoples.

India is also, as everyone knows, rich in historical remains and varied, sometimes fabulous, natural scenery. Isabelle and I took the opportunity to see everything tourists should see in Delhi and the surrounding region, particularly the Taj Mahal in Agra, but also the first foothills of the Himalayas in Himachal Pradesh on the road to fabulous Srinagar, capital of Indian Kashmir. The Ganges Valley that we traveled through by train, making sure to stop at the important places—Allahabad, Varanasi, Patna—looked a lot like the countryside of the Nile Delta in Egypt. There was the same richness of the soil, same types of crops, same alarming population density, same abysmal rural poverty in the villages, although considerably even more terrible in India (due to the agrarian reforms of the Nasserist regime, many sights of the past have disappeared), hordes of beggars, children with trachoma-infected eyes, men and women in rags, cripples and lepers, just like I remembered from my childhood.

From Hyderabad to Bangalore, we traveled across the Deccan by automobile. The scenery here was totally different than in the north, reminiscent of the Sudanian savannah of West Africa. The villages gave the impression of being a little less poverty-stricken. The architectural vestiges of the past were quite different. In the north, there were Mongol remains and the styles imported by the ruling class of the Muslim government—mosques and forts. In the south, Hindu temples abound. I was not very receptive to their style—the architecture was not really to my liking, too often overloaded with mediocre sculptures. But I must say that some of these great temples—Lapakshi, some sixty kilometers north of Bangalore, the one in Mysore, a few in Madras—were very pleasing due to the blend of stone (here with beautiful sculptures) and the invading tropical vegetation.

Hyderabad was an interesting city, notably the ruins of the old dead city. Bangalore, like Madras, offered the pleasant spectacle of a somewhat organized urban area, unusual in the Indian subcontinent. Apparently, Pondicherry, on a small scale, and Goa, on a larger one, were built according to actual plans (I have not, however, had the pleasure of seeing these cities). The British did not accomplish anything like that. They always neglected "indigenous" towns and cities, treated with the greatest contempt. The small number of colonists isolated themselves in the "suburbs," wealthy in terms of their residences, but always horrible in their lack of taste and racist arrogance. Bangalore—at least the city center—was clean and tidy. This was also an exception in India.

And I must admit that, for many reasons—the temperament of the people, less poverty perhaps, and the filth was not as predominant—I like southern India better than northern India. Mumbai must be seen. Economic capital of the country—the Shanghai of India—Mumbai was the only large Indian city that immediately plunged you into an urban atmosphere, not into an enormous village. Its dominant comprador class, just like its English administrators, lacked fine tastes and the mixture of the two have given the horrors of what I call "the Bushir and Company" style to products spread across the Gulf region, the Sea of Oman, and the coast of East Africa. The pleasant corniche was worth a look. There was a more active cultural life in Mumbai than elsewhere—including Delhi. Thanks to my Indian friends, I had the chance to drink a beer or had a bite to eat in several of the "cafés," not well known to foreigners, where original, unconventional, and interesting artists, poets, filmmakers, journalists, and politicians gathered. In Delhi, social and cultural life was more stilted. Perhaps this was so because it was the capital, or maybe it was a difference in temperament.

Guest House International held way too many events and symposia—to its benefit, of course—including those in which I participated, such as the meetings of Forum work groups. Nevertheless, I appreciate the comfort provided by this institution, compared with the dilapidated guesthouses at the universities!

### *India: A Great Power?*

I give particular importance to the presence of our WFA and TWF networks in India, for obvious reasons. This presence is facilitated by the quality and number of our Indian friends who actively participated in our meetings, just as we frequently participated (and I do personally) in meetings they organized in Delhi, Kolkata, and elsewhere in India. I shall consider here six large meetings in which we participated between 2000 and 2013. Some of the participants were: Amiya Bagchi (Vice President of the World Forum for Alternatives), Jayati Ghosh (who heads the IDEAs network at the Jawaharlal Nehru University in Delhi, one of my best sources of information for critical economic analysis), Ahmad Ayjaz, Sunandra Sen, Seema Mustafa, Prabhat and Utsa Patnaik, the late Vinod Raina, and many others. I should also mention the Secretary of the WFA, P. K. Murthy, the director of Action Aid, Sandeep Chachra, Indian publishers that distribute our works, and the Indian communist parties (CPI-M and various branches of the former CPI-ML). I presented the following text during these meetings and took into account as much as possible the observations it provoked:

Having already passed the mark of a billion inhabitants and showing economic growth rates better than the world average, India has quickly been ranked among the rising powers of the twenty-first century. I have doubts on this conjecture.

The reason for these doubts lies in the decisive importance that I give to the fact that independent India has not dealt with the major challenge with which it is confronted: radically transforming the structures it inherited from colonial capitalism. British colonialism essentially transformed ancient India into a dependent agrarian capitalist country. To this end, the British systematically constructed clear-cut forms of private property in agricultural land that excluded access to it by the majority of the peasantry. These forms made possible the formation of large properties dominant in the north of the country, and were more favorable to the medium-sized properties of a relatively well-to-do peasantry in the south. The majority of the peasants found themselves transformed into members of a poor peasantry, practically without land. The price paid for choosing this "capitalist path" of agricultural development is the incredible poverty that afflicts the vast majority of the Indian people. Indian communists originally predicted that this heritage would be called into question and included a radical agrarian reform in their program ("the land to those who work it"—in practical terms, to all the peasants). The bourgeois in the Congress Party never made such a reform. In India, progress is blocked by this colonial heritage and reinforced by the effects of the persistence (worsened in some ways) of the ideology of castes. The "lower castes" (today called the dalits) and the assimilated (tribal) populations account for a quarter of the population (around 250 million people). Deprived of all rights, in particular access to the land, they form a mass of quasi-slaves that are the collective property of the "others." Their inferior status, somewhat analogous to that of the Helots in ancient Sparta, allows others to draw from this mass of available workers those they need for a particular task and a particular period of time, paying them a pittance. The persistence of this condition reinforces the reactionary ideas and behaviors of the "others," and encourages the exercise of power by and for the benefit of the privileged minority, and contributes to attenuating, even neutralizing, the possible protests of those of the exploited—the majority—whose status places them between the exploiters (the minority) and the oppressed of dalit status.

Of course, British colonialism had refrained from questioning this organization, hiding behind the hypocritical pretension of "respecting traditions" (which the English had not respected when it was convenient to them, such as when they privatized landed property!). The governments of independent India have continued this tradition. The Hindu right, of course, has nothing to say on the subject. The United States—by means of NGOs that "defend human rights"—attempts to manipulate the protests of the dalits in the same way and contain them within harmless spaces to facilitate the overall management of capitalism. This situation is, perhaps, on the way to being surpassed by the radicalization of struggles, particularly the "Naxalite" Maoist peasant insurrections. These insurrections have certainly been defeated in the sense that they have not succeeded in establishing and stabilizing popular power in liberated regions. They have nonetheless initiated a qualitative leap in challenging both the property structures inherited from colonialism and the organization of castes and, in that sense, could perhaps be only a prelude to future revolutionary mobilizations. The sudden emergence of dalits on the political scene, a major social occurrence of the last two decades, is undoubtedly a result of Naxalism, at least in part.

The Congress governments of independent India implemented a national project that suffered from the ambiguities of the liberation movement itself. This project claimed to be anti-imperialist, and it was in the sense that modernization and development required national liberation beforehand. But it stopped there and believed it possible to impose on the dominant world system—globalized capitalism—the adjustments indispensable for Asian and African nations to assert themselves as equal partners in this system and, by this means, gradually overcome the handicaps of their "delay." The communists have often expressed a clear awareness of this contradiction and the limitations that it imposed on the possible achievements of the system. But, for various reasons, among others the influence of the Soviets (the "non-capitalist path"), the majority of communists in Asia and Africa ended up offering more or less "critical" support to the national populist projects. The fissure created by the opposition between Maoists and the Soviets sometimes attenuated the scope of this support, particularly in Asia. In this context, the Indian communists (the CPI-M as well as the Maoist CPI-ML) have, as a whole, kept their distance from the Congress Party's national populist project.

Despite its limitations, the successes of India's national populist project under Jawaharlal Nehru and Indira Gandhi were not negligible, on the economic as well as political levels. Colonialism had, from the beginning, carried out a systematic deindustrialization of India—then quite advanced—to the benefit of an industrializing Great Britain. Independent India thus gave first priority to industrialization. This was systematically designed to a certain extent, at least during the first plans under the Nehru governments, and combined private Indian large industrial capital with public sector companies, which were promoted to make up for the inadequacies of the productive system inherited from colonialism, and to speed up growth and strengthen basic industries. The project was capitalist as a whole, in the sense that the relations of production and the technologies selected did not call into question the fundamental logic of capitalism. But it could be said that, in this sense, the experiences of really existing socialism (including China) were not that different, despite the exclusivity of public property. The Indian project was, all the same, less radical in the sense that the degree of delinking its productive system from the dominant world system was less systematic than it was in the USSR or China, where wages and prices—planned in principle—were actually detached from any comparison with those of the world capitalist system. This characteristic of the Indian project—which is found in the other non-communist national populist experiences (in the Arab world, for example)—was closely linked to the fact that the social structures inherited from colonialism were not called into question.

These differences between Indian national populism and Chinese communism account for the visible differences in the results allowed by each model. The rates of growth of industrial and agricultural production in India were not, at the time, "bad": they were much higher than they had been in the colonial era, and were above the world average for postwar capitalism at the time in a phase of rapid expansion. But they remained, in broad terms, below those of China. Moreover, while Chinese growth was accompanied by an obvious improvement in living standards for most of the working classes, that was not the case in India, where growth exclusively benefited the new middle classes—a minority, even though they grew in numbers to the point of rising from 5 to 15 percent of the total population of the country in thirty years—while the poverty of the majority working classes remained unchanged, even marginally worsened.

Liberal rhetoric ignores all these fundamental facts. That is why I do not subscribe to the "optimistic" conclusions that many "futurologists" have drawn: India will be on the way to achieving accelerated growth that will raise it to the status of a modern great power, like China. China retains up to now the advantage of the heritage of its radical revolution whereas India is saddled with the handicap of its heritage from a colonialism that has not been called into question.

Of course, independent India's political successes are not unimportant. India is, unlike China, a multinational country and British colonialism had succeeded in imposing its power only by exploiting the diversity of Indian peoples (and states). The success of the national liberation movement in this area, unparalleled elsewhere in the colonial world, is to its credit. The movement actually succeeded in uniting the ten or so large nations of which the country is composed into a single "nation." It is not important that the label given to this nation, "Bharat," from which the concept of Bharatva, or "Indianness," is derived, might be debatable from a scientific (or para-scientific) viewpoint. India is now a nation, the lived reality of which prevails over all its components. Up to now, the feeling of belonging together has won out over the assertion of local identities (linguistic, among others). The national liberation movement suffered only one setback, and that was in its desire to include Muslims in the creation of the new Indian nation. Here the British succeeded in foiling the Indian national project and forcing the creation of the artificial states of Pakistan and Bangladesh. Yet it remains the case that the Muslims who remained in India (around 15 percent of the total population), even if sometimes they appear to "pose problems" (problems that the Hindu culturalists exploit, when they do not provoke them), are properly integrated in all aspects of the social and political life of the country. The secularism of the Indian state, which even the Hindu culturalist wave has not succeeded in calling into question, lies behind this success. The comparison between the behavior of governments and the majority Indian society with regard to their Muslim "minority," and the behavior of Muslim-dominated governments and societies (with regard to their Christian minorities, for example), demonstrates the positive importance of secularism, a democratic advance that is not found in other regions of the world (in the Arab and Muslim world in particular). Undoubtedly, this overall positive judgment could be qualified. The repression of Sikh demands (which cost Indira Gandhi her life) and the Kashmiri mess demonstrate the limitations of the system's capacity to manage "national questions" properly (even if they are described as something else). But it remains the case that the Delhi governments have found ways to correctly manage problems with all the great nations of the "Indo-Aryan" north and the Dravidian south, and consequently give a solid reality to federal unity (which is much more centralized than the terms of the constitution would lead you to believe). The experience of contemporary India demonstrates the indisputable superiority of the democratic option and the hollowness of arguments in favor of supposedly more effective autocratic management. That is the case despite the obvious limitations and the class content of both bourgeois democracy in general and its actual practice in India. This option, to the credit of the national liberation movement (the Congress Party and the communists), was probably the only effective means to manage diverse social and regional interests—even if they be limited to those of the privileged classes—and bring about popular support for the project of the minority making up the hegemonic bloc.

On the international plane, independent India attempted to give substance to the "front of the South" in the Non-Aligned Movement that came out of the Afro-Asian conference in Bandung (1955) without allowing its border conflict with China to call this openly anti-imperialist strategy into question.

The erosion of the national populist project necessarily had to happen in India as elsewhere for the same reasons: the specific limitations and contradictions of this project. This erosion and the delegitimation of the government that accompanies it have given an opportunity to obscurantist forces to launch an offensive, supported by the dominant comprador class and a large portion of the middle classes (as soon as their expansion slowed down or even gave way to growing difficulties), encouraged by the rhetoric (and maneuvering) of U.S. imperialism. In India, these obscurantist illusions have a name: Hindutva. This term designates the claim that priority should be given to adherence to the Hindu religion in defining the "authentic identity" of the country's peoples. It is opposed to the concept of Bharatva, which refers to the nation. Of course, the assertion of Hindu identity in question does not entail calling into question the colonial heritage in the areas of landed property and respect for the hierarchies of caste. In this sense, as Indian communists have continued to point out, the obscurantist illusions perfectly serve the interests of comprador power and imperialism. The "specificities" that they liberally sprinkle throughout their "para-national," even para-anti-imperialist rhetoric, are completely empty. They encourage a revival of communitarian practices (here anti-Muslim) that the colonial government had used in its time to deal with the rising aspirations for a unified, modern, democratic, and secular national liberation. Nothing in this context distinguishes this regression from that which affects other societies in the periphery that are victims of the same erosion of the populist national project, in particular Arab and Muslim societies. The parallel with political Islam is striking.

The construction of a socially progressive alternative as part of an authentic alter-globalization remains difficult. It will be a long march. For India, building such an alternative necessarily implies that adequate responses be given to four challenges, even if only gradually.

First challenge: provide a radical solution to the peasant problem, based on recognition of the right of all the country's peasants to have access to the land in the least unequal conditions possible, which implies, in turn, abolition of the caste system and the ideology that justifies it. In other words, India needs to accomplish a revolution as radical as the one that occurred in China (!), or at least commit itself to major changes that move the country in that direction. Current peasant struggles are certainly not insignificant; the frequency, geographic extent, and violence of those struggles are visible. But they remain confused and pursue diverse and sometimes contradictory objectives. The best organized struggles, those that sometimes win victories or at least force the authorities to retreat, are those of the middle peasantry whose demands are clearly confined within the logic of capitalism and the market; these demands concern the management of prices and conditions of access to inputs and credit. Consequently, these struggles are often led by rich peasants, who are also victims, in the current phase, of the demands imposed by global capitalism, the comprador class, and the subservient state. The struggles of the poor and landless—including the dalits—still manifest themselves, on the whole, as explosions without any long-term strategy.

Second challenge: construct the unity of a labor front by bringing together segments of the relatively stable working classes and those that are in a more precarious position. This is a challenge common to all countries in the contemporary world, more particularly to countries in the system's periphery, characterized by the tremendous destructive effects of the new pauperization (massive unemployment, precariousness, growth of the impoverished informal sector). It must be recognized that the working-class organizations that the national liberation movement—including communists—had succeeded in mobilizing with some effectiveness, and which consequently formed the social base for the political forces of the older "left," are today confronted with a challenge of unprecedented scope. The social compromises of the past between capital, state, and fractions of the working classes (the unionized ones in particular) are today called into question by the offensive of imperialism and comprador elements, while new social structures have resulted in a loss of effectiveness by older forms of organization and action. Trade unionists, communists, and popular movement militants have the responsibility to open debate on these questions and invent new forms of struggle that will lead to advances in participatory democracy and make it possible to define together the steps of a joint strategy for the long term.

Third challenge: maintain the unity of the subcontinent and renew the forms of association of the different peoples that make up the Indian nation on reinforced democratic foundations. It is imperative to thwart imperialism's strategies that always pursue, beyond tactical choices, the objective of breaking up "large states," which are better able to resist imperialism than microstates.

Fourth challenge: articulate international political choices around the reconstruction of a "front of peoples from the South" (in the first place, the solidarity of Asian and African peoples) in conditions that, of course, are no longer those that existed during the formation of the Non-Aligned Movement in the Bandung era (1955–1979). First priority must be given in the current phase to defeating the U.S. project for military control of the planet. Also, Washington's political maneuvering, which aims at hindering a serious rapprochement among India, China, and Russia, must be thwarted.

The political and social forces that present an obstacle to India's commitment to the directions mentioned above are sizable. They form a hegemonic bloc that brings together one-fifth of the population—behind the large industrial, commercial, and financial bourgeoisie and large landowners are the great mass of rich peasants, the middle classes, and the upper ranks of the bureaucracy and technocracy. These 200 million Indians have been the exclusive beneficiaries of the national project as it has developed up until now. Doubtless, in the current moment of triumphant extreme liberalism, this bloc is breaking up under the effect, among other things, of the check put on the rising social mobility of the lower middle classes, threatened with casualization, even impoverishment if not pauperization. This conjuncture offers to the left the possibility of developing tactics—if it knows how to take advantage of the situation—likely to weaken the cohesiveness of these reactionary forces in general, and more specifically their comprador orientation as transmission belt for the domination of globalized imperialism. But it also offers opportunities to the Hindu right, in case the left fails.

It is often said in India that this "nation of 200 million individuals"—which alone forms a large market comparable in size to that found in several large European countries—represents the future of the country while the majority of 800 million miserable Indians is a millstone! This reactionary opinion, beyond its odious character (the poor should be exterminated), is completely stupid. The "privileged minority" has that status only because it has access to the exploitation of the country's resources and the over-exploitation of its workers, which make up the majority. The minority forming this bloc, then, is in a situation that excludes the possibility of reproducing in India a historical capital/labor compromise similar to the social democrat option of the developed West. The view that likens "peripheral Fordism" to the Fordism characteristic of the developed centers proceeds from a mistaken assessment of the import of each of these two situations: Western Fordism connects the majority of the working classes to the benefits of capitalist expansion whereas Fordism in the peripheries operates solely to the benefit of the middle classes. India is not the only example of this; Brazil and contemporary China are in similar situations. The fact that the cohesiveness of this hegemonic bloc is managed by political democracy as it is practiced in India does not attenuate its reactionary class nature. On the contrary, it is an effective means of asserting it. This hegemonic bloc is integrated into the logic of dominant capitalist globalization. Up to now, none of the diverse political forces through which this hegemony is practiced have called it into question. It can now be understood why the "Indian national project" remains fragile and vulnerable, ultimately incapable of achieving its self-assigned objective: to make India a "modern capitalist great power."

This vulnerability results in frequent opportunist behavior by the Indian political class, most often justified in terms of short-term *realpolitik*. This opportunism is not only destructive, in the long run, of conditions for constructing both a progressive national alternative and an alter-globalization that supports it, it also blinds its defenders to the extent that they lose sight of the vulnerability of Indian unity and the possible maneuvers of imperialism that aim at destroying it. There should be no illusions on this score. Even if today Washington's diplomacy chooses—for a moment and for tactical reasons—to "support India and its unity," its longer term project is to break up this large country and thereby destroy its capacity to become a great power. Subjection to the requirements of inclusion in global capitalist expansion reinforces centrifugal tendencies. This subjection accentuates the "regional" inequalities of development. Do we not already hear the "privileged" in Bangalore (favored by the expansion of new technologies) say that an independent Karnataka would derive greater profits from globalization than Karnataka as an Indian state?

Currently, there are elements of a sovereign policy in India, notably in the industrial policies of the private national industrial monopolies, supported by the state. But there is nothing more. General economic policies remain wedded to liberalism, dramatically accelerating the pauperization of the majority of peasants.

NEPAL

*Nepal 2008: A Promising Revolutionary Advance*

During our trips to India, Isabelle and I took the opportunity to take a few vacations in Kathmandu, Nepal's capital. A tourist hub in the Himalayas, it offers the most magnificent mountain scenery imaginable. The city has its charm, despite the grime. At the time, it was also the place where human wrecks from drug use came to live out the agony of what remained of their lives. Young people, boys and girls, hippies from Europe, the United States, and Australia, offered a sad spectacle: thin as cadavers with pale complexions, lying in filthy hovels, awaiting the end of their earthly journey.

I had always closely followed the struggle led by the Maoists in Nepal just as I had the Naxalites in India. Their strategy appeared to me to be the only one capable of responding to the central challenge: the peasant question, which is closely linked to the problem of the caste structure. Beyond the advances and retreats, and probably errors—as someone not involved in these struggles, I do not consider myself able to offer any judgment; to do so would appear as pure and simple arrogance—I saw no fundamental choice possible other than the one they chose: connect the peasant revolution with the abolition of castes. The victory won in Nepal thus appeared to me as the beginning of possibly significant revolutionary advances, in that country as well as the Indian subcontinent. I thus responded immediately to the invitation from the political bureau of the CPN (Maoist) in 2008. In Kathmandu, I was received by Prime Minister Prachanda and by Chandra Prakash Gajurel, member of the political bureau, who subsequently participated in some of the meetings organized by the WFA/TWF. I was also able to make a general survey of the important questions confronting the country and the party, with the trade unions, peasant organizations (brought together by the Rural Reconstruction service), the Forum for Democratic Media, and the magazine *Red Star*.

I must say that the in-depth—and lengthy—discussions in which I participated, sometimes with leaders and sometimes with rank-and-file activists, taught me much more than I could have expected. But when, back in India—in Hyderabad, Delhi, and Kolkata—I attempted to continue these discussions, I most often encountered a wall of absolute refusal on the part of most, even among the leaders of the Indian CPI-M.

What follows is thus more a "mission report," which I submitted to the party leaders.

A liberation army that supports a widespread revolt of the peasantry reaches the gates of the capital where the people, in turn, rise up, drive away the royal government, and welcome as their liberator the CPN (Maoist)—the effectiveness of this revolutionary strategy no longer needs to be demonstrated. This is the most radical victorious revolutionary advance of our era and, as such, the most promising. Just imagine—for comparison—that the FARC of Colombia had succeeded in mobilizing the entire peasantry of the country (impossible to imagine), had coordinated their victory with an urban popular uprising chasing Uribe away from Bogotá (equally impossible to imagine), and were thus able to lead a new revolutionary government!

This victory in Nepal created the conditions for the initial success of a national, popular, and democratic revolution, characterized as an anti-feudal/anti-imperialist revolution by the CPN (Maoist) itself. The widespread urban revolt, combining the working and middle classes, forced all political parties to proclaim themselves to be "revolutionary/republican." That had never been what they thought several weeks earlier, before the Maoist victory, having made the choice of "peaceful struggle" and "reformism," placing their hope in "elections." The other communist party, the CPN (UML), had itself joined the reformist camp and denounced the "adventurism" of the Maoists.

The CPN (Maoist) deliberately chose to make a compromise agreement with the parties in question—the Congress Party of Nepal, the CPN (UML), and others—concluding that they had gained a minimum of legitimacy by their support for revolution, which could not be contested in the aftermath.

This compromise—described as a "peace accord" by the UN authorities that advocated it—transferred the responsibility for drafting the new republican, democratic, and popular constitution to a Constituent Assembly. The multiparty elections gave the Maoists first place in the formation of a victorious coalition (and thus confided responsibility for the reins of government to their leader, Prachanda). For the first time in the country's history, and in the history of the entire Indian subcontinent, authentic elected representatives of the people—poor peasants, informal urban workers, ordinary women—were seated in the Assembly.

### Future Major Challenges

The compromise agreement does not settle future problems; on the contrary, it reveals their full significance. The challenges confronting the revolutionary popular forces are huge.

#### 1. AGRARIAN REFORM

The peasant uprising resulted from a correct analysis of the agrarian question made by the Maoists. The strategic conclusions they drew from that analysis were also correct: the great majority of the peasantry, made up of the landless (often dalits in some regions of the country), overexploited tenant farmers, and poor, small property owners, could be organized into a united front and go over to the armed struggle, land occupation (including giving dalits access to the land, refused by the caste system in India), reduced land rents paid to property owners, etc. For these reasons, the uprising organized by the Maoists gradually spread throughout the country as its army inflicted defeats on the state's armed forces. But it is true that the moment the revolt in the capital opened the gates to the CPN (Maoist), the people's army had not (or not yet) succeeded in disintegrating the state's armed forces, strongly supported and equipped by the Indian government and the imperialist powers. In the current period of "compromise," two lines are advanced by the political forces represented in the Assembly: (i) the line defended by the Maoists—a radical revolutionary agrarian reform, guaranteeing access to the land (and to the means necessary to live on it) to all of the poor peasantry (the large majority), without yet touching the property of rich peasants; and (ii) the imprecise line defended by the other parties of a "moderate" reform, which would require, moreover, even before the law determines its contours, the return of the old order in the regions liberated by the peasant revolt.

## 2. The Future of the Armed Forces

Two armed forces coexist at the present time. This coexistence obviously cannot be continued indefinitely. The CPN (Maoist) suggests that the two should merge. Its opponents fear (they say so publicly) that such a merger might result in the soldiers of the state armed forces being "corrupted" by Maoist ideology (!), but they propose nothing, and dare not demand the dissolution of the people's army.

## 3. Bourgeois Democracy or People's Democracy?

This is a major question, and it lies behind all debates in the Constituent Assembly, in the political parties, in the people's organizations of peasants, women, and students, in the unions, and in various associations in which the politicized sections of the middle classes are mainly found. There are defenders of the conventional view of democracy, reduced to the existence of multiple parties, elections, the formal separation of powers (the independence of the judiciary, among other things), and the proclamation of fundamental human and political rights. This is, moreover, the general formula in which the dominant ideology on the world scale, relayed by the major media (including those of the Western countries), attempts to confine the debate. The Maoists observe that the fundamental rights on which the proposed "democracy" is based place respect for private property at the top of the hierarchy of so-called human rights. In counterpoint, the Maoists defend the priority of social rights without the effective implementation of which no social progress is possible: the right to life, food, housing, work, education, and health. Private property is not "sacred." Respect for it should be limited by the requirements for the implementation of social rights. In other words, some defend the concept of democracy separated from questions of social progress (the bourgeois and dominant concept of democracy), whereas others defend the concept of democracy linked to social progress.

The debate in Nepal is not confused, but it is often polemical. The defenders of Western-style democracy include in their ranks authentic reactionaries who, even yesterday, hardly protested against royal autocracy, or were content with minor protests, hoping ultimately to be more favored by the autocracy. But they also include in their ranks undoubtedly sincere democrats who are not very attentive to the real miseries the working classes suffer. The NGOs that defend democratic rights, mobilized en masse within this context, and are widely supported from outside the country, speak on behalf of the "moderate" cause. Some are content to say that conventional and limited democracy is better than nothing, as if more are impossible. Others impugn the motives of the Maoists, calling them "inveterate communists," "Stalinists," "totalitarians," imitators of the Chinese autocratic model, and the like.

The Maoists do defend themselves rather well in the face of these pernicious attacks. They remind their critics that they do not challenge the private property of peasants, artisanals, or even capitalists, whether national or foreign. However, this stance would not prevent nationalization if national interest demands it (for example, prohibiting foreign banks from imposing integration of the country into the globalized financial market). They challenge only "feudal" landed property, whose beneficiaries had been clients of successive kings, authorized to dispossess peasant communities. They do not challenge personal rights or the independence of the judiciary charged with guaranteeing respect for them. In fact, they wish to add to this program, without reducing it to those additions, by inviting the Constituent Assembly to formulate not only the broad principles of social rights, but also the institutional forms necessary for their implementation. The people's democracy that they define in this way remains, of course, something to be invented gradually through the intervention of both the self-organized working classes and the state.

Obviously, there is no "guarantee" that protects the future from the risks of slipping either into an autocracy of state power or, equally possible, an opportunist alignment on what appears to be "possible" for the moment, thereby showing support for the "moderate" line of their competitors. But by what right should experimentation be condemned in advance when it is well known that the questions raised here are the focus of a serious debate within the party, where multiple opinions are accepted? The Maoists of Nepal have developed an innovative view of the question of socialism. They abstain from reducing the "construction of socialism" to the achievement of all aspects of their current program, that is, radical agrarian reform, people's army, people's democracy. They describe this program as "national popular democratic," opening the way (but no more) to the long (possibly centuries long) transition to socialism. They do not use the expression "socialism of the twenty-first century."

## 4. THE QUESTION OF FEDERALISM

The extreme diversity of Nepal's peasant communities expresses the diverse physical and human geography of the Himalayan valleys. It is not a question of two, three, or four ethnicities, but of a hundred communities, certainly related by language (Nepali or Tibetan) and religion (Hindu or Buddhist), but nevertheless proud of their distinctive characteristics. The peoples of these communities want (i) to recover the use of their lands, which was expropriated by the supporters of conquering generals serving the kings; (ii) recognition of their dignity; and (iii) equality of treatment. But they harbor no aspiration for secession. The federal republic system, advocated by the Maoists, can certainly meet the demands of the Nepalese peoples. It nonetheless carries the danger of being used by opponents of the central government, if need be.

## 5. The Question of the Country's Economic Independence

The United Nations classifies Nepal in the category of "less developed countries." The "modern" administration of the state and social services, as well as the infrastructure, consequently depend on foreign aid. The current government is aware, it seems, of the necessity of freeing itself from this extreme dependence. But it knows that this can only be done gradually. Food sovereignty is not the major problem in Nepal, although self-sufficiency in this area is associated with often-deplorable food rations. The organization of more efficient and less costly marketing networks for peasant producers and urban consumers is, on the contrary, a problem because it involves the interests of intermediaries. The organization of small-scale production (half-artisanal, half-industrial) capable of reducing dependence on imports will require difficult work and time to produce acceptable results. Maoist views on an "inclusive" model of development, that is, benefiting the working classes directly at each of the stages of its deployment, as opposed to the "Indian" model of growth associated with an "exclusive" social model—benefiting only 20 percent of the population and condemning the other 80 percent to stagnation, if not pauperization—is evidence of a principled choice that one can only support. Its translation into effective implementation programs has yet to be worked out.

### Who Will Prevail?

Revolutionary Nepal must deal with the fierce hostility of India whose ruling class fears spillover effects. The endemic revolt of the Naxalites could, drawing upon the lessons learned from the victories achieved in Nepal, seriously challenge the stability of current modes of exploitation and oppression in the Indian subcontinent.

This hostility should not be underestimated. It is one of the reasons for the military rapprochement between India and the United States. India is capable of mobilizing considerable material and political resources. Among other things, it is financing the formation of a political Hindu "alternative" on the model of the Indian BJP, similar to the political Islam in Pakistan and elsewhere, or the political Buddhism of the Dalai Lama and others. Support from the United States and other Western powers—particularly Great Britain— is focused on these reactionary projects. A powerful Nepalese political Hinduism would have an opportunity to crystallize if the achievements— even modest—of the new Nepal began to stagnate for too long. Outside intervention could then also mobilize Nepali reactionaries and even provoke "secessionist" movements. The use of foreign aid, always conditional even if it is not acknowledged, and the demagogic rhetoric on "human rights" and democracy, supported by NGO networks, have a role in the enemy's strategy.

The current compromise delays the implementation of the radical reform program that lies behind the popularity of the Maoists. It tends to encourage a certain willingness—in the ranks of the political leadership itself—to be content with what the compromise allows, thereby preparing the terrain for the reactionary counteroffensive. But there is no reason to despair. The Maoists repeat publicly that the working classes have the right to remain mobilized and continue their struggle to achieve their program, whatever the results of deliberations are in the Constituent Assembly. The Maoists have not fallen into the trap of electoralism. They carefully distinguish what they call their social base (social constituency), consisting of the majority (poor peasants, urban workers from the lower classes, students and youth, women, patriotic and democratic parts of the middle classes) from their electoral base (electoral constituency) that, like all electoral bases, fluctuates. To transform this grassroots social base into a dominant and organized social bloc as an alternative to the feudal-comprador bloc of the overthrown government is the objective of the long-term struggle of the CPN (Maoist).

I shall say no more about this. Of course, I follow changes in the situation as much as possible and take note of what might appear to be retreats, but I maintain my confidence in the future of the struggles in this beautiful Himalayan country. I shall not go into the two magnificent hikes that Isabelle and I made at the feet (at 3,500 meters!) of Annapurna and Everest.

## SRI LANKA

I was given an opportunity to become acquainted with Sri Lanka in 1976 when I was invited to the Non-Aligned Movement summit held in Colombo.

The Forum has always paid a lot of attention to the development of nonalignment, and the Secretariat of the Movement has frequently "consulted" us, whatever that term might mean. But, as is well known, the NAM has never succeeded in creating a permanent secretariat. Perhaps it has not wanted to do so to avoid the possibility of internal contradictions coming to light. From that point of view, perhaps it made a reasonable choice. But still, its ministerial conferences and summits have never been sufficiently prepared.

Some good national secretariats have more or less compensated for this weakness. This was the case with the Indian secretariat that, on several occasions, invited me to come and discuss some of the important problems of the moment. The latest, in February 1998, was a working session on the Southeast Asian financial crisis in which some of the most distinguished names in economic and political thinking in India participated. On that occasion, I offered a few points for consideration aimed at reviving the Movement by retaining its name, but supplementing it in order to adapt its meaning to the new situation: *Non-Alignment on Globalization*. I had had other opportunities to discuss these problems with Chinese leaders—a mixed group from the Academy, the Party, and the Government—in response to the question they had posed to me: is there a lowest common denominator that would make it possible to reconstruct a front of countries from the South (states and peoples) against U.S. hegemony? In Africa, Zimbabwe had earlier had responsibility for preparing one of the NAM summits. Nathan Shamuyarira, then Minister for Foreign Affairs, had invited me to discuss with him the Movement's "crisis" and the requirements needed to adapt to global changes.

The 1976 Colombo Summit was held soon after the Movement and the Group of 77 presented a proposal for a "New International Economic Order" to UN organizations, particularly UNCTAD. At that time, we had formed a discussion group within the new Forum—and in the IDEP—to which I had submitted a working paper. The NAM Secretariat had asked me to come to Colombo and present the content of this document to a group of experts and ministers charged, in turn, to inform the Summit about it. Indira Gandhi, who had come unexpectedly to hear the conclusions of the group—at the end of a long session of perhaps eight hours of discussions—had impressed me, and everyone else, I believe, as a politician of the highest intelligence. She asked three or four short but crucial questions, formulated on the spot, and offered two or three short but remarkable comments that brought out weaknesses or contradictions in speeches on the subject. This summit was, for me, extremely interesting because of what I was able to learn through discussions with various people. But the outcome could not have been other than the adoption of the "New International Economic Order" project. I considered the chances of its being accepted by the Western powers to be exactly zero. It was really no more than a pious hope, expressing the desire of the ruling classes in the periphery to see the capitalist centers adjust to the requirements of the peripheries' populist model, which was beginning to run out of steam. Unfortunately, history quickly proved me right on this point. In opposition to this strategic option, I proposed a program that emphasized internal reforms that expanded the space for action by the working classes, which could thereby strengthen the autonomy of the Third World and its capacity to negotiate with the North from a stronger position. I presented this proposal in terms that were the most acceptable for the audience.

I seized the opportunity of my invitation to prolong my stay in Sri Lanka and, after the summit, get to know the country's critical intellectuals. Most of them were aligned with the populist strategy of the country's left: "Openness [to the market] and accelerated growth (with a human face, as will be said later) combined with vigorous social programs (education and health in particular)." But already some saw the contradictions and limitations of this strategy, the risk of getting bogged down, which could lead to an explosion. History proved them right. Several years later, the "Sri Lankan miracle" (more a miracle of the World Bank that led to disaster) came to an end, and the ruling classes, hard-pressed, chose to divert popular protest by organizing the ethnic conflict from which the country has never recovered.

SOUTHEAST ASIA

## *Are They Emergent Countries?*

The functions given to some Asian countries are not different from those given to African colonies subjected to the pillage of their resources. Suharto's Indonesia was a colony for pillage, of its forest resources in particular, and post-Suharto Indonesia remains so today. The World Bank rhetoric that respectable growth rates associated with such pillage are indices of "emergence" is something of a bad joke. I do not believe that the fate reserved to countries that I know only from my readings (Myanmar, Laos, Cambodia) is any different.

The huge explosions of people's anger that chased out Suharto in Indonesia, Marcos in the Philippines, or Moussa Traoré in Mali have not changed anything. The working classes were not prepared to effectively face the challenges involved with getting their country out of its status as a pillage colony. But the major responsibility of public opinion in the wealthy countries of the West should not be glossed over. The dictatorships were supported until the very end by the imperialist powers and the criminal repression they carried out was never the subject of visible protests in Europe and the United States. After these dictatorships had been overthrown by their peoples, and them alone, the Western powers continued their economic, financial, and political interventions with the aim of maintaining these countries in their miserable status, using the World Bank, the IMF, and the European Union as intermediaries. This criminal policy has elicited no visible protest from the public, which has been taken in by the empty rhetoric of the newly arrived "democracy." Some ecologists point out, here and there, the negative effects on a global scale of the destruction of the natural resources in question. But we hear hardly more than that.

*Thailand*

In Thailand, I was greeted by a good team (Khien Theeravit, Suthy Prasartset, and others) in 1973. Thailand is certainly not exclusively a paradise of sexual tourism for Europeans, Americans, and Japanese, or just a country of magnificent beaches (where we spent some enjoyable days, I admit). It is also a country of an open, active, and combative people whose "Indochinese" culture—a mixture of civilizational elements from the west and the north—that I was able to begin to understand better thanks to my local friends. This mixture has been successful on some levels, in my opinion, but not so much on others, at least according to my personal taste and that of Isabelle. The palaces and groups of pagodas appeared over-ornate to us, a little like the "caravanserai" style! The canals are frequently admired in Bangkok, but not all visitors see the poverty of the people who travel about on them and often live there.

Despite the system's economic success—up to the financial crisis that struck in 1997—social inequalities have continued to worsen. And it can be seen. No statistic is necessary to convince you when you have visited the country on several occasions over the course of the last twenty-five years, as I have done. Traffic congestion is the biggest success of this "miracle." The city—charming in its own way, at the outset—is ruined by the construction of huge urban highways, as ugly as can be imagined, and made worse by aggressive advertising in U.S.-style bad taste. But these transportation routes surround islands of people abandoned to poverty—without streets or sidewalks worthy of the name. The bourgeois and "consumerist" middle classes—the social base of the regime—do not really care. They never travel on foot, always on the highways (despite the congestion) to go from the island fortress of their homes—palace villas for the wealthiest or blocks of flats available for those with middle-class incomes, protected by walls and armed guards—to another island fortress—the business district. That always takes hours, to the point that those traveling on the highways have invented a system of mobile toilets that can be transported in the vehicle!

Thailand—in spite of the horror of its dominant comprador bourgeois class—has sizable assets, in my opinion. It is a genuine nation that also has had the good fortune of never having been traumatized by colonialism. Thus there is no neurotic rhetoric about asserting "identity." There is a ruling class that does not hide its willing acceptance of the wealth offered to it by capitalism without, of course, granting any room for democratic values. There are the working classes who know perfectly well that they can expect nothing from the system and, to the extent possible, fight it. An intelligentsia that sides with the people is present, and has always been so in modern times. It has provided anti-fascist officers for the army, and leaders for the Communist Party and Maoist guerillas. It now provides cadres for a powerful democratic movement, which combines a critique of the capitalist options of the ruling class and of the regionally and globally dominant system with progressive social proposals and their democratic management.

It is probably the active presence of a modern and critical intelligentsia that explains the important place that the student movement continues to occupy in the life of the country, in contrast with the situation in most Third World countries, which are characterized by a strong political and cultural degeneration of the university and student world. The "financial crisis," which arrived in 1997, was not a surprise for the analysts of the Forum's working group. Seven years earlier, in a study published by our Forum, an analysis of the "miracle's" contradictions led to the prediction of a crisis that, up to the last detail, was subsequently confirmed. I am certainly proud of my colleagues whose most celebrated competitors—experts from the World Bank and others—could never understand the subtlety of their analysis.

I am, like everybody, closely monitoring the battle in Thailand between the "yellow shirts," who are mobilizing the openly anti-democratic and comprador middle classes, and the "red shirts," who defend the interests of the working classes, even though the political leadership of their movement can be criticized. But no surprise: the Western media take sides against democracy, even in its basic electoral form, when the results are not acceptable to the imperialist monopolies.

### Malaysia

Malaysia, which I have visited on several occasions beginning in 1973, has experimented over the past twenty-five years with a capitalist development similar to that of Thailand, with similar "successes" (according to the criteria of dominant conventional opinion, that of the World Bank) and weaknesses, brilliantly highlighted by its critical intellectuals (Jomo Sundaram and Hussein Ali, among others).

But it was obvious—for me, at least—that Malaysia does not benefit from the same advantages as Thailand does. There is no nation in the strong sense of the term, but only a country shared between different "communities." The Chinese community monopolizes (capitalist) entrepreneurship and supplies the majority of the qualified workers, while the Malays monopolize political power. That functions well enough so long as the interests of the political ruling class and those of the capitalists converge. That has been the case up to now, since the state's active intervention has aimed at supporting private accumulation. That did not prevent the Chinese of Singapore, who are the overwhelming majority of the population in this city, from deciding that it was better to separate from the former Malaysia to form their own government and make this city-state into an industrial and financial center for the region.

If the crisis were to continue and deepen, if dominant international capital were to succeed in imposing its views, forcing a "retreat of the state" in the name of the principles of globalized neoliberalism—which would be perfectly fine for the multinationals and the comprador Chinese bourgeoisie, but not the Malay political ruling class—the unity of the dominant local bloc could be seriously threatened. These internal tensions could become all the more dangerous since social struggles could be expected to become more radical. How will the Malay peasants, the "feudal" classes that often control them, the proletarians of the cities (often Chinese and Indian) and plantations, and the middle strata found in all communities react to these new challenges? It is difficult to say, but historical experience teaches us that a recourse to "communitarianism," or even to Islamic fundamentalism for the Malays, could be the means by which some political forces might hope to renew lost legitimacy.

The current crisis is not, in my opinion, a "conjunctural" one to be overcome by reviving the model responsible for the growth of the last twenty-five years, but rather it is the signal that this model has exhausted its potential. All of Malaysia's progressive and democratic forces should expend some energy in analyzing this crisis. Such forces exist, fortunately, despite the repression that accompanied the "miracle" praised to the heavens by the World Bank. The illusions fostered by this miracle have now dissipated so we can hope to see these forces flourish again. In the immediate post–Second World War period, these forces crystallized around a combination of the efforts necessary for achieving national independence and those necessary for socialist revolution, following the model of communism current at that time. The defeat of this project—in common with all of Southeast Asia, except for Vietnam, Cambodia, and Laos—did not lead to the disappearance of the aspiration for both freedom and social justice among the peoples of the region. Of course, a "remake" of the past is not the appropriate response to the new challenge, which has arisen in local and global conditions that are quite different from those that characterized the postwar period. Fortunately, no one thinks along those lines and there is no nostalgia for the past (as there still exists, perhaps, in the Philippines). It is difficult to say, then, how a program of democratization and social progress could be reformulated for the coming period.

Nevertheless, Malaysia and Thailand are today put forward as emergent countries. I have already expressed my reservations about this. The model of industrial delocalization from which these countries supposedly benefit is not synonymous with constructing an autonomous and integrated industrial system. And the term "ersatz capitalism" to which I have sometimes referred is still accurate.

In recent meetings organized by the WFA/TWF, I have had the possibility of discussing these questions with new Malaysian participants: Francis Loh, Tian Chua, Choo Chon Kai, activists with new political parties (Parti Sosialis Malaysia and the People's Justice Party), along with my old acquaintants (Jomo Sundaram and Hussein Ali). These discussions have taught me much about the resurgence of promising struggles in the country.

## The Philippines

Successive complications had always delayed my trips to the Philippines, until 1997. I was finally able to accept an invitation from some liberation theologians. George Aseniero, at the time coordinator for the Forum's activities in Southeast and East Asia, is himself Filipino and I have had the opportunity to discuss his country's problems with him, of course, but also with Renato Constantino—key figure of the postwar progressive revival—and his son-in-law Randolf David, who was active in the fall of Marcos, and with Francisco Nemenzo and others encountered in our working groups.

The history of the Philippines is tragic. Filipinos summarize it humorously in one sentence: "Four hundred years in a Spanish convent, forty years in a Hollywood musical comedy, four years in a Japanese concentration camp." I will add: "Flung into capitalist globalization at the end of this glorious preparation." The extremely bloody and corrupt Marcos dictatorship, established and supported by Washington—which never gave one thought to human rights violations and the absence of any elementary form of democracy—came to an end, though it was not actually brought down. The end of the dictatorship was brought about mainly by an urban rebellion organized by the "new social movement," a combination of grassroots organizations for defense of democracy, environmental groups, feminists, and religious groups (belonging to the liberation theology current). There is no shadow of doubt that the dominant local comprador bourgeoisie and, behind it, the diplomacy of the United States, succeeded in containing this movement by getting it to support the questionable figure of Corazon Aquino, if it did not manipulate the movement altogether.

That is why another fraction of the country's historical left, which had taken the initiative to lead a rural guerilla struggle under the leadership of a more or less traditional Communist Party that began to move toward Maoism in the 1960s, has remained severely critical toward this rather heterogeneous "new left." It accuses the latter of lacking a defined doctrine, of being based mainly on the middle classes, of having no strategy, and, consequently, of being manipulated by the local ruling classes and Washington. This guerilla movement, established in the mountains of Luzon Island, has never been successfully driven out; it continues to fight. The defenders of the new urban strategy argue that the guerillas simply survive without any prospect of being able to liberate the country—the cities and rich rural plains.

I listened to the two viewpoints defended by militants for whom I retain the highest respect. The arguments of both are solid, as are, ultimately, the critiques they make of each other. I do not have the temperament of a "sermonizer"—there are, unfortunately, too many of those. I thus always refrain from deciding in favor of one group or another and always respect their opinions and courage. I was thus always satisfied with saying what I really think and hope: Would it not be possible to overcome the inadequacies of both positions—supposing that the crucial points of the mutual critiques are correct, and I believe they are—through a rapprochement rather than continuing a polemic that encourages mutual stubbornness?

Manila is a disaster, just like Bangkok: crisscrossed by urban highways that surround appalling slums, bourgeois quarters organized into fortresses, crazy traffic, etc. What remains of the old Spanish colonial city—minuscule compared to the Metro-Manila agglomeration—is quite pretty and makes you nostalgic . . . for a Spanish convent.

The revolt of the "Moros"—the Muslims of Mindanao—does not make much sense to me. The Moros are not victims of any discrimination. The idea that, because they are Muslims, they should have their own independent state only convinces those who accept the ideological rhetoric of Islamism and "communitarianism." It is, then, a movement able to be manipulated, and one that probably is manipulated (by Washington). The small war ultimately pits only criminal bandits, on the Moro side, against the brutal army of a system that, by nature, is incapable of responding properly to a challenge of this type. This works out quite well for those who want to reap the benefits of such a conflict. Once again, I am referring to Washington.

## INDONESIA

Indonesia has been, for me, a country almost completely off limits since 1966. I had known the leaders of the Communist Party at the beginning of the 1960s. I had also listened to the functionaries of the Sukarno government in meetings of the Non-Aligned Movement. The relationship between these two dominant forces that had emerged from the war of liberation reminded me of what happened in Egypt during the same time period. For the communists, the choice was between aligning with the populism of the government or seriously attempting to go beyond it. And in the communists' case, there would have to be some decision about the means to be used. Sukarno reminded me a lot of Nasser. Fundamentally anti-communist, these two heads of state sought to counterbalance the influence of the popular left by similar means—depoliticize the population by banning debate, corrupt and flatter the tendencies of the petite bourgeoisie on which their power was based, and encourage reactionary currents, particularly Islamism. The biggest difference was that the Indonesian Communist Party (Partai Komunis Indonesia) was much more powerful than the Egyptian party and, consequently, had to be accepted as an equal partner—legally recognized even though it was subject to a surreptitious repression. In a certain way, Syria and Iraq stood between the Egyptian model and the Indonesian one. In any case, the clever game these anti-communist populist leaders thought they were playing was turned against them: in the end, they were brought down by the right, supported by imperialist interventions. In Indonesia, precisely because the Communist Party was so powerful, the overthrow of Sukarno's populist regime required a bloodbath unparalleled in contemporary history. Suharto did not act alone. The Islamists participated, as did the CIA, which carefully planned the massacre of at least 500,000 people—men, women, children, and the elderly. If today it is a question of setting up an "international tribunal" for this type of crime, then the government in Washington should be the principal accused. But of course no such thing would be considered, as if it is possible to imagine the president of the United States offering his apologies to the Indonesian people, which would be the least of it. Among the criminals of our time, such an "international tribunal" will only try those who have not given complete satisfaction to the imperialist masters.

Nevertheless, in 1973, I attempted to contact survivors who had not transferred their allegiance to the combined dictatorship of Suharto and Washington after Sukarno's fall in 1966. This was very difficult given that the horror of the recent massacre and the terror—perpetrated, among other things, by the systematic practice of torture on the least suspicion, using lists supplied by the United States—paralyzed scattered individuals. It is in these conditions that I met some people whose names it is now possible for me to reveal, after Suharto's fall. The main person was Adi Sasono, at the time a fighter for democracy and social justice and a critic of the dependent capitalist development strategy advocated by Washington via the World Bank. But gradually, Adi Sasono moved closer to the government and particularly to B. J. Habibie, who took over for a time after Suharto. It is not unimportant that Habibie proclaimed himself to be the protector of the Islamists. That was the condition Washington set to support him and, by this means, attempt to stop the popular fervor that ended Suharto's dictatorship. The economic and financial crisis was not, as the dominant media claim, the cause of the dictatorship's collapse. Rather, it became a means of managing such a crisis in the interests of international capital and the local comprador bourgeoisie. Underlying this was the refusal by the working classes to pay the price of that type of management—and, in support of this refusal, the powerful mobilization and massive intervention of the youth and the students ended Suharto's power. Unprepared to face the challenge of a mass democratic and social movement, the dictator—as is often the case—reacted "incorrectly" (for the United States): he attempted a last-ditch demagogic nationalist "reversal." It is at that point that those who suddenly discovered he had flouted democratic norms abandoned him. Then, the questionable Habibie was pushed to the forefront. It remains the case that nothing is yet settled in this country in turmoil, despite the apparent stability brought by the election of Sukarno's daughter. No way of managing the crisis has appeared up to now that would satisfy either the imperialist masters or the popular social movement, which has not abated.

In any case, returning to the year 1973, a visa for Indonesia had been granted for Isabelle and me for a tourism trip. We landed at Denpasar and spent several days of vacation on Bali's splendid beaches. At the time, Bali was not yet overrun by hordes of Japanese, Australians, and others. There were a few hippies. Visiting this island, whose population has remained Hindu, also helped us understand the true history of the Indonesian people, the pre-Islamic roots that the fundamentalists, here as elsewhere, want to erase. This would, of course, result in a trauma, as I pointed out earlier. The alliance of U.S. diplomacy and the fundamentalists is thus preparing other horrors and massacres to come. This is certainly known in Washington, but it is desired. It is the most effective way to make sure that Indonesia never becomes a stable country, thus potentially autonomous and capable of rejecting U.S. hegemony. Once again, the official rhetoric of Western diplomacy on democracy, manipulated by the media, does not have the least credibility.

## The Question of Timor Leste

I am returning to the question of Timor Leste that I broached in an incidental way in the first [French] edition of volume 2 of these memoirs. I had the opportunity to discuss the question with the leaders of the liberation movements of this country. I refer here to the work published by Araujo in 2014 on the subject.[35] The oppression to which the odious Suharto government had subjected this people recalls the practices of the government in Khartoum, no less odious, toward the peoples of South Sudan. It should be remembered that the imperialist powers—led by Australia—supported the annexation made in these conditions. They feared that the choice of armed struggle by the Timor Leste movement, inspired by the movements in the Portuguese colonies of Africa, would favor radicalization. But it is clear that when the Western powers and Australia changed tack and came around to supporting the cause of independence, they did so because they no longer feared such radicalization. Their intervention, via the UN, ended this possibility and allowed for the establishment of a compliant government, as in the former Portuguese colonies of Africa. This government now sees to it that Timor Leste continues in its destructive colonial status.

The inability of populist governments and rightist dictatorships in the Third World to resolve this type of problem appropriately is almost congenital and bears a decisive share of responsibility in the revolt of the victims of their dictatorship. But is separation the solution, or will it almost inevitably create countries that are too vulnerable to be able to resist imperialist-dominated globalization while large countries (like Indonesia) are capable of asserting themselves—on condition, of course—and moving in a genuinely popular and democratic direction? The support of independence demands by public opinion in the imperialist countries, profoundly influenced by government manipulation, is, for me, a cause for real concern.

Australia, following Washington's lead, has ambitions to be a regional imperialist power. Government and public opinion intervenes with that in mind, which convinces me even more that this danger is real. Such interventions are really quite shameless. What credence can be given to campaigns by the Australian government and press against "French colonialism" in

New Caledonia? If Australia does not have a problem with "indigenous" inhabitants, is that not simply because it systematically exterminated them and refused all citizenship rights to the few survivors until recently (1967, I believe)? The genocide of the Tasmanians is well known for having been the most "perfect" in history: there were no survivors, not even a single infant (racist Australians did not consider adopting them), which created a problem for linguists since nothing is now known of the language that disappeared with its people. And Australia wants to preach to others!

### KOREA

The economic development of South Korea is different from that of the Southeast Asian countries. However, lumping the two development paths together is frequently done. The World Bank, of course, ignores the concept of peripheral capitalism and consequently makes no distinction between the economic model found in peripheral capitalist societies and models characteristic of central capitalist societies. Its view of the world is flat and without subtlety: the most diverse forms of capitalist expansion are all put into the same category and classified by reference to a single criterion—the growth rate of the GDP. In this way, Korea, Thailand, and Malaysia are all presented as "success stories" (miracles), attributed, without any distinctions, to the virtues of the "market." No effort is made to understand how the market in question is regulated by state policies that are different from one country to another, and one time period to another. But most left activists—in Asia and elsewhere—make the same mistake, though with different arguments. Since they oppose the pro-capitalist and pro-United States options of the Seoul government, they reduce the Korean model to a variant of dependent capitalist development, thus essentially similar to the development found in the countries of Southeast Asia. Most left activists in the Western world treat China's capitalist development in the same way and lump it together with other models from East and Southeast Asia, even other Third World countries. In my opinion, I think this way of lumping together different models of capitalist development is trivial. It is just a polemical procedure that eliminates the central questions concerning the nature of the hegemonic bloc, its relations to the dominated classes and, therefore, its strategies vis-à-vis imperialism.

The hegemonic blocs in Southeast Asia are compradors, and they open their countries to penetration by multinational companies. Yet the state policies implemented fulfill important functions in the system. First, they maintain, through severe repression, low-cost labor power while ensuring that the middle strata benefit from the economic expansion, inviting them to the joys of "consumerism" and to support the choice of an anti-democratic political system. Second, they force dominant international capital, principal beneficiary of the arrangement, to associate the local comprador bourgeoisie with its pillaging operations and thereby lend support to the prodigious enrichment of that bourgeoisie, whether that be through pure and simple corruption or through the creation of reserved and protected companies. This type of growth—even if it were strong for two decades—has not caused Indonesia to leave behind the traditional quasi-colonial model, based mainly on the destructive exploitation of natural resources (forests, in particular). In Thailand and Malaysia, growth has been based more on the expansion of manufacturing industries with the participation of local private capital (Chinese, in the case of Malaysia). The vulnerability and fragility of these models—whether the results have been quite mediocre (the Philippines) or apparently brilliant (Thailand and Malaysia)—are obvious. Work groups from the Forum demonstrated this, and the crisis confirmed it. Depending largely on foreign financing and technology, having developed no expertise in these areas in order possibly to take them over, the model deserves to be called "ersatz capitalism."

The hegemonic bloc in Korea is completely different. Its leading element is statist, in the sense that the dominant class and the state are practically merged. This state's strategy, then, is nationalist, and if it resorts to multinational corporations and their technologies, it does so in accordance with the imperatives of a plan that outlines the stages of a rise through the hierarchy of production, the development of capacities to absorb technologies (through the emphasis put on training and the rules imposed on multinationals in these areas), the construction of a system of monopolies (*chaebols*) that could be called either private or public and are a means to maintain control over ownership of capital, etc. Korea, through its choices for international alliances, is the only case of a "non-socialist" Third World country that is attempting to leave peripheral capitalism and set itself up as a genuinely new center. The United States accepted this choice—for a certain time—and even supported it (by unilaterally opening its market to Korean exports, for example) for specific geostrategic reasons. Washington tolerated here what it fought elsewhere. The Korean War (1950–53) had also forced the local ruling class to make concessions to its people that were not very likely elsewhere, particularly an agrarian reform aimed at satisfying peasants attracted until then by the competing model of North Korea. These conditions allowed the working class to undertake successful struggles that resulted first in an improvement in wages, then led to an attack on the anti-democratic system of political power.

I was thus not very surprised when an invitation reached me in 1984 from Korean intellectuals and academics. I immediately realized that I had been attentively read, in Japanese (my main works are always translated into this language with larger print runs than in French or English!) or even in Korean (translations for university use, later taken over by commercial publishers) or Chinese (an odd circulation of translations made by the Academy of Sciences in Beijing). I also realized that, in spite of very harsh repression, the left (and even Marxism) had a strong presence in the intellectual world and was, moreover, not isolated but, on the contrary, able to maintain organized relations with the worker and peasant worlds, mediated by students of working class origin. Our discussions were thus extremely interesting and tackled all aspects of the problem. In Korea, I met militants who, while declaring themselves to be Marxists and Maoists in general, had been able to avoid many of the simplifications widespread elsewhere. Without the existence of all this intellectual ferment, it would be difficult to understand the extent of the social and political movement that has shaken the country in recent years. Having become friends with these comrades, I was able to visit this very beautiful country, in their company, traveling by rail and road from Seoul through inland cities, such as Daegu, to its southern coasts and the port of Busan (where I visited the impressive naval shipyards).

Korea's success is a real danger for imperialism. This country can become a competing power, all the more so since its reunification is probable and will occur in conditions that have nothing in common with those that allowed Bonn to annex East Germany. This country could shift to the left in a way that is difficult to specify in advance, but significant social and political forces, which have continued to strengthen in recent years, are fighting to move the country in this direction.

There was nothing surprising, then, for me, that the 1997 financial crisis was the opportunity for Washington and its Japanese and European allies to attempt to ruin Korean potential. The financial crisis Korea is experiencing is a minor one—no different, for example, than what France and Great Britain have experienced at least ten times over the postwar decades, without the authorities in Washington resorting to what they are attempting to impose on Korea today. It is minor in the sense that the Korean external deficit, measured in relative terms, in reference to the GDP, for example, and in terms of longevity (over how many years) is below that of the United States. Now, what do we see? The IMF attributes the crisis simply to the existence of monopolies in Korea (as if the large U.S., Japanese, and European companies were not the same!) and proposes their dismantlement and the transfer of the most lucrative parts to American monopolies. In the same way, then, we should expect the IMF to propose—to resolve the American crisis—to cede Boeing (which is a monopoly, as far as I know) to Airbus, its European competitor (which is also a monopoly). Bill Clinton would have ordered Michel Camdessus (former Managing Director of the IMF) removed from office at the very moment he attempted to implement such a ludicrous proposal. Is it surprising, then, that the Korean press unhesitatingly speaks of a new Korean war, with Washington as the designated aggressor? In my opinion, this war is likely to last. It will probably experience ups and downs. But it is not certain that the United States and its allies will end up victors.

The crisis has caused Korea to step back from its project of emergence. The liberalism imposed by the United States and Japan has encouraged the *chaebols* to free themselves from control by the national state. No longer instruments of the state, they have become its masters. The *chaebols* have been transformed into a financial oligarchy, similar to what is occurring elsewhere. And, like elsewhere, the interpenetration of the private interests of this oligarchy with those that dominate the United States and Japan has caused the prospects for Korea's emergence to recede.

## And North Korea?

There is certainly no reason to be enthusiastic about Pyongyang's political model. But is the principle of president-for-life, and even a dynastic transmission of the office, so different from what exists in other countries that are not subject to nasty criticism from the Western media clergy? We have never heard this clergy call for the trial of Cameroon's Paul Biya, for example.

North Korea was, until the end of the 1950–53 war, proceeding along a more promising development path than South Korea. An agrarian reform and industrialization were the foundations and led to a higher per capita GDP and growth rate than in the South. This is why subsequently the United States and Japan (with President Park) were forced to tolerate the commitment of the new national state to the path that made possible the "Korean miracle," while they fought the same choice elsewhere in the Global South.

Unfortunately, particularly after the collapse of the USSR, North Korea has severely regressed. It was unable, like Cuba, to rise to the challenge. But in some areas it has moved ahead (nuclear technology and ballistic missiles). These achievements would have been impossible without an excellent education system and support industries. The Western media never say that, though.

The question of Korean unity is central today. If it happens tomorrow, it will not follow the German model, with the pure and simple annexation of the North and its subjection to the system currently established in the South. This unity will be better balanced and will thus give Korea the possibility of becoming a genuine emergent nation. The United States and Japan know and fear this. That is why they fight the aspirations for unity of these two parts of a single historical nation and, for that reason, raise military tension, and impose sanctions.

# 4

# LATIN AMERICA
## End of the Monroe Doctrine?
## Popular Advances

Latin America and the Caribbean have had a very different history from that of the Asian and African countries. All modern societies of the American continent result from a particular form of colonization that fulfilled decisive functions in the mercantilist system of Atlantic Europe, at that time the nascent center of global capitalism. This history has very little in common with the history of African and Asian societies subjected to a later expansion of triumphant industrial capitalism. In Africa and Asia, societies preserved their earlier national and cultural identities, their languages, and, to a large extent, their (non-Christian) religions. Their systems—called tributary or communal in my analysis—were subjected to, and de-formed to serve, the expanding industrial capitalism; thus these societies retained for a long time distinctive features described as "feudal" in the simplified analyses of modern national liberation movements. The formation of modern America resulted in the far more complete destruction of indigenous societies, or in the most extreme case, their outright elimination through systematic genocides, as the one carried out by English in North America. All of America was Christianized (at least formally) and adopted the use of European languages (even if this observation has to be qualified when discussing the Creole Caribbean and the regions with dense Indian populations in the Andes and Mexico).

The participation of the English, French, and Dutch in the conquest of America, and the establishment of a mercantilist system is easy to understand. These three countries were in the avant-garde of nascent capitalism. Since the continual wars of the seventeenth and nineteenth centuries between these three mercantilist powers ended in the resounding victory of the British, it is not surprising that the French and the Dutch were all but expelled from the continent to the evident benefit of English colonization. But how do we explain the expansion of Spain and Portugal in America when, at the end of the fifteenth century, these two countries could hardly be characterized as mercantilist capitalist societies? I believe that the *Reconquista* is behind this incredible conquest of America. The year 1492 saw both the expulsion of the Muslims from Andalusia and Christopher Columbus's voyage. The *Reconquista* had given rise to the formation of large feudal armies led by warlords throughout the Iberian Peninsula. After having chased out the Muslims, these armies would probably have continued their conquests into North Africa. The "discovery" of America offered them an alternative area for expansion, which turned out, moreover, to be immensely wealthier. But these armies had not been formed on the basis of mercantile capitalist relations similar to those that had crystallized in Northwest Europe. They thus carried to Iberian America a different mindset, still widely marked by European feudalism. It is these forms that posed a problem for the later characterization of Latin American societies.

The core of the mercantilist system lay in the plantation slavery colonies (mainly for growing sugarcane and cotton). This was a Portuguese invention developed in the Cape Verde Islands and then spread on a large scale throughout the Antilles, the English colonies in the southern part of North America, and the Brazilian Northeast. The importing of African slaves influenced the creation of this main mercantilist periphery.

In areas with dense Indian populations—Mexico and the Andes—the Spanish subjected the indigenous inhabitants to a slave-like status in connection with mines rather than plantations, and spread a form inspired by the Iberian feudal tradition, the *encomienda*, which was gradually transformed into latifundia, which were integrated to various degrees into the expanding world capitalism. A similar system of large holdings was established where there were no indigenous populations, or where they did not exist in large numbers, in the southern cone—Brazil, Uruguay, Argentina—relying on immigration from the Iberian Peninsula, Italy, Germany, and elsewhere. In Indian regions, this system "integrated" the Christianized indigenous inhabitants to varying degrees, in its own (brutal and extreme) way. But it was only in Mexico that this integration increased in any real sense of the term due to the peasant revolution of 1910–20. A true, Hispano-Indian nation resulted from the agrarian reform, and populism was built by the PRI on the foundation of this authentically popular revolution.

The development of capitalism in Northwest Europe also produced, particularly in England, an excess proletarianized population that provided large numbers for the colonizing of America. The formation of New England was due to this. This settler colony of small landholders built a self-reliant commodity economy that was of little interest to the dominant mercantilist system, which thought it had no future. The successful colonies, the ones that the "experts" of that time described as "miracles" (for reasons quite similar to those invoked by World Bank experts today), became Haiti and Northeast Brazil, whereas the self-reliant and poor New England produced the United States.

The "revolutions" of the late eighteenth and early nineteenth centuries hardly merit that characterization although they are central in modern American ideology. They were only revolts by the local ruling classes against administration by the mother country and involved no social transformation. Thus it is not by chance that the leaders of the North American war for independence—Washington and the others—were all slave owners and remained so in the United States they created. It was the same with the Creoles of Latin America. The only true social revolution of that time was the slave revolt in Saint-Domingue (Haiti).

Undoubtedly, during the wars of independence in Latin America, there were progressive leaders who envisaged more than just a transfer of power from the mother country to the local ruling classes and said as much. Bolívar is one of those, and the glorification of his name by Venezuela's Bolívarian Revolution is a case in point. Yet it remains the case that the wars of independence were what they were, and ended in a simple transfer of power to the benefit of local property-owning classes without the people themselves seeing their lot improved in any significant way.

In these conditions, the nineteenth century had to end in the emergence of a new center (and only one for the entire hemisphere), the United States, which began in New England and then integrated into industrial capitalism the other parts of the Americas, as peripheries providing agricultural and mineral raw materials. Gradually, the latifundia lost their original para-feudal characteristics to become a form of capitalist property in land. Ultimately, the various American societies became peripheral capitalist. In this sense, the socioeconomic structures in Latin America became more like those of Asia and Africa, which also were transformed into forms of peripheral capitalism. It is within this new context—which has very little to do with centuries of mercantilism—that a cycle of people's revolutions began in the Americas, including the Mexican Revolution of 1910–1920 and the Cuban Revolution that triumphed in 1959.

Certainly, the Latin American people have never lacked courage. The history of the 1920s and 1930s is filled with—often glorious—revolts against the latifundia owners and the lackeys of imperialism. In Nicaragua, Sandino, and in El Salvador, Farabundo Marti led the uprising of their peoples, perhaps inspired by the glorious Mexican Revolution. In Cuba in 1933, inspired by San Martin, a revolution overthrew the pro-Yankee Machado dictatorship. In Peru, APRA attempted to give new strength to Indian peasant masses. In the 1920s, Luís Carlos Prestes in Brazil led a column of landless peasants in revolt in a long march that earned him the name "the knight of hope." But the fact is that none of these revolts succeeded. The dictatorships reconstructed on their ruins—that of Somoza in Nicaragua and Batista in Cuba—lasted peacefully for decades after, until Castro's victory in Cuba in 1959 and the Sandinistas' triumph in Nicaragua twenty years later. (I shall deal with Cuba in chapter 6.)

I do not think it useful to give a quick explanation of these defeats in my memoirs. Each case has its own unique history that was later the subject of serious analyses and debates. Each time I had the good fortune of being involved in these discussions, in the 1970s and 1980s, I found them very rewarding. I do not think that the main cause of the defeat can be attributed to local "communists" in the 1920s and 1930s (there were very few outside of the Southern Cone), as well as the Comintern, which claimed to direct their strategies. Besides, the Comintern understood very little about Latin American societies outside of the Southern Cone, where Spanish and Italian immigrants had brought with them the workers, anarchists, and socialist traditions of Latin Europe. Being sizable, communist parties apparently could be formed here—in Uruguay, Argentina, and Chile—which the Comintern leaders could understand and in which they invested all their hopes. But they also first misled them into hopeless adventures (socialist revolution was thought to be on the agenda everywhere), then forced them to align themselves with the diplomacy of the Stalinist USSR, without taking into account the difference separating the societies of peripheral capitalism from those of the European centers. The Comintern committed the same blunders in Asia and Africa, but the peoples of these continents did not always submit to the strategies it advocated. The communist parties in China and Vietnam were able to assert their independence. National liberation movements, whether led by communist parties or not (as in India, Indonesia, and the Middle East), followed their own path in accordance with the social content of their leading forces.

Thus, I understand the uniqueness of Latin American history in terms of the nature of its ruling classes, fundamentally comprador from the beginning, completely dazzled by the attraction exercised over them by Europe (later the United States). Popular revolts suppressed in these conditions made way for regimes that, from Mexico's southern border to the border separating the Southern Cone from the Andean region, were only vulgar dictatorships established on the basis of relative stagnation. On the other hand, in the Southern Cone, social movements—which remained alive despite revolutionary disillusions—opened the way to various forms of Latin American populism, initially in Brazil and Argentina, and later more widespread after the Second World War. Still, the first two decades of this postwar period turned out to be "calm," since Latin America easily aligned itself with Washington and the communist parties were quiet, while these decades were a great turning point in the modern history of Asia and Africa.

I knew this history only through readings and, in fact, like most Asians and Africans, did not really assess Latin America's specificities, as I mentioned in my 1994 book *Re-Reading the Postwar Period*. My readings had initially led me to become acquainted with *desarrollismo* (developmentalism), proposed as an ideological framework for the development strategy of the 1950s and 1960s. Then, beginning in the second half of the 1960s, I familiarized myself with the first critiques of this theory made by the new Latin American left.

*Desarrollismo* had only ever partly convinced me. Certainly, it advocated a development that could be described as autocentric in a certain way, through local industrialization (called import substitution) protected from the devastating competition of the imperialist oligopolies. But it assumed that the local bourgeoisie would be able to manage such a project, that is, it assumed that this bourgeoisie was "national" in the sense that we give to the term—i.e., anti-imperialist. The theory distinguished the latifundia owners—considered to be the exclusive beneficiaries of integration into the world market and, consequently, opposed to industrialization—from the national bourgeoisie, which the intelligentsia could represent through modernization of the state. It was necessary to accept the "price" of this modernization and the financing of the primitive accumulation it conveyed. This "price" included the absence of democracy, which would come "after" as the natural product of the formation of a new middle class.

What the theory ignored, then, was that the middle classes in question would be the exclusive beneficiaries of the new development and, in order to subject the working classes to the exploitation necessary to this end, they would not at all choose to initiate a democratic transformation of political life. Import substitution merely substituted imports of equipment and technology for the earlier imports of consumption goods. This was, then, a form of integration into the world system—and not a form of delinking—and was quite acceptable to the imperialist oligopolies. In other words, this change replaced the old class, the latifundia owners, that acted as transmission belt for imperialist domination, with a new comprador class of the same kind (the "middle classes" and their state). Modernization became a synonym for modernization of exploitation (replacing the labor of "peons" with wage labor having relatively high modern productivity paid at minimal levels in factories), modernization of poverty (slums taking the place of impoverished villages), and modernization of dictatorship ("scientific" police forces, torture, and death squads taking the place of gangs at the service of caudillos).

The left of Third World Marxism—to which I belonged—could not but reject this theory. We saw in that theory an ideological legitimation of the joint project of imperialism and the local bourgeoisie, comprador by nature, even if it were in new forms corresponding to changes in capitalism. Since we had read Mao's "New Democracy"—at the beginning of the 1950s—we were persuaded that the bourgeoisie of the peripheries could not be national, could not imagine any other development than one incorporated into the requirements of globalization. To break with this dead-end path, which ended in the deepening of polarization between centers and peripheries, synonymous with the contrast between imperialism and dominated peoples, the necessary delinking could only be done under the leadership of the working classes. Here we meant the working class and the poor peasantry who would open the way to contravening the anti-imperialist and anti-feudal bourgeois revolution, and transform it into the first step of a socialist revolution.

The debate around these questions went back to the end of the 1950s in Asia and Africa, quickly following the contours of the Sino-Soviet conflict. On the Soviet side, requirements emanating from the Cold War were privileged: it was necessary to submit to the concessions required by coexistence (the only way to avoid nuclear war, it was claimed in Moscow). Socialism would triumph because the socialist countries would show higher growth rates than those of the capitalist world, thus would "catch up" and even bury it, as Nikita Khrushchev had proclaimed. Mao advanced another theory of world capitalism, focused on the permanence of imperialism. The main enemies of capitalism, then, were those who threatened imperialism, that is, those who, having read "New Democracy" mentioned above, combined national liberation and socialist revolution. From 1957 to 1960, with Maoism, the question was clear-cut from this point of view.

In this debate, which mainly took place in Afro-Asian contexts, Latin America seemed to be absent. *Desarrollismo* satisfied those whom we called "revisionists," and it was not by chance that the Latin American communist parties, who were aligned with Moscow against Beijing, supported it. I explained this situation by the particularities of Latin American history briefly recalled above. The ruling classes of this continent had always belonged to the world capitalist system; they were a product of it. They had thus always turned their attention toward the model represented by the dominant power of the moment: England in the nineteenth century and the United States after 1945. The ideology they conveyed and which was imposed as the dominant ideology in their societies did not call into question the capitalist model, and their belonging to the European cultural tradition certainly facilitated their support for that model. Moreover, capitalism did not appear to include any cultural aggression. On the contrary, it was only by submitting to capitalism that it would be possible to "catch up" and become what was desirable: like Europeans and North Americans. The communist parties and the intellectual left of Latin America joined the partisans of *desarrollismo* on one fundamental point: the enemy of progress (viewed as "catching up") was the hegemonic bloc of latifundia owners (described as feudal, in reference to its presumed ancestor, Iberian feudalism) and not the bourgeoisie.

Then things began to change in Latin America. The triumph of the Cuban Revolution, when Fidel Castro and his forces entered Havana on January 1, 1959, was a definite challenge for *desarrollismo*, as well as the electoral, strategies of the communist parties. The Cuban Revolution had its ups and downs: the break with Che Guevara after 1963, followed by his trips to Africa in 1964, and his death in the Bolivian maquis in 1967. Then 1968 erupted and presented another challenge, on the global level, for all leftist intellectuals. On the level of theoretical analysis, André Gunder Frank's writings also marked the beginning of a break, advancing the thesis that Latin American societies are capitalist and not feudal, have even been capitalist since the mercantilist centuries (mercantilism itself considered to be the first phase of capitalism) and were never feudal. Toward the end of the 1960s—particularly after 1968—a new theory took form that was later known as the "dependency school." In fact, this school gave itself the name, an unfortunate choice in my opinion. In any case, I was interested in these three major changes: the Cuban Revolution, the appearance of a left that declared itself to be to the left of the communist parties in several countries (sometimes even supporting the Maoist view, but that was the exception in Latin America), and the development of new theses concerning peripheral capitalism.

I had already read quite a few of the early writings that came out of this new moment, and the names of the founders of the new Latin American school were no longer unknown to me when I decided to establish meaningful contact with them and subsequently go see what was happening for myself. The first trip, with Isabelle, occurred in the summer of 1971 and led us to Brazil, Argentina, Chile, Peru, and Bolivia. The following year, I attended the General Assembly of CLACSO, the Latin American organization that inspired us to create CODESRIA. Then we organized the first major meeting of critical intellectuals from Africa and Latin America at the IDEP in 1972.[36] Isabelle and I also visited Venezuela and were welcomed by Hector and Adicea Michelena, back home in their country after their stay at the IDEP in Dakar. I also subsequently visited Chile on several occasions—the last time shortly before the fall of Allende in 1973, for our first constituent meeting of the Third World Forum—and also went to Mexico, once at the invitation of President Luis Echeverría Álvarez.[37] But the misfortune of my tight travel schedule forced me to continually postpone the visits I would have liked to have made to the Caribbean. I had the opportunity to visit Jamaica only in 1989, where I met my friend, Norman Girvan, whom I had also invited to the IDEP in Dakar.

The Latin America that I visited in the 1970s was going through one of the darkest periods of its tradition of violent dictatorships, although the system was beginning to weaken. These were nations formed by colonization, nations that did not exist prior to that, as Brazilian scholar Emir Sader has written. Consequently, the ruling classes never imagined themselves as existing outside the globalized capitalist system of which they were the product. The state apparatus (particularly the armed forces) in these countries considered its main function to be repression of the people. These are the characteristics that explain the astonishing submission of these ruling classes to Washington's diktats. In return, Washington and its armed forces never considered Latin America as a "dangerous zone" for its hegemonic project. All of that probably explains the astonishing ease with which the Organization of American States was created in 1948 at Washington's initiative—an organization described by isolated critics at the time as the "United States' ministry of colonies." The Latin American ruling classes took Washington's side during the Cold War without the least hesitation and always refused to support the "non-aligned" camp, which remained strictly Afro-Asian (except for Cuba). From 1945 to 1960, while the Asian and African peoples—and even their bourgeoisie, in part at least—were involved in endless struggles against imperialism, silence reigned in Latin America. When the CIA overthrew President Jacobo Arbenz of Guatemala in 1954 for attempting an agrarian reform, the Latin American states said not a word. The victory of the Cuban Revolution in 1959, however, heralded the beginning of a possible end to the system.

Washington and the Latin American ruling classes immediately worked together to isolate Cuba. In 1961, President John F. Kennedy announced the famous "Alliance for Progress." Of course, this initiative was certainly misnamed because it was really an alliance to maintain the status quo, that is, against progress. The "democrat" Kennedy became, then, the protector of the worst dictatorships, the initiator of their "modernization," and the "intellectuals"—minions for hire such as the illustrious Samuel Huntington, the CIA's sociologist—attempted to "justify" this choice by declaring simply that democracy is the enemy of "progress" (defined, of course, as the expansion of capitalism). Another of these "intellectuals" was the no less illustrious Robert McNamara, then Secretary of Defense and responsible for the intensification of the Vietnam War and massive terrorist bombing campaigns of civilian populations (probably inspired by the strategy the Nazis implemented during the Spanish Civil War). Washington was then at the heart of the worst aggressions against Third World peoples: the CIA organized the massacre in Indonesia in 1966. It did not hesitate to organize assassinations or coups against elected democratic governments, like Chile's Popular Unity government. Washington's true friends in Latin America were the Brazilian and Argentine generals, the Castelo Brancos and Jorge Videlas, who are responsible, among many atrocities, for the thousands of the "disappeared," whose police were trained in "scientific" torture techniques by North American instructors. No public expression of regret has ever come from the "democratic" governments in Washington for these acts of terrorism and massacres. It will never come, we can be sure of that.

The Latin American left began to organize a riposte to the criminal arrogance of Washington and its local accomplices. Splitting from fearful communist parties, it advocated armed struggle. Rural guerillas adopted a simplified version of Maoism—"encircle the cities from the countryside"—without worrying too much about the conditions in which Mao had developed this thesis concerning the military dimension of the revolution. Others opted for urban guerilla action, without always clearly defining the boundary between that and "terrorism." In Central America, the rebellion in Guatemala had continued. Douglas Bravo and the FALN in Venezuela, Camilo Torres and the ELN in Colombia, Carlos Marighella and POLOP in Brazil, the Tupamaros in Uruguay, the Monteneros in Argentina, the MIR in Chile, and others elsewhere took center stage during a large part of the 1960s and 1970s. Obviously, I had followed these developments closely and, through the Maoist journal *Révolution*, sometimes witnessed their first elaborations. I met some of the leaders of these organizations during the 1970s in Latin America.

I must say, without any false modesty, while I have much respect for the courage of these comrades, and despite the friendship I rapidly developed with some of them, I was not especially impressed by their analyses. Their Marxism often seemed superficial, sometimes almost reduced to the caricatural assertion that the "people" are spontaneously revolutionary and await only the courage of a minority to proclaim the revolution and, consequently, act to follow them. The attempt to "theorize" this strategy, undertaken by Régis Debray in his 1967 *Revolution in the Revolution?*, straightaway seemed childish to me.[38] Certainly, the criticism these comrades made of the communist parties seemed correct. The latter had reduced the idea of mass struggle to that of the electoral contest (when it existed) and/or the demand for elections. This gradual alignment on positions almost strictly reduced to the demand for democracy contrasted sharply with the courageous class struggle undertaken by some of these same parties in the 1930s. It certainly corresponded to their failure, but also to the opportunism of postwar Soviet diplomacy. The demand for democracy, if it is not accompanied by a program for social transformation and by activities undertaken with that aim in mind, in my opinion, always remains rather unconvincing. The peoples of the capitalist periphery generally do not believe it very much. This is so, not only because the tradition of the democratic bourgeoisie is absent in these regions, but even more because experience has taught these peoples about the fragility and emptiness of reformist governments that follow electoral victory. But one cannot make a legitimate critique of the electoral strategy by simply replacing the watchword of electoral struggle by that of armed revolution. It is still necessary to combine possible armed struggle with consistent mass struggle—a lengthy preparation without which armed insurrection or guerilla warfare will have little hold over the working classes. I was not convinced that the comrades who were critical of "revisionism" actually combined their call for guerilla warfare with the necessary mass struggles.

But these judgments might appear cut-and-dried and should be nuanced. The "revisionists" (the term used by Maoists to refer to defenders of the official line advocated by communist parties aligned with Moscow) obviously always confused the issue and attributed the origin of this "leftism" to Che Guevara. Che is a much more complex person. We know him a bit better today than at the time he was active, since some of his writings (always brief, usually personal notes) have finally been published. Che's judgment on Soviet society has turned out to be accurate. Well in advance of his time, in the middle of the 1960s, Che had seen that the October Revolution had exhausted its potential, and even that the USSR had lost the battle of the technological revolution underway in the capitalist world. Che had seen that the theory that claimed Latin America was more feudal than capitalist—in which a preliminary passage through "national" capitalist development was seen as necessary and thus the demand for bourgeois democracy justified—served only as an alibi for an actual alignment with the strategies of the dominant comprador bourgeoisie. Che had not been unaware that armed insurrection was only the last phase of a process that mass struggle had begun. But undoubtedly he also felt hurried and consequently overestimated the nature of the advances that mass struggle had been able to produce. Since Asia and Africa had been involved in anti-imperialist movements since 1945, Che took the side of those who, in these movements, set themselves the objective of radicalizing the social content of their struggles. That also allowed him to propose a strategy to break Cuba's isolation.

The collusion of American imperialism, its European allies, and the ruling classes of all Latin America had isolated Cuba since the beginning of the 1960s. To survive, Cuba was forced to rely on the USSR, the only country capable of breaking the blockade (and providing it with the oil without which the local economy could not function) and protecting it against U.S. military attack, which had been planned, then put off after the defeat at the Bay of Pigs and the missile crisis. Cuban diplomacy well understood the importance of the stakes, and Cuba dared to confront the Monroe Doctrine, scrupulously respected by all Latin American ruling classes to this day. It thus took initiatives whose implementation I followed closely, coinciding with the creation of AAPSO and its congresses in Cairo (1958), Accra (the same year), and Conakry (1960, date of the official birth of the organization).[39] But a contradiction had cut across AAPSO from the beginning that totally paralyzed it. On the one hand, the governments that resulted from the radicalized (therefore populist) bourgeois national liberation movements chose a diplomatic alliance with Moscow, which allowed them to reject the diktats the Western powers attempted to impose on them in the name of the supposed necessities of the Cold War they had started. Delhi, Jakarta, Cairo, Damascus, and Moscow, of course, benefited from this. But on the other hand, there were movements that had not yet triumphed (as in Algeria, the Portuguese colonies, South Africa) that naturally sympathized with Beijing's theses, particularly the contention that imperialism was the main enemy. In Winneba, Ghana, in 1965—at a conference I followed closely as I was visiting Ghana at the time—the Sino-Soviet "diatribe" hid a quiet conflict between the representatives of states and those of movements. This was precisely the moment when Che had come to Africa in the hope that some of the movements in question (Lumumba's in particular) could, by becoming more radical, offer better prospects for pursuing liberation from the imperialist yoke. I mentioned above my reactions to Che's proposals, and to his more detailed observations, which were unknown until much later.

It was in this context that Cuba took the initiative to propose a "Tricontinental" conference in Havana in 1966, where Latin America would join Asia and Africa. The procrastination and reservations of some, particularly the non-aligned governments and Soviet diplomacy, led to the creation of a separate organization for Latin America, LASO, established in Havana in 1967, parallel to AAPSO. But unlike the AAPSO, which was supported by the majority of independent Asian and African states, LASO could only unite movements in conflict with Latin American governments, all of which were in Washington's camp. These movements were forced to clash with traditional communist parties and undertake the violent struggles mentioned above. Havana needed to remain on good terms with Moscow, on which Cuba depended for its survival.

I have made this long introduction because what I discussed with our Latin American comrades at the time, and subsequently (up to the present), when the transformations of the world system gathered pace and put an end to the postwar arrangement, only makes sense when placed in this context.

### BRAZIL: A NEW EMERGING POWER?

In Brazil, the first friend to receive me in 1971 was Fernando Henrique Cardoso, who then directed the CEBRAP, and courageously and determinedly faced one of the most savage dictatorships known in our time. At the time, we agreed on most things and I admired—and still do—the work he had written in collaboration with the Chilean Enzo Faletto. We easily agreed that a large Afro-Latin American meeting was necessary, which I organized a year later in Dakar where Fernando Henrique and his wife, Ruth, visited us in turn. Cardoso was one of the originators of the critique of *desarrollismo,* one of the founders of the "dependency school." Breaking with the dominant Marxist tradition, he lucidly analyzed the comprador character of the bourgeoisie in peripheral capitalism, which was based on latifundia owners in the first stage of its formation (which was not feudal, as Eurocentric scholastic Marxists depicted it) and then committed to an industrialization project that was just as dependent. Cardoso would now say "all his youthful writings should be forgotten." If that be true, that is really too bad because these writings count and will continue to count among the strongest analyses produced by modern Latin America.

I met other Brazilians elsewhere, in exile in Europe or in Chile during Allende's time, or even in Mexico: Theotonio dos Santos; the late Ruy Mauro Marini; the young (at the time) Emir Sader, who became one of the leading minds of the renewal in the 1990s; Maria da Conceição Tavares; and the "ancestors," Darcy Ribeiro and Celso Furtado, the first Brazilian I met, along with Jorge Amado, in Paris when I was still a student.

We wandered through several places in this continent-sized country, once again to see for ourselves what it was like, even if quickly: the Northeast (Bahia, its surroundings, and the *sertão*), the incomparable Rio de Janeiro, the terrible São Paulo, and the lamentable new capital, Brasilia. I would have much to say if I knew how to write on these topics. Welcomed by friends, we had the privilege of seeing things that we would not have been able to see as ordinary tourists, whether that be the opportunity to visit the historic churches and buildings of old Bahia or a *candomblé*, the lively cafes in Rio, its chic neighborhoods and favelas, and the astonishing tropical forest in the middle of the city. São Paulo gave us the impression of being a terrible place. Like all the large cities of the Western Hemisphere—including, of course, those in the United States—São Paulo is the result of an unrestrained capitalism that is found only in the Americas. This is the product of a specific history, of course. There were fortress-like residential areas where the tremendously wealthy bourgeois found refuge, (mainly black) working-class districts, run-down and as dangerous as those found in Chicago, New York, or Los Angeles, and intolerable favelas of poverty and shame. Here we found all the vices of the United States—in the first place, racism as a legacy of slavery—and, in addition, the material poverty of the industrialized Third World. At that time, Brasilia presented only the appearance of clean architecture and urban planning, so well ordered that the city appeared lifeless. Several generations will have to pass by before an urban life can be created; that is obvious. The magnificent exhibition "Brazil—500 Years," that we saw in São Paulo in 2000, really brought out the Brazilian problem: all the wealth of its artistic culture is the product of the black and mixed-race Northeast.

Brazil is certainly a captivating country. Yet that does not mean that the horrible aspects of its society should be accepted. Of course, there is the racism that most of the intellectuals do not want to see because that hampers their defense of the Brazilian nation. And then there is the systematic murder of children. Abandoned by the hundreds of thousands, they grow up alone like wild animals and are murdered by gangs of killers (who are not really murderers so much as hunters) paid by shopkeepers and other petite bourgeois quite simply because the petty theft of these children bothers them. There is not a single country in Asia or Africa where such ongoing savagery can even be imagined. For me, this is the proof that "pure capitalism," that is, the unilateral triumph of the "law of the market," is synonymous with pure barbarism. Such barbarism can only be tempered either by the survival of earlier social relations that are alien to pure capitalism (the family in Asia and Africa), or by the successes of popular and democratic struggles (those of the working class in Europe). The entire Western Hemisphere, from Alaska to

Tierra del Fuego, is marked by a savagery that can only be explained by the history of its formation within the context of mercantilism, outlined above.

Isabelle and I discussed these questions with many Brazilian friends and other Latin Americans. We presented our hypothesis to Celso Furtado for his opinion: that this savagery is found more in the behavior of the "newly arrived immigrants," who came to America to make a fortune at any price, than in that of the "old Brazilians." Celso confirmed the soundness of our intuition. The question of why there is so much brutality in the society is certainly one of the most complex, and the phenomenon has so many diverse aspects that no unilateral causality can explain it. One of the devastating results of slavery—usually hardly mentioned—is the destruction of the idea of family. When human beings are treated as beasts, they end up behaving as such. Should we be surprised, then, that in entire segments of society built on the basis of slavery, even one century after its abolition, women and children abandoned by their husbands and fathers, and children even abandoned by their mothers (though this is less frequent), are so numerous?

Savagery under its various forms is certainly not exclusive to the Americas. After all, the world cup for barbarism was won by the Nazis in a European society generally classified as belonging to the "civilized" world. I am not a defender of the pre-capitalist world, reserving the label "savage" only to the effects of the law of capitalist profit. A thousand types of barbarism—in the treatment of "others" (peoples and ethnicities foreign to the group) and/or frequently women—are as old as humanity. But in our era, it frequently happens that manifestations of barbarism in these forms, far from being vestiges of the past, are actually revived by the impasses in which the modernization of peripheral capitalism traps its victims. The violence caused by religious fundamentalism and ethnic genocide is an example of this. Such savagery is undoubtedly less visible today in the societies of central capitalism. If it persists, it is largely only in areas such as the exacerbation of male chauvinism or in the treatment of animals. There is, then, perhaps a transhistorical dimension to the *"carnalitas,"* a term preferred by the late Yves Bénot.

It was the peculiar construction of capitalism in the Americas and the motivations that drove most settler colonialists—whose "pioneer" spirit is often praised—that favored such a barbarous form of capitalist development. Brazil appeared to me to be a typical case in this respect. New immigrants from the end of the nineteenth century, who came above all from Germany, Poland, or more generally Central and Eastern Europe, and incidentally also from Lebanon, had not chosen Brazil and could just as well have landed in the United States. In either case, the same mindset was at work: having given up all hope of collective struggle in their former societies (which is not a reproach; it was the result of circumstances over which they had no control), they clung to hopes of success in an individual struggle within the jungle that was open to them.

I revisited Brasilia in 2002 and it appeared to be the perfect horror. It was not so much that the Corbusier-style collective housing units—imagined at the time as a liberating innovation—then presented the drab appearance of unimaginatively designed French public housing, or that Oscar Niemeyer's architecture did not appear to me to have deserved the praise it received. The horror was the result of the hyper-functionality that was retained as the basic organizational principle: the hotel district, a district for banks, the street for restaurants (!!!) and even one for pharmacies (!!!), etc. It was as if it had been simply forgotten that each district of a real city must itself form a cell where one can live, find a pharmacy, grocery store, café, or restaurant nearby. A visit to the mausoleum of Juscelino Kubitschek quite bluntly clarified the reasons for this urban failure. The populism that dominated the world of the 1930s to the 1950s here was quite manifest in images of an extremely repetitive banality: photographs of the "great leader" addressing admiring crowds; promises of rapid modernization, wealth, and power; a childish worship of the leader (display cases filled with his awards and everyday objects), etc. All of that can be found in Atatürk's mausoleum, for example. Populism views everything from above and kills all spontaneous initiatives—the thing that historically made cities, the real ones, that is.

Manaus was what one would expect: the memory of the crazy era when rubber was king, at the beginning of the last century. Many of the very beautiful vestiges were being restored. But Amazonia revealed to me that the Indian presence in Brazil was much stronger than I had imagined. There was an almost dominant physical presence and unexpected "Asian" cultural traits. The small lodge in the forest seemed to us as if it were managed by Vietnamese, as much by the personal attention as by its perfect organization. Isabelle remarked that the feathers that were used in large numbers and varied colors in Carnaval were probably the contribution of the Indians, since there was nothing equivalent to them in Africa. Carnaval was, for me, more a masquerade than anything else, despite the exuberant and extraordinary imagination the Brazilian people clearly demonstrate in organizing it. The samba could be monotonous, but above all there was a certain hyper-commercialization. The entire Carnaval experience was used by the system to make people forget the reality of poverty, just like the running of the bulls and other circus games. Porto Alegre has become a capital, having already hosted the World Social Forum four times between 2001 and 2005. The Forum in Amazonia, organized in Belém by its sympathetic mayor, Edmilson Rodrigues, in which

Isabelle and I participated in 2003, was also an opportunity to visit São Luís, the Saint Louis of Brazil, founded by Richelieu at the same time as the town of the same name in Senegal—the latter to send the "Negroes" and the former to receive them! The architecture of the two places is similar, understated and beautiful.

In recent years, I have had the opportunity to see a little more closely, thanks to comrades and friends—Emir Sader and Giorgio Romano Schutte— what became of the organized popular forces in this large country, since they seem rarely active at the present moment: the PT, the MST, and the CUT. For me, Brazil is one of the weak links in the world system. That is why one has a duty to be demanding with regard to its avant-garde: the possibility of what could be achieved is large. Will they do it? That is the question. The main danger is, in my opinion, produced by the "European" illusion, which is a strong presence in a large part of the activist leadership, encouraged by the PT's European "friends," who are a bit too numerous. What I mean by the European illusion is the idea that Brazil could "imitate" the "European lefts," of yesterday and today, and maybe of tomorrow, forgetting a little too much that Brazil belongs to the system's periphery, not to its center. There is already more than enough proof that this illusion encourages "electoralist" temptations, which, as always, entail their dose of opportunism. From the Salvador Allende experience in Chile to the permanent crisis in Argentina, this illusion—which finds its roots in the cultural history of the continent, as I pointed out above—has already had devastating effects and led to many aborted movements that could have moved in a different direction.

I met Lula in 2001 and he impressed me as a first-rate politician, intelligent and modest, who knew how to listen and respond with non-stereotypical arguments. But will he and the others resist the temptation? Will the PT avoid, in this case, a break between its leadership and its grassroots activists? There are already indications of such a break. Or will the party succeed in overcoming the heterogeneity of the social interests it has to bring together and invent new methods that allow democratic, social, and anti-imperialist advances? All that is also possible. Brazil is confronted with a threefold challenge: social progress, democracy, and national independence. Advances in these three directions must be simultaneous so they can mutually support one another. Populism had a national and social project, but it was hardly democratic. The (nationalist) dictatorship despised social progress and was horrified by democracy. Fernando Henrique Cardoso sacrificed social aspects and independence for democracy. It was up to Lula, elected and reelected with a large majority, and then up to the president who succeeded him, to push the country in the three directions simultaneously. I am of the opinion that modest, but parallel advances are, in the long run, better than leaps in one direction that sacrifice the others. Brazil, unfortunately, does not currently appear to be committed to this path.

Brazil is often presented too quickly as a good example of emergence and I have a few observations to make about that. I gave priority in my travel plans to visits that would allow me to follow the changes in this large country closely. My repeated visits, among others during the World Social Forums held in Porto Alegre in the beginning of the 2000s, gave me the opportunity to discuss these questions with our Brazilian colleagues, Paulo Nakatani (vice president of the WFA and leader of one of the best working groups on the critique of contemporary capitalism), João Pedro Stedile (MST), Renaldo José (PCB), Plino Sampaio (involved with agrarian reform), and others.

There are certainly elements of a sovereign politics in Brazil, led by large Brazilian private industrial and finance capital and large-scale capitalist agrarian concerns. But here, as in India, the general economic policies remain liberal, providing no solution to the problems of poverty in a country now 90 percent urbanized, although that is attenuated by redistributive measures of social assistance. In Brazil, as in India, the government's hesitation to go further encourages ambiguity in the behavior of large capital, tempted by a search for compromise with international capital. The exploitation of Brazil's fabulous natural wealth in deplorable conditions (destruction of the Amazon Basin) reinforces even more the attempt to insert the country into the established system of globalization. I would add that Brazil is fully subject to the vagaries of financial globalization since the financial management reforms introduced by Cardoso—which have not subsequently been questioned. Paulo Nakatani, who is one of the best specialists on these questions (I will dare to say one of the best in the world), not only has judged the disastrous effects of financial globalization, but has also put forward ideas that would allow Brazil to overcome these effects. The situation was different in India, which had long maintained control of its financial system, but this is now on the way to being reversed.

## ARGENTINA

Isabelle and I have visited Argentina twice, in 1973 and 2003. On our second visit, we hardly recognized the society since it seemed to us that it has changed so much. Argentina's history is unparalleled. In 1900, Argentina was one of the top countries in terms of income per capita. Argentines—despite the most scandalous inequality in the distribution of wealth—believed they had built, once and for all, a new Europe in the American paradise, one where the prosperity contrasted sharply with the poverty of the regions from which the migrants had come.

Our first visit, which coincided with Juan Perón's return in 1973, brought home to us what I do not hesitate to describe as a neurotic political culture produced by the inexorable decline afflicting the country. I do not intend this description as an insult. History is replete with similar declines to which para-religious or para-ethnic fundamentalisms are witness. For me, Argentina is the example of a country in the periphery of world capitalism that refuses to acknowledge its status, under the pretext that it feels itself to be "European." This European dimension did not bother us. Isabelle and I are not lovers of exoticism, and the Europeanness of Buenos Aires—which we expected—was not a disappointment to us.

Most people have much difficulty in understanding that peripheral societies can, in exceptional circumstances, be rather well off. The peripheral character of a society is defined by the fact that it is not an active actor in shaping the world system, to which it must only "adjust itself," through a process of "permanent structural adjustment" (to use the expression I have used for more than fifty years!). The oil-rich countries of the Persian Gulf are a good example. And I can only imagine, with a shiver down my spine, what their reaction might be if they returned to poverty tomorrow (probably much worse than that of the Argentines). I will say that in (ongoing) globalization, there are globalizers (the centers) and the globalized (the peripheries). It is easy to understand that the loss of wealth—if the latter is associated with Europeanness—may be experienced not only as intolerable, but also as inexplicable.

Received by the important novelist Jorge Sabato in 1973, we were literally flabbergasted by his words and actions. An extreme male chauvinist, he seemed anxious to show it through the (imposed?) behavior of women, silent and respectful, carrying dishes of food and ashtrays to the "master," etc. There were illuminating remarks: "We Argentines are pure Europeans, no Negroes or Indians here." So? What a reason to be proud! But maybe Jorge Sabato was only an exception, the type of person who might just as well be encountered elsewhere. Unfortunately, Argentine politics only reinforced my judgment that here it was a question of a neurotic polity. Yet, the decline in Argentina's position in the world resulted in a mass social movement and workers' struggles that had quite a significant impact and produced one of the first great explosions of modern populism, beginning in the 1940s with Perón. Today, we can smile when presented with images of that time, the adulation of the leader. But Argentina had no monopoly over that kind of thing. And the all-too-quick identification of this populism with fascism is not correct. Perónist populism was anti-imperialist and progressive in its own way. The excesses of language and manners by the general and his wife, Eva, should not take anything away from the positive measures made in favor of workers. We can find the later excursions of the aged leader who did not want to be separated from the armored casket of Eva—"*los restos de Eva*"—amusing, or macabre. But there is something more serious that is problematic here: at the time, no one seemed to have gone beyond Peronist populism. I was always, then, worried—and sometimes truly irritated—that all the activists and politicians that I met said they were "Peronists." Peronists of the left, the extreme left, the center, the right, the extreme right, but everyone was always a "Peronist." I do not believe that such a phenomenon—which I have seen nowhere else—can only be explained by political reasons or by the class struggle.

I have known in Argentina many brilliant intellectuals and charming personalities. Enrique Oteiza, the true initiator of CLACSO, who gave to the *dependencia* school its worldwide reputation, is a friend of extreme refinement, which he combines with a flawless activist spirit. Moise Ikonikoff, whom I saw both in Paris and Buenos Aires, was always so generous, even if he chose to make a foolish political career. Oscar Braun, whom I invited to join the IDEP team, was devoted to his teaching, as the best always are. Atilio Boron succeeded Oteiza at CLACSO and brought it back to its glory days after it had succumbed for a time to the charms of triumphant liberalism. But is it by chance that all these friends felt some repugnance toward the Peronist phenomenon? Is it by chance that, consequently, some remained attached to an old Communist Party even when it turned out unable to define any effective strategy whatsoever to go beyond populism, even though it clearly saw its limitations?

All the same, the page of Peronism is, perhaps, on the way to being turned. After the odious Jorge Rafael Videla dictatorship—Washington's man, who bathed in the blood of thousands of the "disappeared," murdered daily by his police, trained by experts from the United States—followed by the Carlos Menem farce, another Washington man, this time from the neoliberal era, the conditions seemed ripe for a renewal of social and political struggles freed from the specter of Perón. Videla, like Saddam Hussein, ended up losing his grip, believing that reconquering the Malvinas would provide a foundation for the national legitimacy of his government. The Malvinas are Argentines, just like Kuwait is Iraqi. Both of these dictators then became, without meaning to, enemies to bring down.

The new democracy, by joining the neoliberal camp, subject to the diktat of U.S. financial capital, could only lead to disaster. Dollarization, hailed by the World Bank as the way to salvation, ended in a resounding failure at the end of 2001. The middle classes were then suddenly pauperized in the extreme, losing all their savings, which were stolen by the banks (U.S. ones, of course—pure and simple pillage). But they did not react as one might have feared, that is, by a move toward fascism and a repudiation of democracy, its credibility undermined in public opinion. On the contrary, and to their honor, they led the gigantic mass movement of the *piqueteros*.

Our second visit to Argentina took place after this movement. The working class itself, fragmented as elsewhere by neoliberal policies, is open to the possibility of renewing its ways of organizing and acting. The new union—the CTA—to which our Cuban-Argentine friend Isabel Rauber introduced me, is working to invent new forms of organization capable of uniting organized workers, the unemployed, and the precarious workers—and, with that in mind, advance and enrich democratic practice. There are pioneering experiments underway (on a world scale). In such conditions, there are serious reasons for optimism. The construction of a united front of workers and the definition of terms for an acceptable social compromise for the middle classes are possible. Their realization would give Argentina the leading role in Latin American liberation and in progressing beyond "low-intensity (bourgeois) democracy."

I must say that, in this atmosphere, I learned much over the cycle of lectures and debates that the CTA organized for me in August 2003, and the excursions from district to district, from Buenos Aires to Rosario and to Neuquén. I shall pass over the delightful excursions to the Tigre district (the splendid delta of the Paraná), to wild Patagonia, and to the Andes where another Fujiyama towers up, almost exactly on the other side of the world from the original. I shall also pass over any discussion of Gardel and the tango, a brilliant Italo-Castilian synthesis.

CHILE

I visited Chile for the first time a little after the electoral victory of the Popular Unity (UP) and President Salvador Allende in 1971. Socialist and communist leaders—particularly Clodomiro Altamira, Gonzalo Martner, and Pedro Vuskovic—opened the doors of ministerial offices where they worked and explained their program to me. It was not a question of a socialist revolution that would completely abolish private property, but only a program of radical reforms: nationalization of the copper mines with fair compensation to the owners (North American oligopolies), an agrarian reform that would reduce the size of latifundia and satisfy the minimal demands of poor peasants and the landless (themselves well organized), as well as laws and reforms in favor of wage workers (also strongly organized). It was a question, then, of a program that would replace the brutal form of capitalism dominant in the Americas with civilized capitalist management by means of advances for the working class. In other words, to do what the best social democrats had done in Europe in the postwar period. It was also a question of strengthening the tools for national management of the economy by reducing the means of action for dominant foreign capital.

From there, it would be possible to examine prospects for the longer term. For the moderates—Christian Democrats like Osvaldo Sunkel and, perhaps, some socialists like Juan Somavia—these reforms were maybe an end in itself, letting history decide the later developments allowed by these reforms. For others, dominant in the socialist and communist organizations, these reforms would open the road to a gradual construction of socialism. The new left was powerful in the country and had played an important role in the mobilization and organization of the working classes. The Christians of MAPU, whom I knew through one of their important ideologues, Franz Hinkelammert, one of the leading figures in the new theology of liberation, was a strong and active wing of this new left. The MIR, whose leaders were introduced to me by André Gunder Frank, his wife, Marta Fuentes, Marta Harnecker (a Chilean who subsequently chose to live and work in Cuba), and numerous Latin American refugees (particularly Brazilians) who followed the same line as this new left, was the dominant leftist organization in Popular Unity.

I was invited everywhere—to the universities, hotbeds of activity in this historic moment, and to very long evenings (night until the early hours of the morning) of discussions organized by different people at their own homes, in the Latin American way. I listened and freely shared my personal opinions. But as I have already said, I am not the type of person who "sermonizes," above all to activists who carry on actual struggles in the field.

At bottom, the only thing that worried me—very much even—was the naïveté of the government leaders about Washington's probable (for me, certain) reaction to their program. It was this naïveté that bothered me and not the limitations of the reforms implemented. The reforms were an imperative first step. One could see afterward if the dynamics of the social movement would make it possible to go further. But even if it would not have been possible—at least immediately, on the heels of the UP's victory— one could be sorry about it, but the reforms would have to be done in any case. History advances as it can. What I feared, then, was that the United States would not even tolerate the UP's reform program. For me, it was obvious that to lay a finger on the excessive profits of the North American oligopolies was to hurt the most sacred part—the only sacred part—of the

U.S. body. Interpreted as a declaration of war in Washington, these reforms were immediately the occasion for a violent intervention by the United States. Neither rhetoric on "democracy," which has no credibility for me when it is orchestrated by the media in service to Washington, nor the least respect for the sovereignty of peoples and nations, would stop the implementation of U.S. aggression. With cynicism, U.S. foreign policy never hesitates to assassinate a president, whether elected democratically or not, to cause the massacre of tens of thousands (even hundreds of thousands, as in Indonesia) of ordinary human beings by a dictatorship established with its support in order to restore the excess profits of its threatened corporations. Of course, the United States looks for—and finds—local allies (and there are always some, particularly in Latin America where the wealthy classes and the armed forces are loyally devoted to it), just as it exploits the possible errors (which even democratic governments can commit!) of its opponents. I continued to repeat this scenario to all my Chilean interlocutors and was astounded that a large majority of them did not believe it. A. G. Frank—a pessimist by nature, but clear thinking and without any illusions about what the leaders of the United States are—and some comrades from the MIR were the only ones to share my fears.

Subsequent events, unfortunately, proved me right. When I visited Santiago again in 1973, a few months before Pinochet's coup d'état, the situation had deteriorated considerably, less from errors committed by the UP government than from the implementation of the strategies of the alliance between Washington and local reactionary forces. The strike by truckers, demonstrations by loud fascist groups, which were not repressed, hailed by U.S. media as demonstrations by "democrats" (!!)—all of that smelled of trouble. The leaders, however, remained phlegmatic and, it seemed to me, maybe even unaware.

Occupied full time by all these discussions, I did not have the possibility of seeing a little of the country, except for a short trip to Valparaiso. There, local comrades invited me to taste the excellent shellfish (the *locos*) in a wooden casino built on the sea, in the style of those we know in Egypt. It was a very enjoyable day. The visit to the fabulous Andes, where the union of copper miners expected me, and to the coastal fjords where students from the provincial university had invited me, had to be put off until later. The "later" never came, of course, because of the Pinochet coup d'état. What I personally regret the most, from a tourist point of view, is not having had the opportunity to see Tierra del Fuego. But who knows, perhaps in the future.

The Chilean people charmed Isabelle and me very much. Even beyond the numerous meetings with comrades and friends, the encounters here or there with students or others were always very friendly. As for the daily earthquakes, one could get used to it quite quickly, it seemed. Yet I remember having been witness to a much more violent jolt. We were meeting in the basement of the ECLAC building. Enrique Iglesias presided. A muffled rumbling, as if it were coming from the beyond, stopped short all discussion. Iglesias quite calmly said after a half minute of cold silence: "Remain calm and in your seats; this building was built to resist the strongest quakes." I can then say that the Third World Forum, born that day in 1973 in Santiago, made the earth shake, or that the earth made it shake. Choose your omen.

I then also visited the ECLAC itself. There were many excellent analysts, talented economists and sociologists. Leftist political refugees (Brazilians and Argentines mainly, but also Peruvians, Colombians, and Bolivians) were always welcomed with kindness, which is all to the credit of the tradition begun by Raúl Prebisch and continued by Iglesias. However, I found the works of the *desarrollismo* school rather insipid in comparison with what the *dependencia* authors were then producing, represented here by the works of political refugees. On this occasion, I met Prebisch, with whom I had a long discussion. I did not hide my critical opinion of *desarrollismo*. I was impressed by his caliber, culture, extraordinary modesty, and his way of listening attentively. His always astute responses displayed a profound doubt, which is often characteristic of real thinkers. He did not dismiss the critiques of *desarrollismo* and seemed indeed to understand its contradictions and limitations. But he did not believe a better alternative was possible. Prebisch continued to age well, becoming more radical with the passing years and the lessons of history. I saw him again some fifteen years later in 1988, in Vienna, where we discussed the Brandt Report and the new prospects for globalization. This time we were on the same page and made the same critique of the naïveté of the European social democrats who dominated the scene. They did not understand the reasons for the failure of *desarrollismo*. "You saw them," he said to me.

## PERU

In 1971, Anibal Quijano, Julio Cotler, and their group in Peru welcomed Isabelle and me. They were probably almost alone at the time in their criticism of Juan Velasco Alvarado's populist government, which had just chased out Washington's traditional lackeys. The atmosphere altogether reminded me of Nasser's Egypt: same rhetorical style, same nationalist emphasis and social indecisiveness, same contempt for democracy.

Lima is a beautiful city and its Plaza de Armas is a monument of Spanish colonization. In spite of the ethnic mixing—the Indian type dominates—the truly urban population of the capital gives the impression of being quite Hispanic. In the slums, which continue to grow, this is maybe not the case, and recent rural immigrants are "more Indian," it was explained to me. The shock comes as soon as one ascends into the Andes. Isabelle and I reached Cuzco by plane—a small DC 3 or 4 that turned in a frightening spiral into the bowl in which the city sits, surrounded by 7,000-meter peaks. From there, we took a marvelous trip to La Paz via train, a boat across Lake Titicaca, and then a taxi from the border to the Bolivian capital. What a landscape! To travel through a pass at an altitude of more than 5,000 meters, on the Altiplano populated by magnificent herds of llamas, leaves an unforgettable impression. At the rail terminus in Puno, we had to spend the night. Although everything had been supposedly arranged by the agency in Lima that had organized our tour, the "hotel"—if the inn where we stayed could be called that—claimed to know nothing. Moreover, the hotel had only a dormitory where Isabelle and I, still completely dressed, were tightly packed together under dubious-looking blankets next to twenty loudly snoring Indian peasants. We traveled over a small part of Lake Titicaca by boat then continued on to La Paz.

From Cuzco, we also visited Machu Picchu. The small train ran along a frightening precipice: to the left, the Andes peaks; to the right, the drop to Amazonia; and in between was a winding embankment two meters at the widest on which the rails were placed. The beauty of the place made up for the fright of the trip. And what a reward: the ruins of Machu Picchu, photos of which are distributed throughout the world on postcards, are even more imposing when seen in person, as was to be expected. But even more astonishing is that the existence of these ruins was held secret for three centuries. The fact that the local Indian peasants, who went there to practice their religion, had maintained such a level of solidarity in keeping silent before the Spanish conquistador, says more about the national reality of the country than all the "scientific" analyses could produce on the subject. My impression that there were still two countries was convincingly confirmed, even if there were nuances that must be pointed out. I shall return to this matter.

BOLIVIA

At the border with Bolivia, there was a long wait while negotiations with customs officials and the police took place. The army was visible everywhere and we were afraid of the stern faces of the Indian peasants that made up its ranks. Finally, we were in the taxi. The road went through the beautiful Altiplano. Halfway between the border and La Paz, completely surrounded by a desert—in the middle of nowhere, as the English say—was a gigantic cathedral. It was abandoned, but not fallen into ruin—testifying both to the madness of the conquistadors and the wealth of the silver mines they plundered. This was an echo of the glorious beginnings of capitalism, built on the corpses of millions of slaves, as Marx recounted in his analysis of primary accumulation.

In La Paz, it was as if we had arrived in another country. The "revolution" had just triumphed. There were red flags everywhere and banners with the usual slogans. Received by the leaders of the revolution, well-known Trotskyist leaders, I took note of their astonishing remarks: "This is a proletarian revolution, comrade. We will not make the same error as those imbeciles, the false communists in China and elsewhere, who united the peasants with their movement and thus caused it to lose its proletarian purity. Here, it is the working class that is in power, and it alone." Peasant leaders had been received by this government, which had straight out refused to promise them anything whatsoever; above all, not an agrarian reform that would make possible the formation of a bloc of property owners hostile to socialism! I contented myself with saying to the Trotskyist leaders: "Your pure revolution will only last the space of one morning. The army of Indian peasants will not revolt against their reactionary officers; they will obey them to crush you."

La Paz lived in a phenomenal illusion. Its sight reminded me of Barcelona in 1936, at the high point of the POUM, some images of which I have seen in documentaries. In the evening, the friends who had welcomed us took us to a popular "cabaret." This was a sort of tavern where you ate a little, drank even more, and listened to a popular singer strumming a guitar. These were amazing songs, partly in Spanish (which I understand) and partly in Quechua (which had to be translated for me). "We have had enough of you [the Spaniards] and your religion, etc.," sang these singers. There were two countries, as I said earlier. But our interlocutors—intellectuals, of course—a little embarrassed, attempted to minimize the meaning of the words. We left La Paz a few days later. One week later, the army carried out the 130th Bolivian coup d'état (or maybe the total was a bit higher), putting an end to the festival. There were mass arrests, assassinations of militants, etc. . . . the well-known song. The Indians ended up winning all the same with the presidency of Evo Morales, which is a truly revolutionary advance.

## VENEZUELA

In Venezuela in 1971, our very dear friend Héctor Silva Michelena and his wife, Adicea, welcomed us with characteristic generosity. The couple had spent two years at the IDEP, at my invitation. Hector is a man of exceptional quality, with wide-ranging knowledge, a subtle reading of Marxism, solid argumentation, and compassion. His two brothers, Ludovico, a brilliant philosopher who died too young as an alcoholic, and the late José Silva, a sound political scientist, also became our friends in Caracas, like all the others of their small group, notably Hein Sonntag and Armando Cordova. Venezuela is certainly not Mexico. And our friend Alonso Aguilar told us in the plane that took us from Caracas to Mexico that the Venezuelan bourgeoisie was *"rastaquera"* (*rastaquouère* in French, a social upstart, especially from a Mediterranean or Latin American country), nothing like that of Mexico. Caracas was famous for businessmen of this type, originally owners of bars and brothels and connected with diverse mafias from around the world rather than managers of less conspicuous businesses and industries. The oil money had not altered things, of course. The nouveau riche–style palatial villas in questionable taste, massive gold bracelets, and white suits and shoes dominated the bourgeois landscape. As for the middle and working classes, McDonald's, plastic, and U.S.-style prefabs had triumphed. The horrible slums were perhaps the most authentically Latin American thing remaining in the country. The Michelenas took us through part of this extensive country. We saw the pretty tropical Caribbean coast, Maracaibo and the horror of the oil boom, the peaks of the Andes, and the small city of Medina de los Andes, a Hispanic haven lost in a wonderful location.

It was forty years later that I returned to Venezuela to participate in the Caracas session of the World Social Forum in 2006. I found a country that had nothing in common with the one I had known. A true social revolution—it is not excessive to say so—had occurred in the sense that, finally, we could see Indians, blacks, and mixed race people—the majority of the population—elsewhere than in the street! Until the arrival of Hugo Chávez, all the powers in the country were reserved for the whitest of the white, strictly European in origin. This change is not, in my opinion, of secondary significance. It is the proof that political power (but nothing more, understand) has passed to the representatives of the Venezuelan people as it really is. It is the proof that the Chávez government is not that of some soldier—one of mixed race, at that—but the result of a real mass movement. That augurs well for many new possibilities that could ultimately be conducive to necessary radical social transformations. That is the new challenge confronting the Venezuelan people. It is well known that a large number of Venezuelan intellectuals, recently of the left, have taken positions that are not critical, but clearly reactionary. This is the case probably because they did not support the emergence of the people from the street as has happened. I was not too surprised at that. The oil rent had truly corrupted the middle classes. To see these intellectuals strut about in sumptuous villas was always unsavory and unacceptable to me.

## MEXICO

In 1973, I was invited to the CLACSO assembly in Mexico. Again, I was confronted with the same phenomenon of two countries in one. Here, however, I shall offer some different comments. I had arrived on Friday and the assembly was not to begin until Monday. On the weekend, I ventured out as a tourist. Equipped with a good map, I visited everything important to see. The cathedral impressed me, not so much by its architecture and size than by the spectacle of the faithful. Men and women, young and old, from the working classes, all or almost all with Indian physiques or at least of mixed race, participated in a half-Spanish, half-Indian liturgy—shaking paper flowers, plastic skeletons, curious objects, and holy images no less unusual because of their Indian faces and feathered heads. On Monday, in the great meeting hall of CLACSO, there was a completely different human landscape: once again we were in Barcelona or Madrid. I had the audacity to say: "Yesterday, I was in Asia, today I am in Spain. This does not cause you any problems?" I believe my remarks were not at all well received.

In visiting this large country a little with Isabelle, I noted all the same that Mexico was neither Peru nor Bolivia. We went to two Indian regions: the superb Oaxaca and in Mayan Yucatán, to Mérida and, nearby, Chichen Itza. I believe that a foreign observer—if he were attentive to this type of thing—would understand that Mexico is one nation—only one, Hispano-Indian, if you wish to call it such. My hypothesis is that this nation is the result of the great revolution of the 1910s and 1920s. Beyond the romanticism inspired by Zapata's peasant cavalcade and others, beyond the fact that the bourgeoisie put an end to this popular revolution, it remains the case that the revolution put an end to the colonial heritage for good. That is not the case in the Andean countries, which have yet to experience a similar transformation.

Mexico is a beautiful country that I believe I know a little better than others. I owe this advantage to my numerous Mexican colleagues, above all to Pablo González Casanova and his wife, Marianne, both our very dear friends. Pablo is, because of his stature, a leading Mexican politician, respected by all democratic and popular forces in his country. Our discussions are always, for me, a way to enrich my knowledge of Mexico and Latin America. Mexican colleagues, such as Alonso Aguilar, and others, also help me find my way through the twists and turns of Mexican politics, which are very complicated. Mexico City was certainly a city well worth knowing, for the liveliness of the historic parts, the richness of its museums, its cultural life, and intense politics. But it was terribly polluted by automobiles fueled with poorly refined gasoline. Perched at an altitude of 2,500 meters, oxygen was thinner there.

Moreover, since it was located at the bottom of a basin, it received all the noxious effects from the suspect smoke and fumes generated by its industries. But, if you were wealthy, you could always escape this hell and find refuge in one of the magnificent small cities nearby, such as Cuernavaca. I went further, to Guadalajara and Puebla, and can no longer remember how many talks I made in the country's universities. The pyramids, well known to all tourists, were certainly worth the trip. The ascent was easy, but the descent was terrifying because of the vertigo.

President Echeverría had shown a stronger interest in intensifying relations between Mexico and Asia and Africa than his predecessors and successors. He sought me out during his official trip to Dakar, in 1992 I believe, and invited me to Mexico to continue the discussion we had barely begun—due to lack of time—in the Senegalese capital. I accepted, simply because I thought all initiatives that set out to strengthen a front of the Global South were always worth supporting even if it was clear that the objective conditions—that is, the social nature of the governments in question—limited the potential scope of such actions. Echeverría had organized a grand fiesta in a fabulous hacienda that Cortés had built on a remarkable site along the route of his conquests. I was seated next to the president who posed many—intelligent and precise—questions to me about the world economy and the problems of Asia and Africa. I responded frankly, as I am used to doing, explaining my arguments. But the music was so loud we could barely hear each other. I then told the president straight off: perhaps our conversation would be a little easier if the musicians were to move farther away from you? Echeverría burst out laughing and responded: "Impossible, I am only the President, and in Mexico, musicians take precedence!" The conversation was thus resumed in the quiet of his office at the presidential palace in Mexico City. Echeverría probably wanted to exploit our Forum in a certain way and the first choice that had been made for our bureau in Latin America was unfortunate and might have encouraged some ambitions of the PRI bureaucracy. We quickly put things right and ended any ambiguity about the Forum's objectives.

During a recent trip to Mexico, I saw firsthand the social and political disaster produced by the country's membership in NAFTA (the common market of the United States, Canada, and Mexico). I even went so far as to speak of the "suicide of the Mexican nation." My friends in the country considered that judgment too harsh. Let me explain myself. The uncontrolled opening to trade and capital (including speculative capital) movements cannot result in anything other than the systematic pillage of Mexico's natural resources, the destruction of its peasantry, and lumpen-development. The fabulous enrichment of the new oligarchy (Carlos Slim and others) does not compensate for this disaster. Mexicans are thus condemned to attempt to cross en masse the most protected border in the world, a wall of shame and crime in comparison to which the Berlin Wall was a joke. Are the immigrants, then, going to reconquer the United States, as it is all too quickly said, or at least the West, which had been stolen from Mexico in the nineteenth century? You would have to be incredibly naive to believe this fairy tale. Immigrants to the United States always end up accepting their submission and subscribe to the "American dream." If I remain optimistic, despite my unreserved judgment that the Mexican dominant class is responsible for nothing less than national treason, it is because I am convinced that the Mexican people, which already made a great revolution, will make a second one. It will combine revolutionary social advances with the reconquest of Mexico's independence. The renewal of creative Marxist thinking, which I have noted among young communists, and the interest they exhibit in participating in debates we organize are good indicators of this.

## THE WEST INDIES

The English-speaking Caribbean and Haiti make up a world that has little in common with Latin America beyond the geographic proximity. Center of the mercantilist slave system, the region is, consequently, among the most ravaged by the history of capitalism.

### *Jamaica*

In Jamaica, I was welcomed by my friend Norman Girvan, one of those I had originally invited to join the IDEP, and by Kari Polanyi, Karl Polanyi's daughter and a longtime friend whom I first met during one of her trips to Dakar at the beginning of the 1970s, and then later at McGill University in Montreal. She split her time between Montreal and Kingston. Right away, I met a group of Anglophone West Indians sparkling with mischief and humor. Norman had been strongly active in supporting the national populist experiment of the first Manley government, and then withdrawn to the university and had no illusions after Michael Manley's return to power in the conditions of the new liberal policies to which the Jamaican government believed it was forced to subscribe (this was in 1989). The subject of our discussions focused on globalization in general, a subject on which Norman always has much to say, having meticulously studied the strategies of the multinationals that pillage his country.

I visited this small country in the company of these good friends. There were beautiful beaches separated from the rest of the country—which was considered too aggressive for tourists—by barbed wire, watchtowers, and U.S.-style armed security officers equipped with all kinds of devices. Isabelle had imagined, in one of her caricatures, this way of organizing tourism in the Third World. Jamaicans recount with humor that, in passing along the barbed wire, they give the finger to the North Americans, but that the latter, upon returning home, say that the people of the country are so hospitable and nice and always wave to them, but in a funny way. I saw desolate scenes of land devastated by an unrestrained plantation agriculture that destroyed the soil (and the human beings, in this context, slaves). Fugitive slaves had taken refuge on these abandoned lands. Along the coast, we could see a U.S. submarine, always there, I was told, in the country's territorial waters without permission, as if to remind Jamaicans that U.S. arrogance had no accountability.

During my stay, an amusing incident occurred. An Air Jamaica plane had been inspected in Miami and found to be transporting drugs. U.S. television—which could be easily viewed in Kingston—questioned the passengers. A good little bourgeois from Jamaica, a housewife who went to shop in Miami every month, declared straight out: "Ah! This is the Wednesday flight, but everyone knows that for many years now this is the one for drugs; there is so much that it smells strong." That the U.S. customs service might be implicated in this traffic (and the search probably due to a fight among mafia gangs—including North American ones—or to a disagreement between them and the corrupt customs officials) was not mentioned or even implied. The role of the media was to attribute responsibility for the traffic solely to the drug suppliers, never to the U.S. importers and their accomplices in the Yankee administration.

## Haiti

I knew Haiti through my readings and my discussions with exiled Haitian activists. Long a refugee in Mexico, the late Gérard Pierre-Charles and his Dominican wife, Suzy Castor, are among my friends (and with whom we stayed in Port au Prince). Having returned to the country as soon as that became possible, with the first election of Jean-Bertrand Aristide, Pierre-Charles invited me there. CRESFED, an institution active in the left opposition, and its leaders, Laennec Hurbon and others, organized the visit. The "mass" conference in which François Houtart and I participated in 1999 reminded me of the best moments of great popular mobilization.

The slave uprising in Saint-Domingue at the end of the eighteenth century was the first revolution in the Americas and it was not until the Mexican Revolution of the 1910s to 1920s, followed by the Cuban Revolution in the 1950s and 1960s, that the continent experienced others. Neither the war of independence of the thirteen English colonies nor those of Latin America that followed were revolutions, since they did not challenge the social relations established by the dominant classes of mercantilist capitalism (including, of course, colonial slavery), but only involved the transfer of political power from the mother countries to the local dominant classes. It is not, then, a coincidence if the leaders of the American "revolution" were all slaveholders and that they did not even see the contradiction between their "democratic" rhetoric and their status. In Saint-Domingue, on the other hand, it was the victims of the system who revolted, not its beneficiaries. But the slaves who freed themselves had no other social aim than to become free peasants, thereby ensuring family self-subsistence, and nothing more. This sympathetic and human project was completely contradictory to that of dominant world capitalism because it did not allow the local ruling classes any way to insert themselves into the dominant system. These classes, then, used state power and terrorist forms of exercising that power to reconstruct large property holdings, tax small peasants, and thus favor the production of what the world market would buy (sugar, coffee). But the strong and continuous resistance of the free Haitian people has never allowed this form of peripheral capitalist exploitation to have any great success, unlike elsewhere in the Americas.

This popular resistance, despite the impasses in which it has often found itself, fueling outbreaks of violence, makes Haiti a captivating country, at least for me. This history gives a particular responsibility to the country's intellectuals because it is up to them to help ensure that this popular will is part of a larger effort worthy of its humanist aspirations. Throughout the nineteenth century, these intellectuals did not do this; they instead offered support to the project of the dominant classes, which was to become part of the world system. The communism of the Third International offered another possibility, that of leaving this system and building socialism. The vicissitudes of historical communism and, in the end, its excesses and collapse could inspire a return to the illusions of integrating into global capitalism, but they could also free socialist thinking and action to take a new step forward. This is all the more so since Cuba, a neighboring country that made a revolution and succeeded in avoiding the collapse we have come to associate with the Soviet model, will perhaps advance in a new direction of this sort, which would be difficult, but not impossible. This might also be the case since, throughout the West Indies, the choices on offer are the same: the peoples of this region have learned to fight, and globalized capitalism has nothing to offer them except tourism and mass emigration.

The subject of these choices was at the center of all the discussions that I had with activists from Haiti, Jamaica, the Dominican Republic, Cuba, and the other Caribbean islands. More than elsewhere, the fault line is visible between those who do not want to give up the possibility of an improved integration into global capitalism, based on serious internal social and political reforms, regional cooperation, and the possible strengthening of a front of the South capable of demanding real negotiations with the imperialist North, and those who fear that such attempts will ultimately only end in new illusions. It is not easy to choose between these two approaches. The "reformists" here are nevertheless radicals and should not be confused with the comprador bourgeoisie that is content to benefit from globalization as it is. The "revolutionaries" are not necessarily irresponsible "adventurers" or outmoded "dogmatists." Both are the products of valiant peoples, courageous in their tradition of struggle. The North American establishment is well aware of this and that is why it considers the Caribbean a "dangerous" region and never hesitates to use the most odious and violent means to intervene and destroy any attempt by these peoples to liberate themselves and achieve social and democratic progress. Its continuous support for the Tontons Macoutes in Haiti; its hypocritical military interventions (in the name of democracy!), aimed at making any democratic progress impossible; its invasion of Grenada; its unconditional support to the contras in Nicaragua; its daily threats and provocations against Cuba; and today its support for Aristide, whom it bought—all these provide daily proof of its true intentions. Faced with that, the attitude of Europeans remains timorous and, in fact, often simply aligns with Washington.

## *The Dominican Republic*

As opposed to Haiti, the Spanish part of Hispaniola (the Dominican Republic) could be integrated into the world capitalist system with less difficulty, for obvious reasons: this part of the island was much less populated during the insurrection of the French colony, it was "liberated" by the Haitians instead of having done so itself, then "protected" by the late preservation of Spanish colonialism, and ultimately integrated into the North American space to which it provides heavy immigration (and some drugs, it goes without saying).

The vestiges of this first Spanish colony (Columbus landed here) and the first capital of the Vice-Royalty of America are impressive, beautiful, and well preserved. As in Cuba, Mexico, and Brazil, the importance of these monuments and ancient cities, in contrast with the desert that is the United States, is testament to the fact that the social project of the Spanish and Portuguese was considerably richer in its cultural aims than that of the English in North

America. The island, which Isabelle and I crossed in a beautiful journey, is obviously magnificent. In the Spanish part, the poverty of the working classes seems less visible than in Haiti. Thanks to Isabelle Rauber, an activist in popular movements in several countries of the region, we could see how the working classes attempt to organize themselves as an autonomous force.

The result of all that is a rather confused government, which could be characterized as a "social democracy of the poor." Yet it has been positively active in an attempt at a North-South dialogue worthy of the name, just as Max Puig demonstrated in the course of discussions between the EU and the ACP for the renewal of the Lomé convention. The academics of the Dominican Republic welcomed me with unexpected pomp and offered me the honorary title of professor at the University of Santo Domingo in 1999. This was a testament to their sincere anti-imperialist feelings.

## The French West Indies

Upon returning from Haiti and the Dominican Republic, the stop in Guadeloupe offered a striking image. The French West Indies, like the other islands, had been subjected to the horrors of slavery and had remained impoverished colonies until the Second World War. The French today have completely forgotten that the transformation was the result of a struggle in favor of "departmentalization-assimilation" (that is, becoming an integral part of France as an overseas department), led by local communists and those of metropolitan France, against the old colonial mindset of the right and social democracy. Without the communists, the West Indies would have remained colonies and, probably, their peoples would have undertaken a struggle for independence as in the English West Indies. The choice of assimilation, that is, the effective application of the laws of metropolitan France in all political, social, and economic areas, marginalized the choice of the pro-independence forces. Today, this choice is expressed through the justified revolt against the vestiges of racism (on the way to extinction anyway) and, above all, against the ravages of tourism. Assimilation has occurred in the conditions of a system that has remained capitalist, although the communists of that earlier time had thought of it in terms of a socialist transformation. As such, it has included the reproduction of the inequality immanent to this system (but attenuated in terms of quality of life by emigration), the opening of services to West Indians by the French Civil Service, tourism, and economic and social subsidies.

In 2003, on our way to Belem, Isabelle and I passed through French Guiana. One must see the space center. Impressive, and reassuring, when one knows that the technology used, French in this case, is equal to that of the United States and could easily surpass it if the importance of the stakes were understood: put an end to Washington's arrogance.

As a student in Paris, I knew a good number of communist militants and leaders from the West Indies (and Réunion) and shared their choice: assimilation. I do not believe they were wrong. Unquestionably, their socialist hopes were disappointed. But the struggle for socialism can and must be continued, today side by side with other segments of French society. This struggle has no less a chance of success than that undertaken by the other West Indians in opposing the American ogre.

The Haitian people originally made a similar choice: to benefit from citizenship in revolutionary France. The Montagnards understood that, to the point that some among them were capable of formulating this superb thought: "They (the slaves of Saint-Domingue) have conquered their liberty; they are citizens." But Napoleon, prisoner of his conservative, and thus colonialist, prejudices was not made to understand this.

EMERGENCE OR INCREASED PILLAGE OF NATURAL RESOURCES?

The functions attributed to certain countries in Latin America and the Caribbean are no different than those the pillage colonies in Africa and Asia fulfill. This status still characterizes Venezuela and Bolivia: suppliers of oil and minerals and nothing more. Certainly, the established governments—Chávez, followed by Nicolás Maduro, in Venezuela, and Morales in Bolivia—which arose from authentic popular advances, are aware of this and would like to promote genuine systematic policies that allow them to get beyond this status of raw materials supplier. Beyond the objective difficulties this aim encounters, there is not only the declared hostility of the imperialist powers, but also that of sizable segments of Western public opinion, once again successfully manipulated by the media clergy that serve the pillaging monopolies.

In the Caribbean, after the sugar-growing era began its decline, the dominant forces on the world scale could propose nothing other than tourism and the super-exploitation of local labor in enclaves—subjected to the direct dictatorship of international capital (beneficiary of exorbitant financial advantages) as new foci of economic activity. I had the opportunity to discuss these questions in 1999 in Jamaica, Haiti, and Cuba. I made the observation that the proposed development path straightaway excluded even a timid beginning to constructing an integrated economy at the national and regional levels, an imperative condition to meet the minimal requirements for social and political progress.

## THE DEMOCRATIZATION OF LATIN AMERICA, 1980–2000

Latin America's political culture was profoundly transformed during the 1980s and 1990s, and its societies began a real democratization far beyond, I believe, anything attempted in Asia, the Middle East, and Africa (except South Africa). I am not speaking here of appearances, that is, the superficial adoption of so-called principles of a multiparty system and elections—sometimes almost honest, usually just a masquerade—and the occasional recognition of some human rights in theory and practice. These "reforms," made fashionable by the dominant media, in no way guarantee the democratization of society, not even really that of political life. They are, to a large extent, only a convenient way to manage the crisis for dominant transnational capital in the current phase of chaos. I am speaking here of serious things, of the democratization of political culture and ideological interpretations.

From this viewpoint, the majority of Latin American societies seem to be on the way to making a qualitative leap. The "traditions" of autocracy in the management of relations between governors and governed, between leaders and masses, between party leaders and rank-and-file activists (including in left, even revolutionary and Marxist parties, of course), between men and women, between central power and local communities, are all being strongly shaken by a growing awareness and multiform actions. I owe my understanding of all this to my friend P. G. Casanova, who emphasizes that this is indeed a new reality crystallizing, and I am convinced of the strength of his arguments. The beginning of this deep democratization is real, it is not a question of pious wishes and illusions nourished by superficial transformations; it is a question of a real groundswell.

Nothing comparable, it seems to me, has been undertaken in Asia and Africa. As a whole, the demand for democratization (and I deliberately say "democratization," considered as a deep and long process, and not "democracy," defined in general as a state of being amounting to some partial concepts with limited significance) remains alien to the political culture of both the ruling classes and the dominated classes. There are even many signs of regression in these areas, such as the support of both the dominant and the dominated for the mirages of fundamentalism, whether that be religious or ethnic. These regressions empty the so-called democratic reforms—when they are implemented—of any serious content. There are unquestionably exceptions of various kinds and of varying scope, in Korea, China, in its own way, India, where a certain dose of democracy in political management appears to be solidly rooted, and South Africa, thanks to the victory over apartheid. But these are only exceptions, still fragile or even threatened.

But in Latin America, as in the Asian and African exceptions, the aspiration of peoples to democratization of social and political relations immediately comes up against the constraints imposed by capitalist globalization. Inequality in income distribution, mass pauperization, and the exclusion of so-called marginalized strata—all fatally generated by submission to the requirements of globalized capitalist liberalism—weaken democratic advances, empty them of any actual content, and, if the submission to liberalism were continued, would reduce their scope to what I have called elsewhere "low-intensity democracy." The imperative task today is to define overall strategies—economic and political—that would secure the mutual reinforcement of democratic aspirations and aspirations to "social justice" (a term I do not like very much because it is elastic and ambiguous, but I use it to designate all of the reforms necessary to ensure maximum equality and social integration). These strategies necessarily imply a refusal to submit to neoliberalism and a willingness to begin with the principle that the "markets," as it is said, should be regulated to serve a real development for the benefit of the working classes. The degree of awareness of this new contradiction and the responses given to it vary from one country to another, and from one political current to another.

I have followed with as much attention as possible the ideological renewals that prepared the ground for this qualitative leap. In particular, I have monitored debates within the revolutionary left, in which I have participated as much as possible. At the center of these debates is the abandonment of all aspects of Stalinist dogma (including those related to the organization of the party and social movements) and the critique of the "revolutionism" promoted by militant movements of the 1965–1975 decade as a substitute for the former. The Zapatistas in Mexico, the PT in Brazil, the neo-Maoists in China (the name they give themselves), and the radical new tendencies that are arising in (and around) the communist parties in India and South Africa, are in the forefront of these debates. I would not say that these new forces have already defined credible, powerful, and effective alternatives. I would only say that they have the potential to do so. In contrast, the Islamic, Arab, and African worlds seem still to be stricken with sterility.

I have followed with equal interest the birth and development of another new radical current represented by liberation theology among the Christians of Latin America and the Philippines. I am among those who think that this current is an important component of a necessary radical transformation. Initiated, it seems to me, by the writings of Gustavo Gutierrez beginning in 1968, this current quickly brought together leading thinkers of the highest quality, such as Leonardo Boff, Franz Hinkelammert, and François Houtart.

I have learned much from the writings of the last, who has become a gentle and reliable friend. I participated in some of the important debates opened by the liberation theologians, in particular as a participant in their congress at Manila in 1997. The important figures I met in these debates—Israël Batista, Sam Kobia, James Oporia Ekwaro, Xavier Gorostiaga—and others, have since become some of my permanent interlocutors. But the movement's success does not lie exclusively at the level of thought. The liberation theology current has not only led lots of "small actions" at the grassroots level (but, of course, all great movements begin with many "small actions"); it has succeeded in becoming a mass movement and, as in Brazil, in asserting its presence at the level of the Conference of Bishops. Unfortunately, this turned out to be only momentary because the counteroffensive launched by the conservative Church under the leadership of the Pope is working to support the construction of a right-wing—and even extreme right-wing, fundamentalist Christian "backfire"—and has succeeded in forcing the movement to retreat. Here, as elsewhere, there are advances and retreats. That is the law of any serious war.

Democratic movements with more strictly and immediately political scope, mainly dominated by the urban middle classes—but supported by the workers—have forced back the dictatorships of the South American cone beginning in 1985. That these movements have benefited from the sympathy of the Western powers, including obviously Washington—if only because these dictatorships were worn out and had lost their usefulness in managing the crisis—does not cancel out the positive character of this evolution in the middle classes. Elsewhere—particularly in the Islamic and African worlds—the middle classes have adopted very different attitudes and have slid toward religious or ethnic fascism, also supported by Washington. In both cases, it is the same: these classes accept submission to the diktat of neoliberal globalization and this is all that interests the dominant powers of large transnational capital. The result of these Latin American democratic movements is simultaneously an advance (political democracy) and a retreat (the neoliberal impasse that weakens the democratic advance). The F. H. Cardoso government, which supported this path—against Lula's PT of that era—is the best example of this impasse. The economic stagnation in which neoliberalism has inevitably trapped Brazil contradicts all the promises that mechanically unite "markets and democracy." The same approach—in a more vulgar version—characterized Menem's Argentina. In Chile, the compromise with the armed forces—which had long remained under Pinochet's command—has attenuated even more the scope of political democratization, here strongly limited.

Three developments appear—or appeared—more promising. First, the doors opened by the neo-Zapatista uprising in Chiapas, the date of which coincided—and not by chance—with the signing of the NAFTA treaty that integrated Mexico into the economic space of the United States. Neo-Zapatism is a victory on two levels. First, the movement has not retreated into regionalism-ethnicism, but has found an immensely favorable response throughout Mexico. This is proof both that the Mexican nation exists (and this is a positive fact) and that the democratic aspiration is a powerful presence in that nation. On another level, the methods of mobilization and organization and the political language that Subcomandante Marcos initiated are an incomparable advance and a true response to the challenges of our era. I shall pass over in silence the "society events" organized by the "friends of Chiapas," in which I refrained from participating. The future will obviously tell us who will ultimately win in this current phase: the democratic alliance inspired by neo-Zapatism, which will have to simultaneously move the country out of the neoliberal impasse imposed by NAFTA and go beyond its original theory ("the objective is not to take power," etc.), or the alliance of conservative Mexican forces and Washington.

I could see for myself the transformations undergone in Latin America during the last two decades, the scope of which is positive, although unquestionably limited, as always. In many respects, the society is no longer the same as the one I had known during my earlier trips and through my readings. But perhaps the same can be said about nearly all societies in the world.

The positive: Latin America appears to have entered into a process of real democratization. Not so much in that governments now, as a whole, are elected (though doubtful in some cases, as in Peru with the forced reelection in 1999 of Alberto Fujimori, who had to flee shamefully a little later) rather than the result of military coups. Much more important is that the working classes are truly beginning to feel a need for autonomous democratic expression. In Mexico, the intelligent strategy adopted by the movement in Chiapas has succeeded in allowing the neo-Zapatistas to escape from the regional indigenous ghetto to become the active avant-garde component for the general democratic demands of the Mexican people. Isabelle and I were in Mexico when the movement organized an "informal popular vote" (not organized by the state) in 1998. Shown through various districts by a group of activists to whom we had been introduced by our friend, P. G. Casanova, we could observe the seriousness of the campaign. That this campaign was as successful as many official elections is an indicator that, I believe, has few equivalents in the contemporary world. The result confirmed the renaissance of a powerful radical leftist force.

This same process of democratization is at work elsewhere. In the Dominican Republic, as in Cuba and Haiti, guided by grassroots activists who were leading multiple activities (in particular, Isabelle Rauber and our friends in Haiti), we could also see how these expressions of the need for political and social democracy effectively contribute to the repoliticization of the working classes, give them a new confidence in themselves, and help them overcome the tradition of following charismatic, or supposedly charismatic, leaders.

Brazil, visited frequently from 2000, provides reasons to be confident about its possible future. Powerful leftist social forces are working everywhere in the country. I had the opportunity to have discussions with some of the leaders from the MST, the CUT, and the PT, and listen to analyses of the challenges and difficulties (I am thinking above all of Emir Sader's analyses). I have fond memories of some of these militants: the metal worker Tarcisio Secoli, organizer of a rural cooperative; Roberto Villela, a senior member of the "Carlos Marighela" group; the union adviser, Giorgio Romano Schutte. F. H. Cardoso's U-turn—I see no other term to describe his allegiance to the Brazilian right—could probably be explained by the personal ambition of a man who was always considered "presidential," and ended up completely submitting to the achievement of this project. Personal character traits, of which I had been well aware and had suspected in the past, appear to me today to explain this change. Faced with this reality, the rose-tinted images of the government that a large number of Europeans (such as Alain Touraine) had propagated through the media should make us smile.

Every coin has a reverse side. Democratic aspirations in Latin America have not been accompanied by an unequivocal rejection of the dominant neoliberal rhetoric. Social struggles are generally defensive and fight a specific unacceptable consequence of the implementation of the neoliberal project by the dominant classes. On the other hand, most of the basic principles of the ideology of contemporary capitalism are accepted either because of a lack of critical thinking or because a socialist alternative does not appear credible. Intellectuals have a particular responsibility in this state of affairs, and their abdication of this responsibility serves to perpetuate dangerous illusions. The Latin American lefts continue the tradition of turning to the "West," the models of central capitalism found in the United States and Europe, which I can explain only by the fact that their historical, cultural, and linguistic origins are found in Europe. Today, these lefts believe it possible to imitate the European social democrats—never mind how miserable they became by switching their allegiance to liberalism—and seek to draw closer to them (by joining the Socialist International, for example). The idea that the challenges confronting their societies are specific to peripheral capitalism and that these challenges should rather encourage them to contribute to an anti-imperialist front with Asia and Africa is not immediately obvious to them. The democratic trajectory followed in Latin America reaches its limitations here. That is why the current efforts at democratization still appear to me to be vulnerable, fragile, and maybe even reversible. It is not only that the masters of the global system—the United States establishment—are quite capable of a reversal in favor of violent dictatorships if maintaining the privileges of capital require it (and I have no confidence in the—conjunctural—"democratic" rhetoric of this establishment). It is also the case that the peoples themselves, disappointed by the low-intensity democracy associated with liberalism, could again plunge into illusions of one kind or another. Yet the election of Chávez in Venezuela, followed by Morales in Bolivia and Rafael Correa in Ecuador, are certainly good revolutionary advances that open the real possibility of a new path in the direction of inventing a socialism for the twenty-first century.

In Latin America, as elsewhere, insofar as the struggle for democratization of society in all its dimensions (which implies the total rejection of the liberal project) is not combined with a strategy to renew the prospects for socialism, then the advances realized here or there will remain fragile. For example, in Mexico, the end of the PRI dictatorship is now complete, but to whose benefit? To an illusion that connects formal democracy and submission to liberalism and Washington's hegemony? What can the Mexican people expect? Is not the alignment of the São Paulo Forum with the so-called Buenos Aires consensus an indication that the threat of this false resolution of the dilemma also concerns other countries of the continent? We are confident that the new radical Mexican left is fully aware of the nature of the challenge.

In the face of these real dangers, the late Celso Furtado was certainly exemplary in his stance. Invited to attend his eightieth birthday celebration in May 2000, I was not surprised to hear him present one of the most radical, coherent, and powerful critiques of liberalism, and he did so, moreover, in the captivating region of the Brazilian Northeast, in its charming historic capitals, Recife and João Pessoa, which I visited on this occasion. In a country like Brazil, which is, perhaps, one of the weak links of the liberal capitalist system, it is important that this voice continue to enjoy the prestige due to it.

Central America has always remained the site of a quasi-permanent rebellion since the 1920s (the early movements of Sandino and Martí) and, despite bloody and long dictatorships—like those of Somoza in Nicaragua and those in Guatemala after the overthrow of Arbenz, firmly supported by Washington, financially and militarily—the fire has never stopped smoldering. The Sandinistas' victory in 1979 and the extension of the struggle with the Farabundo Martí National Liberation Front of El Salvador in the 1980s were not surprising. At least, they were not surprising to me. I had the opportunity to meet militants from these movements before and after their victories and—beyond the natural respect that I have for all courageous combatants of popular anti-imperialist movements—I always, in the main, shared their analyses, which appeared to me to offer a serious critique of Stalinist dogma and of the "leftist" response to the former, and strove to integrate the democratic dimension. They gave some real and important proof of that after their victory. Unfortunately, that did not prevent backsliding by the Nicaraguan government, which encouraged the Washington interventionists in their support for the contras and, in the end, led to the electoral defeat of 1989. I followed the unfolding of this drama quite closely, analyzed with the highest lucidity by our friend Gorostiaga. Also, as a result, the Farabundo Martí Front was forced to agree to a minimal compromise in El Salvador. Daniel Ortega's return to power in 2007 in Nicaragua, even if, obviously, the conditions are not the same as those in the initial revolutionary experience, must nevertheless be considered as a positive indicator.

The hopes invested in this type of affirmative reaction to the challenge of our time should not, for all that, be dismissed out of hand. Under other forms, mass struggles will be able to advance the implementation of strategies that successfully link anti-imperialist liberation and democratization. But for the time being, the defeats in Central America have tilted the balance in favor of the choice to engage in electoral struggles rather than mass struggles (class struggle), started by Lula's PT in Brazil. This choice was crystallized by the formation of the São Paulo Forum, which unites important organizations and parties from most of the major Latin American countries. These parties have, moreover, scored gains in the electoral arena the significance of which it would be wrong to underestimate. Lula had been very close to winning the presidential elections in Brazil against Cardoso—a "luxury candidate for the right," as my old friend Darcy Ribeiro said, and he actually won it several years later. Subsequently, to conquer the councils in gigantic cities such as São Paulo, Porto Alegre, or Montevideo is not within reach of just any movement. But these advances—victories even—cause problems in turn. They encourage electoralist illusions, as always. They hinder the stabilization of coherent and effective offensive strategies that aim at combining democratization and social progress (which implies abandoning neoliberalism). In this area, the Forum of São Paulo and the PT, which forms its spine, have truly disappointed me, I must say. I have found nothing in the debates sponsored by them—which I have followed closely—that has demonstrated sufficient awareness of the nature of the challenge. I was not, then, surprised when this Forum began to show signs of running out of steam, marked both by the crisis within the PT and the position taken by the signatories of the "Buenos

Aires consensus," formed by the main associated parties that believed they were able to win elections in their respective countries, such as the Chilean Socialists, the Argentine Radicals, and the Mexican Democrats. It is well known that all these parties ended up subscribing to the idea that globalized liberalism had become a permanent fact of life for the present and the future. What a huge mistake, in my opinion! At the very moment these large Latin American parties, in which so many hopes had been placed, subscribed to the neoliberal nonsense, the world crisis of neoliberal capitalism broke out in East and Southeast Asia. In these regions, anti-liberal reactions were taking shape (the closure of capital accounts by China and India), implemented by the ruling classes themselves, which are not always particularly democratic. It was at this very moment that the Chilean socialists chose to place themselves to the right of this country's timid Christian democrats, dreaming perhaps of rivaling the zeal of Tony Blair and Gerhard Schröder, their deviation encouraged by the Socialist International!

The Andean countries appear to have remained largely outside the continent's general developments. In Peru, the insurrectional approach of the 1960s and 1970s has been perpetuated under the dramatic form of the (pseudo-Maoist) Shining Path. In Colombia, the civil war seems to be never ending. Dictatorship is, for the government in Washington and the dominant classes, the only way to manage stagnation and the crises in Colombia, Peru, and, of course, Bolivia.

## NEW VICTORIES, NEW CHALLENGES

I shall return later (see appendix in chapter 7: "Is the World Social Forum Useful for Popular Struggles?") to our critique of "social movements" that, since the beginning of the century, are now part of the Forums and to the place the World Forum for Alternatives occupies in the Social Forums.

My responsibilities as an activist within these movements allows me to speak from the inside because I am as close as possible to the debates within all these movements in Europe, Asia, Africa, and Latin America. I stand with all those who think that these movements must become collective actors for the transformation of the world, conscious and clear thinking, capable not only of analyzing, but also, and above all, of organizing what we call "convergence in diversity," of fighting the battles together and winning them. The Bamako Appeal is part of this approach, as Houtart and I pointed out.[40]

From this point of view, Latin America appears to be in advance of the other continents. The movements that have mobilized there are not small, marginal organizations or movements limited to the middle classes, as is still often the case elsewhere. There are large, popular (in the good sense of the term) movements, leading into action masses of people counted in the millions. That is what I call a revolutionary advance. We could discuss the reasons that have allowed this qualitative leap: the benefit of democratic conditions better than elsewhere and independence of the movements from the traditional political parties. The fact is that these movements have initiated changes that have allowed electoral victories hardly imaginable elsewhere. Lula's victory was the first on the list. This was unquestionably a victory of the working classes. That is why a possible defeat of the experiment would be nothing less than disastrous. This victory was followed by that of Néstor Kirchner in Argentina, running against the dominant liberal programs. A large-scale, popular movement in Venezuela carried Chávez to victory, won difficult electoral battles and a referendum, and then defeated the coup d'état fomented by local reactionary forces and the CIA. The Indian people of Bolivia carried Morales to the presidency. Correa was elected in Ecuador and Ortega in Nicaragua. Other victories are possible. In Peru, the candidate of the right just barely won the election in May 2006 over the movement's candidate. In a country that has experienced so many vicissitudes, the excesses and then defeat of the Shining Path, this new situation is not insignificant. In Mexico, the rise of the new left is well advanced.

The emergence of the "indigenous peoples" is occurring in this context. It is not a question of separatist "communitarian" demands, as is so often the case elsewhere. Rather, these are citizen demands that take aim at the fundamental problem of defining the continent's nations, which should now be called Indo-Afro-Latin nations.

Yes, then, these are important victories. But whenever we talk about a victory, we are also talking about new challenges to be met. It is important to assess fully the true extent of these challenges. These victories were not the result of what are ordinarily called "revolutions," which would be in a position to "make a clean sweep" and commit the society to radical transformations. The movements are in the government, but the economic and social power, most of the institutions, such as the judicial system, remain under the control of large local and foreign capital, latifundia owners, and their political servants. In Brazil, faced with Lula's government, these reactionary forces still have a strong presence, in the Congress, the states, and municipalities. It is the same elsewhere, even in Venezuela and Bolivia.

In these conditions, what should be done? How can left forces begin and advance the necessary transformation of social relations in a direction favorable to the working classes? I have no advice to give on these subjects, but maybe some warnings. I am not against the "politics of small steps." I do not think that one can do better and more in the circumstances. But I am one of those who think that the conflict with the dominant interests of oligopolistic world capitalism and its local reactionary allies is inevitable. The choice in favor of "realistic solutions" and "adjustment to the requirements of liberal globalization," as European social liberals, the World Bank, and others advocate, can only be disastrous. Unfortunately, this choice is the one that has the attention of Lula's government, as proven by its rushing to rescue the WTO confronting difficulty in Hong Kong in 2005. The defeat of the WTO would have been an immense victory for the peoples of the South, launching the construction of an authentic multipolar world. Lula's Brazil preferred the illusions of the "emergent countries," flattered by the Western powers and, in the last analysis, defended the interests of its latifundia owners side by side with India!

The construction of a front of Latin American nations against the arrogance of the United States has now become imaginable. That is the aim of ALBA. The organization is founded on political solidarity in which economic relations are based, not on the concept of a "common market" (as with Mercosur), but on that of the construction of complementarities, beginning with those involving access to and use of natural resources.

### PROMISING ADVANCES IN LATIN AMERICA

In Latin America, advances begun in the preceding decades are now confronted with difficult choices that will decide the future. In Venezuela, a major difficulty will be moving beyond the economy of oil rent and building a still nonexistent productive agricultural-industrial system to condition the commitment of the country to the long road of progress toward socialism. In Bolivia and Ecuador, responses to the two issues of going beyond the current model of lumpen-development and settling the national question—more precisely, the institutional definition of multi-nationality—remain uncertain. In Brazil, the central question is this: is the historical compromise established by Lula and the PT, which combines limited social advances and the unquestioned progress of democracy with preservation of the economic (and political) powers of the owning classes—modernized latifundia owners and industrial monopolies—viable in the longer term? In these conditions, the "emergence" of Brazil also remains quite fragile.

My responsibilities in the WFA have permitted me several visits to Caracas during the last few years. I have attempted to follow the development of the struggles more closely, in particular at the invitation of Chávez, several ministers, Marta Harnecker (Centro Miranda), and communist intellectuals (generally critical). I deplore the negative attitude toward this evolving experiment displayed by many intellectuals who, in the past, were on the left—and sometimes on the left of the left. This experiment remains quite capable of further advances, despite the huge character of the challenge: to construct an economy that the oil rent has destroyed from top to bottom. Its possible failure will only set the country further back. The WFA held its congress in Caracas in 2008, thanks to the generous support of Carmen Bohórquez, then Minister of Culture.

The best invitation I received from Latin America came in 2010 from Bolivian Vice President Álvaro García Linera in La Paz: one month to travel around this huge country, from the Altiplano (Isabelle and I have the good fortune to be able to handle high elevations) to the Amazonian forest. I knew about the courageous—and victorious—battles led by the Bolivian people (the water war in Cochabamba, the surrounding of La Paz, forcing the president, Washington's puppet, to flee, and the rebirth of the Indian nations) only through my readings. Very frank discussions with groups of rank-and-file militants and leaders, including Vice President García Linera, Oscar Oliveira, Oscar Vega Camacho, Raul Prada—the staff of the MAS, certainly contributed to helping me better understand the nature of the challenges and the responses given by the various currents of the Bolivian left. David Choquehuanca, Minister of Foreign Affairs, gave me the most beautiful gift: a splendid facsimile of Che's notebooks, a gift that brought Isabelle and me to tears.

My visit to Ecuador had been postponed several times. The WFA working group, led by Napoleon Saltos and Victor Hugo Jijon, is undertaking its activities with much energy and persistence. My reading of recent works by Houtart, who has chosen to live in Quito, concerning "good living" (*buen vivir*) has been highly rewarding. Finally, in 2011, I participated in a meeting of an excellent WFA working group. Concerning problems specific to Ecuador, I shall refrain from passing any judgment about the rightness or wrongness of the claims made by the indigenous movements opposed to Correa's government. I regret only one thing: that time did not permit me (and without Isabelle, it would not have made sense anyway) to visit the exceptional Galápagos Islands.

I shall say no more about any of this in my memoirs. It is really Houtart who has taken on the responsibility of coordinating the activities of the WFA in Latin America. Thanks to his unlimited dedication and keen intelligence, he has succeeded in making the WFA's presence in Latin America a political reality of some importance. To draw up a list of colleagues active in our associated networks and the meetings they have organized is better left to Houtart, not me. For my part, I will say only that I have always learned a lot each time that I have had the opportunity to participate in these meetings. All the same, I should like to call attention to one more name in addition to the comrades mentioned earlier in connection with Brazil, Cuba, Venezuela, Haiti, Mexico, Argentina, and Ecuador: Wim Dierckxsens in Costa Rica.

# 5

# EASTERN EUROPE, THE USSR, AND RUSSIA
## The End of the Tunnel?

REALLY EXISTING SOCIALISM IN EASTERN EUROPE AND THE USSR

I should begin by saying that I do not like the expression "really existing socialism" used in this title. It was invented by Rudolf Bahro and implied that the governments in question were fundamentally socialist, but that they had been subject to deformations, serious for some, less so for others, but able to be overcome so that possible reforms could push these systems toward a better socialism. Such reforms might be guided by a type of "market socialism" or by an approach based on forms of democratization that would lead to a decline in market and economic alienation.

Were the systems in question "reformable" or not? The question is wrongly put. There is no society that is unable to be transformed. The future is always open and depends on social, political, and ideological struggles that are undertaken in response to the problems confronting that society. For me, the "Soviet" systems were condemned to be transformed or disappear, one day or another. I wrote that in 1960. But they could have evolved or even fallen to the right, the center, or the left; and that would have depended on the struggles that might have developed. Obviously, I would have liked it if they had evolved or fallen to the left, that the dominated classes had forced developments to move in that direction or succeeded in reversing the existing situation with a strong movement that opened this alternative. Such a hope was in no way absurd or illusory, and to struggle to make it a reality was the only defensible principle of political action, in my opinion. I would even have considered an evolution to the "center" as positive, that is, a reform that provided stable foundations—for a time—to a "market socialism" that combined collective forms of dominant property and wide recourse to a regulated market. Within the context of the long transition to socialism, such a step is not necessarily absurd. But they fell to the right, in the end; that is, the worst alternative came to triumph. This can be explained, but it was certainly not the only possibility.

Dominant opinion in the Western world never thought that socialism was possible. Having been decreed as "non-reformable," when these systems fell and gave way to a pure and simple capitalist restoration (what I call falling to the right), they said that it was the case because no other alternative could exist. This is why the expression "really existing socialism" pleases them: it both demonstrates that socialism is an impossible utopia and defines the essential character of the systems in question. For me, these systems were not socialist. I shall not go back over the analyses that led me to see them as particular varieties of capitalism—"capitalism without capitalists," I once wrote.

I will add that those who speak of "really existing socialism" never discuss capitalism in the same terms. The dominant so-called liberal ideology speaks of capitalism in abstract terms as a rational ideal-type without a history. That allows it to avoid having to confront the reality of capitalism, and especially the opposition between its central and peripheral forms, immanent to its globalized expansion.

I have already mentioned my early visits, when still a student, to three popular democracies: Czechoslovakia, Poland, and Hungary.[41] I returned to two of these three countries more than thirty-five years later, when their so-called communist governments had collapsed.

In September 1991, in the pretty and small city of Venice, located on a lake southwest of Budapest, I participated in a colloquium in the course of which the infamous Oleg Bogomolov made the curious statement that I commented on in volume 1 of these memoirs.[42] I rediscovered Budapest, the topography of which, I confess, I had forgotten a bit. I remembered only vaguely the beautiful old Buda (today completely restored so apartments can be sold to the new bourgeoisie), the Parliament, which was a copy of Westminster, and the large island in the middle of the superb Danube—the width of the Nile here, not that of the Seine, the Thames, or the Rhine! I also rediscovered, with nostalgia, the famous café "1900," located on a pleasant square in Pest, also completely restored, and the large square decorated with the imaginary statues of the nation's founders—the Hun leaders, Attila and others, well made up as Mongols with beautiful moustaches. Sex shops and "massage parlors" were also flourishing for the use of new German tourists. Isabelle and I were lodged in the extraordinary old hotel (from 1900) in Buda called the Gellert, where I enjoyed the Turkish baths fed by a mineral spring. The hotel was a true masterpiece of the Belle Époque.

My Hungarian friend, Imre Marton, was a longtime communist, a refugee in France fleeing the Horthy regime, a resistance fighter who returned to Hungary in 1945, and an Africanist who stayed in Guinea several times. I always found a way to discuss the problems of socialism with him quite freely. I invited him to one of our large North-South meetings organized by the Third World Forum. Marton fell into a bottomless despair to see the system fall to the right. He died in 1998. Another friend, the economist Tamás Szentes, I met for the first time in Dar es Salaam in the 1970s. In my opinion, he is one of the best analysts of world capitalism and the problems of "really existing socialism." He is also a man of quality with a keen sense of humor. He had occupied important functions within the Party committee charged with reform during the second half of the 1980s. During that time, he had defended tenaciously and with great skill centrist reform positions (market socialism, control over external relations, and a guarantee of reasonable income distribution). He told me in detail how and why the "majority" rejected this plan: the bourgeoisie of the Party quite simply wanted to restore capitalism for its benefit. The left is still alive in Hungary and I have had the opportunity to discuss its prospects with younger militants who are ensuring its continuity: the brilliant young woman Andréa Szego; Andor Laszlo; and Agnes and Gabor Kapitany, who are activists working with the unions and publish a quality journal (to which I contribute from time to time) on the problems of the struggle for socialism. By contrast, most of those who formed the old guard of the fallen system's famous economists have quite simply changed sides and altered the direction of their careers, encouraged by the World Bank (like János Kornai).

I returned to Czechoslovakia a few years ago as a tourist with Isabelle, my daughter, Anna, and her friend, Claire. We spent three days in Prague. I had a precise recollection of this superb city and particularly of the amazing abundance of its Baroque style, which was characteristic not only of its monuments, but was widespread along all the streets of the old city. I rediscovered that. On the other hand, the "university city" of Opletalova—where I had stayed secretively—appeared to me to have been destroyed, or transformed to the point of being unrecognizable. I had no political contact. On the highway, intended for German visitors, the sex tourists followed one another—a new fate for the reestablished protectorate of Moravian Bohemia, probably waiting for the return of the Sudeten Germans. I felt only a profound contempt for the new ruling class, particularly President Vaclav Havel. Celebrated as a democratic liberator, this mediocre individual had never been more than a bad writer of stage plays. Supposedly boycotted by the communist government, these plays are probably not very interesting since they are still not performed. Cynicism and vulgarity characterize the new Czech bourgeoisie. Should we be surprised, then, that the prime minister, later president of the Czech Republic, Vaclav Klaus, a "liberal," declared right up front that the workers would have to give back what they got in the past. In Berlin, at one of the colloquia organized by some German foundations, I met a specimen of these new "liberal managers," who said to me: "We are a small country; we will always be dependent, but it is much better to depend on the rich [like the Germans, he thought] than the poor [like the Russians]." "Yes, you are right," I answered. "Look at Haiti, this country depends on the United States; perhaps that is the paradise of which you are dreaming for the future of the Czech Republic." He was reduced to silence.

I have not returned to Poland. I have warm memories of courageous comrades I had met, often just released from Nazi camps. When Solidarność appeared, I did not share the naive enthusiasm of those who saw in it a renewal of the workers' movement. Did not the CIA openly support the movement? I have learned that the imperialist powers have never supported any progressive movement whatsoever. Never. Subsequent events proved me right. An anti-Russian neurosis, idolatry of the papacy, and admiration for the United States inevitably won out over everything.

I was in the former German Democratic Republic (GDR) only after it had disappeared and was annexed by West Germany. There I met some of the most enlightened and likable intellectuals I have known in Germany, such as the philosopher Joachim Wilke and leaders of the PDS, such as André Brie and Michael Brie, and some others. Most of them had been somewhat critical (often courageously so) of the GDR's "real socialism" and consequently (and not by chance) were held in much more contempt by the dominant forces of unified Germany (by the social democrats as much as by the right) than those who, having belonged to the former nomenklatura, did not hesitate to change sides. Will the PDS succeed in forming a unifying force in the East, sufficient to influence the West a bit and encourage a more socialist-oriented thinking that is not content with a Schröder-type farce? The formation of the Linkspartei (Left Party) is certainly a good sign. Otherwise, the risks of a slide toward "national populism" with a whiff of fascism, as with Jörg Haider in Austria or Fini-Berlusconi-Lega Nord (Northern League) in Italy, would find serious chances for success throughout Germany.

Berlin's historic heart was located in the eastern part of the city, where almost all of the monuments and beautiful old districts (under restoration) are concentrated, making a real contrast with the insignificance of the "American" styles of the western part of the capital. The latter has now been abandoned following the reunification of the country, both by the German political bourgeoisie, proud to rediscover its true capital, and by the world of snobbery, inevitable in the societies of the opulent West. I had not imagined that signs of the Huguenots were so strong in historic Berlin. East Germans—who have remained cultured and imbued with a (good) knowledge of their history and culture—know this. Those of the West are unaware of this, having been educated in U.S. business schools. André Gunder Frank indirectly pointed this out to me one day by saying, "Ask the question in East Germany: who was Frank [André's father]? Anyone can answer you: an anti-Nazi writer. Ask the same question of intellectuals in West Germany, they don't know the name." Is the Marxist culture of historic Germany, which was preserved in the East after a fashion, despite the serious dogmatic reductions imposed on it, and disappeared in the West, going to come alive again? I do not know.

I have followed the evolution of Yugoslavia much better, having visited regularly, specifically for the annual Cavtat conferences between 1977 and 1989. I have already spoken about this.[43] Its market socialism was acceptable to me, on condition that it was viewed as a step in a long transition and not as a "final" system (as it was actually lived, in fact), and on condition that appropriate adjustments were made to withstand the vagaries of internal and international developments. Its limitations and contradictions quickly appeared to me to be dangerous: no real democratization of politics (real power remained concentrated in the hands of the Party nomenklatura) and too much market (linked with too much openness to the outside, which was controlled very little and very poorly, and structured around federalism). In these conditions, only disaster could result: the worsening of inequalities between the constituent republics, vulnerability to conjunctures of global capitalism, the cynical manipulation of power by segments of the nomenklatura, and, in the end, the retreat of the latter into chauvinism as a way to take over companies. These were the questions that I discussed repeatedly year after year with comrades and friends, such as the "Serbs" Milos Nikolic, Radmila Nakarada, Mirjana Jevtic, the "Bosniac" Blagoje Babic, the "Croat" Vjekoslav Mikecin, and the "Slovene" Anton Vratusa, and with many others as well. I remember diverse viewpoints, but generally accompanied with an openness and sincerely held socialist convictions for the most part—to the point that I was relatively optimistic about the ability of the system to remain "social," if not socialist, and save the federation in the face of the challenge from the local and global offensive of capitalism. Events have disappointed my optimism.

I admit I was mistaken about the reactions I expected from the Yugoslav people to the challenges of liberal globalization. I had viewed critically the concessions made in relation to Yugoslavia's insertion into the world market. I had expressed my (well-founded) fears that these concessions, accompanied as they were by increased decentralization of economic power, would only worsen regional inequalities of development, leading to serious problems in the management of a multinational polity. That is indeed what happened.[44] Yet, I was hoping that the working classes and a good part of the Communist Party—which had a fine history behind it—would avoid the worst and that a balance, even if only a relative stability, would be found "at the center," preserving the possibility for a later resumption of a development to the left. The country swung to the right and ethnic chauvinism—which was not necessarily as strongly rooted in the working classes as the media wanted to make us believe—became, in any case, the flag behind which the shattered fragments of the hard-pressed ruling class rallied. I shall not return here to what I have written elsewhere: that the crimes resulting from this choice were committed by all the "national" political leaderships, by the Croats as much as by the Serbs, by the Bosnian Muslims or the KLA as much as by others. These criminal choices were, moreover, encouraged by the United States and the European powers. The systematic distortion of "international" information that attributes to "Serbian chauvinism" the responsibility for having begun the series of events (which is false), and for having done more than the others (which is also false), is simply the product of propaganda from the United States and its subaltern European NATO allies. That this propaganda has succeeded in dominating with such ease should make us think very carefully about the role of the media, whose servility should be a source of grave concern. Unfortunately, this is not the case, in the West, at least. The U.S. operation, barely disguised in NATO and "humanitarian" accoutrements (Bernard Kouchner participated in this farce, as he had already done elsewhere), provisionally attained its objectives.

Isabelle and I had visited Moscow and Leningrad in summer 1964. Here are a few caricatures—conventional images known to everyone—that were yet part of my experience. First, the hotel, called the Ukraina: this was a gigantic palace from the Stalinist era, with armchairs that were so heavy (to use up the raw material, since the Plan set the objective in tons) that they were completely impossible to move. There were *babas* monitoring every floor. Then there was the infinite wait for service in restaurants. An Italian had exploded with anger at this situation and yelled, "There are three 'eights': eight hours for work, eight for sleep, and eight for eating—two in the morning, three at midday, and three in the evening!" A French businessman from the PCF had told us the secret to being served quickly, so long as you were willing to eat in the same restaurant every day: The first day, you order and make sure to indicate that you are pressed for time. Then wait patiently. When, one hour later, the server arrives with the food, you get up abruptly and look at your watch. "Excuse me. I no longer have time. I warned you. Now I must leave." The poor man must redo in the reverse order all the administrative formalities in order to return the plates of food to the kitchen. The next day, you choose the same table, which is served by the same waiter. You are served in five minutes. At the Gum department store—established in a superb 1900-era arcade, then in a deplorable state—the layout was much like the style of colonial trading posts of "Syrians" in the cities of the African bush: shelves, a long table that separated you from them, and the sellers. You asked what you were looking for. "Nyet, there aren't any." That was the automatic response. "But no, there is, there, behind you, on the shelf." What a horrible customer to force the woman to make the effort of turning around. "It's too high." You insist. She has to call a strong fellow who climbed a stepladder. Then she gave you a paper with four or five copies (there is carbon paper between the sheets). You left two copies with her, went to the cashier, where you presented another copy, which was stamped, before returning to the seller to retrieve the object. And then there were the taxis. They were probably paid for the time they hid in the alleys. Having spotted one, you had to approach it nonchalantly (if the taxi sees that you are looking for it, it takes off). Then, when you draw level with it, you suddenly open the door and jump in. Having done that, the cab driver could not believe that I was not a local. All the same, he had a sense of humor and acknowledged: foreigners don't know the trick. Then there was the train from Moscow to Leningrad. There were only five classes. We took the best: "extra-comfortable" (it was not called "first" or "super-first"). It was a magnificent sleeping car, just as in the era of the Orient Express. Cushions and more cushions, small, lovely curtains, a samovar, and always, a *baba* coming and going to fill cups with tea.

Moscow and Leningrad are cities that we liked very much, probably like most visitors. They are not common. Far from it. It is pointless, then, to elaborate on the Kremlin, Red Square, several old convents in the area, the banks of the Neva, the cruiser *Aurora*, the Summer Palace, or the museums, the Bolshoi, etc. There are pretty postcards of all that.

On the political side, reality showed through in spite of the rhetoric. We visited a kolkhoz of the region. The director made a speech—a nice guy who spouted statistics that no one listened to because strawberries (beautiful, unlike the ones in the markets) were brought to us, and the members of our "Third World" group went for them without restraint. I pointed out to the director that if his statistics were correct (90 percent of the collective land provided 50 percent of the production by value, while the 10 percent that represented individual allotments produced the same amount), that would be proof that socialism is not worth it. Unless the statistics were hiding some deception and, in fact, a good part of the harvest from the collective land was redistributed to the kolkhozians and sold, at much better prices, as produce from the individual plots. He looked at me sardonically, smiled, and said nothing.

African students, scholarship holders at Lumumba University—particularly the young (at the time) Malian, Founéké Keita—told us less comical stories. One young man from among his Russian friends chatted with us. "How many students are members of the Komsomol [the political youth organization]?" Isabelle asked him. He said there were 97 percent. "What happens to the remaining three percent?" "A lot of trouble. The professors are more demanding of them on exams. When they leave, they are given less desirable appointments." "Good, these are the three percent who are communists," Isabelle said to him, "the same proportion as elsewhere." At the museum in Leningrad, a young, unconventional painter drew us into a corner to show us hidden paintings. That reminded me of something my friend the Brazilian painter Tiberio said: "What happens to a non-figurative painter when he goes for a walk in Moscow? Two very figurative characters follow him!" At the Gosplan, someone I no longer remember by name met me and told me what was told to everyone: everything is working well. But in walking through the halls, I encountered small functionaries carrying stacks of files while the important functionaries were closely followed by those who carried their briefcases or attaché cases. In the offices, apparently idle women were doing their nails or eyes and, as soon as you entered, shut away their materials as if caught red-handed.

We passed through Moscow in 1991, on the way to and from central Asia. There was a new urban and social landscape, in full disarray. Arbat Street was very lively and cheerful. Everything was being sold, in total disorder. There was a new model of nested dolls for sale: on the outside, Gorbachev, then successively, Brezhnev, Chernenko, Andropov, Khrushchev, Malenkov, Stalin, and the last—the very smallest: Lenin. We got onto a bus. The fare was several kopecks, but because of inflation, there was no longer such small currency, which had become useless. I said to the conductor: "The smallest bill I have is this one—two or five rubles, I don't know anymore." He said to me: "Ah, shit—get on. It is free now for everyone. There is no more money." At the hotel—the Akademicheskaya—we had to spend an extra night, since we had been late for the plane. I asked the price: "100 dollars," was the response. That was a little expensive for the actual quality of the place (equivalent to 0 or 1 star at most), but since it was classed as a luxury hotel, we had to accept it.

Then I had a fantastic idea: "Can we pay in rubles?" I asked. "Yes, of course." "That is how much?" "Fifty rubles." "OK, I'll pay you in rubles." At the time, the dollar was worth 35 rubles. We had then paid one and a half dollars for our room! The system's incoherence did not seem to bother the woman at reception, which was all the better for us.

I knew some of the dignitaries from the system, particularly "academicians," professors and researchers who were members of the Academy of Social Sciences, including the Russianized Armenian Avakov (Avakian), who had worked at UNESCO for a long time. He and his spouse were intelligent and charming people who invited us to dine with them. We chatted freely. Avakov had guided us through the maze of the Academy. The sense was that the system was coming to an end. The probably exclusive concern of the academicians was to get hold of something: an automobile, a dacha, an apartment, or furniture. The discussions centered only on the means of doing so, who to see, etc. When I attempted to lead the discussion to some political problems, I had the impression of profoundly annoying my interlocutors, who completely scorned my attempts. Yet some of them had been fighters against anti-Soviet deviationists. I knew them by name or reputation. They had probably become the worst.

None of that effaces the greatness of the Russian people and the magnificent pages they wrote in 1917 and then saving humanity from the Nazis through their incomparable courage. I cannot hide the fact that I find them a very likable people. Even their flaws, which are obviously the result of their history, this mixture of patience that is often mistaken for absolute resignation (which is not the case), romanticism, anarchism, irrationality, lack of practical sense, an exuberance that is often described as "Slavic"—what pleasure there is, I admit it, in breaking glasses after having emptied them—are not ordinary. They are never horrible and there is nothing comparable to the spirit of submission that an unfortunate history has sometimes encouraged among some peoples or to the conformism and hypocrisy of the dominant Anglo-Saxon ideology. Lumping together communism and fascism in the catchall "totalitarian" makes utterly no sense. Certain apparently similar social phenomena (such as mass demonstrations) were widely common to all industrial societies of the time period, the product of capitalism (and its socialist version) at that stage of its development. The suffering that the peoples of the former USSR are subject to today are, for me, simply appalling.

I had the opportunity to visit Riga, the capital of newly independent Latvia, in 1997. I participated in a symposium organized by a friendly group of scientists—from the hard sciences, physics and others—inquisitive about social affairs. We were housed on the coast—some ten kilometers from Riga, itself located on the estuary of the river Daugava—in a renowned seaside resort, Jūrmala. This Deauville-like place, created at the time of the Tsarist Empire, was quite charming. There were dachas of sculpted wood lost in the forest. To visit Riga, I took a commuter train. It was there that I discovered there were Soviet-era train cars without bathrooms! But even more interesting, I observed that everyone (98 percent) spoke Russian, and everyone read Russian-language newspapers; in fact, all the newspapers were in Russian. I did not hear a single word of Latvian or see a single person reading Latvian. Yet the Russian speakers, which were considered a "minority" (I bet that this minority was around 80 percent in Riga), had no rights! Those were reserved for "pure" Latvians! One specimen of the latter, who came to give his talk to the symposium, appeared to me to be what he most certainly was: a fascist cretin. Fortunately, thanks to his small intelligence, he fell into all the traps from my questions. "Do you expect to give some rights to the Russians?" "Never." "Even those whose ancestors were here since the eighteenth century?" (It was around 1720 that the Baltic countries were annexed by the Russian Empire.) "Even them." I concluded, for my colleagues at the symposium, by calling their attention to the "double standard" (I spoke English) implemented by the dominant Western media. "The Russians came to the Baltic region during the same time period that the Protestant Scots went to Ireland. Did it ever dawn on the media to consider that Ulster should belong only to Irish Catholics and that the Protestants should have no rights? It is said that the Russians do not speak Latvian. Have the media ever demanded that the British in Ulster should learn Gaelic? And why treat the Irish Catholics—who perhaps might like to do what the Latvians are doing—as "terrorists" and characterize the Latvians as 'democrats'? The new ethnocratic (not democratic—the two should not be confused) regime has erected a monument to praise the SS. No comment from the European media! I leave it to you to imagine what would have happened if an Arab country had taken a similar initiative!"

Riga deserves to be seen. Its urban form is typical of Hanseatic trading ports. The Latvian countryside, which I saw during a short car trip, is worth seeing as well. But what a horrible government it is of these "friends of the West" who strut about in a reconquered country!

Let's return to Russian questions. I met a good number of people from the Soviet nomenklatura; I often listened to them. Except for Vladimir Kollontai, I never experienced the least desire to become friends with any of them. There was also the exception of the USSR consul in Port Said, Chikov. I knew pen-pushers, such as Bogomolov, who tried to destroy those they portrayed as deviationists, or even as agents of imperialism. On a more amusing note, occasionally when I hear the name of one or another of the new "great dignitaries" (characterized as democrats, reformers, and the like), or mafia chiefs and billionaires who appropriated one-third of the oil in Siberia or things of that nature, I recognize him as one of those who used to be highly placed in the system and whom I had heard of here or there, or with whom I had actually engaged in a discussion (and sometimes they possessed recognizable intelligence).

Since then, I have met some of the intellectuals from the Marxist new left, who stand to the left of the Communist Party (which is not difficult!). Vladimir Jordanski, whom I already knew, is one of those. He is a man of great integrity. They must be numerous in the former USSR, but they are not talked about and they are never given the opportunity to speak, neither in the new Russia nor in the international media. Others, such as Boris Kagarlitsky or Alexander Buzgalin, were unknown to me. I have had many discussions with them, read their writings, and count on continuing our exchange of views.

The future of Russia and those of the other republics of the former USSR seem quite bleak. Their peoples were not prepared to confront the challenges of global capitalism, let alone grasp the stakes involved. The primary responsibility for this twofold disaster—social and economic regression and the breakup of the USSR—falls obviously on the "communist" nomenklatura, which gradually became the "headquarters of the bourgeoisie," as Mao wrote in 1960, a bourgeoisie that had hastened to grab hold of the public property it had already managed for a long time as quasi-private property owners. The breakup of the Union was also the result of a narrow nationalist-chauvinist choice of ruling classes in desperate straits. The borders of the republics had not been drawn with the idea in mind that they might become independent states. Kazakhstan—mainly Russian, in fact—could have been an autonomous republic of the Russian Federation. Belarusians and Ukrainians, despite some local particularities, are nothing other than two of the constitutive elements of the Russian nation. We can add example after example of the dramatic problems created for various peoples resulting from the absurd breakup of the Union. The systematic depoliticization of the Soviet peoples, systematically implemented to hide the real intentions of the ruling class, lies behind the failure of really existing socialism. The dominant classes of the capitalist centers in the West took advantage of the debacle and made it worse. The rhetoric of "supporting democracy" should not fool us. That is not the real objective pursued by the foreign policies of the NATO countries. The Soviet disaster has served not only to strengthen U.S. hegemony, but also to subject the Europeans more firmly to the latter in the wake of that disaster. All the rest is just for show. Proof of the reality of this strategic choice by NATO is certainly not lacking. I note that Western foreign policies—unanimously—always support the worst candidates to manage the countries of the former USSR (the worst for their peoples, but the best for the interests of dominant capital): Boris Yeltsin versus Mikhail Gorbachev, for example, even if this be at the price of trampling underfoot the democratic principles that supposedly inspired their propaganda, such as when they supported the Yeltsin-ordered military attack on the Russian Duma.[45]

The double standards implemented in relations with Russia are glaringly cynical. The principle of nationalities on which the Soviet Union had been built was far from being perfect in its actual implementation, something I criticized elsewhere and shall not return to here. The dominant media highlight only the system's deficiencies. For example, they emphasize *ad nauseam* the poverty of the Samoyeds and Yakuts of Siberia in widely distributed reports. They refrain from saying—honestly—that the Soviet system had given these peoples of the north the theoretically autonomous management of Siberia. One would love to see the United States and Canada restore half of their territory to the Indians and grant them—even if only on paper—the same degree of autonomy. Rest assured, nothing like that will ever happen. This is clearly a case of seeing the mote in a neighbor's eye, but not the beam in your own! We could multiply to infinity examples of the same kind that characterize the "anti-Soviet" campaigns of the dominant media.

After the collapse of the USSR, the Western powers immediately put themselves at the service of anti-Russian "ethnocrats." The CIA financed the "rose revolution" to establish a bloody dictatorship in Georgia, which was in no way different from that of Shevardnadze, and the "orange revolution" to set up a nauseating mafia in Ukraine. The media reserve their violent critiques for Belarus, simply because its government rejects liberalism and maintains the "social advantages" of the Soviet system, which the working classes appreciate, leading them to cast their votes for the government (even if the percentages involved—more than 90 percent—are reminiscent of an old tradition!). They are careful not to mention the NGO reports that there is no torture in Minsk's prisons, unlike in those of Tbilisi.

A NEW SOUTH IN EUROPE?

Eastern Europe has remained a "black hole" in WFA activities. The reason is certainly the strength of the illusions to which the peoples of the region have clung, persuaded that belonging to Europe would allow them to "catch up" to the living standards of the continent's opulent countries and, consequently, that the structural adjustments imposed on them were an acceptable price for the "transition." In fact—and this is my contention—these adjustments were designed to meet the exact opposite objective: to open Eastern Europe to the expansion of monopolies from the West; in other words, transform Eastern Europe into a sort of Latin America for the capitalist centers of Western Europe, and primarily for Germany. Has awareness of this reality made any progress? I do not see much, despite the efforts expended by some activists with whom we finally succeeded in establishing fruitful contact, such as Ana Bazac in Romania, Kapitany and Agnès Gabor in Hungary, and several others.

It is said that there is no longer a North and South. There is a South (of the poor) and a North (of the rich) everywhere. There is nothing new in that. Moreover, this fact is irrelevant to what concerns us. The South is made up of social formations dominated by dominant capital from social formations in the North. The wealthy in the South are mostly from the comprador classes; they are the minority who benefit from "happy globalization" and are, consequently, complicit with capitalist classes that are not only dominant in the North, but on the world scale.

Who is responsible for the disaster in Eastern Europe? Unquestionably, the communist parties of the region bear primary responsibility. Except in Yugoslavia, these Soviet-type parties had never been able to overcome their original weaknesses—or even their original nonexistence. Still, we need to be careful and avoid confusing the Czech Republic with Romania, for example. But that is not our focus here. One could have expected more in Yugoslavia where the party was the authentic result of a popular war conducted against fascist invaders and their local accomplices.

Looking more closely, we discover the responsibility of Europe, specifically the ruling classes of capitalist and imperialist Western Europe—Great Britain, France, and Germany primarily. Without the forceful intervention of these reactionary forces, the contradictions between the peoples of the different Yugoslav republics would almost certainly have found a better outcome. It has to be said that the European project is a criminal political one. It was never about "liberating" the region from "totalitarianism" (an empty concept). The aim was actually to reduce Eastern Europe to the status of a colony, and that is what was done. We must speak of a political crime here, committed against all European peoples, but first of all against those from the East. This is the same policy that Europe is pursuing today in Ukraine. The crime is, moreover, now extended to other peoples in the European Union, in Greece, Cyprus, and Portugal, though they never "suffered from communism"!

Of course, the reactionary leaders of Europe (whether from the right or the electoral left) have found accomplices in the East, just as they have in Greece and Portugal. In Eastern Europe, the Catholic Church formed a major reactionary force complicit in the destruction of the societies. The beatification of the Polish Pope, who was an active accomplice of the CIA and friend of the Croatian Ustashi and others, is simply indecent. When are we going to see a beatification of the popes of the Inquisition and the Borgias? But this beatification, which made millions of Poles happy, it appears, has its natural place in the plan to strengthen reactionary Europe and the colonization of the East.

Are there signs of an awakening in the East?

In Croatia, Srećko Horvat took the initiative to organize a subversive film festival in Zagreb, an effective way to mobilize the youth and advance their political awareness. I accepted his invitation to visit in 2010 and 2011. I took advantage of my presence to reestablish contacts with our Slovenian comrades at the University of Ljubljana. I also attended the first Balkans Social Forum in 2011.

There is in Eastern Europe a visibly growing nostalgia for the "communist era." A poll in Romania revealed that 80 percent of the people miss Nicolae Ceaucescu. Portraits of Josip Broz Tito are reappearing. Nevertheless, the impression that I get from my visits and discussions, and my semi-tourist trips, recalled earlier, is that we are still far from glimpsing an exit from the tunnel. Are our comrades in Western Europe aware of this?

RUSSIA: OUT OF THE TUNNEL?

*My Contributions to Russian Debates*

In Moscow, at the invitation of some old and new Russian friends, I had the opportunity to discuss all the questions raised in the following pages. But my attempts to make contact with the new Russian Communist Party were not successful. Nevertheless, I heard with great interest the analyses of Alexander and Ludmilla Buzgalin—cultivated, charming, and intelligent people, vestiges of the best of the intelligentsia Russia has always produced. I could extend the list of my new Russian friends (Ruslan Dzarasov and others). Living and creative Marxist thinking has not disappeared in Russia, side by side with the obvious explosion of popular nostalgia for the USSR, including flags and the portraits of Joseph Stalin. "Everything that *Pravda* said about socialism was not true, but everything it said about capitalism was," is often heard. Boris Kagarlitsky had invited me to the counter-G20 in St. Petersburg in 2013. My works are beginning to be published in Russian, which had never been the case in the Soviet past. I even had the surprise of seeing texts written in Arabic translated into Russian (by Said Gafourov)! My nephew, director of the French bank Crédit Agricole in Russia, and his spouse, are settled in Moscow quite close to Arbat Street. They accompanied us on our walks.

But beyond all that, are there embryos of radical left forces in the process of being formed? My latest visits to Moscow (in 2012) were encouraging. The symposia now bring together not only a group of old-timers, but many young people who did not experience the Soviet era yet are convinced that capitalism has nothing to offer their people. These young people had overwhelmingly joined the Communist Party. They were quickly excluded for "various deviations"! Obviously, nothing has changed!

The reader will certainly have noticed that I have emphasized the systematic hostility of the Western powers with regard to the new Russia, even though it is capitalist. This hostility cannot be explained by some kind of paranoia that has suddenly struck Europeans. The explanation is much more ordinary: the strategies implemented by the ruling classes of the triad (the United States, Western Europe, and Japan) are focused on a single objective, that is, to guarantee the continuation of their exclusive control of the planet—an objective that consequently implies such hostility.

The imperialist powers (once again, the triad) intend to maintain their privileges on a global scale by deploying a strategy that combines, on the one hand, globalized neoliberalism (which allows the triad's financialized monopolies to make decisions alone about everything on a global scale and, in that way, maximize their monopoly rents) and, on the other hand, military control of the planet by the United States and its subaltern NATO and Japanese allies, the sole guarantee of the permanence of the globalized neoliberal order. The objective of this strategy is to hold in check any attempt by an Asian, African, or Latin American country to free itself from their control. Consequently, all peoples, all nations, are enemies, at least potentially, even when a country's ruling class in power is aligned with them. The reason for such fear is that it is not possible to "stabilize" the neoliberal system. It is not even stable in its dominant centers, as the current implosion of the euro system and, behind it, the European Union, demonstrates. *A fortiori*, it is not stable in the peripheries, which are condemned to a lumpen-development that reduces the legitimacy of established governments to nothing. Russia is not an exception to the rule. The Ukrainian crisis shows that.

The changes Russia has undergone over the last twenty-five years, as huge as they appear, are not a "revolution" (or a counterrevolution); it instead expresses the acceleration of underlying tendencies that were already at work in the Soviet system itself in the 1930s. On this topic, I shall not be content with noting that the Soviet society was already not (or no longer) "socialist," as the leaders of the 1917 Revolution had envisioned, but was a particular form of capitalism, which I have dubbed "a capitalism without capitalists," likely to become a "normal" capitalism, one with capitalists, which is indeed the project of the new ruling class (itself a product of the preceding one), even if, as we will see, the reality of the system it has established is far from being adequate to the objective.

The 1917 Revolution was a great event in human history that embodied and carried forward a huge amount of potential. My aim in these pages is not to retrace its history in order to make a liquidationist case against it, as it is currently fashionable to do, and still less to imply that the salient traits brought out here were already contained in the Revolution, or in Leninism, or even Stalinism. My sole aim is to clarify the nature of the processes underway and the challenges these now present for the survival of the peoples of the former Soviet Union.

I define the Soviet system by five fundamental characteristics: corporatism, autocratic government, social stabilization, its delinking from the global capitalist system, and its insertion into the latter as a superpower. The concept of "totalitarian regime," popularized by the dominant ideological rhetoric, turns out in this case, as in others, to be unimaginative and hollow, incapable of accounting for the reality of Soviet society, its management techniques, and the contradictions that governed its development and have controlled its current transformation.

One: a corporatist system. By this I mean that the working class (supposed to have become the "ruling" class) had lost its unifying political consciousness, both through deliberate policies implemented by the government and through objective conditions arising from the rapid increase in the workforce produced by equally rapid industrialization. The workers of each company— or group of companies united in an industrial complex—formed, with the administrators and directors, a social/economic "bloc," and jointly defended their place in the system. This corporatism entailed the accentuation of regionalism in negotiations with competing blocs. This regionalism was not primarily founded on "national" diversity (as it had been in Tito's federal Yugoslavia). The relations between Russia—the numerically and historically preponderant nation—and the other nations were not "colonial" relations. This is shown by the redistributional flows of investments and social advantages that took place to the detriment of "Russians" in favor of peripheral regions. I have, in this context, rejected the nonsense that likens the USSR to an "imperial" system, with Russia dominating its internal colonies, despite the feeling of "supremacy" of the Russian nation.

Two: an autocratic government. The choice of this term is not meant to weaken the criticism of the system. It is not difficult to notice the "absence of democracy," whether that be of the representative kind (elections here being only ceremonial without any surprises), or the participative kind—which is more advanced by nature, as the 1917 revolutionaries had envisioned—with unions and all other possible forms of social organization having been domesticated, thereby precluding effective participation in decision making at all levels.

Three: a stabilized social order. The major conflict pitted the defenders of the revolution's original socialist project against the "realists" who, in practice, if not rhetorically, gave absolute priority to "catching up" through industrialization and rapid modernization. This conflict was the inevitable result of the objective contradiction confronting the revolution: it simultaneously had to "catch up" (or at least reduce the gap), since the revolution had inherited a "backward" country (I dislike the term and prefer "peripheral capitalism"), and build "something else" (socialism). I have emphasized this contradiction, which I have placed at the center of the problem of surpassing capitalism on the world scale (the "long transition from capitalism to world socialism"). The victims of this first major reason for recourse to violence were communist militants. A second level of violence accompanied rapid industrialization. This violence was in certain respects comparable to that which accompanied the construction of capitalism in the West. It remains the case that the USSR accomplished its industrialization in record time—a few decades—compared to the century available to the central capitalist countries. The latter had, moreover, distinct advantages due to their dominant imperialist position in the world system and the possibility of allowing their "excess" population to emigrate to the Americas. In addition, we should not forget the violence committed by the global capitalist system: military interventions—of which the Nazi aggression represents the most savage form—and economic blockade.

The Soviet system, as contradictory as it was, succeeded in building a social order that could be stabilized, and was effectively stabilized, during the post-Stalinist period. Social peace was "bought" by moderating the exercise of power—although still autocratic in nature—by improving the material conditions of life, and by tolerating "illegal" deviations.

Undoubtedly, stability of this sort is not likely to be "eternal." But no system has an advantage in this respect, despite the claims of ideological rhetoric (whether that of "socialism" or capitalist "liberalism"). Soviet stability masked the system's contradictions and limitations, epitomized by the difficulty it encountered in passing from extensive forms of accumulation to intensive forms of the latter, and by the difficulty in making a transition from autocracy to democratization of its political management. But this contradiction could have found its solution in an "evolution" toward what I have called the "center-left": the opening of market spaces (without calling into question the dominant forms of collective property) and democratization. That was, perhaps, Gorbachev's intention, but the failure of the attempt—naive and incoherent in many respects—caused the system to fall to the "right" from 1990.

Four: delinking of the Soviet system. The Soviet productive system was actually widely delinked from the dominant world capitalist system. By that I mean that the logic governing the economic decisions of the government (investments and prices) did not proceed from the requirements of an "open" integration into globalization. It is due to this delinking that the system had succeeded in advancing at such a rapid tempo. The system was not, nevertheless, "fully" independent from the "rest of the (capitalist) world." No system can be, and delinking, in my definition of the concept, is not synonymous with "autarky." The USSR occupied a "peripheral" position in the world system, primarily as exporter of raw materials.

Five: a military and political superpower. The USSR, thanks to the successes—and not the failures—of its construction, had succeeded in raising itself to the rank of military superpower. It was the Soviet army that defeated the Nazis. After the war, it succeeded in putting an end to the United States' nuclear and ballistic missile monopoly in record time. These successes were behind its political presence on the post–world war scene. The Soviet government benefited, moreover, from the prestige of its victory over Nazism and the success of the "socialism" of which it claimed to be the proof, regardless of the illusions concerning the reality of this "socialism"—sometimes characterized as "really existing." Yet it only made "moderate" use of these, in the sense that, contrary to the assertions of anti-Soviet propaganda, it proposed neither to "export the revolution" nor to "conquer" Western Europe (the false motive Washington and the European bourgeoisies invoked to force acceptance of NATO). Yet it used its political (and military) power to force imperialism to retreat in the Third World, opening up a degree of autonomy for the dominant classes (and the peoples) of Asia and Africa that they lost with the fall of the USSR. It is not by chance that the United States' militarized offensive has been deployed with such violence since 1990. The Soviet presence imposed—from 1945 to 1990—a "multipolar" organization of the world.

*New Forms of Capitalism in Russia*

The collapse of the Soviet system, combined with the failure of Third World populisms and the erosion of the social democratic compromise in the West, made possible the triumph of so-called liberal ideology and encouraged widespread acceptance of its rhetoric. This was as true in Russia as elsewhere. Elsewhere, I have pointed out the carefully maintained illusion that, just as

Germany and Japan had "lost the war, but won the peace," Russia was, thanks to liberalism, going to embark on an effective (finally) and rapid modernizing development and enter into democracy. It was forgotten—or there was a pretense of forgetting—that Washington's objective was not to allow the rebirth of a strong Russia (anymore than it is going to allow a strong China), even if it be capitalist, but to destroy it.

Have twenty-five years of "reforms" ended up with the establishment in Russia of a capitalist system capable of being "stabilized" and, from there, of actually moving the country onto the path that leads to the fulfillment of liberalism's promises? Reality forces us to respond to this question in the negative. The USSR was broken up and Russia lives under the same threat; none of the established institutions (its private companies, its state) is equipped to carry out the necessary investments to improve the effectiveness of the productive system (quite the contrary, there is massive disinvestment), and the systematic destruction of the positive achievements of the Soviet system (particularly in education) does not augur well for a "better future." It is difficult to understand how a system with these characteristics could be "stabilized," unless we understand "stabilization" to be one of complete poverty and powerlessness.

*1. THE INCLUSION OF THE NEW RUSSIA AS A SUBALTERN PERIPHERY OF THE CONTEMPORARY CAPITALIST-IMPERIALIST SYSTEM*

The "open" Russia is an "exporter of primary commodities" (especially oil), but it tends to be no more than that. Its industrial and agricultural productive systems no longer benefit from any attention on the part of the authorities and interest neither the national private sector nor foreign capital. Who is responsible for this huge decline? First, of course, it is the new ruling class. For the most part, this class has its origins in the former Soviet ruling class and unquestionably has been fabulously enriched by the privatizations/pillages from which it has benefited. This new class is unusually concentrated, so much so that the term "oligarchy" suits it perfectly. This class derives its wealth from three sources: petroleum rent (which depends on the global conjuncture, that is, the higher or lower prices of crude), cannibalization of industries (privatized industrial firms are not intended to form the basis for larger and more efficient production, but only to allow the oligarchs to live off their decline), and commissions in connection with opening the country's markets to imports. Rents and commissions always define a comprador bourgeoisie, not a "national" one. The oligarchy's explosion of wealth led to the formation of a new "middle class," called the "new Russians." The jobs that they hold are completely unproductive, derived from the spending of the oligarchs, whereas the earlier middle class of professionals and technicians, generally much more qualified and certainly productive, are now, along with the working classes, among the victims of this comprador capitalist development. Furthermore, the monopolies of the oligarchy, exclusive beneficiary of the state's generosity, stifle the possible formation of a real class of inventive entrepreneurs, who are hounded by the government and the mafias of the oligarchy, thereby making the formation of a capitalism "from below" impossible.

## 2. *An irresponsible autocratic government*

The capitalist forms of the new Russia exclude any democratic progress. The autocracy is not a "vestige of the past" but the necessary form of the exercise of power by the new comprador oligarchy. What sets apart the new autocracy from the old one is found elsewhere: in the totally irresponsible character of the power it wields. The autocracy is in the service of the oligarchy and participates in the pitched battles in which the oligarchic clans are involved, though it does know how to get paid for its services. Moreover, the autocracy has placed itself at the service of globalized oligopolistic foreign capital, for which it implements, without the least resistance, the diktats formulated by the WTO, the IMF, and even NATO! The recent conflicts between Vladimir Putin and some oligarchs have not led to any significant change in the organization of the system. Putin's objectives have remained limited: "rationalize" the system by separating more distinctly the bureaucracy of the autocratic presidential state from the class that it continues to serve, the oligarchy.

Are the "Russian people" responsible for this state of affairs? In part, they probably are, because of the disarray in which they found themselves following the sudden collapse of Soviet institutions. The new political parties had no social and ideological foundation that would have allowed them to emerge into any semblance of actual existence. The new "rightist forces," reduced to coteries of irresponsible individuals stemming from the old system, have certainly successfully used demagogic rhetoric, which is amplified by corrupt media at their service. Their patter has nevertheless rapidly worn thin in the face of intelligent public opinion, which testifies to the strong politicization of the Russian people. Consequently, the new rightist forces have quickly found themselves prisoners of support from the bureaucratic power of the new autocracy. It remains the case that the Communist Party, despite the hopes placed in it by a strong minority of electors, has been unable to begin a self-reform (and leave behind its own heritage of autocratic government management) or even resist the pressures of the new dictatorship.

## 3. RUSSIA ERASED FROM THE INTERNATIONAL SCENE

Russia now has a minor role in the G7, which has become the G8 (or rather 7.5). But, for all that, it is not an active participant in shaping the world balance of power. In appearance, it retains considerable military power, second in terms of its nuclear and ballistic missile capabilities. Yet the sorry state of its military organization gives rise to some doubt that it would be capable of using its armed forces effectively, if necessary that is, in case of aggression on the part of the United States.

The pressures exerted by the Western powers in Central Asia, the Caucasus, and Ukraine have succeeded up to now in keeping Russia outside of the international great game. Russia could foil the U.S. project (which is aimed at reducing it to a subaltern periphery in the new world order dominated by Washington) by playing a role in the reconstruction of a "front of the anti-imperialist South" and, first and foremost, to that end, moving closer to China. It is not doing that. On the contrary, it often acts in the opposite direction, bolstered by the illusion that its alliance with the United States protects it against possible expansionist moves by Beijing in Central Asia and Siberia. In doing so, Russia reinforces Washington's strategy, which is to isolate its "main potential enemy" (China). We bet that Russia will be not paid in return for this service. On the contrary, it will find itself weakened, and the process of its decline to the rank of subaltern periphery accelerated. It remains the case that all these balances (or imbalances) from which the United States benefits are fragile, and the certain failure of its intervention in Iraq will end up one day or another by calling them into question. Will Russian diplomacy then find its place when the cards are reshuffled? I shall return to this question, which is one of the major aspects of constructing an alternative to the liberal U.S. globalization.

## 4. IDEOLOGICAL POVERTY

Soviet ideology never gave up, even to the last moment, propagating the rhetoric of so-called socialism. The Soviet government, even in its deteriorated state, knew that it derived its legitimacy from the 1917 Revolution. We can be annoyed about that or even ridicule it. The distance that separated the rhetoric from Soviet reality was, moreover, no larger than the one that separates "liberal" rhetoric from really existing capitalism. And since a large number of normal individuals subscribe to such a liberal rhetoric despite the social disaster that accompanies its implementation, there should be no surprise that "socialist" rhetoric had its believers up to the last day.

The new oligarchic autocracy, on the other hand, needs to oppose Soviet rhetoric. But it does not know what to replace it with. All the patter about economic efficiency and democracy is not credible in Russia. "Patriotic" rhetoric is, then, the only mainstay of a hard-pressed government. The rhetoric in question serves to dispose of the real problems (social inequality, the ineffectiveness of the new economic management, the disappearance of the country's international role) by claiming to "unite the entire country behind its leaders," implying that the latter are "resisting" globalized capital. All comprador ruling classes in the contemporary periphery attempt to give themselves a "patriotic" image, while they are responsible for the decline of which their nations are victims and, in fact, act only as transmission belts for the (foreign) domination of international capital.

*Is an Alternative Possible?*

The picture of Russia I have sketched here might give rise to a great deal of pessimism about the country's future. Yet the failure of the new Russian capitalism and its inability to build the conditions for its stabilization, on the contrary, should inspire optimism. Russia is, as on the eve of 1917, "pregnant with a new revolution," it is sometimes said in Moscow—or at least with radical transformations able to rectify the direction of development. What are the local and world prospects for this and what are the conditions?

The basic principles on which the alternative to the current world system should be based are simple, obvious, and widely understood when put forward. On the internal (national) level: (i) a "mixed economy," on the one hand giving the state the means to direct general development and, on the other, offering to private property and the market sufficient margin to allow initiative; (ii) institutionalization of social negotiation among workers, companies, and the state; (iii) the strengthening of representative democracy by fostering initiatives in participatory democracy. On the world level: (i) organizing negotiations over forms of economic management (trade, capital flows, technology transfers, monetary management), based on an acknowledgment of the diversity of interests and inequality of partners; (ii) recognition of the principle of sovereignty of peoples, which is reinforced by the support for the progress of democratization, the foundation for a politically multipolar world. The implementation of all of these principles would make it possible to begin the first step in the "long transition to world socialism."

For Russia to implement them implies (i) the renationalization of large companies, particularly in the areas of oil and energy, mineral production, and banking (hence, it implies expropriating the oligarchy); (ii) the invention of new forms of joint management (workers and directors) of industrial and retail companies, whether the latter are formally public property (state, community, workers' collectives) or private; (iii) the reestablishment and strengthening of public social services, education (which was of high quality in the USSR), and scientific and technological research; (iv) the abolition of the 1993 constitution and the drafting of an authentically democratic one by a large, elected assembly; (v) a support for forms of participatory democracy; (vi) an opening toward large-scale negotiations between the republics of the former USSR, focused on building a regional economic and political space that respects the autonomy of the partners and capable of radically reforming interdependencies to the benefit of all; (vii) a reestablishment of Russian military power (while awaiting a general disarmament, when the United States is ready to agree to such); (viii) a promotion of negotiated trade, technological, and financial relations to begin the process of building a "larger Europe"—from the Atlantic to the Pacific; and (ix) a promotion of an active and independent (from that of the United States in particular) foreign policy that aims at strengthening institutions that can underpin the construction of a multipolar world.

Yevgeny Primakov's government had begun a turnaround in the direction outlined here with, it seems, some determination, but also much prudence in the initial measures it undertook (which is easy to understand). Primakov envisaged the formation of a "center left" economic and political system, as Gorbachev, perhaps, had wished, without knowing how to achieve. Primakov was, first of all, a victim of the (then still powerful) Communist Party's inability to understand and support the initiative. But he was also the victim of international hostility, first and foremost from the United States, but unfortunately also from Europe, which has not departed from its aim of a "Latino-Americanization" of the former USSR (and likewise of Eastern Europe, in the process of being integrated into the European Union).

The result of this failure facilitated the initial success of the United States' offensive and reinforced the subjection of Putin's government to its immediate demands. But perhaps Putin has now understood that the objective of the United States and its European allies is to destroy Russia and not to help it reform itself. Nevertheless, the system on which he bases his government does not allow him to resist effectively the destructive attacks of the imperialist triad. To do that, he would have to give up his support for the oligarchy, which exploits and oppresses the Russian people. Otherwise, the latter will do nothing.

The possible future alternatives for Russia and the states born from the collapse of the USSR are certainly not the same. I had never had a great deal of confidence in Gorbachev's "perestroika" and "glasnost." His unconditional capitulation in Reykjavik to the arrogant Ronald Reagan caused me to fear the worst, which did happen. In 2003, I had accepted a curious invitation to come to Rimini, Italy, in the hope of hearing Gorbachev's comments on my remarks. I phrased my questions about Russia's future in extremely prudent terms, without going over the past. But I did not interest Gorbachev, who was exclusively attentive to (and approving of) the twaddle mouthed by the North American economists. I then understood that Gorbachev had never really known what Marxism was.

I could follow events in capitalist Russia only from afar since the WFA had never succeeded in finding interested correspondents. And then, one day in 2007, I was invited by an odd "Kremlin Organization," close to Putin and headed by Vyacheslav Glazyaev. Europe Publishers, the organization's publishing house, had just published *The Liberal Virus* in Russian, the only one of my works to have been published in that language (whereas all my major writings had always been published quickly in Chinese since the 1970s). The choice led me to understand that this fundamental ideological dimension of the challenge had appeared important to them. The debate, supported by impressive resources (television and journalists), quickly convinced me that the sole concern of my interlocutors relates to geopolitics, understood in conventional bourgeois geostrategic terms, which separates these problems from social questions. The awareness of U.S. hostility to any attempt at "emergence" by Russia was visible, but nothing more. Subsequently, I received a no less curious invitation to participate in an annual conference, held in Rhodes by Russian geopolitical specialists interested in the Middle East. But the approach—"dialogue of civilizations"—seemed too artificial to me to allow for a discussion of the region's real problems.

*The Ukrainian Crisis, the Eurasian Project, and Putin's Balancing Act*

In March 2014, Europe organized a "Euro-Nazi" putsch in Kiev. The Western media clergy's rhetoric crowing about the promises of democracy is purely and simply false. The powers of the triad have promoted democracy nowhere. On the contrary, the triad has always supported the staunchest opponents of democracy, including fascists rebaptized as "nationalists." In the former Yugoslavia, the Europeans supported those who are nostalgic for Croatian fascism, returned from their Canadian exile; in Kosovo, they gave power to drug and prostitution mafias; in the Arab countries they continue to support the most reactionary political Islam, itself financed by the new democratic republics that Saudi Arabia and Qatar have become, and to believe the Western media's endless patter. Military intervention in Iraq and Libya destroyed these countries, without promoting the least possibility of democracy. In Syria, the triad powers' military support for the "Islamists," directly or indirectly through the democratic republics of Saudi Arabia and Qatar, promises nothing better.

In Ukraine, the pro-Nazi junta has not succeeded very well in establishing its despotic government. The obstacle it has come up against is not "ethnic," opposing Russian speakers and Ukrainian speakers. Certainly, the Soviet government had deliberately drawn the borders of the republics of the former USSR to the advantage of non-Russian nationalities, in an attempt to break with Great Russian chauvinism. The example of Crimea, which had never been Ukrainian, demonstrates that. Donetsk and Odessa had never been "ethnically" Ukrainian. Just as with the Yugoslav republics, these borders had never been drawn with the idea in mind that the republics in question would become independent states. Putin is probably not a hero of democratic causes, but in this context, he could not but support all those in Ukraine who reject the Euro-German colonization that Brussels intends to impose, just like it has done in Eastern Europe, Greece, and Cyprus. It is not only the "Russian speakers" of Ukraine who might come to reject the European project, even if the despotic powers exercised by the junta in Kiev do not allow the expression of such opposition to the Euro-German project.

Russia is searching for a place in the current and future world system. Putin appears to have made building a vast alliance among the peoples of the former USSR his project. This project is now known as the alliance of "Euro-Asian" peoples. This is not a recent artificial invention. In an article I wrote a decade and a half ago, I observed that this idea responded to Russia's centuries-long search for its place in the world.[46] I see no reason to refuse this right to the Russians and other peoples of the former USSR.

Moscow's struggle against the imperialist order, in Ukraine and elsewhere, will be victorious only if it is firmly supported by the peoples concerned. This support will be possible only if Russia frees itself from the neoliberal yoke, here as elsewhere the origin of the social disaster. Up to now, Putin has undertaken a perilous balancing act, attempting to combine continuation of his disastrous neoliberal internal policies with defense of the legitimate interests of an independent Russia. Abandoning neoliberalism and moving away from financial globalization are now necessary and possible. Segments of the political class that governs in Moscow are disposed to support a state capitalism that is able, in turn, to open the way to a possible advance in the direction of the democratic socialization of the system's management. But if the comprador fraction of the Russian ruling classes—exclusive beneficiaries of neoliberalism—come to gain the upper hand, then the sanctions with which Europe threatens Russia could bear fruit. Comprador forces are always ready to capitulate to preserve their share of the loot from the plundering of their country. Russia could then not avoid being colonized by the triad's imperialism.

# 6

# CHINA, VIETNAM, AND CUBA
## Fears and Hopes

### CHINA

My political choices have led me to follow China's evolution closely since 1960. Beginning in 1980, Isabelle and I went to China regularly and stayed there for a month each time. We split our time between Beijing, where I was regularly invited by various institutes of the Academy and usually met Party leaders and the country's economic managers, and organized visits elsewhere in this gigantic country. We thus traveled thousands of kilometers, from Beijing to Tianjin, Shanghai, Nanjing, and Hangzhou (the wealthy coastal provinces of the center east); from Hunan to Guilin, Guangzhou, and Hong Kong; from Beijing to Xian (the poor provinces of the northwest); from Sichuan (Chengdu, Chongqing) to Kashgar in the extreme west. We still have not visited three large regions: the northeast (the former Manchuria), Yunnan, and Tibet.

Chinese painters have captured to perfection the essence of the distinctive characteristics of the country's various landscapes, such as the sugarloaf mountains with their peaks lost in the mist. But nothing replaces traveling through these unusual landscapes, unparalleled in my experience. China is immense; it offers the visitor an infinite variety of landscapes because of its diverse climates, which extend from the Siberian to the semi-tropical, from the Pacific of tropical monsoons to the Taklamakan Desert, more fearsome than the Rub el Khali or the Ténéré, and its relief, which descends from Everest to one of the lowest points on earth, and rises from the flat rice plains to Tibet, Qinghai, and Altai.

Sichuan (a province with a population of only 120 million) offered us several beautiful excursions. One was through the rich rice fields supplied with water by a system of dams that dates from very ancient times, constructed by "moving the mountains" with spades and mattocks to "make them fall into the river" and block its passage. Another was on the steep slopes on the eastern side of Tibet, where magnificent Buddhist monasteries were perched. We also traveled from Chongqing to Wuhan on a four-day cruise aboard a beautiful ship along with some foreign tourists, of course, but mainly vacationers from the new Chinese bourgeoisie. We passed through the extraordinary gorges of the Yangtze and its tributaries. We were in the company of Fawzy and Gerda Mansour. This was the last year before the new large dam modified forever the topography of these places. To visit a gorge of one of the most untamed tributaries, we had to leave the large ship and board a canoe, which barely managed the current. On the banks of the river, the Chinese peasants, jovial as always, watched us with amusement. They had set up an entire business in "rescue" products (biscuits, tea, woolen garments, etc.) in expectation of a possible shipwreck. What a beautiful opportunity to sell! The Chinese "organizers" of the trip also had a strong taste for risk, bordering on the irresponsible. One time, we were late and it was not until night that we reached a bank of the Yangtze. Since there was a superb monastery perched on the mountain to visit, they did not hesitate to restart a chairlift and have us get on, despite the violent storm. Then we visited the monastery by flashlight!

I shall not describe in detail the number of diverse landscapes and cities that we visited. In Beijing, beyond the Great Wall, we saw the Forbidden City, the Summer Palace, and many other monuments. In Xian—a superb city still surrounded by its ancient walls—we saw the well-known extraordinary cemetery of statues of the imperial army. In Nanjing, we visited the bridge over the Yangtze and many other things. In cities such as Hangzhou, Suzhou, Shao Xi, and others, we frequented the delightful teahouses built on artificial lake-gardens the Chinese were crazy about. In Shanghai, we saw the imposing port districts of this capital of comprador capitalism, divided into foreign concessions. We traveled through the countryside of dusty loess along the Yellow River on the way to Yan'an, and through rice fields lost to view on the plains of the center east. We marveled at the extraordinary mountains of Guan Xi, around Guilin, traveled on the Li River, then through Guangdong, along the Pearl River. We saw Huangshan, the green mountain—source of inspiration for painters and poets—descending on foot by the stone staircase which climbed to 1,860 meters! Quite fortunately, there was a foot massager at the base of the mountain!

In 1980, we were housed in the main guesthouse for Party guests, outside Beijing. Certainly, we were given special treatment, but subsequently, we liked it much better when we stayed in one of the hotels in the city center, which today have become quite numerous.

During the Maoist era, which we experienced directly, Beijing presented the unforgettable spectacle of a river of bicycles filling the entire width of its immense streets. The "Mao suit" (pioneered by Sun Yat Sen) in blue or green (military colors, adopted by young people who professed to be on the left in the Party), along with the hat that girls wore tilted to one side, which made them look a bit like a mocking street urchin and enhanced their charm, was the uniform of the entire population. I never found this detestable; on the contrary, I think it was a good way to begin to create some of the conditions necessary to affirm the equality of individuals. Moreover, the blue jacket was both sturdy and elegant. Mao Zedong's China had succeeded—without truly wanting to do so—in creating a cultural fashion of worldwide scope as strong as that of American jeans. We stocked up on our Mao jackets—blue, green, and gray—and Isabelle and I continue to wear them almost daily, when the season permits. Some perhaps look at us as "dinosaurs," but that doesn't matter. Today, the uniform is abandoned, replaced by the sadly anonymous suit and tie for men. But giving up the blue or green Mao jacket allows young Chinese females, whom I generally find pretty, to enhance their stylishness: light dresses and small straw hats often decorated by a flower or—for more formal occasions—Chinese dresses slit on the side.

Beijing is an unusual city. Prior to the accelerated modernization of recent years, it had retained its character as austere imperial capital. Long streets, rather narrow, but straight, bordered by uniformly gray walls, behind which the *yamen* were found. A yamen is an aristocratic residence arranged in a square around a courtyard closed to the outside by a beautiful Chinese door. From the street, roofs of colored tiles can be seen. The great variety of colors and the exuberance are enhanced by the contrast with the severe sobriety of the walls. Our friends Sol and Patricia Adler lived in one of these superb yamens on Nancaochang Street (Deng Xiaoping lived there in 1949 when Beijing was liberated). Mao had ordered at the time that all these beautiful houses should be cleared and either used to house foreign friends or as schools and cultural centers. Sol was an American who came with an aid mission to China during the war against Japan. Like Bill Hinton, whom I also knew, he remained in the country and placed all his skills at the service of Maoist China. And he had a lot to offer: cultured, subtle, and knowledgeable about U.S. politics, as well as the strategic views of the U.S. ruling class. The Chinese authorities always treated their foreign friends with the greatest fraternal trust, even during the harshest moments of the Cultural Revolution, when "suspicion" weighed on everyone. From this point of view, there is nothing similar to the behavior of Soviet authorities, who were often more than horrible with foreigners. Sol is dead. But he would have died much sooner if he had not been in China. Afflicted with lung cancer, he underwent successive operations by the best surgeons in Beijing, which gave him several more years of life.

There was in Beijing a street of antique dealers where Isabelle and I liked to stroll. Chinese antique dealers, even those in the public sector, were men of taste and refinement. But there was also in Beijing a sort of grand bazaar (the Chinese Khan Khalili, equivalent of the Cairo bazaar) where anything could be found, including objects of high quality and beauty.

A young Chinese student who had attended my lectures offered to be our guide. A charming boy, he led us to places infrequently visited by foreigners. We also continuously talked about politics with him (he spoke English—not well, but adequately). He was critical from a leftist perspective, but considered that it was still useful to be active in the Party, which remained, according to him, sufficiently open to lively and serious debates. We ate with him in popular and inexpensive restaurants. There was nothing wrong with them; it was rare to eat poorly in China.

Beijing's modernization is not a disaster, and that is something of note. The skyscrapers aside—which pop up like mushrooms, form groups that were distinguished by their diverse architectural styles, but always well spaced—the Chinese are careful to leave a lot of space for trees and gardens where they like to stroll. The old city has undergone some destruction, but, on the other hand, the stylish aristocratic and shopping districts, which had deteriorated, have been renovated—sometimes a little too much! Belatedly, like elsewhere in the Third World, the Chinese have become aware that their heritage should be preserved. Restorations of old cities, like Shao Xi or the old districts of Canton, those of the English and French concessions (magnificent in Canton), are a testament to this awareness. Generally speaking, the new urbanization—China now has 400 million city dwellers, 200 million of which are made up of first-generation inhabitants from rural areas, must be recognized as a definite success both by the quality and true originality of its urban planning and most of its housing developments. Facing Hong Kong, China built a city of the same size in fifteen years: Shenzhen, with seven million inhabitants. This story shows that China was able to build in fifteen years a city the same size as the one it took the English a hundred years to build! A comparison should be made here: Brasilia, a new city, is hideous. The new Chinese cities, like Shenzhen, are beautiful.

The Chinese people are not ordinary, either. It is not difficult to communicate with them, except for the challenging issue of language. The Chinese are, as a whole, curious to meet foreigners and approach them without hesitation. The government has never segregated foreigners from the population, as in the Soviet Union. I like to stroll through the streets of Beijing. One muggy September evening, I went to the Tiananmen Square. The Chinese are peasants and their behavior is very *baladi* (a term from Egyptian popular language to refer to ordinary people). The square was overrun with families that had come to picnic. A plastic covering was placed on the ground and while some people were stretched out on cushions, others were seated on folding stools. There were boxes of biscuits and thermoses of tea, without which no one ever went anywhere. Many were eating watermelon. Someone called to me and invited me to share their picnic. I accepted and attempted to chat. They had to recruit from neighboring picnickers a young man who had learned a little English. We spoke of politics, obviously, and quite freely. As for the "market," it was viewed as good in some respects, but insofar as it had made some people wealthy, that was considered bad.

There is great social diversity in Chinese crowds, unparalleled elsewhere in most areas of the Third World. Boys and girls mix freely and couples do not hide. But scratch a little, as it is said, and you will find the solid core of the patriarchy. That is undoubtedly true, but progress can be seen nonetheless; for example, in the forward characteristics of girls who do not hesitate to put boys in their place when necessary, and who show no timidity in doing so. There is nothing comparable in Japan or Korea where the same original patriarchal customs continue to govern all daily behavior. The same uninhibited behavior is observable between fellow workers. The Chinese, as I have said, are peasants. Thus, they love opportunities to feast as a group. In the numerous restaurants of Chinese cities, at least half of the space is set aside for booths separated by light curtains. Groups can feel at ease and enjoy a certain intimacy in such a setting. Every opportunity is seized to organize a collective or family feast of this type: official celebrations, retirement of a workmate, promotion of another, etc. Social gatherings are always mixed—spouses and work colleagues of both sexes participate. The Chinese are coarse, drink a lot (on these occasions, at least), eat as much as possible, and, according to what I have been told, use straightforward, rather bawdy language.

There are other aspects of Chinese social life that should be noted. Confucianism has not been eradicated, despite the Cultural Revolution. The model of the "perfect" leader remains Confucian: elegant, sober, calm, and polite. When Mao was alive, dressed like the others, he was distinguished only by his understated refinement. The "old" Wang Yué, who had been our guide during our first trip to China, was a perfect model of that; it was the same with Pu Shan. I recognize that Confucian ideology, even if it includes obvious conservative dimensions, also has developed what appear to me to be good qualities. During the Maoist era, leaders were visibly divided into two models—the Confucians, which in no way implies that all Confucians were on the same side, some were on the right, some in the center, others on the left; and the "proletarians." The latter came directly from the working class or the poor peasantry, almost always anti-Confucian in principle, for good reasons (because Confucianism is the ideology of traditional China's dominant class); and, for the peasants, strongly affected by Taoism. The Cultural Revolution recognized only this second type of leader as communist. Today, a third model has openly appeared: the bourgeois. I will add without hesitation: their style is nouveau riche, comprador, and vulgar. In the luxury hotels and on the boat during our cruise on the Yangtse, they were (and are) quite visible. Where do they come from? Most of them are Chinese from abroad who were always that way. Are they taking root in the new Chinese "entrepreneur" circles? Probably.

Other aspects of Chinese life to take note of involve the family, the elderly, and children—"the only child." The family was always a strong basic unit of Chinese society. It remains so. Respect for the elderly goes beyond what is found elsewhere (except for the Chinese cultural area of Vietnam, Korea, and Japan). If you are a leader, you never retire in China. At eighty years old, you are still considered an "active" director. A little later, you are named "president." That way, you keep an office and continue to receive greetings from the young and provide advice. Grandmothers are always present and get together in public gardens or on the sidewalk in front of their houses. They take care of the children. The children are spoiled—due to the law allowing only one child—surrounded by their two parents and up to four grandparents. Many Chinese have told me that they are worried about what will happen in the future because of the egoism developed by this demographic policy.

Two comrades in particular, who occupied relatively high posts in the hierarchy, had invited me to China: Wang Yué and Pu Shan. Now deceased, Wang had been responsible for monitoring the activities of Maoists in the Third World and, among other things, had maintained a relationship with our journal *Révolution*, which I have already spoken about above. Pu and Wang were from the Academy and, in my opinion, were among the most open, astute, and well-informed leaders about what was happening in the world beyond China's borders. I always enjoyed talking with them.

The interpreter who had been assigned to us was the young Li Baoyuan, who had studied at Aix, spoke French perfectly, and, moreover, knew France and its cultural, social, and political life well. Li was well educated and was the best translator possible for the lectures I gave, especially since I did not want my analyses presented with less precision and nuance than elsewhere. I took up difficult questions about Marxist theory and presented my theses on world capitalism and Third World societies, particularly those of Africa and the Arab world. I verified, on this occasion, that my theses were not unknown in China. A lot of my writings had been translated and circulated in the Academy and the Party's Central Committee. Some had been published for the universities and the public. I was unaware of all that. Let me indicate in passing that the Soviets did not translate one line of my writings, which did not prevent the Bogomolovs and others from "denouncing" me in their journals! Li became a friend, obviously. He and his wife, Yiping, subsequently came to Dakar where he was the first secretary to the ambassador. We saw both of them recently in Beijing.

I devised a formula in China that pleased our hosts. I had well understood how tiresome it must be for the Chinese to receive all these foreigners curious to know more about their country, questioning and questioning again, without bringing anything to their hosts in exchange. I put myself in their place. I proposed to my hosts to alternate: one day, I would attend a discussion where China and its problems would be the focus (and I would pose questions, make comments, etc.); on the other day, I would make a presentation on a topic concerning Africa, the Arab world, the world system, or the problems of socialism and Marxism that would be, in turn, the focus of our collective discussion. The approach worked perfectly and allowed me to establish good rapport with the Chinese. I can no longer count the dozens and dozens of discussions in which I participated using this framework, invited by various institutes of the Academy and the management schools in Beijing, Nanjing, Shanghai, and Chengdu. I believe I know fairly well the corridors of all the buildings that are concentrated along the large avenue Jianguomennei Dajie in Beijing. In Shanghai, Isabelle and I were housed in a splendid half-traditional, half-modern house belonging to a rich Chinese merchant and located in the middle of the former French concession, the most attractively urbanized part of Shanghai. Isabelle claims to have recognized places about which she had read a clear description in some novel or other. The house served as a guesthouse for distinguished visitors.

The sometimes quite numerous Chinese participants grouped themselves according to their political affinities, as in a parliament: left, center, and right, as always and everywhere. What struck me is that, in each group, there were men—and fewer women—of all ages, from youths in their twenties to octogenarians. The latter were always treated with great deference by partisans of the viewpoints they represented. We discussed issues quite freely. Nothing comparable with the atmosphere in the Soviet world, where it had been unthinkable that someone would be invited to make a presentation on important issues from a point of view that claimed to be Marxist without necessarily being orthodox. In the Soviet world, it was reactionary U.S. professors who were invited, and their liberal twaddle was attended to with deference, even open admiration. That was the only viewpoint, other than the official cant, that could be heard. In China, it was quite different. The debates were lively, sometimes heated with the thundering proclamations coming from various perspectives. I always expressed my viewpoint unreservedly, though always in courteous language, which I thought was very important.

That has earned me, I believe, the honor of being considered China's sincere friend, which, of course, I really am. I certainly have opinions on most problems. But I do not think I am one of those who believe they have ingested some kind of magic pill that guarantees that their point of view must necessarily be the best. I present my arguments and listen to those from others. In any case, China's future depends, in my opinion, on the Chinese; and the numerous Westerners who sermonize on the virtues of the market, efficiency, or even democracy cannot stand this. The Chinese, like everyone, know all that, or can come to know it on their own. China's choices are, as elsewhere, the result of class struggles and the possible ensuing compromises. One can, of course, consider a given choice, good or bad, and one has the right to say so. But, in my opinion, we can only hope that China is able to assert itself as a strong power, capable of standing up to external attacks. This is, in fact, a necessary condition for the emergence of the best—from the perspective of humanity's socialist future. It is in this precise sense that I am a "friend of China." Consequently, I categorically refuse to back those who ultimately align themselves with the strategic objectives of U.S. hegemony, which are to weaken China and dismember it by supporting Tibet and Sinkiang, encouraging centrifugal tendencies among compradors, and showcasing apparently "democratic" slogans that are capable of being manipulated quite simply to serve the anti-socialist objectives of imperialism. That the inadequacies of the policies implemented by the Party-state create favorable terrain for the imperialist enemy is another matter, and I do not hide my opinion about these inadequacies. The solution advocated by the dominant forces of world capitalism is never the best—on the contrary, it is always the worst.

The debates in which I participated were always continued by discussions with various people, particularly my friends Pu Shan, Wang Yué, and Li Baoyuan, and also with young people. In this way, I came to know those who professed to be "neo-Maoists": faithful to the fundamental principles of Maoism and simultaneously critical of its anti-democratic practices. The conception of democracy that they defend subscribes to the twofold objective of being open to ideological and political pluralism and of allowing the working classes to promote respect for their social demands. This is a conception defended by Lin Chun with strong theoretical and political arguments. This is obviously quite far removed from the view orchestrated by the Western media, which highlights some of the slogans advanced during the occupation of the Tiananmen Square by those who, combining "democracy" with "markets," are attempting to promote the positions of capitalism they represent. For them, "democracy" is only a means, intended to ensure the rapid transition to their domination—and then they can get rid of it subsequently, since their true objective is the triumph of the "market" and hardly anything else.

On other occasions, I had the opportunity to discuss, with some degree of seriousness, I believe, the economic strategies promoted by the state, particularly with Ma Jiantang, the Plan director in the State Council (equivalent of the Council of Ministers). My questions concerned three essential points: social redistribution of income, strengthening the integration of all China's provinces in a single production system, and, within this context, financing of poor provinces by the beneficiaries of opening; in other words, control of external relations. I have commented elsewhere on the responses I received and the supporting documents put at my disposal.

There is one last observation I wish to make in these memoirs concerning Chinese leadership circles. China's ruling class under Deng and his successors is certainly split into different tendencies. Beyond the divergent currents that exist within the Party leadership, we should also include in this class the heads of private companies and the leaders of semi-public companies that belong to provinces, cities, village groups, and the state. Other sociopolitical interests—the army, certainly, and the unions in some cases—are also represented in the ruling class. All of these spheres of influence sometimes (or often?) solidify into blocs to defend provincial interests, even if this is against the central state. Taking into account the country's gigantic size and the immediate prospects for unequal development, these regionalist tendencies could become even more dangerous since external forces (overseas Chinese, U.S. imperialism) are devoted to encouraging such centrifugal propensities. Nevertheless, my feeling is that the central government has succeeded up to now in maintaining the unity of some kind of dominant national bloc through centrist policies, which lean to the center right (encouragement of capitalism). The means implemented are, it seems, effective, due, among other things, to a strong national sentiment.

Despite the regionalisms that the country's size inevitably generates, the (Han) Chinese nation is a reality (and I congratulate them for that). The only national questions managed in a questionable manner are those involving the Tibetans and the Uyghurs, and imperialism is actively involved in exploiting these weaknesses of the government. (Of course, I do not at all share the viewpoint of the supposed "defenders of democracy" who, when it is no longer useful, move on to praising the lamas and the mullahs who, beyond their obscurantism, have always exploited their peoples with the most barbaric violence, until the Chinese Revolution liberated them.) I will go a little further in expressing my insights on this issue. I have had the opportunity to discuss various problems with mid-level leaders (hardly more) who are responsible for diverse functions. My feeling (perhaps too generalizing?) is that those who are in charge of economic management lean to the right, but that those who manage political power remain clear-headed on one point that, for me, is fundamental: they do not like the United States and generally consider its hegemony to be the number one enemy of China (as nation and state, not only because it is "socialist"). They say so easily and often. I remain struck by the difference, in this context, between their language and what I heard (with conviction, it seems) from Soviet political leaders (and *a fortiori* those of the former popular democracies). The latter always appeared to me to be totally unaware of the true objectives of Washington and its Western allies. Gorbachev's rhetoric in Reykjavik, when he proclaimed—with incredible naivety—the "end" of U.S. hostility toward the USSR, is unthinkable in China. By chance, I discussed this a little later in Beijing. All the Chinese were dumbfounded by this "imbecility" and, getting worked up, did not hesitate to conclude: "The United States is and will remain our enemy, our main enemy."

The judgments that I am making about contemporary China, which I know is committed to a capitalist path, will appear curious to those who know my irrevocable commitment to socialism. This is not the place to take up again the political analyses I have made elsewhere on the subject. Up to now, China's capitalist development is not analogous to that which is well known elsewhere in the Third World because the Chinese people have had the experience of a great revolution. Consequently, it has become resolutely—and straightforwardly—modern. There is no pseudo-cultural neurosis about "specificity" as flourishes elsewhere. That is why the Chinese should not be compared to other peoples of the Third World, but rather to those of the First World. That they think they can "catch up" is no doubt a dangerous illusion cherished by the rapidly expanding new middle classes, which well serves the opportunism of the ruling classes. But there is also a positive aspect of this leap forward into modernity: the Chinese working classes know how to fight and have confidence in themselves. There is no submissive attitude as seen elsewhere in many places on a daily basis. There is also a record of social struggles, often violent, and not always defeated, far from it. All of that forces those committed to the capitalist path to accommodate as much as possible the demand for equality carried by the revolution. The Chinese have a sense of equality and social justice as strong as the French, for example (who also made a great revolution), completely unlike the acceptance of injustice and inequality by Americans (who never made a revolution). China is—along with Vietnam, who also made a great revolution—the only country in the world where all rural inhabitants have retained, up to now, a right of equal access to the land that cannot easily be called into question. Of course, I continue to follow as closely as possible the country's development, thanks to our friends in the Forum: Wen Tiejun, Lin Chun, Lau Kin Chi, and Huang Ping.[47]

The result is that China is a poor country (which succeeds in feeding 22 percent of the world's population with only 6 percent of the world's arable land) where few poor people can be seen. It is the diametrical opposite of Brazil, a wealthy country where only the poor are seen. I am choosing my words carefully. I traveled by automobile over thousands of kilometers through both the rich and poor provinces of China. There was nothing comparable to the atrocious poverty encountered at each step in India, Egypt, Mexico, Brazil, or South Africa. There were rich villages, which sustained comparison with those of Japan, and there were poor villages—like there were barely fifty years ago in some areas of Europe—but not millions of people living in slums as there are almost everywhere.

All of that, however, is being threatened, it will be said. Will not capitalist logic eventually win out? Those who are the bearers of capitalism in China gain absolutely no sympathy from me. I view them just as I view all the vulgar comprador bourgeoisies of our time. The depoliticization of the young (no doubt in the middle classes), which the still autocratic government encourages, of course, operates in favor of a possible negative development. Will the Chinese people allow that? I do not think so, and I note that numerous friends whom I have in China, and to whom I continually pose pertinent and difficult questions, share this point of view—which will appear quite optimistic to some.

### China, Emergent Power

Over the last twenty years, I have prioritized making frequent, long visits to China. The latest was a trip of one month in December 2012 from Xian to Chongqing with a WFA/TWF/China group, coordinated by Lau Kin Chi, vice president of the WFA—who did it with faultless efficiency, but still found time to be diligent and full of kindness toward Isabelle and me (Isabelle almost always travels with me to China)—and by Wen Tiejun, an influential person who leads a network for "renovation of the Chinese countryside." The trip allowed us to have discussions with the leaders of grassroots organizations that are independent of the Communist Party, but not hostile to it, in five provinces in the center of the country. It was fascinating. What follows will enlighten the reader on the understanding of the Chinese challenge I gained from these discussions.[48]

I am known in China. A lot of my writings are translated into Chinese, sometimes more quickly than into English (that is the case for the interviews about the "Arab revolutions," political developments in Africa, Russia, and elsewhere). I was thus received by influential leaders in numerous institutions of the country: Institute of Marxism-Leninism and Mao Zedong Thought, Centre for World Politics (Huang Ping), China Center for Comparative Politics and Economics (Li Qing), Tshing Hua University and Beijing University (Wang Hui, Lu Ai Guo, Dai Jinhua), the journals *International Critical Thought*, *Marxism and Reality*, *Beijing Cultural Review*, as well as *China Daily* and television.

Sometimes I am consulted on difficult and controversial questions in the Chinese establishment. For example, this was the case concerning the convertibility of the yuan. Friends submitted two papers on the question to me, one produced by the British bank HSBC (liberal to excess, of course) and the other from a source close to the management of the Central Bank of China. My comments were published in China. The reader can find the English version on the Pambazuka.org website.[49]

Probably the central question of our time concerns China's future. Where does the path chosen by the Chinese government lead? Does it lead to a form of capitalism, even a national one, regulated by an active state, tempered by an agricultural policy that safeguards the access of all (or almost all) peasants to the land? And in this case, what kind of political system can ensure its viability? A slow evolution, on the model of Taiwan, in the direction of limited concessions to some kind of democracy, without calling into question the power of a ruling-party state, should not be ruled out. The discussions on this topic in which I participated in Beijing and Taipei (in 2008) inspired me to put forward the idea—which might appear preposterous—of a Communist Party becoming a sort of Kuomintang. Would the prospect of socialism, then, be permanently remote? I heard that said by some of the participants from think tanks connected with our network of debates. But others do not think so and base their argument on the progress of social struggles by movements that call themselves "neo-Maoist." Such movements might be capable of shifting the evolution of events, of inventing and advancing forms of democratization required for the progressive socialization of the management of a state capitalism that would then become a step, which could be called "market socialism," in a long transition. There is visible awareness that the implosion of globalized capitalism and the rise of conflicts between an emergent China's national interests and those of the imperialist triad could force the government to move in this direction.

China's different possible evolutions will weigh heavily on the future of the world system. China's advantage does not derive solely from its continental size, but above all from the fact that it is just about the only Third World country (along with Korea) to be advanced in the building of a self-reliant economy, which gives it both an appreciable margin of autonomy and considerable bargaining capacity. However, we should not prejudge any guaranteed success for pursuing a project that might finally embark on the long transition to socialism, which would require a real blossoming of popular democracy. That is not impossible, even if this is not the choice of the—nationalist, but autocratic—government or that of the new "pro-Western" comprador bourgeoisie.

The questions I shall examine in the following pages (written in 2014) were the subject of long discussions with my Chinese friends over the course of four one-month visits to the country, in 2002, 2004, 2008, and 2012. Written fragments were sent to one or another of these friends for comment. Lu Aiguo had annotated (in Chinese) his remarks. We had a long exchange that helped me understand why he insisted on what he saw as a necessary distinction between "state socialism" and "state capitalism." Wen Tiejun is the best expert on conditions in rural China, from whom I learned everything found on the topic in these memoirs. He also shares with me the same understanding of the importance of China's resisting financial globalization, a condition of success for any "sovereign project" worthy of the name. Wang Hui, published and known abroad, clarified for me the Chinese view of long-term history and perspectives on the contemporary world and the challenge it represents. Huang Ping helped me understand better than anyone else the nuances in the conflicts that occur within the ruling political class of the Party and the state. At a distance, I have learned much, not only from reading Lin Chun's works, but also from my discussions with her.

I make no long-term predictions such as Western futurologists like to do. Will China "inevitably" be the number one world economy—capitalist and imperialist, of course—even without being the number one military power? I doubt that it is possible to be one without the other. Or will this colossus with feet of clay collapse like the USSR, which, in the 1930s, appeared to be building a superior system in opposition to the crisis-ridden United States and

Europe? I am not going to answer this false question. For me, history remains open. The best and the worst are both possible. All depends on the development of the political consciousness of the partners and opponents battling in a society, in China as elsewhere.

The debates about the present and future of China—"emergent" power—leave me unconvinced. Some consider that China has permanently chosen the "capitalist path" and are pleased about that; they only hope that this "return to normal" will be accompanied by an evolution toward Western-style democracy. Others deplore this in the name of the values of a "betrayed socialism." In fact, the question of whether China is capitalist or socialist is poorly formulated because China has actually been involved on an original path since 1950 and maybe even since the Taiping Revolution in the nineteenth century.

Mao described the nature of the revolution in China led by its Communist Party as an anti-imperialist/anti-feudal revolution aimed at achieving socialism. He always characterized this as the first phase of a long route to socialism. I believe it is necessary to emphasize that the Chinese Revolution initiated a special response to the agrarian question. Distributed (agricultural) land was not privatized; it remained the property of the nation represented by village communities and was only given to rural families for use. That had not been the case in Russia where V. I. Lenin, presented with the *fait accompli* of the peasants' insurrection in 1917, recognized the private property rights of the distribution's beneficiaries. This "Chinese uniqueness"—the effects of which are of major importance—strictly prohibits describing China today (in 2014) as "capitalist." The capitalist path is based on the transformation of land into a commodity.

The principle (land as common property, support for small production without small land ownership) is the source of these unparalleled results. It has allowed a relatively controlled rural to urban migration. Compare that with a capitalist approach, such as Brazil, for example. Private property in agricultural land has emptied the Brazilian countryside. Today, 11 percent of the population lives in rural areas. But at least 50 percent of the urban population lives in slums (the favelas) and survive only because of the "informal economy" (including organized crime). There is nothing like that in China, where the urban population is, as a whole, properly employed and housed.

The first characteristic an analyst of contemporary China must note is state capitalism. It is capitalism in the sense that the relation between the workers and the authorities that organize production is similar to the worker-capitalist relation that characterizes capitalism: subjected and alienated labor, extraction of surplus labor. Extremely brutal forms of exploitation of laborers exist in China—in the coal mines, and imposed in a furious pace on female workers on the factory floor. Nevertheless, the establishment of a state capitalist system is inescapable, and will remain so everywhere. The socialization and reorganization of the economic system at all levels, from the company (the elementary unit) to the nation and world, require undertaking a long struggle for an entire historical period, one which cannot be shortened.

Chinese state capitalism has been constructed to achieve three objectives: (i) construction of an integrated and sovereign modern industrial system; (ii) management of the interaction between this system and small rural production; and (iii) control of how China is inserted into the world system, which is itself dominated by the generalized monopolies of the imperialist triad (United States, Europe, and Japan).

China entered globalization beginning in 1990 through the rapid development of manufactured exports. The triumph of neoliberalism facilitated the success of this choice during a fifteen-year period (1990 to 2005). Continuing with this choice is not only questionable because of its political and social effects, but also because it is threatened by the implosion of neoliberal globalized capitalism beginning in 2007. To say, as I have heard *ad nauseam*, that China's success should be attributed to the abandonment of Maoism, external openness, and the entry of foreign capital is quite simply idiotic. The Maoist construction established the foundations without which the opening would not have ended in the well-known success. A comparison with India, which has not undergone a comparable revolution, demonstrates this. To say that China's success is mainly (and even completely) owed to the initiatives of foreign capital is no less idiotic. It is not the capital of multinationals that has built the Chinese industrial system and achieved the objectives of urbanization and infrastructure; 90 percent of the success is owed to the sovereign Chinese project. Certainly, the opening to foreign capital has fulfilled useful functions, such as increasing the importation of modern technology. But through its partnership arrangements, China has absorbed these technologies and now controls their development. There is nothing similar elsewhere, even in India or Brazil, and *a fortiori* in Thailand, Malaysia, or South Africa.

China's integration into globalization has remained, by the way, partial and controlled (or at least controllable if desired). China has remained outside of financial globalization. Management of the yuan is still the result of China's sovereign decisions. Beijing can say to Washington: "The yuan is our money, the problem is yours," just like Washington said to Europeans in 1971: "The dollar is our money, the problem is yours." What is more, China retains a considerable reserve for the deployment of its public credit system. The public debt is negligible compared to the debt ratio deemed intolerable in the United States, Europe, Japan, and a lot of countries in the South. China can thus increase the expansion of its public expenditures without serious danger of inflation.

The influx of foreign capital from which China has benefited is not behind the success of its project. On the contrary, it is the success of this project that has made investment in China attractive for Western multinational corporations. The countries of the South that have opened their doors much wider than China and unconditionally accepted their subjection to financial globalization have not become attractive to the same degree. In those countries, transnational capital is attracted only because it can plunder natural resources or relocate production and benefit from cheap labor. But there is no technology transfer or positive effects from training and integration of relocated units into a national production system that is still nonexistent. The other reason multinational capital might be attracted is because of the possibility of conducting a financial raid, thereby allowing imperialist banks to dispossess national savings, as happened in Mexico, Argentina, and Southeast Asia.

For my part, I contend that if China is indeed an emergent power, it is precisely because it has not chosen the capitalist path of development, pure and simple. Consequently, if it were to be won over completely to that path, its project of emergence would itself be in serious danger of failing. Mao understood—better even than Lenin—that the capitalist path would lead to nothing, and that the revival of China could only be the work of communists. The Qing emperors at the end of the nineteenth century, followed by Sun Yat Sen and the Kuomintang, had already cherished the project of a Chinese revival in response to the challenge of the West. But they could not imagine any other path than that of capitalism and did not have the intellectual tools available that would have allowed them to understand what capitalism really is and why this path was already closed for China, as for all the peripheries of the world capitalist system. Mao, a Marxist independent spirit, understood that. Personally, I have always shared Mao's analysis and I refer you to what I have written on the role of the Taiping Revolution, which I consider the distant origin of Maoism. China has been involved on a particular path not since 1980, but since 1950, although this path has passed through contrasting phases in many respects. China has developed a coherent and unique sovereign project that is certainly not that of capitalism, in which agricultural land must in principle be treated as a commodity. This project remains sovereign insofar as China stays outside of contemporary financial globalization. Because the Chinese project is not capitalist does not mean that it "is" socialist, but only that it opens the possibility to advance on the long road to socialism. Yet, there is always another possibility: China might deviate from its project and end up simply returning to capitalism.

The success of China's emergence is completely owed to this sovereign project. In this sense, China is the only authentically emergent country (with Korea and Taiwan). None of the numerous other countries awarded a certificate of emergence by the World Bank is really emergent. That is because none of them persistently pursues a coherent sovereign project. All subscribe to the fundamental principles of capitalism, including for possible segments of their state capitalism. All have accepted submission to every aspect of contemporary globalization, including financial. On this latter point, Russia and India are still (partial) exceptions, but not Brazil, South Africa, or the others. Sometimes there are segments of "national industrial policies," but nothing comparable with the systematic Chinese project of constructing a complete, integrated, and sovereign industrial system (notably in terms of technological mastery). For all these reasons, the appearances of emergence—respectable growth rates, capability of exporting manufactured goods—are always combined with processes of pauperization that affect the majority of the population (particularly the peasants), which is not the case for China. Certainly, the growth of inequality is visible everywhere, including in China, but this observation is superficial and deceptive. Inequality in the distribution of the benefits from a model of growth that nevertheless excludes no one (and is even accompanied by a reduction of pockets of poverty—that is the case in China) is one thing, but inequality associated with growth that benefits only a minority (from 5 to 30 percent of the population, depending on the case), while the lot of others remains desperate is another thing altogether.

Korea and Taiwan are the only two examples of successful authentic emergence in and through capitalism. These two countries owe their success to geostrategic considerations, which have led the United States to accept that they can achieve what Washington has prevented others from doing. Contrasting U.S. support to the state capitalism of Korea and Taiwan with the violent opposition of the United States to Nasser's Egypt or Boumedienne's Algeria is quite illuminating in this regard.

To understand the nature of the challenges confronting China today, it is important to realize that the conflict between the Chinese sovereign project and North American imperialism (and its subaltern European and Japanese allies) is going to increase in intensity to the extent that the project is successful. There are multiple areas of conflict: China's control of modern technologies, access to natural resources, the strengthening of China's military capabilities, and China's pursuit of the objective of reconstructing international politics on the basis of recognizing the sovereign right of people to choose their political and economic system. The preventive wars by the United States in the Middle East are part of the objective to counter China and, in this sense, are a preliminary step in the (nuclear) preventive war against China, coldly considered as possibly necessary by the North American establishment. Keeping hostility toward China active by supporting the oppressors of Tibet and Sinkiang, strengthening the U.S. naval presence in the South China Sea, and lavishing encouragement on Japan—who is involved in the reconstruction of its military forces—is inseparable from U.S. global strategy toward China. Simultaneously, Washington is working to mollify the possible ambitions of China and other so-called emergent countries by creating the G-20, aimed at giving the countries involved the illusion that their support for liberal globalization would serve their interests. The so-called G-2 (United States and China) is, with that in mind, a trap—which, by making China complicit in the imperialist adventures of the United States, would cause China's peaceful foreign policy to lose all credibility.

The only effective response possible to this strategy must be "to walk on two legs": (i) reinforce China's military capacities and equip them with the ability to counterattack as a deterrent; and (ii) tenaciously pursue the objective of reconstructing a multipolar international political system, respectful of all national sovereignties, and in this sense act to rehabilitate the UN, which has been marginalized by NATO. I insist on the decisive importance of this second objective, which implies, first and foremost, the reconstruction of a "front of the South" (the second Bandung?) capable of supporting the independent initiatives of the peoples and states of the South. It also implies, in turn, that China realizes that it does not have the means for a possible absurd alignment with the predatory practices of imperialism (the pillage of the earth's natural resources), since it lacks a military power comparable to that of the United States—which guarantees the success of imperialist projects. On the other hand, China has much to gain by developing its offer to support the industrialization of countries in the South, which the club of imperialist "donors" is working to make impossible.

The other aspect of the challenge concerns the question of democratizing the country's political and social management. Mao had devised and implemented a general principle for the political management of the new China, which he had summarized in the following terms: rally the left, neutralize (I add: and not eliminate) the right, govern from the center left. In my opinion, that is the most effective way to conceive of progress by successive advances, understood and supported by the large majority. Mao had in this way given a positive content to the concept of democratization of society, combined with social progress on the long road to socialism. He had formulated the method to implement it: "the mass line" (go down into the masses, learn about their struggles, return back to the summits of power). Lin Chun has precisely analyzed the method and the results it has allowed. The question of democratization linked to social progress—in contrast with "democracy" separated from social progress (and even frequently associated with social regression)—does not concern only China, but all of the world's peoples. In any case, the system advocated by Western media propaganda—multiple parties and elections—should simply be rejected. The "democracy" fostered by that system turns to farce, even in the West and *a fortiori* elsewhere. The "mass line" was the means to produce consensus on successive strategic objectives in a continual advance. It contrasts with the "consensus" obtained in the Western countries by media manipulation and the electoral farce, a consensus that is nothing other than aligning with the demands of capital. But today, where does the process of reconstructing the equivalent of a new mass line in new social conditions begin? This is not easy because the leadership passed largely to the right in the Communist Party and established a stable management based on depoliticization and the naive illusions that accompany it. The very success of the development policies reinforces the spontaneous tendency to go in this direction. It is widely believed in the Chinese middle classes that the royal road to catching up to the lifestyle of the opulent countries is now open without any obstacles. It is believed that the states of the triad will offer no opposition. The American way of life is even admired uncritically.

China's government is not insensitive to social questions, not only because of a Marxist tradition, but also because the Chinese people, who have learned to fight and continue to do so, oblige it to give some consideration to such questions. Whereas in the 1990s this social dimension had retreated before the immediate priorities of speeding up growth, today the tendency is reversed. Repoliticization and the creation of conditions favorable to the invention of new responses cannot be achieved by "propaganda" campaigns. These objectives can only be reached through social, political, and ideological struggles. That implies prior recognition of the legitimacy of such struggles and legislation based on collective rights—of organization, expression, and leadership. That implies, in turn, that the Party itself be involved in these struggles; in other words, that it reinvents the Maoist formula of the mass line. Repoliticization is meaningless if it is not combined with procedures that encourage the gradual assumption of responsibility by workers in the management of society at all levels—company, town, and nation. A program of this type does not exclude recognition of individual rights. To the contrary, it supposes their institutionalization. Its implementation would make it possible to reinvent new ways of using elections to choose leaders.

## A Brief Note about Hong Kong, Macao, and Taiwan

When Isabelle and I first visited Hong Kong in 1972, it was still under British colonial control. For ninety-five years, the colony had been subject to a ruthless police regime that did not grant Chinese habeas corpus or any elementary rights. Militants, trade unionists, and above all "communists" were subjected daily to arbitrary arrests and torture, and sometimes cold-bloodedly assassinated. It was only a few years before the restitution of the territory to China (July 1997) that the British granted the colony "democratic" status and accepted elections. This move was totally transparent and its intent was immediately obvious.

We visited Hong Kong as tourists. As everyone knows, the location is splendid. The impression I had from this visit was that once the British left nothing would remain of their century-long presence. This impression was fully confirmed on our second visit in 2002. There were some large, Victorian-style buildings—banks—like the ones in Shanghai along the banks of the Huangpu River, but nothing more. The total segregation that predominated in the territory, the isolation of the small English colony, their deep racism, and the contempt in which they held the Chinese had deprived them of any cultural influence whatsoever. The Chinese who had continued living there once again became ordinary Chinese, just like their fellow citizens. For this reason, among others, I never believed that Hong Kong's return to China would pose any particular problem whatsoever, contrary to the opinion of probably a majority of observers, including journalists who claimed to be specialists in the affairs of the Orient, and even a large number of leftist intellectuals. In Hong Kong, just as in Shanghai, the future will depend essentially on the evolution of China's internal relations, specifically between its working classes and ruling classes, between its peasantry and proletariat, on the one hand, and its old and new bourgeoisie (from Shanghai, Hong Kong, and elsewhere), on the other, and on how their conflicts are settled—whether that be by the triumph of "socialism" (and its statist form, more specifically), or by a form of capitalism (national or comprador), or even by a historic compromise as a step along the way.

We made the most of our 1972 trip to visit Macao as well, and we revisited in 2002. This mini-colony had a totally different appearance than Hong Kong. Here, as in Goa (India), the Portuguese really mixed with the indigenous inhabitants, producing an original, ethnically diverse culture. For example, there is a Sino-Portuguese cuisine in which dishes combine Cantonese traditions, olive oil, and wine. There is the same mixture—successful also—in architecture.

It was only in 2008 that I first traveled to Taiwan. I was not surprised to observe that, despite their justified reservations with regard to the Chinese system, in particular concerning freedoms, attachment to the mother country and solidarity with it against foreign countries (United States and Japan) are strong. Beijing's slogan—"One nation, two systems"—finds a real echo, not only among businessmen who benefit from trade with China but also among ordinary people and the political classes stemming from the old Kuomintang. The comments of the Minister of Relations with Beijing, who received me, convinced me of that.

An amusing note: Lin Shenjing (who translated my French into Chinese), whom Lau Kin Chi had introduced to me and who had organized our symposium, was someone whom Isabelle immediately recognized. She had seen him in Paris street demonstrations in 1995, which Lin confirmed. The world is truly small! Lin also took us out into the beautiful countryside of this island, which certainly merits the admiring name given to it by the Portuguese: Formosa.

## VIETNAM

My first visit to Vietnam, with Isabelle, dates back to 1997. Just like in Cuba, Vietnam's leadership had adopted a clear "pro-Soviet" line, to the point that the abrupt collapse of the Soviet system in 1991 completely surprised them, as it did many others. I was certainly not delighted with the collapse, but it certainly did not surprise me. For thirty years, I said and wrote that if the system did not engage in leftist reforms (democratization and real socialization of public property), it was condemned to hasten its evolution—even if it were disastrous (which is what happened)—toward the pure and simple restoration of a "normal" capitalism to which its ruling class had completely rallied. After the fall of the USSR, the Vietnamese system, which remained somewhat trapped by its dogma and under severe pressure, seemed strongly tempted by the Southeast Asian capitalist models (Thailand and Malaysia). The crisis that struck the region—which had just begun when we visited Vietnam—gave pause for reflection and provided an opportunity to embark on a different path.

The Vietnamese people were irresistibly likable. Isabelle and I thus immediately liked Vietnam very much. I was invited to the Francophone Conference held in Hue, a preparatory meeting for the summit held in Hanoi two months later. We first went to Hanoi. Our trip had been prepared by the contacts our close friend, the late Ngo Manh Lan, had established and consequently went off in superb conditions.

Pham Xuan Phuong, a retired army colonel, welcomed us and acted as our guide. Pham had joined the liberation army barely out of adolescence in 1946 and had retired only after the liberation of Saigon in May 1975: thirty years of continual war, first the war against the French—Pham was a captain at Dien Bien Phu and had conquered one of the forts, taking high-ranking French officers prisoner—then the war against the United States. It is unnecessary to say that a person like him could not but immediately become our friend. We discussed everything at length, and Isabelle especially questioned him in detail. On the personal side, his mother had remarried during the colonial period to a Corsican and had a son. Pham's half brother had made a career in the French army—not in the Vietnam War, of course—in which he, also, had become a colonel. Pham recently went to Corsica to visit his mother's tomb.

General Bigeard had recently gone to Vietnam and Pham had accompanied him to Dien Bien Phu. With all the thoughtlessness and tactlessness that often characterizes soldiers of colonial armies, Bigeard insisted that a monument be erected on the spot to the French dead. The Vietnamese authorities put up a column for all the dead. Furious, Isabelle wrote to Bigeard to ask him how he would have reacted to a request from the Germans to build a monument to their dead on the beaches of Normandy. She then pointed out to him the disgracefulness of his writing about their treatment as prisoners: the prisoners received the same ration as the Vietnamese soldiers, who were content with that because they knew why they were fighting. Bigeard replied in such a way that his sad story came out: he was an army child with no political education (and he appeared to be aware of it).

That being the case, the Vietnamese make a distinction between the French and Americans. The French war was a vile colonial war. But the professional army—the opposition of the French people made it impossible to send conscripts to Vietnam—was content to make war, with all of the accompanying brutality (summary executions, torture). The Americans, on the other hand, did not make war. They learned from the Nazi bombardment of Guernica that it is much better to subject an "enemy" people to terrorist bombing campaigns made possible by its technological superiority. Pham explained to us that they were ill disciplined: as soon as they were surrounded, it was chaos; they killed one another. Their commanders avenged their defeat by a massive bombardment of villages in the area. That did not prevent the U.S. authorities from having the nerve to demand that the Vietnamese government return the bodies of all their soldiers, missing and dead, most often from hunger, thirst, or wounds because all prisoners were treated properly. This was not the case for Vietnamese prisoners, always executed in the field by U.S. soldiers, their officers, and their paid henchmen. Moreover, the Vietnamese make a distinction between the opposition of the French people to a war in which they refused to participate because of the political conviction that the war was a just cause for the Vietnamese, and the opposition of the American people who were motivated only by the fear of "dying in Vietnam." On the long road we traveled by automobile from north to south in Vietnam, we could not help but notice, every five kilometers perhaps, the cemeteries of combatants and massacred civilians. This is a density of deaths found only in Champagne and around Verdun. Consequently, I felt, and still feel, an unconditional hatred toward the U.S. ruling class. It is the main enemy of all peoples, the most dangerous criminal class of our time.

With a guide like Pham, we obviously could reach a mutual understanding straightaway and establish an ambitious program. In Hanoi, we stayed in the center of the old city, a few meters from the Rue de la Soie, in a cute, small hotel that was perfectly comfortable. This imperial city has great charm. Moreover, the French left behind beautiful colonial buildings—as in Saigon—maintained with all the care the Vietnamese are capable of, which is to say to perfection. The military museum must certainly be seen, and the commentated reproduction of the battle of Dien Bien Phu provides a lesson that should be understood. In Saigon, we also visited, for the same reasons, the military museum and looked at the scene reproducing the liberation of the capital of the south. Chance had it that I was in New York on the very day of this liberation in 1975. What joy in following live on television the debacle of the U.S. Army. And what an incredible spectacle—though quite predictable—of officers (U.S. officers, of course) rushing madly, shoving aside women and children to be the first to jump into the helicopters, holding under their arms works of art stolen from the country. What joy to see the amused look of Vietnamese soldiers observing the scene and checking watches to see if the time they had given to the fleeing Americans had expired or not.

What I did not know—and discovered at the museum of modern art—is that there is a high-quality Vietnamese painting of the scene, a creative synthesis of tradition (Chinese style) and modernity brought by the French. There is nothing comparable in China or even in Hong Kong. It is one of the signs—and they are numerous—of the complex relations between Vietnam and France. Vietnam, a strong nation that has never suffered from any inferiority complex in relation to others, has continually fought against colonial domination. Consequently, because it has no inferiority complex (which is not always the case among the colonized) and thus has no neurotic need to assert its "specificity," the Vietnamese people see France—and the rest of the world—as they are, in all the various facets of their reality. This is an advantage that can very well be decisive in knowing how to face the challenges of the modern world.

We also visited Ha Long Bay by boat. The bay is so well known through the abundance of beautiful images available that we had the bizarre feeling of having already been there. But this in no way takes anything away from the beauty of the place and the wonder we experienced when we toured it. In a good little restaurant in the coastal village near the hotel where we were staying, we overheard a young man—a Vietnamese from New Caledonia who had returned—share fond memories of the comings and goings of the French actress Catherine Deneuve, who had come to Vietnam to make the film *Indochine*. From Hanoi, we also took a short trip to the mountainous province of Son La in the northwest, near the border with Laos. We stopped in the Thai village of Moc Chau on the road to the Dien Bien Phu basin. We wanted to go further and see more, but there was not always enough time to see everything.

Hue, where the Francophone Conference was held, is a place of great importance in Vietnam's history: it was the imperial capital in the nineteenth century. You must see its extraordinary old imperial cemeteries and its baroque monuments, built by order of the emperors during the protectorate period, mixing traditional and modern styles. You should also see what remains of the old imperial palace, destroyed by the hateful and vicious U.S. bombing, fortunately now in the process of being restored. You also simply have to try its incomparably exquisite cuisine—and this is saying a lot since Vietnamese cuisine in general is exquisite—particularly the twenty kinds of banh cuon (rice pasta raviolis).

We traveled the road from Hue to Saigon in a hired taxi with a nice guide whom a friend of Ngo Manh Lanh had recommended. We passed through the superb Ocean Clouds Pass, along Da Nang Bay, ravaged by U.S. destruction, just like Cam Ranh further south. It was long the main naval and air base from which the U.S. bombers took off for their infamous missions. All of the surrounding vegetation had been ruthlessly destroyed with chemical weapons to prevent infiltration by Vietnamese soldiers. Let's praise the American defenders of the environment! We are waiting for Greenpeace to initiate proceedings and bring before its court the criminals, some of whom are still active, Robert McNamara first of all, since it is this "friend of the people" (as he was presented at the World Bank when he was made president) who ordered this destruction. Shortly after Da Nang, we passed through the old port city of Hoi An. This is a marvelous small city, which experienced its greatest prosperity during the eighteenth century, when Chinese and Japanese merchant navigators came to procure "exotic" products—mother-of-pearl, among other things. Further south, we stopped in the seaside resort of Nha Trang. There we visited a magnificent beach, not at all crowded, facing islands that were no less magnificent to visit. We were about the only foreigners. There were a few beach umbrellas, a respectable distance from one another, under which Vietnamese families had gathered to enjoy the sea. From Nha Trang, we headed inland toward Dalat. Along the highway, we saw the Champa Towers, impressive vestiges of the civilization that existed prior to the more recent conquest of the country by the Vietnamese. Dalat is reminiscent of French-style spa towns, which is what it was in the colonial period. A mountain resort, it enjoys a dry and cool climate that contrasts sharply with the heat and humidity of the coastal plains that make up rural Vietnam. But we are used to tropical climates, they don't bother us. From Dalat to Saigon, we passed alongside enormous rubber plantations, the main beneficiaries of colonization. Saigon is certainly very different from Hanoi. The commercial and economic capital during the colonial period—and it remains so, in part—the city has benefited from a modern urbanization that, in my opinion, is simply very successful. Isabelle and I loved Saigon as much as Hanoi, but in a different way. Its beautiful colonial monuments—the Hotel de Ville, the Opera—are well maintained. Its very Parisian cafés are quite pleasant for visitors on foot, as we were.

I do not hide the extreme sympathy that Isabelle and I have toward Vietnam and Cuba, its peoples, and the beautiful pages of history their revolutions have written. Thus, I wanted to respond to the invitation extended by their authorities to participate in some international symposia they were organizing. Even more—and a sign of confidence—I tried to respond to their expectations in internal debates directly concerning the problems with which they were confronted. I made two memorable visits to Hanoi in 2007 and 2009, and three to Havana in 1999, 2003, and 2009.

I did not hesitate to open the debate on the most difficult questions (the future of socialism, reforms, and, through them, the requirements for safeguarding the future) in the discussions organized in Hanoi by the Peace and Development Foundation (then directed by Madame Binh, and of which my friend, Tran Dac Loi, was long the active secretary), the powerful Ho Chi Minh National Academy of Politics (center for the ideological education of the Party's political cadres), and the Institute of World Economics and Politics. The first Secretary of the Central Committee of the Party—Truong Tan Sang—and other high-ranking cadres also participated. Madame Binh, Isabelle, and I shared a mutual immediate friendship. I wish to say how much Madame Binh's personal gestures of friendship meant to me. Collaboration between Vietnamese institutions and the TWF/WFA networks is ongoing.

Madame Binh had organized a meeting with a limited group of high-ranking leaders (including from the political bureau and administrative staff).

That session lasted for more than five hours. I was expected to present some of my thoughts on revived imperialism and its strategic objectives, strengths and weaknesses, and its military interventions in the Middle East and Africa, which I did by focusing on difficult issues. I was not there to "preach," but to clarify arguments and counterarguments. The comments of the Vietnamese were quite astute. Then, the subject exhausted, I allowed myself to go further and straight out raise the question of the conflict with China in the South China Sea. In substance, this is what I said: "If I were president of Vietnam or China—and since the probability of that is nil, you can see that my remarks will have no real impact—I would do this. I would say: we Vietnamese and Chinese together will control this sea that we will call the Southern Sea, without any other qualifier, just as we say "the Gulf" to avoid calling it Arab or Persian. Our two navies will patrol it together. A senior Vietnamese officer will be on board on each Chinese ship and vice versa. We will prohibit intruders—Japan and the United States—from being there. And then, concerning the exploitation of the sea's resources, we will form a high commission charged with laying out the forms and conditions of that exploitation." I did not expect a response, and I didn't get one. But I could read on their faces: *this man is a dreamer; he is totally unrealistic.* My conclusion: Yes, people in positions of power, everywhere, even now, think they are realists, but their realpolitik is not realistic. Realism is being revolutionary, acting to change things and not make day-by-day adjustments.

CUBA

Cuba is certainly a special case in Latin America. The Cuban government had long "boycotted" me personally. I was considered to be pro-Chinese, but above all, I held opinions that differed from those of Moscow—which Havana adopted without much restraint, by conviction or under pressure—on various questions concerning strategies for liberation in Africa during the debates mentioned previously. Things have changed since then. My discussions with Isabel Monal, Marta Harnecker, and others I met abroad helped me to follow a little more closely the internal debates that had long been delayed, but that circumstances had now brought to the forefront.

Comrades from the Association of Cuban Economists (Roberto Verrier), and more particularly my friend Dario Machado and his Argentine wife—and charming militant—Isabelle Rauber, organized my visit to Cuba in 1999. A busy program of two or three substantial discussions every day in the main institutions of the state and Party left little time for rest. I was still able to snatch a few quick visits here and there. That gave us an opportunity to observe that the old colonial city of Havana had escaped intact. It had been slated for destruction by the comprador bourgeoisie and North American tourism multinationals, who dreamt only of skyscrapers. Socialism saved it, even if this meant it was left to deteriorate for a long time because of a lack of resources. Today, it is in the process of being restored, and Isabelle and I could appreciate its magnificence. A visit to the old colonial city of Trinidad allowed us to glimpse the island's beauty. In Santa Clara, one could see the very beautiful statue of Che. A visit to the memorial where his remains and those of his companions were laid to rest was very moving. At the city's cultural center, we met a cartoonist with whom we got on very well and who reminded us that humor remains a progressive political weapon in Cuba. It was also a great pleasure to meet again our old friend Jacqueline Meppiel in Havana, who, along with Isabelle, was fined by a Parisian court for the same infraction: distributing anti-imperialist tracts![50]

The Cuban people are open, welcoming, and friendly. They are also truly courageous and know that they must accept many sacrifices to resist the Yankee vulture. Without this patriotism, the system would have succumbed to the Soviet collapse. The Soviet Union had become its protector both because of circumstances, that is, the geostrategic reality, and through the errors of the revolutionary leadership—won over at the time to Soviet concepts of constructing socialism. Friends and enemies predicted that the system would not survive the terrible years from 1992 to 1995, when the food ration had to be reduced below sustenance level. Cuba has succeeded in bouncing back. But now what should it do? That was obviously the focus of all our discussions. What concessions should be made to triumphant globalized capitalism? How can the dangers of an internal social deviation necessarily entailed by such concessions be managed? The opinions I heard expressed, or sometimes guessed, seemed to cover a fairly broad spectrum, the obvious expression of real and conflicting social interests and of diverse social and ideological views.

The dangers are obvious. To get out of a difficult situation, Cuba has opened itself to tourism—the devastating effects of which are not only cultural, as always, but also political and social. Throughout the Caribbean, the choices made to "stimulate growth" through a new type of insertion into the world system to replace the declining sugar industry are identical: emigration (and the transfer of money payments back to families), tourism, free trade zones open to the establishment of light export industries whose profits—derived from low-wage labor and tax exemptions—are captured by the multinationals that control the technologies and dominate the markets. These activities have not become the development poles promised by the World Bank, but scourges that do not carry along the rest of the economy and society, and gnaw away at them. The currency and profits produced in these sectors are either re-exported or reinvested exclusively back into the same sectors. The comprador bourgeoisie, the only local beneficiary of this type of unbalanced maldevelopment, is strengthened politically and can thus assume its function as a conduit for the management of peripheral capitalism.

Will Cuba be able to avoid a similar fate? A fraction of the "new class" resulting from bureaucratic socialism in the preceding decades openly aspires, through privatization and the dollar economy, to carry out comprador functions of this type. But other voices are making themselves heard in Cuban society. Not all cadres educated in the spirit of Marxism are nostalgic for a simple and dogmatic interpretation of socialism. Some (or many? I don't really know) understand that the working classes will defend socialism only if they exercise effective control over decision making at all levels. Thanks to my Cuban friends who share this viewpoint, we have noticed that there are indeed, here and there, the beginnings of autonomous organizations of the working classes. Enough to tilt the balance in their favor, make it possible to expand their reach, or even assert themselves on the political scene? That is difficult to say. And what will happen after Fidel Castro? Enjoying an undisputed and deserved aura (and certainly not the object of any "personality cult," which is absent in Cuba), Castro can maintain a balance between competing currents that could, once he is gone, end up confronting one another in dubious clashes.

Still, in light of some of the discussions I had, it seemed that the "senior leaders" were somewhat aware of the danger that the "tourism-free trade zones-reliance on foreign capital-dollarization" complex would represent, as well as risk, that this kind of development would become an excrescence on Cuban society. Measures have been encouraged to avoid it, mandating currency transfers and that profits be retained on the island in favor of financing the development of other activities aimed at strengthening the relative autonomy of the country in relation to the world system (food self-sufficiency, maybe energy self-sufficiency as well, for example). Are they really being implemented and, if so, strongly enough? That is difficult to say. In any case, good signs are not lacking, such as an exit from dollarization, which is well underway. On the question of the Cuban involvement in Africa, my visits also allowed me to hear the viewpoint of some of the most senior officials involved, including in particular the very likable comrade Risquet. There is not the least shadow of doubt about their fundamental internationalist conviction. I will even say that this choice has all my sympathy as a counterpoint to the attraction that Europe exercises over almost all of the Latin American left, causing it to forget that Latin America belongs, with Asia and Africa, to the peripheral capitalist world.

However, whatever the opinions of various people may be concerning the best strategy for Cuba to safeguard its gigantic social gains (in comparison with the rest of Latin America), to adapt to the new conditions of global imbalance, and to keep the door open to favorable development for the future, I maintain (and I repeat on every possible occasion) that the strict duty of all the world's democrats is to support Cuba against its North American aggressor, from which nothing should be expected, despite all the possible "democratic" rhetoric it spews. The Latin American democratic parties and those of the European socialist left have major responsibilities in this area. They alone could force the aggressor to retreat and give the Cuban people the time and means to make progress in solving their problems. Unfortunately, they are not doing that. The Latin American parties remain quiet, believing they can justify their silence by saying things such as "Cuba is no longer a model." Certainly, but that is not the point. The European social democrats and socialists are in this case, just like for the countries of the East, aligned with the rhetoric of the global right led by Washington and its instruments (the World Bank, the IMF, and the WTO). None of these groups give the least importance to the fact that Cuba has resolved basic problems that none of the Latin American countries—even those that are far wealthier—has even begun to deal with. Further, these groups accord no importance to the fact that the "liberal" solution that Washington wants to impose by any means will necessarily end in an incredible regression on every front, both social and democratic.

In Cuba, I have had the possibility of participating in internal discussions on the same difficult subjects. I even had the good fortune to hear Fidel give his opinions on these questions in a select committee. I have already pointed out that there was no "personality cult" for Fidel. His colleagues did not hesitate to tap him on the shoulder gently and say "don't repeat yourself, answer our questions."

Rémy Herrera, executive secretary of the WFA, offers us a collection of excellent studies on Cuba, produced by the country's best intellectuals.[51]

### Cuba: An Authentic Revolution

The Cuban Revolution is the third authentic popular revolution on the North American continent, after that of the slaves in Saint-Domingue (Haiti, at the end of the eighteenth century) and the peasants in Mexico (1910–1920). On the other hand, the American revolutions in the English and Spanish colonies were nothing more than wars of independence led by local ruling classes, themselves the product of European mercantilist colonization.

The Cuban Revolution, considerably more radical than earlier ones, was called socialist for this reason, and not without good reasons. In this sense, it is part of the first wave of struggles for the liberation of workers and peoples, alongside the Russian, Chinese, and Vietnamese revolutions.

The growth of sugar production in Cuba, which maintained a slave system in the nineteenth century, was accelerated even more when U.S. colonization replaced that of Spain. Colonial proletarianization was more prevalent than elsewhere in Latin America, the origin of a radicalization that naturally combined the anti-imperialist dimension of the national struggle and the socialist ambitions of the working classes and intelligentsia. The Cuban Revolution traces its origin back to José Martí. He must be distinguished from the heroes of independence in the Americas by his acute sense of social equality and his awareness that the question of emancipation cannot be reduced to the conquest of independence and "liberty," but requires a radical transformation of social relations. To the horror of the U.S. colonizers, Cuba responded rapidly by organizing the working classes and supporting communism.

The authentic radicalness of the Cuban Revolution was exhibited internally by the effective implementation of revolutionary reforms and political structures of a socialist character inspired by Marxism and exhibited internationally by the consistent assertion of theoretical and practical anti-imperialist positions. In contrast many earlier and later American "revolutions" often used violent rhetoric toward Washington, but simultaneously took care to weigh their words when it was a question of calling into question the interests of the privileged national classes, Cuba directly confronted its local classes right away. Cuba has never nourished the illusion of an "independent national capitalism."

Committed to the path of building socialism, Cuba has immense real achievements to its credit, including not only in the areas of education and health, but even in areas affecting the daily lives of the working classes (housing, food). This is unparalleled anywhere in the Americas. Cuba is the only country in the Americas that does not offer the spectacle of the most distressing poverty, common everywhere else. It remains the case that the Cuban people and its communist militants rightly expect more than to do better than the rest of the continent. They have chosen to build a new society, without classes, freed from all forms of oppression and exploitation. They have implemented for that purpose various means, inspired by the experience of others or invented by themselves. Certainly, these means have not always benefited from the expected effectiveness, but ultimately have always given rise to useful critiques for the future.

Certainly, the "Soviet model" provided broad inspiration for Cuba. Its influence was all the more real since the support of the Soviet Union—economic (petroleum) and politico-military—was necessary to face the blockade and ongoing military interventions of the United States and its allies. But Cuba was able to maintain a certain distance from this model in terms of the economic and political management of its system. The single party was here the result of the liberation and the merging of the Castroist movement and the older Communist Party, two partners that understood the demands imposed by history. Despite limitations in the theory and practice of this new party, the government has never fallen into a personality cult or into other extreme deviations of the Soviet model. Cuba's responses to the challenges that followed the collapse of the USSR demonstrated its capacity to reassess its policies and projects. At that time, it was widely assumed the Cuban government was lost for good. Against this expectation, Cuba was able to get out of the difficult situation in five years, between 1990 and 1995, and succeeded in getting back on its feet again. But since then, Cuba has faced new challenges, to which I shall return.

Voices critical of the chosen model were always expressed from inside the Cuban system. Che Guevara was one of those. Che, Mao, and Palmiro Togliatti, each in his own way, had understood that the Soviet model had exhausted its capacity to innovate and move society along the path to socialism. Each in his own way had understood that the deviation led to a capitalist restoration, the inevitability of which was clearly revealed in the years 1985–91. We should analyze Che's writings on this deviation closely and make them the focus of careful debates rather than reach any hasty judgments, which I shall avoid here.

From the beginning, Cuba adopted a consistent anti-imperialist and internationalist line of thought and action. Cuba was the only country in Latin America to realize the importance of the liberation front that started in Bandung (1955) and was continued by the Non-Aligned Movement (NAM). The latter was formed by Asia and Africa, plus Cuba, as was said. Cuba rightly sought to integrate Latin America into this front of the South and, for this purpose, took the initiative in creating the Tricontinental (1966). However, while the Bandung Conference united the peoples of Asia and Africa and their states represented by governments that then benefited from the legitimacy conferred on them from liberation struggles, in Latin America, the Tricontinental grouped together popular movements that were involved in a struggle against established governments that were dominated by the United States. Che attempted to shape the armed struggles in which the Tricontinental was engaged. History has demonstrated that the objective conditions were not in place at that time for these struggles to succeed in overcoming their isolation.

Latin America had to wait until much later to make its contribution to transforming the world in the form of civil grassroots movements at the same time that the national/popular wave begun in Bandung was becoming exhausted. This new wave of expanding grassroots movements and the resulting victories in Brazil, Argentina, Uruguay, Venezuela, Bolivia, and Ecuador released Cuba from the isolation in which the United States and the Organization of American States (Washington's Ministry of Colonies) had confined it for forty years. The success of the assistance operations by Cuban doctors and teachers throughout the continent, combined with the response to the creation of ALBA by Venezuela, has reversed the balance of power. Today, it is the United States and not Cuba that is isolated throughout the Americas. Years earlier, Cuba had demonstrated its support for the anti-imperialist cause through its military support for Angola in a war against the combined intervention of South Africa and "friends" of the imperialist camp. The Cuban defeat of the South African army had other effects, among which was speeding up the implosion of the apartheid regime.

Cuba is today confronted by new challenges. The Cuban Revolution occurred in the aftermath of the first wave of struggles for the liberation of workers and peoples, which shaped the twentieth century. This first wave is now behind us. But already the first signs of the formation of a new wave of struggles can be seen. Cuba, which survived when the other participants of the first wave collapsed, could be the link between the past and future. Cuba hosted the Non-Aligned summit (now non-aligned on imperialist globalization) in Havana in 2007. It reminded the countries of the South that they can defeat the dictatorship of the financialized plutocracy of the imperialist oligopolies and the deployment of their project for military control of the planet.

This imperialist system itself entered into crisis in autumn 2008 with the collapse of its integrated monetary and financial market. Behind this collapse, the systemic crisis of obsolete capitalism/imperialism can be clearly discerned. At the same time, the conditions for a humanist, popular, and democratic response are becoming apparent, with the initial victorious advances of the Latin American and Nepalese peoples. Karl Marx has returned. The second wave of workers' and peoples' liberation struggles is now on the agenda. This possible better future will become an imperative reality if the forces of progress, in Cuba and elsewhere in the world, learn from the limitations in the first wave's theoretical approaches and practices.

Twenty-first-century socialism must be democratic, not only in the bourgeois sense of the term, which separates political democracy—limited to multiparty (or allegedly multiparty) electoralism—from social progress, but in a richer and deeper sense, capable of combining democratization of societies with social progress. Cuba can innovate in this direction. Cuba has already provided the example of a democratic life that, despite its inadequacies, was incomparably more real than the false electoral democracies elsewhere, which were invariably combined with social regression. That being said, Cuba must move forward, overcome the inadequacies, and invent adequate legal and institutional forms that are able to combine respect for individual rights with social progress.

The conceptions of the Third International, which were behind the twentieth-century revolutions, did not sufficiently take into account the consequences that the polarization inherent in globalized capitalist/imperialist expansion implied for the "construction of socialism." We must understand that the polarization produced by the history of really existing capitalism requires another view of the long transition (over centuries) from capitalism to socialism. For the peoples of the South, this long transition must be formed from successive phases of implementing national, popular, and democratic structures. These alone are capable of combining the contradictory requirements of an effective development of the productive forces, which is still imperative, and the step-by-step progress of new social practices—those of socialism—able to give complete respect to democracy in all its social dimensions and meet the requirements of life on the planet, threatened by the irrationality of the logic of capitalist accumulation. Creative Marxism should strive to produce adequate theoretical concepts and stimulate the formulation of the necessary transition strategies for the development of twenty-first-century socialism. Cuba is well placed to participate in this human creation.

# 7

# THE WORLD FORUM FOR ALTERNATIVES AND THE SOCIAL FORUMS

BIRTH OF THE WORLD FORUM FOR ALTERNATIVES, 1996–1999

Capitalism celebrated its triumph during the first half of the 1990s. The Soviet Union had disappeared, Eastern Europe had been reconquered, Deng Xiaoping's famous sentence—"It doesn't matter if a cat is black or white, as long as it catches mice"—was interpreted as synonymous with saying "why not the capitalist path," and the countries of the South had, one after another, been subjected to "structural adjustment" policies. At this point, it is good to clarify that while some easily accepted the new order, having always been faithful representatives of local compradors and nothing more, others understood the scope of the disaster that awaited them. Abdou Diouf, the president of Senegal, literally burst into tears when he was told of the cuts, "Senegal is going to be destroyed by this." But still, his French friends forced him to capitulate. I have already said that those heirs of the national popular governments (Arab, among others) who were still in charge chose to capitulate in order to preserve their positions.

All our cowardly intellectuals, concerned about protecting their careers, took up the easy phrases heard at the time: "End of history"; "There is no alternative" (TINA); and the like. The rest of us were sad, obviously. Some took refuge only in nostalgia for the past. At the time, I met some people in

Egypt and Yugoslavia who confided to me, saying that we have been beaten once and for all. It is sad, but nothing more is possible. Others obviously—and this is normal—sunk into a confused revisionism: "Marxism has been surpassed by history," etc. There were very few (and without arrogance, I am proud of having been one) who said (I actually wrote it): "We are only in the trough of a long wave just like at other times in history." I recalled Gramsci: "The old is dying and the new cannot be born; in this interregnum a great variety of morbid symptoms appear."

History quickly proved us right. The triumph of imperialist monopoly capitalism was that of a colossus with clay feet. The horrors that accompanied its triumph—the rapid increase in poverty, NATO's wars of aggression—brought about a quick rise in resistance of all kinds, spontaneous and disorganized (but it is always this way at the beginning). As for France, with the large demonstrations in 1995, Isabelle said to me: "This horror is over, the people will not accept it."

It was imperative to provide an organized form to critical analysis, one capable of advancing a correct analysis of the challenge and, consequently, able to contribute to defining consistent and effective strategies for struggle. A small group of intellectuals who had been active over the preceding decades—and who had been aware of the obvious problems with existing challenges to capitalism (and had offered critiques of Sovietism and national popular regimes)—gathered together in 1996 in Louvain la Neuve, at the CETRI, then led by François Houtart, and decided to create a "World Forum for Alternatives." Houtart and Pablo Gonzales Casanova, if I am not mistaken, suggested the idea and the name. I instinctively supported the initiative. But how could we translate intention into action?

Upon returning to Cairo, I contacted the Afro-Asian People's Solidarity Organization. This institution had been created during the height of the Bandung era and Nasserism, then had fallen into decay, but was still in existence—a building and a few employees, nothing more. Its president was Mourad Ghaleb, Nasser's former ambassador to Moscow. Despite our political disagreements—which appeared small with the passage of time—we maintained strong mutual respect. When I proposed the idea to him, he jumped at the chance, "We can organize some kind of congress for the organization and you can invite whomever you want."

Thus, the World Forum for Alternatives (WFA) was born in Cairo in 1997. The Assembly did me a great honor by appointing me to be the president of the WFA. A working group—in which I voluntarily abstained from participating—drafted the WFA's Manifesto, which the reader will find in Appendix A.

An initial, very restricted executive committee was set up. Houtart was the executive secretary. He gave everything to his responsibility. It is due to him, and to no one else, that the WFA has not remained an institution that exists only on paper, "stillborn" like so many others. He ran to the right and the left (as did I) to collect whatever necessary assistance he could to organize a minimum of meetings and activities. At the time, there were still a few (Nordic) donors that had not yet been won over to the neoliberal pack.

The expansion of our activities convinced us to better reorganize ourselves. We ended up establishing the system still in force: nine vice presidents (Houtart, John Bellamy Foster, Bernard Founou, Issa Shivji, Lau Kin Chi, Amiya Bagchi, Mamdouh Habashi, Paulo Nakatani, and Wim Dierckxsens), two executive secretaries (Rémy Herrera and P. K. Murthy), and a website administrator (Carlos Tablada).

The WFA first appeared on the international stage when it organized the "anti-Davos" in January 1999, on the occasion of the annual elite conference in Davos. We were, of course, denied access to the holy precinct itself, but we took up a position fifty meters away, on the other side of the snow-covered street in this beautiful winter resort. Our small group included a number of committed intellectuals and figures from mass movements in the five continents, chosen for their high degree of representativeness: the farmers' organizations of Burkina Faso, Brazil, and India; the labor unions of South Africa, Korea, and Brazil; the neo-Zapatistas of Chiapas in Mexico; the activists of the World March of Women; the "Sans" in France and the ATTAC group. Helped into Davos by *Le Monde diplomatique*, we were there to say that it was we, not the club of billionaires, who represented the real world. The Davos organizers, like the narrow-minded Swiss authorities, were so furious that it was impossible to produce the surprise a second time around. Hence the idea of a World Social Forum, on a different scale, for which Porto Alegre seemed a natural choice due to the considerable resources that the Brazilian Workers' Party (PT) could mobilize for it there. A collective work, rapidly published in several languages, offers a report on this "anti-Davos at Davos."

The WFA and the Third World Forum (which still exists, fortunately) operate in a close symbiosis. They have a relatively strong network of committed intellectuals in each of the three continents (Asia, Africa, and Latin America), which in no way excludes the importance of other networks, whether of tricontinental scope (such as Via Campesina, Third World Network, IDEAs in Delhi), regional scope (such as CLACSO or Forum de São Paulo in Latin America, CODESRIA in Africa, ARENA and Focus on Global South in Southeast Asia, the Taegu Forum in East Asia, the Arab networks coordinated by the Centre d'Études Arabes in Cairo), or even national scope (no less important in large countries such as India or Brazil). The committed intellectuals who sustain these networks of course maintain close relations, often organizational, with numerous social organizations that, in their respective countries, bring together sometimes millions of activists (such as the unions in Korea or South Africa, the Landless Movement in Brazil, or the neo-Zapatistas in Mexico). The same is true in many countries in the "first world": in France (CEDETIM, ATTAC, M'Pep), in Switzerland (CETIM), in Italy (*Il Manifesto, Punto Rosso*), in Germany (Rosa Luxemburg Foundation), in Europe (the Transform network), in Japan (AMPO: *Japan-Asia Quarterly Review*), in Canada (Alternatives), and elsewhere. The current electronic means of communication have increased the capability and speed of exchanging views on a massive scale and, among other things, facilitate contact between movements that belong to quite diverse political and ideological traditions, such as those in Europe (where the political life is mainly dominated by the large parties and unions) and the United States (where "civil society" is formed from a large number of small local organizations, which are distant from the two identical, or almost identical, establishment parties).

The WFA is located within a complex universe. It is therefore a forum in the true sense of the term—that is, a place of mutual encounter and debate, not an "International" (Communist, Socialist, Christian Democrat, Islamic, or Liberal), still less a centralized international like the Third Communist International was. It brings together currents of thought and action which, though totally independent of one another (a good thing, in my opinion), share critical points of view about the application of liberal policies to such areas of social management as relations between the sexes, environmental issues, human rights or inter-communal problems. All these currents have a place in the WFA, whatever their ideological inspirations or practical choices. The WFA program for debate on the objectives, instruments, and achievements of social movements around the world—whether it is a question of regional balance sheets, the stimulation of alternatives to agribusiness, or systematic reflection on universal values concerning individual, social and collective rights—testifies to its openness, which is a matter of principle for the Forum. The group of coordinators who appointed me chairman of the WFA did me a great honor, which is perhaps justified, if at all, by the fact that my activities over forty years familiarized me with a large number of organizations and leading personalities around the world.

### *The World Forum for Alternatives and Third World Forum as "Networks of Networks"*

The WFA's role is to serve as a center for systematic analyses of alternatives to the present world order. Our enemy recognizes the importance of such systematic analyses without which no effective action strategy is possible. I am referring here to the Mont Pelerin Society (MPS), founded in 1947, with members like Milton Friedman, Lionel Robbins, Ludwig von Mises, Friedrich von Hayek, and Karl Popper—all advocates of today's liberalism. I am also thinking of the Trilateral Commission, founded in 1973, which includes David Rockefeller, Zbigniew Brzezinski, Cyrus Vance, Andrew Young, and Paul Volcker among its members, all of whom have participated in designing the North American establishment's strategy. The enemy recognizes that the major problem confronting it today is managing the criminal and impossible system it is attempting to foist on everyone. In the accepted jargon, this management is called "governance," which has been made into the dominant concern for the programs of international institutions. Unfortunately, a large number of NGOs have adopted this concern as their own, in the best of cases for lack of critical reflection, in most cases out of opportunism. It is not clear at the present moment exactly what the enemy's analysis is, though Susan George has attempted to evoke it with humor and sagacity in her 2006 *Le Rapport Lugano*.[52]

## THE SOCIAL FORUMS

The first meeting of the WSF was organized by a mainly Brazilian committee, which benefited from sizable financial support, in cooperation with ATTAC-France and *Le Monde diplomatique* (Bernard Cassen). Others have written the history of the WSF.

The success of Porto Alegre I, in January 2001, did not feature on the front pages of the major Western newspapers. The enemy's chosen strategy was to boycott the whole initiative. Nevertheless, the rich gentlemen in Davos grew a little worried and suggested opening a "dialogue" with us on the occasion of Porto Alegre II in 2002. I was lucky enough to take part in the ten minutes of airtime set aside for it on the radio. *"Monsieur,"* asked my Davos partner, "how does it happen that an economist like yourself is not with us in Davos?" My answer was simple: "There are three reasons. One: I don't have $20,000 to spend on entering paradise for three days. Two: I wasn't invited—which doesn't surprise me, as my opinions are well enough known. Three: if by some mistake I had been invited, I wouldn't have accepted, as I am not a billionaire and have no interest in joining the club of their servants." "But, *monsieur*," he countered, "I am not a billionaire." "I know, you are the public relations director of a company whose owners are billionaires." "What have you got against billionaires?" "Simple arithmetic, *monsieur*. Their profits doubled in the 1990s, but the incomes of all the non-billionaires—and there are a lot of them—obviously did not increase in the same proportion. You want inequality, and I, equality. So, we are enemies, and I don't see what we could have a dialogue about." Even so, Davos will not fail to "make an effort" in the future, and from the wide spectrum of social organizations it will find some "left-wing figures" to go, consciously or unconsciously, on a journey to the mountain of reconciliation.

In January 2002, Porto Alegre II took a great step forward that was well expressed in the "appeal" adopted at the final rally. The "social movements" have been growing more political—in the good sense of the term. Beyond the organization of struggle against the disastrous social effects of neo-liberalism, they are taking the measure of a system that already entails, and will increasingly entail, "military" barbarism on the pretext of a "war on terrorism." The aftermath of 9/11 had demonstrated this amply. The TWF and the WFA were very active at Porto Alegre, leading five major seminars at which the whole criminal political logic of global neoliberalism was subjected to analyses and commentaries by hundreds of the most lucid intellectuals in the contemporary world.

I shall return later to subsequent events, specifically, the developments (we have to speak in the plural here) that led diverse and numerous "movements" involved with the social forums to advance on some occasions and retreat (from my perspective) on others.

Participation of the WFA/TWF in social forums, whether at the world or other levels, is not our main objective. What is a priority for us, first of all, is organizing meetings by ourselves, for ourselves, in order to advance our own analyses of the requirements for the theoretical and practical construction of positive and real alternatives leading to popular and democratic advances. The reader will see in our current program (see Appendix B) how we define the questions we are asking. The reader will also find in preceding chapters my accounts of internal debates that I consider to be important, and participated in in China, Russia, Egypt, Algeria, South Africa, India, Senegal, Mali, Niger, Tanzania, Zambia, Nepal, Latin America, and the Caribbean. These genuinely productive debates have provided the main material for our analyses.

Yet we do not ignore the social forums and intend to participate in them. It is a not unimportant means, among others, to disseminate the results of our own analyses. In fact, the WFA/TWF has probably been in attendance at all, or almost all, social forums held throughout the world, even if this presence has been more obvious in some cases, less so in others. I have personally participated in many activities of so-called civil society.

A complete agenda for the social forums should exist. Perhaps the WSF Secretariat could provide this. I shall recall here only those forums in which

I have personally participated, most often with others active in our networks. Reading through the list might be tedious, but for these memoirs, I believe I should do it.

I have participated (as part of WFA/TWF teams) in the World Social Forums of Porto Alegre (2001, 2002, 2005), Mumbai (2004), Bamako and Caracas (2006), Nairobi (2007), Belem (2009), Dakar (2011), and Tunis (2013 and 2015). I have participated in some of the regional forums, which often are preparatory to the World Forums: Hyderabad (2003, Indian and Asian Forum), Lusaka (2004, African Forum), and Zagreb (2011, Balkans Forum). I have also participated in more topical forums: Amazonia in Belem, Brazil (2003), and Via Campesina in Valencia, Spain (2004). I have attended all the European Forums since Florence (2002), followed by Paris, London, Athens, and Malmo. I have personally participated in several Egyptian, Arab, and African Forums, but not unfortunately at those of the network that called itself the "Mashreq-Maghreb Forum."

At each of the forums mentioned, we have always led four to ten roundtables, led by six to ten of us who seemed the most competent in the areas in question. In some cases, the miserable working conditions certainly considerably reduced—for us as well as for others—the reach of our messages. For example, in Nairobi, the forum was held in a stadium and it was impossible to isolate the voices in our roundtable from those in neighboring roundtables. What can be said about the real effect of debates held in these conditions? However, in Dakar in 2011 and in Tunis in 2013 and 2015, we benefited from much better conditions. Many participants and observers at these forums have noted the high quality of our roundtables. The interested reader can find reports on these roundtables at numerous internet sites.

*Responses to Our Enemies*

The active members of our WFA/TWF networks, and I personally, have been invited to respond to the declarations of our enemies, the leading lights of "happy globalization." To make an exhaustive list of these speeches would require some archival work, which I have not done. I shall restrict myself here to singling out a few of these speeches. An account of those of many other major actors in the WFA—particularly Houtart—would certainly make the WFA's work better known to the reader. A more exhaustive report of the WFA's activities, which I am not attempting in my memoirs, would be very useful. I shall indicate, then, in chronological order, the speeches that I remember.

The UN had organized in Copenhagen in 1995 one of the large conferences of its series, pompously described as preparatory for the renewal of civilization for the 2000s, or something like that. The topic was "reduction of poverty"! This conference, like the others in the series, was "intergovernmental," that is, delegates with the right to vote were selected by member states. But members of "civil society" were invited as observers, sometimes with the right to speak, but nothing more. Our opportunity arose because the African states chose us—the TWF—to draft and present a report on poverty in Africa. I jumped at this magnificent opportunity to respond to our "partners"—in fact, enemies—the World Bank, the European Community, U.S.-AID, etc. Our report was drafted from the contributions of twenty active members in Africa. Each of them provided a good report that, instead of drawing up an "inventory" of the poor and of poverty, focused the analysis on a critique of the policies implemented, which had inevitably led to a worsening of poverty in the countries concerned. The synthesis report assembled these contributions into a document of around two-hundred pages.

The report had an impact. Some of the official African delegates praised it officially. Our enemies were furious. They simply insulted me and attempted to prevent me from crossing certain barriers (in the physical sense of the term), separating officials from others in the conference.

In 2001, the World Bank had considered commemorating its fiftieth anniversary in Barcelona. The Bank had proposed to conduct a dialogue on its policies with a group of carefully selected NGOs. We were invited to present a contrary opinion. At the last minute, the Bank called off its planned "dialogue," out of fear that some troublemakers—we and some others—might pose some awkward questions. A meeting was held all the same, organized by Spanish "civil society," without the Bank. I personally presented the "list of charges." We put on trial the neoliberal policies that are the cause of the poverty that the Bank claimed to want to fight. A collection of documents had been assembled for that purpose under the scathing title *Fifty Years Is Enough*.[53]

The last of the major UN conferences of this kind was held in Durban in 2001 on the very general topic of the "struggle against discrimination." The dominant establishment and the UN bureaucracy had previously controlled the expressions of "civil society" that were invited to participate in these international conferences; it had managed to do this through its hold on the purse strings and its manipulation of NGOs sufficiently apolitical to sign up to the mainstream proposals, which in effect cancelled any impact of the protests and demands of the peoples in the countries where the NGOs originated. The protest against "racism and all other forms of discrimination" was to be an innocuous event at which all participants, both governments and NGOs, would be called upon to perform some breast-beating over the "vestiges" of discrimination afflicting "indigenous peoples," "non-Caucasian races" (to use the official U.S. language), women and "sexual minorities." Some highly general recommendations were drawn up, in the spirit of North American legalism according to which an act of legislation is all that is required to solve a problem. The social and international inequalities generated by the logic of globalized capitalism, which are the essential causes of the main forms of discrimination, were left out of the original considerations.

This strategy of Washington and its allies was defeated by the massive participation of African and Asian organizations determined to pose the real questions. The issue of racism and discrimination, they argued, is not synonymous with the behavior of people still suffering from "outmoded" prejudices, who sadly are still present in large numbers in every society on earth. Contemporary racism and discrimination are produced and reproduced by the expansionist logic of actually existing capitalism, especially in its so-called liberal form. The forms of "globalization" imposed by dominant capital and its political intermediaries (above all, the triad governments, United States, Western Europe, and Japan) can result in nothing other than "global apartheid."

On two issues—that of "reparations" due to the victims of slavery and that of Israeli colonization—the two opposing camps quickly took shape: the Africans and Asians in the majority in one camp, whereas in the other, unfortunately, were almost all the Europeans, lined up behind Israel (any criticism of Israel is anti-Semitic!). Having sensed the danger during the lively debates in the preparatory committee, the G7 governments had already decided to boycott the conference and decreed its "failure" in advance. The Africans and Asians stood their ground and held the conference anyway. In keeping with the strategy they had adopted, they forced discussion of the two questions the Western diplomats did not want to hear.

The first question raised concerned "reparations" for the damage caused by the black slave trade. I have used quotation marks because, on this topic, American and European diplomats tried to undermine the whole discussion by condescending remarks about the "amount" of reparations and the "professional beggars" who were claiming them on behalf of formerly colonized peoples. Africans certainly did not see things in that way. For them the issue was not "money," but a recognition that colonialism, imperialism, and slavery were largely responsible for the "underdevelopment" of the continent and the legacy of racism. It was these arguments that provoked the ire of the representatives of Western powers.

The second conflict concerned Israel's continual settlement colonization. Here the Africans and Asians were clear and precise: the continuation of

Israeli settlement in the occupied territories, the eviction of Palestinians in a process of veritable ethnic cleansing, the Bantustanization plan for Palestine directly inspired by the defunct apartheid regime in South Africa—these were but the latest chapter in its long history of evidently "racist" imperialism. Characteristically, the Palestinian question unites people in Africa and Asia, whereas it divides them in other parts of the world.

The WFA/TWF is always invited to participate in the counter-G7 or G8 or G20 conferences. We are almost always in attendance, and I personally have attended twice (Lyon and Saint Petersburg). I regret having missed the counter-G7 in Genoa, where Silvio Berlusconi's police won notoriety by killing a youth.

I have only a vague memory of the Lyon meeting. The conference had been organized by a panoply of "nice" French and European NGOs for which it was imperative to avoid turning critiques of the policies of the large imperialist powers into a trial of "Europe." For them, since Europe as a community was not imperialist by nature, it should not have to bear responsibility for such policies. Thus nothing was said at the conference that is worth remembering. A small number of participants from the Third World, including me, found this emptiness amusing. But the French had organized things well, culinarily speaking. At low prices, we could enjoy excellent dishes typical of Lyonnaise cuisine. A Moroccan, a Chinese, and I enjoyed a delicious meal together.

In Saint Petersburg in 2013 (I referred to this event in chapter 5 on Russia), Boris Kagarlitsky succeeded in getting financing to invite foreigners—including me—who would come to reinforce the Russian delegation. This was a G20 and the topic was "reform" of the international financial system. But we all knew that developments in Syria (the allegation that chemical weapons had been used by the Syrian government) were going to occupy most people's attention. Obama and Putin, moreover, had discussed nothing else. This was true of the Chinese, Brazilians, and several others also. The organizers of this counter-G20 had invited for our debates an assistant to the Brazilian Minister of Finance—at least for the financial question (we had, like the G20, put Syria on the agenda for our discussions). Pedro Paez questioned the financial system with his well-known talent and presented his counterproposal for reform of the international monetary and financial system. Very good, but the Brazilian in our group refrained from commenting. For my part, I had chosen another method to launch our discussion. I was content to say, "You know, you Brazilians and other representatives from the emerging countries, we will never get a good reform of the system, since the G7 does not want it. We are going to be kept waiting around, from G20 to G20, from Stiglitz Commission 1 to Stiglitz Commission 2, with anodyne proposals that will change nothing.

So why take part in this game? We should move the debate, locate it outside of the G20 and organize it among ourselves, the BRICS (Brazil, Russia, India, China, and South Africa), to advance, not an impossible international reform, but the construction of a space for us, as distant and autonomous as possible from the influence of the Western powers." The Minister's assistant warmly approved of what I had said.

In some situations, I have declined an invitation to participate in undertakings to which I had been personally invited. I refused to participate in the Stiglitz Commission formed by the UN Secretary-General in 2010. I knew that it was a maneuver to impress and fool public opinion by leading people to believe that it was possible to reform the globalized system. Joseph Stiglitz, who has never ventured outside of the strictures of neoliberalism and is a specialist in window-dressing reforms, was chosen for that purpose. History has proved me right. The "Stiglitz Report," delightfully empty, has ultimately, and fortunately, been remembered by no one. On the other hand, an UNCTAD committee proposed the beginning of a real reform. Obviously, its report was rejected by the Western powers.

*Solidarity among the Peoples, Nations, and States of the South*

For all regions of the capitalist Third World, the construction of an auto-centered economy is the unavoidable precondition for any further progress. This requires that external relations be subordinated to the priorities of internal development, not that the internal economy be "adjusted" to external constraints (as mainstream economic discourse repeats ad nauseam). On the topic of delinking, I have not changed my opinion. On the contrary, a half-century of history has strengthened my fundamental conviction even more. It remains the case—but this is really just an uninteresting commonplace—that the concrete forms of delinking are not set once and for all. Yet the construction of an auto-centered economy—which remains indispensable at the national level—would encounter serious obstacles if forms of regional integration capable of enhancing its positive effects were not organized to reinforce it. I am speaking here not of regionalization as envisioned by conventional economists—common markets, etc.—who are incapable of imagining anything other than the logic of capitalist accumulation, but rather of regionalization where the political dimensions are decisive and can challenge the scientific, financial, and military monopolies through which the First World imposes its project of world capitalist expansion. Regions such as the Arab world, Latin America, Africa, and Southeast Asia, or vast countries such as India or Brazil, can capitalize on certain advantages that history has bequeathed to them (a common language or culture, for example), but also, and above all, on the fact they have a common enemy.

The ruling classes of countries in the South have always had ambiguous positions on this major question. When the comprador tendency is dominant, South-South solidarity is certainly not encouraged. The local beneficiaries of integration into imperialist globalization seek to strengthen their positions (for them that means enriching themselves even more) to the detriment of the weaker states in the South and, consequently, accept joining in imperialism's strategic game, which counts on unequal competition among countries in the South. On the other hand, the defenders of the national tendency in these ruling classes are able to understand the advantages of solidarity against the imperialist North. This was the case during the Bandung era.

This is why, at that time, the TWF and I had pursued our collaboration with the Bandung institutions: the NAM, the OAU (later transformed into the African Union, a union in name only), the AAPSO (headquartered in Cairo), and more recently, the Asia-Pacific Peoples' Organization, which has demonstrated its real strength at various official meetings of APEC. We were aware, without illusions, of the NAM's limitations and contradictions. We knew that the OAU expressed the solidarity of African peoples through its support for the liberation movements in the Portuguese colonies, South Africa, and Rhodesia (the future Zimbabwe), but nothing more. We knew that, on the level of economic cooperation, the Bandung secretariats and the non-aligned states of that era envisioned little more than promoting regional (that is, continental) and sub-regional integration by means of "common markets." We criticized this capitalist path that, contrary to its declared objective, reinforced inequalities among partners in the South and, consequently, weakened the prospects for asserting their solidarity. But we understood that what happened in Bandung could evolve in the right direction; there were forces that worked for that. We also understood that the movement, despite its limitations, strengthened the governments of states in the South against the North. For example, the Gabon of Léon M'ba, and later Omar Bongo, would never have been able to recover a fraction of the oil rent without OPEC. What the Gabonese government used this rent for is a different question (we know that a part of it was used to buy French politicians!).

At the time, the UN system itself was sensitive to the pressures brought to bear by the Bandung institutions. This was true particularly for UNCTAD, which was created by Raúl Prebisch and run by a number of directors known personally to me: Kenneth Dadzie, Gamani Corea, and Rubens Ricupero. This was also true for the UNU at the time that Kinhide Mushakoji was vice-rector, or for UNESCO when Mahtar M'bow, in advance of his time, was waging the struggle for a "new international communications order." The UN at that time offered its services to the pursuit of successful initiatives that advanced international law and the rights of peoples (to self-determination, development, and social and collective rights). I personally participated in some of these progressive initiatives, particularly those promoted by my Italian friend Lelio Basso, with the support of Algeria under the NLF/Boumedienne. I have referred to some of these moments in the history of the Bandung Conference, as well as my modest interventions in these debates.

The situation was turned upside down beginning in 1990 with the neo-imperialist offensive that set out to eliminate the role of the United Nations—and succeeded. Unfortunately, then Secretary-General Kofi Annan (whom I had known as a different person when he worked for Nkrumah!) joined in this operation. His "Millennium Report" seemed to come straight from the offices of the U.S. State Department. Now, the UN no longer represents the international community. The new self-proclaimed "international community" formed by the G7 (the major imperialist powers) and by the two new democratic republics (Saudi Arabia and Qatar!) has replaced these institutions. For the media clergy, who bore us to tears every day with "information" about the views of this international community, there is no other one. China, Russia, Egypt, Tanzania, India, Venezuela, and all the other countries of the world do not exist for this "international community."

Thus, what do we do now?

The WFA and TWF are today participating in the fight to restore the rights of the only international community possible, the UN. In my recent speech to the congress of the IADL in Brussels in 2014, I commented on this.

On the other side of the world, in Hanoi, the Vietnam Peace and Development Foundation took the initiative in 2009 to establish a network charged with formulating proposals for strengthening South-South cooperation. Madame Binh and her talented collaborator, Tran Dac Loi, invited me to participate in this initiative. Many colleagues in the WFA/TWF and I responded enthusiastically, of course.

I speak in these pages of solidarity among the peoples, nations, and states of the South. I know quite well that states are what they are and are not always true representatives of their peoples. But I am not one of those who believe that we can "change the world" without modifying established states. Solidarity among peoples, and the struggle of peoples in their home countries, must and can have the objective of forcing states to change in ways likely to support popular advances.

## Relations of Cooperation between the WFA Networks and Networks from Countries of the North

I am now going to broach delicate and difficult questions.

The TWF is, as its name indicates, a network of the South. At first, it was strictly Asian and African, as was the NAM (Asia, Africa, plus Cuba, as it was said). Then it was enlarged to include Latin America and the Caribbean by conducting activities in common as frequently and systematically as possible, linking African and Asian networks with networks in Latin American countries that had worked together closely for a long time. Yet the TWF did not intend to forget the North. We thought it was more than useful—necessary, in fact—to make our voices heard in New York, Paris, London, or Tokyo. To draw up a list of meetings between the TWF in the South (or me personally) and persons and organizations in the North would require that I immerse myself into difficult archival work (all the more so because, as I have said, I did not keep a regular datebook that would facilitate the task).

When the WFA was created, we well understood that it was different because it is a world forum that includes the North in its network of collaborators. The task was and is difficult, and we knew it. Without the slightest intention of being malicious, I will say that the historical experience of North-South relations did not make the task easy. Relations among the world's states are unequal by definition. There are dominant imperialists, on the one hand, and dominated peripheries, on the other. Certainly, outside of these relations, there are other relations among persons, organizations, even political parties from the North and the South. To be brief, I will note that the Communist Internationals, just like the churches, formed places for such encounters. Later, with the independence gained by the nations of Asia and Africa, conditions were created that permitted the emergence of—socialist or liberal—internationals and facilitated meetings between organizations from the South (Bandung-affiliated) and some political forces from the North (Europe and Japan, the United States to a lesser degree) that put themselves forward as friends of nations from the South. But the organizations and parties of the South of that era—with national-popular tendencies—prioritized their relations with the East of that time, the Soviets and Chinese. That is understandable.

The dominant imperialist establishment had, for its part, formed non-governmental (in appearance at least) organizations that were allegedly worldwide. The Society for International Development (headquartered in Rome) is a good example. These "networks" were formed—pushed by the World Bank—as North to South transmission belts. Decision-making powers were reserved for persons from the North or those from the South who were their devotees; the other "representatives" from the South occupied only minor roles. For that reason, I refused to join the SID, as was suggested to me.

Of course, we had no intention of reproducing an unequal North-South relation in the formation of the WFA. To avoid this danger, we even bent the stick in the other direction, as it is said. That is, we gave to the South a representation that more accurately reflected the reality (the South is the "minority" that makes up 80 percent of the global population!). There are, thus, eight vice presidents in the WFA from the South and two from the North; there is one executive secretary from the South and one from the North.

Immediately after its creation, the WFA contacted a large number of European organizations and individuals that we knew were sincere friends of peoples from the South. These include, for example, groups from the European left (and the Greens that are linked to them) in the European Parliament and in their respective countries; CEDETIM (France), CETIM (Switzerland), IEPALA (Spain), *Punto Rosso* and *Il Manifesto* (Italy), the Rosa Luxemburg Foundation (Germany), the Communist Party and Syriza (Greece), and the European network Transform-Europe. We often found ourselves side by side with them in the World Social Forums and European Forums.

The results of our meetings are, nevertheless, quite meager, and there is no reason to deny it. Responsibilities are shared, and I do not say that out of diplomatic courtesy. I remain severe in my judgments of the new European left, but I am no less so with regard to our lefts in the South.

Personally, I am an internationalist along with others, of course, in our WFA/TWF networks. I am among those who believe that a better world can only be built together, when and if the radical lefts of the North and South are able to define jointly common strategic objectives and ultimately succeed, through the struggles they undertake, in producing advances in this direction, that is, win victories (not necessarily the "final victory") in their own countries.

In my analysis of the history of the twentieth century, I reached what I consider to be a sad conclusion: major progressive transformations on the world scale were initiated by struggles of peoples in the peripheries of the world system, through the socialist revolutions (Russia, China, Vietnam, and Cuba) and national-popular liberation movements (of the Bandung era). It was actually these advances that made possible those of the workers in the centers. There would have been no true social democracy (whose achievements I do not denigrate, on the contrary) without the "communist threat." Nevertheless, the truly anti-imperialist political forces in the North—by that

I mean the communist parties of the Third International—did not succeed in overcoming the relative isolation to which they were condemned in their own societies. The tragedy of the twentieth century is precisely there, in my opinion: the isolation of the USSR, China, and the countries of the South active in the Bandung era. These countries suffered terribly from the systematic hostility against them from the states of the North and the inability of the radical lefts in those countries to prevent this hostility from reaching full strength. This situation is mainly what lay behind the limitations of what could be achieved in the twentieth century in the larger East and South, and even behind the abuses and excesses, the stifling and ultimate collapse of this first wave of attempts to "go beyond capitalism and imperialism."

To see a repeat of this same failure to achieve effective solidarity in the development of peoples' struggles in the North and South today, in the twenty-first century, would be even more tragic. That is why I am an internationalist, to avoid adding to the risks of a tragic failure for everyone.

If I judge our European comrades harshly, it is for this reason: their awareness of the importance of anti-imperialist action is, in large part, far short of what is required. There are several explanations for this state of affairs, none of which justifies it: (i) excesses in countries of the South (and East), which do not encourage solidarity with their peoples; (ii) the drift of the left in Europe (which originated in historical communism) toward a "humanist-social democrat" view of the world; and (iii) the focus of Europeans on the problems involved in the construction/reform/reconstruction of the European Union.

I made my own analysis of the European situation.[54] I am not going to return to that analysis and, moreover, obviously do not demand that others agree with me. I am not that presumptuous. It is up to Europeans to define their strategic objectives: to "reform" (and how to succeed in doing so) or "deconstruct" (without going back to the old nationalism) the European Union. But whatever the response (or responses) that progressive Europeans give to this challenge, it should in no way reduce their active and determined opposition to the interference and interventions that their imperialist states, aligned with the United States, undertake in the South and East. Europeans should know that, for us, NATO is the enemy. Its interventions, regardless of the pretext invoked, humanitarian or otherwise, are really in pursuit of only one objective: to perpetuate the domination of Western financial monopoly capital in our countries. For me, the alternative is a Europe that is non-imperialist in its relations with the rest of the world. That would be a Europe that places itself outside the triad, that would no longer be subject to orders from Brussels, the Central European Bank, and NATO.

I have devoted some space here to assessing the difficult relations between the TWF/WFA and Europe, and the insufficient results from those relations. I believe that as far as relations between Asia (including China) and Japan are concerned, our Asian comrades (Lau Kin Chi and others) are better placed than I to make a correct assessment. As for the relations between Latin America and the Caribbean, on one side, and the United States and Canada, on the other, our Latin American colleagues are better placed than I to speak of that.

If the European reader finds my judgments too harsh, I will respond that they do not appear unjust. Moreover, I am no less harsh in my assessment of struggles in the greater South. These memoirs should convince any reader of that.

### Toward an Assessment of the WFA/TWF's Activities

The most favorable conjunction of factors for getting out of the current impasse involves combining a widespread demand for democracy with a widespread demand for social management that benefits the working classes. The geometry of these two dimensions is different from one place to another, and from one moment to another; they are variable in space and time. The art of politics in the noble sense of the term is not merely to become part of a particular spatiotemporal arrangement—whether passively or even actively—as do politicians who are avid for power and nothing else, but to act to change the established articulation of these dimensions. In other words, the point should be not to act within the established relations of force, but to act to change them. As always, the future remains uncertain. It is not programmed in advance by any linear determinism whatsoever (such as that of the rationality of the market). History is not written before having been lived. The worst and the best are equally possible. Breakthroughs in the right direction are likely to occur—here and there—without its being possible to predict them with more than an average degree of probability. If these breakthroughs occur in enough places and in a short enough time frame, then perhaps they will snowball and could overturn the world conjuncture. We must work toward that.

All of the recent developments, subsequent to the writing of these memoirs, illustrate what I call the "autumn of capitalism." But this has not coincided with (or not yet) a true "springtime of peoples." The temporal distance between the two defines the nature of our era's tragedy.

All societies on earth, without exception, find themselves in an impasse where the only future ahead seems to be the destruction of human civilization. The reader of my writings will doubtless have come to the same conclusion—if, that is, he or she accepts the analyses I have offered of the Third World, the former socialist countries, and the First World. It may seem pessimistic in the extreme, but that is not how I see it. The point, rather, is that the world capitalist system has reached the end of its historical trajectory and can no longer produce anything positive, if we assume that circumstances will allow it to survive at all. Human civilization is therefore at a dangerous crossroads: it can avoid destruction only by embarking on a new road, an "alternative," as they say, which for me is synonymous with the long transition to world socialism. The neoliberal view of the world, though seemingly triumphant, is not viable. But the certainty of its collapse does not guarantee that what follows will automatically take the right path; the demise of liberal capitalism might produce only indescribable chaos, with consequences impossible to predict. This is not, however, the only exit from the impasse in which obsolescent capitalism imprisons humanity. Real forces exist more or less everywhere in the world that might be able to initiate positive changes—forces visible today in the numerous struggles the scale of which has already shaken neoliberal triumphalism.

Capitalism has built a world system and can really be overcome only at the level of the planet. Although national struggles have to be the starting point, without which no progress can be achieved at the level of the world, they are not sufficient because the scope for change that they can unleash is inevitably limited by the constraints of globalization. It is therefore absolutely necessary that these struggles should converge and open a way beyond the logic of capitalist accumulation, both in its national bases and at the regional and global levels.

The WFA has a major intellectual responsibility. Our moment is characterized by "treason of the intellectuals," in the sense that the overwhelming majority of the "experts" (including academic ones) no longer seek an alternative for the current system. They close their eyes, not without a degree of cynicism, to the destructive dimensions of this system. Some act to make a fortune in the tradition of pure and simple opportunism. Others busy themselves sterilizing their own "critiques" by reducing them to the minimum compatible with the main requirements of the authorities. This treason is not surprising. It is always so in all the important moments of "the end of an era," when the established society declines, but the new has not yet crystallized from qualitative changes.

The strongest argument for pessimism about the future is based on the lack of visible subjects capable of undertaking the necessary historical transformation to put an end to the hugely destructive dimensions of obsolescent capitalism. To say that "the workers"—or even wage and salary earners more generally—constitute such a subject is likely to cause smiles all round. But the optimist that I am will reply that active subjects appear only for relatively brief periods in history, when a favorable combination of circumstances allows the different logics of social existence (economic, political, geostrategic, etc.) to converge with one another. At such moments, in ways impossible to predict in advance, potential subjects may crystallize into decisive agents of change. Who could have foretold two thousand years ago that the great religions (Christianity, Islam, Buddhism) would become decisive subjects of history? Who predicted that the nascent bourgeoisie of the Italian and Dutch towns would become the decisive subject of modern history, a class for itself with a keen awareness of what it wanted and what it was capable of achieving, which its opponent—the "proletariat"—had acquired only here and there in short moments of its struggles? And who predicted that certain "peoples" in the periphery—the Chinese and Vietnamese—were going to take up the challenge and become the most decisive subjects of transformation in the postwar world? This is not to say that present-day social movements will not occasionally constitute themselves into active subjects, whose precise shape is difficult to imagine. We need to give constant thought to the precise situations that might permit this, and to the strategies that would make it easier for their different elements to come together.

These questions will find adequate answers only out of developments that take shape in the contexts defined by the state (or nation-state), within which political and social choices are decided. But as I have already said, I believe that the current stage of globalization demands that the most important possible breakthroughs acquire at least a regional presence. Europe, China, India, Southeast Asia, the Arab world, Africa, and Latin America are the major regions of the modern world where, it seems to me, it is possible to envisage the crystallization of alternatives.

I will not offer here an appraisal of the WFA/TWF's organized activities in response to the challenges described in the preceding analyses. I believe that such an appraisal would be quite useful and a WFA working group would be capable of doing it.

I will content myself with indicating two milestones through which our progress and our weaknesses can be assessed: (i) the WFA Assembly held at Bamako in 2006 that produced the Bamako Appeal (see Appendix C); and (ii) the Congress held in Caracas in 2008, the committee reports from which are available on numerous internet sites.

We had advanced despite everything, but we noticed that the World Social Forum stagnated. The approach of the great majority of NGOs that set the tone for the WSF does not go beyond the framework of what the existing system can tolerate. The critique of the WSF, laid out in a collective letter drafted in 2005 (available on numerous websites), was not listened to and, consequently, the WSF appears to have exhausted its capacities for organizing responses equal to what is required. The text presented later as a conclusion to this chapter reproduces the terms of our critique.

*Some Moving Commemorations*

I have turned eighty years old. Comrades and friends who are very dear to me thoughtfully organized moving ceremonies to celebrate my eightieth birthday.

In September 2011, on the occasion of my birthday, my comrades in Cairo organized a colloquium in my honor in which twenty dear friends from five continents participated. Beyond the quality of the discussions, this colloquium, which took place on a Nile cruise ship between Aswan and Luxor, brought me much joy and happiness. The Egyptian left also honored me by instituting the "Samir Amin Prize" awarded to researchers or activists contributing to the elaboration of common objectives for struggles. It was thus with great emotion that I had the pleasure to award the first prize in October 2012 to Ahmad El Naggar, who produced a remarkable work of synthesis on the demands of various segments of the Egyptian popular movement.

In Dakar, on the occasion of the WSF of February 2011, in the course of which the excellent participation of the TWF/WFA networks was duly noted, CODESRIA also honored me by organizing a session devoted to my written work and to the initiatives I have taken over the course of the preceding decades to establish Pan-African institutions as an integral part of the liberation of the continent's peoples and nations. The Executive Secretary, Ebrima Sall, and my friend Moussa Dembélé published on this occasion a work dedicated to my activities, which touched me greatly.[55]

The preceding year, Issa Shivji organized an event of the same kind, accompanied by lectures, in Dar es Salaam within the framework of the Julius Nyerere Foundation whose activities he coordinated. On this occasion, I wanted to offer to a large audience of thousands of young people a general survey of the challenges confronting the continent's peoples with a view to beginning a second wave of struggles for liberation and progress, taking up the torch of the Bandung era to advance the clear definition of objectives and means. The youth of Dar had prepared banners with my portrait and that of Julius Nyerere. As this was in the middle of an electoral campaign, I pointed out that I was not a candidate for the presidency!

In Bamako in 2010, on the occasion of the fiftieth anniversary of Mali's independence, the UM-RDA (originally U.S.-RDA) and Aminata D. Traoré brought together some "old-timers" who were still alive, but also many young people who did not want to forget the lessons of their history. They did me the honor of requesting that I present the 1960–1965 Malian Plan and its achievements.

In 2009, the Committee of the Ibn Rushd Prize in Berlin, made up of well-known and respected Arab thinkers, writers, and artists, did me the honor of awarding me the prize. This recognition of my modest contributions to the cause of the liberation and progress of Arab peoples deeply moved me.

## APPENDIX 1, CHAPTER 7: IS THE WORLD SOCIAL FORUM USEFUL FOR POPULAR STRUGGLES?

### Is the Social Forum Approach Useful?

[THE AUTHOR DRAFTED THE FOLLOWING TEXT IN 2008 IN CLOSE CONSULTATION WITH FRANÇOIS HOUTART.]

1. The undeniable success of the World Social Forums (WSFs) as well as the national and regional forums, from the first one (Porto Alegre, 2001) up to the seventh (Nairobi, 2007), shows that the approach met an actual objective need, felt by many activists and movements involved in fighting against neoliberalism and the aggressions (including military) of imperialism. In these struggles, movements and activists have made many reforms to their forms of organization and ways of actively intervening in society.

Yes, the left's dominant political culture in the nineteenth and twentieth centuries had been characterized by the hierarchical vertical organization of parties, unions, and associations. In the circumstances of that time, the movements they led transformed the world in a direction that was generally favorable to the working classes—radical and reformist social transformations, revolutions, and national liberations.

Nevertheless, the limitations and contradictions characteristic of these forms of action appeared forcefully beginning in the 1980s and 1990s. The democratic deficit of these forms, with organizations going as far as proclaiming themselves to be an "avant-garde" armed with "scientific" knowledge and "effective" strategy, lies behind the later disappointments. The least that can be said about the regimes carried to power by these reforms and revolutions is that they frequently did not keep their promises and often degenerated, sometimes in criminal directions. These failures made possible the resumption of the offensive by dominant capital and imperialism.

2. The moment of euphoria for capital and imperialism, which moved onto the offensive under the banner of neoliberalism and globalization, was short lived (1990-1995). The working classes quickly began to resist this offensive.

Yes, generally speaking, this first wave of struggles is situated on terrains of resistance to the offensive in all of its many dimensions: resistance to economic neoliberalism, the dismantling of social achievements, police repression, and the military aggressions by U.S. imperialism and its allies. The chain of these terrains of resistance is continuous and, depending on the circumstances of place, the struggles are conducted on the main terrain of the immediate challenge confronting the peoples in question. In this sense, the demand in one place to regulate the market, in another to protect the rights of women, or in yet another to defend the environment, to support public services, or to protect democracy, along with armed resistance to the aggression of the United States and its allies in regions such as the Middle East (Iraq, Palestine, Lebanon), are all connected to one another.

Peoples have been innovative in these resistance struggles. Many of the older political forces of the organized left have remained aloof and tentative in the face of aggressions, sometimes even moving to support liberal and imperialist choices. "New forces" began the movement, sometimes in an almost "spontaneous" way. As these forces have developed, they have promoted the fundamental principle of democratic practice. They reject a vertical hierarchy and promote horizontal forms of cooperation in action. This advance in democratic awareness should be considered a "civilizational" advance. To the extent that it is reflected in the social forums, the latter should then be considered to be perfectly "useful" to the development of current struggles.

3. Resistance struggles have recorded undeniable victories. They have only begun the defeat of the offensive of capital and imperialism. This setback is clear in every aspect of the offensive.

The U.S. project for military control of the planet—which is indispensable to guarantee the "success" of existing globalization—along with the "preventive" wars undertaken to ensure its effectiveness (invasion of Afghanistan and Iraq, occupation of Palestine, aggression against Lebanon) have already visibly suffered a political defeat.

The so-called neoliberal economic and social project, designed to provide a strong and stable foundation for capital accumulation—to ensure the maximum rate of profit at any price—is incapable of imposing its conditions, even according to the institutions that are its originators (the World Bank, the IMF, the WTO, the European Union). The project has "broken down": the Doha cycle of the WTO is at an impasse, the IMF is in financial collapse, etc. The threat of a violent economic and financial crisis is on the agenda.

4. Nevertheless, there is no room to be too self-congratulatory on these successes. They will remain insufficient to transform the social and political relations of force in favor of the working classes and, consequently, remain vulnerable so long as the movement does not pass from defensive resistance to the offensive. Only going on the offensive can open the way to the construction of a positive alternative—that is, "another possible world," and a better one, of course.

The challenge confronting the peoples in struggle is entirely found in the response that they choose to give to the question posed here, in terms strongly expressed by Houtart: to pass from the collective awareness of the challenges to building active social agents for transformation.

This challenge obviously involves, beyond the Forums, the peoples themselves. To what extent does collective awareness find expression in the Forums? Such awareness is certainly present, but in unequal levels of maturity, as always in history, depending on the moments, the places, and the movements concerned. But beyond that, do the Forums contribute to the necessary progress from this awareness to the building of agents of transformation? I shall attempt to answer this question later.

Progress is and will be difficult because it implies (i) radicalization of struggles and (ii) their convergence in diversity (to use the expression of the WFA) in common action plans, which imply a strategic political vision and the definition of immediate and more distant objectives (the "perspective" that defines the alternative).

Radicalizing struggles is not the equivalent of radicalizing their rhetoric; rather, it is the articulation of these struggles with the alternative project proposed as a substitute for the established systems of social power. In other words, it is necessary to build social hegemonies (class alliances and compromises) that aim to be alternatives to the social hegemonies in power (the alliances dominated by capital, imperialism, and the local comprador classes serving the latter). A vague "coordination" of struggles (or even simply exchanges of views) does not in itself create the conditions to transcend fragmentation and the consequent weakness. Convergence can only be the result of a "politicization" (in the good sense of the term) of fragmented movements. This requirement is actively countered by the rhetoric of "apolitical civil society," an ideology imported directly from the United States, which continues to wreak havoc.

Convergence in diversity and the radicalization of struggles will find their expressions in the inescapable construction of "stages" (some do not even want to hear the term evoked, as it appears to them synonymous with compromise and opportunism) that allows (i) advances in democratization (understood as a process without an end and not as a system established once and for all with Western representative political democracy as model) combined with (and not separate from) social progress, and (ii) assertion of the sovereignty of states, nations, and peoples, requiring forms of globalization that are negotiated and not unilaterally imposed by capital and imperialism.

Certainly, not everyone accepts these definitions of the content of an alternative construction.

Some consider that democracy (multiple parties and elections), even if dissociated from the "social question" (subject to market requirements), is "better than nothing." It remains the case that the Asian and African peoples do not, as a whole, appear disposed to fight for this form of democracy dissociated from social progress (and even linked to social regression at the present time). They often prefer to join para-religious/ethnic movements that are not at all democratic. We can lament this, but it would be more helpful to ask why. "Democracy" can neither be exported (by Europe) nor imposed (by the United States). It can only come about through struggles for social progress by the peoples of the South, just as the European peoples did, and still do.

The very mention of the nation, national independence, and sovereignty causes some people's skin to crawl. "Sovereigntism" is almost always considered to be a "defect of the past." The nation should be thrown in the garbage; besides, globalization has already made it obsolete. Popular in the European middle classes (for obvious reasons linked to the problems of constructing the EU), this thesis finds no echo in the South (or, moreover, in the United States and Japan!).

Transformation by steps does not exclude the affirmation of a long-term prospect. For some, like the author of these lines, that prospect is "socialism for the twenty-first century"; others reject "socialism," now permanently contaminated for them by its practice in the past century.

But even if the principle of convergence is accepted, its implementation will remain difficult because it is necessary to reconcile (i) advances in the practice of democracy achieved in and through struggles (necessarily giving up any nostalgia for movements controlled by "avant-gardes"), and (ii) the requirements for unity in action, modest or ambitious depending on local (national) conjunctures.

Not everyone accepts the principle of a necessary convergence. Some so-called "autonomist" currents, more or less inspired by "postmodernist" ideas, reject it. The movements they lead should be respected as such; they are part of a common struggle. Some go as far as claiming that the movement, even if it be fragmented, itself constructs the alternative, to the point of contending that the "individual subject" is already on the way to becoming the agent of transformation (Antonio Negri's theoretical view). One can, of course, not support this thesis. That is probably the case for most of the powerful popular movements involved in large and important struggles. We can also expect (hope?) that organizations inherited from the past—political parties, unions, etc.—are capable of transforming themselves in the direction of required democratic practices. The thinkers of the autonomist currents assert that it is possible to change the world without taking power. History will say whether that is possible or illusory.

In any case, whether we are talking about large organizations or small ones, the main line of conflict pits the "logic of struggle" (which privileges the requirements of the latter) against the "logic of organization" (which privileges the interests represented by established leaderships, or those aspiring to become leaders, who wish to participate in established power structures and, consequently, encourages opportunism).

Convergence cannot be built on the world and regional levels if it is not first established on the national level because, whether one likes it or not, the latter defines and frames concrete challenges; and it is at this level that a radical change in the social and political relations of force benefiting the working classes will or will not occur. Regional and world levels can reflect national advances and certainly facilitate them (or at least not be a handicap), but not much more.

5. Advances in the direction of opening the way to building an alternative are taking place right now, in Latin America. This is an evident contrast with their absence—or near absence—in Europe, Asia, and Africa.

These advances in Brazil, Argentina, Venezuela, Bolivia, and Ecuador, and their visible success, which might become possible elsewhere—Mexico, Peru, Nicaragua—are precisely the result of the radicalization of movements that have achieved an effective critical mass and political convergence. These are "revolutionary advances" in the sense that they have begun a change in social and political relations in favor of the working classes. Their success is due to their practice, which combines democratic management of the movements with the political crystallization of their projects, thereby overcoming the fragmentation still dominant elsewhere.

Who would deny that the state powers produced by these advances "pose a problem," that they might sink under pressure from external constraints and from local privileged classes? Must we then spurn the possibilities that these changes (of power!) open to popular movements? These powers make possible other advances, based on combining (and not keeping separate) assertion of national independence (vis-à-vis the United States), democratization, and social progress.

Elsewhere, the reality, despite the struggles undertaken, is less advantageous.

In Europe, the priority given to "construction of the European Union" encourages a shift toward social liberalism and the illusions maintained by the rhetoric of the "third way" and "capitalism with a human face." Will the "movement" succeed in overcoming these weaknesses on its own? Personally, I strongly doubt it and I think that decisive changes in the orientation of political power are a precondition, particularly a break with Atlanticism (NATO is the enemy of the European peoples). Others do not think so. In Eastern Europe, which is becoming in its actual relations with Germany and Western Europe similar to what Latin America was (and still is) in its relations with the United States, the illusions are even greater.

In Asia and Africa, we are currently witnessing deviations that can only be described as "culturalist." These nourish the illusion of supposed civilizational projects based on para-religious or ethnic organizations. In this context, the rhetoric on "cultural diversity" often comes to the aid of those trapped in such impasses. This rhetoric is completely tolerated (and even encouraged) by capital and imperialism.

It is necessary to find out more about how the advances were made in some places, on the one hand, and more about the reason for the movement's relative stagnation, even decline or defeat, on the other. That should be an essential focus for numerous debates, in the Forums and elsewhere. The World Forums, essentially meeting places, are poorly equipped to offer an adequate framework for extending these debates. National (or even regional) forums are much better, or could be.

6. The proposals drawn up in the Bamako Appeal (January 2006) intentionally called for giving more importance to extensive debates of this kind. These are only proposals, and not imposed decisions (besides, who would have the audacity to do that without the actual power to follow up on them!). Naturally, they were rejected in principle by extreme autonomist currents and the huge number of "apolitical" NGOs. But they are gaining ground elsewhere.

The WSF Charter does not prohibit in any way initiatives like the Bamako Appeal, which was, by the way, endorsed by the Assemblies of Movements. Yet this initiative has irritated the WSF "Secretariat." Why? Perhaps because it does not fundamentally share the proposals contained in the Appeal. Must we conclude from this that the Secretariat has in fact sided with the "apolitical"

NGOs (and maybe the extreme autonomist currents) to close the Forum to other currents of action? Who would deny that the Appeal—drafted by two hundred participants in one day and night—has inadequacies, even contradictions? But is it necessary to accuse its drafters of "intellectual arrogance," of outmoded "avant-gardist" attitudes, even of dangerous political motives? It would have to be demonstrated that the extreme autonomist currents produce nothing that is not the spontaneous, eloquent, and coherent result of the direct expression of the masses; that the "intellectuals" that formulate the theses of these currents do not exist! It would have to be demonstrated that the "apolitical" NGOs do not use language that has an obvious political meaning by embracing the rhetoric of government institutions: reduction in poverty, good governance, exacerbated culturalism, etc.

7. The World Forums have a history and a pre-history. They did not suddenly appear without any preparation. Houtart, Bernard Cassen, and others have recalled the essential stages of this history since the anti-Davos at Davos (1999) and other initiatives. To offer an evaluation of their development over the last seven years is not the purpose of this paper. Even if it is thought that their success is certain and their impact real (which is what we think), it remains the case that the emphasis should be placed, not on self-congratulations, but on the weaknesses.

The institutions responsible for the actual management of the Forums are diverse (Secretariat, International Council, "leaderships" of the main movements and NGOs represented). They are sites of power, by definition and as always (and it would be naive to ignore this). The often-dominant concern is to self-evaluate with regard to internal criteria of performance, often quite banal (number of participants, number—perhaps quality—of debates, material questions of organization). The real criterion of evaluation is external to the Forums: do they contribute to the progress of, rather than stagnation of, even decline in, struggles? It would be desirable if this dimension of evaluation were to find a wider echo in the assemblies and meetings organized by these institutions.

Carrying the critique a little further, we dare to say that the World Forums suffer from a (growing?) imbalance in the nature of their participants. Attendance is extremely costly in both money and intellectual work. Thus it is not surprising that the Forums attract more NGOs (sometimes obviously devoted to supporting struggles) with the personnel and financial means—from the North, but also, to be blunt, from their "clients" in the South—than large movements in struggle. Hundreds of millions of peasants involved in ferocious battles, or entire peoples facing the machine guns and bombs of the imperialist occupier, occasionally make their voices heard in a "workshop." But many other organizations—sometimes insignificant given the scope of their activities—have "ten workshops" to present their "propaganda." Quite frankly, some of these organizations are part of the system (and are "safety valves") rather than being part of the alternative. The question of "opening up the Forums" (the principle of which should not be questioned) is problematic. However, the way this is managed should be subject to closer scrutiny.

These "flaws" of the world Forums are also found in the national Forums. But here the immediate proximity of the forces fighting against the existing order favors overcoming the weaknesses mentioned here, at least potentially. Any balance sheet—positive or less positive—depends on the concrete conditions of locale and the nature of the handicaps (national political competition) as well as favorable factors (radicalization of struggles).

8. Reconstructing a "front of countries and peoples of the South" is one of the fundamental conditions for the emergence of "another world" not founded on imperialist domination.

Without underestimating the importance of all kinds of transformations originating in the societies of the North in the past and present, it should be emphasized that they have remained, up to now, tied to imperialism. It should not be surprising, then, that the great transformations on the world scale originated in the revolt of peoples in the peripheries, from the Russian Revolution (the weak link of that time) to the Chinese Revolution and the Non-Aligned Movement (Bandung) that, for a time, forced imperialism to "adjust" to demands that conflicted with the logic of its expansion. The page of the Bandung Conference and the Tricontinental (1955–1980), of a globalization that was multipolar, has turned.

The conditions of existing globalization prohibit a remake of the Bandung Conference. The current ruling classes in the countries of the South are attempting to be part of this globalization, which they sometimes hope to bend in their favor, but which they do not fight. These can be divided into two groups: those who have a "national" project, the nature of which—mainly capitalist, but nuanced by concessions (or not) to the working classes, yet in open or muted conflict with imperialism—should be discussed on a case-by-case basis, such as China or the emergent countries of Asia and Latin America; and those who do not have such a project and accept having to adjust unilaterally to imperialist requirements (these, then, are comprador ruling classes).

Various kinds of alliances are emerging between states (governments), some of which can be seen within the WTO. We should not spurn the possibilities that such alliances might open for movements of the working classes (without, of course, having any illusions).

Is a front of the peoples of the South possible, one that goes beyond the rapprochements between the ruling classes? The construction of such a front is difficult since it is set back by the "culturalist" deviations mentioned above, and results in confrontations between peoples of the South (on pseudo-religious or pseudo-ethnic bases). It will be less problematic if and insofar as the states that have a project could—under pressure from their peoples—move in a more resolutely anti-imperialist direction. But that implies that their projects set aside any illusions that "national capitalist" governments are resolutely and exclusively able to modify imperialist globalization in their favor and become active agents in that globalization, participating in forming the world system (and not unilaterally adjusting to it). These illusions are still widespread and reinforced by the rhetoric that flatters the "emergent countries," on the way to "catching up," developed by institutions in the service of imperialism. But insofar as facts come to contradict these illusions, national popular and anti-imperialist blocs might once again pave the way to an internationalism of peoples. We can only hope that progressive forces in the North will understand and support this.

9. In conclusion, one could say that the future of the Forums depends less on what might happen within them than what might develop elsewhere, in the struggles of peoples and the evolution of the geostrategy of states.

This conclusion should not lead to any pessimism concerning the Forums, but it should lead to a degree of modesty when evaluating their achievements.

Other forms of intervention are necessary at the same time as (and not in conflict with) undertaking actions within the Forums. This should allow an expansion of debates and discussions with a view toward organizing joint actions beyond a day of world protest against the debt, or against preventive wars, or in favor of women's rights, or in support of access to water, etc.

The WFA has been committed to this path since its inception in 1997. A network of numerous think tanks directly connected with social and political forces struggling against the system, it attempts to organize working groups (and not only exchanges of views), and perhaps facilitates the emergence of joint action fronts. For your information, these are groups of union members ("reconstruct the united front of labor"), peasant movements ("mandate access to the land for the benefit of all peasants"), and political forces non-aligned on the global politics of capital and imperialism (working on questions of international law or for reform of the United Nations and systems for economic management of globalization, etc.).

Many other national, regional, and world "networks" are developing praiseworthy efforts moving in comparable directions. I shall not list them all here, but mention only, as examples, ATTAC in France, the work of "Focus on the Global South," and ARENA.

As a way to strengthen the effectiveness of the Forums, it would be highly desirable if these programs found a greater presence there.

## Appendix 2, Chapter 7: Audacity, More Audacity

[THE FOLLOWING TEXT TAKES UP, IN A SHORTENED FORM, PROPOSITIONS DEVELOPED IN MY BOOK *THE IMPLOSION OF CONTEMPORARY CAPITALISM*. THE READER SHOULD ALSO READ THE "PROGRAM OF THE WFA/TWF FOR 2014/15" (APPENDIX B).]

The historical circumstances created by the implosion of contemporary capitalism require the radical left, in the North as well as the South, to be bold in formulating its political alternative to the existing system. This system is visibly incapable of overcoming its growing internal contradictions and is condemned to continue on its insane path. But up to now, the strategy deployed by the monopolies has always given the desired results: "austerity" plans are always successfully imposed, in spite of resistance. The initiative has always remained, up to now, in the hands of the monopolies (the markets) and their political servants (the governments that submit their decisions to the so-called requirements of the market).

Faced with the war declared by monopoly capital, workers and peoples must develop strategies that allow them to move to the offensive. This conjuncture of social war is necessarily accompanied by the proliferation of international political conflicts and military interventions by the imperialist powers of the triad. The strategy of "military control of the planet" by the armed forces of the United States and its subordinate NATO allies is ultimately the only way in which the imperialist monopolies of the triad can expect to continue their domination over the peoples, nations, and states of the South.

Faced with this challenge, what alternatives are being proposed?

*First response: "Market regulation" (financial and otherwise):* These are initiatives that monopolies and governments claim they are pursuing. It is only empty rhetoric, designed to mislead public opinion. These initiatives cannot stop the mad rush for financial return that is the result of the logic of accumulation controlled by monopolies. They are, therefore, a false alternative, and the Stiglitz Commission was designed to promote it.

*Second response: A return to the postwar models*: This response fuels three forms of nostalgia: (i) the rebuilding of a true "social democracy" in the West, (ii) the resurrection of "socialisms" founded on the principles that governed those of the twentieth century, and (iii) the return to formulas of popular nationalism in the peripheries of the South. These nostalgias imagine that it is possible to roll back monopoly capitalism, forcing it to regress to what it was in 1945. But history never allows such returns to the past. Capitalism must be confronted as it is today, not as what we would have wished it to be by imagining the blocking of its evolution. However, these longings continue to haunt large segments of the left throughout the world.

*Third response: The search for a "humanist" consensus:* I define this pious wish in the following way: the illusion that a consensus among fundamentally conflicting interests would be possible. Naive ecology movements, among others, share this illusion.

*Fourth response: The illusions of the past:* These illusions invoke "specificity" and "right to difference" without bothering to understand their scope and meaning. In this view, the past has already answered future questions. These "culturalisms" can take many para-religious or ethnic forms. Theocracies and ethnocracies become convenient substitutes for the democratic social struggles that have been cleared from the agenda.

*Fifth response: The priority of "personal freedom":* The range of responses based on this priority, considering the exclusive "supreme value," includes in its ranks the diehards of "representative electoral democracy," which they equate with democracy itself. The formula separates the democratization of societies from social progress, and even tolerates a de facto association with social regression in order not to risk discrediting democracy, now reduced to the status of a tragic farce. But there are even more dangerous forms of this position. I am referring here to some common "postmodernist" currents (such as that of Negri in particular) who imagine that the individual has already become the subject of history, as if communism—which will allow the individual to be emancipated from alienation and actually become the subject of history—were already here!

The war declared by the generalized monopoly capitalism of contemporary imperialism has nothing to fear from the false alternatives I have just outlined. So what is to be done? This moment offers us the historic opportunity to go much further; it demands, as the only effective response, a bold and audacious radicalization in the formulation of alternatives capable of moving workers and peoples to take the offensive to defeat their adversary's strategy of war.

### AUDACIOUS PROGRAMS FOR THE RADICAL LEFT

I will organize the following general proposals under three headings: (i) socialize the ownership of monopolies, (ii) de-financialize the management of the economy, and (iii) de-globalize international relations.

#### *Socialize the Ownership of Monopolies*

The effectiveness of the alternative response necessarily requires the questioning of the very principle of private property of monopoly capital. Monopolies are institutional bodies that must be managed according to the principles of democracy, in direct conflict with those who sanctify private property. Although the term "commons," imported from the Anglo-Saxon world, is itself ambiguous because it is always disconnected from the debate on the meaning of social conflicts (Anglo-Saxon language deliberately ignores the reality of social classes), the term could be invoked here specifically to call monopolies part of the "commons." The abolition of the private ownership of monopolies takes place through their nationalization. This first legal action is unavoidable. But audacity here means going beyond that step to propose plans for the socialization of the management of nationalized monopolies and the promotion of democratic social struggles on this long road.

I shall give here a concrete example of what could be involved in these socialization plans:

"Capitalist" farmers (those of developed countries), like "peasant" farmers (mostly in the South), are all prisoners of both the upstream monopolies that provide inputs and credit, and the downstream ones on which they depend for processing, transportation, and marketing of their products. Therefore they have no real autonomy in their decisions. In addition, the productivity gains they make are siphoned off by the monopolies that have reduced producers to the status of subcontractors. What is the possible alternative?

Public institutions working within a legal framework that would set the mode of governance must replace the monopolies. These would constitute the representatives of: (i) farmers (the principal interests), (ii) upstream units (manufacturers of inputs, banks) and downstream units (food industry, retail chains), (iii) consumers, (iv) local authorities (interested in the natural and social environment—schools, hospitals, urban planning and housing, transportation), and (v) the State (citizens). Representatives of these components would be self-selected according to procedures consistent with their own mode of socialized management, such as units of production of inputs that are themselves managed by directorates of workers directly employed by the units concerned, as well as those who are employed by subcontracting units, and so on. These structures should be designed to associate management personnel with each of these levels, such as centers for independent and appropriate scientific and technological research. We are therefore talking about institutional approaches that are more complex than the "self-managed" or "cooperative" forms we have known. Ways of working need to be invented that allow the exercise of genuine democracy in the management of the economy, based on open negotiation among all interested parties. The proposed procedure abolishes the power by which the monopolies exploit workers and subcontractors using the mandatory system of prices. This monopoly power is replaced with social power based on solidarity and an authentically just price system based on an equal rate of profit for everyone. This system, then, allows "another development," one that is more effective and more rational because it responds to the collective choices of society and thereby involves the entire productive system in real progress, and avoids the destruction characteristic of monopoly capitalism. This system opens the state capitalist model toward further evolution toward socialism; it could be considered a form of "market socialism" necessary at this stage.

This is only a particular example from one sector of the economy, in this case agricultural production.

In the proposals I am making, I am respecting the constraints in which we find ourselves at present, particularly the "large production" units. The proposed methods of social reorganization are aimed at a single objective: to abolish the control of capital (today, the generalized monopolies) over production, and begin to substitute forms of management based on democracy and negotiation among the partners in the modern, extensive division of labor.

The nationalization/socialization of monopolies addresses a fundamental need at the central axis of the challenge confronting workers and peoples under the contemporary capitalism of generalized monopolies. It is the only way to stop the accumulation by dispossession that is driving the management of the economy by the monopolies. This solution does not intend to define the fundamental nature of any future communism. It simply responds to the immediate challenge: to begin the process of ending capitalism by building the first stage of the long transition to socialism. This socialism has hardly left the "entrails of capitalism," as Marx said; and the proposed step still bears traces of it. Nevertheless, based on the abolition of monopoly capitalist property, it is what I call a revolutionary advance that, by means of the democratic debate it fosters, prepares the terrain for later advances on the long road to communism.

### De-Financialization: A World Without Wall Street

Of course the nationalization/socialization of monopolies also applies to banks, at least the major ones. But the socialization of their intervention (credit policies) has specific characteristics that require an appropriate design in the constitution of their directorates. Nationalization in the classical sense of the term implies only the substitution of the state for the boards of directors formed by private shareholders. This would permit, in principle, implementation of bank credit policies formulated by the state—which is no small thing. But it is certainly not sufficient when we consider that socialization requires the direct participation in the management of the bank by the relevant social partners. Here the "self-management" of banks by their staff would not be appropriate. The staff concerned should certainly be involved in decisions about their working conditions, but little else, because it is not their place to determine the credit policies to be implemented.

If the directorates must deal with the conflicts of interest of those who provide loans (the banks) and those who receive them (the enterprises), the formula for the composition of directorates must be designed to take into account what the enterprises are and what they require. A restructuring of the banking system, which has become overly centralized since the regulatory frameworks of the past two centuries were abandoned over the past four decades, is necessary. There is a strong argument to justify the reconstruction of banking specialization according to the requirements of the recipients of their credit as well as their economic function (provision of short-term liquidity, contributing to the financing of investments in the medium and long term). We could then, for example, create an "agriculture bank" (or a coordinated ensemble of agriculture banks) whose clientele is composed not only of farmers and peasants but also those involved in the "upstream and downstream" of agriculture described above. The bank's directorate would involve, on the one hand, the bankers (staff officers of the bank—who would have been recruited by the directorate) and, on the other, clients (farmers or peasants, and other upstream and downstream entities). We can imagine other sets of articulated banking systems, appropriate to various industrial sectors, in which the directorates would involve the industrial clients, centers of research and technology, and services to ensure control of the ecological impact of the industry, thus ensuring minimal risk (while recognizing that no human action is completely without risk), and subject to transparent democratic debate.

The de-financialization of economic management would also require two sets of legislation. The first concerns the authority of a sovereign state to ban speculative fund (hedge funds) operations in its territory. The second concerns pension funds, which are now major operators in the financialization of the economic system. These funds were designed, first in the United States of course, to transfer to employees the risks normally incurred by capital—which are the reasons invoked to justify capital's remuneration. So this is a scandalous arrangement, in clear contradiction even with the ideological defense of capitalism! But this "invention" is an ideal instrument for the strategies of accumulation dominated by monopolies. The abolition of pension funds is necessary and they should be replaced by distributive pension systems, which, by their very nature, require and allow democratic debate to determine the amounts and periods of assessment and the relationship between the amounts of pensions and salaries. In a democracy that respects social rights, these pension systems are universally available to all workers.

De-financialization certainly does not mean the abolition of macroeconomic policy, and in particular the macro management of credit. On the contrary, it restores its efficiency by freeing it from its subjugation to the strategies of rent-seeking monopolies. The restoration of the powers of national central banks, no longer "independent" but dependent on both the state and markets regulated by the democratic negotiation of social partners, gives the formulation of macro credit policy its effectiveness in the service of socialized management of the economy.

### At the International Level: Delinking

Here I use the term "delinking" that I proposed half a century ago, a term that the contemporary discourse appears to have replaced with the synonym "de-globalization." I have never conceptualized delinking as an autarkic retreat, but rather as a strategic reversal in the face of both internal and external forces in response to the unavoidable requirements of self-determined development. Delinking promotes the reconstruction of a globalization based on negotiation, rather than submission to the exclusive interests of the imperialist monopolies. It also makes possible the reduction of international inequalities.

Delinking is necessary because the measures advocated in the two previous sections can never really be implemented at the global scale, or even at a regional level, for example, Europe. They can only be initiated in the context of states/nations with advanced radical social and political struggles, committed to a process of socialization of the management of their economy.

Imperialism, in the form that it took until just after the Second World War, had created the contrast between industrialized imperialist centers and dominated peripheries, where industry was prohibited. The victories of national liberation movements began the process of the industrialization of the peripheries, through the implementation of delinking policies required for the option of self-reliant development. Associated with social reforms that were at times radical, these delinking policies created the conditions for the eventual "emergence" of those countries that had gone furthest in this direction—with China leading the pack, of course. But the imperialism of the current era, the imperialism of the triad, was forced to retreat and "adjust" itself to the conditions of this new era, rebuild itself on new foundations, based on the "advantages" (or monopolies of control) through which it sought to hold on to the privilege of exclusivity. I have classified these monopolies of control into five categories: (i) technology; (ii) access to natural resources of the planet; (iii) global integration of the monetary and financial system; (iv) systems of communication and information; and (v) weapons of mass destruction.

The main form of delinking today is thus defined precisely by the challenge to these five privileges of contemporary imperialism. Emerging countries are engaged in delinking from these five privileges, with varying degrees of control and self-determination, of course. While earlier success in delinking over the past two decades enabled them to accelerate their development, in particular through industrial development within the globalized "liberal" system using "capitalist" means, this success has fueled delusions about the possibility of continuing on this path—that is to say, emerging as new "equal capitalist partners." The attempt to co-opt the most prestigious of these countries with the creation of the G20 has encouraged these illusions. But with the current ongoing implosion of the imperialist system (called globalization), these illusions are likely to dissipate. The conflict between the imperialist powers of the triad and emerging countries is already visible, and is expected to worsen. If they want to move forward, the societies of emerging countries will be forced to turn more toward self-reliant modes of development through national plans and by strengthening South-South cooperation. Audacity, under such circumstances, involves being committed vigorously and consistently toward achieving this goal, bringing together the required measures of delinking with the desired advances in social progress.

The goal of this radicalization is threefold: the democratization of society; the consequent social progress achieved; and the taking of anti-imperialist positions. A commitment to this direction is possible, not only for societies in emerging countries, but also in the "abandoned" or the "written-off" countries of the Global South. These countries had been effectively recolonized through the structural adjustment programs of the 1980s. Their peoples are now in open revolt, whether they have already scored victories (South America) or not (in the Arab world). Audacity here means that the radical left in these societies must have the courage to assess the challenges they face and to support the continuation and radicalization of the necessary struggles that are in progress.

The delinking of the South prepares the way for the deconstruction of the imperialist system itself. This is particularly apparent in areas affected by the management of the global monetary and financial system, since it is the result of the hegemony of the dollar. But beware: it is an illusion to expect to substitute for this system "another world monetary and financial system" that is better balanced and favorable to the development of the peripheries. As always, the search for a consensus over international reconstruction from above is mere wishful thinking akin to waiting for a miracle. What is on the agenda now is the deconstruction of the existing system, that is, its implosion, and a reconstruction of national alternative systems (for countries or continents or regions), as some projects in South America have already begun. Audacity here is to have the courage to move forward with the strongest determination possible, without too much concern about the reaction of imperialism.

This same issue of delinking or dismantling is also of relevance to Europe, which is a subset of globalization dominated by monopolies. The European project was designed from the outset and built systematically to dispossess its peoples of their ability to exercise their democratic power. The European Union was established as a protectorate of the monopolies. Its submission to these monopolies effectively abolishes democracy, reduced to a farce. Now, with the implosion of the eurozone, this submission takes on extreme forms: how are the "markets" (that is, the monopolies) reacting? That is the only question posed now. How the people might react is no longer given the slightest consideration. It is thus obvious that here, too, there is no alternative to audacity: "disobeying" the rules imposed by the European Constitution and the imaginary central bank of the euro. In other words, there is no alternative to deconstructing the institutions of Europe and the eurozone. This is the unavoidable prerequisite for the eventual reconstruction of "another Europe" of peoples and nations.

### *In Conclusion: Audacity, More Audacity, Always Audacity*

What I mean by audacity is therefore: For the radical left in the societies of the imperialist triad to engage in building an alternative anti-monopoly social bloc.

For the radical left in the societies of the peripheries to engage in building an alternative anti-comprador social bloc.

We are in a crucial period of history. The only legitimacy of capitalism is to have created the conditions for passing on to socialism, understood as a higher stage of civilization. Capitalism is now an obsolete system, its continuation leading only to barbarism. No other capitalism is possible. The outcome of a clash of civilizations is, as always, uncertain. Either the radical left will succeed through the audacity of its initiatives to make revolutionary advances, or the counterrevolution will win. There is no lasting compromise between these two responses to the challenge.

All the strategies of the non-radical left are non-strategies; they are merely day-to-day adjustments to the vicissitudes of the imploding system. And while the powers that want, like le Guépard (the Leopard), to "change everything so that nothing changes," the candidates of the left believe it is possible to "change life without touching the power of monopolies"![56] The non-radical left will not stop the triumph of capitalist barbarism. They have already lost the battle because they do not want to take it on.

Audacity is necessary so that we can make sure the autumn of capitalism, announced by the system's implosion, that coincides with a genuine springtime of peoples, has now become possible.

# 8

# THE NORTH AND THE QUESTION OF IMPERIALISM

The conflict between the North (centers) and the South (peripheries) is an inherent part of the entire history of capitalist development. Historical capitalism (there is no other except in the unreal world of liberal doctrine) merges with the history of world conquest by Europeans and their descendants, who made the United States and Canada and Australia. This conquest was victorious for four centuries—from 1492 to 1914—before which the resistance of victim peoples had always failed. Such success made it possible to legitimize the conquest by citing the obvious superiority of the European system, synonymous with modernity, progress, and happiness—to use the terms from English utilitarianism—the foundation of Eurocentrism. The successful conquest persuaded the peoples of the imperialist centers (originally all Europeans, to which were added the Japanese, who chose to imitate their predecessors, but excluding the Latin Americans) that they have a "preferential" right to the world's wealth. This is really a type of deep-seated racism, one that no longer takes on the elementary form of belief in the inequality of "races."

This phase of history is coming to an end, called into question by the awakening of the South. This awakening began in the twentieth century with the revolutions carried out in the name of socialism, first in the Russian semi-periphery, followed by China, Vietnam, and Cuba in the periphery, and with the national liberation movements in Asia and Africa, plus advances in Latin America. I have offered, practically throughout all my writings, concrete analyses of these challenges as well as more theoretical and general analyses of their connection with transformations of the capitalist/imperialist system. Gabriela Roffinelli's small book, published in 2013, offers an excellent synthesis of my theses.[57] In these memoirs, I have added a more personal note to all that.

The struggle of the peoples of the South for their liberation—now victorious overall—is closely connected with the challenge to capitalism. The conjunction is inevitable. The conflicts between capitalism and socialism and between the North and the South are inseparable. No socialism is conceivable outside of universalism, which implies equality of peoples. In the countries of the South, the majority are victims of the system, whereas in those of the North, they are the beneficiaries. Both know this perfectly well, although often they are resigned to it (in the South) or pleased about it (in the North). Thus, it is not by chance that the radical transformation of the system is not on the agenda in the North, whereas the South continues to be the "zone of storms"—repeated revolts, some of which are potentially revolutionary. Consequently, initiatives of peoples from the South have been decisive in transforming the world, as the entire history of the twentieth century clearly demonstrates. Class struggles in the North have primarily been focused on economic demands that, in general, do not call into question either the ownership of capital or the imperialist world order. That is particularly visible in the United States, which I explain by the effects of successive waves of immigration that prevented the politicization of social struggles and led instead to the assertion of "communitarianism" within the context of a political culture of consensus. The situation is more complex in Europe because of its political culture of conflict between right and left, beginning with the Enlightenment and the French Revolution, then followed by the formation of a socialist workers' movement and the Russian Revolution.[58] Nevertheless, the Americanization of European societies, underway since 1950, has gradually attenuated this contrast. Therefore, the changes in comparative competitiveness in the economies of central capitalism—associated with the unequal development of social struggles—do not deserve to be placed at the center of transformations of the world system or at the heart of the different possible variations in the relations between the United States and Europe, as many partisans of the European project think. As for the revolts in the South, when they become more radical, they come up against the challenges of underdevelopment. Consequently, their "socialisms" always include contradictions between initial intentions and the realities of the possible. The possible, but difficult, conjunction between the struggles of peoples in the South with those in the North is the only way to go beyond the limitations of both. This conjunction defines my reading of Marxism, which begins with Marx, but refuses to stop at him, Lenin, or Mao. In my view, Marxism is conceptualized as a method of analysis and action, and not as a group of propositions drawn from use of that method. Hence, there is no hesitation to reject some conclusions, even if they come from Marx himself. Ultimately, then, this Marxism is unbounded and always incomplete.

This possible conjunction also explains why I am an internationalist. Since capitalism is a global system and not the simple juxtaposition of national capitalist systems, I have always thought that for political and social struggles to be effective, they should be undertaken simultaneously in the national sphere, which remains decisive because the social and political conflicts, alliances, and compromises are formed there, and on the world level. This viewpoint—rather commonplace, in my opinion—appears to have been that of Marx and historical Marxisms ("Proletarians of the world unite," or in the expanded Maoist version: "Proletarians of all countries, oppressed peoples, unite"). The debates and struggles in which I have participated—the reader will have realized—are simultaneously located on these different levels. This obviously implies not a "Third Worldism," but a "worldism" (or internationalism), an essential nuance about which I have often spoken. I have even defended the necessity of a Fifth International.[59] The nature of the organizations fostering the debates in which I have participated—whether the IDEP, the TWF, or the WFA—implied that we were seeking to build effective bridges for international action.

At the present moment, the page of the South's liberation appears, nevertheless, to have turned. The South's ruling classes seem to accept being subjected to the requirements of globalization, some because they hope to profit, others because they are forced to do so. The Westernization of the world is underway. The liberal doctrine is triumphing and believes that it has found proof for the correctness of its vision: because of the homogenization of the world, "catching up" is possible within capitalism; its achievement depends on the intelligence of the ruling classes involved. I believe I have provided good arguments demonstrating why this is not so, that polarization will continue to govern the system in the future just as it has in the past. The liberation of peoples in the South is thus inseparable from constructing a socialist perspective and progressing from capitalism to world socialism.

But it is widely held that this is an illusion, illustrated by the ultimate collapse of the Soviet and Maoist models. To those who think that socialism is impossible, I say: capitalism did not emerge at a single moment from the London-Amsterdam-Paris triangle of the seventeenth century; three centuries earlier, it had crystallized in the Italian city-states in an early form that foundered, but without which its much later ultimate form would have been unthinkable. It will probably be the same for socialism. But this probability will only become reality if the connection between the liberation of the South and the invention of stages for the long transition to world socialism is created with the effectiveness necessary to "change the world." This implies that Marxism's "Afro-Asian vocation" must take shape, as I have written. Certainly, the South does not appear to be moving on this path. On the contrary, backward-looking illusions are dominant among many of its peoples. Will Latin America, but above all China, which are exceptions, move away from such illusions? I believe that is possible. A new "front of the South" can bring together the states and peoples of the South in various ways. This would be a better-equipped Bandung Conference than the first since the countries of the South now have many more fruitful possibilities for cooperation.

To believe the repetitive chatter from the Western media, the idea of reviving non-alignment would be a pipe dream. In this narrative, everything that happened in the world between 1945 and 1990 can only be explained by the Cold War, and nothing else. The USSR has disappeared, and the Cold War along with it, so any position similar to those known at that time makes no sense. Consider the absurdity of this attitude and the incredibly contemptuous—even racist—prejudice that underlies it. The true history of the Bandung Conference and the non-alignment that emerged from it demonstrated that the Asian and African peoples undertook an initiative at the time by themselves and for themselves. The reader will find in what I have written on the subject a demonstration that non-alignment was already "non-alignment on globalizaton," on the model of globalization that the imperialist powers wanted to impose on newly independent countries by means of neocolonialism as a replacement for defunct colonialism. Non-alignment proceeded from a refusal to submit to the requirements of this reasserted imperialist globalization. This initiative won the battle and forced imperialism to retreat for a while. It was thus, by itself, a positive factor in transforming the world for the better in spite of all its limitations. The Soviet Union understood at that time the benefit that it could derive by supporting the non-aligned. The Soviet Union was also in conflict with the dominant system of globalization and suffered from the isolation in which the Atlanticist powers imprisoned it. Moscow understood that it could break this isolation by moving closer to the non-aligned. On the other hand, the imperialist powers fought against non-alignment precisely because it was "non-alignment on globalization." Today, the countries of the South are again confronted with an imperialist globalization project of which they would be the victims. Their willingness not to submit to its requirements places a "rebirth" of non-alignment on globalization back on the agenda. We can call that "Bandung 2," if we want. Of course, the world has changed since the days of the original non-aligned movement (such an observation is really quite commonplace). Consequently, the new imperialist globalization is not a copy of the one with which the original Bandung was confronted.

The narrative that reduces non-alignment to an avatar of the Cold War proceeds from a stubborn prejudice in the West: the peoples of Asia and Africa were not capable of taking the initiative by themselves, anymore than they are capable of doing so today or tomorrow! They are condemned to being endlessly manipulated by the major powers—first and foremost the West, of course. This contempt poorly conceals a profound racism. In this view, it is as if the Algerians, for example, had taken up arms to please Moscow, or maybe Washington; that they had been manipulated to this end by some leaders who had chosen to turn toward one power or another. No, their decision derived simply from their desire to be freed from colonialism, the form globalization took at that time. When they implemented their own decision, the two sides were formed around those who supported them and those who fought them. That is the historical reality.

It is impossible to project the trajectory that will emerge from the unequal advances produced by struggles in the South and the North. My feeling is that the South is currently going through a moment of crisis, but a crisis of growth in the sense that pursuing the objective of liberating its peoples is irreversible. The peoples of the North should take stock of this objective, and it would be even better if they were to offer their support for it as part of the construction of socialism. Solidarity of this kind existed during the Bandung era. At that time, young Europeans displayed their "Third Worldism," undoubtedly naive, but much more admirable than their current sole focus on Europe.

There is no need to go back over the analyses of really existing capitalism that I have developed elsewhere, but I would like to emphasize one conclusion from them: humanity will be able to undertake the construction of a socialist alternative to capitalism only if things change in the developed West too. That does not mean that the countries of the periphery must wait for this change and, until that happens, be content to "adjust" to the possibilities offered by capitalist globalization. On the contrary, it is more likely that when things begin to change in the peripheries, societies in the West would be forced to change as well, and they could be led to move in the direction required for the progress of all of humanity. Without that, the worst—that is, barbarism and the suicide of human civilization—remains the most probable outcome. I locate the desirable and possible changes in both the centers and peripheries of the global system within the context of what I have called "the long transition." Here, I refer the reader to my 2014 article "Popular Movements Toward Socialism."[60]

My analyses also led me to view China, and maybe Europe, as places with the greatest probability of developing possible favorable changes. Yet, I recognize that the part played by intuition in this type of futuristic analysis can never be eliminated. Each of us knows, or believes we know, the societies of the developed West, the inertial forces produced by the advantage of their central position in the world system, the relative stability that this inertia provides to these societies, but also the openness that characterizes them, their creative imagination; in other words, their capacities to respond to challenges by often difficult to predict, but no less astonishing advances. Each of us knows the immense knowledge—good and not so good—accumulated in the universities and research centers of the First World.

My memoirs essentially concern the Global South. Nevertheless, my universalist and internationalist political position demands that, even if only as an epilogue, I clarify my view of the North. My political position and the exercise of my functions required that my contacts and exchanges of views were extensive. Inevitably, my choices led me to spend more time with the scientific, intellectual, and political circles of the First World whose concerns were close to ours in critical analyses of globalization and development. At the same time, I had to devote some time to seeking out sources that might be likely to support our work with financial contributions.

My experience with "donors" (Western or international), as they are called in the rather vulgar language of the profession, was certainly mixed. Some institutions are clearly in the service of imperialism: USAID, the large North American foundations, but also most of the development assistance services of the large Western powers. It was pointless, and would have been politically unacceptable, for us to approach them. Others, at certain moments, can be possible partners capable of accepting viewpoints that do not reflect the dominant currents through which the unilateral requirements of capitalist expansion are expressed. This is either because the makeup of the leadership at a particular moment makes that possible or even, in some cases, because some organizations are authentically democratic and manifest genuine openness. Such was the case, for us, with some development assistance institutions in the Netherlands, Norway, Sweden (up to the time this country turned to the right in its views on international politics), Italy (before the rise of the new right, which has the wind in its sails now), Luxemburg, some institutions of Christian inspiration, a few uncommon organizations clearly on the left (such as the Rosa Luxemburg Foundation of the German Social Democratic Party), and some institutions of the United Nations (particularly the UNU and UNCTAD in some circumstances). The United Nations system is now largely a vassal of the United States—this is particularly true of the UNDP, without mentioning the World Bank, obviously. I do not believe it is helpful to say more about this; it would be tedious and uninteresting.

What are the conditions in which the countries of the North might very well move away from the path on which they embarked five centuries ago, that is, the continuing war against the peoples of the South and no less permanent wars among themselves to determine distribution of the spoils?

My thesis is that the imperialist system has moved to a new stage in its development, in which a collective imperialism of the triad has come to replace a multiplicity of imperialisms in permanent conflict characteristic of an earlier stage in the history of capitalism. Produced by the growing centralization of capital, this transformation puts a fundamentally anti-democratic financial plutocracy in positions of leadership.[61] Having become obsolescent, capitalism must be surpassed by the invention of twenty-first-century socialism. But capitalism will not die a quiet death; on the contrary, the current plutocracy has no other choice than to attempt to destroy the South, which has become capable of developing itself. Will the peoples of the North participate in this criminal undertaking of their ruling classes? To answer that question, my analysis does not emphasize, as others do, the contradictions that oppose the oligopolies of the centers to one another (particularly those of the United States and Europe), but rather focuses on the particularities of the political cultures of the peoples concerned, which allows us to perceive possible cracks in the front of the triad's plutocracies. In my opinion, these particularities explain both the paths followed in the past and the future prospects, just as much as general economic and social conditions do. Bourgeois thought, dominated by economism, ignores these considerations. Marx paid close attention to them. But that is not true of simplified Marxism, as can be seen in the rhetoric of numerous segments of the European extreme left, content with denouncing "exploiting capital" without taking the time to develop political strategies for struggle, which necessarily implies that the force of the concrete political cultures in question cannot be ignored.

The reader of what follows might consider my judgments a little too severe. They are indeed. My earlier analyses of the Global South were no less so. It should be noted that political cultures are not transhistorical invariants. They change, sometimes for the worse, but just as often for the better. I consider that the construction of "convergence in diversity" toward the prospect of socialism demands it.

## UNITED STATES

I have explained why I do not see how the wind of change could find its point of departure in the "most advanced" center of capitalism.[62] This is so precisely because the "perfection" of the capitalist model means that the people here are, as a whole, deeply alienated in a political culture dominated by the idea that the "market is king" and by the illusion that the "individual" is also king. The power of the vulgar ideology of capitalism, here accepted by everyone, then makes possible the particular vulgarity of the ruling class. In the ideology of the Enlightenment, the values of liberty and equality are associated as if they were naturally convergent, whereas they are actually in conflict and building their possible complementarity requires a social system "beyond capitalism." In the United States, more than elsewhere, the value of "liberty" is imposed unilaterally, legitimizing inequality. The system's victims seem willing to accept that liberty in these conditions is deprived of any creative potential, becoming instead easily manipulated consensual submission, that the "individual" sanctified in the rhetoric is in reality no more than a boneless puppet incapable of participating in building their future. Moreover, politicization of class struggles was here weakened by communitarianism resulting from the succession of waves of immigration. I have offered my analyses on these questions, which were also the focus of major discussions with many friends in the United States. It is always the case that this situation allows the dominant class in the United States to manage the society in its exclusive interest, by formidable means that combine cynicism in action with extreme hypocrisy in rhetoric. Like Noam Chomsky, I believe that the United States is the actual leading "rogue state," to use Clinton's term, in the contemporary world. And I always expect the worst from U.S. presidents (including genocide of opponents, as the very courageous Daniel Ellsberg demonstrated). Those who know this class well—from the inside (like Paul Sweezy)—confirm my fears. George W. Bush's (questionable) election was a quasi-coup d'état and a true junta of war criminals now governs the United States, giving powers to the police similar to those found only in the police states of modern history. In the short term, nothing indicates that the American people are capable of realizing the tragedy inherent in the outrageous and criminal project of this junta—military control of the planet—which leads the world into a permanent war and deprives democracy, which has become laughable, of any meaning.

Personally, since the U.S. "leading lights" have held very little attraction for me, I have always declined the tempting offers of positions at certain major universities in the country (Harvard, Yale, UCLA, Denver). But generally speaking, expressing this viewpoint immediately earns you the label of "simple-minded anti-American," a facile anathema that illustrates the cowardly capitulation of media-friendly intellectuals.

From the Atlantic to the Pacific, the United States offers up nothing but an urban desert, which would be absolute if it were not for the inspired invention of Manhattan in the 1920s. Of course, there is Los Angeles, which Barbara Stuckey had us tour via the freeways, only to say, with humor, at the end: "You have visited everything." This inspired an article.[63] Then there is the ultimate: Las Vegas, with its cardboard reconstruction of Rome as third generation Italian-Americans imagine it, with a giant statue of a cross between Bacchus and Nero, spinning and speaking American. We shouldn't forget Disneyland in Los Angeles, where you can admire a world tour sponsored by Bank of America, proudly announcing: "Wherever Bank of America operates, the people are happy!" There is a documentary film—seen by more than a hundred million spectators—"You came here to get rich, you will be rich...." I cannot believe that, if shown in Europe, such a cartoon would be greeted with anything other than whistles from the viewers. More examples can be found of such a ridiculous repertoire unique in the world.

All these sad realities are nothing other, in my opinion, than the ravages of a capitalism that is, unfortunately, purer here than anywhere else. But behind this facade of plastic kitsch, there is still a people, in spite of its political stupidity. Beyond personal friends whom I hold in the highest esteem (such as Sweezy, Harry Magdoff, and Harry Braverman at *Monthly Review*, or Immanuel Wallerstein, Giovanni Arrighi, and A. G. Frank), my feeling—and Isabelle's as well—is that these people are nice (in the positive sense of the term, that is, not nasty). Wandering through the incredible West, stopping at Bagdad Café-type establishments where everything is run-down as in a Third World country, we did not meet embittered, petite bourgeois–type owners as there would have been in Europe in similar situations but rather calm, carefree people—a lot of crazed ones, too! It should be remembered, after all, that the American people are one of only three (with the French and the Swedes) who reacted to the 1930s crisis by moving to the left. The welcome given to José Bové in January 2000 in Seattle reminds us of this people's possibilities.

Yet my intuition is that the initiative for change will not come from the United States, even if it is not impossible that the U.S. wagon might subsequently become hitched to others that will initiate the movement. I had, like others, placed some hope in American blacks. Invited to their caucus during the heroic Black Panther era, which was ultimately held in 1972 in Montreal because it had become impossible to meet openly in the United States, I was able to assess the extent of the intellectual, cultural, and political disaster of which they were the victims, and their inability to formulate the means to overcome it. There were many likable, even amusing actions (such as putting up portraits of Mao in the corridors of the prestigious Hotel Elizabeth II using strong glue!). But no analysis, just purely emotional attitudes interiorizing racism, accepted and returned. Our friend Abdou Moumouni from Niger was seated at Isabelle's feet in a packed room. Some of the caucus organizers were outraged, persuaded that the posture could be interpreted only as a sign of submission. Moreover, Isabelle had to "pass an exam" before being allowed to enter the room. "Would you dare to fire on a white police officer who was attacking us?" Isabelle's matter-of-fact response, "yes, of course," was baffling: in the United States, this was unthinkable. This testifies to the immense depth of racism in this society. I have always thought that the devastating effects of internal colonialism exceeded those of external colonialism. The slavery practiced in the United States thus produced terrible effects compared with those caused by the slavery practiced by Europeans in distant colonies.

Can Canada be something other than an external province of the United States, like Australia? This economist by nature is unable to imagine a different Canada, in spite of English Canada's political traditions and Quebec's cultural rejection of the status quo. But the country's most lucid thinkers not only imagine it, but are working to raise awareness of this requirement. The road will be long and difficult. No matter how likable the people of Quebec are (for Isabelle and me) and however just and important their cultural struggle is, the major political forces of the country—their resistance polarized around the linguistic dimension—do not envisage any delinking of their economy from that of their large neighbor to the south. Obviously, these conditions make a mockery of any autonomy or even independence for Quebec. The United States will be able to continue plundering Canada's immense natural resources until they are exhausted—water, among other items.

### JAPAN

This is a country that is in the exact opposite position: a dominant capitalist economy and a non-European cultural ancestry. Which of these two dimensions will prevail: solidarity with the partners of the triad (the United States and Europe) against the rest of the world, or the desire for independence, sustained by "Asianism"? Analyses—even rambling rhetorical pieces—on this topic could alone make up an entire library.

An economic and geopolitical analysis of the contemporary world leads me to conclude that Japan will continue to follow Washington, just as Germany has done up to now for the same reasons. The currently fashionable globalization is built on an asymmetry between the main partners of the world economy—which is almost never pointed out. The United States continues to show a growing structural deficit in its external trade balance, whereas China and other major capitalist competitors (particularly Germany and Japan) have sizable surpluses. A solidarity of the partners in misfortune is based on this asymmetry. If this asymmetry were to disappear, the entire capitalist structure would sink into indescribable chaos, which humanity could overcome only by beginning to build another system. In addition, this solidarity appears very solid: not only are the ruling classes in Japan and Germany clearly aware of the stakes involved, but even their peoples seem to be willing to accept the price. Why, and until when?

A too easy answer points to the autocratic traditions of these countries, the spirit of submission, the willingness to accept the principle of inequality, and the like. These are historical realities, but like all such realities they are not destined to last forever. A better approach, in my opinion, stresses Washington's strategic options following the Second World War. The United States had then chosen not to "destroy" its two enemies—the only ones to have threatened the inexorable rise of the United States to world hegemon—but, on the contrary, to help them reconstruct and become faithful allies. The obvious reason is that there was, at the time, a real "communist" threat from the USSR and China. By the way, the leaders of the new Russia have not understood this. I heard some of them say that, having chosen capitalism, Russia was now in a similar situation to that of Japan and Germany: it had lost the war, but could win the peace and the economic battle. They ignored the fact that, no longer having any dangerous competitors, the U.S. establishment in this case opted for total destruction of its vanquished enemy. It did so with all the more cynicism since Europe followed suit, not really understanding that it was thereby contributing to making it much more difficult to challenge U.S. hegemony.

Returning to Japan, are there any indications of a popular (not populist in the demagogic sense of the word) and national (not nationalist in the chauvinistic sense of the term) reaction? What do the Japanese people think behind the facade of a glaring conformism so easily caricatured, a facade seemingly hardly touched by the "end of the miracle" and the stagnation of the single ruling party? Japanese society is difficult to understand. The obstacle is partly linguistic. The Japanese translate almost everything written elsewhere (more of my books are sold in Japanese than in French!), but no one or almost no one translates from Japanese. To pierce the mystery, it is necessary to know the Japanese and know them well. I was lucky to be able to get to know the Japanese a little thanks to Kinhide Mushakoji, Masao Kitazawa, Muto Ichiyo, Yoko Kitazawa, and the activists connected to the journal AMPO, and to hear the analyses of old (and young) orthodox and Maoist communists (unknown outside of Japan). Once one has broken through the somewhat rigid formality, one obviously discovers a people like any other. It is a vulnerable people, never sure of itself. The repetitive use of the term "*ne*," the equivalent of "isn't it?" or "isn't that right?," which is characteristic of everyone's speech, probably attests to that.

Invited to the theater—where a dreadful melodrama was playing, which was easy to follow—I observed high-ranking bureaucrats in their coats and ties take out handkerchiefs or tissues because of their profuse tears. Another example of extreme Japanese sensitivity: One day I bought bus tickets for a trip to the interior of the country—into the beautiful mountains around Fujiyama. I had mentally calculated the cost more accurately than the ticket seller with his useless calculator. I pointed this out to him. I believed that he was either going to kill me on the spot or commit suicide. It was a big effort to reassure him that I did not think he was a half-wit. The super-hot baths—which I liked very much—perhaps could also be put down to the permanent anxiety of culturally, if not naturally, worried human beings.

Here are a couple more examples of Japanese character. In a meeting of a UNU committee, a North American was lording it over everyone with all the arrogance of a dimwit. My neighbor—a high-level Japanese academic—began to roar like a lion. I expected him to pull out a samurai sword and slit the throat of that pompous ignoramus. In a low voice, I suggested that very thing as a way of expressing my solidarity. That made him laugh out loud to the point that all the participants were surprised!

I admit not only do I appreciate, but even love Japanese punctuality (I must share the same neurosis). I had been scheduled for an appointment at 3:03 and, obviously, I arrived at exactly that time. I realized that my host had wanted, out of extreme politeness, to put me at ease. The train that served the station arrived at 3:00 and it took two minutes to go from the station to the place of the appointment. If he had invited me to arrive at 3:00, I would had to have run to be on time; if the invitation had specified 3:15, I would have walked around for twelve minutes!

I had the opportunity to systematically visit the country's largest universities (in Tokyo, Yokohama, Nagoya, Kyoto, Osaka) and participated in discussions that I do not think were either commonplace or limited to "technical" questions (scholarly economics, political economy, etc.), to which the Japanese usually limit their foreign guests (with the open intention of benefiting from others without giving anything in return). What I believe I came to understand is that the complacent certitudes suggested by the mask of conformism are less solid than is often thought. Among other things, an "inferiority complex" in relation to China seems to return frequently. We have messed up our modernization, having aped the Westerners; the Chinese will do better (the second part is perhaps questionable, but that is another matter).

Chinese remains the language of cultural reference, a bad English is used only for business relationships. One of my books appeared to me at first sight to be printed in Chinese rather than Japanese. My translator said to me proudly: "This is an important book; I thus wrote it just like the Emperor writes his annual address to the Diet, in Japanese, but with Chinese characters!" Another time, invited to talk to the director of a large newspaper (with an enormous circulation of several million per day), I was surprised that his English was totally inadequate. I asked him, "You don't know a foreign language?" I certainly got a reply to my stupid question: "Yes, like everyone, Chinese and Korean!" Yet the rapprochement with China that this type of thinking might suggest remains quite difficult. First, because the dominant capital in Japan, like dominant capitals everywhere, remains what it is: imperialist. On top of that, the Chinese and Koreans know this, beyond their (justified) mistrust of yesterday's enemy.

### EUROPE

Would there be more of a chance for change to begin in Europe than in the United States or Japan? I think so—intuitively—without underestimating the difficulties given the diversity of the "Europeans." I shall attempt to explain my intuition here.

The first reason for this relative optimism is due to the fact that European nations have a rich and varied history, which can be seen in the incredible accumulation of their imposing medieval remains. My interpretation of this history is certainly quite different from that of the dominant Eurocentrism. I have rejected (and, I believe, refuted) the latter's myths, developing the counter-thesis that the same contradictions found in medieval society, which were overcome by the invention of modernity, existed elsewhere. Yet I equally reject the "anti-European" ranting of some Third World intellectuals who probably want to convince themselves that their societies were richer, more advanced, and even better than those of "backward" medieval Europe. This is to forget that the myth of the backward Middle Ages is itself a product of the later view of European modernity. In fact, if the premodern history of Europe is not better than that of other regions of the world—the historical trajectories are more similar than many think, in my opinion—it is certainly not "worse" or "inferior." In any case, having crossed the threshold of modernity first, Europe acquired advantages that it is absurd to deny.

Europe is, of course, diverse, despite a certain homogenization underway and the "European" rhetoric. Many European observers of the particular characteristics of others, even if they do not reduce them to the common denominator of the empty descriptor "Oriental," nevertheless attempt to relate the observed differences to European "models" taken as reference points. This is due to Eurocentrism. Thus, it is often said for example that Japan is the Prussia of Asia. I had the good fortune to discuss these problems concerning the general and the particular in history with Asian intellectuals (from China and Japan specifically) whose analyses were of great interest. This was partly because they spontaneously reversed the terms of comparison and saw, for example, in Germany a Japanese model, in France and Russia the "China of Europe." This reversal, which was not always subconscious, but deliberate, forces us to think both generalities and particularities in universal terms. This is the method I have tried to implement. What are the positive and negative elements affecting the potential for change in Europe?

England and France are the pioneers of modernity, the two societies that systematically constructed it. This blunt assertion does not mean that modernity did not have earlier roots, particularly in the Italian cities and later in the Netherlands. The contributions of England and France to the construction of the final form of capitalist modernity, far from being similar, developed along different axes even if they can be viewed ultimately as complementary.

England went through a very tumultuous period of its history during the period of the birth of the new (mercantilist) capitalist relations. It changed from medieval "Merry England" into somber Puritan England, executed its king, and proclaimed a republic in the seventeenth century. Then everything was calm. It invented modern democracy in the eighteenth century, albeit with restrictions, and then experienced an accumulation of capital through the Industrial Revolution in the nineteenth century without major upheavals. Certainly this did not happen without class conflict, which culminated in the Chartist movement in the middle of the nineteenth century. But these conflicts were not politicized to the point of calling the entire system into question. And this characteristic appears to have continued up to our time.

France, on the other hand, crossed the same stages through an uninterrupted series of violent political conflicts. It is the French Revolution that invented the political and cultural dimensions of capitalism's contradictory modernity. The French working classes were not as clearly developed as in England, which had the only true proletarians of the time. Yet their struggles were more politicized, beginning in 1793, and then in 1848, 1871, and much later in 1936, when they were organized around socialist objectives, in the strong sense of the term. There was no 1968 in England. There have certainly been many explanations given for these different paths. Marx was quite aware of them and it is no accident that he devoted most of his attention to analyzing these two societies, offering a critique of the capitalist economy from England's experience and a critique of modern politics from France's experience.

Britain's past, perhaps, explains the present, and the patience with which the British people endure the degradation of their society—from the trains (which travel between London and Edinburgh in five and a half hours, which is as long as during Marx's day, and he marveled at it!), poorly heated apartments, prevalent junk food, and visible poverty to the deterioration of education. It is true that education in England had always been more unequal than in France or Germany, and long reserved solely for the aristocracy, which gave it a snobbish tone that persists in its most prestigious universities (Oxford and Cambridge). Industrial England was behind France and Germany in primary education and even in ordinary literacy. Certainly, contemporary England is in the forefront of research in some areas. But at the same time, there is a hollow conventionalism, particularly in the social sciences. All of that has convinced me that the origin of the degradation lies not so much in the "decline of the Empire" and industry (the decline of the latter is more a consequence than cause) than in the weak attachment the British have to the values of equality. In the immediate postwar period, the Labour Party had attempted to get back on course. That page appears to be turned now. Perhaps this passivity is explained by the way British national pride has been shifted to the United States. The latter is not, for the British, a foreign country like others. It remains their prodigal child, though somewhat monstrous. Since 1945, England has chosen to align itself unconditionally with Washington. The extraordinary world domination of the English language helps the English people live this decline without, perhaps, even feeling it to the fullest extent. The English relive their past glory by proxy through the United States. Great Britain remains a key power for Europe's future. While much of its "new left" has slid to the right without hesitation—but that phenomenon is very widespread throughout Europe—a group of British intellectuals are actively contributing to the revival of critical thinking. They should certainly not be considered "dinosaurs" by anyone who sees that neoliberal chaos has no future. This is obviously true of Eric Hobsbawm and some others.

Moreover, London is, in my opinion, one of only three global metropolises, along with Paris and New York. The city by itself is, in my opinion, rather ugly, a result of the demolitions and absence of taste during early Victorian capitalism. But it is a genuine cosmopolitan capital. All the other capitals of the First World—Berlin, Rome, Madrid, Tokyo—are provincial in comparison with the three world cities. The same is true of the Third World megalopolises: Beijing, Mexico City, São Paulo, Cairo, or Mumbai. The number of foreigners in the city is not the criterion for my classification; there are lots of immigrant workers in the whole First World. The cosmopolitanism of the three world capitals has roots in history, and not only colonial and imperial history. You cannot understand Paris without knowing the role this city played in modern painting, for example. You cannot say you know London today and not know about the contribution of foreigners, not know about the problems confronting the innumerable Africans and Asians who move in and out of London, just as others do in Paris. The question of coexistence with the new masses of immigrant workers is a completely different problem. The general tendency is to ghettoize them. But we should note the subtle differences. In England and Germany, as in the United States with the blacks and Hispanics, the separation is more pronounced than it is in France. To be convinced of that, it is sufficient to watch children leaving school at the end of the school day (mixed in France, almost never elsewhere) or the relative number of mixed couples. The effects of France's traditional assimilationist doctrine—unfortunately attacked today in the name of the absurd reactionary right to "difference"—contrasts strongly with the effects of the "communitarian" or even "ethnicist" traditions. Opinion polls are here particularly misleading, belied by the actual facts.

Yet history has no more reached its end in Great Britain than elsewhere. But my feeling is that this country will be able to join any movement of change only if and when it breaks the umbilical cord that still attaches it to the United States. I do not see the least sign of that, for the moment. I asked Hobsbawm about this and he seemed to share my fears.

Could Germany make the move toward genuine change? The parallel I made above between it and Japan, both reliable lieutenants of the United States, the three forming the real triad, the G3 (United States, Germany, and Japan—rather than North America, Europe, and Japan) would not seem to imply that.

Neither Germany nor Italy nor Russia would have succeeded in reaching capitalist modernity without the paths pioneered by England and France. That statement should not be understood to mean that the peoples of these countries would have been, for some mysterious reason, incapable of inventing capitalist modernity, solely reserved to Anglo-French genius. Rather, the possibilities for a similar invention existed only in other areas of the world—China, India, or Japan, for example. But once a people entered into capitalist modernity, it shaped its own path, whether as a new center (as with the European countries mentioned above and Japan) or a dominated periphery.

I interpret the history of Germany—and other countries—using that fundamental method. In this way, I understand German nationalism, pushed by

Prussian ambitions, as a compensation for the mediocrity of the bourgeoisie, deplored by Marx. The result was an autocratic form of managing the new capitalism. Yet despite its ethnicist tone, this nationalism (in contrast with the universalist ideologies found in England and, above all, in France, and later Russia) did not succeed in uniting all Germans (hence the eternal problem of the Austrian Anschluss, still unresolved today). This, then, became a factor that favored the criminal and demented excesses of Nazism. But there was also, after the disaster, a powerful motivation for constructing what some have called "Rhenish capitalism," supported by the United States. This is a capitalist form that deliberately chose democratization copied from the Anglo-French-American model. But it is without deep, local historical roots, even considering the brief existence of the Weimar Republic (the only democratic period of German history) and the ambiguities, to say the least, of socialism in the German Democratic Republic (GDR). Many German friends have confirmed my feelings on the subject, particularly my very dear friend from the former GDR, Joachim Wilke, but also, to a certain extent, the late Otto Kreye and his colleagues at Starnberg: Elmar Altvater, Wolfgang and Frieda Haug, and others.

My explanation is historical, not "atavistic," and history has no end. Today, Germany is facing serious problems. "Rhenish capitalism" is not a "good capitalism" in contrast with the Anglo-American extreme liberal model or the statism of Jacobin France. Each is different, but all suffer from the same illness, that is, a capitalism that has reached a stage characterized by predominance of its destructive aspects. Faced with this challenge, what are the possible German reactions?

In the short term, Germany's position in globalization under U.S. hegemony, just like Japan's, seems to be comfortable. The resumption of expansion to the East through a type of "Latino-Americanization" of the Czech Republic, Poland, Hungary, the Baltic countries, Slovenia, Croatia—the bone with a little meat thrown to Germany by the United States—can nourish the illusion that Berlin's path is sustainable. This choice is easily satisfied with low-intensity democracy and economic and social mediocrity, and is reinforced by support for the European Union and the euro. If the political classes on the Christian Democrat and liberal right and the Social Democrat left continue in their stubborn pursuit of this dead end, we should not exclude the emergence of right-wing, even fascist-type, populisms—of which Haider in Austria is only a prototype—though this does not mean they would necessarily be remakes of Nazism The Berlusconi-Fini-Bossi trio in Italy is not much better. The electoral successes of the National Front in France illustrate the reality of the general danger in Europe. In France, the Bonapartist tradition has triumphed again with Sarkozy, who interprets the Fifth Republic's very reactionary constitution in that way. In the longer term, Germany's difficulties will probably worsen, not improve. German fragility can be summarized in two observations: a declining population (in a quarter of a century, Germany's population will be no greater than that of France and Great Britain) and very limited inventiveness. The German educational system produces good executing agents, but few with creative capacities, as Joachim Wilke pointed out to me, observing further that his small, failing country (the GDR) was better in this area than the prosperous Federal Republic. Germany's current economic assets are based on standard industrial production (mechanical, chemical) that modernize by increasingly incorporating software invented elsewhere. Germany recognizes this, declaring that it is ready to open its doors to Indian computer scientists and mathematicians. Then what? What will happen? The generations pass and the negative past fades. There is always the possibility that the German people will become aware of the necessity of initiating a real change off the beaten track. I believe that if France and Russia were to take more initiative, another future for Europe would be possible. This choice could also lead to a resumption of positive movements for change in Mediterranean and Nordic Europe, which have failed up to now.

Southern Europe was momentarily thrust into the center of critical analysis and action during the "long 1968" of the 1970s. I followed these developments as closely as possible, visited Italy regularly, supported by the networks of *Il Manifesto* beginning in 1970–72 (Luciana Castellina, Rossana Rossanda, Lucio Magri, Valentino Parlato), the critical left, the Lelio Basso Foundation—I had known Lelio well during the period of his active support for liberation movements—the *Punto Rosso* (Giorgio Riolo, Luigi Vinci), and many others. The movement had sufficient power to influence to a certain degree the "center-left" state of the time, despite the withdrawal of the PCI into itself, which did not bode well. Therefore, the Third World Forum succeeded in obtaining support (including financial) from the Italian state, thanks to the dynamic Giuseppe Santoro, whose career was subsequently destroyed in a dubious operation of so-called independent justice that in Italy, as in France, probably implemented a systematic strategy of destroying the political independence of the left. The magnificent seminar organized in Naples at the Castel dell'Ovo in 1983, which I discussed previously, was one of the results of the sympathy expressed by Italian officials for a different policy toward the South than the dominant one found in other countries of the North. Perhaps this was "Third Worldism," as in Portugal, Greece, and Sweden.[64] Yet they were exceptions in Europe.

There were some amusing sides to my visits to Italy. Invited to sign the protocol of financial support to the TWF, my Roman hosts—Andreotti himself, accompanied by others—received me in an incredibly splendid hotel on the coast near Naples: developed from a beautiful old monastery, the bathrooms overlooked the sea that one could admire while soaking in a bath-pool. At dinner, the neighboring table was occupied by two men with white shoes, wearing their Borsalino fedoras during dinner and talking in a low voice, accompanied by two blonde women of glamorous vulgarity. The Mafia, here in its caricatured version, is still present. In Sicily, I traveled through Corleone's famous village with my friend Nicola Cipolla and the mayor of Palermo during a hot afternoon. The streets were deserted, but it was certain that our passage was noted by eyes that continued to watch us from behind closed shutters. But Sicily is not only the country of the Mafia. It is also the country of those who resisted it and, in 1944, were massacred with the open complicity of U.S. authorities. A monument was erected for them: a magnificent block of stone was placed on each spot where one of the hundred victims fell. I found this to be an immensely beautiful idea. In traveling from Palermo to Catania, I made a prolonged stop in the curious "plain of the Albanians" to visit Giorgio Riolo, whose family is originally from this place, where Albanian is still spoken. Sicily is also the only Italian province that makes you feel that you are somewhere else than in Italy: the coincidence of three cultures—Latin, Byzantine, and Arab—has no parallel anywhere else in the Mediterranean world, and produces a moment of exceptional cultural richness. My most moving memory of Italy is the "diploma" I was awarded in 1975 by miners in Sardinia. Their cultural association had chosen to reward me for my book *Unequal Development*.[65] That an association of this type—which usually honors a regional poet or an amateur archaeologist of the area—made their choice a testament to the serious politicization of that time.

This phase of Italian history has probably come to an end. Now we can only examine the weaknesses of the society that made it possible. Our friend Carla de Benedetti explains the incompletely developed sense of national citizenship by the fact that the rulers of the Italian states were most often foreigners. The people generally saw in them only opponents to deceive as much as possible. The Italian nation—which does exist—has not sufficiently overcome this weakness, and perhaps weakened, it has left the door open to the unbelievable involution of the Lombard League. This disaster is linked with the emergence of a populism that feeds on a rising fascism. In Italy, as in France, the struggle for liberation during the Second World War had also been a quasi-civil war. Consequently, the fascists were forced to hide in the decades following 1945 without ever having really disappeared. Yet such an involution is difficult to understand without calling attention to two factors. First, the country's economy, despite the "miracle" that had given Italians a good standard of living—better than that of the British—up until the current crisis, remains fragile. The sometimes eulogistic rhetoric on the "third Italy" and its exceptional "social capital" maintain too much silence on this fragility. Second, European integration as presently constituted (since Maastricht above all) has encouraged the deviation and its illusions. Unreserved support for the European choice, which completely dominates the entire Italian political space, I believe, is the main reason for the dead end in which the country finds itself.

The same unthinking support for the European project as it is has frustrated the radical potential of the popular movements that put an end to fascism in Spain, Portugal, and Greece.

This potential was, it is true, limited in Spain where Francoism simply died from the quiet death of its leader while the transition was being well prepared by the same bourgeoisie that had formed the main support of Spanish fascism. The three components of the workers' and popular movement—socialist, communist, and anarchist—had been eradicated by a dictatorship that continued its bloody repression until the late 1970s, supported by the United States in exchange for anti-communism and the concession of bases to the U.S. military. In 1980, Europe set as a condition for Spain's joining the European Community that it should also join NATO, so that it should accede to the complete formalization of its submission to Washington's hegemony! The workers' movement, which I met as soon as it was possible, attempted to play a role in the transition through its "workers' committees" that formed underground in the 1970s. The Izquierda Unida and its heirs are friends that are still active. It was unfortunately obvious that, not having succeeded in gaining the support of other segments of the popular and intellectual classes, this radical wing of the movement could not prevent the reactionary bourgeoisie from controlling the transition. The feeling of helplessness, perhaps even the change of direction, of former communists like Jorge Semprún (who invited me to Madrid when he was Minister of Culture) or Fernando Claudín (an old acquaintance from the time of his exile in France) can then be understood.

On the other hand, the radical potential of the forces that truly brought down fascism in Portugal and Greece was substantial. The revolt of the armed forces in Portugal that ended Salazarism in April 1974 was followed by a huge popular explosion the backbone of which was formed by communists, both from the official Communist Party and from Maoist currents. The atmosphere in Lisbon, which I visited in the summer of 1974, demonstrated that. Welcomed by the Da Nobregas, family friends from our Bamako days, Isabelle and I visited the magnificent city of Lisbon. For me, this was an opportunity to hold discussions with many of the grassroots leaders of that time, particularly Otelo Carvalho, and to assess the effect that the reading of my works might have on the formation of their strategic thinking. Carvalho led the globalist-internationalist tendency of the Portuguese ruling group and was suspicious—rightly—of "Europe" as it is. The defeat of this tendency within the ruling group and Carvalho's arrest earned me sometime later a strange reception in Lisbon. The police at the airport hesitated to allow me to enter the country. I suggested that they telephone the presidential palace, which was done. Admitted to the country, two days later President Antonio Ramalho Eanes received me and explained (or attempted to do so) that the "European" and "internationalist" choices were not contradictory. He was not very convincing. The reversal played into the hands of the right and replaced the dominance of Lisbon and the country's south, where the left was stronger, with that of the traditional Catholic peasants of the north, which provided most of the Portuguese emigrants in Europe. The leadership of the left consequently passed to all-too-timid socialists. Since then, the political sphere has settled back into sleep and what remains of the revolutionary movements live in nostalgia for the years 1974–75. It would not be a coincidence if the publisher (led by active comrades of "Abril em Maio," Bruno da Ponte, Rodrigues Martines, and Ana Barradas) that published my works in Portuguese decided to call itself "O Dinosauro."

In Greece also, the choice in favor of Europe was not obvious following the fall of the colonels. The Greek people had not forgotten that the fascist regime had, in fact, been supported by the United States and Europe—even if France welcomed, as political refugees, a large number of intellectuals. I got to know them at the Université de Vincennes and my friendship with Kostas Vergopoulos dates back to this time. Among them was also the late Nicos Poulantzas. I met up with them again, as well as others, in leadership positions in Athens. Andreas Papandreou, founder of PASOK, who won the 1980 elections, himself had been the Greek translator of my 1974 *Accumulation on a World Scale* during his Canadian exile.[66] The international choices he made at the time were not, then, without a carefully considered foundation. Even if the communists of the two parties (internal and external) expressed reservations about the person of Papandreou—a "patriarchal-type" leader—and the ill-assorted nature of PASOK, they all shared the heritage of the EAM. During the Second World War, the Communist Party had succeeded, just as in Yugoslavia, in forming a single anti-fascist front. Greece and Yugoslavia not only "resisted" the German invaders, like others did; they continually fought a real war that played a decisive role in the instantaneous collapse of the

Italian armies in 1943, thereby forcing the Germans to station a large number of troops on their territories. The Greek resistance, which became a revolution in 1945, was defeated by the joint intervention of the United States and Great Britain. The Greek right was established in this way, with the approval of Western Europe. It not only had no part in the resistance, but was responsible for integrating the country into NATO (alongside Turkey!), within which the European project was taking shape. That the Greek working classes and their political leaders were suspicious toward the advances made by the EEC from 1980 is thus neither difficult to understand nor groundless.

The large crisis that globalized capitalism has now entered, along with the strategy implemented by the dominant financial monopolies (transfer the brunt of the crisis onto the weaker partners of the system, Greece, among others, in this case), should cause us to examine the strategic error of those who thought, in Greece and elsewhere, that adherence to the European project would offer an unexpected historical chance.

The economic difficulties experienced by Greece under PASOK, combined with pressures from Europe, ended up eroding the hopes placed in the internationalist, neutralist choice, with Third Worldist undertones. Little by little, Greece moved toward closer integration into the new Europe, an integration that, in turn, strengthened the "cosmopolitan" (in the negative sense of the term) comprador bourgeoisie, of which the (sometimes dubious) ship-owners are typical models, and in the face of which PASOK became a powerless socialist party, like elsewhere in Europe. Yet there are some bones that stick in the craw of the Greek people: the dominant position of Turkey in NATO, which has forgiven its aggression against Cyprus without much fuss, and NATO's aggression against Yugoslavia. The dominant media present the people's protests as a manifestation of "orthodox solidarity." That exempts them from analyzing reality—specifically, the contradiction felt by the Greek people between Europe's democratic rhetoric and its alignment with the arch-reactionary United States.

I witnessed a similar turn in the small island of Malta. An interesting and likable country where Arabic is spoken and Catholicism, which returned with the *Reconquista* and the Order of the Knights of Malta, is the dominant religion. Memory of the past is still sufficiently alive for the Maltese to call Lent, the Christian fast before Easter, "Ramadan." The few English words of the current language have been totally Arabized, the plurals "broken." For a cash payment, the word "cash" is used in the singular, but the plural is *cawash* (an Arab reader will understand)! A party of the popular left (the Labor Party), more radical than the members of the socialist family, tinged with communism and in the majority, nourished the hope of a rapprochement with the Arab world. The contempt in which the English held this "semi-Arab" people perhaps encouraged this feeling. But the Arab states—quite insensitively—never responded to the expectations of the Maltese. The only memory they have of the latter is of the second-class colonists who accompanied the British Army. Invited in 1991 by its leader, Mifsud Bonnici, to discuss these problems with the political leadership of the party and government, I felt the wind changing direction. Would Malta be able to resist the European sirens? A few months later, the new Catholic right majority opted for Europe. Cyprus ended up succumbing in the same way, after the era of Patriarch Makarios, friend of the Soviet Union and Nasser, was past. The Cypriot people must miss him today.

For different reasons, the Nordic countries have maintained, up to now, a suspicious attitude with regard to the European project. Sweden was outside of NATO by choice, Finland outside of it by obligation, while Norway and Denmark chose to join NATO.

Under the leadership of Olof Palme, Sweden attempted to follow a globalist, internationalist, and neutralist path. I shall not go over what I have written elsewhere about my early contacts with this country, my participation in the Conference on the Environment (1972), my relations with Palme and SAREC beginning in 1975, and the lecture series that I gave in the country's universities.[67] Sweden at that time was a unique figure in Europe, which I summarized in a brief phrase: "a civilized Soviet Union." My intention was to note that its "state socialist" choice as well as its internationalist sense broke with the dominant tendencies in European social democracy. I made numerous friends in Sweden during this turbulent era. Rolf Gustavson, who had introduced me to various circles, has passed over to liberalism. The TWF owes much to my friend Gerhard Hulcrantz, who always passionately defended our project before SAREC.

The reversal has been quite abrupt, beginning with the country's more recent European choice and the rightward drift of its social-democratic forces. The current rhetoric is well known: the time of the Welfare State is over, we must be like other Europeans, etc. There is nothing original in all this nonsense. This reversal, however, forces us to look more closely at the weak points of Sweden's exceptional experience: Palme's perhaps too personal role, the illusions of the youth who, long confined to this relatively isolated country, belatedly discovered the world with a good dose of naïveté after 1968, but also its somewhat tarnished, and long-hidden, past during the Second World War.

Norway, Finland, and the Netherlands have resisted better, it seems, for various reasons. Institutions in these three countries had, in the past, provided generous support for the Forum.

Norwegian society was formed from small peasants and fishers, without the presence of an aristocratic class as in Sweden or Denmark. Thus it is very much alive to questions of equality. This undoubtedly explains the relative power of its left (communist) party, the AKP, and the radical proclivities of social democratic forces that, up to now, have resisted the European and neoliberal sirens. The Greens appeared in this country before organizing in others and the Norwegian Johan Galtung was a pioneer in ecological thinking. I must mention here Tertit Aasland, who lucidly defended the Forum's project before NORAD with the idea of strengthening the universalist-globalist tendency active in public opinion. In contrast, the country's membership in NATO and the financial affluence from North Sea oil (an affluence that is somewhat corrupting in the long term) certainly counteract these positive tendencies.

The independence that Finland gained without a struggle during the Russian Revolution (Lenin had already unhesitatingly accepted it) was less the product of a unanimous demand than is often admitted. The Grand Duchy already benefited from a large degree of autonomy in the Russian Empire, which was considered quite satisfactory by opinion at the time. Its ruling classes served the tsar with as much sincerity as those of the Baltic countries (the tsar's statue in Helsinki was never removed). The working classes were not oblivious to the program of the Russian Revolution. That is why independence did not settle the country's problems, which were dealt with only at the end of the civil war, in the end barely won by the reactionary forces (with the support of imperial Germany and later the Allies). These forces later drifted toward fascism and became allies of the fascist powers during the Second World War. However, given what the Soviet Union became, Finland's independence was certainly positive in the end. What is called "Finlandization," which NATO propaganda presented as unacceptable, was only a neutralism (certainly imposed originally by the peace treaty) that could have formed one of the bases for a better European reconstruction than that of the Atlanticist alliance. The presence today of a Finnish left grouped in the Left Wing Alliance is, in my opinion, the expression of a potential that has not disappeared. I have had the opportunity to discuss all these problems with the leaders of this group. Will European pressures, which have triumphed in the monetary area (with Finland's participation in the euro), succeed in eating away at this interesting historical heritage?

Can one expect anything from Denmark with an economy that is too dependent on Germany? This dependence is experienced neurotically, as can be seen in the ambiguous and confused series of votes on the question of the euro. But it does not seem that it can be called into question by a quite standard social democracy. My friends Jacques and Hélène Hersch, like those of the "red-green alliance," are rather isolated.

It is well known that the Netherlands was the site of the original bourgeois revolution in the seventeenth century, before England and France. But the modest size of the United Provinces prevented this country from achieving what its competitor students were able to do. Yet the heritage of this history is far from being lost. The Netherlands is not only a democracy that, although bourgeois, is at the forefront of tolerance and freedom, but it is also a cosmopolitan country (in the positive sense of the term) and Amsterdam is—on a small scale—what London and Paris are, world capitals, not so much because of the proliferation, now quite common, of "exotic" restaurants and immigrants as by its atmosphere and some of its institutions, such as the Institute for Social Studies, the Transnational Institute, and the Amsterdam School for Social Research. I have not, then, been surprised to find effective support for the Forum's activities in this country (the Forum owes much to my friend Hans Slot). Nevertheless, today the economic and financial system of the Netherlands functions within the mark/euro environment.

In the 1970s and 1980s, I thought that the formation of a north-south "neutralist" axis in Europe, made up of Sweden, Finland, Austria, Yugoslavia, and Greece, was possible, with positive effects on the countries of both Western and Eastern Europe. It could have encouraged the former to rethink their Atlanticist alignment and might have found a favorable echo in France. Unfortunately, de Gaulle was no longer there and the Gaullists had completely forgotten the general's reservations about NATO. Such an axis might have opened up possibilities for East European countries to move toward center left positions and thereby avoid their later fall to the right. This project might have initiated the construction of an authentic "other Europe," truly social and thus open to the formulation of a socialism for the twenty-first century that respected its national components, was independent of the United States, and facilitated a reform worthy of the name in Soviet Bloc countries. This construction was possible, concomitant with the Europe of Brussels, at that time consisting only of a still limited economic community. I was even able to present these ideas to the leadership of Finland's united left and Swedish social democracy, to Chancellor Bruno Kreisky in Vienna, the Yugoslav government, and PASOK in Greece. I even had the impression that the idea did not displease them. But there was no follow-up.

The European lefts have not properly assessed the stakes and have supported the development of the European project led by Brussels. This has been a reactionary project from the beginning, devised by Monnet (whose fiercely anti-democratic opinions are well known, as shown in the 2006 writing of Jean-Pierre Chevènement).[68] The European project, along with the Marshall Plan devised by Washington, was designed to rehabilitate rightist forces (under the cover of "Christian democracy") or even fascists, reduced to silence by the Second World War, so as to nullify any scope for the practice of political democracy. The communist parties understood that. But at the time, the alternative of a "Soviet" Europe was already no longer credible. Their later unconditional adherence to the project was no better, even though it was disguised as "Eurocommunism."

Today, not only has the European Union trapped the peoples of the continent in an impasse, consolidated by the "liberal" and Atlanticist (NATO) choice, but it has even become the instrument for the "Americanization" of Europe, substituting the U.S. culture of "consensus" for the European tradition's political culture of conflict.[69] The ultimate adherence of Europe to Atlanticism is not unthinkable, based on the awareness of the advantages from exploiting the planet for the benefit of the triad's collective imperialism. The "conflict" with the United States turns around sharing the booty, hardly more. What I call the "alter-globalization of the *bobos*" (to use a term from Parisian jargon that refers to segments of the middle classes from the opulent countries in question) perhaps clearly expresses this tendency. If ever the project were carried out against everyone, then the European institutions would become the main obstacle to the progress of Europe's peoples. My long-held thesis is that the more a society is impregnated with capitalist "values" (the market as king; the individual that is formed by that market viewing him or herself as supreme), the more difficult it will be to overcome them.

European reconstruction, then, requires the deconstruction of the current project. Is it thinkable today to question the European-Atlanticist project such as it is and construct an alternative Europe that would be both social and non-imperialist with regard to the rest of the world? I think so, and even think that the beginning of an alternative project originating from anywhere would find favorable echoes throughout Europe in a short period of time. An authentic left, in any case, should not think otherwise. If it dares to do so, then I am one of those who believe that the European peoples can demonstrate that they still have an important role to play in shaping a future world. Short of that, the strongest probability is the collapse of the European project into chaos, which would not displease Washington. In any case, whether with its "constitution" or in chaos, Europe is busily eliminating its place in the world. Europe will be socialist, if the left forces dare to make it so, or it simply will not be.

THIS TEXT WAS ORIGINALLY WRITTEN at the beginning of the 2000s, and I have only made minor updates that did not change the central argument. I did not imagine at the time that subsequent events were going to lend force to my fears so quickly. I refer here to the chapter that I devoted to the crisis of the euro and, behind it, the crisis of the European system itself in *The Implosion of Contemporary Capitalism*. Yet how are the European peoples reacting to the challenge? It is clear that in the opinion of most people, it is not necessary to deconstruct the European system; they prefer to bury their heads in the sand and convince themselves that the current European system is reformable.

# APPENDICES

## MANIFESTO OF THE WORLD FORUM FOR ALTERNATIVES

## PROGRAM FOR THE WFA/TWF FOR 2014–2015

## THE BAMAKO APPEAL

## Manifesto of the World Forum for Alternatives: It Is Time to Reclaim the March of History

**It is time to reclaim the march of history.**
Humanity's future is at stake. Scientific progress and technical advances, the supreme achievements of knowledge, fortify the privilege and comfort of a minority. Instead of contributing to the well-being of all, these feats are used to crush, marginalize, and exclude countless human beings. Access to natural resources, especially in the South, is monopolized by the few and is subject to political blackmail and threats of war. *It is time to reclaim the march of history.*

**It is time to make the economy serve the peoples of the world.**
The economy provides goods and services mainly to a minority. In its contemporary form, it forces the majority of the human race into strategies for abject survival, denying tens of millions of people even the right to live. Its logic, the product of neoliberal capitalism, entrenches and accentuates grotesque inequalities. Propelled by faith in the market's self-regulating virtue, it reinforces the economic power of the rich and exponentially increases the number of the poor. *It is time to make the economy serve the peoples of the world.*

**It is time to break down the wall between the North and the South.**
Monopolies of knowledge, scientific research, advanced production, credit and information, all guaranteed by international institutions, create a relentless polarization both at the global level and within each country. Trapped in patterns of development that are culturally destructive, physically unsustainable, and economically submissive, many people throughout the world can neither define for themselves the stages of their evolution, establish the basis of their own growth, nor provide education for their younger generations. *It is time to break down the wall between the North and the South.*

**It is time to confront the crisis of our civilization.**
The confines of individualism, the closed world of consumption, the supremacy of productivism, and, for many, an obsessive struggle for sheer daily survival obscure humanity's larger objectives: the right to live liberated from oppression and

exploitation, the right to equal opportunities, social justice, peace, spiritual fulfillment and solidarity. *It is time to confront the crisis of our civilization.*

### It is time to refuse the dictatorship of money.

The concentration of economic power in the hands of multinational corporations weakens, even dismantles, the sovereignty of States. It threatens democracy—within single countries and on global scale. The dominance of financial capital does more than imperil the world's monetary equilibrium. It transforms states into mafias. It proliferates the hidden sources of capitalist accumulation, drug trafficking, the arms trade, and child slavery. *It is time to refuse the dictatorship of money.*

### It is time to replace cynicism with hope.

Stock prices soar when workers are laid off. A competitive edge is gained when mass consumerdom is replaced with elite niche markets. Macroeconomics indicators react positively as the ranks of the poor multiply. International economic institutions coax and compel governments to pursue structural adjustment, widening the chasm between classes and provoking mounting social conflict. International humanitarian aid trickles to those reduced to despair. *It is time to replace cynicism with hope.*

### It is time to rebuild and democratize the state.

The program of dismantling the state, reducing its functions, pilfering its resources, and launching sweeping privatizations leads to a demoralized public sector, weakened systems of education and health, and the eventual usurping of the state by private economic interests. Neoliberal globalization divorces the state from the population and encourages corruption and organized venality on an unprecedented scale: The state becomes a repressive instrument policing the privilege of the few. *It is time to rebuild and democratize the state.*

### It is time to re-create the citizenry.

Millions of people are deprived of voting rights because they are immigrants. Millions more fail to vote because they are angry or discouraged, because parties are in crisis or because they feel impotent and excluded from political life. Elections are often distorted by influence-mongering and deceit. But democracy is about more than elections. Democracy means participation at every level of economic, political, and cultural life. *It is time to re-create the citizenry.*

### It is time to salvage collective values.

Modernity, conveyed by capitalism and ideologized by neoliberalism, has destroyed or profoundly corrupted existing cultures. It has imploded solidarities and dismantled convictions, extolling instead the high-performance individual evaluated on the basis of economic success. Rather than bringing emancipation to the peoples of the world, modernity is generating a crisis in education, fueling social violence, and triggering an explosion of insular movements that seek salvation and protection in nationalist, ethnic, or religious identity politics. *It is time to salvage collective values.*

### It is time to globalize social struggles.

In all this, it is not the internationalization of the economy per se that is to blame. It could represent a dramatic step forward for material, social, and cultural exchanges between human beings. But in its neoliberal form it becomes a nightmare lived by the victims of unemployment, young people traumatized by the future, workers shut out of the productive system, and nations subjected to structural adjustment, labor deregulation, the erosion of social security systems, and the elimination of networks serving the poor. It purports to link and unite, yet separates and imprisons. *It is time to globalize social struggles.*

### It is time to build on peoples' resistance.

Across the world, people are organizing resistance, engaging in social struggles and creating alternatives. Women, men, children, unemployed people, excluded and oppressed people, workers, landless peasants, communities suffering from racism, impoverished city dwellers, indigenous peoples, students, intellectuals, migrants, small business people, outcasts, declining middle classes—citizens—are asserting their dignity, demanding respect for their human rights and natural heritages, and practising solidarity. Some have given their lives for these causes. Others practice heroism in their day-to-day existence. Some are rebuilding knowledge on the basis of the concrete situations, some are trying out new economic forms, some are creating the basis of a new kind of politics, and some are inventing new cultures. *It is time to build on peoples' resistance.*

### Now is the time for joining forces.

Convergence of struggles, of knowledge, of resistances, of innovations, of minds and hearts for a world of justice and equality, invention and material progress, optimism and spiritual development. We can build this world by seeking and discovering viable alternatives to neoliberalism and unilateral globalization, alternatives based on the interests of peoples and respect for national, cultural and religious differences. *Now is the time for joining forces.*

### A time of creative universal thought has arrived.

Honest, probing analysis of the current economic organization and its economic, social, ecological, political, and cultural consequences can only delegitimize this phenomenon which is paraded to the world as the paragon of progress. The search for a balance between personal initiative and the pursuit of collective goals—based on a celebration of human diversity and creativity—must open the way to new models. Studies of expanding non-market sectors, productive techniques that respect the well-being of those who use them, and the organization and nature of work will help create more human forms of organization. *A time of creative universal thought has arrived.*

**The time to rebuild and extend democracy is here.**
Democracy is no longer merely a goal for the organization of societies. It is also the key for the functioning of communities, social movements, political parties, businesses, institutions, nations and international bodies. It is progressively experienced as an essential contribution to the respect of popular interests, and the preservation of national and international security. By prising open spaces for all cultures—not patronizingly, but because they represent humanity's endowment—we can reverse the retreat into enclaves of narrow self-interest and the seclusion of identity politics. The existence of democratic, competent, and transparent states is considered the basis for restoring their power to regulate. Regional economics and political groupings based on international complements are viable answers to the real needs of the population and a necessary alternative to neoliberal globalization. Strengthening and democratizing regional and international institutions is a realistic imperative. It is a condition for progress in international law and the indispensable regulation of economic, social, and political relations at the global level, particularly in the fields of financial capital, taxation, migration, information, and disarmament. *The time to rebuild and extend democracy is here.*

—CAIRO, 1997

# Program for the WFA/TWF for 2014–2015
*From the Algiers Conference, September 2013*

This symposium resulted in rich discussions that revolved around a central axis: the question of the "sovereign project," understood as the need for the peoples and states of the contemporary world to overhaul their policy choices (economic, social cultural, management of power, etc.) in a way that allows them to distance themselves from the pattern of globalization unilaterally imposed by the monopolies of the imperialist centers of the historically and still dominant triad, raising themselves to the rank of active agents in shaping the world, in initiating new forms of just and sustainable development.

The symposium provided an overview of the multiple facets of the challenges of building a "sovereign project": defining the means by which economic policies can end the processes of dispossession and impoverishment that are intrinsic to the logic of capitalism, ensuring instead the sharing of the benefits of development in favour of the popular classes; defining the means of exercising political power that paves the way for real and progressive democratization of societies; defining the means for guaranteeing the sovereignty of peoples and states, paving the way for a polycentric negotiated globalization and not one unilaterally imposed by the powerful for their own exclusive profit.

The discussions revealed that the "sovereign projects" of those countries of the South, referred to as "emerging," leaving aside the diversity of their origin and the efficiency of their results, fall far short of the requirements of social development, as they emerge from pathways that are based on the fundamental logic of capitalism, a logic that is itself founded on forms of development of productive forces that are destructive of human beings and nature.

The order in which the five following themes are presented here does not imply an order of priority.

### Theme 1: What do we mean by "sovereign projects"?

The very notion of the "sovereign project" must be a subject for discussion. Given the level of penetration of transnational investments in all sectors and in all countries, one cannot avoid the question: what kind of sovereignty is being referred to?

i. The global conflict for access to natural resources is one of the main determinants of the dynamics of contemporary capitalism. The examination of this particular aspect should not be embedded in other general considerations. The dependence of the United States for numerous resources and the growing demands of China constitute a challenge for South America, Africa, and the Middle East, which are particularly well endowed with resources and shaped by the history of the pillage of those resources. Can we develop national and regional policies in these domains as the beginning of a rational and equitable global management of resources that would benefit all peoples? Can we develop new relations between China and the countries of the South that subscribe to such a perspective, linking access to these resources by China with support for the industrialization of the countries concerned (that which the so-called donors of the OECD refuse to do)?

ii. The framework for the deployment of an effective sovereign project is not limited to the fields of international action. An independent national policy remains fragile and vulnerable if it does not have real national and popular support, which requires it to be based on economic and social policies that ensure that the popular classes are beneficiaries of "development." This is the price of the social stability that is the condition for the success of the sovereign project against the political destabilization of the imperialist project. We must therefore examine the nature of relationships between existing or potential sovereign projects and the social bases of the system of power: a national, democratic, and popular project, or an illusory project of national capitalism?

iii. We will attempt to provide, in this context, a "balance sheet" of "sovereign projects" that have been implemented by "emerging" countries. Among other things, we consider:

- The characteristics of the project of China: their various possible futures. State capitalism based on the illusion of a leader of the national bourgeoisie, or state capitalism with a social dimension, evolving toward a "state socialism," itself a step on the long road to socialism?
- Is there a sovereign project being implemented in India and Brazil? Contradictions and limitations.
- Can we say that there is no sovereign project in South Africa? What are the conditions for a sovereign project to emerge in this country? Relationship with the rest of Africa?
- Can non-continental countries develop sovereign projects? What are their limits? What forms of regional coming together could facilitate such progress?

### Theme 2: Exiting from financial globalization

Warning: this is only on the financial aspect of globalization, not globalization in all its dimensions, in particular, commercial.

One assumes that this is the weak link in the established neoliberal globalized system. We therefore consider:
- The question of the future of the dollar as the universal currency, taking account of the growing external debt of the United States.
- The question related to the perspectives of "full convertibility" of the yuan, ruble, and rupee (see paper by Samir Amin on the debate about the yuan).
- The issue of "exit convertibility" of certain currencies in emerging countries (Brazil, South Africa).
- Measures that could be taken in the field of management by fragile countries of their national currency (particularly in Africa).

### Theme 3: Thwarting the geopolitical and geostrategic plans of the United States and its allies of the triad

Our starting point is the following: the pursuit of global domination by the capitalist monopolies of the historic imperialist powers (United States, Europe, Japan) is threatened by the growing conflicts between (1) the objectives of the triad (to maintain its domination); and (2) the aspirations of emerging countries and the revolt of the peoples who are the victims of neoliberalism.

Under these conditions the United States and its subordinate allies, partners in the "collective imperialism of the triad," have chosen the headlong rush ahead through the use of violence and military interventions:
- Deployment and strengthening of U.S. military bases (Africom and others)
- Military interventions in the Middle East (Iraq, Syria, tomorrow Iran?)
- Military encirclement of China, provocations by Japan, issues of the conflicts of China / India and China / Southeast Asia

But though it seems that violent interventions by imperialist powers remain on the agenda, evidence of them being part of a coherent strategy as a condition for eventual success is increasingly hard to find. Is the United States at bay? Is the decline of this power a passing phase or decisive? The responses of Washington, which are apparently decided from one day to the next, do not make them less dangerously criminal.

What political (including military) strategies could reduce the United States' project of military control of the planet?

### Theme 4: The civilization project, toward a second wave of the emergence of states, nations, and peoples of the peripheries

Preparations for the future, even if far away, begin today. It is good to know what we want. What model of society do we want? Founded on what principles? The destructive competition between individuals or the affirmation of the advantages of solidarity? The liberty that gives legitimacy to inequality or the liberty associated with equality? The exploitation of the planet's resources without regard for the future or by taking into consideration the precise measure of what is needed for the reproduction of the conditions of life on the planet?

The future must be seen as the realization of a higher stage of universal human civilization, not merely a more "fair" or more "efficient" model of civilization as we know it (the "modern" civilization of capitalism).

First hurdle for the organization of the debate: the risk of staying on the ground of wishful thinking, a remake of the utopian socialism of the nineteenth century. To avoid this we should ensure the participation of highly competent people on the following topics:

- What anthropological and sociological scientific knowledge today interrogates the "utopias" formulated in the past?
- What is our new scientific knowledge about the conditions for the reproduction of life on the planet?
- Can we integrate this knowledge in an open Marxist thought?

Second pitfall: avoiding dealing with only these problems while dealing with those concerning the ways and means for advancing in this direction.

In this framework we give space to projects on the emergence of states and of peoples in Asia, Africa, and Latin America. The first wave of emergences, which was successfully deployed between 1950 and 1980, was exhausted. The new situation resulted in the imperialist powers seeking to regain the initiative and impose their "diktat" (not the so-called consensus) of Washington. In its turn this savage globalization project is imploding, giving the peoples of the peripheries an opportunity to engage in a second wave of liberation and progress. What could the objectives of this second wave be? Different political and cultural visions (reactionary, illusory, progressive) compete here. We will need to study the opportunities. We subscribe to the radical alternative perspective paving the way for overcoming capitalism.

### Theme 5 : Organization of struggles: the unity and diversity of active progressive forces

We come back here to the ongoing and major political questions concerning political parties, unions, movements, and struggles, leadership, the vanguard, etc.

These ongoing issues of modern history have always inspired various theoretical and practical responses, even conflicting ones. In certain periods, the ambition to unite all the progressive forces in action has taken front stage. At other times, as in our times, diversity has paralyzed the effectiveness of struggles and left the opposition the advantage of taking the initiative. The present is characterized, in my (Samir Amin's) opinion, by the deployment of the process of "generalized proletarianization, segmented and diversified in the extreme," concretely different from one I refer to here in my writings concerning these transformations and the audacious strategies needed to address the challenge.

## Modalities of Implementation

The project for continuing our discussions, based on our discussions in Algiers, and avoiding reproducing once again another "colloque d'Alger," is to propose a series of meetings to deepen the analysis and proposals for action on some specific questions. We will keep to the five themes mentioned above for the moment, without prejudice to any other suggestions offered by colleagues of our networks.

The format of these meetings should be designed to lead to breakthroughs in our thinking. The number of participants should be limited (15?), chosen on the basis of their competence in the relevant field. Preparation for the meeting will require drafting and circulation of introductory papers for discussion.

# The Bamako Appeal

More than five years of worldwide gatherings of people and organizations who oppose neoliberalism have provided an experience leading to the creation of a new collective conscience. The social forums—world, thematic, continental, or national—and the Assembly of Social Movements have been the principal architects of this conscience. Meeting in Bamako, Mali's capital, on January 18, 2006, on the eve of the opening of the Polycentric World Social Forum, the participants during this day dedicated to the fiftieth anniversary of the Bandung Conference have expressed the need to define alternate goals of development, creating a balance of societies, abolishing exploitation by class, gender, race, and caste, and marking the route to a new relation of forces between North and South.

The Bamako Appeal aims at contributing to the emergence of a new popular and historical subject, and at consolidating the gains made at these meetings. It seeks to advance the principle of the right to an equitable existence for everyone; to affirm a collective life of peace, justice and diversity; and to promote the means to reach these goals at the local level and for all of humanity.

In order that a historical subject come into existence—one that is diverse, multipolar, and from the people—it is necessary to define and promote alternatives capable of mobilizing social and political forces. The goal is a radical transformation of the capitalist system. The destruction of the planet and of millions of human beings, the individualist and consumerist culture that accompanies and nourishes this system, along with its imposition by imperialist powers are no longer tolerable, since what is at stake is the existence of humanity itself. Alternatives to the wastefulness and destructiveness of capitalism draw their strength from a long tradition of popular resistance that also embraces all of the short steps forward indispensable to the daily life of the system's victims.

The Bamako Appeal, built around the broad themes discussed in subcommittees, expresses the commitment to:

i. Construct an internationalism joining the peoples of the South and the North who suffer the ravages engendered by the dictatorship of financial markets and by the uncontrolled global deployment of the transnational firms;
ii. Construct the solidarity of the peoples of Asia, Africa, Europe and the Americas confronted with challenges of development in the twenty-first century;

iii. Construct a political, economic, and cultural consensus that is an alternative to militarized and neoliberal globalization and to the hegemony of the United States and its allies.

## THE PRINCIPLES

1. **Construct a world founded on the solidarity of human beings and peoples.** Our epoch is dominated by the imposition of competition among workers, nations and peoples. However, historically the principle of solidarity has played a role much more conducive to the efficient organization of intellectual and material production. We want to give to this principle of solidarity the place it deserves and diminish the role of competition.

2. **Construct a world founded on the full affirmation of citizenship and equality of the sexes.** The politically active citizen must ultimately become responsible for the management of all the aspects of social, political, economic, and cultural life. This is the condition for an authentic affirmation of democracy. Without this, the human being is reduced by the laws imposed on him or her to a mere provider of labor power, an impotent spectator confronted with decisions handed down by those in charge, a consumer propelled toward the worst waste. The affirmation, in law and in deed, of the absolute equality of sexes is an integral part of authentic democracy. One of the conditions of this democracy is the eradication of all forms of the patriarchy, either admitted or hidden.

3. **Construct a universal civilization offering in all areas the full potential of creative development to all its diverse members.** For neoliberalism, the affirmation of the individual—not that of the politically active citizen—allows the spread of the best human qualities. The capitalist system's unbearable isolation, imposed on the individual, produces its own illusory antidote: imprisonment in the ghettos of alleged common identities, most often those of a para-ethnic and/or para-religious type. We want to construct a universal civilization that looks to the future without nostalgia; one in which the political diversity of citizens and cultural and political differences of nations and peoples become the means of reinforcing individual creative development.

4. **Construct socialization through democracy.** Neoliberal policies aim to impose as the sole method of socialization the force of the market, whose destructive impact on the majority of human beings no longer needs to be demonstrated. The world we want conceives sociability as the principle product of a democratization without boundaries. In this framework, in which the market has a place but not the predominant place, economy and finance should be put at the service of a societal program; they should not be subordinated to the imperatives of dominant capital that favor the private

interests of a tiny majority. The radical democracy that we want to promote reestablishes the creative force of political innovation as a fundamental human attribute. It bases social life on the production and reproduction of an inexhaustible diversity, and not on a manipulated consensus that eliminates all meaningful discussions and leaves dissidents weakened and trapped in ghettoes.

5. **Construct a world founded on the recognition of the non-market-driven law of nature and of the resources of the planet and of its agricultural soil.** The capitalist neoliberal model aims at submitting all aspects of social life, almost without exception, to the status of a commodity. The process of privatization and marketization to the ultimate degree brings with it devastating results on a scale without precedent in human history: the threat to the fundamental biogeochemical processes of the planet; destruction of biodiversity through the undermining of ecosystems, the waste of vital resources (oil and water in particular); the annihilation of peasant societies threatened by massive expulsion from their land. All these areas of society-nature metabolism must be managed as the common wealth and in accordance with the basic needs of all of humanity. In these areas, the decisions must be based not on the market but on the political powers of nations and peoples.

6. **Construct a world founded on the recognition of the non-market-driven status of cultural products and scientific acquisitions, of education and of health care.** Neoliberal policies lead to turning cultural products into commodities and to the privatization of the most important social services, notably those of health and education. This option is accompanied by the mass production of low-quality para-cultural products, the submission of research to the exclusive priority of short-term profits, the degradation of education and health care for the poorest sectors of the people, including even their exclusion. The reinstatement and expansion of these public services should reinforce the satisfaction of needs and rights essential to education, health care, and providing food.

7. **Promote policies that closely associate democracy without preassigned limits, with social progress and the affirmation of autonomy of nations and peoples.** Neoliberal policies deny the preconditions of social progress—that some claim are a spontaneous product of the market—preconditions such as the autonomy of nations and peoples, necessary to the correction of inequalities. Under the regime of market hegemony, democracy is emptied of all effective content, made vulnerable and compromised in the extreme. To affirm an authentic democracy demands giving to social progress its determining place in the management of all aspects of social, political, economic, and cultural life. The diversity of nations and of peoples produced by history, in all its positive aspects along with the inequalities that accompany them,

demands the affirmation of autonomy of peoples and nations. There does not exist a unique universal recipe in the political or economic spheres that would permit any bypassing of this autonomy. The task of building equality necessarily requires a diversity of means to carry it out.

8. **Affirm the solidarity of the people of the North and the South in the construction of an internationalism on an anti-imperialist basis.** The solidarity of all the peoples—of the North and of the South—in the construction of a universal civilization cannot be founded on the illusory notion that it is possible simply to ignore the conflicts of interest that separate different classes and nations that make up the real world. Such genuine solidarity must necessarily transcend the antagonisms inherent to capitalism and imperialism. The regional organizations behind the alternative globalization movement must seek to strengthen the autonomy and the solidarity of nations and of peoples on the five continents. This perspective is in contradiction to that of the present dominant model of regionalization, conceived as consisting of mere building blocks of neoliberal globalization. Fifty years after Bandung, the Bamako Appeal calls for a Bandung of the peoples of the South, victims of really existing capitalism, and the rebuilding of a peoples' front of the South able to hold in check both the imperialism of the dominant economic powers and U.S. military hegemony. Such an anti-imperialist front would not oppose the peoples of the South to those of the North. On the contrary, it would constitute the basis of a global internationalism associating them all together in the building of a common civilization in its diversity.

## LONG-TERM OBJECTIVES AND PROPOSALS FOR IMMEDIATE ACTION

In order to progress from a collective conscience to the building of collective, popular, plural, and multipolar actors, it has always been necessary to identify precise themes to formulate strategies and concrete proposals. The themes of the Bamako Appeal deal with the following ten fields, including both long-term goals and proposals for immediate action: the political organization of globalization; the economic organization of the world system; the future of peasant societies; the building of a workers' united front; regionalization for the benefit of the peoples; the democratic management of the societies; gender equality; the sustainable management of the resources of the planet; the democratic management of the media and the cultural diversity; democratization of international organizations.

The Bamako Appeal is an invitation to all the organizations of struggle representative of the vast majorities that comprise the working classes of the globe, to all those excluded from the neoliberal capitalist system, and to all people and political forces who support these principles to work together in order to put into effect the new collective conscience, as an alternative to the present system of inequality and destruction.

### PROPOSALS OF THE BAMAKO APPEAL

Only by building synergies and solidarity beyond geographical and regional borders is it possible to find methods of action that can lead to real alternatives in this globalized world. Working groups will continue during the year to inquire further into and concretize the topics addressed below, to prepare for the next meeting and to propose strategic priorities for action.

*1. For a Multipolar World System Founded on Peace, Law, and Negotiation*

In order to imagine an authentic multipolar world system that rejects the control of the planet by the United States of America and guarantees the whole gamut of rights for politically active citizens, allowing the people to control their destinies, it is necessary to do the following:

1. Reinforce the movement protesting against war and military occupations, as well as solidarity with the people engaged in resistance in the hot spots of the planet. In this respect, it is crucial that the world demonstration against the war in Iraq and the military presence in Afghanistan envisaged for March 18 and 19, 2006, coincide with:
   - calls for the prohibition of the use and the manufacture of nuclear weapons and destruction of all the existing arsenals;
   - calls to dismantle all the military bases outside of national territory, in particular the base in Guantánamo (U.S.-occupied Cuba);
   - calls for the immediate closing of all the CIA-run prisons.
2. Reject any interventions by NATO outside Europe and require that the European partners dissociate themselves from U.S. "preventive" wars, while engaging in a campaign intended to dissolve NATO.
3. Reaffirm solidarity with the people of Palestine, who symbolize resistance to world apartheid, as expressed by the wall establishing the divide between "civilization" and "barbarism." For this purpose, to give priority to reinforcing the campaigns that demand the demolition of the wall of shame and the withdrawal of Israeli troops from the occupied territories.
4. Widen the solidarity campaigns with Venezuela and Bolivia, since these are places where people are building new alternatives to neoliberalism and crafting Latin-American integration. Besides these campaigns, it would also be advisable to:
   - set up of a network of researchers, working in close connection with associations of militants acting at the local level, to build extensive and up-to-date databases concerning U.S. and NATO military bases.

Precise information on these military and strategic questions would make it possible to increase the effectiveness of the campaigns carried out to dismantle them;
- create an observer group, an "Imperialism Watch," which would not only denounce wars and war propaganda, but also expose all operations and pressures, economic and otherwise, exerted on the peoples of the world;
- create a worldwide anti-imperialist network that could coordinate a variety of mobilizations throughout the planet.

### 2. For an Economic Reorganization of the Global System

With the goal of developing an action strategy for transforming the global economic system, it is necessary to:
1. Reinforce the protest campaigns against the current rules of operation of the World Trade Organization (WTO) and to define alternative rules (for the removal of the WTO from agriculture, services, intellectual property);
2. Create working groups, which build relations with existing social associations and movements that have already undertaken this work over an extended period, to establish, in the most serious and exhaustive manner possible, an inventory of proposals for alternative measures in the most fundamental economic areas:
   - the organization of the transfer of capital and technology;
   - the proposal for regulations (codes of investments, for example) specifying the rights of nations and workers;
   - the organization of the monetary system: control of the flow of capital (in particular speculative capital), suppression of tax havens, construction of regional systems of management of the stock exchanges and their connection to a renovated world system (calling in question the role of the IMF and the World Bank, returning to the principle of the rule of national laws to define the local economic system, overcoming the obstacles imposed by the unnegotiated decisions of international organization, etc.);
   - the development of a true legislation concerning foreign debts (requiring that national states provide audits allowing people to identify illegitimate debts) and the reinforcement of the mobilization, in the very short term, for the cancellation of Third World debt;
   - the reform of social services and their financing, including education, health, research, retirements.
3. Create groups of expert researchers who can follow the evolutions of the movements of capital and mechanisms of dependence of national financial capital on international financial capital.

4. Create working groups, with internet site and news groups, by country and area, for the study of the structures of capitalist property, and the mechanisms by which capitalism operates in each country and its relationship with the international financial system.
5. Create places to educate journalists and inform them about the complex mechanisms of neoliberal globalization.
6. Establish contacts, in the form of connected internet sites, between various associations of economists, progressives, and militants engaged in the search for alternatives to neoliberal globalization in each world region (Asia, Africa, Latin America, Oceania, Europe, North America).

### 3. For Regionalizations in the Service of the People and to Reinforce the South in Global Negotiations

Starting from the assumption that free trade, while supporting strongest countries and transnational monopolies, is the enemy of genuine regional integration and that the latter cannot be carried out according to the rules of free trade, it is necessary to create the conditions for an alternative means of cooperation within each great area; for example, a revival of the Tricontinental, always in close connection with the action of the social movements.

In Latin America, to confront the aggression of the multinationals the workers have proposed the demand for regional integration from a new point of view, based on cooperative advantages, instead of on comparative advantages. Such is the case of the alternative experiments of cooperation in the South regarding oil (Petrocaribe), reduction of the debt (repurchase of debts between countries of the South) or of education and health (Cuban doctors), for example. In fact, this cooperation, meant to support the growth and solidarity of all countries, must be based on political principles and not on the rules imposed by the WTO.

In Africa, hopes for unity are very strong, as is the consciousness that resistance and development are impossible while countries are isolated and confronted with pressures from neoliberal globalization. The many institutions of integration, however, are ineffective there, and the most active are those inherited from the periods of colonization and apartheid. The African Union and its economic and social program (NEPAD) do not include any idea of collective resistance. It is in this context that civil societies must become aware of the need to overcome their divisions.

For the North African countries bordering the Mediterranean Sea, the Euro-Mediterranean Accords constitute an additional example of regionalization carried out to impose dependency on the South.

In Asia, to confront neoliberal globalization, despite the difficulties, popular initiatives to carry out another type of regional integration have succeeded in beginning to join together a number of civil society organizations and NGOs in the majority of the countries, leading in particular to the development of a popular charter aiming to reinforce cooperation in trade.

Consequently, it seems appropriate to recommend, besides an intensification of the campaigns against wars and the threats of wars, the following proposals:

1. For Latin America: to widen the support campaigns to the ALBA to make sure the U.S. strategy of ALCA fails; to promote independence and the development in justice and equity among peoples and to integrate based on cooperation and solidarity and with the ability to adapt to specific needs of these two latter characteristics; to mobilize the social movements so as to broaden and deepen the processes of alternative integration, such as with Petrocaribe or Telesur; to promote trade in the context of a logic of cooperation; and to strengthen the coordination of social and political action organizations to implement these recommendations.
2. For Africa: to sensitize the movements of civil society to the need to formulate alternative proposals for African initiatives; to take into account the need for coordinating actions undertaken on regional and national levels; to launch campaigns for peace to put an end to the existing conflicts or to prevent the risks of new conflicts; to depart from designs of integration founded on race or culture.
3. For Asia: to thwart the expansion and the competition of capital among countries and to reinforce solidarity between working classes of the various countries; to promote the local circuit between production and consumption; to promote sciences for rural reconstruction.

To be effective, cooperation among countries of the South must express solidarity with the peoples and governments that resist neoliberalism and seek alternatives from the point of view of a multipolar world system.

### 4. For the Democratic Management of the Planet's Natural Resources

The concept of "natural resources" must be subordinated to that of sustainability, and thus of the right to a decent life for both present and future generations, with the goal of stopping the devastation and plunder of the planet. What is involved here is a vital principle and not a simple management of natural resources. These resources cannot be used beyond their renewal or replacement capacity, and should be employed in accordance with the needs of each country. Criteria for their use must be defined so as to guarantee genuine sustainable development, which means preserving biodiversity and intact ecosystems. It is also necessary to encourage the development of substitutes for nonrenewable resources. The commodification of life results in wars over oil, water, and other essential resources. Agribusiness gives the advantage to the culture of exploitation and profits over the culture of ecological sustainability (and the meeting of subsistence needs). It imposes technical methods which produce dependency and destruction of the environment (contracts of exploitation to impose certain material methods of production: machinery, chemical fertilizers and pesticides, and imperial seeds—along with GMO).

Concretely, two levels of actions on the environment must be combined: micro and macro. At the macro level, which relates to the national governments, it would be desirable that an interstate framework of multilateral dialog should have the ability to put political pressure on the national governments to take global measures. The micro level concerns local or regional actions, where civil society has an important role to play, in particular to disseminate information and to change practices in order to save resources and protect the environment. The local level must be at all times be reinforced, as decisions are too often considered only at the macro level. The following actions could result from this:

1. Constitute an international court charged with considering ecological crimes: the countries of the North and their local clients could then be sentenced to pay reparations to the countries of the South (ecological debts);
2. Disallow as illegal contracts that force farmers to be dependent on the suppliers of seeds, a situation that leads to technological slavery and the destruction of biodiversity;
3. Abolish "pollution rights" and their sale and purchase and oblige the rich countries to decrease their production rate of carbon dioxide (now 5.6 tons per person per year in the United States) and allow the poor countries (now 0.7 tons per person per year for the non-G8 countries) to industrialize;
4. Prohibit the building of dams (insofar as they are really necessary) without compensation for the displaced populations (economic refuges);
5. Protect the living and genetic resources from being patented by the North, which impoverishes the countries of the South. This process constitutes a colonial-type theft;
6. Fight against the privatization of the water, which the World Bank promotes, even in the form of private-public partnership (PPP) and to guarantee a minimum quantity of water per person while respecting the rhythm of renewal of groundwater;
7. Create a group to Observe the Environment (Ecology Watch) prepared to denounce and respond to those actions characterized as aggression against the environment.

### 5. For a Better Future for Peasant Farmers

In the domain of peasant agriculture, there are initially medium- and long-term objectives related to food sovereignty, which are simultaneously at the national, international, multilateral (that of the WTO) and bilateral levels (Economic Partnership Agreements or EPA, negotiated between the African, Caribbean, and

Pacific or ACP countries and the European Union). Then, at the national level, this also involves agricultural pricing and marketing policy (more than structural policy)—the access of the farmers to the means of production and first of all, the land. In the very short term, in 2006, what is necessary is preventing the completion of the Doha Round, and the refusal to conclude the EPAs. For this purpose, the proposals here relate to two axes: the means to achieve food sovereignty in the medium term and as a precondition imposing a setback on the Doha Round and EPAs.

**Proposals to assure food sovereignty:** Food sovereignty involves granting to each national state (or group of states) the right to define its internal agricultural policy and the type of connection it wishes to have with the world market, along with the right to protect itself effectively from imports and to subsidize its farmers—with the proviso that it is prohibited from exporting agricultural produce at a price lower than the average total production cost excluding direct or indirect subsidies (upstream or downstream). Food sovereignty is the lever that makes it possible for all countries to regain their national sovereignty in all areas. It is also a tool to promote democracy since it requires the participation of all the various forces in agro-alimentary production in defining its objectives and means, starting with the family farmers. It thus implies regulatory action on the national, subregional, and international levels.

**At the national level:** The national states must guarantee access of the peasant producers to the productive resources, and first of all to the land. It is necessary to stop promoting agribusiness and the monopolization of the land by the national bourgeoisies (including government officials) and transnational firms to the detriment of the peasant producers. That implies facilitating investments in family farms and improving the local products to make them attractive to consumers. Access to land for all the peasants of the world must be recognized as a basic right. Implementing this right requires adequate reforms of the land systems and sometimes agrarian reform.

To share the objective of food sovereignty with the urban consumers—an essential condition to have the governments participate—three types of actions should be carried out:

1. Restrict actions of the merchants that penalize the farmers and consumers.
2. Hold public awareness campaigns for consumers regarding the immense harm done to agriculture and to the economy as a whole by dependence on imported products, which are virtually the only products sold, for example, in the supermarkets of West Africa.
3. Gradually raise farm prices by promoting the right to import, but only in such a way as to avoid penalizing consumers with very limited purchasing power.

This must be accompanied by the distribution of coupons to the poorer consumers that allows them to purchase local foodstuffs at the old price, similar to what is done the United States, India and Brazil—while awaiting an increase in productivity of the farmers to cause a drop in their unit production costs, enabling them to lower their selling prices to the consumers.

**At the subregional level:** So that the national states can recover their full sovereignty, and first of all their food sovereignty, regional political integration is unavoidable for the small countries of the South. For this purpose, it is necessary to reform the current regional institutions, in particular, in Africa, the West African Economic and Monetary Union, and the Economic Community of West African States (UEMOA and CEDEAO in their French initials), which are much too dependent on the various mega-powers.

**At the international level:** To pressure the United Nations to recognize food sovereignty as a basic right of national states, one essential to implement the right to food as defined in the Universal Declaration of Human Rights of 1948 and the International Treaty of 1996 relating to economic, social, and cultural rights. At this level, four regulatory instruments of international agricultural trade should be established to make food sovereignty effective:

1. Protect against irresponsible, socially destructive imports, one founded on variable deductions that can guarantee a high-enough fixed entrance price to assure minimum domestic farm prices adequate to secure farmers' investments and banks' loans; customs duties alone are insufficiently protective with regard to strongly fluctuating world prices, a fluctuation worsened by that of fluctuating exchange rates.
2. Eliminate all forms of dumping, by prohibiting any export priced below the total average production cost of the exporting country, excluding direct or indirect subsidies.
3. Set the mechanisms of international coordination of price controls, so as to avoid structural overproduction and to minimize conjunctural overproduction that collapses farm prices.
4. Get agriculture away from WTO control by entrusting the international regulation of agricultural trade to an institution of the United Nations, possibly the Food and Agricultural Organization (FAO). In particular, reform its organization on the tripartite model of the International Labor Organization (ILO), which would associate to this regulation the representatives of agricultural trade unions (International Federation of Agricultural Producers and Via Campesina) besides representatives of the agro-alimentary firms (which act already in the shadows on the governments negotiating with the WTO) and of the national states.

APPENDIX                                                                                              453

**Short-term proposals to prevent the Doha Round and the Economic Partnership Agreement:** A major lesson of the ministerial Conference of the WTO in Hong Kong is that the governments of Brazil and India, and with them G-20, abandoned the interests of the populations of the Third World and appeared the most determined promoters of neoliberal globalization. Since the Doha Round is a "total package" (individual undertaking), there is a way to cause its failure. International civil society, and first of all the country-wide organizations of the North and the South, will be able in a media campaign to show that these subsidies (particularly of the "green box"), are an instrument of dumping much more significant than the explicit subsidies for exports, and they will be still more significant starting in 2014 when the export subsidies are eliminated.

*6. To Build a Workers' United Front*

Two of the principal weapons in the hands of workers are the right to vote and the right to form trade unions. Up to now democracy and trade unions were built mainly within the national states. Now, however, neoliberal globalization has challenged the workers the world over, and globalized capitalism cannot be confronted at the national level alone. Today, the task is twofold: to strengthen organizing on a national level and simultaneously globalize democracy and reorganize a worldwide working class.

Mss unemployment and the increasing proportion of informal work arrangements are other imperative reasons to reconsider the existing organizations of the laboring classes. A world strategy for labor must consider not only the situation of workers who work under stable contracts. Employment out of the formal sectors now involves an increasing portion of workers, even in the industrialized countries. In the majority of the countries of the South, the workers of the informal sector—temporary labor, informal labor, the self-employed, the unemployed, street salespeople, those who sell their own services—together form the majority of the laboring classes. These groups of informal workers are growing in the majority of the countries of the South because of high unemployment and a two-sided process: on the one hand, the decreasing availability of guaranteed employment and increased informal employment, and on the other hand, the continuous migration from the rural areas to the towns. The most important task will be for workers outside the formal sector to organize themselves and for the traditional trade unions to open up in order to carry out common actions.

The traditional trade unions have had problems responding to this challenge. Not all the organizations of the workers—except in the formal sectors—will necessarily be trade unions or similar organizations and the traditional trade unions will also have to change. New perspectives for organizing together, based on horizontal bonds and mutual respect, must develop between the traditional trade unions and the new social movements. For this purpose, the following proposals are submitted for consideration:

1. An opening of the trade unions toward collaboration with the other social movements without trying to subordinate them to the traditional trade-union structure or a specific political party.
2. The constitution of effectively transnational trade-union structures in order to confront transnational employers. These trade-union structures should have a capacity to negotiate and at the same time have a mandate to organize common actions beyond national borders. For this purpose, an important step would be to organize strong trade-union structures within transnational corporations. These corporations have a complex network of production and are often very sensitive to any rupture in the chains of production and distribution, that is, they are vulnerable. Some successes in the struggles against the transnational corporations could have a real impact on the world balance of power between capital and labor.
3. Technological development and structural change are necessary to improve living conditions and eradicate poverty, but the relocations of production are not carried out today in the interest of the workers; instead, they are exclusively profit-driven. It is necessary to promote a gradual improvement of the wages and working conditions, to expand local production along with local demand and a system of negotiation to carry out relocation in other ways than simply following the logic of profit and free trade. These relocations could fit under transnational negotiation in order to prevent workers of the various countries from being forced to enter in competition with each other in a relentless battle.
4. Consider the rights of migrant worker as a basic concern by ensuring that solidarity among workers in trade unions is not dependent on their national origin. Indeed, segregation and discrimination on ethnic or other bases are threats to working-class solidarity.
5. Take care so that the future transnational organization of the laboring class is not conceived as a unique, hierarchical and pyramidal structure, but as a variety of various types of organizations, with a network-like structure with many horizontal bonds.
6. Promote a labor front in reorganized structures that also include workers outside the formal sector throughout the world, capable of taking effective coordinated actions to confront globalized capitalism.

Only such a renewed movement of workers, worldwide, inclusive and acting together with other social movements will transform the present world and create a world order founded on solidarity rather than on competition.

## 7. For a Democratization of Societies as a Necessary Step to Full Human Development

Progressive forces must reappropriate the concept of democracy, because an alternative, socialist society must be fully democratic. Democracy does not come from on high. It is a process of cultural transformation, because people change through their practice. It is thus essential that activists in popular movements and in left or progressive governments understand that it is necessary to create spaces for real participation both in workplaces and in neighborhoods. Without the transformation of people into protagonists of their history, the problems of the people—health, food, education, housing—cannot be solved. The lack of political participation contributed to the fall of the socialist countries of Eastern Europe. The citizens of these countries were hardly motivated to defend regimes where they were observers and not actors.

The struggle for democracy must also be linked to the struggle to eradicate poverty and all forms of exclusion. Indeed, to solve these problems, the people must become wielders of power. That implies waging a struggle against the logic of capitalist profit and erecting in its place, in whatever areas that can be won, a different, humanist logic of solidarity. It is no longer enough to just assert the need for an alternative society; it is necessary to propose popular initiatives that are alternatives to capitalism and that aim to break the logic of commerce and the relations that this dynamic imposes.

But this also involves organizing struggles that cannot be reduced to simple economic demands, as necessary as these are, and that put forward an alternative social project, including real levels of authority and democracy, going beyond the current forms of parliamentary representative democracy and its elections. We must struggle for a new type of democracy, coming from below, for those on the lowest levels of society, through local governments, rural communities, workers fronts, politically active citizens. This democratic practice of solidarity will be the best way to attract new sectors of society to the struggle for a fully democratic alternative society.

In order to concretize these principles, the following broad outline is proposed:

- Insert democracy into the totality of the conditions that characterize movements of emancipation and liberation, in their individual and collective dimension.
- Recognize that the failures of the Soviet system and the regimes that arose from decolonization resulted largely from their denial of freedom and their underestimation of the value of democracy. The development of alternatives must integrate this fact and give preeminence to building democracy.
- Contest the hypocritical words of the dominant powers, which are all too ready to give lessons in democracy. U.S. imperialism's cynicism is

particularly unbearable, as its agents reveal themselves as torturers, warmongers, and violators of liberty. Despite this, U.S. cynicism should not serve as a pretext to limit freedom and the exercise of democracy.

- Reject the dominant conception of democracy advanced by the United States and the Western powers. Democracy cannot be defined as accepting the rules of the market, subordinating oneself to the world market, to multiparty elections controlled from abroad, and to a simplistic ideology of human rights. This type of neoliberal democracy blocks genuine democracy by arbitrarily tying the importance of free elections and the respecting of human rights to demands for an expansion of the market economy. The curtailment of democracy in this way, which puts the market first, perverts its meaning.
- Recognize that there is a strong dialectic between political democracy and social democracy, because political democracy is incomplete and cannot last if inequalities, exploitation, and social injustice persist. Social democracy cannot progress without struggle against oppression and discrimination, while still keeping in mind that no social policy can justify the absence of freedom and disrespect of basic rights.
- Affirm that democracy requires an effective and increasing participation of the population, producers, and inhabitants. This implies transparency in decision making and in responsibilities. It does not diminish the importance of representative democracy. On the contrary, it completes and deepens it.
- Since democracy must facilitate the struggle against poverty, inequalities, injustice, and discrimination, it must reserve a strategic position for the poor and oppressed, their struggles and their movements. In this sense democracy in the operation of these movements contributes to their survival and successes.
- Democracy in the anti-globalization (or other-globalization) movement is an indication of the importance the movement attaches to democracy in its orientations. It indicates a renewal of the political and organizational culture, with particular attention given to the question of authority and hierarchy. For this purpose, one proposal for immediate action is to lead a campaign so that the movements for popular education have an important role in civic education in democracy and that this dimension be present in teaching.

Let us recall, indeed, that the anti-globalization movement is carrying a fundamentally democratic project. It asserts the access for all to fundamental rights. These include civil and political rights, in particular the right to freedom of organization and expression that are the bases of democratic freedoms. It also asserts the economic, social, cultural and environmental rights that are the foundation of social democracy. It finally asserts collective rights and the rights of the people to struggle against oppression and violence imposed on them. It is a question here of defining a program to implement democracy.

The anti-globalization movement also recognizes the importance of public services as one of the essential means to guarantee access to equal rights for all. It defends the struggles of workers and users of these public services. It promotes proposals coming out of movements to defend them, in education and health. For example, in health, access to a list of free drugs, the rejection of monopolies, the dictatorship of patents and their attempts to put living organisms under control of a patent.

The struggle for democracy must take account of various levels of intervention. We will examine five of these levels: enterprise, local democracy, national democracy, larger regions, and worldwide democracy. For each of these levels, an action can be proposed as illustration. The choice of the priorities will be the result of debate over strategy:

1. Democracy in the enterprise is a major demand. It implies the recognition of the authority of workers, users and territorial and national collectives. It necessitates the rejection of the shareholders' dictatorship and the destructive logic of finance capital. It leads to control of decisions, and in particular to making them on a local level. The development of innovative forms of self-organization and mutualization is one way to assert the plurality of forms of production and to reject the false evidence that private capitalist enterprises are the most efficient. The movement demanding social and environmental responsibility from companies is of great interest, in spite of the risks of cooptation, on the condition that it leads to putting enforceable public standards into international law.

2. Local democracy responds to the demand for proximity and participation. It bases itself on local institutions that must guarantee public services and that provide an alternative to neoliberalism. It puts the satisfaction of the needs at the local level ahead of arrangements for companies on the world market. It makes the acquisition of citizenship possible, in particular through residence, and its consequences in terms of voting rights.

3. National democracy remains the strategic level. The questions of identities, borders, respect of the rights of minorities and the legitimacy of institutions form the bases of popular sovereignty. Public policies can be the arena of confrontation against neoliberalism. The progressive redistribution of wealth based on taxation should be defended and extended. Measures like a minimum income and retirement based on solidarity between the generations are not reserved for the rich countries, but flow from the division between profits and the income of labor specific to each society.

4. The larger regions can spread neoliberal policies everywhere, as in the European Union, or can demonstrate counter-tendencies or provide sites

of resistance, as the development of Mercosur and the failure of the Free Trade Area of the Americas (FTAA—English, ALEA—French, ALCA—Spanish, Portuguese) shows. From this point of view, the continental social forums have considerable responsibility.

5. Worldwide democracy is a prospect for response to widespread neoliberal policies. In the current situation, the mobilizations with the highest priorities to be carried by the anti-globalization movement are: cancellation of the debt, fundamental questioning of World Trade Organization (WTO—English, OMC—French), suppression of tax havens, international taxation particularly on financial capital (transfers of capital, profits of the transnational firms, etc.), a radical reform of the international financial institutions (with in particular the principle of one country, one vote), the reform of the United Nations in respect of the rights of the people and the rejection of preventive war.

We should create a Democracy Observation Post, which is able to resist the hegemony of the dominant countries, primarily the United States, with its duplicitous discourse on democracy; to encourage citizen control; to promote the democratic forms invented and implemented by the social movements and politically active citizens.

## 8. For the Eradication of All Forms of Oppression, Exploitation, and Alienation of Women

The forms of the patriarchy are multiple, like its bonds with imperialism and neoliberalism. It is important and necessary to analyze its impact on women. Patriarchy refers to the domination of the father/patriarch and is used to describe a family model dominated by men, who have authority over all other members of the family. This model is certainly not universal, a number of African societies having been matrilineal or dual, with paternal and maternal lineages, each having their own roles for an individual. This patriarchal system expanded with the rise of monotheistic religions along with colonial ideologies and legislation.

Today, patriarchy specifically designates domination by males and inequality between genders to the detriment of women, and their multiple forms of subordination. The family, which socializes the child, remains primarily for the "domestication" of girls and women. This imposition of a hierarchy of the genders is all the more marked in that it is supported by cultural standards and religious values leading to the appropriation of women's productive and reproductive capacities. The state reinforces this patriarchal structure with its policies and family codes. Discrimination persists in relations within the family, in education, in access to material, financial and natural resources, in employment, in participation in political power, etc. Despite a perceptible advance in women's rights, male domination is still firmly in place with the "masculinization" of institutions that constitute neoliberal organizations.

The analysis of the relationship between patriarchy and imperialism and the balance sheet of the struggles of women against these systems leads us to propose several actions:

1. Break with the practice of placing the women's question on the side. This practice leads to a political and scientific apartheid. Since the question of gender cuts across many arenas, it must be taken into account in every recommendation.
2. Continue lobbying organizations of civil society and the political community, in order to reinforce the alliance between feminist organizations and progressive forces and to insert in the progressive agenda appeals in favor of women, including:
   - Struggle against the image of their inferior position in the social, political, cultural and religious discourse of the global society;
   - Develop education and training of women in order to break the internalization of this position of inferiority;
   - Spread a better consciousness of their active roles in society;
   - Encourage men to question this masculine domination in order to deconstruct its mechanisms;
   - Reinforce legal provisions for an effective equality between the genders;
   - Increase women's equal representation in institutions (parity).
3. Render visible the history of women, their individual and collective actions, notably:
   - The nomination of Mille women, established by some associations in Hong Kong, for the 2005 Nobel Peace Prize;
   - The campaign of Women Say No to War against the war in Iraq;
   - Various campaigns on current subjects or social projects.
4. Promote the basic right of the women to control their bodies and their brains, to control decisions relating to their life choices: education, employment, various activities, but also sexuality and child-bearing (right to contraception, choice to have a child, right of abortion)—as women's bodies are the site for all sorts of oppression and violence.
5. Support theoretical reflection, starting from feminine experiences, to counter male domination in order to reinforce the perspectives of women on various questions affecting society and in order to open new horizons for research and action. Women's perspectives need to be cultivated particularly on matters of population (such as the Population Conference in Cairo in 1994), or environment (as in the Earth Summit in Rio de Janeiro in 1992), where women demanded the right to live in a healthy environment.

6. Develop databases and an internet site on the relationship between women and imperialism and neoliberalism.

*9. For the Democratic Management of the Media and Cultural Diversity*

**For the right to education:** Before the right to culture, the right to information and the right to inform, the fundamental problem of the right to education arises. This right, though it is officially recognized everywhere, remains ineffective in many countries, and particularly for young women. It is thus a priority for all social movements to pressure governments to fulfill their most elementary obligations in this field.

**For the right to information and the right to inform:** The right to obtain information and the right to inform enter in contradiction with the general logic of how the media are structured. Through their increasing concentration on a worldwide scale, the media are not only the direct recipients of the benefits of neoliberal globalization, but also the carriers of its ideology. It is thus necessary to fight tooth and nail to throw sand into the gears of this machinery for "formatting" the human spirit, machinery whose goal is to make the neoliberal order appear not only inevitable but even desirable. For this purpose, campaigns must be launched in each country, within the framework of an international coordination:

- for legislative initiatives aimed at fighting against media concentration;
- for legislative initiatives aimed at guaranteeing the autonomy of the editors as opposed to the shareholders and owners, by encouraging, where they do not exist, the creation of journalists' associations with real power to act;
- for education encouraging criticism of the media in the school system and popular organizations.

**To support the alternative media:** The alternative media and the nonprofit media, in all their forms (print, radio, television, internet), already play an important role in delivering pluralist information not subject to the diktats of finance capital and multinational corporations. This is why it is necessary to demand that governments create legal and tax conditions from which these media can benefit. A watchdog group of the Alternative Media could identify the most advanced laws existing in the world today. Just as the owners and directors of the large media do, it would be useful for the alternative media to organize each year a worldwide meeting of the people responsible for the alternative media, possibly within the framework of the process of the World Social Forums.

**Don't allow the television networks of the North a monopoly of the images broadcast to the world:** The large networks of international television of North, like CNN, have profited for a long time from a de facto monopoly and have presented a view of the world corresponding to the interests of the dominant powers. In the Arab world, the creation of Al-Jazeera, with great professionalism, made it possible to break with the one-sided vision of Middle Eastern conflicts. The recent launching of Telesur makes it possible for Latin America to be seen not exclusively through the prism of the North American media. The creation of an African network meets an identical need, and all effort must be made to assure that it is born.

**For the right to express oneself in one's language:** The first way to recognize all the expatriate elites of the planet is by their use of English. There is a logical bond between the voluntary or resigned submission to the U.S. superpower and the adoption of its language as the sole tool for international communication. Today Chinese and the Romance languages have the right—if one promotes mutual comprehension within the large family that they form—and tomorrow Arabic will have as much a right to play in parallel the role English does. It is a question of political will. To fight against "all-English," the following measures should be encouraged:

- Create a goal within the educational systems, if conditions allow, of teaching two foreign languages (and not only English) for active and passive competence (understand, speak, read, write) and one or two other languages for passive competence (to read and understand orally).
- Put into practice, in the education systems, methods to teach mutual comprehension of the Romance languages (Spanish, Catalan, French, Italian, Portuguese, Romanian—which are official languages in sixty countries). When each one speaks his/her own language and understands that of the conversational partner that communication is most efficient.
- Make teaching and promotion of the national languages a political priority of the African Union.
- Create an international fund to support the translation of the maximum number of documents in the languages of the countries that have low incomes, in particular so that they are present on the internet.

*10. For the Democratization of International Organizations and the Institutionalization of a Multipolar International Order*

The United Nations is a peoples' institution, and for this reason represents a step forward. But it also reflects the balance of power among national states, whose impact can prove to be ambivalent, even negative, regarding certain peoples or under certain circumstances. Changes in the UN are thus necessary, insofar as the hegemony of the most powerful countries enables them to use the UN for their own purposes. Consequently, we propose the following initiatives:

1. Democratize the area referred to as the United Nations.

2. Initiate "reforms" of the UN with a goal of limiting the inequalities of the balance of power among national states.
3. Act on the governments that constitute the UN, and for this reason, constitute within each country an observer group that permits a demonstration of the actions of the governments within the United Nations, its specialized organizations, and the authorities created by the Bretton Woods meeting (the IMF, the World Bank, WTO).
4. Refinance the specialized organizations such as the FAO or the WHO, to avoid their dependence upon transnational corporations.
5. Ensure a wide and effective presence of social movements and non-governmental organizations within the international institutions.
6. Promote International Courts of Justice, in particular concerning the economic crimes, while preventing them from being manipulated by the dominant powers, and, at the same time, constitute courts of popular opinion in order to promote alternative means of establishing justice.
7. Democratize the United Nations, increase the power of the General Assembly, and democratize the Security Council in order to break the monopolies (right of veto, nuclear powers).
8. Promote a United Nations that allows for regionalization that is equipped with real powers on the various continents. It is in particular proposed to promote a Middle East Social Forum, gathering the progressive forces of the countries of the area to seek alternative solutions instead of the U.S. project of the Greater Middle East.
9. Promote inside the UN respect for the sovereignty of national states, especially vis-á-vis the actions undertaken by the IMF, the World Bank, and the WTO.
10. Promote a world Parliament of the People to bring humanity out of the vicious circle of poverty.

# Notes

1. Samir Amin, *L'Éveil du sud: L'Ère du Bandoung, 1955–1980: Panorama politique et personnel de l'époque* [The South's Awakening: The Bandung Era, 1955–1980: Political and Personal Panorama of the Era] (Pantin: Le Temps des Cerises, 2008).
2. Samir Amin, *A Life Looking Forward: Memoirs of an Independent Marxist*, trans. Patrick Camiller (London: Zed, 2006).
3. Ibid., 169–81.
4. See Samir Amin, "Révolution ou décadence? La crise du système impérialiste contemporain et celle de l'Empire romain" [Revolution or Decadence: The Crisis of the Contemporary Imperialist System and That of the Roman Empire], *Review: A Journal of the Fernand Braudel Center* 4/1 (1980): 155–67.
5. See Samir Amin, *Ending Capitalism or Ending the Crisis of Capitalism?*, trans. Victoria Bawtree (Oxford, UK: Pambazuka Press, 2011).
6. Samir Amin, *Beyond US Hegemony: Assessing the Prospects for a Multipolar World*, trans. Patrick Camiller (London: Zed, 2006); see the chapter on India.
7. Samir Amin, *The Law of Worldwide Value*, trans. Brian Pearce and Shane Mage (New York: Monthly Review Press, 2010), 135–44.
8. See Mathis Wackernagel and William Rees, *Our Ecological Footprint: Reducing Human Impact on the Earth* (Gabriola Island, Canada: New Society Publishers, 1996); François Houtart, *Agrofuels: Big Profits, Ruined Lives and Ecological Destruction*, trans. Victoria Bawtree (New York: Pluto Press, 2010); John Bellamy Foster, *Marx's Ecology: Materialism and Nature* (New York: Monthly Review Press, 2000).
9. Samir Amin, *Eurocentrism*, 2nd ed., trans. Russell Moore and James Membrez (New York: Monthly Review Press, 2009).
10. Samir Amin and Ali El Kenz, *Le Monde arabe: Enjeux sociaux, perspectives méditerranéennes* [The Arab World: Social Issues and Mediterranean Perspectives] (Dakar: Forum du Tiers Monde/Forum mondial des alternatives; Paris: L'Harmattan, 2003), 6–8, 61–71.
11. Samir Amin, *L'hégémonisme des États-Unis et l'effacement du projet euro-*

*péen: Face à l'OTAN, le combat pour un monde multipolaire et démocratique* [U.S. Hegemony and the Failure of the European Project: The Fight for a Multipolar and Democratic World Against NATO] (Paris: L'Harmattan, 2000).

12. Gilbert Achcar, *The Arabs and the Holocaust: The Arab–Israeli War of Narratives*, trans. G. M. Goshgarian (London: Saqi, 2011).
13. Samir Amin, *The Reawakening of the Arab World: Challenge and Change in the Aftermath of the Arab Spring* (New York: Monthly Review Press, 2016).
14. Hassan Riad [Samir Amin], *L'Égypte nassérienne* [Nasser's Egypt] (Paris: Minuit,)
15. Samir Amin and Karim Mroué, *Communistes dans le monde arabe* [Communists in the Arab World] (Pantin: Le Temps des Cerises, 2006).
16. Samir Amin, *The Maghreb in the Modern World*, trans. Michael Perl (Baltimore: Penguin, 1970).
17. Samir Amin, *Re-Reading the Postwar Period: An Intellectual Itinerary*, trans. Michael Wolfers (New York: Monthly Review Press, 1994).
18. Samir Amin, *The Reawakening of the Arab World*.
19. Bahar Kimyongur, *Syriana: La conquête continue* [Syriana: The Ongoing Conquest] (Brussels: Investig'Action; Charleroi: Couleur Livre, 2011).
20. Samir Amin and Catherine Coquery, *Histoire économique du Congo, 1880–1968: Du Congo français à l'Union douanière et économique d'Afrique centrale* [Economic History of the Congo, 1880–1968: From the French Congo to the Customs and Economic Union of Central Africa] (Paris: Anthropos, 1974).
21. See Amin, *A Life Looking Forward*, 74, 184.
22. Samir Amin, "The Future of Southern Africa," *Journal of Southern African Affairs* 2/3 (1977): 355–70.
23. See Amin, *A Life Looking Forward*, 70.
24. Ibid., 204.
25. Samir Amin and Joseph Vansy, *L'Ethnie à l'assaut des nations: Yougoslavie, Éthiopie* [Ethnicism versus the Nation: Yugoslavia and Ethiopia] (Paris: Harmattan, 2002).
26. Samir Amin, ed., *Les Luttes paysannes et ouvrières face au defies du 21ème siècle* [Peasant and Worker Struggles in the Face of 21st Century Challenges] (Paris: Les Indes Savantes, 2005).
27. Amin, *A Life Looking Forward*, 13.
28. Ibid., 117.
29. Yash Tandon, *Ending Aid Independence* (Oxford: Fahamu, 2008).
30. Hein Marais, *South Africa: Limits to Change* (London: Zed, 2001).
31. Anna Bednik, "Bataille pour l'uranium au Niger" [Battle for Niger's Uranium], *Le Monde diplomatique* 651 (June 2008): 16.
32. See Amin, *Eurocentrism*.
33. Samir Amin, *Le Défis de la mondialisation* [The Challenges of Globalization] (Paris: L'Harmattan, 1996).
34. See Amin, *Beyond U.S. Hegemony*, chapter on India.
35. Benjamin Araújo, Christine Cabasset-Sémédo, and Frédéric Durand, *Timor-Leste contemporain* [Contemporary Timor Leste] (Paris: Les Indes Savantes, 2014).

36. See Amin, *A Life Looking Forward*, 224–25.
37. Ibid., 225–27.
38. Régis Debray, *Revolution in the Revolution? Armed Struggle and Political Struggle in Latin America* (New York: Monthly Review Press, 1997).
39. See Amin, *A Life Looking Forward*, 221–22.
40. Samir Amin and François Houtart, "Trois defis pour les Forums sociaux" [Three Challenges for the Social Forums], *Le Monde diplomatique* 624 (May 2006): 31.
41. See Amin, *A Life Looking Forward*, 42–46.
42. Ibid., 63.
43. Ibid., 191–92.
44. See Amin and Vansy, *L'Ethnie à l'assaut des nations: Yougoslavie, Éthiopie*.
45. See Amin, *Beyond US Hegemony*.
46. Samir Amin, "La Russie dans le système mondiale: Géographie ou histoire?" [Russia in the World System: Geography or History?] *Review: A Journal of the Fernand Braudel Center* 21/2 (1998): 207–19.
47. See Amin, *Beyond US Hegemony*, chapter on China.
48. For more insights, see Samir Amin, "China 2013," *Monthly Review* 64/10 (March 2013): 14–33.
49. Samir Amin, "The Chinese Yuan and HSBC Bank," *Pambazuka News*, August 13, 2013, https://www.pambazuka.org/global-south/chinese-yuan-and-hsbc-bank.
50. See Amin, *A Life Looking Forward*, 66.
51. Rémy Herrera, ed., *Cuba révolutionnaire* [Revolutionary Cuba], 2 vols. (Paris: L'Harmattan, 2003–2006).
52. Susan George, *Le Rapport Lugano: Jusqu'où ira le capitalisme?* [The Lugano Report: How Long Will Capitalism Last?] (La Tour d'Aigues, France: Éditions de l'Aube, 2006).
53. Kevin Danaher, ed., *Fifty Years Is Enough: The Case Against the World Bank and the International Monetary Fund* (Boston: South End Press, 1994).
54. Samir Amin, *The Implosion of Contemporary Capitalism* (New York: Monthly Review Press, 2013), see the chapter on the implosion of the European project.
55. Dembélé, Demba Moussa, *Samir Amin: Intellectuel organique au service de l'émancipation du Sud* [Samir Amin: Organic Intellectual Working on Behalf of the South's Liberation] (Dakar: CODESRIA, 2011).
56. Referring to the main character in Visconti's 1963 Italian film *Il Gattopardo* (*The Leopard*), which was based on Giuseppe Tomasi di Lampedusa's novel of the same title.
57. Gabriela Roffinelli, *Samir Amin: La Théorie du système capitaliste, critique et alternatives* [Samir Amin: Theory of the Capitalist System, Critique, and Alternatives] (Lyon: Parangon, 2013).
58. Samir Amin, *The Liberal Virus*, trans. James Membrez (New York: Monthly Review Press, 2004).
59. See Amin, *The World We Wish to See*.
60. Samir Amin, "Popular Movements Towards Socialism: Their Unity and Diversity," *Monthly Review* 66/2 (June 2014): 1–32.
61. See Amin, *The Implosion of Contemporary Capitalism*.

62. See Amin, *The Liberal Virus*.
63. Samir Amin and Isabelle Eynard, "Los Angeles, United States of Plastika," *L'Homme et la Société* 33/1 (1974): 181–210.
64. See Amin, *A Life Looking Forward*, 234.
65. Samir Amin, *Unequal Development: An Essay on the Social Formations of Peripheral Capitalism*, trans. Brian Pearce (New York: Monthly Review Press, 1976).
66. The English edition: *Samir Amin, Accumulation on a World Scale: A Critique of the Theory of Underdevelopment*, trans. Brian Pearce (New York: Monthly Review Press, 1974).
67. See Amin, *A Life Looking Forward*, 231–32.
68. Jean-Pierre Chevènement, *La Faute de Monsieur Monnet* [Monsieur Monnet's Offense] (Paris: Fayard, 2006).
69. See Amin, *The Liberal Virus*.

# Index

AAPSO (Afro-Asian Peoples' Solidarity Organization), 269
Aasland, Tertit, 426
Accra Action Agenda (2008), 181
Achcar, Gilbert, 54–55
Adler, Patricia, 333
Adler, Sol, 333, 334
Afghanistan, 57, 203–6, 214
Africa, 105–7; conference of liberation movements in (1957), 52; Cuban involvement in, 358, 362; foreign aid for, 181–82; land tenure systems in, 31–32, 34, 37–40; neocolonialism in, 151–67; "Renaissance of," 180
African Development Bank, 147
African Institute for Economic Development and Planning, *See* IDEP
African Social Forum, 165
African socialism: in Angola and Mozambique, 141–43; in Benin, 117–19; in Burkina Faso, 119–22; in Cape Verde and Guinea-Bissau, 139–40; in Congo-Brazzaville, 114–17; in Ethiopia, 132–38; in Ghana, 112–14; in Madagascar, 127–32; in Mali, 107–9; in Portuguese colonies, 138; in Sahelistan project, 109–12; in Tanzania, 122–26; in Zambia, 165; in Zimbabwe, 144–46
Africom (U.S. military command for Africa), 100, 166
Afro-Asian People's Solidarity Organization, 366
agrarian question and agrarian reform, 30–42, 185; in Afghanistan, 205–6; in China, 344; in Egypt, 93; in Iran, 200; in Madagascar, 130; in Nepal, 239–40; in South Africa, 176–77; in Zimbabwe, 144, 145
agriculture, 41, 185–86; in Africa, 183; in India, 230; in Iran, 201; plantation slavery for, 260; in Turkey, 192
Aguilar, Alonso, 284, 285
Ahidjo, Ahmadou, 153
Ahmad, Eqbal, 208
Ahmad, Feroz, 208
AIDS, 177
ALBA (Bolivarian Alliance for the Peoples of Our America), 302, 362
Alexander (the Great; king, Macedon), 217
Algeria, 69–73; elections of 2014 in, 94–96; Sahelistan and, 110
Algerian Communist Party, 69

Ali, Haydar Ibrahim, 102
Ali, Hussein, 248
Allende, Salvador, 266, 278
Alliance for Progress, 266–67
al-Qaida, in Yemen, 103
al-Qaida in the Islamic Maghreb (AQIM), 109
Altamira, Clodomiro, 278
Alvarado, Juan Velasco, 281
Amado, Jorge, 270
Americas: *Reconquista* of, 260; *See also* Latin America and Caribbean; United Sates
Amharic (language), 134
Amin, Idi, 164
Amin, Isabelle, 366, 411; in Argentina, 275; at Black Panther meeting, 412; in Bolivia, 303; in Brazil, 272–74; in Cape Verde, 139; in Central African Republic, 153; in Central Asia, 212, 214, 216; in Chile, 280; in China, 331–34, 337, 341–42; in Cuba, 357; in Czechoslovakia, 307; in French West Indies, 291–92; in Hong Kong, 350; in Hungary, 306–7; in India, 226, 228; in Indonesia, 252; in Jamaica, 288; in Latin America, 265, 266; Lau Kin Chi and, 351; in Mexico, 285, 296; in Mongolia, 219, 221, 223, 224; in Nepal, 237, 243; in Niger, 161; Parisian arrest of, 357; in Peru, 282; in Portugal, 423; in Saudi Arabia, 78; in Soviet Union, 310, 312; in Tanzania, 126; in Thailand, 246; in Turkey, 188, 189; in Vietnam, 351, 352, 355; in Zambia, 165
Amoa, Kwame, 112–14, 165
Amsterdam (Netherlands), 427
Anatolia, 188, 191
ANC (African National Congress), 177, 178
Andrade, Mario de, 141–43
Andrade, Pinto de, 141
Andreotti, 421
Angola, 141–43, 362
Anis, Mona, 84
Annan, Kofi, 377
Anyang, Peter, 150
apartheid, 175
Aquino, Corazon, 250
Arab and African Research Centre, Samir Amin Prize awarded by, 91, 384
Arab Islamic *Nahda*, 53–55
Arab League, 171
Arab Spring, 85

Arab world: failure of *Nahda* in, 53–56; historical trajectory of, 51–52; modernity, democracy, secularism, and Islam in, 56–58; nationalism in, 66; Palestinians in, 64–65; revolutions predicted in, 83–103; Turkey and, 192–93; U.S. military interventions in, 58–64
Araujo, Benjamin, 253
Arbenz, Jacobo, 266
Argentina, 108, 267, 275–78
Aristide, Jean-Bertrand, 288, 290
Armenia, genocide in, 191
Arrighi, Giovanni, 411
Arusha Accords (1993), 170
Arusha Declaration (1967), 123
Aseniero, George, 249
Asia, 187
Asian Social Forum, in Hyderabad (2003), 227–28
Asia-Pacific Peoples' Organization, 376
Asmara (Ethiopia), 137, 138
assimilation, in French West Indies, 291, 292
Ataturk, Mustafa Kemal, 190, 191
austerity policies, 20
Australia, 253–54
Avakov (Avakian), 313

Baath Party: Iraqi, 59–62; Syrian, 101
Babu, 122, 124–26
Bagchi, Amiya, 229, 367
Baghdad Pact, 193
Bahrain, 77
Bahro, Rudolf, 305
Bali (Indonesia), 252
Baluchis (people), 208
Bamako (Mali), 107–9
Bamako Appeal (2006), 300, 383, 390–91
Bandung Conference (1955), 65, 361, 406; African countries in, 105; global struggles following, 16–18; India-China dispute at, 233–34
Bandung system, 17
Bangladesh, 207
Bank of America, 411
banks and banking, 398
Bantustans, 144, 175, 176, 179
barbarism, 271–72
Barre, Siad, 172–74
al-Bashir, Omar, 85
Başkaya, Fikret, 189
Basso, Lelio, 377, 420
el Baz, Sshahida, 84
Bazac, Ana, 317

Bédié, Henri Konan, 149
Bednik, Anna, 184
Bedoui, Abdeljalil, 97
Beijing (China), 333, 335
Beirut (Lebanon), 82–83
Belaid, Choukri, 97
Belarus, 316
Ben Bella, Ahmed, 72–73
Bendjedid, Chadli, 72
Benedetti, Carla de, 421
Bengalis (people), 209
Benguerrah, Abderrahmane, 85
Benin, 117–19
Bénot, Yves, 272
Berktay, Ayse, 189
Berlin (Germany), 308–9
Berlusconi, Silvio, 374
Berthelot, Jacques, 186
Bharatva, 227, 233, 234
Bhutto, Benazir, 208
Bhutto, Zulfikar Ali, 208
Bigeard (general), 352
Binh (madame), 355, 377
Bin Laden, Osama, 205
biofuels, 183
Biya, Paul, 153, 257
Black Panther Party (U.S.), 411–12
blacks: in Mali, 111; in South Africa, 175–77; in Zanzibar, 123
Blondin Diop, Oumar, 161
Boff, Leonardo, 294
Bogomolov, 314
Bogomolov, Oleg, 306
Bohórquez, Carmen, 303
Bokassa, Jean-Bédel, 153
Bolívar, Simón, 261
Bolivia, 282–83, 292, 302, 303
Bonnici, Mifsud, 425
Borisov, Boyko, 100
Boron, Atilio, 277
Botchwey, Kwesi, 113
El Boudi, Fatma, 84
Boumedienne, Houari, 71–72
bourgeois civilization, 24–25
bourgeoisie: in Kenya, 150; transformation of, 20
Bourguiba, Habib Ben Ali, 68, 97
Bouteflika, Abdelaziz, 72, 95, 96
Boutillier, Jean-Louis, 78
Bové, José, 411
Bragança, Aquino de, 143
Brancos, Castelo, 267
Brasilia (Brazil), 271, 273, 334

INDEX 469

Braun, Oscar, 277
Braverman, Harry, 411
Bravo, Douglas, 267
Brazil, 224, 262, 267, 270–75, 298; Fordism in, 236; future of, 297; liberation theology in, 295
Brie, André, 308
Brie, Michael, 308
Britain, *See* Great Britain
Brito, José, 148
Budapest (Hungary), 306–7
Buddhists, 216, 224
Bujra, Abdallah, 125, 150
Burkina Faso, 119–22
Bush, George W., 410
Buzgalin, Alexander, 315, 318
Buzgalin, Ludmilla, 318

Cabral, Amílcar, 39, 121, 139, 140
Camdessus, Michel, 257
Cameroon, 153
Canada, 412
Cape Town (Soth Africa), 179
Cape Verde, 139–40, 260
capitalism, 306; apartheid and, 175; as barbarism, 271–72; in China, 340, 344; crony capitalism, in Egypt, 90–91; democracy and, 43–45; development, in Northwest Europe of, 261; European Renaissance and, 53–54; generalized monopoly capitalism, 18–25; green, 47; implosion of, 394–96; as market economy, 182; in peripheries, 254; Rhenish, 419; in Russia, 319–20, 322–26; tied to historic conquests, 403; in Turkey, 190–91; in U.S., 410
Cardoso, Fernando Henrique, 270, 274, 275, 295, 297, 299
Caribbean: Cuba, 356–63; Dominican Republic, 290–91; French West Indies, 291–92; Haiti, 288–90; Jamaica, 287–88; *See also* Latin America and Caribbean
Carnaval (Brazil), 273
Carvalho, Otelo, 423
Casablanca group (Africa), 105
Casanova, Pablo González, 285, 293, 296, 366
Cassen, Bernard, 369, 391
caste system: in India, 225, 230–31, 234; in Nepal, 238
Castor, Suzy, 288
Castro, Fidel, 262, 358, 359; Cuban Revolution led by, 265; on East African confederation, 138, 173, 174
Catholic Church: in Eastern Europe, 317–18; liberation theology and, 295; in Malta, 424

CEAO (Economic Community of West Africa), 148
Ceaucescu, Nicolae, 318
centers/peripheries conflicts, 21; between North and South, 403
Central Africa, 151–53
Central African Republic, 153, 171
Central America, 267, 298–99
Central Asia: former Soviet provinces of, 216–19; Mongolia, 219–24; Xinjiang (China) in, 212–16
Central Intelligence Agency (CIA): in Georgia, 316; in Guatemala, 266; in Indonesian massacre, 251, 267; Mossadegh overthrown in Iran by, 200; Muslim Brotherhood and, 57–58; September 11th terrorist attacks and, 205
Ceu Carmoreis, Maria do, 143
Chachra, Sandeep, 229
*chaebols* (Korean monopolies), 255, 257
Chagula, Wilbert, 123
Chalaq, Nazhat, 67
Chanda, Donald, 180
Charaffeddine, Fahima, 79
Chávez, Hugo, 284, 301, 302
Chege, Michal, 150
Chevènement, Jean-Pierre, 428
Chikh, Karim, 85
Chikov, 314
children: in Brazil, 271; Chinese policy on, 336
Chile, 266, 267, 278–81, 295
China, 331–41; African projects of, 125–26; on Angola, 142; capitalism in, 254; conflicts between Vietnam and, 356; emergence in, 28; as emergent power, 341–49; Fordism in, 236; Hong Kong returned to, 350; India compared with, 225–26, 232; Japan and, 414–15; land management in, 34–35; Russia versus, 325; Syria and, 102; Xinjiang in, 212–16; Zambia and, 180
Chinese (language), 415
Chinese Communist Party, 29
Chipeta, Chinyama, 150–51
Chitala, Derrick, 165
Chomsky, Noam, 410
Choquehuanca, David, 303
Christianity: liberation theology in, 294–95; in Madagascar, 129; salvation sects in, 158–59
Cipolla, Nicola, 421
civil society, 182
CLACSO (Latin American Council of Social Science), 266, 277, 285
Claudín, Fernando, 422

Clinton, Bill, 123, 257
CODESA (Convention for a Democratic South Africa), 177
CODESRIA (Council for the Development of Social Science Research in Africa), 266, 384
Cold War, 406, 407
Colombia, 267
colonialism: in Africa, 105; in Brazil, 272; development of, 261; in India, caste system in, 225, 230; in Latin America and Caribbean, 259–60; neocolonialism and, 106, 406; in Portuguese colonies, 138; in Southeast Asia, 33; victims of, 45
Columbus, Christopher, 260
Comintern, *See* Third International
commons, 396
Commonwealth of Independent States (CIS), 219
communism and communists: in Afghanistan and South Yemen, 57; in French West Indies, 291, 292
Communist Parties: of Algeria, 69; of China, 29, 344, 349; of Cuba, 361; of Dahomey, 117; of Eastern Europe, 317; of Greece, 423; of India, 229, 231; of Indonesia, 251; of Iraq, 62; isolation of, 380; of Latin America, 264–65, 268, 270; of Lebanon, 65; of Nepal, 238–39; of Philippines, 250; of Portugal, 422; of Russia (current), 318, 319, 324; of South Africa, 126, 145–46, 177; of Sudan, 75–76; of Syria, 83; of Yugoslavia, 310
Conceição Tavares, Maria da, 270
Confucianism, 336
Congo-Brazzaville, 114–17
Congo-Kinshasa (Democratic Republic of the Congo), 153–59, 170
Congolese Rural Code (2008), 183
Congress Party (India), 207, 226, 227, 230, 231, 233
Constantino, Renato, 249
Coptic Christians, 86, 132, 133
Coquery, Catherine, 151
Cordova, Armando, 284
corporatism, 320
Correa, Rafael, 193, 301
COSATU (Congress of South African Trade Unions), 177
Costa, Da, 114
Côte d'Ivoire, 119, 120, 146–49, 166
Cotler, Julio, 281
Cotonou Convention, 163
crony capitalism, 21, 90–91
Cruz, Viriato da, 141

CTA (Argentine Workers' Central Union), 278
Cuba, 262, 269–70, 289, 356–59; in Angola, 143; emergence in, 28; isolation of, 269; Revolution in, 265, 266, 359–63
culturalism, 150, 395
Cultural Revolution (China), 336
currencies, 162–63
Cyprus, 424, 425
Czechoslovakia, 307–8

Dacko, David, 153
Dalai Lama, 116
Dalat (Vietnam), 355
dalits (caste in India), 230–31
Da Nobregas family, 422–23
David, Randolf, 249
Davos (Switzerland), 367
Debray, Régis, 268
debts, sovereign, 20
de-financialization of economic system, 398–99
de Gaulle, Charles, 109, 427
Delhi (India), 229
Dembélé, Moussa, 384
democracy and democratization, 42–47; in China, 339, 349; in Latin America and Caribbean, 293–300; modernity, secularism, Islam and, 56–58; needed for African-Arab unity, 70; in Nepal, 240–41; World Social Forums on, 388
Democratic Republic of the Congo (Congo-Kinshasa), 153–59, 170
Deneuve, Catherine, 354
Deng Xiaoping, 35, 365
Denise, Auguste, 147
Denmark, 425–27
dependency school, 265, 270
depoliticization: of former Soviet citizens, 315; in political Islam, 88–89
DERG (Ethiopia), 136
*desarrollismo* (developmentalism), 263–65, 281
Development Assistance Committee, 166
Development Cooperation Forum (DCF), 184–85
Diabaté, Moustapha, 146
diamonds, 155
Diarrassouba, Charles Waly, 146
Diawara, Mohamed, 146
Diaware, Ange, 114
Diène, Doudou, 211–12, 217, 219, 222, 223
Dierckxsens, Wim, 304, 367
Dikoumé, Cosme, 153
Diori, Hamani, 162, 163
Diouf, Abdou, 365

INDEX

Dominican Republic, 290–91, 296–97
drug trade, 288
Druon, Maurice, 219

Eastern Europe, 316–18; really existing socialism in, 305–16
Echeverría Álvarez, Luis, 266, 286
ECLAC (Economic Commission for Latin America and the Caribbean), 281
ecology, Marxism and, 47–49
economism, 409
ECOWAS (Economic Community of West African States ), 112
Ecuador, 302, 303
Egypt, 66, 84–85; Algeria compared with, 95–96; under Britain, 60; lumpen development in, 90–91; modern emergence of, 85–90; proposals for, 91–94; under Wafd, 57
Egyptian Social Forums, 65
Egyptian Socialist Party, 84
Ekbatani, 194
elderly people, in China, 336
elections: in Algeria (2014), 94–96; in Iran (1999), 197; in Latin America, 296, 299–300; in Turkey (1950), 192
Ellsberg, Daniel, 410
El Salvador, 262, 298–99
emergence, 24–29, 187; of China, 341–49; of Iran, 199–203; in Latin America and Caribbean, 292; in Southeast Asia, 245–46
*encomienda*, 260
England, *See* Great Britain
Ennahda (party, Tunisia), 97
environmentalism, 48–49
EPLF (Eritrean People's Liberation Front), 136
Eritrea, 132–35, 137
Ethiopia, 79, 132–38, 166; Somalia and, 174
Eurocentrism, 49
Eurocommunism, 428
Europe, 390, 415–28; avoiding criticism of, 374; globalization in, 401; Renaissance in, 53–54; represented in WFA, 379; Turkey and, 190–91; world conquest by, 403
European Union, 193, 390, 401, 428
exports, emergence not tied to, 27
Eyadéma, Gnassingbé, 118

Fahmy, Mansour, 80–81
Falachas (Ethiopian Jews), 132–33
Faletto, Enzo, 270
family, in China, 336
Farabundo Martí National Liberation Front (El Salvador), 298–99

fascism, 328, 421, 422
Fifth International, 405
financialization of economic system, 19; definancialization and, 398–99
Finland, 425, 426
First, Ruth, 126
FIS (Islamic Salvation Front; Algeria), 72, 95
FLN (National Liberation Front; Algeria), 71, 72
FNLA (National Liberation Front of Angola), 141
food, 41
Fordism, in India, 236
foreign aid: for Africa, 181–82; donor organizations, 408; Nepal dependent on, 242
Formosa (Taiwan), 351
Foster, John Bellamy, 47, 367
Foté, Memel, 146, 148
Founou, Bernard, 367
fourth world, 175, 176, 187
FPI (Ivorian Popular Front), 149
FPR (Rwandan Popular Front), 170
France, 416–20; African currencies and, 163; Algeria under, 71; in conquest of Americas, 259–60; demonstrations of 1995 in, 366; French West Indies under, 291–92; Sahelistan project of, 109–12; in war with Vietnam, 352–53
Frank, André Gunder, 279, 280, 309, 411; on capitalism in Latin America, 265; on lumpen-development, 28
FRELIMO (Mozambique Liberation Front), 143
French Guiana, 291–92
French Revolution, 416
French West Indies, 291–92
Front Line States, 123
Fuentes, Marta, 279
Fujimori, Alberto, 296
Furtado, Celso, 270, 272, 298

Gabon, 152
Gabor, Agnès, 317
Gaddafi, Muammar, 99, 100
Gafourov, Said, 318
Gajurel, Chandra Prakash, 238
Galtung, Johan, 426
Gamal, Mostafa, 84
Ganao, Charles, 114
Gandhi, Indira, 231, 233, 244
Ganzion, Aba, 114
Garang, John, 102
García Linera, Álvaro, 303

Garnier, Melle, 146
Gbagbo, Laurent, 146, 149
gender: in peasant families, 40; *See also* women
generalized monopoly capitalism, 18–25
Genghis Khan (Mogol ruler), 220, 222
George, Susan, 369
Georgia, Republic of, 316
German Democratic Republic (GDR; East Germany), 308–9, 419, 420
Germany, 308–9, 418–20
Ghai, Dharam, 150
Ghaleb, Mourad, 366
Ghana, 112–14, 146, 269
Ghosh, Jayati, 229
Gide, André, 152
Girvan, Norman, 266, 287
Glazyaev, Vyacheslav, 328
globalization, 19; in Africa, 182; in China, 345; de-globalization and, 399; in Europe, 401; in Germany, 419; non-aligned movement on, 406; sovereignty and, 388
Gnidéhou, Justin, 117
Goma (Zaire), 157
Gorbachev, Mikhail, 216, 316, 322, 327; perestroika and glasnost policies of, 328; on U.S. attitudes toward Soviet Union, 340
Gorostiaga, 299
governance, 182
Gramsci, Antonio, 52, 366
Great Britain (United Kingdom), 416–18; Afghanistan under, 203; in conquest of Americas, 259–60; Egypt under, 60, 85–87; enclosures in, 31; Hong Kong returned to China by, 350; India under, 225, 228, 230; Uganda under, 164
Greater Middle East, 64–66
Greece, 423–24
green capitalism, 47
Greenpeace (organization), 354
Grenada, 290
Guadeloupe, 291
Guatemala, 266, 267
Guéï, Robert, 149
Guevara, Che, 156, 265, 268–69, 361
Guinea-Bissau, 139–40
Gulf countries, 77–78
Gustavson, Rolf, 425
Gutierrez, Gustavo, 294

Habashi, Mamdouh, 84, 367
Habibie, B. J., 252
Habyarimana, Juvénal, 169, 170
Haider, Jörg, 308

Haiti, 261, 288–90, 292, 308
Ha Long Bay (Vietnam), 354
Hama, Boubou, 160
Hanoi (Vietnam), 353
Hansen, Emmanuel, 113–14
Haratins (people), 74
Hardallu, Adlan, 102
Hariri, Rafic, 65
Harnecker, Marta, 279, 302, 356
Havana (Cuba), 357; Non-Aligned Movement conference in, 362
Havel, Vaclav, 307–8
Herrera, Rémy, 359, 367
Hersch, Hélène, 427
Hersch, Jacques, 427
Hezbollah, 65
Hinduism, 48; caste system in, 230–31; in India, 225–27, 234; in Nepal, 243
Hindutva, 227, 234
Hinkelammert, Franz, 279, 294
Hinton, Bill, 333
Hobsbawm, Eric, 417, 418
Hoi An (Vietnam), 354
Hong Kong, 350
Horvat, Srećko, 318
Houphouët-Boigny, Félix, 147–49
Houtart, François, 171, 294–95; on Bamako Appeal, 300; on green capitalism, 47; in Haiti, 288; as WFA executive secretary, 366–67; WFA's Latin American activities coordinated by, 303–4; on World Social Forum approach, 385, 387; at World Social Forums, 371, 391
Huang Ping, 341, 343
Hue (Vietnam), 354
Hulcrantz, Gerhard, 425
humanism, 395
Hungary, 306–7
Huntington, Samuel, 267
Hurbon, Laennec, 288
Hussein, Saddam, 59, 62; U.S. support for, 202
Hutu (people), 157, 168–70
Hydén, Göran, 150
Hyderabad (India), 227–28

Ibn Rushd Prize, 385
Ibro, Abdou, 109, 184
Ichiyo, Muto, 413
IDEP (African Institute for Economic Development and Planning), 15; Algiers seminar by, 71; Bamako seminar by, 107; Brazzaville seminar by, 115; Brussels congress of (2014), 377; Cotonou seminar by,

INDEX    473

117; Dar es Salaam semimar by, 123–26; Douala seminar by, 153; Ibadan seminar by, 164; International African Institute and, 167; Latin American intellectuals in, 266; Madagascar conference of, 129
Iglesias, Enrique, 281
Ikonikoff, Moise, 277
immigration and immigrants, 119, 272–73; in cosmopolitan cities, 417–18; to U.S., 287, 404
imperialism, 400; in Africa, 166; globalization and, 406; new stage in, 409
India, 209, 224–37; emergence in, 28–29; Nepal and, 242–43; Pakistan and, 207; traditional land policies in, 32–33
indigenous peoples ("Indians"): in Bolivia, 283; in Brazil, 273; in Latin America and Caribbean, 259, 301; in Mexico, 285; in Peru, 282
Indonesia, 245, 251–54, 267
Indonesian Communist Party, 251
industrialization: in Africa, 166; during Bandung era, 17; in India, 231–32; required for development, 185; in South Africa, 175; in Soviet Union, 321
International African Institute (IAI), 167
internationalism, 405
International Monetary Fund (IMF), 113
*intifada*, 81–82
Iran, 194–203
Iraq, 62–64, 80–81; U.S. war on, 59–60; in wars with Iran, 202
Iraqi Communist Party, 62
Iskandari, 194
Islam: in Afghanistan, 203; in Anatolia, 191; in Egypt, 89; in Iran, 196–98, 201–2; in Mauritania, 74; modernity, democracy, secularism, and, 56–58; *Nahda* in, 53–55; in Pakistan, 207–10, 226–27; in Sudan, 76
Israel, 64–65; Egypt and, 88; Ethiopian Jews in, 133; Lebanon invaded by (1982), 81; Turkey as ally of, 193; in war of 1967, 87; WFA on, 373–74
Italy, 420–22
Izquierda Unida (Spain), 422

Jalil, Mustafa Muhammad Abdul, 100
Jamaica, 266, 287–88
Jamal, Amir, 123
Jaona, Monja, 129
Japan, 412–15
Jews, Falachas (Ethiopian Jews), 132–33
Jijon, Victor Hugo, 303

Jonglei Canal (Sudan), 77
Jordanski, Vladimir, 315
José, Renaldo, 275
Julius Nyerere Foundation, 384

Kaara, Wahu, 150
Kabila, Laurent, 156–58, 171
Kabinda, Wynter, 180
Kachoukh, Mounir, 97
Kagame, Paul, 169, 170
Kagarlitsky, Boris, 315, 318, 374
Kalonji, Albert, 154
Kane, Abdussalam, 161
Kapitany, Gabor, 307
Karakorum (Mongolia), 224
Karume, 125
Kashgar (China), 214–15
Kathmandu (Nepal), 237
Kaunda, Kenneth, 165, 179
Kautsky, Karl, 37
Kaya, Paul, 116
Kazakhstan, 315
Keita, Ibrahima, 107
Keita, Madeira, 107
Keita, Michel, 161
Kemalism (Turkey), 57, 189, 192, 93, 195
Kennedy, John F., 266–67
Kenya, 149–50
Kenyatta, Jomo, 149
Kérékou, Mathieu, 117–18
Khaddam, Abdul Halim, 101
Khadra, Yasmina, 72
Khoja, Abdallah, 70
Khomeini (Ayatollah, Iran), 200–203
Khrushchev, Nikita, 264
Kimyongur, Bahar, 101
Kinshasa (Congo), 156, 157
Kirchner, Néstor, 301
Kitazawa, Masao, 413
Kitazawa, Yoko, 413
Klaus, Vaclav, 308
Kobdo (Mongolia), 219–20
Kollontai, Vladimir, 314
Konaré, Alpha, 108
Korea, 28, 254–58
Korean War (1950-53), 255
Kouchner, Bernard, 310
Kourouma, Ahmadou, 147
Kreisky, Bruno, 427
Kubitschek, Juscelino, 273
Kurds (people), 62; in Turkey, 188, 189, 193
Kuwait, 77

Labor Party (Malta), 424–25
labor unions: in Côte d'Ivoire, 120; in Egypt, 92
Labour Party (Great Britain), 417
Lancaster House Agreement (1980; for Zimbabwe), 126, 144
La Paz (Bolivia), 282–83
Lara, Lúcio, 141
LASO (Latin American Solidarity Organization), 270
Las Vegas (Nevada), 411
Laszlo, Andor, 307
Latin America and Caribbean, 259–70; advances in, 302–4; Argentina, 275–78; Bolivia, 282–83; Brazil, 270–75; Chile, 278–81; Cuba, 356–63; democratization in, 293–300; emergence in, 292; Mexico, 285–87; new victories and challenges for, 300–302; Peru, 281–82; political advances in, 389–90; Venezuela, 283–84; West Indies, 287–92
Latvia, 313–14
Lau Kin Chi, 341–42, 351, 367, 381
Lebanese Communist Party, 65
Lebanon, 81–83
Left Wing Alliance (Finland), 426
Lelio Basso Foundation, 420
Lemonnier, 156
Lenin, V. I., 29–30; on agrarian question, 344; on Finish independence, 426; on land reform, 37
Léonard, Willy, 129
Li Baoyuan, 336–38
liberation theology, 56, 250, 294–95
Liberia, 167–68
Libya, 99–100
Lin Chun, 339, 341, 343, 349
Linkspartei (Left Party; Germany), 308
Lin Shenjing, 351
Lisbon (Portugal), 423
Lissouba, Pascal, 114–17
Lomé convention, 291
London (Great Britain), 417–18
Lopez, Henri, 114
Los Angeles (California), 411
Lu Aiguo, 343
Lula, 274, 295, 299, 301, 302
lumpen-development, 28–29; in Africa, 166; in Egypt, 90–91; in Iran, 203
Lumumba, Patrice, 154
Lusaka (Zambia), 165

Macamo, Eugenio, 143
Macao (China), 350

MacFadden, Patricia, 150
Machado, Dario, 356
Machel, Samora, 143
Machili, Carlos, 143
Machu Picchu (Peru), 282
Madagascar, 127–32, 183
Mafia, 421
Magdoff, Harry, 411
Maghreb, 99
Mahiou, Ahmad, 70
Ma Jiantang, 339
Makarios (patriarch, Cyprus), 425
Malawi, 150–51
Malays (people), 248
Malaysia, 224, 247–49
Mali, 107–12, 166
Malta, 424–25
Mamadou Gologo, 107
Mamdani, Mahmood, 165
*mameluk* regime, 52
Mandaza, Ibo, 144
Mandela, Nelson, 123, 178
Manila (Philippines), 250
Manley, Michael, 287
Mansour, Fawzy, 332
Mansour, Gerda, 332
Maoism, 29–30, 264; in India, 231; in Latin America, 267; in Napal, 237–43; of neo-Maoists, 338–39; origins sof, 346; on path to liberation, 18; in Philippines, 250
Mao Zedong, 70–71, 264, 315; agrarian revolution under, 34; on Chinese Revolution, 344; fashions of, 333, 335; political strategy of, 348–49; Soviet model rejected by, 361
Al-Maqaleh, Abdel Aziz, 78
Marais, Hein, 158, 177, 178
Marcos (Subcomandante), 296
Marcos, Ferdinand, 249–50
Mariam, Mengistu Haile, 136
Marighella, Carlos, 267
Marini, Ruy Mauro, 270
market economy, 182
market regulation, 394–95
market socialism, 305, 306; in China, 342; in Yugoslavia, 309
Marti, Farabundo, 262
Martí, José, 360
Martner, Gonzalo, 278
Marton, Imre, 307
Marx, Karl, 398, 405; on capital accumulation, 48; on economism, 409; on enclosures, 31; on England and France, 416–17; on land reform, 37; proletariat defined by, 22

INDEX

Marxism, 405; ecology and, 47–49; stages of development theories in, 29
Marzouki, Moncef, 98
Mashreq, 67, 77, 99
Mashreq-Maghreb Forum, 371
Maududi, Maulana, 207
Maures (people), 74–75
Mauritania, 68–69, 73–75
Mawdudi (Egypt), 58
Mazrui, Ali, 150
Mbaya, Kankwenda, 171
M'bow, Mahtar, 377
Mbuji Mayi (Congo), 154–55
McNamara, Robert, 267, 354
Mehmed the Conqueror, 190
Menderes, Adnan, 192
Menem, Carlos, 277
Meppiel, Jacqueline, 357
mercantilist system: expansion to Americas of, 260; in Latin America, 265
Mexico, 260, 266, 285–87, 301; end of PRI in, 298; neo-Zapatista uprising in, 295–96; Revolution in, 261
Mexico City (Mexico), 285–86
Michelena, Adicea, 266, 283
Michelena, Héctor Silva, 266, 283–84
Middle East: Turkey and, 193–94; *See also* Arab world
migrations: from Africa, 106; agrarian question and, 40–41; *See also* immigration and immigrants
MIR (Revolutionary Left Movement; Chile), 279
Mkandawire, Mjedo, 150–51
Mobutu Sese Seko, 123, 154, 156–59
modernity, 53; in Britain and France, 416; democracy, secularism, Islam and, 56–58; limits of, 55–56
Modibo Keïta, 107
Moi, Daniel, 149
Monal, Isabel, 356
Mongolia, 219–24
Monnet, Jean, 427–28
monopoly capitalism, 18–25; in Koarea, 255; socialization of, 396–98
Monroe Doctrine, 269
Monrovia group (Africa), 105
Mont Pelerin Society (MPS), 369
Morales, Evo, 283, 301
Morel, Michelle, 180
Moreno, Isabelle, 222
Morocco, 68–70
Moros (people), 250–51

Morqos, Samir, 84
Morsi, Mohamed, 94
Moscow (Russia), 310–13, 319
Mossadegh, Mohammad, 194, 200
Moumouni, Abdou, 412
Moyo, Sam, 145
Mozambique, 143
MPLA (People's Movement for the Liberation of Angola), 141–43
Mubarak, Hosni, 87, 88
Mudenda, Gilbert, 165
Mugabe, Robert, 145
Muhajir (people), 208
Muhammad Ali (ruler of Egypt), 85, 95
Mulele, 156
Mumbai (India), 227–29
Murthy, P. K., 229, 367
Muscat (Sultanate of Muscat and Oman), 78
Museveni, Yoweri, 125, 164
Mushakoji, Kinhide, 376, 413
Muslim Brotherhood (Egypt): history of, 57–58, 86–87; in Morsi government, 94
Muslims: expelled from Andalusia, 260; in India and Pakistan, 207–8, 227, 233; Moros, 250–51; in Turkey, 191; *See also* Islam

Nabudere, Dan, 165
NAFTA (North American Free Trade Agreement), 286, 296
el Naggar, Ahmad, 84, 91–92, 384
*Nahda* (Arab Renaissance), 52; failure of, 53–56
Nairobi (Kenya), 150
Najibullah, Mohammad, 206
Nakatani, Paulo, 275, 367
Napoleon Bonaparte (emperor, France), 292
Nasser, Gamal Abdel, 87–88
Nasserism, 80, 86, 87, 90, 94
National Front (France), 419–20
nationalization, 396–98
national populist movements, 106; in Congo-Kinshasa, 154; in India, 232, 234
National Transitional Council (NTC; Libya), 100
nations: sovereignty of, 388; states distinguished from, 30
NATO (North Atlantic Treaty Organization): as enemy of South, 380, 390; Greece in, 424; Nordic countries and, 425; Spain in, 422; Turkey in, 62, 192
natural resources: in Africa, 183; in Latin America and Caribbean, 292; in Niger, 184; *See also* oil
Naxalism, 231, 242

Ndiaye, Samba, 147
Negri, Antonio, 389, 395
Nehru, Jawaharlal, 231
Nemenzo, Francisco, 249
neocolonialism, 106, 406
neoliberalism: in China, 345; in Latin America, 295, 296
neo-Maoists, 338–39
neo-Zapatism (Mexico), 295–96
Nepal, 237–43
Netherlands, 259–60, 427
Neto, Agostinho, 141
neutralism, 427
New International Economic Order (proposed), 52, 71, 244–45
new left: in Chile, 279; in Great Britain, 417; in Philippines, 250; in Russia, 315
Ngo Manh Lan, 351
Ngombale-Mwiru, Kingunge, 123–24
Nicaragua, 262, 290; Sandinistas in, 298–99
Niemeyer, Oscar, 273
Niger, 159–63, 184
Nigeria, 110, 163–64
Nimeiry, Gaafar, 85
Njonjo, Apolo, 150
Nkomati Accord (1984), 143
Nkrumah, Kwame, 122
Non-Aligned Movement (NAM): African countries in, 105; Arab world in, 52; Bandung conference of (1955), 233–34; Colombo conference of (1976), 243–44; Cuba allied with, 361; Havana conference of (2007), 362; IDEP's Madagascar conference and, 129; Indonesia in, 251; rebirth of, 406–7
non-governmental organizations (NGOs), 183–84
Nordic countries, 425
North Korea, 257–58; in Korean War, 255
North Yemen, 78
Norway, 425, 426
Noumazalaye, Ambroise, 114
Ntogolo, 152
Nyerere, Julius, 123–25
Nzé, Pierre, 114
Nzongola, George Ntalaja, 171

Obama, Barack, 374
Obeng, P. V., 113, 114
Obote, Milton, 164
Occupy movements, 23
Odhiambo, Thomas, 150
Ogaden war, 173

oil (petroleum): in Iran, 200; in Iraq, 60; rising profits from, 52; in Russia, 323
Oliveira, Oscar, 303
Organization for African Unity (OAU), 70, 105; on Angola, 142
Organization of American States (OAS), 266, 362
Organization of Solidarity with the People of Asia, Africa, and Latin America, 52
Ortega, Daniel, 299, 301
Oteiza, Enrique, 277
Ottoman Empire, 188, 190
Ouattara, Alassane, 112
Ould Cheikh, Abdel Wedoud, 73
Ovanissian, Vazguen, 194–95

Paez, Pedro, 374
Pahlavi, Mohammad Reza (Shah of Iran), 200, 201
Pahlavi, Reza (Shah of Iran), 199–200
PAICV (African Party for the Independence of Guinea and Cape Verde), 140
Pakistan, 206–11; Afghanistan and, 203; India compared with, 226–27
Palestine Liberation Organization (PLO), 64
Palestinians, 64–65; Sabra and Shatila massacre of, 81; WFA on, 374
Palme, Olof, 425
Papandreou, Andreas, 423
Paris Declaration on Aid Effectiveness (2005), 181–82, 185
Pasha, Enver, 193
PASOK (Panhellenic Socialist MovementMouvement; Greece), 424
Pathans (people), 209
Patriotic Front (Zambia), 180
PCT (Congolese Labor Party), 116
Peace and Development Foundation (Vietnam), 355
peasants: in Ethiopia, 133; in India, 234–35; in liberation struggles, 42; in Mali, 108; in Nepal, 238–40; in South Africa, 175; in Zimbabwe, 144
peasant society, 30–31; gender in, 40
peripheries: Argentina in, 276; Brazil in, 274; capitalism in, 254; Fordism in, 236; generalized monopoly capitalism in, 19; Global South as, 403; local ruling classes in, 21–22; popular democracy in, 46; proletariat in, 22–23; Russia as, 323–24
Perón, Evita, 277
Peronism, 276–77
Persian Empire, 194

# INDEX

Peru, 262, 281–82, 300, 301
petite bourgeoisie: Cabral on, 121, 139; in Cape Verde, 140; in Ethiopia, 132–35
petroleum, *See* oil
Pham Xuan Phuong, 352
Philippines, 249–51
Pierre-Charles, Gérard, 288
Pires, Pedro, 140
PKK (Kurdistant Workers Party), 189
plutocrats, 20–21
Poland, 308
Polanyi, Kari, 287
political Islam, 52; in Algeria, 95–96; depoliticization and, 88–89; in Egypt, 87, 89; in Libya, 99; in Mali, 109; Taliban and, 206; U.S. support for, 58
Polo, Marco, 224
pornography, 77–78
Porto Alegre (Brazil), 367, 369–70
Portugal, 422–23; African colonies of, 138; in Americas, 260; Cape Verde colony of, 139; Macao under, 350
postmodernism, 45, 89, 388, 395
Poulantzas, Nicos, 423
poverty, 182; in India, 225–26, 228; in Siberia, 316; in Thailand, 246; UN conference on, 372
power (political), 47
Prachanda (Pushpa Kamal Dahal), 238, 239
Prada, Raul, 303
Prasartset, Suthy, 246
Prebisch, Raúl, 281, 376
Prestes, Luís Carlos, 262
PRI (Institutional Revolutionary Party; Mexico), 260, 298
Primakov, Yevgeny, 327
private property, 396; traditional land policies and, 31–33
privatization, in Egypt, 90, 92
profiteers, 22
proletariat: in peripheries, 22–23; *See also* working classes
Puig, Max, 291
Pu Shan, 336, 338
Putin, Vladimir, 324, 327, 374
Pygmies (people), 115

Qarmatian Revolution, 77
*qat,* 78–79
Quijano, Anibal, 281

Rabesahala, Gisèle, 128
Rabevazaha, Céline, 129

race, in Zanzibar, 123
racism: in apartheid South Africa, 175; in Brazil, 271; UN on, 372–73; World Conference against Racism (2001) on, 177–78
Rajaona, François, 129
Rakotonirina, Manandafy, 129
Ramadan, Tariq, 97
Ramalho Eanes, Antonio, 423
Ramsis, Amal, 84
Rasolomanana, Léon, 129
Ratsimandrava, Richard, 129–30
Ratsiraka, Didier, 127, 130–31
Rauber, Isabelle, 278, 291, 297, 356
Ravalomanana, Marc, 131
Rawlings, Jerry, 112–14
Reagan, Ronald, 328
"really existing socialism," 305, 306
*Reconquista,* 260
Rees, William, 47
Refaa, Magda, 84
religion, 46; in Iran, 201–2; liberation theology, 294–95; in Madagascar, 129; salvation sects, 158–59
Renaissance (European), 53
RENAMO (Mozambican National Resistance), 143
Rey, Pierre Philippe, 114
Rhenish capitalism, 419
Rhodes, Cecil, 144
Rhodesia (Zimbabwe), 144
Ribeiro, Darcy, 270, 299
Riga (Latvia), 313–14
Riolo, Giorgio, 421
Roberto, Holden, 141
Rodney, Walter, 125
Rodrigues, Edmilson, 273
Roffinelli, Gabriela, 404
Rumelia, 191
Russia, 312–16, 318–22, 413; agrarian reform in, 37; alternatives for, 326–28; capitalism in, 322–26; Revolution in, 29; Syria and, 102; Ukranian crisis and, 328–30
Russian Revolution, 29, 37, 320, 325
Rwanda, 168–69; genocide in, 157, 167, 169–71

Sabahi, Hamdin, 84
Sabato, Jorge, 276
Sadat, Anwar, 87, 88, 90
Sader, Emir, 266, 270, 274, 297
Sahelistan project, 109–12
Saigon (Vietnam), 353, 355
Salah, Ben, 67

Saleh, Ali Abdallah, 103
Sall, Alioune, 148, 161
Sall, Ebrima, 384
Saltos, Napoleon, 303
salvation sects, 158–59
Samarkand (Uzbekistan), 216–17
Samir Amin Prize (Arab and African Research Centre), 91, 384
Sampaio, Plino, 275
Sandinistas (Nicaragua), 298–99
Sandino, 262
Sangaré, Dramane, 146
Sankara, Thomas, 39, 108, 120–22
Sanogo, Amadou, 112
Santoro, Giuseppe, 420
Santos, Marcelino dos, 143
Santos, Theotonio dos, 270
São Luís (Brazil), 274
São Paulo Forum, 298–300
Sarkozy, Nicolas, 110, 420
Sasono, Adi, 252
Sassou Nguesso, Denis, 116–17
Saudi Arabia, 77–78, 211; Yemen feared by, 79
Savak (Iranian political police), 200
Savary, Alain, 160
Savimbi, Jonas, 141, 158
Schutte, Giorgio Romano, 274, 297
science, 48–49
Secoli, Tarcisio, 297
secularism: in India, 227, 233; modernity, democracy, Islam and, 56–58
Sedky Pasha, Ismail, 86, 87
Selassie, Haile, 105, 132
Semprún, Jorge, 422
Senegal, 110–11, 365
Senghor, Léopold, 148
September 11th terrorist attacks, 205
Sertel, Yildiz, 189
Shaarawi, Helmy, 84
Shamuyarira, Nathan, 244
Sharon, Ariel, 205
Shia Islam, 62; in Iran, 201–2
Shining Path (Peru), 300, 301
Shivji, Issa, 367, 384
Siberia (Russia), 316
Sichuan (China), 332
Sicily (Italy), 421
Sierra Leone, 167–68
Sikhs, 233
Silk Roads program (UNESCO), 211–12, 217, 219, 220
Silva, José, 284
Silva, Ludovico, 284

Sindis (people), 208
Slaoui, Driss, 68
slavery: in Cape Verde, 139; family destroyed under, 272; in French West Indies, 291; in Haiti, 289; in Jamaica, 288; in Mauritania, 74; in mercantilist system, 260; in U.S., 412; in Zanzibar, 122
Slovo, Joe, 126
Smith, Ian, 144
socialism: African, 107–46; of Cuban Revolution, 360; in Eastern Europe and Soviet Union, 305–16; in Global South, 404–5; of Nepali Maoists, 241; in twenty-first century, 362–63, 409; *See also* African socialism
social movements, 300–301
Society for International Development, 378–79
Solidarność (Poland), 308
Somalia, 166, 172–75
Somavia, Juan, 279
Sonntag, Hein, 284
South Africa, 180, 224; in Angola, 142; apartheid in, 148; Congo and, 158; after end of apartheid, 175–79
South African Communist Party (SACP), 126, 145–46, 177
South China Sea, 356
Southeast Asia, 245–46; financial crisis in, 244, 256; Philippines, 249–51; Thailand, 246–49
Southern Africa Association of Political Science, 165
South Korea, 254–58
South Yemen, 57
sovereign debt, 20
sovereignty, 388
Sovietism, 17
Soviet Union, 126, 320–22; Afghanistan invaded by, 204; on Angola, 142; Central Asian provinces of, 116–219; Comintern under, 262; Cuba allied with, 269, 356, 357, 360–61; Ethiopia and, 136; Finland and, 426; Guevara on, 268–69; non-alignment movement and, 406; really existing socialism in, 310–16; Vietnam allied with, 351
Spain, 260, 422
Sri Lanka, 243–45
Stalin, Joseph, 318
state capitalism, in China, 344–45
states: dominant ideology on, 182; nations distinguished from, 30
state socialism, in Sweden, 425
Stedile, João Pedro, 275
Stiglitz, Joseph, 375

INDEX 479

Stiglitz Commission, 180, 375, 395
Stuckey, Barbara, 411
Sudan, 75–77, 85, 102–3
Sudanese Communist Party, 75–76
Suharto, 159, 245, 251–53
Sukarno, 251
Sultanate of Muscat and Oman, 78
Sundaram, Jomo, 248
Sunkel, Osvaldo, 279
Sunni Islam, in Iraq, 60
sustainable development, 45
Sweden, 425
Sweezy, Paul, 410, 411
Syria, 65, 82, 83, 101–2, 329; chemical weapons used in, 374; Turkey in, 193
Syrian Communist Party, 83
Szego, Andréa, 307
Szentes, Tamás, 307

Tablada, Carlos, 367
Taiping Revolution, 346
Taiwan, 28, 342, 351
Taliban: in Afghanistan, 205, 206; CIA and, 57–58
Tandon, Yash, 166, 181
Tanzam railway, 179–80
Tanzania, 122–26
Tasmanians (people), 254
el Tawil, Saad, 84
taxes, in Egypt, 91–93
Tchangari, Moussa, 184
Tchicaya, Thystère, 116
Termez (Uzbekistan), 217
terrorism: September 11th terrorist attacks, 205; in Syria, 101
Thailand, 224, 246–47, 249
Theeravit, Khien, 246
Third International (Comintern), 262, 289, 363, 380
Third World Forum (TWF), 84–85, 184, 367, 378; activities of, 381–84; in Chile, 266; Italian support for, 420, 421; in Karachi (1974), 206–7; as network of networks, 368–69; in Porto Alegre (2002), 370; United Nations and, 377; *See also* World Social Forums
Tiberio, 312
Tibet, 116
Tigray (people), 133, 135
Timor Leste, 253–54
Tito (Josip Broz), 318
Togliatti, Palmiro, 361
Togo, 118

Tontons Macoutes (Haiti), 290
Torres, Camilo, 267
Toucouleurs (people), 74–75
Toumi, Khalida, 85
Touré, Amadou Toumani, 107–8, 112
tourism: in Cuba, 357; in French West Indies, 291; in Jamaica, 288; in Kenya, 150; in Thailand, 246
Tran Dac Loi, 355, 377
Transoxiana (Uzbekistan), 217, 219
trans-Saharan highway, 160–61
Traoré, Ali, 146
Traoré, Aminata D., 109, 384–85
Traoré, Moussa, 110
Tricontinental (1966), 361
Trilateral Commission, 369
Trotskyism, 283
Truong Tan Sang, 355
Tshombe, Moise, 154
Tsikata, Kojo, 113, 114
Tsiranana, Philibert, 127
Tuaregs (people), 111
Tudeh Party (Iran), 194, 196, 200, 201
Tunisia, 67–70, 96–99
al-Turabi, Hassan, 76, 102
Turkey, 101, 187–94; Kurds in, 62; in NATO, 424
Turkish (language), 188
Turpan (China), 214
Tutsis (people), 157, 167–70

Uganda, 164–65
Ujamaa, 124
Ukraine, 317, 328–30
UNCTAD (United Nations Conference on Trade and Development), 376
UNESCO, 377; Silk Roads program of, 211–12, 217, 220, 222
Union Soudanaise (Mali), 111
UNITA (AssemblyNational Union for the Total Independence of Angola), 141, 142, 158
United Arab Emirates, 77
United Kingdom, *See* Great Britain
United Nations, 184, 348, 377; under control of U.S., 408–9; Copenhagen conference (1995) of, 371–72; World Conference against Racism (2001) organized by, 177–78
United Sates, 409–12; access to oil as objective of, 52; Afghanistan and, 206; Africom, military command for Africa, of, 100, 166; on Angola, 142, 143; Chinese views of, 340; development of industrial capitalism in, 261; Ethiopia and, 138; immigration to, 287, 404;

in Indonesian massacre, 251–52; intervention in Chile by, 279–80; Iran and, 201–2; Korea and, 255; Latin American policies of, 266–67; Liberia and, 167; military interventions in Arab world by, 58–64; policies toward China of, 348; political Islam supported by, 58; Revolutionary War of, 289; Somalia and, 174; Syria and, 101–2; Turkey and, 192; in Vietnam War, 352–54; Yemen and, 103
United States Africa Command (U.S. AFRICOM), 100, 166
UNU (United Nations University), 376
UP (Popular Unity; Chile), 279
Upper Volta, 119
Urdu (language), 208
Uruguay, 267
USFP (Socialist Union of Popular Forces; Morocco), 68
USSR, *See* Soviet Union
Uyghurs (people), 215

Van den Reysen, Antoine, 114
Van den Reysen, Joseph, 114
Vega Camacho, Oscar, 303
Venezuela, 266, 267, 283–84, 292, 302
Vergopoulos, Kostas, 423
Verhaegen, Benoit, 156
Verrier, Roberto, 356
Videla, Jorge Rafael, 267, 277
Vieira, Sérgio, 143
Vietnam, 351–56; emergence in, 28; land management in, 34–35
Vietnam Peace and Development Foundation, 377
Vietnam War, 267, 352–54
Villela, Roberto, 297
Vuskovic, Pedro, 278

Wackernagel. Mathis, 47
Wafd (Egypt), 57, 86, 87
Wallerstein, Immanuel, 411
Wamba, Wamba Dia, 158
Wang Hui, 343
Wang Yué, 335–36, 338
wars of national liberation, in Portuguese colonies, 138
Wen Tiejun, 341–43
Western Sahara, 68–69
West Indies: Dominican Republic, 290–91; French West Indies, 291–92; Haiti, 288–90; Jamaica, 287–88
whites: in South Africa, 175, 176; in Zanzibar, 123

Wilke, Joachim, 308, 419, 420
Wilson, Amrit, 122
Wodié, Francis, 146
women: in Iran, 201; in Islam, 56; in Madagascar, 128; in peasant families, 40; in Tunisia, 68
workers' rights, in Egypt, 92
working classes, 264; in Arab national liberation movements, 88; in India, 235
World Bank: Ghana and, 113; on Malawi, 151; on peripheral capitalism, 254
World Conference against Racism (2001), 177–78
World Forum for Alternatives (WFA): activities of, 381–84; creation of, 366–68; Eastern Europe and, 316–17; in Latin America, 300, 302–4; as network of networks, 368–69; relations between North and, 378–81; United Nations and, 377; World Social Forums and, 393
World Social Forums, 84–85; in Caracus (2006), 284; creation of, 367; in Mumbai (2004), 227–28; in Nairobi (2007), 150; Porto Alegre conferences of, 369–71; responses from, 371–75; in Tunis (2013), 97; usefulness of approach of, 385–94
World Trade Organization (WTO), 31, 41, 302; attack on peasantry promoted by, 106

Xian (China), 213
Xinjiang (China), 212–16

Yaméogo, Maurice, 120
Yeltsin, Boris, 316
Yemen, 78–80, 103
Young Turks, 190
Yugoslavia, 317; fascists in, 328; globalization and, 309–10; NATO aggression in, 424; World War II in, 423–24

Zaire, 123
Zambia, 164–65, 179–80
Zanzibar, 122–23
Zapata, Emiliano, 285
Zasulich, Vera, 37
Zennadi, Samia, 85
Zéroual, Liamine, 72
Zhall, Hussein, 67
Zimbabwe, 144–46; Lancaster House Agreement for, 126